D1330574

PEARSON BACCALAUREATE

STANDARD LEVEL

Chemistry

2nd Edition

BROWN • MIKE FORD

Supporting every learner across the IB continuum

58

Published by Pearson Education Limited, Edinburgh Gate, Harlow, Essex, CM20 2JE.

www.pearsonglobalschools.com

Text © Pearson Education Limited 2014
Project Management by Alison Nick
Edited by Sara Hulse
Proofread by Eilidh McGregor
Designed by Astwood Design
Typeset by Phoenix Photosetting, Chatham, Kent
Original illustrations © Pearson Education 2014
Illustrated by Tech-Set Ltd and Phoenix Photosetting
Cover design by Pearson Education Limited

The rights of Catrin Brown and Mike Ford to be identified as authors of this work have been asserted by them in accordance with the Copyright, Designs and Patents Act 1988.

First published 2014

20 19 18 17 16
IMP 10 9 8 7 6 5

British Library Cataloguing in Publication Data
A catalogue record for this book is available from the British Library

ISBN 978 1 447 95906 9
eBook only ISBN 978 1 447 95907 6

Printed in Slovakia by Neografia.

Acknowledgements
We would like to thank David Moore and Dr. Garth Irwin for their invaluable help with and feedback on this title.

The authors wish to thank Professor Colin Oloman, of the University of British Columbia, Canada for his valuable input and professional advice on the text.

We are grateful also to the following IB senior educators who provided useful feedback on the manuscript: Dr. Karen Mclean and Oksana Jajecznyk.

The authors and publisher would like to thank the R. Bruce Weisman laboratory at Rice University for permission to use their fullerene ozonide kinetics data.

The authors and publisher would like to thank the following individuals and organizations for permission to reproduce photographs:
(Key: b-bottom; c-centre; l-left; r-right; t-top)

123RF.com: Olga Miltsova 576bl; **Asset Library (AL):** Sojaijiten 633c, Trevor Clifford 634c; **Catrin Brown:** 27bc, 152b, 155tr, 163bc, 202b, 217cr, 252tc, 303t, 498bl; **Corbis:** David Lees 539br, Ted Levine 304c; **DK Images:** Clive Streeter 211tc; **Eva Campbell:** 135b, 137br, 146bl, 281br, 317b, 320t, 321t, 321tr, 327t, 330t, 498cl; **Fotolia:** Aaron Ama 42tc, Africa Studio 114br, alessandrozocc 333tr, Andrej Kaprinay 614b, bilderstoeckchen 168bc, Can Balcioglu 170tl, Cosma 298cr, goodluz 170tr, GoodMood 11r, Jürgen Fälchle 233br, Kzenon 638, nikesidoroff 344c, Nikolai Sorokin 164c, quayside 196c, SAS 175b, Tiero 143, TTstudio 506c; **Glow Images:** Adam Gault 591tr; **Rick Eppler Estate:** 11bc; **Science Photo Library Ltd:** A. Dex, Publiphoto

Diffusion 586cl, Adam Hart-Davis 269cl, Adrienne Hart-Davis 427br, AJ Photo/Hop Americain 297bl, Alexis Rosenfeld 545cr, Alfred Pasieka 92cl, 113cr, 145tl, 153tr, 172bl, 267br, 387br, 392tr, 449br, 509cr, 574t, Andrew Lambert Photography 10tl, 18bc, 21cr, 23br, 39bc, 48c, 49r, 74tl, 92tc, 104tr, 105c, 106cl, 106br, 107tr, 109c, 116tc, 116cl, 209c, 218tl, 228tl, 247tr, 251c, 251b, 278cl, 280bc, 288cl, 290c, 322tl, 330bl, 332tl, 336cl, 336br, 337b, 347cr, 443cr, 478t, 574bl, 625cr, Argonne National Laboratory 413tr, 414c, Astrid & Hanns-Frieder Michler 386c, 403cr, 427c, Biophoto Associates 495cl, Bjorn Svensson 555tr, Bob Edwards 603c, Brian Bell 461t, BSIP VEM 480tl, BSIP, Chassenet 608tl, Carol and Mike Werner 535c, Charles D. Winters 2c, 5br, 16c, 28bl, 39tr, 88c, 104cl, 106tr, 219tr, 230tl, 241tr, 245tr, 246bl, 269tr, 279b, 335tr, Chemical Design Ltd., Oxford 423br, Chemical Heritage Foundation 59tr, Chris Knapton 345tr, Clive Freeman, The Royal Institution 323bc, 412cl, 469tr, Clive Freeman/Biosym Technologies 518tl, Cordelia Molloy 108tl, 173tl, 261tr, 484cl, 628br, Cristina Pedrazzini 348c, D. Phillips 216c, 479c, David A. Hardy 70bc, David Hay Jones 191tr, David McCarthy 412br, David Scharf 147tl, David Taylor 69br, 435c, Digital Instruments/Veeco 434t, Dirk Wiersma 397cr, Dr David Wexler, Coloured by Dr Jeremy Burgess 626tl, Dr Juerg Alean 531br, Dr Mark J. Winter 76c, 76b, 77tc, 77bc, 462b, Dr P. Marazzi 592tl, Dr Tim Evans 139tc, 465br, 497br, Edward Kinsman 37tr, EFDA-JET 533tr, Equinox 622bl, Equinox Graphics 600bl, Eye of Science 147bc, 272b, 305br, Frans Lanting, Mint Images 507br, Franz Himpsel 432b, Friedrich Saurer 625cl, Geoff Tompkinson 375tr, 561br, George Bernard 12cr, Hank Morgan 62tc, Hazen Group, Lawrence Berkeley National Laboratory 502c, Heine Schneebeli 277tc, Hewlett-Packard Laboratories 435tr, Hybrid Images 31br, Hybrid Medical Animation 480c, IBM 438b, J-L Charmet 293bc, James Bell 416tl, James King-Holmes 440br, 604c, James Prince 347c, Jean-Claude Revy, ISM 399br, Jean-Loup Charmet 627tl, Jeremy Walker 516c, Jerry Mason 69tr, 69cr, 536c, Jim Dowdalls 572cl, Jim Edds 8bc, John Bavosi 582bl, 587br, John McLean 328tl, John Mead 509b, Juergen Berger 562bl, Kenneth Eward/Biografx 75tr, 141tc, 185tr, 437br, Kevin Curtis 626br, Laguna Design 57bc, 119tr, 435b, 598b, 601cr, Lawrence Berkeley National Laboratory 107br, 129br, 197b, Lawrence Livermore National Laboratory 392tl, M. H. Sharp 417cr, Manfred Kage 403br, Mark Thomas 284c, Martin Bond 263cr, Martyn F. Chillmaid 6tl, 12cl, 13br, 48tl, 104tl, 104tc, 159br, 204tl, 209br, 257cr, 258c, 266c, 402tl, 425cr, 495cr, 630bl, Massimo Brega 481c, Mauro Fermariello 628tr, Maximilian Stock Ltd 294c, Mehau Kulyk 345br, Mere Words 541t, Michael Donne 565cr, Michael Szoenyi 246br, N K D Miller 581br, NASA 339bc, Natural History Museum 448c, NYPL 4l, Patrick Landmann 393b, 497cr, 534tl, 540bl, Paul J. Fusco 623cr, Paul Rapson 310bc, 455b, 501c, 518bl, Peggy Greb/US Department of Agriculture 630br, Philippe Plailly 56c, Philippe Psaila 120bc, 239cr, Photostock-Israel 503br, Physics Dept., Imperial College 58bc, 71bc, Physics Today Collection/American Institute of Physics 432cl, Pierre Philippon 293tr, Power And Syred 472t, Ramone Andrade 3Dciencia 560c, 597tr, Ray Ellis 515t, Ria Novosti 65cr, 89tr, 400b, 522bl, 537t, Rich Treptow 157c, Robert Brook 440tl, 441b, Russell Kightley 123tr, 436cl, 563tr, 595b, 597c, Saturn Stills 477b, Science Photo Library 59br, 89bc, 92cr, 165cr, 169tr, 232bl, 322br, 333c, 406tl, 578cl, 588cl, 606c, 627tr, Scientifica, Visuals Unlimited 398c, Scott Camazine 589br, Sheila Terry 4bc, 405tr, Simon Fraser 235tr, 238c, 261cr, 512tl, Simon Fraser/Mauna Loa Observatory 552b, Simon Fraser/Northumbrian Environmental Management Ltd. 440cl, Sinclair Stammers 465tr, St Mary's Hospital Medical School 577b, St Bartholomew's Hospital 570cl, Steve Gschmeissner 458cl, Steve Horrell 420bl, Susumu Nishinaga 112c, 117tr, 143br, 579cr, TEK Image 364cl, Tom McHugh 442cl, Tony Craddock 443br, US Department of Energy 533b, 605t, 605b, Victor de Schwanberg 299tc, Wladimir Bulgar 476b; **Shutterstock.com:** Dmitry Lobanov ifc, Susan Santa Maria 46bc

Cover images: Front: Science Photo Library Ltd: Power And Syred

All other images © Pearson Education

We are grateful to the following for permission to reproduce copyright material:

Figures

Figure on page 202 adapted from www.vernier.com, with kind permission from Vernier Software & Technology; Figure on page 361 adapted from University of California Museum of Paleontology's *Understanding Science* (http://www.understandingscience.org), copyright 2006 by The University of California Museum of Paleontology, Berkeley, and the Regents of the University of California; Figure on page 500 adapted from 'Fluorescent Guest Molecules Report Ordered Inner Phase of Host Capsules in Solution' Author(s): Dalgarno, S. J. DOI: 10.1126/SCIENCE.1116579 Date: Sep 23, 2005 Volume: 309 Issue: 5743, reprinted with permission from AAAS; Figure on page 500 adapted from 'Challenges to achievement of metal sustainability in our high-tech society'. *Chemistry Society Review*, 10.1039/C3CS60440C (Izatt, R. M.; Izatt, S. R.; Bruening, R. L.; Izatt, N. E.; Moyer, B. A.) (Jan 27, 2014) with permission of The Royal Society of Chemistry; Figure on page 580 adapted from 'ß-lactamase enzymes identified during the age of antibiotics', Professor Karen Bush with permission.

Text

Quote on page 622 from 'What Is Science?', *The Physics Teacher*, Vol. 7, issue 6, pp. 313–320, (Feynman, Richard 1969) reproduced with permission from American Association of Physics Teachers (c)1969;

Quote on page 630 from *Physics and Philosophy: The Revolution in Modern Science ISBN-13: 978-0141182155* Penguin Modern Classics (Heisenberg,Werner) p.25, with kind permission from Penguin Books Ltd and HarperCollins Publishers.

Every effort has been made to contact copyright holders of material reproduced in this book. In some instances we have been unable to trace the owners of copyright material, and we would appreciate any information that would enable us to do so. Any omissions will be rectified in subsequent printings if notice is given to the publishers.

The Understandings, Applications and skills, Guidance, Essential ideas, past exam questions, corresponding mark schemes provided on the eBook, assessment criteria and prescribed essay titles have been reproduced from IB documents and past examination papers. Our thanks go to the International Baccalaureate for permission to reproduce its intellectual copyright.

This material has been developed independently by the publisher and the content is in no way connected with or endorsed by the International Baccalaureate (IB). International Baccalaureate® is a registered trademark of the International Baccalaureate Organization.

There are links to relevant websites in this book. In order to ensure that the links are up to date and that the links work we have made the links available on our website at www.pearsonhotlinks.co.uk. Search for this title or ISBN 9781447959069.

eBook System requirements

System requirements supported are listed below:

Windows	Macintosh	iPad	Android
• Windows 7, Windows 8 • Intel® Pentium® II 450 MHz or faster processor (or equivalent) • 128 MB available RAM (256 MB or higher recommended) • 20 MB hard drive space • Supported browsers: IE 9.0, IE 10, IE 11 (Desktop Version), Chrome 25.0 or higher, and Firefox 19.0 or higher	• OS X version 10.6.x, 10.7.x, 10.8.x, 10.9.x • Intel Processor • 256 MB or higher RAM • 20 MB hard drive space • Supported browsers: Safari 5.1, Safari 6, and Firefox 19.0 or higher, Chrome 25 or higher * One-finger and two-finger swipe gestures are not supported	• iPad1, iPad2, iPad3, iPad4 or iPad mini • iOS 5, iOS 6, iOS 7 or higher * One-finger and two-finger swipe gestures are not supported	• Android 7" and 10" tablets • OS v4.0.x (Ice Cream Sandwich), v4.1 (Jelly Bean), v4.4 (Kit Kat) or higher • Accessible via Google Play only

Other requirements:

- Adobe Flash Player 11.2 or higher
- Javascript enabled in your browser to view and use the online Help
- Screen resolution: Minimum 1024 pixels wide x 768 pixels high
- Internet connection: Broadband cable, high-speed DSL, or other equivalent is recommended.

Contents

Introduction

Authors' introduction to the second edition

Welcome to your study of IB Standard Level chemistry. This book is the second edition of the market-leading Pearson Baccalaureate SL chemistry book, first published in 2008. It has been completely rewritten to match the specifications of the new IB chemistry curriculum, and gives thorough coverage of the entire course content. While there is much new and updated material, we have kept and refined the features that made the first edition so successful.

Our personal experience and intimate knowledge of the entire IB chemistry experience, through teaching and examining, curriculum review, moderating internal assessment and leading workshops for teachers in different continents, has given us a unique understanding of your needs in this course. We are delighted to share our enthusiasm for learning chemistry in the IB programme with you!

Content

The book covers the core part of the syllabus (Topics 1–11) and the four possible options, of which you will study one. Each chapter in the book corresponds to a topic or option in the IB guide, in the same sequence. The sub-topics

within each chapter are listed in the contents page.

Each chapter starts with a list of the Essential ideas from the IB chemistry guide, which summarize the focus of each sub-topic.

Essential ideas

3.1 The arrangement of elements in the Periodic Table helps to predict their electron configuration.

This is followed by an introduction, which gives the context of the topic and how it relates to your previous knowledge. The relevant sections from the IB chemistry guide for each sub-topic are then given

as boxes showing Understandings, and Applications and skills, with notes for Guidance shown in italics where they help interpret the syllabus.

Understandings:

- Atoms contain a positively charged dense nucleus composed of protons and neutrons (nucleons).

  Guidance
  Relative masses and charges of the sub-atomic particles should be known, actual values are given in section 4 of the IB data booklet. The mass of the electron can be considered negligible.

Applications and skills:

- Use of the nuclear symbol notation $^{A}_{Z}X$ to deduce the number of protons, neutrons, and electrons in atoms and ions.

The text covers the course content using plain language, with all scientific terms explained and shown in bold as they are first introduced. It follows IUPAC nomenclature and definitions throughout.

We have been careful also to apply the same terminology you will see in IB examinations in all worked examples and questions.

The nature of science

Throughout the course you are encouraged to think about the nature of scientific knowledge and the scientific process as it applies to chemistry. Examples are given of the evolution of chemical theories as new information is gained, the use of models to conceptualize our understanding, and the ways in which experimental work is enhanced by modern technologies. Ethical considerations, environmental impacts, the importance of objectivity, and the responsibilities regarding scientists' code of conduct are also considered here. The emphasis is not on learning any of these examples, but rather appreciating the broader conceptual themes in context. We have included at least one example in each sub-section, and hope you will come up with your own as you keep these ideas at the surface of your learning.

Key to information boxes

A popular feature of the book is the different coloured boxes interspersed through each chapter. These are used to enhance your learning as explained using examples below.

 Nature of science

This is an overarching theme in the course to promote concept-based learning. Through the book you should recognize some similar themes emerging across different topics. We hope they help you to develop your own skills in scientific literacy.

 NATURE OF SCIENCE

The story of Fleming's discovery of penicillin is often described as serendipitous – a fortunate discovery made by chance or by accident. But it was more than that. Would not the majority of people who noticed the plates were contaminated simply have thrown them away, likely disappointed at the 'failed experiment'? The difference was that Fleming had the insight to observe the plates carefully and ask the right questions about why a clear ring appeared around the fungal growth. Scientists are trained to be observant and to seek explanations for what they see, and this must include the unexpected. As Louis Pasteur once famously said, 'Chance favours only the prepared mind'. Consider to what extent scientific discoveries are only possible to scientists who are trained in the principles of observation and interpretation.

The disposal of plastics is a major global problem. The very features that make plastics so useful, such as their impermeability to water and low reactivity, mean they are often non-biodegradable and so remain in landfill sites for indefinite periods of time. It is estimated that about 10% of plastics produced end up in the ocean, causing widespread hazards to marine life. Measures to try to address this problem include developments of more efficient recycling processes, biodegradable plastics, and plastic-feeding microorganisms. A reduction in the quantities of plastic produced and used is also urgently needed – which is something for which every individual can share responsibility.

  International-mindedness

The impact of the study of chemistry is global, and includes environmental, political and socio-economic considerations. Examples of this are given to help you to see the importance of chemistry in an international context.

 Utilization

Applications of the topic through everyday examples are described here, as well as brief descriptions of related chemical industries. This helps you to see the relevance and context of what you are learning.

Freeze-drying is an effective process for the preservation of food and some pharmaceuticals. It differs from standard methods of dehydration in that it does not use heat to evaporate water, but instead depends on the sublimation of ice. The substance to be preserved is first frozen, and then warmed gently at very low pressure which causes the ice to change directly to water vapour. The process is slow but has the significant advantage that the composition of the material, and so its flavour, are largely conserved. The freeze-dried product is stored in a moisture-free package that excludes oxygen, and can be reconstituted by the addition of water.

The person who researched and patented tetraethyl lead as a petroleum additive was the same person who later was responsible for the discovery and marketing of chlorofluorocarbons (CFCs) as refrigerants. Thomas Midgley of Ohio, USA, did not live to know the full extent that the long-term impact his findings would have on the Earth's atmosphere. He died in 1944, aged 55, from accidental strangulation after becoming entangled in ropes and pulleys he had devised to get himself in and out of bed following loss of use of his legs caused by polio. Perhaps his epitaph should have been 'The solution becomes the problem'.

  ## Interesting fact

These give background information that will add to your wider knowledge of the topic and make links with other topics and subjects. Aspects such as historic notes on the life of scientists and origins of names are included here.

 ## Laboratory work

These indicate links to ideas for lab work and experiments that will support your learning in the course, and help you prepare for the Internal Assessment. Some specific experimental work is compulsory, and further details of this are in the eBook.

 Experiment to determine the empirical formula of MgO

Full details of how to carry out this experiment with a worksheet are available on your eBook.

A sample of magnesium is heated and the change in mass recorded. From this, the ratio of moles of magnesium to oxygen can be determined.

Hess's law is a natural consequence of the law of conservation of energy. If you know the law of conservation of energy, do you automatically know Hess's law?

  ## TOK

These stimulate thought and consideration of knowledge issues as they arise in context. Each box contains open questions to help trigger critical thinking and discussion.

 ## Key fact

These key facts are drawn out of the main text and highlighted in bold. This will help you to identify the core learning points within each section. They also act as a quick summary for review.

 The concentrations of H^+ and OH^- are inversely proportional in an aqueous solution.

In writing the ionization reactions of weak acids and bases, it is essential to use the equilibrium sign.

Hints for success

These give hints on how to approach questions, and suggest approaches that examiners like to see. They also identify common pitfalls in understanding, and omissions made in answering questions.

Challenge yourself

These boxes contain open questions that encourage you to think about the topic in more depth, or to make detailed connections with other topics. They are designed to be challenging and to make you think.

CHALLENGE YOURSELF

6 Explain why oxygen behaves as a free radical despite having an even number of electrons.

eBook

In the eBook you will find the following:

- Interactive glossary of scientific words used in the course
- Answers and worked solutions to all exercises in the book

- Fast facts and labs worksheets
- Interactive quizzes
- Animations
- Videos

For more details about your eBook, see the following section.

Questions

There are three types of question in this book:

1. Worked example with Solution

These appear at intervals in the text and are used to illustrate the concepts covered.

They are followed by the solution, which shows the thinking and the steps used in solving the problem.

Worked example

Calomel is a compound once used in the treatment of syphilis. It has the empirical formula HgCl and a molar mass of 472.08 g mol^{-1}. What is its molecular formula?

Solution

First calculate the mass of the empirical formula:

$$\text{mass(HgCl)} = 200.59 + 35.45 = 236.04 \text{ g mol}^{-1}$$

$$(236.04) \times x = M = 472.08$$

$$\therefore x = 2$$

$$\text{molecular formula} = Hg_2Cl_2$$

2. Exercises

These questions are found throughout the text. They allow you to apply your knowledge and test your understanding of what you have just been reading.

The answers to these are given in the eBook, at the end of each chapter.

Exercises

64 Calculate the mass of potassium hydroxide, KOH, required to prepare 250 cm^3 of a 0.200 mol dm^{-3} solution.

3. Practice questions

These questions are found at the end of each chapter. They are mostly taken from previous years' IB examination papers. The mark-schemes used by examiners when marking these questions are given in the eBook, at the end of each chapter.

Practice questions

1 How many oxygen atoms are in 0.100 mol of $CuSO_4.5H_2O$?

   A 5.42×10^{22} **B** 6.02×10^{22} **C** 2.41×10^{23} **D** 5.42×10^{23}

Answers and worked solutions

Full worked solutions to all exercises and practice questions can be found in the eBook, as well as regular answers.

 Hotlink boxes can be found at the end of each chapter, indicating that there are weblinks available for further study. To access these links go to www.pearsonhotlinks.com and enter the ISBN or title of this book. Here you can find links to animations, simulations, movie clips and related background material, which can help to deepen your interest and understanding of the topic.

We truly hope that this book and the accompanying eBook resources help you to enjoy this fascinating subject of IB Standard Level chemistry. We wish you success in your studies.

Catrin Brown and Mike Ford

Jump to any page

Switch from single- to double-page view

Highlight parts of the text

Create notes

Search the whole book

Zoom

Browse   My Searches   Search...   Go

Page 174   107%

05 Energetics and thermochemistry

It takes considerably more heat energy to increase the temperature of a swimming pool by 5 °C than boil a kettle of water from room temperature. The swimming pool contains more water molecules and so has a larger heat capacity.

The water in the kettle has a higher temperature but the water in the swimming pool has more heat energy. Temperature is a measure of the average kinetic energy of the molecules.

Video

Select the icon to watch a video

A temperature rise of 1 K is the same as a temperature rise of 1 °C.

Worksheets

Select the icon to view a worksheet with further activities

W   PDF

Our shared knowledge is passed on from one generation to the next by language. The language we use today is often based on the shared knowledge of the past which can sometimes be incorrect. What do such phrases as "keep the heat in and the cold out" tell us about previous concepts of heat and cold? How does the use of language hinder the pursuit of knowledge?

TOK

Note

This relationship allows the heat change in a material to be calculated from the temperature change.

When considering the relationship between different objects the **heat capacity** is often a more convenient property. The heat capacity (C) is defined as the heat needed to increase the temperature of an object by 1 K.

$$\text{heat capacity } (C) = \frac{\text{heat change } (q)}{\text{temperature change } (\Delta T)}$$

A swimming pool has a larger heat capacity than a kettle.

- The specific heat capacity (c) is defined as the heat needed to increase the temperature of unit mass of material by 1 K.

$$\text{specific heat capacity } (c) = \frac{\text{heat change } (q)}{\text{mass } (m) \times \text{temperature change } (\Delta T)}$$

- The heat capacity (C) is defined as the heat needed to increase the temperature of an object by 1 K.

$$\text{heat capacity } (C) = \frac{\text{heat change } (q)}{\text{temperature change } (\Delta T)}$$

NATURE OF SCIENCE

Although heat is a concept that is familiar to us all – we need it to cook our food and to keep us warm – it is a subject that has proved to be difficult for science to understand. We are equipped by our sense of touch to distinguish between high and low temperature but heat has proved challenging on a more fundamental level. The development of different temperature scales was an important technological and scientific step as it recognized the need for objectivity in scientific measurement, and the need to calibrate the instruments to one or more one fixed points. However, scientific understanding in this area was still confused at the time. The original Celsius scale, for example, had the boiling point of water at a lower temperature than its melting point, so it was not clear what it was quantifying and other scales used arbitrary fixed points such as the melting points of butter, or the temperatures of the Paris wine cellars.

The observation that heat can be added to melting ice or boiling water without changing its temperature was a significant observation in the distinction between the heat and temperature.

Our modern distinction is based on our particulate theory of matter. Temperature is a measure ... gy is transferred.

PRIVATE NOTE   Close

Do exercises 1–6, and worksheet for homework.   at capacity of

Edit

170

See definitions of key terms in the glossary

reate a bookmark

Switch to whiteboard view

Animation

Select the icon to see a related animation

Solution

$$\text{heat change} = m \times c \times \Delta T$$
$$= 10.0 \text{ g} \times 0.385 \text{ J g}^{-1}\,°\text{C}^{-1} \times -60.0\ °\text{C} \text{ (the value is negative as}$$
$$\text{the Cu has lost heat)}$$
$$= -231 \text{ J}$$

Exercises

1 When a sample of NH_4SCN is mixed with solid $Ba(OH)_2.8H_2O$ in a glass beaker, the mixture changes to a liquid and the temperature drops sufficiently to freeze the beaker to the table. Which statement is true about the reaction?

A The process is endothermic and ΔH is −
B The process is endothermic and ΔH is +
C The process is exothermic and ΔH is −
D The process is exothermic and ΔH is +

2 Which one of the following statements is *true* of all exothermic reactions?

A They produce gases.
B They give out heat.
C They occur quickly.
D They involve combustion.

3 If 500 J of heat is added to 100.0 g samples of each of the substances below, which will have the largest temperature increase?

	Substance	Specific heat capacity / J g^{-1} K^{-1}
A	gold	0.129
B	silver	0.237
C	copper	0.385
D	water	4.18

Quiz

Select the icon to take an interactive quiz to test your knowledge

4 The temperature of a 5.0 g sample of copper increases from 27 °C to 29 °C. Calculate how much heat has been added to the system. (Specific heat capacity of Cu = 0.385 J g^{-1}K^{-1})

A 0.770 J   B 1.50 J   C 3.00 J   D 3.85 J

5 Consider the specific heat capacity of the following metals.

Metal	Specific heat capacity / J g^{-1} K^{-1}
Al	0.897
Be	1.82
Cd	0.231
Cr	0.449

1 kg samples of the metals at room temperature are heated by the same electrical heater for 10 min. Identify the metal which has the highest final temperature.

A Al   B Be   C Cd   D Cr

6 The specific heat of metallic mercury is 0.138 J g^{-1} °C^{-1}. If 100.0 J of heat is added to a 100.0 g sample of mercury at 25.0 °C, what is the final temperature of the mercury?

CHALLENGE YOURSELF

2 Suggest an explanation for the pattern in specific heat capacities of the metals in Exercise 3.

Worked solutions

Select the icon at the end of the chapter to view worked solutions to exercises in this chapter

Enthalpy changes and the direction of change

There is a natural direction for change. When we slip on a ladder, we go down, not up. The direction of change is in the direction of lower stored energy. In a similar way, we expect methane to burn when we strike a match and form carbon dioxide and water. The chemicals are changing in a way which reduces their enthalpy (Figure 5.5).

Answers

Select the icon at the end of the chapter to view answers to exercises in this chapter

171

01

Stoichiometric relationships

Essential ideas

1.1 Physical and chemical properties depend on the ways in which different atoms combine.

1.2 The mole makes it possible to correlate the number of particles with the mass that can be measured.

1.3 Mole ratios in chemical equations can be used to calculate reacting ratios by mass and gas volume.

The birth of chemistry as a physical science can be traced back to the first successful attempts to quantify chemical change. Carefully devised experiments led to data that revealed one simple truth. *Chemical change involves interactions between particles that have fixed mass.* Even before knowledge was gained of the atomic nature of these particles and of the factors that determine their interactions, this discovery became the guiding principle for modern chemistry. We begin our study with a brief introduction to this particulate nature of matter, and go on to investigate some of the ways in which it can be quantified.

The term **stoichiometry** is derived from two Greek words – *stoicheion* for element and *metron* for measure. Stoichiometry describes the relationships between the amounts of reactants and products during chemical reactions. As it is known that matter is conserved during chemical change, stoichiometry is a form of book-keeping at the atomic level. It enables chemists to determine what amounts of substances they should react together and enables them to predict how much product will be obtained. The application of stoichiometry closes the gap between what is happening on the atomic scale and what can be measured.

In many ways this chapter can be considered as a toolkit for the mathematical content in much of the course. It covers the universal language of chemistry, **chemical equations**, and introduces the **mole** as the unit of amount. Applications include measurements of mass, volume, and concentration.

You may choose not to work through all of this at the start of the course, but to come back to these concepts after you have gained knowledge of some of the fundamental properties of chemical matter in Chapters 2, 3, and 4.

The reaction between ignited powdered aluminium and iron oxide, known as the thermite reaction:

$$2Al(s) + Fe_2O_3(s) \rightarrow Al_2O_3(s) + 2Fe(s)$$

Significant heat is released by the reaction, and it is used in welding processes including underwater welding. The stoichiometry of the reaction, as shown in the balanced equation, enables chemists to determine the reacting masses of reactants and products for optimum use.

1.1 Introduction to the particulate nature of matter and chemical change

Understandings:

- Atoms of different elements combine in fixed ratios to form compounds, which have different properties from their component elements.

  ### Guidance
  Names and symbols of the elements are in the IB data booklet in section 5.

- Mixtures contain more than one element and/or compound that are not chemically bonded together and so retain their individual properties.
- Mixtures are either homogeneous or heterogeneous.

Applications and skills:

- Deduction of chemical equations when reactants and products are specified.

  Guidance
  Balancing of equations should include a variety of types of reactions.

- Application of the state symbols (s), (l), (g), and (aq) in equations.
- Explanation of observable changes in physical properties and temperature during changes of state.

  Guidance
  - *Names of the changes of state – melting, freezing, vaporization (evaporation and boiling), condensation, sublimation and deposition – should be covered.*
  - *The term 'latent heat' is not required.*

Antoine-Laurent Lavoisier (1743–1794) is often called the 'father of chemistry'. His many accomplishments include the naming of oxygen and hydrogen, the early development of the metric system, and a standardization of chemical nomenclature. Most importantly, he established an understanding of combustion as a process involving combination with oxygen from the air, and recognized that matter retains its mass through chemical change, leading to the law of conservation of mass. In addition, he compiled the first extensive list of elements in his book Elements of Chemistry (1789). In short, he changed chemistry from a qualitative to a quantitative science. But, as an unpopular tax collector in France during the French Revolution and Terror, he was tried for treason and guillotined in 1794. One and a half years after his death he was exonerated, and his early demise was recognized as a major loss to France.

Chemical elements are the fundamental building blocks of chemistry

The English language is based on an alphabet of just 26 letters. But as we know, combining these in different ways leads to an almost infinite number of words, and then sentences, paragraphs, books, and so on. It is similar to the situation in chemistry, where the 'letters' are the single substances known as **chemical elements**. There are

Antoine-Laurent Lavoisier, French chemist (1743–1794).

A chemical element is a single pure substance, made of only one type of atom.

Pictographic symbols used at the beginning of the 18th century to represent chemical elements and compounds. They are similar to those of the ancient alchemists. As more elements were discovered during the 18th century, attempts to devise a chemical nomenclature led to the modern alphabetic notational system. This system was devised by the Swedish chemist Berzelius and introduced in 1814.

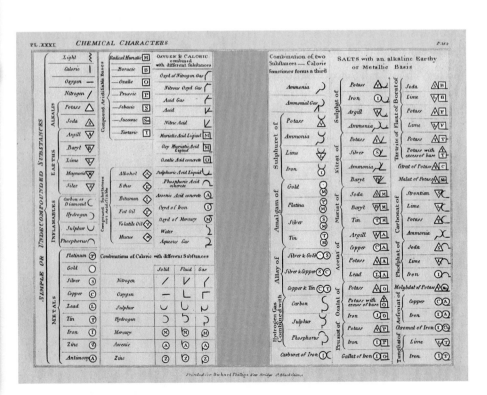

only about 100 of these, but because of the ways in which they combine with each other, they make up the almost countless number of different chemical substances in our world.

In Chapter 2 we will learn about atomic structure, and how each element is made up of a particular type of atom. The atoms of an element are all the same as each other (with the exception of isotopes, which we will also discuss in Chapter 2), and are different from those of other elements. It is this distinct nature of its atoms that gives each element its individual properties. A useful definition of an atom is that it is the smallest particle of an element to show the characteristic properties of that element.

To help communication in chemistry, each element is denoted by a **chemical symbol** of either one upper case letter, or one upper case letter followed by a lower case letter. A few examples are given below.

Name of element	Symbol
carbon	C
fluorine	F
potassium	K
calcium	Ca
mercury	Hg
tungsten	W

You will notice that often the letter or letters used are derived from the English name of the element, but in some cases they derive from other languages. For example, Hg for mercury comes from Latin, whereas W for tungsten has its origin in European dialects. Happily, these symbols are all accepted and used internationally, so they do not need to be translated. A complete list of the names of the elements and their symbols is given in section 5 of the IB data booklet.

Chemical compounds are formed from more than one element

Some elements, such as nitrogen and gold, are found in **native** form, that is uncombined with other elements in nature. But more commonly, elements exist in chemical combinations with other elements, in substances known as **chemical compounds**. Compounds contain a fixed proportion of elements, and are held together by chemical bonds (discussed in Chapter 4). The bonding between atoms in compounds changes their

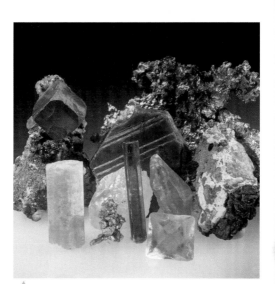
▲ Assorted minerals, including elements such as sulfur and silver, and compounds such as Al_2O_3 (sapphire) and CaF_2 (fluorite). Most minerals are impure and exist as mixtures of different elements and compounds.

The International Union of Pure and Applied Chemistry (IUPAC) was formed in 1919 by chemists from industry and academia. Since then it has developed into the world authority on chemical nomenclature and terminology. It has succeeded in fostering worldwide communications in the chemical sciences and in uniting academic, industrial, and public sector chemistry in a common language.

Chemistry is a very exact subject, and it is important to be careful in distinguishing between upper and lower case letters. For example, Co (cobalt, a metallic element) means something completely different from CO (carbon monoxide, a poisonous gas).

The number of elements that exist is open to change as new ones are discovered, although there is often a time-lag between a discovery and its confirmation by IUPAC. During this time a provisional systematic three-letter symbol is used, using Latin abbreviations to represent the atomic number. The letters u (un) = 1, b (bi) = 2, t (tri) = 3 and so on are used. So the provisional element of atomic number 118 will continue to be known as ununoctium or uuo until it is confirmed and a name formally agreed according to the process established by IUPAC.

A compound is a chemical combination of different elements, containing a fixed ratio of atoms. The physical and chemical properties of a compound are different from those of its component elements.

properties, so compounds have completely different properties from those of their component elements.

A classic example of this is that sodium, Na, is a dangerously reactive metal that reacts violently with water, while chlorine, Cl_2, is a toxic gas used as a chemical weapon. Yet when these two elements combine, they form the compound sodium chloride, NaCl, a white crystalline solid that we sprinkle all over our food.

Compounds are described using the chemical symbols for elements. A subscript is used to show the number of atoms of each element in a unit of the compound. Some examples are given below. (The reasons for the different ratios of elements in compounds will become clearer after we have studied atomic structure and bonding in Chapters 2 and 4.)

Name of compound	Symbol	Name of compound	Symbol
sodium chloride	NaCl	water	H_2O
potassium oxide	K_2O	glucose	$C_6H_{12}O_6$
copper bromide	$CuBr_2$	ammonium sulfate	$(NH_4)_2SO_4$

A combustion spoon holding sodium, Na, is lowered into a gas jar containing chlorine, Cl2. The vigorous reaction produces white crystals of sodium chloride, NaCl.

$2Na(s) + Cl_2(g) \rightarrow 2NaCl(s)$

The properties of the compound are completely different from those of its component elements.

A chemical equation shows:

direction of change

reactants ⟶ products

Chemical equations are the universal language of chemistry. What other languages are universal, and to what extent do they help or hinder the pursuit of knowledge?

TOK

Chemical equations summarize chemical change

The formation of compounds from elements is an example of **chemical change** and can be represented by a **chemical equation**. A chemical equation is a representation using chemical symbols of the simplest ratio of atoms, as elements or in compounds, undergoing chemical change. The left-hand side shows the **reactants** and the right-hand side the **products**.

For example: calcium + chlorine → calcium chloride

$$Ca + Cl_2 \rightarrow CaCl_2$$

As atoms are neither created nor destroyed during a chemical reaction, *the total number of atoms of each element must be the same on both sides of the equation*. This is known as **balancing the equation**, and uses numbers called **stoichiometric coefficients** to denote the number of units of each term in the equation.

For example: hydrogen + oxygen → water

$$2H_2 + O_2 \rightarrow 2H_2O$$

coefficients

	total on left side	total on right side
hydrogen atoms	4	4
oxygen atoms	2	2

$2H_2 + O_2 \rightarrow 2H_2O$

Figure 1.1 When hydrogen and oxygen react to form water, the atoms are rearranged, but the number of atoms of each element remains the same.

Note that when the coefficient is 1, this does not need to be explicitly stated.

Early ideas to explain chemical change in combustion and rusting included the 'phlogiston' theory. This proposed the existence of a fire-like element that was released during these processes. The theory seemed to explain some of the observations of its time, although these were purely qualitative. It could not explain later quantitative data showing that substances actually gain rather than lose mass during burning. In 1783, Lavoisier's work on oxygen confirmed that combustion and rusting involve combination with oxygen from the air, so overturning the phlogiston theory. This is a good example of how the evolution of scientific ideas, such as how chemical change occurs, is based on the need for theories that can be tested by experiment. Where results are not compatible with the theory, a new theory must be put forward, which must then be subject to the same rigour of experimental test.

Chemical equations are used to show all types of reactions in chemistry, including reactions of decomposition, combustion, neutralization, and so on. Examples of these are given below and you will come across very many more during this course. Learning to write equations is an important skill in chemistry, which develops quickly with practice.

Worked example

Write an equation for the reaction of thermal decomposition of sodium hydrogencarbonate ($NaHCO_3$) into sodium carbonate (Na_2CO_3), water (H_2O), and carbon dioxide (CO_2).

Solution

First write the information from the question in the form of an equation, and then check the number of atoms of each element on both sides of the equation.

$$NaHCO_3 \rightarrow Na_2CO_3 + H_2O + CO_2$$

	total on left side	total on right side
sodium atoms	1	2
hydrogen atoms	1	2
carbon atoms	1	2
oxygen atoms	3	6

In order to balance this we introduce coefficient 2 on the left.

$$2NaHCO_3 \rightarrow Na_2CO_3 + H_2O + CO_2$$

Finally check that it is balanced for each element.

Exercises

1 Write balanced chemical equations for the following reactions:

  (a) The decomposition of copper carbonate ($CuCO_3$) into copper(II) oxide (CuO) and carbon dioxide (CO_2).

  (b) The combustion of magnesium (Mg) in oxygen (O_2) to form magnesium oxide (MgO).

  (c) The neutralization of sulfuric acid (H_2SO_4) with sodium hydroxide (NaOH) to form sodium sulfate (Na_2SO_4) and water (H_2O).

  (d) The synthesis of ammonia (NH_3) from nitrogen (N_2) and hydrogen (H_2).

  (e) The combustion of methane (CH_4) to produce carbon dioxide (CO_2) and water (H_2O).

2 Write balanced chemical equations for the following reactions:

  (a) $K + H_2O \rightarrow KOH + H_2$

  (b) $C_2H_5OH + O_2 \rightarrow CO_2 + H_2O$

  (c) $Cl_2 + KI \rightarrow KCl + I_2$

  (d) $CrO_3 \rightarrow Cr_2O_3 + O_2$

  (e) $Fe_2O_3 + C \rightarrow CO + Fe$

An equation by definition has to be *balanced*, so do not expect this to be specified in a question. After you have written an equation, *always* check the numbers of atoms of each element on both sides of the equation to ensure it is correctly balanced.

When a question refers to 'heating' a reactant or to 'thermal decomposition', this does not mean the addition of oxygen, only that heat is the source of energy for the reaction. If the question refers to 'burning' or 'combustion', this indicates that oxygen is a reactant.

Remember when you are balancing an equation, change the stoichiometric coefficient but never change the subscript in a chemical formula.

When balancing equations, start with the most complex species, and leave terms that involve a single element to last.

3 Use the same processes to balance the following examples:

(a) $C_4H_{10} + O_2 \rightarrow CO_2 + H_2O$
(b) $NH_3 + O_2 \rightarrow NO + H_2O$
(c) $Cu + HNO_3 \rightarrow Cu(NO_3)_2 + NO + H_2O$
(d) $H_2O_2 + N_2H_4 \rightarrow N_2 + H_2O + O_2$
(e) $C_2H_7N + O_2 \rightarrow CO_2 + H_2O + N_2$

A chemical equation can be used to assess the efficiency of a reaction in making a particular product. The **atom economy** is a concept used for this purpose and is defined as:

$$\% \text{ atom economy} = \frac{\text{mass of desired product}}{\text{total mass of products}} \times 100$$

Note that this is different from % yield discussed later in this chapter, which is calculated using only one product and one reactant. Atom economy is an indication of how much of the reactants ends up in the required products, rather than in waste products. A higher atom economy indicates a more efficient and less wasteful process. The concept is increasingly used in developments in green and sustainable chemistry. This is discussed further in Chapters 12 and 13.

Mixtures form when substances combine without chemical interaction

A mixture is composed of two or more substances in which no chemical combination has occurred.

Air is described as a **mixture** of gases because the separate components – different elements and compounds – are interspersed with each other, but are not chemically combined. This means, for example, that the gases nitrogen and oxygen when mixed in air retain the same characteristic properties as when they are in the pure form. Substances burn in air because the oxygen present supports combustion, as does pure oxygen.

Another characteristic of mixtures is that their composition is not fixed. For example, air that we breathe in typically contains about 20% by volume oxygen, whereas the air that we breathe out usually contains only about 16% by volume oxygen. It is still correct to call both of these mixtures of air, because there is no fixed proportion in the definition.

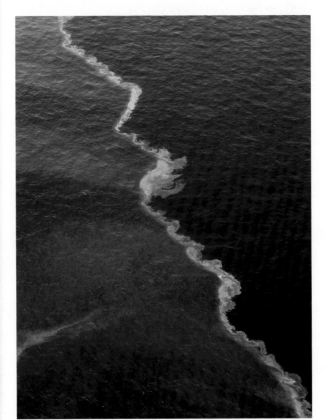

Tide of oily water heading towards Pensacola Beach, Florida, USA, after the explosion of the offshore drilling unit in the Gulf of Mexico in 2010. The oil forms a separate layer as it does not mix with the water.

Air is an example of a **homogeneous mixture**, meaning that it has uniform composition and properties throughout. A solution of salt in water and a metal alloy such as bronze are also homogeneous. By contrast, a **heterogeneous mixture** such as water and oil has non-uniform composition, so its properties are not the same throughout. It is usually possible to see the separate components in a heterogeneous mixture but not in a homogeneous mixture.

Because the components retain their individual properties in a mixture, we can often separate them relatively easily. The technique we choose to achieve this will take advantage of a suitable difference in the physical properties of the components, as shown in the table below. Many of these are important processes in research and industry and are discussed in more detail in the following chapters.

Mixture	Difference in property of components	Technique used
sand and salt	solubility in water	solution and filtration
hydrocarbons in crude oil	boiling point	fractional distillation
iron and sulfur	magnetism	response to a magnet
pigments in food colouring	adsorption to solid phase	paper chromatography
different amino acids	net charge at a fixed pH	gel electrophoresis

Matter exists in different states determined by the temperature and pressure

From our everyday experience, we know that all matter (elements, compounds, and mixtures) can exist in different forms depending on the temperature and pressure. Liquid water changes into a solid form such as ice, hail, or snow, as the temperature drops and it becomes a gas, steam, at high temperatures. These different forms are known as the **states of matter** and are characterized by the different energies of the particles.

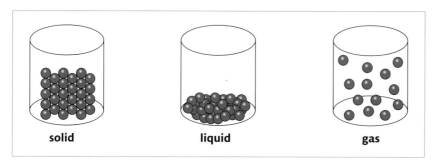

solid   liquid   gas

increasing temperature

increasing kinetic energy of particles

- particles close packed
- inter-particle forces strong, particles vibrate in position
- fixed shape
- fixed volume

- particles more spaced
- inter-particle forces weaker, particles can slide over each other
- no fixed shape
- fixed volume

- particles spread out
- inter-particle forces negligible, particles move freely
- no fixed shape
- no fixed volume

Figure 1.2 Representation of the arrangement of the particles of the same substance in the solid, liquid, and gas states.

Depending on the chemical nature of the substance, matter may exist as atoms such as $Ar(g)$, or as molecules such as $H_2O(l)$, or as ions such as Na^+ and Cl^- in $NaCl(aq)$. The term **particle** is therefore used as an inclusive term that is applied in this text to any or all of these entities of matter.

Temperature is a measure of the average kinetic energy of the particles of a substance.

This is known as the **kinetic theory** of matter. It recognizes that the average kinetic energy of the particles is directly related to the temperature of the system. The state of matter at a given temperature and pressure is determined by the strength of forces that may exist between the particles, known as **inter-particle forces.** The average kinetic energy is proportional to the temperature in kelvin, introduced on page 37.

Worked example

Which of the following has the highest average kinetic energy?

A   He at 100 °C   B H_2 at 200 °C

C O_2 at 300 °C   D H_2O at 400 °C

Solution

Answer = D. The substance at the highest temperature has the highest average kinetic energy.

Liquids and gases are referred to as **fluids,** which refers to their ability to flow. In the case of liquids it means that they take the shape of their container. Fluid properties are why **diffusion** occurs predominantly in these two states. Diffusion is the process by which the particles of a substance become evenly distributed, as a result of their random movements.

Kinetic energy (KE) refers to the energy associated with movement or motion. It is determined by the mass (*m*) and velocity (*v*) of a substance according to the relationship:

$$KE = \tfrac{1}{2}mv^2$$

As the kinetic energy of the particles of substances at the same temperature is equal, this means there is an inverse relationship between mass and velocity or speed. This is why substances with lower mass diffuse more quickly than those with greater mass, when measured at the same temperature. This is discussed in more detail in Chapter 14, Option C: Energy.

▲ Bromine liquid, $Br_2(l)$, had been placed in the lower gas jar, and its vapour has diffused to fill both jars. Bromine vaporizes readily at room temperature and the gas colour allows the diffusion to be observed. Because gas molecules can move independently of each other and do so randomly, a gas spreads out from its source in this way.

State symbols are used to show the states of the reactants and products taking part in a reaction. These are abbreviations, which are given in brackets after each term in an equation, as shown below.

State	Symbol	Example
solid	(s)	Mg(s)
liquid	(l)	$Br_2(l)$
gas	(g)	$N_2(g)$
aqueous (dissolved in water)	(aq)	HCl(aq)

For example:

$$2Na(s) + 2H_2O(l) \rightarrow 2NaOH(aq) + H_2(g)$$

Exercises

4   Classify the following mixtures as homogeneous or heterogeneous:

   (a) sand and water   **(b)** smoke   **(c)** sugar and water
   (d) salt and iron filings   **(e)** ethanol and water in wine **(f)** steel

5   Write balanced equations for the following reactions and apply state symbols to all reactants and products, assuming room temperature and pressure unless stated otherwise. If you are not familiar with the aqueous solubilities of some of these substances, you may have to look them up.

   (a) $KNO_3 \rightarrow KNO_2 + O_2$ (when heated (500 °C))
   (b) $CaCO_3 + H_2SO_4 \rightarrow CaSO_4 + CO_2 + H_2O$
   (c) $Li + H_2O \rightarrow LiOH + H_2$
   (d) $Pb(NO_3)_2 + NaCl \rightarrow PbCl_2 + NaNO_3$ (all reactants are in aqueous solution)
   (e) $C_3H_6 + O_2 \rightarrow CO_2 + H_2O$ (combustion reaction)

6   A mixture of two gases, X and Y, which both have strong but distinct smells, is released. From across the room the smell of X is detected more quickly than the smell of Y. What can you deduce about X and Y?

7   Ice floats on water. Comment on why this is not what you would expect from the kinetic theory of matter.

! It is good practice to show state symbols in all equations, even when they are not specifically requested.

Matter changes state reversibly

As the movement or kinetic energy of the particles increases with temperature, they will overcome the inter-particle forces and change state. These state changes occur at a fixed temperature and pressure for each substance, and are given specific names shown below.

sublimation

melting   evaporating/boiling

| solid | | liquid | | gas |

freezing   condensing

deposition

Sublimation, the direct inter-conversion of solid to gas without going through the liquid state, is characteristic at atmospheric pressure of some substances such as iodine, carbon dioxide, and ammonium chloride. Deposition, the reverse of sublimation that changes a gas directly to solid, is responsible for the formation of snow, frost, and hoar frost.

Note that evaporation involves the change of liquid to gas, but, unlike boiling, evaporation occurs only at the surface and takes place at temperatures below the boiling point.

▲
Drying clothes. The heat of the Sun enables all the water to evaporate from the clothes.

Ice crystals, known as Hair Ice, formed by deposition on dead wood in a forest on Vancouver Island, Canada.

Boiling, on the other hand, is a volume phenomenon, characterized by particles leaving throughout the body of the liquid – which is why bubbles occur. Boiling occurs at a specific temperature, determined by when the vapour pressure reaches the external pressure. The influence of pressure on the temperature at which this occurs is demonstrated in Figure 1.3.

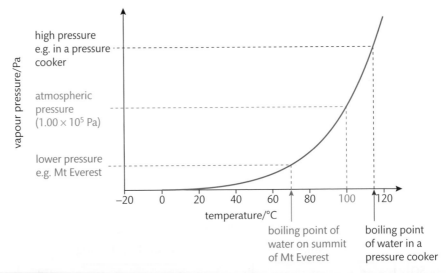

Figure 1.3 Graph showing the increase in vapour pressure with temperature. This explains why boiling point changes with pressure. The boiling point of water at three different pressures is shown.

A pressure cooker is a sealed container in which a higher pressure can be generated. This raises the boiling point of water and so cooking time decreases. Conversely, at altitude, where the atmospheric pressure is lower, the boiling point of water is reduced so it takes much longer to cook food.

A butane gas camping stove. Butane, C_4H_{10}, is stored as a liquid because the high pressure in the canister raises its boiling point. When the valve is opened the release of pressure causes it to boil, releasing a gas that can be burned.

Macrophotograph of freeze-dried instant coffee granules.

CHALLENGE YOURSELF

1 Propane (C_3H_8) and butane (C_4H_{10}) are both commonly used in portable heating devices. Their boiling points are butane –1 °C and propane –42 °C. Suggest why butane is less suitable for use in very cold climates.

Freeze-drying is an effective process for the preservation of food and some pharmaceuticals. It differs from standard methods of dehydration in that it does not use heat to evaporate water, but instead depends on the sublimation of ice. The substance to be preserved is first frozen, and then warmed gently at very low pressure which causes the ice to change directly to water vapour. The process is slow but has the significant advantage that the composition of the material, and so its flavour, are largely conserved. The freeze-dried product is stored in a moisture-free package that excludes oxygen, and can be reconstituted by the addition of water.

At night as the temperature is lowered, the rate of condensation increases. As the air temperature drops below its saturation point, known as the **dew point**, the familiar condensed water called **dew** forms. The temperature of the dew point depends on the atmospheric pressure and the water content of the air – that is, the relative humidity. A relative humidity of 100% indicates that the air is maximally saturated with water and the dew point is equal to the current temperature. Most people find this uncomfortable, as the condensation inhibits the evaporation of sweat, one of the body's main cooling mechanisms.

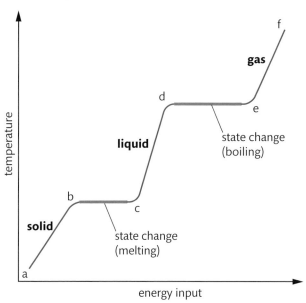

Figure 1.4 Temperature change versus energy input at fixed pressure as a solid substance is heated. The flat regions shown in red are where the state change is occurring, as heat energy is used to overcome the inter-particle forces.

A fourth state of matter, plasma, exists only at conditions of very high temperatures and pressures, such as are commonly found in space. It is characterized by atoms that have been stripped of their electrons, and so exist as positively charged ions in loose association with their electrons. Plasma is a fluid, like liquid and gas, but also generates electromagnetic forces due to the charged particles present. All matter in the stars, including our Sun, exists in the plasma state.

Simple experiments can be done to monitor the temperature change while a substance is heated and changes state. Figure 1.4 shows a typical result. The graph can be interpreted as follows:

a–b As the solid is heated, the vibrational energy of its particles increases and so the temperature increases.

b–c This is the melting point. The vibrations are sufficiently energetic for the molecules to move away from their fixed positions and form liquid. Energy added during this stage is used to break the inter-particle forces, not to raise the kinetic energy, so the temperature remains constant.

c–d As the liquid is heated, the particles gain kinetic energy and so the temperature increases.

d–e This is the boiling point. There is now sufficient energy to break all of the inter-particle forces and form gas. Note that this state change needs more energy than melting, as all the inter-particle forces must be broken. The temperature remains constant as the kinetic energy does not increase during this stage. Bubbles of gas are visible throughout the volume of the liquid.

e–f As the gas is heated under pressure, the kinetic energy of its particles continues to rise, and so does the temperature.

Experiment to measure the change in temperature of water using a temperature probe. In this example, the temperature of the water is decreasing as it cools from about 90 °C.

The global demand for refrigeration and air-conditioning systems is increasing sharply with increases in population and industrialization. It is estimated that world consumption of energy for cooling could increase tenfold by 2050, and that China will surpass the USA as the world's biggest user of energy for cooling by 2020. The increased energy demand has significant consequences for the environment, as both the energy use and the release of refrigerants such as HFCs contribute to greenhouse gas emissions, linked to climate change.

The process of refrigeration is usually based on energy changes during the evaporation and condensation cycle under changing pressure of a volatile liquid known as the **refrigerant**. At low pressure the liquid vaporizes and absorbs heat, causing cooling of the surroundings. Chlorofluorocarbons (CFCs) were commonly widely used as refrigerants, but these are now mostly phased out owing to their harmful role in causing ozone depletion. This is discussed further in Chapter 4. CFCs are largely replaced by hydrofluorocarbons (HFCs).

Exercises

8 A closed flask contains a pure substance, a brown liquid that is at its boiling point. Explain what you are likely to observe in the flask, and distinguish between the inter-particle distances and the average speeds of the particles in the two states present.

9 During very cold weather, snow often gradually disappears without melting. Explain how this is possible.

10 Explain why a burn to the skin caused by steam is more serious than a burn caused by the same amount of boiling water at the same temperature.

11 Which of the following occurs at the melting point when solid sulfur is converted to its liquid form?

  I   movement of the particles increases
  II   distance between the particles increases

  A I only   **B** II only   **C** Both I and II   **D** Neither I nor II

12 You are given a liquid substance at 80 °C and told that it has a melting point of 35 °C. You are asked to take its temperature at regular time intervals while it cools to room temperature (25 °C). Sketch the cooling curve that you would expect to obtain.

The SI (Système International d'Unités) refers to the metric system of measurement based on seven base units. These are metre (m) for length, kilogram (kg) for mass, second (s) for time, ampere (a) for electric current, kelvin (K) for temperature, candela (cd) for luminous intensity and mole (mol) for amount. All other units are derived from these. The SI system is the world's most widely used system of measurement.

1.2 The mole concept

Understandings:

- The mole is a fixed number of particles and refers to the amount, *n*, of substance.

  ### Guidance
  The value of the Avogadro's constant (L or N_A) is given in the IB data booklet in section 2 and will be given for Paper 1 questions.

- Masses of atoms are compared on a scale relative to ^{12}C and are expressed as relative atomic mass (A_r) and relative formula/molecular mass (M_r).
- Molar mass (*M*) has the units g mol⁻¹.

  ### Guidance
  The generally used unit of molar mass (g mol⁻¹) is a derived SI unit.

- The empirical and molecular formula of a compound give the simplest ratio and the actual number of atoms present in a molecule respectively.

Applications and skills:

- Calculation of the molar masses of atoms, ions, molecules, formula units.
- Solution of problems involving the relationship between the number of particles, the amount of substance in moles, and the mass in grams.
- Interconversion of the percentage composition by mass and the empirical formula.
- Determination of the molecular formula of a compound from its empirical formula and molar mass.
- Obtaining and using experimental data for deriving empirical formulas from reactions involving mass changes.

The International Bureau of Weights and Measures (BIPM according to its French initials) is an international standards organization, which aims to ensure uniformity in the application of SI units around the world.

The Avogadro constant defines the mole as the unit of amount in chemistry

A problem in studying chemical change is that atoms are too small to measure individually. For example, even a relatively large atom like gold (Au) has a mass of 3.27×10^{-25} kg – not a very useful figure when it comes to weighing it in a laboratory. But it's not really a problem, because all we need to do is to weigh an appropriately large number of atoms to give a mass that will be a useful quantity in grams. And in any case, atoms do not react individually but in very large numbers, so this approach makes sense. So how many atoms shall we lump together in our base unit of amount?

To answer this, let's first consider that atoms of different elements have different masses because they contain different numbers of particles, mostly **nucleons** in their nucleus, as we will discuss in Chapter 2. This means we can compare their masses with each other in relative terms. For example, an atom of oxygen has a mass approximately 16 times greater than an atom of hydrogen, and an atom of sulfur has a mass about twice that of an atom of oxygen. Now the good news is that these ratios will stay the same when we increase the number of atoms, *so long as we ensure we have the same number of each type.*

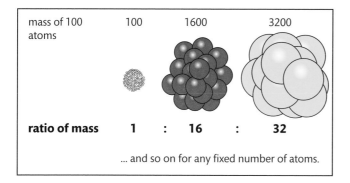

... and so on for any fixed number of atoms.

Now if we could take 6×10^{23} atoms of hydrogen, it happens that this would have a mass of 1 g. It follows from the ratios above, that *the same number of atoms* of oxygen would have a mass of 16 g while *the same number of atoms* of sulfur has a mass of 32 g. So we now have a quantity of atoms that we can measure in grams.

Amedeo Avogadro (1776–1856) was an Italian scientist who made several experimental discoveries. He clarified the distinction between atoms and molecules, and used this to propose the relationship between gas volume and number of molecules. His ideas were not, however, accepted in his time, largely due to a lack of consistent experimental evidence. After his death, when his theory was confirmed by fellow Italian Cannizzaro, his name was given in tribute to the famous constant that he helped to establish.

Figure 1.5 One hundred atoms of H, O, and S have the same mass ratio as one atom of each element, 1:16:32.

Figure 1.6 6.02×10^{23} atoms of H, O, and S have the same mass ratio by mass as one atom of each element. This number of atoms gives an amount that we can see and measure in grams. (Note that this is illustrative only; in reality hydrogen and oxygen do not occur stably as single atoms, but as diatomic molecules – as explained in Chapter 4.)

This number, accurately stated as $6.02214129 \times 10^{23}$, is known as the **Avogadro number**, and it is the basis of the unit of **amount** used in chemistry known as the **mole**. In other words, a mole of a substance contains the Avogadro number of particles. Mole, the unit of amount, is one of the base units in the SI system and has the unit symbol **mol**.

So 'mole' is simply a word that represents a number, just as 'couple' is a word for 2, 'dozen' is a word for 12, and 'score' is a word that was commonly used for 20. A mole is a very large number, bigger than we can easily imagine or ever count, but it is nonetheless a fixed number. So a mole of any substance contains that Avogadro number, 6.02×10^{23}, of particles. You can refer to a mole of atoms, molecules, ions, electrons, and so on – it can be applied to any entity as it is just a number. And from this, we can easily calculate the number of particles in any portion or multiple of a mole of a substance.

Each beaker contains one mole, 6.02×10^{23} particles, of a specific element. Each has a characteristic mass, known as its molar mass. From left to right the elements are tin (Sn), magnesium (Mg), iodine (I), and copper (Cu).

Avogadro's constant is so large that we cannot comprehend its scale. For example:
- 6.02×10^{23} pennies distributed to everyone alive would make everyone on Earth a dollar trillionaire;
- 6.02×10^{23} pencil erasers would cover the Earth to a depth of about 500 m;
- 6.02×10^{23} drops of water would fill all the oceans of the Earth many times over.

TOK What ways of knowing can we use to grasp the magnitude of Avogadro's constant even though it is beyond the scale of our everyday experience?

In Paper 1 of the IB examinations you are not allowed to use a calculator, so you may well be asked questions that you can solve by simple arithmetic and by manipulating expressions using scientific notation.

Worked example

A tablespoon holds 0.500 moles of water. How many molecules of water are present?

Solution

1.00 mole of water has 6.02×10^{23} molecules of water

$\therefore$ 0.500 moles of water has $\dfrac{0.500}{1.00} \times 6.02 \times 10^{23}$ molecules

$= 3.01 \times 10^{23}$ molecules of water

When doing multiplication or division, the answer is given to the same number of significant figures as the data value with the least number of significant figures. When doing addition or subtraction, the answer is given to the same number of decimal places as the data value with the least number of decimal places.

Worked example

A solution of water and ammonia contains 2.10×10^{23} molecules of H_2O and 8.00×10^{21} molecules of NH_3. How many moles of hydrogen atoms are present?

Solution

First total the number of hydrogen atoms:

from water H_2O: number of H atoms $= 2 \times (2.10 \times 10^{23})$
$= 4.20 \times 10^{23}$

from ammonia NH_3: number of H atoms $= 3 \times (8.00 \times 10^{21})$
$= 0.240 \times 10^{23}$

$\therefore$ total H atoms $= (4.20 \times 10^{23}) + (0.240 \times 10^{23})$
$= 4.44 \times 10^{23}$

To convert atoms to moles, divide by the Avogadro constant:

$$\frac{4.44 \times 10^{23}}{6.02 \times 10^{23}} = 0.738 \text{ mol H atoms}$$

divide by Avogadro constant, L

number of particles (N) ⟷ number of moles (n)

multiply by Avogadro constant, L

Exercises

13 Calculate how many hydrogen atoms are present in:

(a) 0.020 moles of C_2H_5OH

(b) 2.50 moles of H_2O

(c) 0.10 moles of $Ca(HCO_3)_2$

14 Propane has the formula C_3H_8. If a sample of propane contains 0.20 moles of C, how many moles of H are present?

15 Calculate the amount of sulfuric acid, H_2SO_4, which contains 6.02×10^{23} atoms of oxygen.

Dealing with Avogadro's constant to calculate the number of particles in a sample has its uses, but it still leaves us with numbers that are beyond our comprehension. What is much more useful, as you have probably realized, is the link between the Avogadro number and the mass of one mole of a substance, which is based on the relative atomic mass.

Relative atomic mass is used to compare the masses of atoms

On page 15 the numbers used to compare the masses of the elements H, O, and S are only approximate. A slight complexity is that most elements exist naturally with atoms that differ in their mass. These different atoms are known as **isotopes**, and we will look at them in Chapter 2. So a sample of an element containing billions of atoms will include a mix of these isotopes according to their relative abundance. The mass of an individual atom in the sample is therefore taken as a **weighted average** of these different masses.

Number of particles (N) = number of moles (n) × Avogadro constant (L).

Relative atomic mass, A_r, is the weighted average of one atom of an element relative to ½ of an atom of carbon-12.

The nomenclature and the reference point used for describing atomic mass have been a subject for debate since John Dalton's work on atomic structure in the early 1800s. The original term 'atomic weight' is now considered largely obsolete. Chemists and physicists previously used two different reference points for mass based on isotopes of oxygen, but since the 1960s the unified scale based on carbon-12 (^{12}C) has gained wide acceptance. The current IUPAC definition of the *unified atomic mass unit* is one-twelfth of the mass of a carbon-12 atom in its ground state with a mass of 1.66×10^{-27} kg.

A_r values are often rounded to whole numbers for quick calculations, but when using values from the IB data booklet for calculations it is usually best to use the exact value given in section 6.

CHALLENGE YOURSELF

2 Three of the compounds in the photograph are hydrated, containing water of crystallization, as described on page 23. Use the formulas given in the caption and the masses marked on the photograph to deduce which compounds are hydrated, and the full formula of each.

The relative scale for comparing the mass of atoms needs a reference point. The international convention for this is to take the specific form of carbon known as the **isotope carbon-12** (see Chapter 2) as the standard, and assign this a value of 12 units. In other words, one-twelfth of an atom of carbon-12 has a value of exactly 1.

Putting this together, we can define the **relative atomic mass** as follows:

$$\text{relative atomic mass } A_r = \frac{\text{weighted average of one atom of the element}}{\frac{1}{2}\text{ mass of one atom of carbon-12}}$$

Values for A_r do not have units as it is a relative term, which simply compares the mass of atoms against the same standard. As they are average values, they are not whole numbers; the IB data booklet in section 6 gives A_r values to two decimal places. Some examples are given below.

Element	Relative atomic mass (A_r)
hydrogen, H	1.01
carbon, C	12.01
oxygen, O	16.00
sodium, Na	22.99
sulfur, S	32.07
chlorine, Cl	35.45

You will notice that the A_r of carbon is slightly greater than the mass of the isotope carbon-12 used as the standard, suggesting that carbon has isotopes with masses slightly greater than 12. In Chapter 2 we discuss how relative atomic mass is calculated from isotope abundances, using data from mass spectrometry.

Relative formula mass is used to compare masses of compounds

We can extend the concept of relative atomic mass to compounds (and to elements occurring as molecules), to obtain the **relative formula mass**, M_r. This simply involves adding the relative atomic masses of all the atoms or ions present in its formula. Note that M_r, like A_r, is a relative term and so has no units.

One mole of different compounds, each showing the molar mass. The chemical formulas of these ionic compounds are, clockwise from lower left: NaCl, FeCl$_3$, CuSO$_4$, KI, Co(NO$_3$)$_2$ and KMnO$_4$.

Worked example

Use the values for A_r in section 6 of the IB data booklet to calculate the M_r of the following:

(a) chlorine, Cl_2

$$M_r = 35.45 \times 2 = 70.90$$

(b) ammonium nitrate, NH_4NO_3

$$M_r = 14.01 + (1.01 \times 4) + 14.01 + (16.00 \times 3) = 80.06$$

(c) aluminium sulfate, $Al_2(SO_4)_3$

$$M_r = (26.98 \times 2) + [32.07 + (16.00 \times 4)] \times 3 = 342.17$$

Molar mass is the mass of one mole of a substance

The Avogadro number is defined so that the mass of one mole of a substance is exactly equal to the substance's relative atomic mass expressed in grams. This is known as the **molar mass** and is given the symbol **M** with the unit $g\ mol^{-1}$, which is a derived SI unit. Using the examples discussed already in this chapter, we can now deduce the following:

Element or compound	Molar mass (M)
hydrogen, H	$1.01\ g\ mol^{-1}$
oxygen, O	$16.00\ g\ mol^{-1}$
sulfur, S	$32.07\ g\ mol^{-1}$
chlorine, Cl_2	$70.90\ g\ mol^{-1}$
ammonium nitrate, NH_4NO_3	$80.06\ g\ mol^{-1}$
aluminium sulfate, $Al_2(SO_4)_3$	$342.17\ g\ mol^{-1}$

From our knowledge of molar mass we can state the definition of the mole as the mass of substance that contains as many particles as there are atoms in 12 g of carbon-12.

Now we are truly able to use the concept of the mole to make that all-important link between the number of particles and their mass in grams. The key to this is conversions of grams to moles and moles to grams. In the calculations that follow, we use the following notation:

• n = number of moles (mol);
• m = mass in grams (g);
• M = molar mass ($g\ mol^{-1}$).

Note that the term *relative molecular mass* was previously used for M_r, but can accurately be applied only to substances that exist as molecules. This excludes all ionic compounds, so the term *relative formula mass* is preferred as it is a more inclusive term, not dependent on the bonding present.

Relative formula mass, M_r, is the sum of the weighted average of the masses of the atoms in a formula unit relative to one-twelfth of an atom of carbon-12.

The molar mass of a substance, M, is its relative atomic mass, A_r, or its relative formula mass, M_r, expressed in grams. It has the unit $g\ mol^{-1}$.

One mole is the mass of substance that contains as many particles as there are atoms in 12 g of carbon-12.

Dimensional analysis, or the factor-label method, is a widely used technique to determine conversion factors on the basis of cancelling the units. This method is not specifically used in the examples here, but the units are shown through the calculations. This method can be helpful to check that the units on both sides of the equation are balanced, and are appropriate for the answer, which is often a useful check on the steps taken. As in all cases, there is no one correct way to set out calculations, so long as the steps are clear.

Worked example

What is the mass of the following?

(a) 6.50 moles of NaCl

(b) 0.10 moles of OH^- ions

Solution

In all these questions, we must first calculate the molar mass, M, to know the mass of one mole in $g\ mol^{-1}$. Multiplying M by the specified number of moles, n, will then give the mass, m, in grams.

(a) $M(NaCl) = 22.99 + 35.45 = 58.44\ g\ mol^{-1}$

$$n(NaCl) = 6.50\ mol$$

$$\therefore m(NaCl) = 58.44\ g\ mol^{-1} \times 6.50\ mol = 380\ g$$

(b) OH^- ions carry a charge because electrons have been transferred, but the change to the mass is negligible and so can be ignored in calculating M.

$$M(OH^-) = 16.00 + 1.01 = 17.01\ g\ mol^{-1}$$

$$n(OH^-) = 0.10\ mol$$

$$\therefore m(OH^-) = 17.01\ g\ mol^{-1} \times 0.10\ mol = 1.7\ g$$

Note the units cancel to give the correct units for mass. This is often a useful check that we are using the terms correctly in a calculation.

Worked example

What is the amount in moles of the following?

(a) 32.50 g $(NH_4)_2SO_4$

(b) 273.45 g N_2O_5

Solution

Again we calculate the molar mass, M, to know the mass of one mole. Dividing the given mass, m, by the mass of one mole will then give the number of moles, n.

(a) $M((NH_4)_2SO_4) = [14.01 + (1.01 \times 4)] \times 2 + 32.07 + (16.00 \times 4) = 132.17\ g\ mol^{-1}$

$$m((NH_4)_2SO_4) = 32.50\ g$$

$$\therefore n((NH_4)_2SO_4) = \frac{32.50\ g}{132.17\ g\ mol^{-1}} = 0.2459\ mol$$

(b) $M(N_2O_5) = (14.01 \times 2) + (16.00 \times 5) = 108.02\ g\ mol^{-1}$

$$m(N_2O_5) = 273.45\ g$$

$$\therefore n(N_2O_5) = \frac{273.45\ g}{108.02\ g\ mol^{-1}} = 2.532\ mol$$

These simple conversions show that:

$$\textbf{number of moles (amount)} = \frac{\textbf{mass}}{\textbf{molar mass}} \qquad n\ (\textbf{mol}) = \frac{m\ (\textbf{g})}{M\ (\textbf{g mol}^{-1})}$$

This is a very useful relationship, but it is hoped that you understand how it is derived, rather than rote learn it.

$$amount = \frac{mass}{molar\ mass}$$

$$n\ (mol) = \frac{m\ (g)}{M\ (g\ mol^{-1})}$$

We can now put together the conversions shown on pages 17 and 19, to see the central role of the mole in converting from number of particles to mass in grams.

Figure 1.7 Summary of the central role of the number of moles, n, in converting between the number of particles and the mass in grams.

> ! Calculations involving mass in chemistry always involve converting grams to moles and moles to grams. Think of these conversions as fundamental tools for chemists, and so make sure you are fully comfortable with carrying them out effectively.

Exercises

* indicates you should be able to do this question without a calculator.

Note that you should refer to section 6 of the IB data booklet for the values of A_r.

16 Calculate the molar mass of the following compounds:

  (a) magnesium phosphate, $Mg_3(PO_4)_2$ **(b)** ascorbic acid (vitamin C), $C_6H_8O_6$
  (c) calcium nitrate, $Ca(NO_3)_2$ **(d)** hydrated sodium thiosulfate, $Na_2S_2O_3.5H_2O$

17 Calcium arsenate, $Ca_3(AsO_4)_2$, is a poison which was widely used as an insecticide. What is the mass of 0.475 mol of calcium arsenate?

18* How many moles of carbon dioxide are there in 66 g of carbon dioxide, CO_2?

19 How many moles of chloride ions (Cl^-) are there in 0.50 g of copper(II) chloride, $CuCl_2$?

20 How many carbon atoms are there in 36.55 g of diamond (which is pure carbon)?

21* What is the mass in grams of a 0.500 mol sample of sucrose, $C_{12}H_{22}O_{11}$?

22* Which contains the greater number of particles, 10.0 g of water (H_2O) or 10.0 g of mercury (Hg)?

23* Put the following in descending order of mass.

  1.0 mol N_2H_4 2.0 mol N_2 3.0 mol NH_3 25.0 mol H_2

The empirical formula of a compound gives the simplest ratio of its atoms

Magnesium burns brightly in air to form a white solid product, and we might ask how many atoms of magnesium combine with how many atoms of oxygen in this reaction? Thanks to the mole, and its central role in relating the number of particles to a mass that can be measured, we can find the answer to this quite easily.

All we have to do is:

- burn a known mass of Mg, and from this calculate the moles of Mg;
- calculate the mass of oxygen that reacted from the increase in mass, and from this calculate the moles of O;
- express the ratio of moles Mg to moles O in its simplest form;
- the ratio of moles is the ratio of atoms, so we can deduce the simplest formula of magnesium oxide.

Magnesium burns with a bright white flame, combining with oxygen from the air to form the white solid magnesium oxide.

Figure 1.8 Apparatus used to investigate mass changes on burning magnesium.

Experiment to determine the empirical formula of MgO

Full details of how to carry out this experiment with a worksheet are available on your eBook.

A sample of magnesium is heated and the change in mass recorded. From this, the ratio of moles of magnesium to oxygen can be determined.

Sample results

	Mass / g ± 0.001	Observations
mass of crucible + lid	19.777	
mass of crucible + lid + Mg	19.820	magnesium metal has grey, shiny appearance
mass of crucible + lid + white solid product	19.849	metal burned with bright flame, leaving grey-white powder

Processed data

	Magnesium, Mg	Oxygen, O
mass / g ± 0.002	0.043	0.029
M / g mol^{-1}	24.31	16.00
moles / mol	0.00177	0.00181

ratio moles Mg : moles O = 1 : 1.02

So the ratio atoms Mg : atoms O approximates to 1 : 1

So the formula of magnesium oxide is MgO.

The fact that the experimental result is not exactly 1 : 1 indicates there are some errors in the experiment. We can consider possible systematic errors here, such as:

- the Mg weighed is not all pure;
- not all the Mg weighed reacted;
- the product was not magnesium oxide only;
- loss of Mg or of product occurred;
- change in the mass of the crucible occurred during handling and heating.

Modifications to the experimental design can be considered, which help to reduce the experimental error.

NATURE OF SCIENCE

Scientific investigations based on quantitative measurements are subject to errors, both random and systematic. Analysis of the impact of these errors is inherent in the practice of science. It is good practice in all experimental work to record the sources of errors, consider their effect on the results, and suggest modifications that aim to reduce their impact. This is discussed in detail in Chapter 11. Scientists have the responsibility to communicate their results as realistically and honestly as possible, and this must include uncertainties and errors.

The empirical formula is the simplest whole-number ratio of the elements in a compound.

From the result of this experiment, we conclude that the formula of magnesium oxide is MgO. This is known as an **empirical formula**, which gives the simplest whole-number ratio of the elements in a compound.

Worked example

Which of the following are empirical formulas?

I C_6H_6

II C_3H_8

III N_2O_4

IV $Pb(NO_3)_2$

Solution

Only II and IV are empirical formulas, as their elements are in the simplest whole-number ratio. I has the empirical formula CH; III has the empirical formula NO_2.

The formulas of all ionic compounds, made of a metal and a non-metal such as magnesium oxide, are empirical formulas. This is explained when we look at ionic bonding in Chapter 4. But as we see in the worked example above, the formulas of covalently bonded compounds, usually made of different non-metal elements, are not always empirical formulas. This is explained in the next section on molecular formulas.

Empirical formulas can be deduced from experimental results, usually involving combustion, that give the masses of each of the elements present in a sample. It is a similar process to the one we used for magnesium oxide.

Worked example

A sample of urea contains 1.210 g N, 0.161 g H, 0.480 g C, and 0.640 g O. What is the empirical formula of urea?

Solution

• Convert the mass of each element to moles by dividing by its molar mass, M.
• Divide by the smallest number to give the ratio.
• Approximate to the nearest whole number.

	Nitrogen, N	Hydrogen, H	Carbon, C	Oxygen, O
mass / g	1.121	0.161	0.480	0.640
M / g mol^{-1}	14.01	1.01	12.01	16.00
number of moles / mol	0.080	0.159	0.0399	0.0400
divide by smallest	2.00	3.98	1.00	1.00
nearest whole number ratio	2	4	1	1

So the empirical formula of urea is N_2H_4CO, usually written as $CO(NH_2)_2$.

A modification of this type of question is to analyse the composition of a **hydrated salt**. These are compounds that contain a fixed ratio of water molecules, known as **water of crystallization**, within the crystalline structure of the compound. The water of crystallization can be driven off by heating, and the change in mass used to calculate the ratio of water molecules to the **anhydrous salt**. The formula of the hydrated salt is shown with a dot before the number of molecules of water, for example $CaCl_2.4H_2O$.

It is common for the composition data to be given in the form of percentages by mass, and we use these figures in the same way to deduce the ratio of atoms present. Percentage data effectively give us the mass present in a 100 g sample of the compound.

Experiment to determine the formula of hydrated barium chloride, $BaCl_2.xH_2O$

Full details of how to carry out this experiment with a worksheet are available on your eBook.

Hydrated copper(II) sulfate, $CuSO_4.5H_2O$, is blue due to the presence of water of crystallization within the structure of the crystals. The anhydrous form is white, as shown in the lower part of the tube. Heating removes the water molecules, leading to the colour being lost. The process is reversible, and the addition of water to the anhydrous crystals restores their blue colour.

▼

Fertilizers contain nutrients that are added to the soil, usually to replace those used by cultivated plants. The elements needed in the largest quantities, so-called **macronutrients**, include nitrogen, phosphorus and potassium. Fertilizers are often labelled with an N-P-K rating, such as 30-15-30, to show the quantities of each of these three elements. The numbers indicate respectively the percentage by mass N, percentage by mass diphosphorus pentoxide, P_2O_5, and percentage by mass potassium oxide, K_2O. The percentage data for P_2O_5 and K_2O represent the most oxidized forms of elemental phosphorus and potassium present in the fertilizer. Ammonium salts are the most common source of nitrogen used in fertilizers.

CHALLENGE YOURSELF

3 A fertilizer has an N-P-K rating of 18-51-20. Use the information in the box above to determine the percentage by mass of nitrogen, phosphorus and potassium present.

When working with percentage figures, always check that they add up to 100. Sometimes an element is omitted from the data and you are expected to deduce its identity and percentage from information given.

GENERAL PURPOSE 20-10-20 **(For continuous liquid feed programs)**	
Guaranteed analysis	**F1143**
Total nitrogen (N)	20%
7.77% ammoniacal nitrogen	
12.23% nitrate nitrogen	
Available phosphate (P_2O_5)	10%
Soluble potash (K_2O)	20%
Magnesium (Mg)(Total)	0.05%
0.05% Water soluble magnesium (Mg)	
Boron (B)	0.0068%
Copper (Cu)	0.0036%
0.0036% Chelated copper (Cu)	
Iron (Fe)	0.05%
0.05% Chelated iron (Fe)	
Manganese (Mn)	0.025%
0.025% Chelated manganese (Mn)	
Molybdenum (Mo)	0.0009%
Zinc (Zn)	0.0025%
0.0025% Chelated zinc (Zn)	

Derived from: ammonium nitrate, potassium phosphate, potassium nitrate, magnesium sulfate, boric acid, copper EDTA, manganese EDTA, iron EDTA, zinc EDTA, sodium molybdate. Potential acidity: 487 lbs. calcium carbonate equivalent per ton.

Figure 1.9 The label on a fertilizer bag shows the percentage by mass of macro- and micro-nutrients that it contains.

Worked example

The mineral celestine consists mostly of a compound of strontium, sulfur and oxygen. It is found by combustion analysis to have the composition 47.70% by mass Sr, 17.46% S, and the remainder is O. What is its empirical formula?

Solution

Here we need first to calculate the percentage of oxygen by subtracting the total given masses from 100.

$$\% \, O = 100 - (47.70 + 17.46) = 34.84$$

	Strontium, Sr	Sulfur, S	Oxygen, O
% by mass	47.70	17.46	34.84
M / g mol^{-1}	87.62	32.07	16.00
number of moles / mol	0.5443	0.5444	2.178
divide by smallest	1.000	1.000	4.001

So the empirical formula of the mineral is $SrSO_4$.

An understanding of percentage by mass data helps us to evaluate information that we commonly see on products such as foods, drinks, pharmaceuticals, household cleaners as well as fertilizers. For example, a common plant fertilizer is labelled as pure sodium tetraborate pentahydrate, $Na_2B_4O_7.5H_2O$ and claims to be 15.2% boron. How accurate is this claim?

Percentage composition by mass can be calculated from the empirical formula

We can see in the example above that, even though the mineral celestine has only one atom of strontium for every four atoms of oxygen, strontium nonetheless accounts for 47.70% of its mass. This, of course, is because an atom of strontium has significantly greater mass than an atom of oxygen, and the percentage by mass of an element in a compound depends on the *total* contribution of its atoms. We can calculate this as follows.

Worked example

What is the percentage by mass of N, H, and O in the compound ammonium nitrate, NH_4NO_3?

Solution

First calculate the molar mass M

$$M(NH_4NO_3) = 14.01 + (1.01 \times 4) + 14.01 + (16.00 \times 3) = 80.06 \text{ g mol}^{-1}$$

Then for each element total the mass of its atoms, divide by M and multiply by 100:

$$\% N = \frac{14.01 \times 2}{80.06} \times 100 = 34.99\% \text{ by mass}$$

$$\% H = \frac{1.01 \times 4}{80.06} \times 100 = 5.05\% \text{ by mass}$$

$$\% O = \frac{16.00 \times 3}{80.06} \times 100 = 59.96\% \text{ by mass}$$

(alternatively, this last term can be calculated by subtraction from 100)

Finally check the numbers add up to 100%.

The molecular formula of a compound gives the actual number of atoms in a molecule

The empirical formula gives us the simplest ratio of atoms present in a compound, but this often does not give the full information about the actual *number* of atoms in a molecule. For example, CH_2 is an empirical formula. There is no molecule that exists with just one atom of carbon and two atoms of hydrogen, but there are many molecules with multiples of this ratio, such as C_2H_4, C_3H_6 and so on. These formulas, which show all the atoms present in a molecule, are called **molecular formulas**.

The molecular formula can be deduced from the empirical formula if the molar mass is known.

$$x \text{ (mass of empirical formula)}_x = M \text{ where } x \text{ is an integer}$$

> The molecular formula shows all the atoms present in a molecule. It is a multiple of the empirical formula.

Worked example

Calomel is a compound once used in the treatment of syphilis. It has the empirical formula HgCl and a molar mass of 472.08 g mol^{-1}. What is its molecular formula?

> **TOK** Assigning numbers to the masses of elements has allowed chemistry to develop into a physical science. To what extent is mathematics effective in describing the natural world?

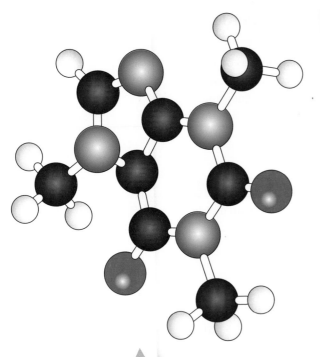

Figure 1.10 A molecular model of the stimulant caffeine. The atoms are colour coded as follows: black = carbon, grey = hydrogen, red = oxygen, blue = nitrogen. Can you deduce the molecular formula, the empirical formula, and the molar mass of caffeine?

Solution

First calculate the mass of the empirical formula:

$$\text{mass(HgCl)} = 200.59 + 35.45 = 236.04 \text{ g mol}^{-1}$$

$$\text{So } (236.04)_x = M = 472.08$$

$$\therefore x = 2$$

$$\text{molecular formula} = Hg_2Cl_2$$

Combustion analysis usually gives data on the mass of compounds formed

The data presented so far may suggest that combustion analysis directly gives information on the relative masses of individual elements in a compound. In fact this is rarely the case, but instead elements are converted into new compounds, typically their oxides, by reaction with oxygen. So the primary data obtained are the masses of carbon dioxide, water, sulfur dioxide, and so on, which are measured by infra-red absorption, as described in Chapter 11. Processing these data simply involves an extra step.

Worked example

A 0.5438 g sample of a compound known to contain only carbon, hydrogen, and oxygen was burned completely in oxygen. The products were 1.0390 g CO_2 and 0.6369 g H_2O. Determine the empirical formula of the compound.

Solution

First we must convert the mass of each compound to moles in the usual way. From the number of moles of CO_2 and H_2O we can deduce the number of moles of C atoms and H atoms.

$$n(CO_2) = \frac{1.0390 \text{ g}}{12.01 + (16.00 \times 2) \text{ g mol}^{-1}} = 0.02361 \text{ mol } CO_2 \Rightarrow 0.02361 \text{ mol C atoms}$$

$$n(H_2O) = \frac{0.6369 \text{ g}}{(1.01 \times 2) + 16.00 \text{ g mol}^{-1}} = 0.03534 \text{ mol } H_2O \Rightarrow 0.03534 \times 2$$
$$= 0.07068 \text{ mol H atoms}$$

In order to know the mass of O in the original sample, we must convert the number of moles of C and H atoms to mass by multiplying by their molar mass, M:

$$\text{mass C} = 0.02361 \text{ mol} \times 12.01 \text{ g mol}^{-1} = 0.2836 \text{ g}$$

$$\text{mass H} = 0.07068 \text{ mol} \times 1.01 \text{ g mol}^{-1} = 0.07139 \text{ g}$$

$$\therefore \text{ mass O} = 0.5438 - (0.2836 + 0.07139) = 0.1888 \text{ g}$$

$$\text{mol O atoms} = 0.1888 \text{ g}/16.00 \text{ g mol}^{-1} = 0.01180 \text{ mol}$$

Now we can proceed as with the previous examples, converting mass of O to moles and then comparing the mole ratios.

	Carbon, C	Hydrogen, H	Oxygen, O
mass / g			0.1888
number of moles / mol	0.02361	0.07068	0.01180
divide by smallest	2.001	5.999	1.000
nearest whole-number ratio	2	6	1

So the empirical formula is C_2H_6O.

Exercises

24 Give the empirical formulas of the following compounds:

(a) ethyne, C_2H_2 (b) glucose, $C_6H_{12}O_6$ (c) sucrose, $C_{12}H_{22}O_{11}$
(d) octane, C_8H_{18} (e) oct-1-yne, C_8H_{14} (f) ethanoic acid, CH_3COOH

25 A sample of a compound contains only the elements sodium, sulfur and oxygen. It is found by analysis to contain 0.979 g Na, 1.365 g S and 1.021 g O. Determine its empirical formula.

26 A sample of a hydrated compound was analysed and found to contain 2.10 g Co, 1.14 g S, 2.28 g O and 4.50 g H_2O. Determine its empirical formula.

27 A street drug has the following composition: 83.89% C, 10.35% H, 5.76% N. Determine its empirical formula.

28 The following compounds are used in the production of fertilizers. Determine which has the highest percentage by mass of nitrogen: NH_3, $CO(NH_2)_2$, $(NH_4)_2SO_4$.

29 A compound has a formula M_3N where M is a metal element and N is nitrogen. It contains 0.673 g of N per gram of the metal M. Determine the relative atomic mass of M and so its identity.

30 Compounds of cadmium are used in the construction of photocells. Deduce which of the following has the highest percentage by mass of cadmium: CdS, CdSe, CdTe.

31 Benzene is a hydrocarbon, a compound of carbon and hydrogen only. It is found to contain 7.74% H by mass. Its molar mass is 78.10 g mol^{-1}. Determine its empirical and molecular formula.

32 A weak acid has a molar mass of 162 g mol^{-1}. Analysis of a 0.8821 g sample showed the composition by mass is 0.0220 g H, 0.3374 g P and the remainder is O. Determine its empirical and molecular formulas.

33 ATP is an important molecule in living cells. A sample with a mass of 0.8138 g was analysed and found to contain 0.1927 g C, 0.02590 g H, 0.1124 g N, and 0.1491 g P. The remainder was O. Determine the empirical formula of ATP. Its formula mass was found to be 507 g mol^{-1}. Determine its molecular formula.

34 A 0.30 g sample of a compound that contains only carbon, hydrogen and oxygen was burned in excess oxygen. The products were 0.66 g of carbon dioxide and 0.36 g of water. Determine the empirical formula of the compound.

35 You are asked to write your name on a suitable surface, using a piece of chalk that is pure calcium carbonate, $CaCO_3$. How could you calculate the number of carbon atoms in your signature?

How many atoms of calcium are in Avogadro's name written in chalk?

1.3 Reacting masses and volumes

Understandings:

- Reactants can be either limiting or excess.
- The experimental yield can be different from the theoretical yield.
- Avogadro's law enables the mole ratio of reacting gases to be determined from volumes of the gases.
- The molar volume of an ideal gas is a constant at specified temperature and pressure.

Guidance
Values for the molar volume of an ideal gas are given in the IB data booklet in section 2.

- The molar concentration of a solution is determined by the amount of solute and the volume of solution.

Guidance
The use of square brackets to denote molar concentration is required.

- A standard solution is one of known concentration.

Applications and skills:

- Solution of problems relating to reacting quantities, limiting and excess reactants, theoretical, experimental and percentage yields.
- Calculation of reacting volumes of gases using Avogadro's law.
- Solution of problems and analysis of graphs involving the relationship between temperature, pressure and volume for a fixed mass of an ideal gas.
- Solution of problems relating to the ideal gas equation.

Guidance
The ideal gas equation, $PV = nRT$, and the value of the gas constant (R), are given in the IB data booklet in sections 1 and 2.

- Explanation of the deviation of real gases from ideal behaviour at low temperature and high pressure.
- Obtaining and using experimental values to calculate the molar mass of a gas from the ideal gas equation.
- Solution of problems involving molar concentration, amount of solute and volume of solution.

Guidance
Units of concentration to include $g\ dm^{-3}$, $mol\ dm^{-3}$ and parts per million (ppm).

- Use of the experimental method of titration to calculate the concentration of a solution by reference to a standard solution.

Chemical equations show reactants combining in a fixed molar ratio

Chemical change, as summarized in chemical equations, is simply an expression of reactants combining in fixed ratios to form products. The most convenient means to express this ratio is as moles, as that gives us a means of relating the number of particles that react to the mass that we can measure. So, for example, when methane, CH_4, burns in air, we can conclude the following, all from the balanced chemical equation.

	$CH_4(g)$	$+$	$2O_2(g)$	$\rightarrow$	$CO_2(g)$	$+$	$2H_2O(g)$
Reacting ratio by mole:	1 mole		2 moles		1 mole		2 moles
Reacting ratio by mass:	16.05 g		64.00 g		44.01 g		36.04 g

80.05 g reactant   80.05 g product

(The figures for total mass of reactant and product are just a check, as we know something would be wrong if they did not equate.)

The Bunsen burner controls the combustion of methane, CH_4, and is often used as a source of heat in the laboratory.

This simple interpretation of equations, going directly from coefficients to molar ratios, opens the door to a wide range of calculations involving reacting masses.

Worked example

Calculate the mass of carbon dioxide produced from the complete combustion of 1.00 g of methane.

Solution

Write the balanced equation and deduce the mole ratio as above. Then pick out from the question the terms that we need to analyse – these are marked in red, and are the species where we need to convert moles to grams.

$$CH_4(g) + 2O_2(g) \rightarrow CO_2(g) + 2H_2O(g)$$

Reacting ratio by mole:	1 mole	1 mole
Reacting ratio by mass / g:	16.05	44.01
For 1.00 g methane:	1.00	x

Now solve the ratio, shown here using cross-multiplication, to determine the value of x.

$$\frac{g\ CH_4}{g\ CO_2} = \frac{16.05}{44.01} = \frac{1.00}{x}$$

$$x = \frac{1.00 \times 44.01}{16.05}\ g\ CO_2 = 2.74\ g\ CO_2$$

All questions on reacting ratios involve a variation of this approach:

- write the balanced equation;
- work out the mole ratio for the species identified in the question;
- work out the reacting ratio by mass for these species, using $m = nM$;
- insert the data from the question and solve the ratio.

Worked example

Iodine chloride, ICl, can be made by the following reaction:

$$2I_2 + KIO_3 + 6HCl \rightarrow 5ICl + KCl + 3H_2O$$

Calculate the mass of iodine, I_2, needed to prepare 28.60 g of ICl by this reaction.

Solution

The relevant terms from the question are I_2 and ICl, so these are our focus.

$$2I_2 + KIO_3 + 6HCl \rightarrow 5ICl + KCl + 3H_2O$$

reacting ratio by mole:	2 moles	5 moles
reacting ratio by mass:	$2 \times (126.90 \times 2)$	$5 \times (126.90 + 35.45)$
	= 507.60 g	= 811.75 g
For 28.60 g ICl:	x	28.60 g

$$\frac{g\ I_2}{g\ ICl} = \frac{507.60}{811.75} = \frac{x}{28.60}$$

$$x = \frac{507.60 \times 28.60}{811.75}\ g\ I_2 = 17.88\ g\ I_2$$

Remember to convert between mass and moles by using $n = \dfrac{m}{M}$ or $m = nM$.

It is common for people to waste time solving questions like this by doing the mole to gram conversions for all the species represented in the equation. You can save yourself a lot of trouble by focusing only on the terms indicated in the question, as shown in this example.

The theoretical yield is determined by the limiting reactant

Imagine that you are following a recipe to make 12 cookies. It calls for you to mix two eggs with four cups of flour. The problem is that you only have one egg. You will quickly realize that this means you can use only two cups of flour and end up with only six cookies. We could say that the number of eggs *limited* the amount of product.

In many chemical reactions the relative amounts of reactants available to react together will similarly affect the amount of product. The reactant that determines the quantity of product is known as the **limiting reactant**. Other reactants will therefore not be fully used, and are said to be in **excess**. Identifying the limiting reactant is therefore a crucial step before we can calculate the expected quantity of product. The **theoretical yield**, which is usually expressed in grams or moles, refers to the maximum amount of product obtainable, assuming 100% of the limiting reactant is converted to product.

Note that identification of the limiting reactant depends on the *mole ratios* in the balanced chemical equation for the reaction. This means that if reactant quantities are given in grams, they must first be converted to moles.

The concept of limiting reactant is often useful in the design of experiments and synthetic processes. By deliberately making one reactant available in an amount greater than that determined by its mole ratio in the balanced equation, it ensures that the other reactant is limiting and so will be fully used up. For example, in order to remove lead ions in lead nitrate from a contaminated water supply, sodium carbonate, Na_2CO_3, is added to precipitate lead carbonate as shown in the equation:

$Pb(NO_3)_2(aq) + Na_2CO_3(aq)$
limiting   excess

$\rightarrow PbCO_3(s) + 2NaNO_3(aq)$

By using excess Na_2CO_3, this ensures that *all* the lead ions react and so are removed from the water supply.

Worked example

Nitrogen gas, N_2, can be prepared from this reaction:

$$2NH_3(g) + 3CuO(s) \rightarrow N_2(g) + 3Cu(s) + 3H_2O(g)$$

If 18.1 g NH_3 are reacted with 90.40 g CuO, determine the mass of N_2 that can be formed.

Solution

First we must determine the limiting reactant. We convert the mass of reactants to moles, and then compare the mole ratio in the balanced equation with the mole ratio of reactants given.

$$n(NH_3) = \frac{18.1 \text{ g}}{14.01 + (3 \times 1.01) \text{ g mol}^{-1}} = 1.06 \text{ mol NH}_3$$

$$n(CuO) = \frac{90.40 \text{ g}}{63.55 + 16.00 \text{ g mol}^{-1}} = 1.14 \text{ mol CuO}$$

mole ratio from equation: $\frac{NH_3}{CuO} = \frac{2}{3} = 0.667$

mole ratio from given masses: $\frac{NH_3}{CuO} = \frac{1.06}{1.14} = 0.930$

As the ratio $NH_3 : CuO$ of the given masses is *larger* than the required ratio in the equation, it means NH_3 is in excess and CuO is the limiting reactant.

This means that the amount of N_2 that can form will be determined by the amount of CuO. This is now similar to the earlier questions, where we write out the equation and focus on the terms identified in the question.

$$2NH_3(g) + 3CuO(s) \rightarrow N_2(g) + 3Cu(s) + 3H_2O(g)$$

reacting ratio by mole: 3 moles   1 mole

for 1.14 moles CuO: 1.14 x

mole ratio $\frac{CuO}{N_2} = \frac{3}{1} = \frac{1.14}{x}$ $\therefore x = \frac{1.14 \times 1}{3} = 0.380 \text{ mol N}_2$

$\therefore$ mass $N_2 = 0.380 \text{ mol} \times M(N_2) \text{ g mol}^{-1} = 0.380 \text{ mol} \times 28.02 \text{ g mol}^{-1} = 10.7 \text{ g N}_2$

There are alternate approaches to determining the limiting reactant, such as calculating which given amount of reactant would yield the smallest amount of product. But in essence, all questions on limiting reactant and theoretical yield involve comparing the mole ratio of given masses of reactants with the coefficients in the equation. This is a summary of the steps:

- write the balanced equation and focus on the mole ratio of reactants;
- convert the given mass of reactants to moles;
- compare the given mole ratios with the ratio of coefficients in the equation;
- identify the limiting reactant from the above ratios;
- calculate the moles of product from the given moles of limiting reactant.

The limiting reactant determines the amount of product that can form. The theoretical yield is the quantity of product that can form from the complete conversion of the limiting reactant.

Sometimes it is useful to measure how much excess reactant will remain when all the limiting reactant has been used up and the reaction stops. One example of this is a technique called **back-titration**, which analyses excess acid or alkali after a reaction is complete, and so indirectly measures the amount of a limiting reactant. This is explained on page 50.

A simple example of how to calculate the excess is shown below using an example of burning CH_4, when 1 mole of CH_4 and 1 mole of O_2 are supplied.

$$CH_4(g) \; + \; 2O_2(g) \; \rightarrow \; CO_2(g) \; + \; 2H_2O(g)$$

reacting ratio by mole:	1	2	
reactant ratio given:	1	1	

$\Rightarrow O_2$ is limiting reactant

mole ratio at the end of reaction: 0.5   0   0.5   1

So 0.5 moles CH_4 will be unreacted at the end of the reaction.

We will study more examples of this type of question in the next section.

The percentage yield can be calculated from the experimental and theoretical yields

The answer to the Worked example above, 10.7 g N_2 is known as the theoretical yield, because it assumes that *all* of the CuO was converted to N_2 with no loss, impurities present, wastage or incomplete reaction. In reality, all of the above happen to different extents in most chemical reactions, and so the theoretical yield is usually different from the actual or **experimental yield**.

When we compare the experimental yield with the theoretical yield, we get a measure of the efficiency of the conversion of reactants to products. This is usually expressed as the **percentage yield**, defined as follows:

$$\text{percentage yield} = \frac{\text{experimental yield}}{\text{theoretical yield}} \times 100\%$$

In your own experiments, you may often be able to calculate the percentage yield of product in evaluating the results. In industry, this is a very important calculation for determining the efficiency of a process such as the synthesis of a drug in the pharmaceutical industry. Many aspects of green chemistry focus on ways to increase the yield of product by reducing wastage.

▲
Industrial plants such as this oil refinery need to be able to track the efficiency of the chemical reactions taking place. Measuring the yield of product is an essential part of this.

Worked example

The previous Worked example on the synthesis of N_2 from NH_3 and CuO had a theoretical yield of 10.7 g N_2 from the starting amounts of reactants. Under the same conditions, an experiment produced 8.35 g N_2. Determine the percentage yield.

Solution

$$\text{percentage yield} = \frac{\text{experimental yield}}{\text{theoretical yield}} \times 100\%$$

$$\therefore \text{percentage yield} = \frac{8.35 \text{ g}}{10.7 \text{ g}} \times 100 = 78.0\%$$

Exercises

36 Iron ore can be reduced to iron by the following reaction:

$$Fe_2O_3(s) + 3H_2(g) \rightarrow 2Fe + 3H_2O(l)$$

  (a) How many moles of Fe can be made from 1.25 moles of Fe_2O_3?
  (b) How many moles of H_2 are needed to make 3.75 moles of Fe?
  (c) If the reaction yields 12.50 moles of H_2O, what mass of Fe_2O_3 was used up?

37 Lighters commonly use butane, C_4H_{10}, as the fuel.

  (a) Formulate the equation for the combustion of butane.
  (b) Determine the mass of butane that burned when 2.46 g water were produced.

38 Booster rockets for the space shuttle use the following reaction:

$$3Al(s) + 3NH_4ClO_4(s) \rightarrow Al_2O_3(s) + AlCl_3(s) + 3NO(g) + 6H_2O(g)$$

Calculate the mass of NH_4ClO_4 that should be added to this fuel mixture to react completely with every kilogram of Al.

39 Limestone is mostly calcium carbonate, $CaCO_3$, but also contains other minerals. When heated, the $CaCO_3$ decomposes into CaO and CO_2. A 1.605 g sample of limestone was heated and gave off 0.657 g of CO_2.

  (a) Formulate the equation for the thermal decomposition of calcium carbonate.
  (b) Determine the percentage mass of $CaCO_3$ in the limestone.
  (c) State the assumptions that you are making in this calculation.

40 Methanol, CH_3OH, is a useful fuel that can be made as follows:

$$CO(g) + 2H_2(g) \rightarrow CH_3OH(l)$$

A reaction mixture used 12.0 g of H_2 and 74.5 g of CO.

  (a) Determine the theoretical yield of CH_3OH.
  (b) Calculate the amount of the excess reactant that remains unchanged at the end of the reaction.

41 The dry-cleaning solvent 1,2-dichloroethane, $C_2H_4Cl_2$, is prepared from the following reaction:

$$C_2H_4(g) + Cl_2(g) \rightarrow C_2H_4Cl_2(l)$$

Determine the mass of product that can be formed from 15.40 g of C_2H_4 and 3.74 g of Cl_2.

42 Calcium carbonate, $CaCO_3$, is able to remove sulfur dioxide, SO_2, from waste gases by a reaction in which they react in a 1 : 1 stoichiometric ratio to form equimolar amounts of $CaSO_3$. When 255 g of $CaCO_3$ reacted with 135 g of SO_2, 198 g of $CaSO_3$ were formed. Determine the percentage yield of $CaSO_3$.

43 Pentyl ethanoate, $CH_3COOC_5H_{11}$, which smells like bananas, is produced from the esterification reaction:

$$CH_3COOH(aq) + C_5H_{11}OH(aq) \rightarrow CH_3COOC_5H_{11}(aq) + H_2O(l)$$

A reaction uses 3.58 g of CH_3COOH and 4.75 g of $C_5H_{11}OH$ and has a yield of 45.00%. Determine the mass of ester that forms.

44 A chemist has to make a 100 g sample of chlorobenzene, C_6H_5Cl, from the following reaction:

$$C_6H_6 + Cl_2 \rightarrow C_6H_5Cl + HCl$$

Determine the minimum quantity of benzene, C_6H_6, that can be used to achieve this with a yield of 65%.

Avogadro's law directly relates gas volumes to moles

All the examples above use mass as a way to measure amount, the number of moles. But in the laboratory we often work with liquids and gases, where *volume* is a more convenient measure. So what is the relationship between gas volume and number of moles?

Consider the following demonstration where two gas jars are each filled with different gases – hydrogen (H_2) in flask A and bromine (Br_2) in flask B. The flasks are at the same temperature and pressure and have equal volumes.

It is known, from many experimental measurements on gas volumes, that the number of particles in the two flasks above is the same. At first this might seem surprising – after all bromine molecules are much larger and heavier than hydrogen molecules.

But we need to consider the nature of the gaseous state, and as we learned on page 9, remember that the particles in a gas are widely spaced out with only negligible forces between them. In simple terms, most of a gas volume is empty space. And for this reason the chemical nature of the gas is irrelevant to its volume. Gas volume is determined only by the number of particles, and by the temperature and pressure.

This understanding is known as Avogadro's law, which states that:

Equal volumes of all gases, when measured at the same temperature and pressure, contain an equal number of particles.

Alternatively, it can be stated that equal numbers of particles of all gases, when measured at the same temperature and pressure, occupy equal volumes.

Using V for volume and n for number of moles

$$V \propto n$$

This relationship enables us to relate gas volumes (of any gas) to the number of moles, and so to reacting ratios in equations.

A   B

Figure 1.11 Flask A contains hydrogen molecules, flask B contains bromine molecules. The two flasks are under the same conditions of temperature and pressure.

 Airbags have become a standard safety fitting in many vehicles. They are designed to act as a cushion or shock absorber by inflating rapidly on sudden impact of the vehicle during a collision. Airbags work on the principle of a chemical reaction triggered by the impact producing a gaseous product that causes a sudden volume change. The key reaction used is the conversion of sodium azide, NaN_3, to nitrogen gas, N_2. To avoid the production of dangerously reactive sodium metal, potassium nitrate, KNO_3, and silicon dioxide, SiO_2, are also included so that harmless silicates are produced instead.

Illustration of an airbag and seatbelt in action during a car accident. On impact, the airbag inflates and the seatbelt slows the forward force of the body, protecting the driver's head and chest.

Worked example

40 cm³ of carbon monoxide are reacted with 40 cm³ of oxygen in the reaction:

$$2CO(g) + O_2(g) \rightarrow 2CO_2(g)$$

What volume of carbon dioxide is produced? (Assume all volumes are measured at the same temperature and pressure.)

CHALLENGE YOURSELF

5 Use the explanation on page 33 to deduce the chemical equations for the reactions taking place in a deployed air bag.

Figure 1.12 These four balloons are all filled with 1 dm³ of gas. At 25 °C and 100 kPa, they each contain 0.044 mol or 2.65 × 10²² atoms or molecules. Which balloon is the heaviest?

Note that STP (standard temperature and pressure) is not the same as the 'standard state', which is used in thermodynamic data and explained in Chapter 5.

STP refers to a temperature of 273 K and a pressure of 100 kPa.

Solution

First identify the mole ratios in the equation:

$$2CO(g) + O_2(g) \rightarrow 2CO_2(g)$$
$$\text{2 moles} \quad \text{1 mole} \quad \text{2 moles}$$

The mole ratio is equal to the ratio of reacting gas volumes, so:

$$2CO(g) + O_2(g) \rightarrow 2CO_2(g)$$
$$40\,cm^3 \quad 20\,cm^3 \quad 40\,cm^3$$

Therefore 40 cm³ of carbon dioxide are produced. (Oxygen is in excess by 20 cm³.)

Worked example

When 10 cm³ of a gaseous hydrocarbon (a compound containing only carbon and hydrogen) is burned in excess oxygen, the products consist of 30 cm³ of carbon dioxide and 30 cm³ of water vapour, measured under the same conditions of temperature and pressure. Determine the molecular formula of the hydrocarbon.

Solution

'Excess' oxygen indicates that the combustion reaction is complete.

$$C_xH_y + \text{excess } O_2 \rightarrow CO_2 + H_2O$$

| volumes: | 10 cm³ | 30 cm³ | 30 cm³ |
| ratio of volumes / mole ratio: | 1 | 3 | 3 |

∴ 1 molecule hydrocarbon → 3 molecules CO₂ + 3 molecules H₂O
3 C atoms   6 H atoms

The molecular formula is C_3H_6.

All gases under the same conditions have the same molar volume

On the basis of Avogadro's law, the volume occupied by one mole of any gas, known as the **molar volume**, must be the same for *all* gases when measured under the same conditions of temperature and pressure.

At standard temperature and pressure (STP), one mole of a gas has a volume of $2.27 \times 10^{-2}\,m^3\,mol^{-1}$ ($22.7\,dm^3\,mol^{-1}$). The conditions at STP are:

• temperature of 0 °C (273.15 K);

• pressure of 100 kPa.

The molar volume can be used to calculate the amount of gas in a similar way to the use of molar mass earlier in this chapter. Here though the calculations are easier, as all gases have the same molar volume under the same conditions.

$$\text{number of moles of gas } (n) = \frac{\text{volume } (V)}{\text{molar volume}}$$

Worked example

What volume of oxygen at standard temperature and pressure would be needed to completely burn 1 mole of butane, C_4H_{10}?

Solution

As always, start with the balanced equation and pick out the terms from the question.

$$2C_4H_{10}(g) + 13O_2(g) \rightarrow 8CO_2(g) + 10H_2O(g)$$

mole / volume ratio:　　1　　　　6.5

6.5 moles of gas at STP have volume = $6.5 \text{ mol} \times 22.7 \text{ dm}^3 \text{ mol}^{-1} = 147.6 \text{ dm}^3$

Worked example

Calculate the volume occupied by 0.0200 g of He at standard temperature and pressure.

Solution

First convert the mass of He to moles:

$$n = \frac{m}{M} = \frac{0.0200 \text{ g}}{4.00 \text{ g mol}^{-1}} = 0.00500 \text{ mol}$$
$$\text{volume} = 0.00500 \text{ mol} \times 22.7 \text{ dm}^3 \text{ mol}^{-1} = 0.114 \text{ dm}^3$$

A note about units of volume

The metric unit m^3 is widely used in industrial and engineering calculations, but is too large to be convenient for many volume measurements in the laboratory. Instead, dm^3 and cm^3 are commonly used, so it is important to be able to interconvert these.

$$1 \text{ dm}^3 = 10^{-3} \text{ m}^3 \qquad\qquad 1000 \text{ dm}^3 = 1 \text{ m}^3$$
$$1 \text{ cm}^3 = 10^{-3} \text{ dm}^3 \qquad\qquad 1000 \text{ cm}^3 = 1 \text{ dm}^3$$

divide by 1000 　　　　　　divide by 1000

cm³ ⟶ **dm³** ⟶ **m³**
　　　⟵　　　　　　⟵

multiply by 1000 　　　　　multiply by 1000

The litre (l or L) is widely used in place of dm^3, and millilitre (ml or mL) in place of cm^3. You will not be penalized for the use of these terms in an examination, but they will not be used in examination questions so it is essential that you know the correct use of m^3, dm^3 and cm^3.

The value of the molar volume and the conditions for STP are given in section 2 of the IB data booklet.

CODATA (Committee on Data for Science and Technology) is an interdisciplinary scientific committee of the International Council of Science. It was established in 1966 to promote the worldwide compilation and sharing of reliable numerical data, such as the molar volume of a gas.

Figure 1.13 The three cubes shown are not to scale. 1 m³ = 1000 dm³ = 1 000 000 cm³. In the laboratory, volumes are usually measured in cm³ or dm³ and often these measurements need to be converted to m³ in calculations.

Exercises

45 How many moles are present in each of the following at STP?

(a) 54.5 dm³ CH₄   (b) 250.0 cm³ CO   (c)   1.0 m³ O₂

46 What is the volume of each of the following at STP?

(a) 44.00 g N₂   (b) 0.25 mol NH₃

47 Pure oxygen gas was first prepared by heating mercury(II) oxide, HgO.

$$2HgO(s) \rightarrow 2Hg(l) + O_2(g)$$

What volume of oxygen at STP is released by heating 12.45 g of HgO?

48 Which sample contains more molecules, 3.14 dm³ of bromine, Br₂, or 11.07 g of chlorine, Cl₂ when measured at the same temperature and pressure?

49 Calcium reacts with water to produce hydrogen.

$$Ca(s) + 2H_2O(l) \rightarrow Ca(OH)_2(aq) + H_2(g)$$

Calculate the volume of gas at STP produced when 0.200 g of calcium reacts completely with water.

50 Dinitrogen oxide, N₂O, is a greenhouse gas produced from the decomposition of artificial nitrate fertilizers. Calculate the volume at STP of N₂O produced from 1.0 g of ammonium nitrate, when it reacts according to the equation:

$$NH_4NO_3(s) \rightarrow N_2O(g) + 2H_2O(l)$$

NATURE OF SCIENCE

Early ideas on gas behaviour were suggested from the postulates of the kinetic theory, but could not advance without scientific evidence. This was provided by experimental work, mainly that of Boyle and Mariotte, Charles and Gay-Lussac who contributed quantitative data based on testable predictions of how gases would respond to changes in temperature, volume and pressure. In a fairly classic example of scientific process, the data supported the theory, and the theory explained the data. As a result there was wide acceptance of what became known as the 'gas laws' by the 18th century.

It is interesting to consider on the other hand why Avogadro's hypothesis was not widely accepted initially. Experiments led him to suggest that equal volumes of all gases at the same temperature and pressure contain the same number of molecules, but data to confirm this were somewhat lacking. In addition, his ideas conflicted with Dalton's atomic theory, which suggested that particles in gases could be only single atoms, not molecules as Avogadro proposed. It took the logical argument of Cannizzaro nearly 50 years later to show that Avogadro's hypothesis could be explained, and moreover used as a means to determine molecular mass. Following this, the relationship between gas volume and number of molecules became widely accepted and known as Avogadro's law. History has shown that the acceptance of scientific ideas by the scientific community is sometimes influenced by the time and manner of their presentation, as well as by their power to explain existing ideas.

The gas laws describe pressure, volume and temperature relationships for all gases

The kinetic theory of matter, summarized on pages 9–10, describes gases as largely empty space containing free moving particles of negligible volume having no inter-particle forces. This is often referred to as the **ideal gas** model. In effect it is an approximation, as no gas fits this description exactly, but it is nonetheless a useful means for predicting and interpreting the physical properties of gases under typical conditions of temperature and pressure. Later in this section we will explore situations when gas behaviour deviates from this ideal model.

You will be familiar with some behaviour of gases through everyday experiences such as blowing up a balloon, or inflating a bicycle tyre to increase the pressure. Perhaps you have noticed how inflated balloons shrivel in colder conditions and expand when it is warmer? The interesting thing about these simple observations of the volume, pressure and temperature of a gas is that they are not dependent on the chemical nature of the gas. In fact, all gases respond in the same way to changes in volume, pressure and temperature when the mass of gas is fixed. These relationships are summarized as the **gas laws** and are discussed on the following pages.

An ideal gas is one that obeys the ideal gas laws.

The ideal gas equation can be deduced from a small number of assumptions of ideal behaviour. What is the role of reason, perception, intuition and imagination in the development of scientific models?

TOK

A note about units of temperature

In all work on gases, it is essential to use values for temperature recorded in kelvin (K), not in Celsius (°C). Temperature in kelvin is known as the **absolute temperature**, and is based on a scale where absolute zero, 0 K, is the point of zero kinetic energy of particles. This coincides with −273.15 °C. As the interval on the Kelvin scale is the same as that on the Celsius scale, conversion between the two simply involves addition or subtraction of 273.15 (commonly approximated to 273).

$$\text{temperature (K)} = \text{temperature (°C)} + 273.15$$

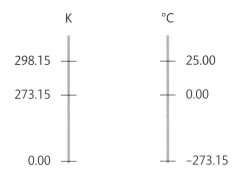

William Thomson (1824–1907), who became known as Lord Kelvin later in life, completed most of his work at the University of Glasgow, Scotland. His concept of the absolute temperature scale followed from his recognition of the relationship between heat energy and the ability to do work. The existence of a minimum possible temperature at which no heat can be extracted from the system and so no work done, led him to the definition of absolute zero in 1848. This in turn led to the formulation of the laws of thermodynamics. Kelvin is considered one of the great scientists of the 19th century, and is buried next to Isaac Newton in London.

A note about units of pressure

The SI unit of pressure is the Pascal (Pa), which is equal to N m^{-2}. Pressure is now commonly given in bars, where 10^5 Pa = 1 bar, as this is conveniently close to 1 atmosphere pressure.

1 Relationship between volume and pressure

The volume of a gas is always the volume of its container as the particles spread out fully. Its pressure is the result of the particles colliding with the walls of the container, and will increase when the frequency or energy of these collisions increases.

If the temperature is held constant, it is found that increasing the pressure on a fixed mass of gas decreases its volume. In other words, the pressure of a gas is inversely proportional to its volume, and the product of pressure and volume is a constant.

The so-called mentos-soda fountain reaction. Dissolved carbon dioxide in the soda changes quickly into gas in the presence of the candy mint mentos. The sudden pressure change causes the soda to be ejected in a fountain of foam.

Different countries continue to use a variety of units for pressure, including millimetres of mercury (mmHg), torr, pounds per square inch (psi), and atmosphere (atm).

In all the examples here, use of the term 'pressure' assumes 'absolute pressure', which is referenced against a perfect vacuum. This is in contrast to 'gauge pressure', which is measured relative to atmospheric pressure.

Figure 1.14 As the pressure on a gas is increased, its volume decreases proportionately.

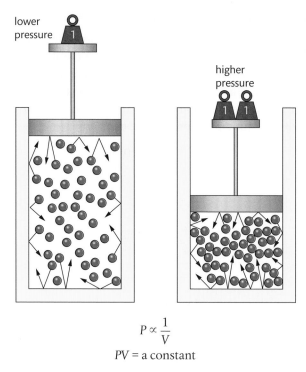

$$P \propto \frac{1}{V}$$

$$PV = \text{a constant}$$

This relationship is often known as **Boyle's law**, as it was first established by Robert Boyle in 1662. Application of this relationship is found in the compression of gases under pressure, often useful in transport and storage.

Figure 1.15 Boyle's law. Gas pressure is inversely proportional to its volume.

$$P \propto \frac{1}{V}$$
$$PV = \text{a constant}$$

2 Relationship between volume and temperature

An increase in temperature represents an increase in the average kinetic energy of the particles. If the pressure is held constant, it is found that increasing the temperature of a fixed mass of gas increases its volume. In other words, the volume of a gas is directly proportional to its absolute temperature, and volume divided by absolute temperature is a constant.

Figure 1.16 Charles' law. Gas volume is proportional to the absolute temperature. Note the dotted line represents an extrapolation, as data at temperatures down to 0 K are not obtainable.

$$V \propto T$$
$$\frac{V}{T} = \text{a constant}$$

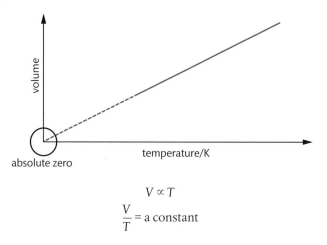

$$V \propto T$$

$$\frac{V}{T} = \text{a constant}$$

TOK The SI base unit of temperature is the kelvin, which has a natural basis for its definition of zero. By contrast, zero in the imperial scale of degrees Celsius is arbitrarily defined. What are the implications of using a scale based on natural or arbitrary values?

This relationship is often known as **Charles' law**, as it was first established by Frenchman Jacques Charles in the late 18th century. You can demonstrate this relationship by immersing dented table tennis balls in warm water. As the air inside the ball equilibrates to the temperature of the water, it expands, pushing the dents out on the surface.

3 Relationship between pressure and temperature

An increase in temperature increases the average kinetic energy of the particles. The particles move faster and collide with the walls of the container with more energy and more frequency, raising the pressure. If the volume is held constant, it is found that increasing the temperature of a fixed mass of gas proportionately raises its pressure. In other words, the pressure of a gas is directly proportional to the absolute temperature, and pressure divided by temperature is a constant.

$$P \propto T$$
$$\frac{P}{T} = \text{a constant}$$

Balloons dipped in a mixture of dry ice (solid CO_2) and water rapidly deflate as the air inside contracts at low temperature.

Figure 1.17 Gas pressure is proportional to the absolute temperature.

 Be certain to use temperature in kelvin only when applying these relationships.

$$P \propto T$$
$$\frac{P}{T} = \text{a constant}$$

The label on the aerosol can warns of the dangers of exposing the pressurized contents to high temperature.

UN No. 1950

Automotive Paint

FLAMMABLE

Keep out of reach of children.
Keep away from sources of ignition –
No smoking.
Do not breathe spray.
Avoid contact with skin and eyes.
Use only in well ventilated areas.
Caution: Pressurised container. Protect from sunlight and do not expose to temperatures exceeding 50°C. Do not pierce or burn even after use. Do not spray on a naked flame or any incandescent material.

Automotive Chemicals Ltd.,
Bury, Lancashire, England. Tel. 061 764 5981

400 ml

TWO STAGE
COLOURS
1. First apply
metallic base
colour as normal
on can and allow
dry.
2. Seconds apply
protective
ClearCoat
(available
paint stand)
be applied
your vehicle
original finish
Check in the
Colour Guide
your vehicle
'Two Stage'

NATURE OF SCIENCE

Scientists work to contribute to a common body of knowledge. Results are shared through publication, considered and used as the basis for further studies by other scientists. Although many scientific discoveries, such as the gas laws, are named after the key scientist involved, in reality the theories and laws of science stand apart from the individual discoverers. Without Charles and Boyle, the relationships between pressure, volume and temperature of a gas would still exist. This is very different from the arts. Without Shakespeare, there would have been no Hamlet, without Picasso, no Guernica.

Pressurized cans, such as soda or beer, often carry a warning to be stored in a cool place. This is because at higher temperatures, the pressure inside the can at fixed volume is able to rise to the point of causing the can to explode.

These three gas laws applied to a fixed mass of gas can be summarized as follows:

$$P \propto 1/V \text{ at constant temperature}$$

$$V \propto T \text{ at constant pressure}$$

$$P \propto T \text{ at constant volume}$$

These can be combined to give one equation for a fixed mass of gas:

$$\frac{PV}{T} = \text{a constant or } \frac{P_1V_1}{T_1} = \frac{P_2V_2}{T_2},$$

where 1 and 2 refer to initial and final conditions respectively.

Application of this enables gas volume, pressure and temperature to be calculated as conditions change.

$$\frac{P_1V_1}{T_1} = \frac{P_2V_2}{T_2}$$

Worked example

What happens to the volume of a fixed mass of gas when its pressure and its absolute temperature are both doubled?

Solution

$$\frac{P_1V_1}{T_1} = \frac{P_2V_2}{T_2}$$

$P_2 = 2 \times P_1$ and $T_2 = 2 \times T_1$, so these can be substituted into the equation:

$$\frac{P_1V_1}{T_1} = \frac{2P_1V_2}{2T_1}$$

cancelling P_1 and T_1 from both sides, and 2s on the right side:

$$V_1 = V_2$$

The volume does not change.

Note that temperature must be in kelvin in these calculations, but the units of volume and pressure are not specified, so long as they are consistent on both sides of the equation.

Worked example

The molar volume of a gas at STP is 22.7 dm³ mol⁻¹. Calculate the molar volume at 25 °C at the same pressure.

Solution

As the pressure is not changing, we do not need to insert P_1 and P_2 into the combined gas equation. Temperature must be converted from °C to K.

$$T_1 = 273 \text{ K}, T_2 = 25 + 273 = 298 \text{ K}$$

$$\frac{V_1}{T_1} = \frac{V_2}{T_2}$$

$$\frac{22.7 \text{ dm}^3}{273 \text{ K}} = \frac{V_2}{298 \text{ K}}$$

$$V_2 = \frac{298 \times 22.7 \text{ dm}^3}{273} = 24.8 \text{ dm}^3$$

The ideal gas equation is derived from the combined gas equation and Avogadro's law

The combined gas equation tells us that

$$\frac{PV}{T} = \text{a constant}$$

The value of the constant is directly proportional to the fixed mass of gas, or the number of moles, n.

So $\frac{PV}{T} \propto n$

This can be made into an equation by introducing a constant, **R**, known as the **universal gas constant**.

$\therefore \frac{PV}{T} = nR$, usually written as $PV = nRT$

This equation is known as the **ideal gas equation**, and is given in section 1 of the IB data booklet. The value of R can be calculated by substituting known values into the equation, such as those for the molar volume of a gas at STP. In this case:

$$P = 10^5 \, \text{Pa} \, (\text{N m}^{-2}), \, V = 2.27 \times 10^{-2} \, \text{m}^3, \, T = 273 \, \text{K}, \, n = 1$$

$$\therefore 10^5 \, \text{N m}^{-2} \times 2.27 \times 10^{-2} \, \text{m}^3 = 1 \, \text{mol} \times R \times 273 \, \text{K}$$

$$R = 8.31 \, \text{N m K}^{-1} \, \text{mol}^{-1} \, \text{or} \, 8.31 \, \text{J K}^{-1} \, \text{mol}^{-1}$$

This value for R, the gas constant, is given in section 2 in the IB data booklet, and should be used for all calculations involving the ideal gas equation.

Use of the ideal gas equation enables us to calculate how systems respond to changes in pressure, volume and temperature, and to calculate molar mass. Gas density can also be derived by applying the relationship, density = mass/volume. These calculations usually involve simply substituting values into the equation, but the use of units needs special attention here. The guidelines below, based on the use of SI units only, should help you avoid some of the common mistakes that arise.

- **Pressure** P: must be in Pa (N m^{-2}); if kPa are given, multiply by 10^3.
- **Volume** V: must be in m^3; if dm^3 are given divide by 10^3, if cm^3 are given divide by 10^6.
- **Number of moles** n: this is often derived by application of $n = \frac{m}{M}$.
- **Temperature** T: must be in kelvin; if °C is given, add 273.15.

Worked example

A helium party balloon has a volume of 18.0 dm^3. At 25 °C the internal pressure is 108 kPa. Calculate the mass of helium in the balloon.

Solution

First ensure all data are in SI units:

$$P: 108 \, \text{kPa} = 108 \times 10^3 \, \text{Pa}$$

$$V: 18.0 \, \text{dm}^3 = 18.0 \times 10^{-3} \, \text{m}^3$$

$$T: 25 \, °\text{C} = 298 \, \text{K}$$

$PV = nRT$

$108 \times 10^3 \, \text{Pa} \times 18.0 \times 10^{-3} \, \text{m}^3 = n \times 8.31 \, \text{J K}^{-1} \, \text{mol}^{-1} \times 298 \, \text{K}$

$\therefore n(\text{He}) = 0.785 \, \text{mol}$

$\therefore \text{mass (He)} = nM = 0.785 \, \text{mol} \times 4.00 \, \text{g mol}^{-1} = 3.14 \, \text{g}$

The ideal gas equation is $PV = nRT$

Many sources give data for ideal gas law questions in non-SI units such as atmospheres, which require a mathematical conversion. You will not be expected to be familiar with these conversions in IB examinations.

As this example shows, if pressure is given in kPa *and* volume is given in dm^3, the same answer is obtained if these values are used directly in the ideal gas equation in place of Pa and m^3.

Blowing up a balloon increases its volume as the number of particles increases. What do you think would happen to this inflated balloon on the top of a very high mountain?

Worked example

A sample of gas has a volume of 445 cm³ and a mass of 1.500 g at a pressure of 95 kPa and a temperature of 28 °C. Calculate its molar mass.

Solution

Substitute $n = \dfrac{m}{M}$ into the ideal gas equation, and rearrange to solve for M.

$$M = \frac{mRT}{PV}$$

Ensure all data are in SI units:

P: 95 kPa = 95 × 10³ Pa

V: 445 cm³ = 445 × 10⁻⁶ m³

T: 28 °C = 301 K

$$\therefore M = \frac{1.500 \text{ g} \times 8.31 \text{ J K}^{-1}\text{ mol}^{-1} \times 301 \text{ K}}{95 \times 10^3 \text{ Pa} \times 445 \times 10^{-6} \text{ m}^3} = 89 \text{ g mol}^{-1}$$

Worked example

A gas has a density of 1.65 g dm⁻³ at 27 °C and 92.0 kPa. Determine its molar mass.

Solution

density data ⇒ 1.65 g occupies 1.00 dm³

As in the example above, substitute data with correct units into $M = \dfrac{mRT}{PV}$

$$\therefore M = \frac{1.65 \text{ g} \times 8.31 \text{ J K}^{-1}\text{ mol}^{-1} \times 300 \text{ K}}{92.0 \times 10^3 \text{ Pa} \times 1.00 \times 10^{-3} \text{ m}^3} = 44.7 \text{ g mol}^{-1}$$

Experiment to calculate the molar mass of carbon dioxide by application of the ideal gas equation

Full details with a worksheet are available on your eBook.

A known mass of $CuCO_3(s)$ is heated and the gas evolved collected by displacement of water. The volume of the gas, the room temperature and pressure are recorded.

$$CuCO_3(s) \rightarrow CuO(s) + CO_2(g)$$

gas collects here

stand

copper carbonate, $CuCO_3(s)$

calibrated glass tube

Bunsen burner

water

trough

Figure 1.18 Experiment to calculate the molar mass of carbon dioxide.

Sample results

	Trial 1	Observations
mass of boiling tube + $CuCO_3$ before heating / g ± 0.001	33.910	$CuCO_3$ is a green powder
mass of boiling tube + $CuCO_3$ after heating / g ± 0.001	33.822	the contents of the tube are black after heating
mass change (mass CO_2) / g ± 0.002	0.088	
volume of gas collected / cm³ ± 0.1	38.1	the gas collected is colourless
temperature / K ± 0.1	293.0	
pressure / kPa ± 0.1	101.3	

Processed data

$$M(CO_2) = \frac{mRT}{PV} = \frac{0.088\,\text{g} \times 8.31\,\text{J mol}^{-1}\,\text{K}^{-1} \times 293.0\,\text{K}}{101.3\,\text{kPa} \times 0.0381\,\text{dm}^3}$$

experimental value $M(CO_2) = 55.5$ g mol^{-1}

theoretical value $M(CO_2) = 44.01$ g mol^{-1}

$\therefore$ % error = 26.1%

The percentage error can be analysed in consideration of systematic errors such as:

- gas collected may not be pure CO_2;
- CO_2 may be soluble in water;
- air in the tube is collected with the gas;
- gas collected has not equilibrated to room temperature.

Modifications to the experimental design should suggest ways to reduce the impact of these errors. Note that repeat trials and error propagation are not shown here.

Exercises

51 A 2.50 dm³ container of helium at a pressure of 85 kPa was heated from 25 °C to 75 °C. The volume of the container expanded to 2.75 dm³. What was the final pressure of the helium?

52 After a sample of nitrogen with a volume of 675 cm³ and a pressure of 1.00×10^5 Pa was compressed to a volume of 350 cm³ and a pressure of 2.00×10^5 Pa, its temperature was 27.0 °C. Determine its initial temperature.

53 The absolute temperature of 4.0 dm³ of hydrogen gas is increased by a factor of three and the pressure is increased by a factor of four. Deduce the final volume of the gas.

54 To find the volume of a flask, it was first evacuated so that it contained no gas at all. When 4.40 g of carbon dioxide was introduced, it exerted a pressure of 90 kPa at 27 °C. Determine the volume of the flask.

55 An unknown noble gas has a density of 5.84 g dm⁻³ at STP. Calculate its molar mass, and so identify the gas.

56 A 12.1 mg sample of a gas has a volume of 255 cm³ at a temperature of 25.0 °C and a pressure of 1300 Pa. Determine its molar mass.

57 Which has the greater density at STP, hydrogen or helium?

58 Calculate the volume of oxygen at STP required for the complete combustion of 125 g of octane, C_8H_{18}, to form carbon dioxide and water.

59 A sample of an unknown gas with a mass of 3.620 g occupied a volume of 1120 cm³ at a pressure of 99 kPa and a temperature of 25.0 °C. The sample contained 2.172 g O and 1.448 g S. Determine the empirical and molecular formula of the gas.

60 A road cyclist pumps his tyres up very hard before a trip over a high mountain pass at high altitude. Near the summit one of his tyres explodes. Suggest why this may have occurred.

NATURE OF SCIENCE

Scientists often use models, which may be simple or complex, to explain concepts that are not observable. By their nature, models are thinking tools and so they all have limitations. Models are often tested against experimental results, and should be able to explain phenomena that are seemingly different from the ones used to develop the model. Sometimes, when a model does not seem consistent with data or observations, it may need to be modified or replaced. At other times it can be retained, with limitations to its usefulness agreed.

The ideal gas model has all of these characteristics. While it provides a useful conceptual image of gas behaviour, and is consistent with some testable predictions, there are limitations to this, as we will see below. These do not mean, however, that the model should be discarded – rather they alert us to the fact that the model is in some ways an over-simplification, and cannot apply accurately under all conditions.

Real gases show deviation from ideal behaviour

An ideal gas is defined as one that obeys the ideal gas law $PV = nRT$ under all conditions. This means that for one mole of gas, the relationship PV/RT should be equal to one. So a graph of PV/RT against P for one mole of an ideal gas is a horizontal line of intercept 1.

Figure 1.19 For one mole of an ideal gas, the relationship PV/RT is a constant at all pressures.

But as we noted earlier, there is no such thing as an ideal gas and all gases, known as **real gases**, deviate to some extent from ideal behaviour. So, for real gases the value of PV/RT for 1 mole will vary. An example of the extent of this variation from 1 at different conditions is shown in Figure 1.20.

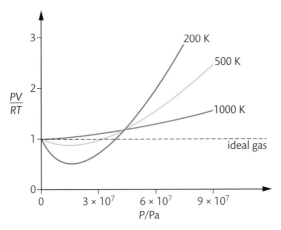

Figure 1.20 The deviation from ideal behaviour of nitrogen at different temperatures and pressures.

We can draw the following conclusions from the graph:

- the gas behaves most like an ideal gas at low pressure and shows the greatest deviation at high pressure;
- the gas behaves most like an ideal gas at high temperature and shows the greatest deviation at low temperature.

To interpret these findings, it will be helpful to question the validity of two assumptions made in describing an ideal gas in the kinetic molecular theory:

1   the volume of the gas particles is negligible;
2   there are no attractive forces between the particles.

1. At relatively low pressure, such as 1×10^5 Pa (STP), the volume occupied by the particles of a typical gas is only about 0.05% of the total volume, so it is reasonably valid to describe this as negligible. But with increasing pressure as the space between the particles is reduced, this percentage increases and with a pressure of 5×10^5 Pa, the volume of the particles is about 20% of the total volume – certainly not negligible. As a result, the volume of a real gas at high pressure is larger than that predicted from the ideal gas law and $PV/nRT > 1$.

2. When a gas is at moderately low pressure, the particles are so widely spaced that interactive forces are highly unlikely, so this assumption is valid. But at pressures up to about 3×10^7 Pa, as the particles approach more closely, attractive forces strengthen between them. These have the effect of reducing the pressure of the gas, so $PV/nRT < 1$. Low temperatures increase this deviation because the lower kinetic energy of the particles increases the strength of inter-particle forces. At even higher pressures, the non-zero volume of the particles becomes more important and this effect dominates where the graph rises.

Overall, we can conclude that real gases deviate from ideal behaviour when either or both of the assumptions above are not valid. This occurs at high pressure and low temperature. It makes sense intuitively that a gas behaves in a less perfect way under these conditions, which are the closest to it changing into a liquid.

Attempts to modify the ideal gas equation to take these factors into account and make it apply accurately to real gases led to the **van der Waals' equation**, formulated in 1873. This has correction terms for both the volume of the particles and the inter-particle attractions, and these are specific to different gases. Happily, for a wide range of conditions under which gases are studied, the ideal gas equation is a sufficiently accurate expression, and has the big advantage that it is a single equation for all gases.

One form of the van der Waals' equation is:
$$\left(p + \frac{n^2a}{V^2}\right)(V - nb) = nRT$$
where a is a measure of the attraction between the particles, and b is the volume excluded by a mole of particles.

Real gases deviate most from ideal behaviour at high pressure and low temperature.

61 (a) List the main features of the kinetic theory for ideal gases.

(b) Explain the reason for the difference in behaviour between real and ideal gases at low temperature.

62 Ammonia, NH_3, forms a relatively strong type of intermolecular attraction known as a hydrogen bond, whereas methane, CH_4, does not. Explain the relative deviation from ideal behaviour that each gas is likely to show.

63 Gases deviate from ideal gas behaviour because their particles:

A have negligible volume **B** have forces of attraction between them

C are polyatomic **D** are not attracted to one another

The concentration of a solution depends on moles of solute and volume of solution

Liquids, like gases, can conveniently be quantified by measuring their volume rather than their mass. Some liquids in common use are pure substances, such as water (H_2O), bromine (Br_2), and hexane (C_6H_{14}), but more commonly liquids are **solutions** containing two or more components.

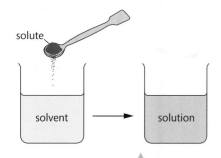

A solution is a homogeneous mixture of two or more substances, which may be solids, liquids or gases, or a combination of these. The **solvent** is the component present in the greatest quantity, in which the **solute** is dissolved. Some examples of solutions include:

- solid/solid: metal alloy such as brass (copper and zinc);
- solid/liquid: seawater (salts and water), copper sulfate(aq) (copper sulfate and water);
- liquid/liquid: wine (ethanol and water);
- gas/liquid: fizzy drinks (carbon dioxide and water).

Figure 1.21 A solution is made by dissolving a solute in a solvent.

In this section we will be considering solutions made by dissolving a solid solute in a liquid solvent.

Unlike gases, the volume of a liquid is not directly related to its amount. Instead, for solutions, we express the amount through its **concentration**. The concentration of a solution (c) is determined by the amount of solute (n) and the volume of solution (V). It is usually expressed as $mol\ dm^{-3}$.

> The concentration of a solution refers to the amount of solute per volume of solution. It has the units $mol\ dm^{-3}$ or $g\ dm^{-3}$.

$$\text{concentration of solution (mol dm}^{-3}) = \frac{\text{amount of solute (ml)}}{\text{volume of solution (dm}^3)} \quad \text{or} \quad c = \frac{n}{V}$$

$\therefore$ amount of solute (mol) = conc. ($mol\ dm^{-3}$) × volume (dm^3) or $\boldsymbol{n = cV}$

Square brackets are often used to represent 'concentration of' a particular substance, such as [HCl] = $1.0\ mol\ dm^{-3}$.

Different types of laboratory glassware, which are identified in Figure 1.22. Note that beakers and conical flasks are generally not used for measuring volume.

Chemists routinely prepare solutions of known concentration, known as **standard solutions**. The mass of solute required is accurately measured and then transferred carefully to a volumetric flask, which is accurately calibrated for a specific volume. The solvent is added steadily with swirling to help the solute to dissolve, until the final level reaches the mark on the flask.

Figure 1.22 Glassware commonly used in the laboratory: (a) conical or Erlenmeyer flask – its shape makes it easy to mix liquids as the flask can be easily swirled; (b) beaker; (c) measuring cylinder; (d) volumetric flask; (e) pipette; (f) burette. Standard solutions are prepared using volumetric flasks.

> Note that concentration is specified per volume of final *solution*, not per volume of *solvent* added. This is because volume changes occur on dissolving the solute.

CHALLENGE YOURSELF

6 When sodium hydroxide pellets (NaOH) dissolve in water, there is a *decrease* in the total volume of the solution. Explain what might cause this.

> The term *molarity*, M, has been widely used to express amount concentration, but it is falling out of common usage. It will not be used in IB examination questions, so make sure you are fully familiar with the terms mol dm^{-3} and g dm^{-3}. (Note that M is used specifically to refer to molar mass.)

A standard solution is one of accurately known concentration.

Number of moles of solute (mol) = concentration of solute (mol dm^{-3}) × volume of solution (dm^3) or $n = cV$.

Worked example

Explain how you would prepare 100 cm^3 of a 0.100 mol dm^{-3} solution of NaCl.

Solution

Ensure that cm^3 are converted to dm^3 by dividing by 1000.

$$n = cV$$

$$n = 0.100 \text{ mol dm}^{-3} \times \frac{100}{1000} \text{ dm}^3 = 0.0100 \text{ mol}$$

M(NaCl) = 22.99 + 35.45 = 58.44 g mol^{-1}

∴ mass required = 0.0100 mol × 58.44 g mol^{-1} = 0.584 g

Add 0.584 g NaCl(s) to a 100 cm^3 volumetric flask, and make up to the mark with distilled water.

Concentration can also be expressed in mass (g dm^{-3}).

Worked example

Calculate the concentration of a 0.0400 mol dm^{-3} solution of sodium carbonate, Na$_2$CO$_3$, in g dm^{-3}.

Solution

M(Na$_2$CO$_3$) = (22.99 × 2) + 12.01 + (16.00 × 3) = 105.99 g mol^{-1}

$m = nM$ ∴ m = 0.0400 mol × 105.99 g mol^{-1} = 4.24 g

∴ [Na$_2$CO$_3$] = 4.24 g dm^{-3}

Label on sparkling water
listing the mineral content in
milligrams per dm³.

The increased popularity in many countries of bottled water over tap water for drinking has raised several concerns, including the environmental costs of transport and packaging, and the source of the water and its solute (dissolved mineral) content. Significant differences exist in the regulation of the bottled water industry in different countries. In the USA, the FDA (Food and Drug Administration) requires that mineral waters contain between 500 and 1500 mg dm^{-3} of total dissolved solids. In Europe, mineral water is defined by its origin rather than by content, and the EU (European Union) prohibits the treatment of any water bottled from a source. The global cost of bottled water exceeds billions of dollars annually. As the United Nations General Assembly has explicitly recognized that access to safe, clean and affordable drinking water is a human right, there is an urgent need for money and technology to be diverted to improving tap water supplies globally to help make this a reality for all.

A different unit of concentration is known as **ppm**, parts per million. It denotes one part per 10^6 by mass, and is useful in describing very low concentrations such as found in air and water pollution.

$$\text{parts per million (ppm)} = \frac{\text{mass of component}}{\text{total mass of solution}} \times 10^6$$

A concentration of 1 ppm for a substance means that each kilogram of solution contains 1 milligram of solute. Assuming a density of 1 g cm^{-3}, 1 ppm also means that each dm^3 of solution contains 1 mg of solute. An advantage of these values based on mass is that they are not temperature dependent.

Dilutions of solutions reduce the concentration

A common practice in laboratory work is to make a **dilution** from a more concentrated starting solution called the **stock solution**, by adding solvent. For all aqueous solutions, distilled water, rather than tap water, must be used.

Series of dilutions of cobalt(II) chloride solutions. In coloured solutions such as these, the effect of lowering the concentration of the solution can be observed.

As a solution is diluted, the number of moles of solute remains the same, but as they become spread through a larger volume, the concentration is decreased. In other words, the number of moles n equals a constant, and as $n = cV \Rightarrow cV$ must be constant through dilution.

$$\therefore c_1V_1 = c_2V_2$$

where c_1V_1 refer to the initial concentration and volume and c_2V_2 refer to the diluted concentration and volume.

This equation provides an easy way to calculate concentration changes on dilution.

Worked example

Determine the final concentration of a 75 cm³ solution of HCl of concentration 0.40 mol dm⁻³, which is diluted to a volume of 300 cm³.

Solution

$$c_1V_1 = c_2V_2$$

$c_1 = 0.40$ mol dm⁻³, $V_1 = 75$ cm³, $V_2 = 300$ cm³

∴ (0.40 mol dm⁻³) (75 cm³) = c_2 (300 cm³)

c_2 diluted concentration = 0.10 mol dm⁻³

A quick check shows that the volume has increased four times, so the concentration must have decreased four times.

In precise work, dilution should be carried out using volumetric flasks so the final volume of the solution is measured, taking account of volume changes that may occur on dilution.

The concentration of a solution can be determined by volumetric analysis

Suppose we have an unlabelled bottle of hydrochloric acid, HCl, and want to know its concentration. We can find this out by reacting the acid with a standard solution of an alkali such as NaOH, and determining the exact volumes that react together. From the stoichiometry of the reaction, when we know the volumes of both solutions and the concentration of one of them, we can use the mole ratio to calculate the unknown concentration as follows.

$$HCl(aq) \quad + \quad NaOH(aq) \rightarrow NaCl(aq) + H_2O(l)$$

mole ratio:	1 :	1
volume:	known	known (by titration)
conc.:	unknown = x	known (standard solution)

- moles NaOH can be calculated as follows:
  $n(NaOH) = c(NaOH) \times V(NaOH)$
- from the mole ratio in the equation:
  $n(NaOH) = n(HCl)$
- ∴ concentration of HCl, x, can be calculated from:
  $n(HCl) = x \times V(HCl)$

This is an example of a process called **volumetric analysis**. Most commonly, a technique called **titration** is used to determine the reacting volumes precisely. A **pipette** is used to measure a known volume of one of the solutions into a **conical flask**. The other solution is put into a **burette**, a calibrated glass tube that can deliver precise volumes into the conical flask through opening the tap at the bottom. The point at which the two solutions have reacted completely, the **equivalence point**, is usually determined by an **indicator** that is added to the solution in the conical flask and changes colour at its **end point**. Different indicators are chosen for specific titrations, so that their end point corresponds to the equivalence point of the titration.

Note that in the equation $c_1V_1 = c_2V_2$, volume terms appear on both sides of the equation and so their units will cancel. This means that any units of volume can be used directly (there is no need to convert them to dm³), so long as they are consistent on both sides of the equation.

▲
Redox titration experiment. The burette tap controls the flow of the orange potassium dichromate(VI) solution into the conical flask containing iron(II) ions. The equivalence point occurs when the exact volumes of the two solutions have reacted completely.

Titration is widely used in acid–base chemistry (Chapter 8), and in redox chemistry (Chapter 9). Its applications include industrial chemical processing, chemical research, quality control checks in the food and pharmaceutical industries and aspects of environmental monitoring.

Burettes generally read to ±0.05 cm³, so be sure to record your results to this precision. Readings such as 0, 12.0 or 3.5 are not acceptable but should be recorded as 0.00, 12.00 and 3.50 respectively.

Titration usually involves multiple trials to obtain a more accurate result of the volume required to reach the equivalence point known as the **titre**. A good titration result is one that gives consistent results within 0.05 cm³ of each other.

Worked example

25.00 cm³ of 0.100 mol dm⁻³ sodium hydrogencarbonate, $NaHCO_3$, solution were titrated with dilute sulfuric acid, H_2SO_4.

$$2NaHCO_3(aq) + H_2SO_4(aq) \rightarrow Na_2SO_4(aq) + 2H_2O(l) + 2CO_2(g)$$

15.20 cm³ of the acid were needed to neutralize the solution. Calculate the concentration of the acid.

Solution

We can calculate the amount of $NaHCO_3$ as we are given both the volume and the concentration.

$$n = cV$$

$$n(NaHCO_3) = 0.100 \text{ mol dm}^{-3} \times \frac{25.00}{1000} \text{ dm}^3 = 2.500 \times 10^{-3} \text{ mol}$$

Look at the mole ratio in the equation:

$$2n(NaHCO_3) = n(H_2SO_4)$$

$$\therefore n(H_2SO_4) = 0.5 \times 2.500 \times 10^{-3} \text{ mol} = 1.250 \times 10^{-3} \text{ mol}$$

$$c = \frac{n}{V} = \frac{1.250 \times 10^{-3} \text{ mol}}{15.20/1000 \text{ dm}^3} = 0.0822 \text{ mol dm}^{-3}$$

$$\therefore [H_2SO_4] = 0.0822 \text{ mol dm}^{-3}$$

Here is a summary of steps in volumetric analysis calculations:

- first write the equation for the reaction;
- look for the reactant whose volume and concentration are given and calculate its number of moles from $n = cV$;
- use this answer and the mole ratio in the equation to determine the number of moles of the other reactant;
- use the number of moles and volume of the second reactant to calculate its concentration from $c = \frac{n}{V}$.

Back titration

As the name implies, a back titration is done in reverse by returning to the end point after it is passed. It is used when the end point is hard to identify or when one of the reactants is impure. A known excess of one of the reagents is added to the reaction mixture, and the unreacted excess is then determined by titration against a standard solution. By subtracting the amount of unreacted reactant from the original amount used, the reacting amount can be determined.

An antacid tablet with a mass of 0.300 g and containing $NaHCO_3$ was added to 25.00 cm^3 of 0.125 mol dm^{-3} hydrochloric acid. After the reaction was complete, the excess hydrochloric acid required 3.50 cm^3 of 0.200 mol dm^{-3} NaOH to reach the equivalence point in a titration. Calculate the percentage of $NaHCO_3$ in the tablet.

Solution

original reaction: $NaHCO_3(s) + HCl(aq) \rightarrow NaCl(aq) + H_2O(l) + CO_2(g)$
mole ratio: 1   1

First calculate the total amount of HCl added, which is a known excess.

$$n(HCl \text{ total}) = \frac{25.00}{1000} dm^3 \times 0.125 \text{ mol dm}^{-3} = 0.00313 \text{ mol HCl total}$$

titration reaction: $HCl(aq) + NaOH(aq) \rightarrow NaCl(aq) + H_2O(l)$
mole ratio: 1   1

$$n(NaOH) = 0.00350 \text{ dm}^3 \times 0.200 \text{ mol dm}^{-3} = 0.000700 \text{ mol}$$

$n(NaOH) = n(HCl \text{ unreacted}) = 0.000700 \text{ mol HCl unreacted}$

$\therefore n(HCl \text{ reacted}) = 0.00313 - 0.000700 = 0.00243 \text{ mol}$

$\therefore$ from the mole ratio in the first equation $n(NaHCO_3) = 0.00243 \text{ mol}$

$M(NaHCO_3) = 22.99 + 1.01 + 12.01 + (16.00 \times 3) = 84.01 \text{ g mol}^{-1}$

$$m = nM = 0.00243 \text{ mol} \times 84.01 \text{ g mol}^{-1} = 0.204 \text{ g}$$

percentage by mass in tablet $= \dfrac{0.204 \text{ g}}{0.300 \text{ g}} \times 100 = 68.0\%$

Note that there are several assumptions made in this calculation. These include the fact that all the $NaHCO_3$ did react with the acid, and that the only component of the tablet that reacted with HCl is $NaHCO_3$. You may like to think how you could test the validity of these assumptions in the laboratory.

64 Calculate the mass of potassium hydroxide, KOH, required to prepare 250 cm^3 of a 0.200 mol dm^{-3} solution.

65 Calculate the mass of magnesium sulfate heptahydrate, $MgSO_4.7H_2O$, required to prepare 0.100 dm^3 of a 0.200 mol dm^{-3} solution.

66 Calculate the number of moles of chloride ions in 0.250 dm^3 of 0.0200 mol dm^{-3} of zinc chloride, $ZnCl_2$, solution.

67 250 cm^3 of a solution contains 5.85 g of sodium chloride. Calculate the concentration of sodium chloride in mol dm^{-3}.

68 Concentrated nitric acid, HNO_3, is 16.0 mol dm^{-3}. What volume would you need to prepare 100 cm^3 of 0.50 mol dm^{-3} HNO_3?

69 In a titration a 15.00 cm^3 sample of H_2SO_4 required 36.42 cm^3 of 0.147 mol dm^{-3} NaOH solution for complete neutralization. What is the concentration of the H_2SO_4?

70 Gastric juice contains hydrochloric acid, HCl. A 5.00 cm^3 sample of gastric juice required 11.00 cm^3 of 0.0100 mol dm^{-3} KOH for neutralization in a titration. What was the concentration of HCl in this fluid? If we assume a density of 1.00 g cm^{-3} for the fluid, what was the percentage by mass of HCl?

71 Sodium sulfate, Na_2SO_4, reacts in aqueous solution with lead nitrate, $Pb(NO_3)_2$, as follows:

$$Na_2SO_4(aq) + Pb(NO_3)_2(aq) \circledR PbSO_4(s) + 2NaNO_3(aq)$$

In an experiment, 35.30 cm^3 of a solution of sodium sulfate reacted exactly with 32.50 cm^3 of a solution of lead nitrate. The precipitated lead sulfate was dried and found to have a mass of 1.13 g. Determine the concentrations of the original solutions of lead nitrate and sodium sulfate. State what assumptions are made.

Practice questions

1 How many oxygen atoms are in 0.100 mol of $CuSO_4.5H_2O$?

A 5.42×10^{22} **B** 6.02×10^{22} **C** 2.41×10^{23} **D** 5.42×10^{23}

2 What is the sum of the coefficients when the following equation is balanced using whole numbers?

$$\_\_\_ Fe_2O_3(s) + \_\_\_ CO(g) \rightarrow \_\_\_ Fe(s) + \_\_\_ CO_2(g)$$

A 5   **B** 6   **C** 8   **D** 9

3 Four identical containers under the same conditions are filled with gases as shown below. Which container and contents will have the highest mass?

nitrogen	oxygen	ethane	neon
A	**B**	**C**	**D**

4 1.0 dm^3 of an ideal gas at 100 kPa and 25 °C is heated to 50 °C at constant pressure. What is the new volume in dm^3?

A 0.50   **B** 0.90   **C** 1.1   **D** 2.0

5 What is the amount, in moles, of sulfate ions in 100 cm^3 of 0.020 mol dm^{-3} $FeSO_4(aq)$?

A 2.0×10^{-3} **B** 2.0×10^{-2} **C** 2.0×10^{-1} **D** 2.0

6 1.7 g of $NaNO_3$ ($M_r = 85$) is dissolved in water to prepare 0.20 dm^3 of solution. What is the concentration of the resulting solution in mol dm^{-3}?

A 0.01   **B** 0.1   **C** 0.2   **D** 1.0

7 What mass, in g, of hydrogen is formed when 3 mol of aluminium react with excess hydrochloric acid according to the following equation?

$$2Al(s) + 6HCl(aq) \rightarrow 2AlCl_3(aq) + 3H_2(g)$$

A 3.0   **B** 4.5   **C** 6.0   **D** 9.0

8 The relative molecular mass of a gas is 56 and its empirical formula is CH_2. What is the molecular formula of the gas?

A CH_2 **B** C_2H_4 **C** C_3H_6 **D** C_4H_8

9 What is the sum of all coefficients when the following equation is balanced using the smallest possible whole numbers?

$$\_\_\_ C_2H_2 + \_\_\_ O_2 \rightarrow \_\_\_ CO_2 + \_\_\_ H_2O$$

A 5   **B** 7   **C** 11   **D** 13

10 What is the total number of hydrogen atoms in 1.0 mol of benzamide, $C_6H_5CONH_2$?

A 7   **B** 6.0×10^{23} **C** 3.0×10^{24} **D** 4.2×10^{24}

11 Chloroethene, C_2H_3Cl, reacts with oxygen according to the equation below:

$$2C_2H_3Cl(g) + 5O_2(g) \rightarrow 4CO_2(g) + 2H_2O(g) + 2HCl(g)$$

What is the amount, in mol, of H_2O produced when 10.0 mol of C_2H_3Cl and 10.0 mol of O_2 are mixed together, and the above reaction goes to completion?

A 4.00   **B** 8.00   **C** 10.0   **D** 20.0

12 What is the concentration of NaCl, in mol dm^{-3}, when 10.0 cm^3 of 0.200 mol dm^{-3} NaCl solution is added to 30.0 cm^3 of 0.600 mol dm^{-3} NaCl solution?

A 0.450   **B** 0.300   **C** 0.500   **D** 0.800

13 On analysis, a compound with molar mass 60 g mol^{-1} was found to contain 12 g of carbon, 2 g of hydrogen, and 16 g of oxygen. What is the molecular formula of the compound?

A CH_2O **B** CH_4O **C** C_2H_4O **D** $C_2H_4O_2$

14 300 cm^3 of water is added to a solution of 200 cm^3 of 0.5 mol dm^{-3} sodium chloride. What is the concentration of sodium chloride in the new solution?

A 0.05 mol dm^{-3} **B** 0.1 mol dm^{-3} **C** 0.2 mol dm^{-3} **D** 0.3 mol dm^{-3}

15 What is the approximate molar mass, in g mol^{-1}, of $MgSO_4.7H_2O$?

A 120   **B** 130   **C** 138   **D** 246

16 Which is both an empirical and a molecular formula?

A C_5H_{12} **B** C_5H_{10} **C** C_4H_8 **D** C_4H_{10}

17 Airbags are an important safety feature in vehicles. Sodium azide, potassium nitrate, and silicon dioxide have been used in one design of airbag.

Two students looked at data in a simulated computer-based experiment to determine the volume of nitrogen generated in an airbag.

Sodium azide, a toxic compound, undergoes the following decomposition reaction under certain conditions.

$$2NaN_3(s) \rightarrow 2Na(s) + 3N_2(g)$$

Using the simulation program, the students entered the following data into the computer.

Temperature (T) / °C	Mass of NaN$_3$(s) (m) / kg	Pressure (p) / atm
25.00	0.0650	1.08

(a) State the number of significant figures for the temperature, mass, and pressure data. (1)

(b) Calculate the amount, in mol, of sodium azide present. (1)

(c) Determine the volume of nitrogen gas, in dm^3, produced under these conditions based on this reaction. (4)

(Total 6 marks)

18 An important environmental consideration is the appropriate disposal of cleaning solvents. An environmental waste treatment company analysed a cleaning solvent, **J**, and found it to contain the elements carbon, hydrogen, and chlorine only. The chemical composition of **J** was determined using different analytical chemistry techniques.

Combustion reaction:

Combustion of 1.30 g of J gave 0.872 g CO_2 and 0.089 g H_2O.

Precipitation reaction with $AgNO_3$(aq):

0.535 g of J gave 1.75 g AgCl precipitate.

(a) Determine the percentage by mass of carbon and hydrogen in **J**, using the combustion data. (3)

(b) Determine the percentage by mass of chlorine in **J**, using the precipitation data. (1)

(c) The molar mass was determined to be 131.38 g mol^{-1}. Deduce the molecular formula of **J**. (3)

(Total 7 marks)

19 Nitrogen monoxide may be removed from industrial emissions via a reaction with ammonia as shown by the equation below:

$$4NH_3(g) + 6NO(g) \rightarrow 5N_2(g) + 6H_2O(l)$$

30.0 dm^3 of ammonia reacts with 30.0 dm^3 of nitrogen monoxide at 100 °C. Identify which gas is in excess and by how much and calculate the volume of nitrogen produced. (2)

20 The percentage by mass of calcium carbonate in eggshell was determined by adding excess hydrochloric acid to ensure that all the calcium carbonate had reacted. The excess acid left was then titrated with aqueous sodium hydroxide.

(a) A student added 27.20 cm^3 of 0.200 mol dm^{-3} HCl to 0.188 g of eggshell. Calculate the amount, in mol, of HCl added. (1)

(b) The excess acid requires 23.80 cm^3 of 0.100 mol dm^{-3} NaOH for neutralization. Calculate the amount, in mol, of acid that is in excess. (1)

(c) Determine the amount, in mol, of HCl that reacted with the calcium carbonate in the eggshell. (1)

(d) State the equation for the reaction of HCl with the calcium carbonate in the eggshell. (2)

(e) Determine the amount, in mol, of calcium carbonate in the sample of the eggshell. (2)

(f) Calculate the mass and the percentage by mass of calcium carbonate in the eggshell sample. (3)

(g) Deduce one assumption made in arriving at the percentage of calcium carbonate in the eggshell sample. (1)

(Total 11 marks)

21 A 2.450 g sample of a mixture of sodium chloride and calcium chloride was dissolved in distilled water. The chloride solution was treated with excess silver nitrate solution, $AgNO_3$(aq). The precipitated silver chloride, AgCl(s), was collected, washed, and dried. The mass of the dried silver chloride was 6.127 g. Calculate the per cent by mass of the sodium chloride and calcium chloride in the original mixture. (2)

22 A hydrate of potassium carbonate has the formula $K_2CO_3.xH_2O$. A 10.00 g sample of the hydrated solid is heated, and forms 7.93 g of anhydrous salt.

(a) Calculate the number of moles of water in the hydrated sample. (1)

(b) Calculate the number of moles of anhydrous salt that form. (1)

(c) Determine the formula of the hydrate. (1)

(d) How could you determine when all the hydrated salt has been converted into anhydrous form? (1)

(Total 4 marks)

23 625 cm^3 of ammonia, NH$_3$, at 42 °C and 160 kPa is combined with 740 cm^3 of hydrogen chloride at 57 °C and 113.3 kPa. The reaction produces ammonium chloride as follows:

$$NH_3(g) + HCl(g) \rightarrow NH_4Cl(s)$$

(a) Which reactant is in excess? (1)

(b) Which reactant is limiting? (1)

(c) What mass of ammonium chloride forms? (1)

(Total 3 marks)

24 Sulfur dioxide, SO$_2$, is one of the gases associated with the formation of acidic deposition. It is released during the process of extracting lead from lead ore, when lead sulfide, PbS, is roasted to form lead oxide, PbO.

(a) Write an equation for the reaction of roasting lead sulfide. (1)

(b) What mass of sulfur dioxide is produced when one tonne of lead sulfide is used in this reaction? (2)

(c) What assumption have you made in this calculation? (2)

(Total 5 marks)

25 Aluminium metal reacts with copper(II) sulfate solution, CuSO$_4$(aq), to produce aluminium sulfate solution, Al$_2$(SO$_4$)$_3$(aq), and copper metal.

(a) Write an equation for this reaction. (1)

(b) How many moles of aluminium are needed to react with 10.38 moles of copper(II) sulfate? (1)

(c) How many moles of copper are produced if 3.95 moles of copper(II) sulfate react with aluminium? (1)

(d) What changes might be observed during this reaction? (2)

(Total 5 marks)

 To access weblinks on the topics covered in this chapter, please go to www.pearsonhotlinks.com and enter the ISBN or title of this book.

02 Atomic structure

Essential ideas

2.1 The mass of an atom is concentrated in its minute, positively charged nucleus.

2.2 The electron configuration of an atom can be deduced from its atomic number.

'All things are made from atoms.' This is one of the most important ideas that the human race has learned about the universe. Atoms are everywhere and they make up everything. You are surrounded by atoms – they make up the foods you eat, the liquids you drink and the fragrances you smell. Atoms make up you! To understand the world and how it changes you need to understand atoms.

The idea of atoms has its origins in Greek and Indian philosophy nearly 2500 years ago, but it was not until the 19th century that there was experimental evidence to support their existence. Although atoms are too small ever to be seen directly by a human eye, they are fundamental to chemistry. All the atoms in a piece of gold foil, for example, have the same chemical properties. The atoms of gold, however, have different properties from the atoms of aluminium. This chapter will explain how they differ. We will explore their structure and discover that different atoms are made from different combinations of the same sub-atomic particles.

This exploration will take us into some difficult areas because our everyday notion of particles following fixed trajectories does not apply to the microscopic world of the atom. To understand the block structure of the Periodic Table we need to use **quantum theory** and adopt a wave description of matter. These ideas are revolutionary. As Niels Bohr, one of the principal scientists involved in the development of quantum theory said, 'Anyone who is not shocked by quantum theory has not understood it.'

Picture of individual atoms. This is a scanning tunnelling micrograph of gold atoms on a graphite surface. The gold atoms are shown in yellow, red, and brown and the graphite (carbon) atoms are shown in green.

TOK

Richard Feynman: '…if all of scientific knowledge were to be destroyed, and only one sentence passed on to the next generation of creatures, what statement would contain the most information in the fewest words? I believe it is the atomic hypothesis…that *all things are made of atoms.*' Are the models and theories which scientists create accurate descriptions of the natural world, or are they primarily useful interpretations for prediction, explanation and control of the natural world?

The hydrogen atom shown as a nucleus (a proton, pink), and an electron orbiting in a wavy path (light blue). It is necessary to consider the wave properties of the electron to understand atomic structure in detail.

A billion of your atoms once made up Shakespeare, another billion made up Beethoven, another billion St. Peter and another billion the Buddha. Atoms can rearrange in chemical reactions but they cannot be destroyed.

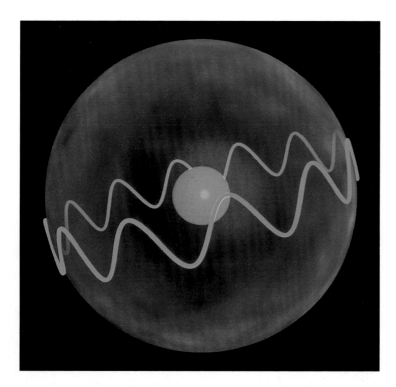

2.1 The nuclear atom

Understandings:

- Atoms contain a positively charged dense nucleus composed of protons and neutrons (nucleons).

  Guidance
  Relative masses and charges of the sub-atomic particles should be known, actual values are given in section 4 of the IB data booklet. The mass of the electron can be considered negligible.

- Negatively charged electrons occupy the space outside the nucleus.
- The mass spectrometer is used to determine the relative atomic mass of an element from its isotopic composition.

  Guidance
  The operation of the mass spectrometer is not required.

Applications and skills:

- Use of the nuclear symbol notation $^A_Z X$ to deduce the number of protons, neutrons, and electrons in atoms and ions.
- Calculations involving non-integer relative atomic masses and abundance of isotopes from given data, including mass spectra.

  Guidance
  Specific examples of isotopes need not be learned.

Dalton's model of the atom

One of the first great achievements of chemistry was to show that all matter is built from about 100 **elements**. As mentioned in Chapter 1, the elements are substances which cannot be broken down into simpler components by chemical reactions. They are the simplest substances and their names are listed in your IB data booklet (section 5). Different elements have different chemical properties but gold foil, for example, reacts in essentially the same way as a single piece of gold dust. Indeed if the gold dust is cut into smaller and smaller pieces, the chemical properties would remain essentially the same until we reached an **atom**. This is the smallest unit of an element. There are only 92 elements which occur naturally on Earth and they are made up from only 92 different types of atom. (This statement will be qualified when isotopes are discussed later in the chapter.)

An element is a substance that cannot be broken down into simpler substances by a chemical reaction.

The word 'atom' comes from the Greek words for 'not able to be cut'.

Scanning tunnelling microscope (STM) image of the surface of pure gold. STM provides a magnification of 250 000 times, which records the surface structure at the level of the individual atoms. Gold exists in many forms – gold foil, nuggets, blocks, etc., which all contain the same type of atoms. The 'rolling hills' structure seen here is the result of changes in the surface energy as the gold cooled from its molten state. STM is based on quantum mechanical effects.

NATURE OF SCIENCE

The idea that matter is made up from elements and atoms dates back to the Indian philosophy of the sixth century BCE and the Greek philosophy of Democritus (460 BCE to 370 BCE). These ideas were speculative as there was little evidence to support them. A significant development for chemistry came with the publication of Robert Boyle's *Skeptical Chemist* of 1661 which emphasized the need for scientific knowledge to be justified by evidence from practical investigations. Boyle was the first to propose the modern concept of an element as a substance which cannot be changed into anything simpler.

The modern idea of the atom dates from the beginning of the 19th century. John Dalton noticed that the elements hydrogen and oxygen always combined together in fixed proportions. To explain this observation he proposed that:

• all matter is composed of tiny indivisible particles called atoms;
• atoms cannot be created or destroyed;
• atoms of the same element are alike in every way;
• atoms of different elements are different;
• atoms can combine together in small numbers to form **molecules**.

Using this model we can understand how elements react together to make new substances called **compounds**. The compound water, for example, is formed when two hydrogen atoms combine with one oxygen atom to produce one water molecule. If we repeat the reaction on a larger scale with $2 \times 6.02 \times 10^{23}$ atoms of hydrogen and 6.02×10^{23} atoms of oxygen, 6.02×10^{23} molecules of water will be formed. This leads to the conclusion (see Chapter 1) that 2.02 g of hydrogen will react with 16.00 g of oxygen to form 18.02 g of water. This is one of the observations Dalton was trying to explain.

NATURE OF SCIENCE

Dalton was a man of regular habits. For fifty-seven years... he measured the rainfall, the temperature... Of all that mass of data, nothing whatever came. But of the one searching, almost childlike question about the weights that enter the construction of simple molecules – out of that came modern atomic theory. That is the essence of science: ask an impertinent question: and you are on the way to the pertinent answer. (J. Bronowski)

Dalton was the first person to assign chemical symbols to the different elements.

CHALLENGE YOURSELF

2 It is now known that some of these substances are not elements but compounds. Lime, for example, is a compound of calcium and oxygen. Can you find any other examples in this list and explain why the elements had not been extracted at this time?

John Dalton's symbols for the elements.

Although John Dalton (1766–1844) was a school teacher from Manchester in England, his name has passed into other languages. The internationally recognized term for colour-blindness, *Daltonisme* in French, for example, derives from the fact the he suffered from the condition.

TOK 'What we observe is not nature itself but nature exposed to our mode of questioning.' (Werner Heisenberg). How does the knowledge we gain about the natural world depend on the questions we ask and the experiments we perform?

A compound is a substance made by chemically combining two or more elements. It has different properties from its constituent elements.

59

▲
Figure 2.1 A model of a water molecule made from two hydrogen atoms and one oxygen atom. Dalton's picture of the atom as a hard ball is the basis behind the molecular models we use today.

▲
Figure 2.2 Thomson's 'plum pudding' model of the atom. The electrons (yellow) are scattered in a positively charged sponge-like substance (pink).

When Geiger and Marsden reported to Rutherford that they had seen nothing unusual with most of the alpha particles passing straight through the gold and a small number being deflected by small angles, he asked them to look and see if any of the alpha particles had bounced back. This was a very unusual suggestion to make at the time, with little logical justification. What is the role of intuition in the pursuit of scientific knowledge?

Following his example, the formation of water (described above) can be written using modern notation:

$$2H + O \rightarrow H_2O$$

But what are atoms really like? It can be useful to think of them as hard spheres (Figure 2.1) but this tells us little about how the atoms of different elements differ. To understand this, it is necessary to probe deeper.

NATURE OF SCIENCE

Dalton's atomic theory was not accepted when it was first proposed. Many scientists, such as Kelvin for example, considered it as nothing more than a useful fiction which should not be taken too seriously. Over time, as the supporting evidence grew, there was a general shift in thinking which led to its widespread acceptance. These revolutions in understanding or '**paradigm shifts**' are characteristic of the evolutions of scientific thinking.

Atoms contain electrons

The first indication that atoms were destructible came at the end of the 19th century when the British scientist J. J. Thomson discovered that different metals produce a stream of negatively charged particles when a high voltage is applied across two electrodes. As these particles, which we now know as **electrons**, were the same regardless of the metal, he suggested that they are part of the make-up of all atoms.

NATURE OF SCIENCE

The properties of electrons, or cathode rays as they were first called, could only be investigated once powerful vacuum pumps had been invented – and once advances had been made in the use and understanding of electricity and magnetism. Improved instrumentation and new technology have often been the drivers for new discoveries.

As it was known that the atom had no net charge, Thomson pictured the atom as a 'plum pudding', with the negatively charged electrons scattered in a positively charged sponge-like substance (Figure 2.2).

Rutherford's model of the atom

Ernest Rutherford (1871–1937) and his research team working at Manchester University in England, tested Thomson's model by firing alpha particles at a piece of gold foil. We now know that alpha particles are helium nuclei, composed of two protons and two neutrons, with a positive charge. They are emitted by nuclei with too many protons to be stable. If Thomson's model was correct, the alpha particles should either pass straight through or get stuck in the positive 'sponge'. Most of the alpha particles did indeed pass straight through, but a very small number were repelled and bounced back. Ernest Rutherford recalled that 'It was quite the most incredible thing that has happened to me. It was as if you had fired a (artillery) shell at a piece of tissue paper and it came back and hit you.'

The large number of undeflected paths led to the conclusion that the atom is mainly empty space. Large deflections occur when the positively charged alpha particles collide with and are repelled by a dense, positively charged centre called the **nucleus** (Figure 2.3). The fact that only a small number of alpha particles bounce back suggests that the nucleus is very small.

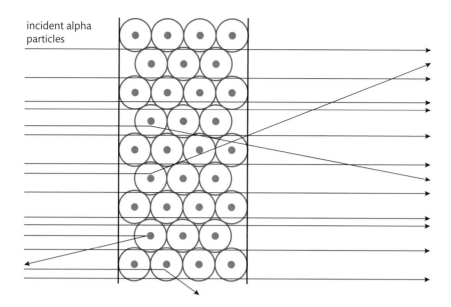

incident alpha particles

Figure 2.3 Rutherford's model of the atom accounts for the experimental observations. Most of the alpha particles pass straight through but a small number collide with and are repelled by a positively charged nucleus.

NATURE OF SCIENCE

Our knowledge of the nuclear atom came from Rutherford's experiments with the relatively newly discovered alpha particles. Scientific knowledge grows as new evidence is gathered as a result of new technologies and instrumentation.

The European Organization for Nuclear Research (CERN) is run by twenty European Member States, with involvements from scientists from many other countries. It operates the world's largest particle physics research centre, including particle accelerators and detectors used to study the fundamental constituents of matter.

Sub-atomic particles

A hundred years or so after Dalton first proposed his model, these experiments and many others showed that atoms are themselves made up from smaller or **sub-atomic** particles. The nucleus of an atom is made up of **protons** and **neutrons**, collectively called **nucleons**. Both the protons and neutrons have almost the same mass as a hydrogen nucleus and account for the most of the mass of the atom. **Electrons**, which have a charge equal and opposite to that of the proton, occupy the space in the atom outside of the nucleus.

These particles are described by their *relative* masses and charges which have no units. The absolute masses and charges of these fundamental particles are given in section 4 of the IB data booklet.

Particle	Relative mass	Relative charge
proton	1	+1
electron	0.0005	−1
neutron	1	0

PET (positron-emission tomography) scanners give three-dimensional images of tracer concentration in the body, and can be used to detect cancers. The patient is injected with a tracer compound labelled with a positron-emitting isotope. The positrons collide with electrons after travelling a short distance (≈1 mm) within the body. Both particles are destroyed with the production of two photons, which can be collected by the detectors surrounding the patient, and used to generate an image.

NATURE OF SCIENCE

The description of sub-atomic particles offered here is sufficient to understand chemistry but incomplete. Although the electron is indeed a fundamental particle, we now know that the protons and neutrons are both themselves made up from more fundamental particles called quarks. We also know that all particles have anti-particles. The positron is the anti-particle of an electron; it has the same mass but has an equal and opposite positive charge. When particles and anti-particles collide they destroy each other and energy in the form of high-energy photons called gamma rays. Our treatment of sub-atomic particles is in line with the principle of Occam's razor, which states that theories should be as simple as possible while maximizing explanatory power.

As you are made from atoms, you are also mainly empty space. The particles which make up your mass would occupy the same volume as a flea if they were all squashed together, but a flea with your mass. This gives you an idea of the density of the nucleus.

None of these sub-atomic particles can be (or ever will be) directly observed. Which ways of knowing do we use to interpret indirect evidence gained through the use of technology?

Figure 2.4 The simplest atom. Only one proton and one electron make up the hydrogen atom. The nuclear radius is 10^{-15} m and the atomic radius 10^{-10} m. Most of the volume of the atom is empty – the only occupant is the negatively charged electron. It is useful to think of the electron orbiting the nucleus in a similar way to the planets orbiting the sun. The absence of a neutron is significant – it would be essentially redundant as there is only one proton.

Figure 2.5 A helium atom. The two neutrons allow the two protons, which repel each other, to stay in the nucleus.

The atomic number is defined as the number of protons in the nucleus.

Bohr model of the hydrogen atom

The Danish physicist Niels Bohr pictured the hydrogen atom as a small 'solar system', with an electron moving in an orbit or energy level around the positively charged nucleus of one proton (Figure 2.4). The electrostatic force of attraction between the oppositely charged sub-atomic particles prevents the electron from leaving the atom. The nuclear radius is 10^{-15} m and the atomic radius 10^{-10} m, so most of the volume of the atom is empty space.

The existence of neutrally charged neutrons is crucial for the stability of nuclei of later elements, which have more than one proton. Without the neutrons, the positively charged protons would mutually repel each other and the nucleus would fall apart.

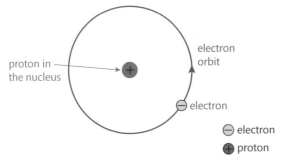

proton in the nucleus

electron orbit

electron

⊖ electron
⊕ proton

⊖ electron
⊕ proton
ⓝ neutron

Atomic number and mass number

We are now in a position to understand how the atoms of different elements differ. They are all made from the same basic ingredients, the sub-atomic particles. The only difference is the recipe – how many of each of these sub-atomic particles are present in the atoms of different elements. If you look at the Periodic Table, you will see that the elements are each given a number which describes their relative position in the table. This is their **atomic number**. We now know that the atomic number, represented by **Z**, is the defining property of an element as it tells us something about the structure of the atoms of the element. The atomic number is defined as the number of protons in the atom.

As an atom has no overall charge, the positive charge of the protons must be balanced by the negative charge of the electrons. The atomic number is also equal to the number of electrons.

The electron has such a very small mass that it is essentially ignored in mass calculations. The mass of an atom depends on the number of protons and neutrons only. The **mass number**, given the symbol A, is defined as the number of protons plus the number of neutrons in an atom. An atom is identified in the following way:

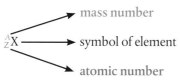

mass number

$^{A}_{Z}X$ ⟶ symbol of element

atomic number

Make sure you have a precise understanding of the terms identified in the subject guide. The atomic number, for example, is defined in terms of the number of protons, not electrons.

The mass number (A) is the number of protons plus the number of neutrons (total number of nucleons) in an atom. As it gives the total number of nucleons in the nucleus it is sometimes called the nucleon number.

We can use these numbers to find the composition of any atom.

number of protons (p) = number of electrons = Z

number of neutrons (n) = A – number of protons = $A - Z$

Consider an atom of aluminium:

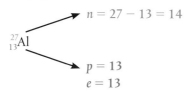

$n = 27 - 13 = 14$

$^{27}_{13}Al$

$p = 13$
$e = 13$

An aluminium atom is made from 13 protons and 13 electrons. An atom of gold on the other hand has 79 protons and 79 electrons. Can you find gold in the Periodic Table?

Isotopes

Find chlorine in the Periodic Table. There are two numbers associated with the element, as shown below.

Atomic number = 17

Relative atomic mass = 35.45

How can an element have a fractional relative atomic mass if both the proton and neutron have a relative mass of 1? One reason is that atoms of the same element with different mass numbers exist, so it is necessary to work within an average value – as discussed in Chapter 1.

To have different mass numbers, the atoms must have different numbers of neutrons – all the atoms have the same number of protons as they are all chlorine atoms. Atoms of the same element with different numbers of neutrons are called **isotopes**.

The isotopes show the same chemical properties, as a difference in the number of neutrons makes no difference to how they react and so they occupy the same place in the Periodic Table.

Isotopes are atoms of the same element with different mass numbers.

The word 'isotope' derives from the Greek for 'same place'. As isotopes are atoms of the same element, they occupy the same place in the Periodic Table.

A common error is to misunderstand the meaning of 'physical property'. A difference in the number of neutrons is not a different physical property. A physical property of a substance can be measured without changing the chemical composition of the substance, e.g. melting point, density.

Radioisotopes are used in nuclear medicine for diagnostics, treatment, and research, as tracers in biochemical and pharmaceutical research, and as 'chemical clocks' in geological and archaeological dating.

Radioactive isotopes are extremely hazardous and their use is of international concern. The International Atomic Energy Agency (IAEA) promotes the peaceful use of nuclear energy. The organization was awarded the Nobel Peace Prize in 2005.

When an atom loses electrons, a positive ion is formed and when it gains electrons, a negative ion is formed. Positive ions are called cations and negative ions are called anions.

Chlorine exists as two isotopes, ^{35}Cl and ^{37}Cl. The average relative mass of the isotopes is, however, not 36, but 35.45. This value is closer to 35 as there are more ^{35}Cl atoms in nature – it is the more abundant isotope. In a sample of 100 chlorine atoms, there are 77.5 atoms of ^{35}Cl and 22.5 atoms of the heavier isotope, ^{37}Cl.

To work out the average mass of one atom we first have to calculate the total mass of the hundred atoms:

$$\text{total mass} = (77.5 \times 35) + (22.5 \times 37) = 3545$$

$$\text{relative average mass} = \frac{\text{total mass}}{\text{number of atoms}} = \frac{3545}{100} = 35.45$$

The two isotopes are both atoms of chlorine with 17 protons and 17 electrons.

- ^{35}Cl; number of neutrons = 35 – 17 = 18
- ^{37}Cl; number of neutrons = 37 – 17 = 20

Although both isotopes essentially have the same chemical properties, the difference in mass does lead to different physical properties such as boiling and melting points. Heavier isotopes move more slowly at a given temperature and these differences can be used to separate isotopes.

Exercises

1 State two physical properties other than boiling and melting point that would differ for the two isotopes of chlorine.

2 Explain why the relative atomic mass of tellurium is greater than the relative atomic mass of iodine, even though iodine has a greater atomic number.

Uranium exists in nature as two isotopes, uranium-235 and uranium-238. One key stage in the Manhattan Project (the development of the atomic bomb during World War II) was the enrichment of uranium with the lighter and less abundant isotope, as this is the atom which splits more easily. It is only 0.711% abundant in nature. First the uranium was converted to a gaseous compound (the hexafluoride UF_6). Gaseous molecules with the lighter uranium isotope move faster than those containing the heavier isotope at the same temperature and so the isotopes could be separated. Isotope enrichment is employed in many countries as part of nuclear energy and weaponry programmes. This is discussed in more detail in Chapter 14.

NATURE OF SCIENCE

Science is a collaborative endeavour and it is common for scientists to work in teams between disciplines, laboratories, organizations, and countries. The Manhattan Project, which produced the first nuclear bomb, employed more than 130 000 people working in secret at different production and research sites. Today such collaboration is facilitated by virtual communication which allows scientists around the globe to work together.

Ions

The atomic number is defined in terms of number of protons because it is a fixed characteristic of the element. The number of protons identifies the element in the same way your fingerprints identify you. The number of protons and neutrons never changes during a chemical reaction. It is the electrons which are responsible for chemical change. Chapter 4 will examine how atoms can lose or gain electrons to form **ions**. When the number of protons in a particle is no longer balanced by the number of electrons, the particles have a non-zero charge. When an atom loses electrons it forms a positive ion or **cation**, as the number of protons is now greater than the number of electrons. Negative ions or **anions** are formed when atoms gain electrons. The magnitude of the charge depends on the number of electrons lost or gained. The loss or gain of electrons makes a very big difference to the chemical properties. You swallow sodium ions, Na^+, every time you eat table salt, whereas (as you will discover in Chapter 3) sodium atoms, Na, are dangerously reactive.

An aluminium ion is formed when the atom loses three electrons. There is no change in the atomic or mass numbers of an ion because the number of protons and neutrons remains the same.

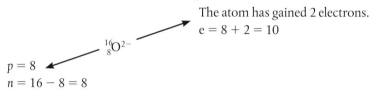

The atom has lost 3 electrons.
$e = 13 - 3 = 10$

$^{27}_{13}Al^{3+}$

$p = 13$
$n = 27 - 13 = 14$

Oxygen forms the oxide ion when the atom gains two electrons.

The atom has gained 2 electrons.
$e = 8 + 2 = 10$

$^{16}_{8}O^{2-}$

$p = 8$
$n = 16 - 8 = 8$

Worked example

Identify the sub-atomic particles present in an atom of ^{226}Ra.

Solution

The number identifying the atom is the atomic number. We can find the atomic number from the IB data booklet (section 5).

We have $Z = 88$ and $A = 226$

In other words:

- number of protons (p) = 88
- number of electrons (e) = 88
- number of neutrons (n) = 226 − 88 = 138

Worked example

Most nutrient elements in food are present in the form of ions. The calcium ion $^{40}Ca^{2+}$, for example, is essential for healthy teeth and bones. Identify the sub-atomic particles present in the ion.

Solution

We can find the atomic number from the IB data booklet (section 5). We have $Z = 20$ and $A = 40$:

- number of protons (p) = 20
- number of neutrons (n) = 40 − 20 = 20

As the ion has a positive charge of 2+ there are two more protons than electrons:

- number of electrons = 20 − 2 = 18

Worked example

Identify the species with 19 protons, 20 neutrons and 18 electrons.

Solution

- the number of protons tells us the atomic number; $Z = 19$ and the element is potassium: K
- the mass number = $p + n = 19 + 20 = 39$: $^{39}_{19}$K
- the charge will be = $p - e = 19 - 18 = +1$ as there is one less electron: $^{39}_{19}$K$^+$

Exercises

3 Use the Periodic Table to identify the sub-atomic particles present in the following species.

	Species	No. of protons	No. of neutrons	No. of electrons
(a)	^{7}Li			
(b)	^{1}H			
(c)	^{14}C			
(d)	^{19}F$^-$			
(e)	^{56}Fe^{3+}			

4 Isoelectronic species have the same number of electrons. Identify the following isoelectronic species by giving the correct symbol and charge. You will need a Periodic Table.

The first one has been done as an example.

	Species	No. of protons	No. of neutrons	No. of electrons
	^{40}Ca^{2+}	20	20	18
(a)		18	22	18
(b)		19	20	18
(c)		17	18	18

5 Which of the following species contain more electrons than neutrons?

   A $^2_1$H   **B** $^{11}_5$B   **C** $^{16}_8$O^{2-} **D** $^{19}_9$F$^-$

6 Which of the following gives the correct composition of the ^{71}Ga$^+$ ion present in the mass spectrometer when gallium is analysed.

	Protons	Neutrons	Electrons
A	31	71	30
B	31	40	30
C	31	40	32
D	32	40	31

Relative atomic masses of some elements

An instrument known as a mass spectrometer can be used to measure the mass of individual atoms. The mass of a hydrogen atom is 1.67×10^{-24} g and that of a carbon atom is 1.99×10^{-23} g. As the masses of all elements are in the range 10^{-24} to 10^{-22} g and these numbers are beyond our direct experience, it makes more sense to use relative values. The mass needs to be recorded relative to some agreed standard. As carbon is a very common element which is easy to transport and store because it is a solid, its isotope, ^{12}C, was chosen as the standard in 1961. As discussed in Chapter 1 this is given a relative mass of exactly 12, as shown below.

Element	Symbol	Relative atomic mass
carbon	C	12.011
chlorine	Cl	35.453
hydrogen	H	1.008
iron	Fe	55.845

Standard isotope	Symbol	Relative atomic mass
carbon-12	^{12}C	12.000

Carbon-12 is the most abundant isotope of carbon but carbon-13 and carbon-14 also exist. This explains why the average value for the element is greater than 12.

Mass spectra

The results of the analysis by the mass spectrometer are presented in the form of a **mass spectrum**. The horizontal axis shows the mass/charge ratio of the different ions on the carbon-12 scale, which in most cases can be considered equivalent to their mass. The percentage abundance of the ions is shown on the vertical axis.

The mass spectrum of gallium in Figure 2.6 shows that in a sample of 100 atoms, 60 have a mass of 69 and 40 have a mass of 71. We can use this information to calculate the relative atomic mass of the element.

total mass of 100 atoms = $(60 \times 69) + (40 \times 71) = 6980$

relative average mass = $\dfrac{\text{total mass}}{\text{number of atoms}} = \dfrac{6980}{100} = 69.80$

The relative atomic mass of an element (A_r) is the average mass of an atom of the element, taking into account all its isotopes and their relative abundance, compared to one atom of carbon-12.

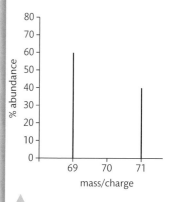

Figure 2.6 Mass spectrum for gallium. The number of lines indicates the number of isotopes (two in this case), the value on the x-axis indicates their mass number (69 and 71) and the y-axis shows the percentage abundance.

Worked example

Deduce the relative atomic mass of the element rubidium from the data given in Figure 2.7.

Solution

Consider a sample of 100 atoms.

total mass of 100 atoms = $(85 \times 77) + (87 \times 23) = 8546$

relative atomic mass = average mass of atom = $\dfrac{\text{total mass}}{\text{number of atoms}} = \dfrac{8546}{100} = 85.46$

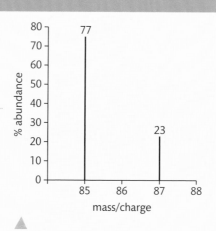

Figure 2.7 Mass spectrum for rubidium.

Worked example

Boron exists in two isotopic forms, ^{10}B and ^{11}B. ^{10}B is used as a control for nuclear reactors. Use your Periodic Table to find the abundances of the two isotopes.

Solution

Consider a sample of 100 atoms.

Let x atoms be ^{10}B atoms. The remaining atoms are ^{11}B.

number of ^{11}B atoms $= 100 - x$

total mass $= x \times 10 + (100 - x) \times 11 = 10x + 1100 - 11x = 1100 - x$

$$\text{average mass} = \frac{\text{total mass}}{\text{number of atoms}} = \frac{1100 - x}{100}$$

From the Periodic Table, the relative atomic mass of boron $= 10.81$.

$$10.81 = \frac{1100 - x}{100}$$
$$1081 = 1100 - x$$

$$x = 1100 - 1081 = 19$$

The abundances are $^{10}B = 19\%$ and $^{11}B = 81\%$

Exercises

7 What is the same for an atom of phosphorus-26 and an atom of phosphorus-27?

    A atomic number and mass number
    B number of protons and electrons
    C number of neutrons and electrons
    D number of protons and neutrons

8 Use the Periodic Table to find the percentage abundance of neon-20, assuming that neon has only one other isotope, neon-22.

9 The relative abundances of the two isotopes of chlorine are shown in this table:

Isotope	Relative abundance
^{35}Cl	75%
^{37}Cl	25%

Use this information to deduce the mass spectrum of chlorine gas, Cl_2.

10 Magnesium has three stable isotopes – ^{24}Mg, ^{25}Mg and ^{26}Mg. The lightest isotope has an abundance of 78.90%. Calculate the percentage abundance of the other isotopes.

11 The Geiger–Marsden experiment, supervised by Ernest Rutherford, gave important evidence for the structure of the atom. Positively charged alpha particles were fired at a piece of gold foil. Most of the particles passed through with only minor deflections but a small number rebounded from the foil.

How did this experiment change our knowledge of the atom?

    A It provided evidence for the existence of discrete atomic energy levels.
    B It provided evidence for a positively charged dense nucleus.
    C It provided evidence that electrons move in unpredictable paths around the nucleus.
    D It provided evidence for the existence of an uncharged particle in the nucleus.

In 1911, a 40 kg meteorite fell in Egypt. Isotopic and chemical analysis of oxygen extracted from this meteorite show a different relative atomic mass to that of oxygen normally found on Earth. This value matched measurements made of the Martian atmosphere by the Viking landing in 1976, showing that the meteorite had originated from Mars.

Electron configuration

Understandings:

- Emission spectra are produced when photons are emitted from atoms as excited electrons return to a lower energy level.
- The line emission spectrum of hydrogen provides evidence for the existence of electrons in discrete energy levels, which converge at higher energies.

Guidance
The names of the different series in the hydrogen line spectrum are not required.

- The main energy level or shell is given an integer number, n, and can hold a maximum number of electrons, $2n^2$.
- A more detailed model of the atom describes the division of the main energy level into s, p, d and f sub-levels of successively higher energies.
- Sub-levels contain a fixed number of orbitals, regions of space where there is a high probability of finding an electron.
- Each orbital has a defined energy state for a given electronic configuration and chemical environment and can hold two electrons of opposite spin.

Applications and skills:

- Description of the relationship between colour, wavelength, frequency, and energy across the electromagnetic spectrum.

Guidance
Details of the electromagnetic spectrum are given in the IB data booklet in section 3.

- Distinction between a continuous spectrum and a line spectrum.
- Description of the emission spectrum of the hydrogen atom, including the relationships between the lines and energy transitions to the first, second, and third energy levels.
- Recognition of the shape of an s orbital and the p_x, p_y, and p_z atomic orbitals.
- Application of the Aufbau principle, Hund's rule, and the Pauli exclusion principle to write electron configurations for atoms and ions up to $Z = 36$.

Guidance
- *Full electron configurations (e.g. $1s^2 2s^2 2p^6 3s^2 3p^4$) and condensed electron configurations (e.g. [Ne] $3s^2 3p^4$) should be covered.*
- *Orbital diagrams should be used to represent the character and relative energy of orbitals. Orbital diagrams refer to arrow-in-box diagrams, such as the one given below.*

- *The electron configurations of Cr and Cu as exceptions should be covered.*

Atoms of different elements give out light of a distinctive colour when an electric discharge is passed through a vapour of the element. Similarly, metals can be identified by the colour of the flame produced when their compounds are heated in a Bunsen burner. Analysis of the light emitted by different atoms has given us insights into the electron configurations within the atom.

To interpret these results we must consider the nature of electromagnetic radiation.

The electromagnetic spectrum

Electromagnetic radiation comes in different forms of differing energy. The visible light we need to see the world is only a small part of the full spectrum, which ranges from low-energy radio waves to high-energy gamma rays. All electromagnetic waves

(a)

(b)

(c)

▲
Flame tests on the compounds of (a) sodium, (b) potassium, and (c) copper.

Flame colours can be used to identify unknown compounds.

Figure 2.8 Snapshot of a wave at a given instant. The distance between successive crests or peaks is called the wavelength (λ).

The distance between two successive crests (or troughs) is called the wavelength (λ). The frequency (ν) of the wave is the number of waves which pass a point in 1s. The wavelength and frequency are related by the equation $c = \nu\lambda$ where c is the speed of light.

travel at the same **speed** (*c*) but can be distinguished by their different **wavelengths** (λ) (Figure 2.8). Different colours of visible light have different wavelengths; red light, for example, has a longer wavelength than blue light. The full electromagnetic spectrum is given in section 3 of the IB data booklet.

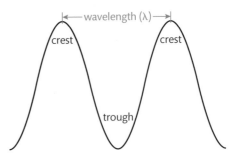

The number of waves which pass a particular point in 1 s is called the **frequency** (*v*); the shorter the wavelength, the higher the frequency. Blue light has a higher frequency than red light.

The wavelength and frequency are related by the equation:

$$c = v\lambda$$

where *c* is the speed of light.

White light is a mixture of light waves of differing wavelengths or colours. We see this when sunlight passes through a prism to produce a **continuous spectrum** or as a rainbow when light is scattered through water droplets in the air.

A continuous spectrum is produced when white light is passed through a prism. The different colours merge smoothly into one another. The two spectra below the illustration of the prism show, (top) a continuous spectrum with a series of discrete absorption lines and (bottom) a line emission spectrum.

As well as visible light, atoms emit infrared radiation, which has a longer wavelength than red light, and ultraviolet radiation, with a shorter wavelength than violet light. The complete electromagnetic spectrum is shown in Figure 2.9.

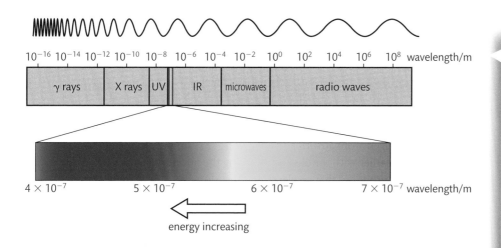

10^{-16} 10^{-14} 10^{-12} 10^{-10} 10^{-8} 10^{-6} 10^{-4} 10^{-2} 10^{0} 10^{2} 10^{4} 10^{6} 10^{8} wavelength/m

| γ rays | X rays | UV | IR | microwaves | radio waves |

4×10^{-7} 5×10^{-7} 6×10^{-7} 7×10^{-7} wavelength/m

⟵ energy increasing

Figure 2.9 The changing wavelength (in m) of electromagnetic radiation through the spectrum is shown by the trace across the top. At the short wavelength end (on the left) of the spectrum are *γ* rays, X rays and ultraviolet light. In the centre of the spectrum are wavelengths that the human eye can see, known as visible light. Visible light comprises light of different wavelengths, energies, and colours. At the longer wavelength end of the spectrum (on the right) are infrared radiation, microwaves, and radio waves. The visible spectrum gives us only a small window to see the world.

Atomic absorption and emission line spectra

When electromagnetic radiation is passed through a collection of atoms some of the radiation is absorbed and used to excite the atoms from a lower energy level to a higher energy level. The spectrometer analyses the transmitted radiation relative to the incident radiation and an **absorption spectrum** is produced.

sample in low energy level

absorption spectrum

sample in high energy level

emission spectrum

Figure 2.10 The origin of absorption and emission spectra. An absorption spectrum shows the radiation absorbed as atoms move from a lower to a higher energy level. An emission spectrum is produced when an atom moves from a higher to a lower level.

When white light is passed through hydrogen gas, an absorption **line spectrum** is produced with some colours of the continuous spectrum missing. If a high voltage is applied to the gas, a corresponding **emission** line spectrum is produced.

🔋 **Investigating flame tests**
Full details of how to carry out this experiment with a worksheet are available on your eBook.

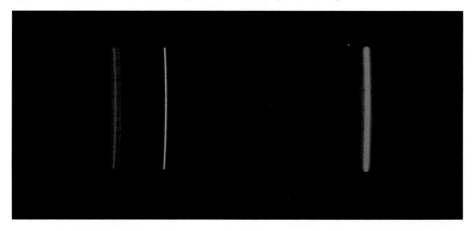

Visible emission spectrum of hydrogen. These lines form the Balmer series and you should note that they converge at higher energies. Similar series are found in the ultraviolet region – the Lyman Series – and in the infrared region – the Paschen series.

The colours present in the emission spectrum are the same as those that are missing from the absorption spectra. As different elements have different line spectra they can be used like bar codes to identify unknown elements. They give us valuable information about the electron configurations of different atoms.

🔋 Emission spectra could be observed using discharge tubes of different gases and a spectroscope.

Electromagnetic waves allow energy to be transferred across the universe. They also carry information. Low-energy radio waves are used in radar and television, for example, and the higher energy gamma rays are used as medical tracers. The precision with which we view the world is limited by the wavelengths of the colours we can see. This is why we will never be able to see an atom directly; it is too small to interact with the relatively long waves of visible light. What are the implications of this for human knowledge?

The elemental composition of stars can be determined by analysing their absorption spectra. This is discussed in more detail in Chapter 14.

Figure 2.11 Emission and absorption spectra are the result of an energy transition between the ground and excited states.

• A continuous spectrum shows an unbroken sequence of frequencies, such as the spectrum of visible light.

• A line emission spectrum has only certain frequencies of light as it is produced by excited atoms and ions as they fall back to a lower energy level.

• A line absorption spectrum is a continuous spectrum except for certain colours which are absorbed as the atoms are excited to higher energy levels.

TOK ⓘ The element helium was discovered in the Sun before it was found on Earth. Some unexpected spectral lines were observed when the absorption spectra of sunlight was analysed. These lines did not correspond to any known element. The new element was named after the Greek word *helios*, which means 'Sun'. Emission and absorption spectra can be used like barcodes to identify the different elements.

Evidence for the Bohr model

How can a hydrogen atom absorb and emit energy? A simple picture of the atom was considered earlier with the electron orbiting the nucleus in a circular energy level. Niels Bohr proposed that an electron moves into an orbit or higher energy level further from the nucleus when an atom absorbs energy. The **excited state** produced is, however, unstable and the electron soon falls back to the lowest level or **ground state**. The energy the electron gives out when it falls into lower levels is in the form of electromagnetic radiation. One packet of energy (quantum) or **photon**, is released for each electron transition (Figure 2.11). Photons of ultraviolet light have more energy than photons of infrared light. The energy of the photon is proportional to the frequency of the radiation.

excited state

ground state

When an atom falls from an excited state to the ground state, light of a specific frequency v is emitted.

When an atom moves from the ground state to an excited state, light of a specific frequency v is absorbed.

The energy of the photon of light emitted is equal to the energy change in the atom:

$$\Delta E_{\text{electron}} = E_{\text{photon}}$$

It is also related to the frequency of the radiation by the Planck equation:

$$E_{\text{photon}} = hv$$

This equation and the value of h (the Planck constant) are given in sections 1 and 2 of the IB data booklet.)

This leads to:

$$\Delta E_{\text{electron}} = hv$$

This is a very significant equation as it shows that line spectra allow us to glimpse the inside of the atom. The atoms emit photons of certain energies which give lines of certain frequencies, because the electron can only occupy certain orbits. The energy levels can be thought of as a staircase. The electron cannot change its energy in a continuous way, in the same way that you cannot stand between steps; it can only change its energy by discrete amounts. This energy of the atom is **quantized**. The line spectrum is crucial evidence for quantization: if the energy were not quantized, the emission spectrum would be continuous.

The idea that electromagnetic waves can be thought of as a stream of photons or quanta is one aspect of quantum theory. The theory has implications for human knowledge and technology. The key idea is that energy can only be transferred in discrete amounts or quanta. Quantum theory shows us that our everyday experience cannot be transferred to the microscopic world of the atom and has led to great technological breakthroughs such as the modern computer. It has been estimated that 30% of the gross national product of the USA depends on the applications of quantum theory. In the modern world our scientific understanding has led to many technological developments. These new technologies in their turn drive developments in science. The implications of the quantum theory for the electron are discussed in more detail later (page 74). Note that 'discrete' has a different meaning to 'discreet'.

The amount of light absorbed at particular frequency depends on the identity and concentration of atoms present. Atomic absorption spectroscopy is used to measure the concentration of metallic elements.

When asked to distinguish between a line spectrum and a continuous spectrum, references should be made to discrete or continuous energy levels and all or specific colours, wavelengths, or frequencies.

The hydrogen spectrum

The hydrogen atom gives out energy when an electron falls from a higher to a lower energy level. Hydrogen produces visible light when the electron falls to the second energy level (*n* = 2). The transitions to the first energy level (*n* = 1) correspond to a higher energy change and are in the ultraviolet region of the spectrum. Infrared radiation is produced when an electron falls to the third or higher energy levels (Figure 2.12).

Figure 2.12 When an electron is excited from a lower to a higher energy level, energy is absorbed and a line in the absorption spectrum is produced. When an electron falls from a higher to a lower energy level, radiation is given out by the atom and a line in the emission spectrum is produced.

The energy of a photon of electromagnetic radiation is directly proportional to its frequency and inversely proportional to its wavelength. It can be calculated from the Planck equation (*E* = hν), which is given in section 1 of the IB data booklet.

The pattern of the lines in Figure 2.13 gives us a picture of the energy levels in the atom. The lines **converge** at higher energies because the energy levels inside the atoms are closer together at high energy. When an electron is at the highest energy *n* = ∞, it is no longer in the atom and the atom has been ionized. The energy needed to remove an electron from the ground state of each atom in a mole of gaseous atoms, ions, or molecules is called the **ionization energy**. Ionization energies can also be used to support this model of the atom.

The first ionization energy of an element is the minimum energy needed to remove one mole of electrons from one mole of gaseous atoms in their ground state.

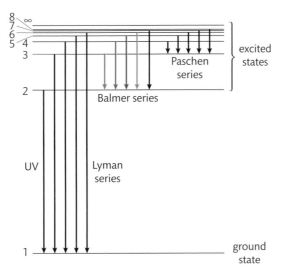

Figure 2.13 Energy levels of the hydrogen atom showing the transitions which produce the Lyman, Balmer, and Paschen series. The transition 1 → ∞ corresponds to ionization:

$$H(g) \rightarrow H^+(g) + e^-$$

This is discussed in more detail later.

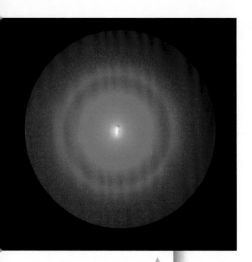

Demonstration of wave–particle duality. An electron gun has been fired at a thin sheet of graphite. The electrons passed through the graphite and hit a luminescent screen, producing the pattern of rings associated with diffraction. Diffraction occurs when a wave passes through an aperture similar in size to its wavelength. Quantum theory shows that electrons have wavelengths inversely proportional to their momentum (momentum is the product of their mass and velocity).

Wave and particle models

Although the Bohr model of the atom was able to explain the emission spectrum of hydrogen with great success, it fails to predict the spectral lines of atoms with more than one electron. The model is a simplification. To develop the model of the atom further, we need to reconsider the nature of light and matter.

We saw earlier that light could either be described by its frequency, v, which is a wave property, or by the energy of individual particles, E (called photons or quanta of light), which make up a beam of light. The two properties are related by the Planck equation $E = hv$. Both wave and particle models have traditionally been used to explain scientific phenomena and you may be tempted to ask which model gives the 'true' description of light. We now realize that neither model gives a complete explanation of light's properties – both models are needed.

- The diffraction, or spreading out, of light that occurs when light passes through a small slit can only be explained by a wave model.
- The scattering of electrons that occurs when light is incident on a metal surface is best explained using a particle model of light.

In a similar way, quantum theory suggests that it is sometimes preferable to think of an electron (or indeed any particle) as having wave properties. The diffraction pattern produced when a beam of electrons is passed through a thin sheet of graphite demonstrates the wave properties of electrons. To understand the electron configurations of atoms it is useful to consider a wave description of the electron.

NATURE OF SCIENCE

Models are used in science to explain processes that may not be observable. The models can be simple or complex in nature but must match the experimental evidence if they are to be accepted. The power of the wave and particle models is that they are based on our everyday experience, but this is also their limitation. We should not be too surprised if this way of looking at the world breaks down when applied to the atomic scale, as this is beyond our experience. The model we use depends on the phenomena we are trying to explain.

When differences occur between the theoretical predictions and experimental data, the models must be modified or replaced by new models. Bohr's model of the hydrogen atom was very successful in explaining the line spectra of the hydrogen atom but had some difficulties. It could not explain the spectra of more complex atoms, or the relative intensities of the lines in the hydrogen spectra. It also suffered from a fundamental weakness in that it was based on postulates which combined ideas from classical and quantum physics in an ad hoc manner, with little experimental justification: ideally models should be consistent with the assumptions and premises of other theories. A modification of Bohr's model could only be achieved at the expense of changing our model of the electron as a particle. Dalton's atomic model and quantum theory are both examples of such radical changes of understanding, often called **paradigm shifts**.

The Uncertainty Principle can be thought of as an extreme example of the observer effect discussed on page 630. The significance of the principle is that it shows the effect cannot be decreased indefinitely by improving the apparatus. There is an inherent uncertainty in our measurements. What are the implications of this for the limits of human knowledge?

TOK

The Uncertainty Principle

Another fundamental problem with the Bohr model is that it assumes the electron's trajectory can be precisely described. This is now known to be impossible, as any attempt to measure an electron's position will disturb its motion. The act of focusing radiation to locate the electron gives the electron a random 'kick' which sends it hurtling off in a random direction.

According to Heisenberg's **Uncertainty Principle** we cannot know where an electron is at any given moment in time – the best we can hope for is a probability picture of where the electron is *likely* to be. The possible positions of an electron are spread out in space in the same way as a wave is spread across a water surface.

Schrödinger model of the hydrogen atom

We have seen that the electron can be considered to have wave properties and that only a probability description of its location is possible

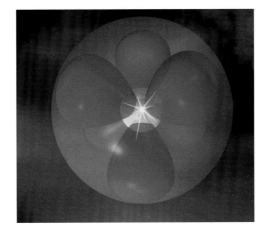

at a given time. Both of these ideas are encapsulated in the Schrödinger model of the hydrogen atom. Erwin Schrödinger (1887–1961) proposed that a wave equation could be used to describe the behaviour of an electron in the same way that a wave equation could be used to describe the behaviour of light. The equation can be applied to multi-electron systems and its solutions are known as **atomic orbitals**. An atomic orbital is a region around an atomic nucleus in which there is a 90% probability of finding the electron. The shape of the orbitals will depend on the energy of the electron. When an electron is in an orbital of higher energy it will have a higher probability of being found further from the nucleus.

Exercises

12 Emission and absorption spectra both provide evidence for:

   A the existence of neutrons   **B** the existence of isotopes
   C the existence of atomic energy levels   **D** the nuclear model of the atom

13 The diagram shows the lowest five electron energy levels in the hydrogen atom.

                ———————————— $n = 5$

                ———————————— $n = 4$

                ———————————— $n = 3$

                ———————————— $n = 2$

                ———————————— $n = 1$

   Deduce how many different frequencies in the visible emission spectrum of atomic hydrogen would arise as a result of electron transitions between these levels.

   A 3   **B** 4   **C** 6   **D** 10

14 Identify which of the following provide evidence to support the Bohr model of the hydrogen atom?

   I   The energy of the lines in the emission spectra of atomic hydrogen.
   II   The energy of the missing lines in the absorption spectra of helium as seen from the sun.
   III The relative intensity of the different spectral lines in the emission spectrum of atomic hydrogen.

   A I only   **B** II only   **C** I and II   **D** I and III

Our model of the atom owes a great deal to the work of Niels Bohr and Werner Heisenberg, who worked together in the early years of quantum theory before World War II. But they found themselves on different sides when war broke out. The award-winning play and film *Copenhagen* is based on their meeting in the eponymous city in 1941 and explores their relationship, the uncertainty of the past, and the moral responsibilities of the scientist.

Representation of atomic orbitals in an atom of neon, Ne. The nucleus is shown by a flash of light and the 1s orbital as a yellow sphere. The 2s orbital is shown as a pink sphere, and the 2p orbitals as blue lobes. According to Heisenberg's Principle, the exact position of an electron cannot be defined; atomic orbitals represent regions where there is a high probability of finding an electron.

 TOK

In our efforts to learn as much as possible about the atom, we have found that certain things can never be known with certainty. Much of our knowledge must always remain uncertain. Some suggest that Heisenberg's Uncertainty Principle has major implications for *all* areas of knowledge. Does science have the power to inform thinking in other areas of knowledge such as philosophy and religion? To what extent should philosophy and religion take careful note of scientific developments?

The progressive nature of scientific knowledge is illustrated by the Nobel Prizes awarded between 1922 and 1933. The Physics prize was awarded to Bohr in 1922, Heisenberg in 1932 and Schrödinger in 1933.

CHALLENGE YOURSELF

3 State **two** ways in which the Schrödinger model of the hydrogen atom differs from that of the Bohr model.

Atomic orbitals

The first energy level has one 1s orbital

We saw that the electron in hydrogen occupies the first energy level in the ground state, which can hold a maximum of two electrons. To highlight the distinction between this wave description of the electron provided by the Schrödinger model and the circular orbits of the Bohr atom, we say the electron occupies a 1s orbital.

Figure 2.14 An electron in a 1s atomic orbital. The density of the dots gives a measure of the probability of finding the electron in this region.

The dots in Figure 2.14 represent locations where the electron is most likely to be found. The denser the arrangement of dots, the higher the probability that the electron occupies this region of space. The electron can be found anywhere within a spherical space surrounding the nucleus.

The first energy level consists of a 1s atomic orbital which is spherical in shape.

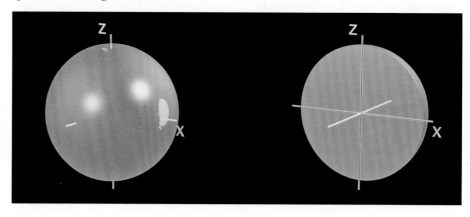

The electrons in the Bohr model occupy orbits, which are circular paths. An orbital, which is a wave description of the electron, shows the volume of space in which the electron is likely to be found.

The second energy level has a 2s and 2p level

The second energy level of the Bohr model is split into two **sub-levels** in the Schrödinger model. Further evidence of sub-shells comes from a consideration of patterns in first ionization energies, which will be discussed on page 97. The 2s sub-level is made up from one 2s orbital and can hold a maximum of two electrons, and the 2p sub-level is made up from three 2p orbitals and can hold six electrons.

The 2s orbital has the same symmetry as a 1s orbital but extends over a larger volume. So electrons in a 2s orbital are, on average, further from the nucleus than electrons in 1s orbitals and are at higher energy.

The 2s electron orbital. Just as a water wave can have crests and troughs, an orbital can have positive and negative areas. The blue area shows positive values, and the gold area negative. As it is the magnitude of the wave, not the sign, which determines the probability of finding an electron at particular positions, the sign is often not shown.

The 2p sub-level contains three 2p atomic orbitals of equal energy which are said to be **degenerate**. They all have the same dumbbell shape; the only difference is their orientation in space. They are arranged at right angles with the nucleus at the centre.

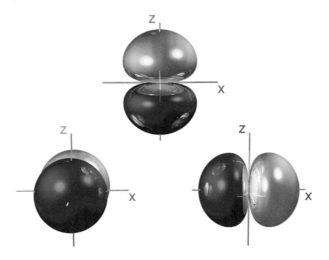

From left to right, the p_y, p_z and p_x atomic orbitals, localized along the y, z, and x-axes respectively (the y-axis comes out of the page). As they have the same energy, they are said to be degenerate. They form the 2p sub-level.

If you wanted to be absolutely 100% sure of where the electron is you would have to draw an orbital the size of the universe.

d and f orbitals

We have seen that the first energy level is made up from one sub-level and the second energy level is made up from three sub-levels. This pattern can be generalized; the nth energy level of the Bohr atom is divided into n sub-levels. The third energy level is made up from three sub-levels: the 3s, 3p, and 3d. The d sub-level is made up from five d atomic orbitals.

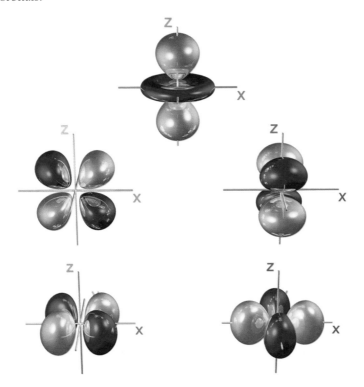

The five electron orbitals found in the 3d sub-level. Four of the orbitals are made up of four lobes, centred on the nucleus.

You are expected to know the shapes and names of the s and p atomic orbitals, but not of the d atomic orbitals.

The labels s, p, d, and f relate to the nature of the spectral lines the model was attempting to explain. The corresponding spectroscopic terms are *sharp, principal, diffuse* and *fine*.

The letters **s**, **p**, **d**, and **f** are used to identify different sub-levels and the atomic orbitals which comprise them. The fourth level ($n = 4$) is similarly made up from four sub-levels. The 4f sub-levels are made up from seven f atomic orbitals, but you are not required to know the shapes of these orbitals.

Worked example

Draw the shapes of a 1s orbital and a $2p_x$ orbital.

Solution

1s orbital   **$2p_x$ orbital**

Figure 2.15 A simple two-dimensional drawing is sufficient.

Electron spin and the Pauli Exclusion Principle

The atomic orbitals associated with the different energy levels are shown in Figure 2.16. This diagram is a simplification, as the relative energy of the orbitals depends on the atomic number. This is discussed in more detail later. The relative energies of the 4s and 3d atomic orbitals are chemically significant.

Figure 2.16 The relative energies of the atomic orbitals up to the 4p sub-level. The 3d sub-level falls below the 4s level for elements $Z > 20$.

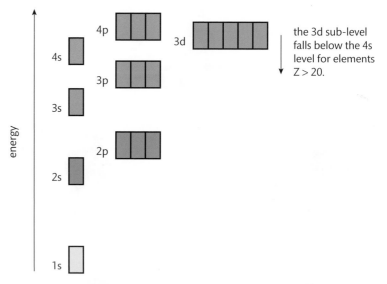

The Pauli Exclusion Principle states that no more than two electrons can occupy any one orbital, and if two electrons are in the same orbital they must spin in opposite directions.

An electron is uniquely characterized by its atomic orbital and spin. If two electrons occupied the same orbital spinning in the same direction, they would be the same electron.

Each atomic orbital can hold a maximum of two electrons. These electrons can occupy the same region of space despite their mutual repulsion as they spin in opposite directions.

Exercises

15 List the 4d, 4f, 4p, and 4s atomic orbitals in order of increasing energy.

16 State the number of 4d, 4f, 4p, and 4s atomic orbitals.

Sub-levels of electrons

The number of electrons in the sub-levels of the first four energy levels are shown in the table below.

Level	Sub-level	Maximum number of electrons in sub-level	Maximum number of electrons in level
$n = 1$	1s	2	2
$n = 2$	2s	2	8
	2p	6	
$n = 3$	3s	2	18
	3p	6	
	3d	10	
$n = 4$	4s	2	32
	4p	6	
	4d	10	
	4f	14	

We can see the following from the table.

- The nth energy level of the Bohr atom is divided into n sub-levels. For example, the fourth level ($n = 4$) is made up from four sub-levels. The letters s, p, d, and f are used to identify different sub-levels.
- Each main level can hold a maximum of $2n^2$ electrons. The 3rd energy level, for example, can hold a maximum of 18 electrons ($2 \times 3^2 = 18$).
- s sub-levels can hold a maximum of 2 electrons.
- p sub-levels can hold a maximum of 6 electrons.
- d sub-levels can hold a maximum of 10 electrons.
- f sub-levels can hold a maximum of 14 electrons.

Aufbau Principle: orbital diagrams

The electron configuration of the ground state of an atom of an element can be determined using the **Aufbau Principle**, which states that electrons are placed into orbitals of lowest energy first. Boxes can be used to represent the atomic orbitals, with single-headed arrows to represent the spinning electrons. The **electron configurations** of the first five elements are shown in Figure 2.17. The number of electrons in each sub-level is given as a superscript.

Aufbau means 'building up' in German.

Figure 2.17 The electron configuration of the first five elements.

The next element in the Periodic Table is carbon. It has two electrons in the 2p sub-level. These could either pair up, and occupy the same p orbital, or occupy separate p orbitals. Following **Hund's third rule**, we can place the two electrons in separate orbitals because this configuration minimizes the mutual repulsion between them. As the 2p orbitals are perpendicular to each other and do not overlap, the two 2p electrons are unlikely to approach each other too closely. The electrons in the different 2p orbitals have parallel spins, as this leads to lower energy. The electron configurations of carbon and nitrogen are shown in Figure 2.18.

Figure 2.18 Electron configurations of carbon and nitrogen.

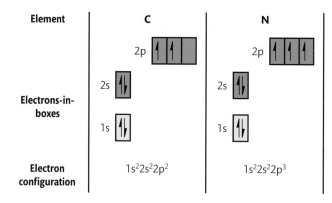

Hund's rule: If more than one orbital in a sub-level is available, electrons occupy different orbitals with parallel spins.

The 2p electrons begin to pair up for oxygen ($1s^22s^22p_x^22p_y^12p_z^1$) and fluorine ($1s^22s^22p_x^22p_y^22p_z^1$). The 2p sub-shell is completed for neon ($1s^22s^22p_x^22p_y^22p_z^2$).

Exercises

17 Apply the *orbital diagram* method to determine the electron configuration of calcium.

18 Deduce the number of unpaired electrons present in a phosphorus atom.

Do you need a useful mnemonic to the order of filling orbitals? Figure 2.19 shows orbitals filled to sub-level 7s. Follow the arrows to see the order in which the sub-levels are filled.

Figure 2.19 Order of filling sub-levels: 1s, 2s, 2p, 3s, 3p, 4s, 3d, 4p, 5s, 4d, 5p, 6s, 4f, 5d, 6p, 7s, 5f, 6d, 7s.

7s	7p	7d	7f	7g	7h	7h
6s	6p	6d	6f	6g	6h	
5s	5p	5d	5f	5g		
4s	4p	4d	4f			
3s	3p	3d				
2s	2p					
1s						

The mathematical nature of the orbital description is illustrated by some simple relationships:

- number of sub-levels at *n*th main energy level = *n*;
- number of orbitals at *n*th energy level = n^2;
- number of electrons at *n*th energy level = $2n^2$;
- number of orbitals at *l*th sub-level = $(2l + 1)$ where *n* and *l* are sometimes known as quantum numbers.

Sub-level	s	p	d	f
l	0	1	2	3

The relative energy of the orbitals depends on the atomic number

The energy of an orbital depends on the attractions between the electrons and the nucleus and inter-electron repulsions. As these interactions change with the nuclear charge and the number of electrons, that is the atomic number, so does the relative energy of the orbitals. All the sub-levels in the third energy level (3s, 3p, and 3d), for example, have the same energy for the hydrogen atom and only become separated as extra protons and electrons are added. The situation is particularly complicated when we reach the d block elements. The 3d and 4s levels are very close in energy and their relative separation is very sensitive to inter-electron repulsion. For the elements potassium and calcium, the 4s orbitals are filled before the 3d sub-level. Electrons are, however, first lost from the 4s sub-level when transitional metals form their ions, as once the 3d sub-level is occupied the 3d electrons push the 4s electrons to higher energy.

When the transition metal atoms form ions they lose electrons from the 4s sub-level before the 3d sub-level.

Worked example

State the full electron configuration of vanadium and deduce the number of unpaired electrons.

Solution

The atomic number of vanadium gives the number of electrons: Z = 23.

So the electronic configuration is: $1s^2 2s^2 2p^6 3s^2 3p^6 4s^2 3d^3$. Note: the 3d sub-level is filled after the 4s sub-level.

It is useful, however, to write the electronic configuration with the 3d sub-shell before the 4s: $1s^2 2s^2 2p^6 3s^2 3p^6 3d^3 4s^2$ as the 3d sub-level falls below the 4s orbital once the 4s orbital is occupied (i.e. for elements after Ca).

Three 3d orbitals each have an unpaired electron. Number of unpaired electrons = 3.

The worked example asked for the full electron configuration. Sometimes it is convenient to use an abbreviated form, where only the outer electrons are explicitly shown. The inner electrons are represented as a noble gas core. Using this notation, the electron configuration of vanadium is written $[Ar] 3d^3 4s^2$, where $[Ar]$ represents the electron configuration of Ar, which is $1s^2 2s^2 2p^6 3s^2 3p^6$.

The electron configurations of the first 30 elements are tabulated below.

TOK The abstract language of mathematics provides a powerful tool for describing the behaviour of electrons in the atom. The shapes and equations it generates have elegance and symmetry. What do such results tell us about the relationship between the natural sciences, mathematics and the natural world?

Element	Electron configuration	Element	Electron configuration	Element	Electron configuration
$_1$H	$1s^1$	$_{11}$Na	$1s^2 2s^2 2p^6 3s^1$	$_{21}$Sc	$[Ar] 3d^1 4s^2$
$_2$He	$1s^2$	$_{12}$Mg	$1s^2 2s^2 2p^6 3s^2$	$_{22}$Ti	$[Ar] 3d^2 4s^2$
$_3$Li	$1s^2 2s^1$	$_{13}$Al	$1s^2 2s^2 2p^6 3s^2 3p^1$	$_{23}$V	$[Ar] 3d^3 4s^2$
$_4$Be	$1s^2 2s^2$	$_{14}$Si	$1s^2 2s^2 2p^6 3s^2 3p^2$	$_{24}$Cr	$[Ar] 3d^5 4s^1$
$_5$B	$1s^2 2s^2 2p^1$	$_{15}$P	$1s^2 2s^2 2p^6 3s^2 3p^3$	$_{25}$Mn	$[Ar] 3d^5 4s^2$
$_6$C	$1s^2 2s^2 2p^2$	$_{16}$S	$1s^2 2s^2 2p^6 3s^2 3p^4$	$_{26}$Fe	$[Ar] 3d^6 4s^2$
$_7$N	$1s^2 2s^2 2p^3$	$_{17}$Cl	$1s^2 2s^2 2p^6 3s^2 3p^5$	$_{27}$Co	$[Ar] 3d^7 4s^2$
$_8$O	$1s^2 2s^2 2p^4$	$_{18}$Ar	$1s^2 2s^2 2p^6 3s^2 3p^6$	$_{28}$Ni	$[Ar] 3d^8 4s^2$
$_9$F	$1s^2 2s^2 2p^5$	$_{19}$K	$1s^2 2s^2 2p^6 3s^2 3p^6 4s^1$	$_{29}$Cu	$[Ar] 3d^{10} 4s^1$
$_{10}$Ne	$1s^2 2s^2 2p^6$	$_{20}$Ca	$1s^2 2s^2 2p^6 3s^2 3p^6 4s^2$	$_{30}$Zn	$[Ar] 3d^{10} 4s^2$

The term 'valence' is derived from the Latin word for 'strength'.

The electrons in the outer energy level are mainly responsible for compound formation and are called **valence electrons**. Lithium has one valence electron in the outer second energy level ($2s^1$), beryllium has two ($2s^2$), boron has three ($2s^2p^1$), etc. The number of valence electrons follows a periodic pattern, which is discussed fully in Chapter 3. Atoms can have many other electron arrangements when in an excited state. Unless otherwise instructed, assume that you are being asked about ground-state arrangements.

For the d block elements three points should be noted:

- the 3d sub-level is written with the other $n = 3$ sub-levels as it falls below the 4s orbital, once the 4s orbital is occupied (i.e. for elements after Ca) as discussed earlier;
- chromium has the electron configuration [Ar] $3d^5 4s^1$;
- copper has the electron configuration [Ar] $3d^{10} 4s^1$.

To understand the electron configurations of copper and chromium it is helpful to consider the orbital diagram arrangements in Figure 2.20. As the 4s and 3d orbitals are close in energy, the electron configuration for chromium with a half-full d sub-level is relatively stable as it minimizes electrostatic repulsion, with six singly occupied atomic orbitals. This would be the expected configuration using Hund's rule if the 4s and 3d orbitals had exactly the same energy. Half-filled and filled sub-levels seem to be particularly stable: the configuration for copper is due to the stability of the full d sub-level.

Figure 2.20 The electron configuration of the 3rd and 4th energy levels for chromium and copper.

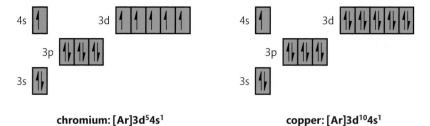

chromium: [Ar]$3d^5 4s^1$ copper: [Ar]$3d^{10} 4s^1$

Exercises

19 Identify the sub-level which does not exist.

    A 5d   **B** 4d   **C** 3f   **D** 2p

20 Which is the correct order of orbital filling according to the Aufbau Principle?

    A 4s 4p 4d 4f   **B** 4p 4d 5s 4f   **C** 4s 3d 4p 5s   **D** 4d 4f 5s 5p

21 State the full ground-state electron configuration of the following elements.

    (a) V   **(b)** K   **(c)** Se   **(d)** Sr

22 Determine the total number of electrons in d orbitals in a single iodine atom.

    A 5   **B** 10   **C** 15   **D** 20

23 Identify the excited state (i.e. not a ground state) in the following electron configurations.

    A [Ne] $3s^2 3p^3$ **B** [Ne] $3s^2 3p^3 4s^1$ **C** [Ne] $3s^2 3p^6 4s^1$ **D** [Ne] $3s^2 3p^6 3d^1 4s^2$

24 Deduce the number of unpaired electrons present in the ground state of a titanium atom.

    A 1   **B** 2   **C** 3   **D** 4

Electron configuration of ions

As discussed earlier, positive ions are formed by the loss of electrons. These electrons are lost from the outer sub-levels. The electron configuration of the different aluminium ions formed when electrons are successively removed are for example:

- Al^+ is $1s^22s^22p^63s^2$
- Al^{2+} is $1s^22s^22p^63s^1$
- Al^{3+} is $1s^22s^22p^6$, etc.

When positive ions are formed for transition metals, the outer 4s electrons are removed before the 3d electrons, as discussed earlier.

For example, Cr is [Ar] $3d^54s^1$ and Cr^{3+} is [Ar] $3d^3$

The electron configuration of negative ions is determined by adding the electrons into the next available electron orbital:

S is $1s^22s^22p^63s^23p^4$ and S^{2-} is $1s^22s^22p^63s^23p^6$

Worked example

State the ground-state electron configuration of the Fe^{3+} ion.

Solution

First find the electron configuration of the atom. Fe has 26 electrons:
$1s^22s^22p^63s^23p^64s^23d^6$

As the 3d sub-level is below the 4s level for elements after calcium we write this as
$1s^22s^22p^63s^23p^63d^64s^2$

Now remove two electrons from the 4s sub-level and one electron from the 3d sub-level.

Electron configuration of Fe^{3+} is $1s^22s^22p^63s^23p^63d^5$

Note the abbreviated electron configuration using the noble gas core is not acceptable when asked for the *full* electron configuration.

Exercises

25 State the full ground-state electron configuration of the following ions.

    (a) O^{2-} **(b)** Cl^- **(c)** Ti^{3+} **(d)** Cu^{2+}

26 State the electron configuration of the following transition metal ions by filling in the boxes below. Use arrows to represent the electron spin.

	Ion	3d					4s
(a)	Ti^{2+}						
(b)	Fe^{2+}						
(c)	Ni^{2+}						
(d)	Zn^{2+}						

27 (a) State the full electron configuration for neon.
    (b) State the formulas of two oppositely charged ions which have the same electron configuration as neon.

Electronic configuration and the Periodic Table

We are now in a position to understand the structure of the Periodic Table (Figure 2.21):

- elements whose valence electrons occupy an s sub-level make up the **s block**;
- elements with valence electrons in p orbitals make up the **p block**;
- the **d block** and the **f block** are similarly made up of elements with outer electrons in d and f orbitals.

Figure 2.21 The block structure of the Periodic Table is based on the sub-levels of the atom. H and He are difficult elements to classify. Although they have electron configurations that place them in the s block, their chemistry is not typical of Group 1 or Group 2 elements.

The *ns* and *np* sub-levels are filled for elements in Period *n*. However the $(n - 1)$d sub-level is filled for elements in Period *n*.

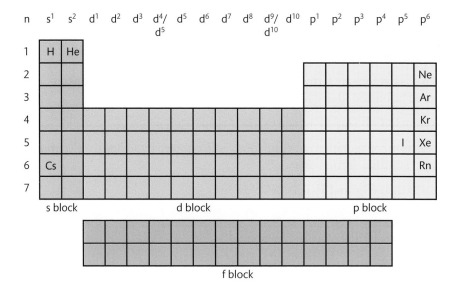

s block   d block   p block

f block

The position of an element in the Periodic Table is based on the occupied sub-level of highest energy in the ground-state atom. Conversely, the electron configuration of an element can be deduced directly from its position in the Periodic Table.

Here are some examples.

- Caesium is in Group 1 and Period 6 and has the electronic configuration: $[Xe]\ 6s^1$.
- Iodine is in Group 17 and in Period 5 and has the configuration: $[Kr]\ 5s^2 4d^{10} 5p^5$.

Placing the 4d sub-level before the 5s gives $[Kr]\ 4d^{10} 5s^2 5p^5$. Iodine has 7 valence electrons in agreement with the pattern discussed on page 82 or see Chapter 3.

Exercises

28 Use the Periodic Table to find the full ground-state electron configuration of the following elements.
   (a) Cl   **(b)** Nb   **(c)** Ge   **(d)** Sb

29 Identify the elements which have the following ground-state electron configurations.
   (a) $[Ne]\ 3s^2 3p^2$ **(b)** $[Ar]\ 3d^5 4s^2$ **(c)** $[Kr]\ 5s^2$
   (d) $1s^2 2s^2 2p^6 3s^2 3p^6 3d^1 4s^2$

30 State the total number of p orbitals containing one or more electrons in tin.

31 How many electrons are there in all the d orbitals in an atom of barium?

32 State the electron configuration of the ion Cd^{2+}.

CHALLENGE YOURSELF

4 Only a few atoms of element 109, meitnerium, have ever been made. Isolation of an observable quantity of the element has never been achieved, and may well never be. This is because meitnerium decays very rapidly.
   (a) Suggest the electron configuration of the ground-state atom of the element.
   (b) There is no g block in the Periodic Table as no elements with outer electrons in g orbitals exist in nature or have been made artificially. Suggest a minimum atomic number for such an element.

5 State the full electron configuration of U^{2+}.

6 Consider how the shape of the Periodic Table is related to the three-dimensional world we live in.
   (a) How many 3p and 3d orbitals would there be if there were only the *x* and *y* dimension?
   (b) How many groups in the p and d block would there be in such a two-dimensional world?

NATURE OF SCIENCE

We have seen how the model of the atom has changed over time. All these theories are still used today. Dalton's model adequately explains many properties of the states of matter, the Bohr model is used to explain chemical bonding, and the structure of the Periodic Table is explained by the wave description of the electron. In science we often follow Occam's razor and use the simplest explanation which can account for the phenomena. As Einstein said 'Explanations should be made as simple as possible, but not simpler.'

Do atomic orbitals exist or are they primarily useful inventions to aid our understanding? What consequences might questions about the reality of scientific entities have for the public perception and understanding of the subject? If they are only fictions, how is it that they can yield such accurate predictions?

Practice questions

1   What is the electron configuration of the Cr^{2+} ion?

   A [Ar] $3d^54s^1$ **B** [Ar] $3d^34s^1$ **C** [Ar] $3d^64s^1$ **D** [Ar] $3d^44s^0$

2   What is the relative atomic mass of an element with the following mass spectrum?

   A   24   **B**   25   **C**   26   **D**   27

3   Which is correct for the following regions of the electromagnetic spectrum?

	Ultraviolet (UV)		Infrared (IR)	
A	high energy	short wavelength	low energy	low frequency
B	high energy	low frequency	low energy	long wavelength
C	high frequency	short wavelength	high energy	long wavelength
D	high frequency	long wavelength	low frequency	low energy

4   An ion has the electron configuration $1s^22s^22p^63s^23p^63d^{10}$. Which ion could it be?

   A Ni^{2+} **B** Cu^+ **C** Cu^{2+} **D** Co^{3+}

5   Which describes the visible emission spectrum of hydrogen?

   A   a series of lines converging at longer wavelength

   B   a series of regularly spaced lines

   C   a series of lines converging at lower energy

   D   a series of lines converging at higher frequency

6 Which statements about the isotopes of chlorine, $^{35}_{17}Cl$ and $^{37}_{17}Cl$, are correct?

   I   They have the same chemical properties.

   II   They have the same atomic number.

   III They have the same physical properties.

   A I and II only   **B** I and III only   **C** II and III only   **D** I, II, and III

7 Which statement about the numbers of protons, electrons, and neutrons in an atom is always correct?

   A The number of neutrons minus the number of electrons is zero.

   B The number of protons plus the number of neutrons equals the number of electrons.

   C The number of protons equals the number of electrons.

   D The number of neutrons equals the number of protons.

8 Which quantities are the same for all atoms of chlorine?

   I   number of protons

   II   number of neutrons

   III number of electrons

   A I and II only   **B** I and III only   **C** II and III only   **D** I, II, and III

9 In the emission spectrum of hydrogen, which electronic transition would produce a line in the visible region of the electromagnetic spectrum?

   A $n = 2 \rightarrow n = 1$ **B** $n = 3 \rightarrow n = 2$ **C** $n = 2 \rightarrow n = 3$ **D** $n = \infty \rightarrow n = 1$

10 How many electrons does the ion $^{31}_{15}P^{3-}$ contain?

   A 12   **B** 15   **C** 16   **D** 18

11 How many protons, neutrons, and electrons does the ion $^{27}_{13}Al^{3+}$ contain?

   A 13 protons, 14 neutrons, and 13 electrons

   B 13 protons, 11 neutrons, and 13 electrons

   C 13 protons, 14 neutrons, and 10 electrons

   D 13 protons, 14 neutrons, and 16 electrons

12 A sample of iron has the following isotopic composition by mass.

Isotope	^{54}Fe	^{56}Fe	^{57}Fe
Relative abundance / %	5.95	91.88	2.17

Calculate the relative atomic mass of iron based on these data, giving your answer to two decimal places.

(2)

13 The electron configuration of chromium can be expressed as $[Ar]4s^x3d^y$.

    (a) Explain what the square brackets around argon, $[Ar]$, represent.   (1)

    (b) State the values of x and y.   (1)

    (c) Annotate the diagram below showing the 4s and 3d orbitals for a chromium atom using an arrow, ↑ and ↓, to represent a spinning electron.

         4s   3d   (1)

                                                       (Total 3 marks)

14 Annotate the diagram below showing the 4s and 3d orbitals for a Cu^{2+} ion using an arrow, ↑ and ↓, to represent a spinning electron.

         4s   3d

15 (a) Explain why the relative atomic mass of cobalt is greater than the relative atomic mass of nickel, even though the atomic number of nickel is greater than the atomic number of cobalt. (1)

    (b) Deduce the numbers of protons and electrons in the ion Co^{2+}.   (1)

    (c) Deduce the electron configuration for the ion Co^{2+}.   (1)

                                                       (Total 3 marks)

To access weblinks on the topics covered in this chapter, please go to www.pearsonhotlinks.com and enter the ISBN or title of this book.

03

Periodicity

Essential ideas

3.1 The arrangement of elements in the Periodic Table helps to predict their electron configuration.

3.2 Elements show trends in their physical and chemical properties across periods and down groups.

The Periodic Table is the 'map' of chemistry; it suggests new avenues of research for the professional chemist and is a guide for students – as it disentangles a mass of observations and reveals hidden order. Chemistry is not the study of a random collection of elements, but of the trends and patterns in their chemical and physical properties.

The Periodic Table is a remarkable demonstration of the order of the subject. It was first proposed in 1869 by the Russian chemist Dmitri Mendeleyev. Previous attempts had been made to impose order on the then known 62 elements, but Mendeleyev had the insight to realize that each element has its allotted place, so he left gaps where no known elements fitted into certain positions. As a scientific idea it was extremely powerful as it made predictions about the unknown elements that fitted these gaps, predictions which could be tested. When these elements were later discovered, the agreement between the predicted properties and the actual properties was remarkable.

Mendeleyev had no knowledge of the structure of the atom, which we discussed in Chapter 2. With the benefit of hindsight it is clear that the periodicity of the elements is a direct consequence of the periodicity of the electron configurations within the atom.

The position of an element in the Periodic Table is based on the sub-level of the highest-energy electron in the ground-state atom.

Water being dripped into a dish containing potassium metal. Potassium reacts violently and exothermically with water, producing potassium hydroxide and hydrogen gas. The reaction is explosive because the generated heat causes the hydrogen to ignite.

Mendeleyev grouped the known elements into families, leaving gaps corresponding to elements that should exist but which had not yet been discovered.

TOK What is the role of imagination and creativity in the sciences? To what extent might the formulation of a hypothesis be comparable to imagining and creating a work of art?

TOK Which attributes of the IB Learner Profile are demonstrated by Mendeleyev's work on the Periodic Table?

Typische Elemente							
			K = 39	Rb = 85	Cs = 133	—	—
			Ca = 40	Sr = 87	Ba = 137	—	—
			—	?Yt = 88?	?Di = 138?	Er = 178?	—
			Ti = 48?	Zr = 90	Ce = 140?	?La = 180?	Tb = 231
			V = 51	Nb = 94	—	Ta = 182	—
			Cr = 52	Mo = 96	—	W = 184	U = 240
			Mn = 55	—	—	—	—
			Fe = 56	Ru = 104	—	Os = 195?	—
			Co = 59	Rh = 104	—	Ir = 197	—
			Ni = 59	Pd = 106	—	Pt = 198?	—
H = 1	Li = 7	Na = 23	Cu = 63	Ag = 108	—	Au = 199?	—
	Be = 9,4	Mg = 24	Zn = 65	Cd = 112	—	Hg = 200	—
	B = 11	Al = 27,3	—	In = 113	—	Tl = 204	—
	C = 12	Si = 28	—	Sn = 118	—	Pb = 207	—
	N = 14	P = 31	As = 75	Sb = 122	—	Bi = 208	—
	O = 16	S = 32	Se = 78	Te = 125?	—	—	—
	F = 19	Cl = 35,5	Br = 80	J = 127	—	—	—

Mendeleyev's Periodic Table of 1869. The noble gas elements had not been discovered. Reading from top to bottom and left to right, the first four gaps were waiting for scandium (1879), gallium (1875), germanium (1886) and technetium (1937).

Understandings:
- The Periodic Table is arranged into four blocks associated with the four sub-levels: s, p, d, and f.
- The Periodic Table consists of groups (vertical columns) and periods (horizontal rows).

Guidance
The group numbering scheme from group 1 to group 18, as recommended by IUPAC, should be used.

- The period number (*n*) is the outer energy level that is occupied by electrons.
- The number of the principal energy level and the number of the valence electrons in an atom can be deduced from its position on the Periodic Table.
- The Periodic Table shows the positions of metals, non-metals and metalloids.

Guidance
The terms alkali metals, halogens, noble gases, transition metals, lanthanoides and actinoides should be known.

Applications and skills:
- Deduction of the electron configuration of an atom from the element's position on the Periodic Table, and vice versa.

Periods and groups

If you have visited a large supermarket you will appreciate the importance of a classification system. Similar products are grouped together to help you find what you want. In the same way, a chemist knows what type of element to find in different parts of the Periodic Table. The elements are placed in order of increasing atomic number (Z), which we now know is a fundamental property of the element – the number of protons in the nucleus of its atoms. As there are no gaps in the sequence of atomic numbers we can be confident that the search for new elements in nature is over.

The only way to extend the Periodic Table is by making elements artificially. Today there are over 110 elements recognized by the International Union of Pure and Applied Chemistry (IUPAC). The columns of the table are called **groups** and the rows **periods**.

In the IB data booklet Periodic Table the main groups are numbered from 1 to 18.

As discussed in Chapter 2, the position of an element is related to the electron configuration of its atoms.

Elements whose valence electrons occupy an s sub-level make up the **s block**, elements with valence electrons in p orbitals make up the **p block**, and the **d block** and **f block** are similarly made up of elements with outer electrons in d and f orbitals. The element sodium, for example, is in Period 3 as it has three occupied principal energy levels, and is in Group 1 of the s block as there is one electron in the valence energy level [Ne] $3s^1$. Bromine is in Period 4 and in Group 17 of the p block as it has seven electrons in the fourth principal energy level, and seventeen more electrons than the previous noble gas, argon: [Ar] $3d^{10}4s^24p^5$ (Figure 3.1).

Mendeleyev is said to have made his discovery after a dream. When he awoke he set out his chart in virtually its final form. He enjoyed playing a form of patience (solitaire) and wrote the properties of each element on cards which he arranged into rows and columns.

IUPAC is an international, non-governmental body with a membership made up of chemists which has the aim of fostering worldwide communication in chemistry.

| s¹ | s² | d¹ | d² | d³ | d⁵s¹ | d⁵ | d⁶ | d⁷ | d⁸ | d¹⁰s¹ | d¹⁰ | p¹ | p² | p³ | p⁴ | p⁵ | p⁶ |

s^1 s^2 d^1 d^2 d^3 d^{5}s^1 d^5 d^6 d^7 d^8 d^{10}s^1 d^{10} p^1 p^2 p^3 p^4 p^5 p^6

| 1 | 2 | 3 | 4 | 5 | 6 | 7 | 8 | 9 | 10 | 11 | 12 | 13 | 14 | 15 | 16 | 17 | 18 |

Period 1: H hydrogen 1; He helium 2

Period 2: Li lithium 3; Be beryllium 4; B boron 5; C carbon 6; N nitrogen 7; O oxygen 8; F fluorine 9; Ne neon 10

Period 3: Na sodium 11; Mg magnesium 12; Al aluminium 13; Si silicon 14; P phosphorus 15; S sulfur 16; Cl chlorine 17; Ar argon 18

Period 4: K potassium 19; Ca calcium 20; Sc scandium 21; Ti titanium 22; V vanadium 23; Cr chromium 24; Mn manganese 25; Fe iron 26; Co cobalt 27; Ni nickel 28; Cu copper 29; Zn zinc 30; Ga gallium 31; Ge germanium 32; As arsenic 33; Se selenium 34; Br bromine 35; Kr krypton 36

Period 5: Rb rubidium 37; Sr strontium 38; Y yttrium 39; Zr zirconium 40; Nb niobium 41; Mo molybdenum 42; Tc technetium 43; Ru ruthenium 44; Rh rhodium 45; Pd palladium 46; Ag silver 47; Cd cadmium 48; In indium 49; Sn tin 50; Sb antimony 51; Te tellurium 52; I iodine 53; Xe xenon 54

Period 6: Cs caesium 55; Ba barium 56; 57–71 see below; Hf hafnium 72; Ta tantalum 73; W tungsten 74; Re rhenium 75; Os osmium 76; Ir iridium 77; Pt platinum 78; Au gold 79; Hg mercury 80; Tl thallium 81; Pb lead 82; Bi bismuth 83; Po polonium 84; At astatine 85; Rn radon 86

Period 7: Fr francium 87; Ra radium 88; 89–103 see below; Rf rutherfordium 104; Db dubnium 105; Sg seaborgium 106; Bh bohrium 107; Hs hassium 108; Mt meitnerium 109; Ds darmstadtium 110; Rg roentgenium 111; Cp copernicium 112; Uut ununtrium 113; Fl flerovium 114; Uup Ununpentium 115; Lv Livemorium 116; Uus Ununseptium 117; Uuo Ununoctium 118

Lanthanides: La lanthanum 57; Ce cerium 58; Pr praseodymium 59; Nd neodymium 60; Pm promethium 61; Sm samarium 62; Eu europium 63; Gd gadolinium 64; Tb terbium 65; Dy dysprosium 66; Ho holmium 67; Er erbium 68; Tm thulium 69; Yb ytterbium 70; Lu Lutetium 71

Actinides: Ac actinium 89; Th thorium 90; Pa protactinium 91; U uranium 92; Np neptunium 93; Pu plutonium 94; Am americium 95; Cm curium 96; Bk berkellium 97; Cf californium 98; Es einsteinium 99; Fm fermium 100; Md mendelevium 101; No nobelium 102; Lr Lawrencium 103

Figure 3.1 The Periodic Table. The rows are called periods. The period number gives the number of occupied electron principal energy levels. The columns in the Periodic Table are called groups. The colours show the blocks formed by the elements with their outer electrons in the same electron sub-level: s block (blue), d block (yellow), p block (red), f block (green). It is these outer electrons that determine an element's chemical properties.

The discovery of the elements was an international endeavour. This is illustrated by some of their names. Some derive from the place where they were made, some derive from the origins of their discoverers, and some derive from the geographical origins of the minerals from which they were first isolated. The Periodic Table of chemical elements hangs in front of chemistry classrooms and in science laboratories throughout the world.

The rows in the Periodic Table are called periods. The period number gives the number of occupied electron principal energy levels. The columns in the Periodic Table are called groups.

Worked example

How many electrons are in the outer shell of iodine?

Solution

Find the element in the Periodic Table. It is Period 5, so has the noble gas core of Kr, with electrons added to 5s, then 4d, and then 5p.

As it is Group 17 it has the configuration: [Kr] $5s^2 4d^{10} 5p^5$ or [Kr] $4d^{10} 5s^2 5p^5$ and so has seven electrons in its valence energy level.

Exercises

1 Use the IB Periodic Table to identify the position of the following elements:

	Element	Period	Group
(a)	helium		
(b)	chlorine		
(c)	barium		
(d)	francium		

2 Phosphorus is in Period 3 and Group 15 of the Periodic Table.

   (a) Distinguish between the terms 'period' and 'group'.
   (b) State the electron configuration of phosphorus and relate it to its position in the Periodic Table.

3 How many valence (outer shell) electrons are present in the atoms of the element with atomic number 51?

CHALLENGE YOURSELF

1 Four elements derive their name from a small town called Ytterby, just outside Stockholm, Sweden. Try to find their names.

Non-metallic elements. Clockwise from top left, they are sulfur (S), bromine (Br), phosphorus (P), iodine (I) and carbon (C). Non-metals are generally poor conductors of both heat and electricity. Graphite, an allotrope of carbon, is unusual in that it is a non-metal that does conduct electricity.

CHALLENGE YOURSELF

2 How many elements in the IB Periodic Table are liquids and how many are gases?

Metals and non-metals

One of the key features of the Periodic Table is that the metals, metalloids, and non-metals occupy different regions. The non-metals are found on the upper right-hand side of the p block. The **halogens**, for example, are a reactive group of non-metals in Group 17 and the **noble gases** are a very unreactive family of non-metals found at the extreme right-hand side in Group 18. Metallic elements are found on the left-hand side of the table in the s block, in the central d block, and the island of the f block. The **alkali metals**, for example, are a reactive group of metals in Group 1 of the s block. The **lanthanoides** and **actinoides** are metals which make up the first and second row of the f block.

The metalloid elements have the characteristics of both metals and non-metals. Their physical properties and appearance most resemble the metals, although chemically they have more in common with the non-metals. In the Periodic Table the metalloid elements silicon, germanium, arsenic, antimony, tellurium, and polonium form a diagonal staircase between the metals and non-metals.

Silicon is a metalloid. There is enough silicon in this piece to make many hundreds of computers.

Europium (Eu), is one of the lanthanoides. It is a hard silvery-white metallic element and is used in television screens and fluorescent light bulbs.

The element europium is used in the security marking of euro notes and other banknotes. When placed in UV radiation europium compounds fluoresce, making the security markers visible.

CHALLENGE YOURSELF

3 Distinguish between the terms 'metalloid' and 'semiconductor'.

The lanthanoides and actinoides both make up the f block of the Periodic Table.

CHALLENGE YOURSELF

4 State the electron configuration of europium.

Exercises

4 Which of the following elements is a metalloid?

   A calcium   **B** manganese   **C** germanium   **D** magnesium

5 Which of the following materials is the best conductor of electricity in the solid state?

   A silicon   **B** graphite   **C** phosphorous   **D** antimony

6 Which of the following properties is used to arrange the elements in the modern Periodic Table?

   A relative atomic mass   **B** number of valence electrons

   C atomic number   **D** effective nuclear charge

NATURE OF SCIENCE

Scientists attempt to discover relationships by looking for patterns, trends, and discrepancies. Classification is an important aspect of scientific work. In the 18th century, Antoine Lavoisier tried to bring order to the confusing number of elements by classifying the elements into groups such as gases, non-metals, and metals. Some classification systems are, however, more useful than others and classifications based on quantitative data are more useful than those on qualitative data. The publication of 1858 by Stanislao Cannizzaro of a list of atomic masses allowed the elements to be placed in some sort of order.

One of the first attempts to classify the elements was made by Johann Döbereiner (1780–1849) who organized the elements into groups of three or 'triads' with similar properties (such as lithium, sodium, and potassium), where the average mass of the first and third element equalled the mass of the second. This pattern is approximately true for several triads of elements. The average relative mass of lithium and potassium, the first and third element in a triad, for example = (6.94 + 39.10/2) = 23.02 which is very close to the relative atomic mass of sodium (22.99), the second element in the triad.

In 1862 Alexandre de Chancourtois wrote a list of the elements on a tape and wound it in a spiral and noticed that chemically similar elements formed vertical groups.

John Newlands developed this idea and noted that many similar elements occur in intervals, rather like the seven notes in a musical scale. His law of octaves stated that any given element will be similar in its properties to the eighth element following it in the table.

Mendeleyev recognized that the breakdown in the periodicity of Newlands' octaves was due to the table's incomplete nature as some elements were yet to be discovered. Mendeleyev left gaps for these elements to ensure that periodicity was maintained, and predicted the physical and chemical properties of these missing elements. This was a key step in the scientific process as his precise predictions could be confirmed or falsified with the discovery of the new elements.

The discovery of elements such as gallium and germanium confirmed Mendeleyev's ideas. One advantage of Mendeleyev's table over previous attempts was that it exhibited similarities not only in small units such as the triads, but showed similarities in an entire network of vertical, horizontal, and diagonal relationships.

Mendeleyev did not propose an explanation for his periodic law. This had to await the discovery of the electron by Thomson in 1897 and the work of Rutherford and Bohr at the beginning of the 20th century.

'Theories' and 'laws' are terms which have a special meaning in science and it is important to distinguish these from their everyday use. Scientific laws are descriptive, normative statements derived from observations of regular patterns of behaviour. They do not necessarily explain a phenomenon. Newlands' law of octaves and Mendeleyev's periodic law, for example, tell us that there is pattern in the properties of the elements but they do not attempt to explain these patterns.

 TOK

The patterns observed in the evolution of the Periodic Table were as a result of inductive reasoning. What do these patterns illustrate about the problems of induction? Is induction ever a reliable source for knowledge?

The development of the Periodic Table took many years and involved scientists from different countries building upon the foundations of each other's work and ideas.

3.2 **Periodic trends**

Understandings:

- Vertical and horizontal trends in the Periodic Table exist for atomic radius, ionic radius, ionization energy, electron affinity, and electronegativity.

  Guidance

  Only examples of general trends across periods and down groups are required. For ionization energy the discontinuities in the increase across a period should be covered.

- Trends in metallic and non-metallic behaviour are due to the trends above.
- Oxides change from basic through amphoteric to acidic across a period.

Applications and skills:

- Prediction and explanation of the metallic and non-metallic behaviour of an element based on its position in the Periodic Table.
- Discussion of the similarities and differences in the properties of elements in the same group, with reference to alkali metals (Group 1) and halogens (Group 17).

  Guidance

  Group trends should include the treatment of the reactions of alkali metals with water, alkali metals with halogens and halogens with halide ions.

- Construction of equations to explain the pH changes for reactions of Na_2O, MgO, P_4O_{10}, and the oxides of nitrogen and sulfur with water.

Physical properties

The elements in the Periodic Table are arranged to show how the properties of the elements repeat periodically. This **periodicity** of the elements is reflected in their physical properties. The atomic and ionic radii, electronegativity, and ionization energy are of particular interest as they explain the periodicity of the chemical properties.

The concept of effective nuclear charge is helpful in explaining trends in both physical and chemical properties.

Effective nuclear charge

The **nuclear charge** of the atom is given by the atomic number and so increases by one between successive elements in the table, as a proton is added to the nucleus. The outer electrons which determine many of the physical and chemical properties of the atom do not, however, experience the full attraction of this charge as they are **shielded** from the nucleus and repelled by the inner electrons. The presence of the inner electrons reduces the attraction of the nucleus for the outer electrons (Figure 3.2). The **effective charge** 'experienced' by the outer electrons is less than the full nuclear charge.

Consider, for example, a sodium atom. The nuclear charge is given by the atomic number of element ($Z = 11$). The outer electron in the 3s orbital is, however, shielded from these 11 protons by the 10 electrons in the first and second principal energy levels ($1s^2 2s^2 2p^6$).

Consider the first four elements in Period 3, as shown in the table on page 95.

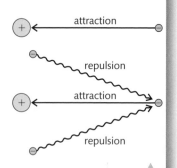

Figure 3.2 An electron in the hydrogen atom experiences the full attraction of the nuclear charge, but in a many-electron atom the attraction for the nucleus is reduced as the outer electron is repelled by inner electrons.

Element	Na	Mg	Al	Si
Nuclear charge	11	12	13	14
Electron configuration	[Ne] $3s^1$	[Ne] $3s^2$	[Ne] $3s^23p^1$	[Ne] $3s^23p^2$
Effective nuclear charge	$\approx 11 - 10$ $\approx +1$	$\approx 12 - 10$ $\approx +2$	$\approx 13 - 10$ $\approx +3$	$\approx 14 - 10$ $\approx +4$

As the period is crossed from left to right, one proton is added to the nucleus and one electron is added to the valence electron energy level. The effective charge increases with the nuclear charge as there is no change in the number of inner electrons, as all the atoms have a noble gas of 10 electrons ([Ne] = $1s^22s^22p^6$).

If we assume that the noble gas core is completely shielding, then the 10 inner electrons of the neon core make the effective nuclear 10 less than the nuclear charge.

The changes down a group can be illustrated by considering the elements in Group 1, as shown in the table below:

Element	Nuclear charge	Electron configuration
Li	3	$1s^22s^1$
Na	11	$1s^22s^22p^63s^1$
K	19	$1s^22s^22p^63s^23p^64s^1$

As we descend the group, the increase in the nuclear charge is largely offset by the increase in the number of inner electrons; both increase by eight between successive elements in the group. The effective nuclear charge experienced by the outer electrons remains approximately +1 down the group.

Atomic radius

The concept of atomic radius is not as straightforward as you may think. We saw in the last chapter that electrons occupy atomic orbitals, which give a probability description of the electrons' locations, but do not have sharp boundaries. The atomic radius r is measured as half the distance between neighbouring nuclei (Figure 3.3). For many purposes, however, it can be considered as the distance from the nucleus to the outermost electrons of the Bohr atom.

Section 8 in the IB data booklet shows that atomic radii increase down a group and decrease across a period. To explain the trend down a group consider, for example, the Group 1 elements – as shown in the table below.

Element	Period	No. of occupied principal energy levels	Radius/10^{-12} m
Li	2	2	152
Na	3	3	186
K	4	4	231
Rb	5	5	244
Cs	6	6	262

The effective nuclear charge experienced by an atom's outer electrons increases with the group number of the element. It increases across a period but remains approximately the same down a group.

Figure 3.3 The atomic radius r is measured as half the distance between neighbouring nuclei.

The atomic radii increase down a group, as the number of occupied electron shells (given by the period number) increases.

The trend across a period is illustrated by the Period 3 elements, as shown below:

Element	Na	Mg	Al	Si	P	S	Cl	Ar
Atomic radius/10^{-12} m	186	160	143	117	110	104	99	–

All these elements have three occupied principal energy levels. The attraction between the nucleus and the outer electrons increases as the nuclear charge increases so there is a general decrease in atomic radii across the period.

The decrease in radii across a period is quite significant; a chlorine atom, for example, has a radius that is about half that of a sodium atom.

Ionic radius

The atomic and ionic radii of the Period 3 elements are shown in the table below.

Element	Na	Mg	Al	Si	P	S	Cl
Atomic radius/10^{-12} m	186	160	143	117	110	104	99
Ionic radius/10^{-12} m	98 (Na^+)	65 (Mg^{2+})	45 (Al^{3+})	42 (Si^{4+}); 271 (Si^{4-})	212 (P^{3-})	190 (S^{2-})	181 (Cl^-)

Five trends can be identified.

• Positive ions are smaller than their parent atoms. The formation of positive ions involves the loss of the outer shell. The Na^+ ion, for example, is formed by the removal of the 3s electron from the Na atom.

• Negative ions are larger than their parent atoms. The formation of negative ions involves the addition of electrons into the outer shell. Cl^- is formed by the addition of an electron into the 3p sub-shell. The increased electron repulsion between the electrons in the outer principal energy level causes the electrons to move further apart and so increases the radius of the outer shell.

• The ionic radii decrease from Groups 1 to 14 for the positive ions. The ions Na^+, Mg^{2+}, Al^{3+}, and Si^{4+} all have the same electron configuration ($1s^2 2s^2 2p^6$). The decrease in ionic radius is due to the increase in nuclear charge with atomic number across the period. The increased attraction between the nucleus and the electrons pulls the outer shell closer to the nucleus.

• The ionic radii decrease from Groups 14 to 17 for the negative ions. The ions Si^{4-}, P^{3-}, S^{2-}, and Cl^- have the same electron configuration ($1s^2 2s^2 2p^6 3s^2 3p^6$). The decrease in ionic radius is due to the increase in nuclear charge across the period, as explained above. The positive ions are smaller than the negative ions, as the former have only two occupied electron principal energy levels and the latter have three. This explains the big difference between the ionic radii of the Si^{4+} and Si^{4-} ions and the discontinuity in the middle of the table.

• The ionic radii increase down a group as the number of electron energy levels increases.

Worked example

Describe and explain the trend in radii of the following ions:

O^{2-}, F^-, Ne, Na^+ and Mg^{2+}.

Solution

The ions and the Ne atom have 10 electrons and the electron configuration $1s^2 2s^2 2p^6$. The nuclear charges increase with atomic number:

O: $Z = +8$

F: $Z = +9$

Ne: $Z = +10$

Na: $Z = +11$

Mg: $Z = +12$

The increase in nuclear charge results in increased attraction between the nucleus and the outer electrons. The ionic radii decrease as the atomic number increases.

Exercises

7 (a) Explain what is meant by the atomic radius of an element.
  (b) The atomic radii of the elements are found in section 8 of the IB data book.
    (i) Explain why no values for atomic radii are given for the noble gases.
    (ii) Describe and explain the trend in atomic radii across the Period 3 elements.

8 Si^{4+} has an ionic radius of 4.2×10^{-11} m and Si^{4-} has an ionic radius of 2.71×10^{-10} m. Explain the large difference in size between the Si^{4+} and Si^{4-} ions.

Ionization energies

First ionization energies are a measure of the attraction between the nucleus and the outer electrons. They were defined in Chapter 2 on page 73. The first ionization energy can be represented by the equation:

$$M(g) \rightarrow M^+(g) + e^-$$

Figure 3.4 First ionization energies of the first 20 elements.

Two general trends can be identified from Figure 3.4.

- Ionization energies increase across a period. The increase in effective nuclear charge causes an increase in the attraction between the outer electrons and the nucleus and makes the electrons more difficult to remove.
- Ionization energies decrease down a group. The electron removed is from the energy level furthest from the nucleus. Although the nuclear charges increase, the effective nuclear charge is about the same, owing to shielding of the inner electrons, and so the increased distance between the electron and the nucleus reduces the attraction between them.

- The small departures from these trends provide evidence for division of energy levels into sub-levels, as discussed in Chapter 2 (page 76). Thus, the Group 3 elements, with the electron configuration ns^2np^1, have lower first ionization energies than Group 2 elements, with the configuration ns^2, as p orbitals have higher energy than s orbitals. The drop between Groups 15 and 16 occurs as the electron removed from a Group 16 element, unlike a Group 15 element, is taken from a doubly occupied p orbital. This electron is easier to remove as it is repelled by its partner.

The trend in ionization energy is the reverse of the trend in atomic radii. Both trends are an indication of the attraction between the nucleus and the outer electrons.

Electron affinity

The first **electron affinity** of an element is the energy change when one mole of electrons is added to one mole of gaseous atoms to form one mole of gaseous ions:

$$X(g) + e^- \rightarrow X^-(g)$$

Values are tabulated in section 8 of the IB data booklet. The noble gases do not generally form negatively charged ions so electron affinity values are not available for these elements. As the added electron is attracted to the positively charged nucleus the process is generally exothermic. The second and third electron affinities are defined similarly. The second electron affinity for oxygen, for example, corresponds to the change:

$$O^-(g) + e^- \rightarrow O^{2-}(g)$$

This process is endothermic as the added electron is repelled by the negatively charged oxide (O^-) ion, and energy needs to be available for this to occur.

The electron affinities of the first 18 elements are shown below. The pattern in electron affinities is related to that observed with first ionization energy but generally displaced to the right by one and inverted. The minimum values for electron affinities occur for the Group 17 elements whereas the values for ionization energy reach a maximum for Group 18.

Electron affinities can be thought of as the negative of first ionization energy of the anion.

- The Group 17 elements have incomplete outer energy levels and a high effective nuclear charge of approximately −7 and so attract electrons the most.
- The Group 1 metals have the lowest effective nuclear charge of approximately +1 and so attract the extra electron the least.

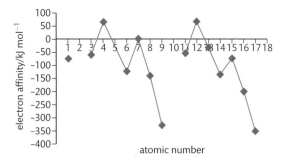

Figure 3.5 The electron affinities of the first 18 elements. Note there are no values assigned to the noble gases.

The electron affinities reach a maximum for Group 2 and Group 5 elements. Group 2 elements have an electron configuration ns^2, so the added electron must be placed into a 2p orbital which is further from the nucleus and so experiences reduced electrostatic attraction due to shielding from electrons in the ns orbital. The value for beryllium is actually endothermic as there is electrostatic repulsion between the electrons of the Be atom and the added electron. The electrons in the 1s and 2s orbitals of Be also shield the added electron from the positively charged nucleus.

Group 15 elements have the configuration $ns^2np_x^1p_y^1p_z^1$ so the added electron must occupy a p orbital that is already singly occupied: the attraction between the electron and atom is less than expected as there is increased inter-electron repulsion. The value is only just exothermic for nitrogen.

Electronegativity

The **electronegativity** of an element is a measure of the ability of its atoms to attract electrons in a covalent bond (see Chapter 4). It is related to ionization energy as it is also a measure of the attraction between the nucleus and its outer electrons – in this case *bonding electrons*.

Figure 3.6 Energy is needed to bring two particles of the same charge closer together as they repel reach other: this is an endothermic process. Particles of the opposite charge attract each other. They will spontaneously move closer together: it is an exothermic process.

An element with a high electronegativity has strong electron pulling power and an element with a low electronegativity has weak pulling power. The concept was originally devised by the American chemist Linus Pauling and his values are given in the IB data booklet. The general trends are the same as those for ionization energy.

• Electronegativity increases from left to right across a period owing to the increase in nuclear charge, resulting in an increased attraction between the nucleus and the bond electrons.
• Electronegativity decreases down a group. The bonding electrons are furthest from the nucleus and so there is reduced attraction.

 Electronegativity is the ability of an atom to attract electrons in a covalent bond.

The most electronegative element is on the top right of the Periodic Table and the least electronegative element on the bottom left. As the concept does not apply to the Group 18 elements, which do not form covalent bonds, Pauling assigned the highest value of 4.0 to fluorine and the lowest value of 0.7 to caesium.

 Linus Pauling has the unique distinction of winning two *unshared* Nobel Prizes – one for Chemistry in 1954 and one for Peace in 1962. His Chemistry Prize was for improving our understanding of the chemical bond and his Peace Prize was for his campaign against nuclear weapons testing.

Although the general trends in ionization energy and electronegativity are the same, they are distinct properties. Ionization energies can be measured directly and are a property of gaseous atoms. Elements with high electronegativities have the most exothermic electron affinities, but again care should be taken to avoid confusion between the terms. Electron affinities are properties of isolated gaseous atoms whereas electronegativity is a property of an atom in a molecule. Electronegativity values are derived indirectly from experimental bond energy data.

Metals have lower ionization energies and electronegativities than non-metals

The ability of metals to conduct electricity is due to the availability of their valence electrons to move away from the atomic nucleus. This can be related to their low ionization energies and electronegativities. There is a transition from metal to metalloid and non-metal from left to right as these properties increase. The diagonal band of metalloids which divides the metals from the non-metals can also be related to the similar electronegativities of these elements.

9 Which of the following is a property of gaseous atoms?

I   ionization energy
II electron affinity
III electronegativity

A I and II   **B** I and III   **C** II and III   **D** I, II, and III

10 Which of the following changes is endothermic?

I $Ca(g) \rightarrow Ca^+(g) + e^-$
II $I(g) + e^- \rightarrow I^-(g)$
III $O^- + e^- \rightarrow O^{2-}(g)$

A I and II   **B** I and III   **C** II and III   **D** I, II, and III

11 Identify the element which is likely to have an electronegativity value most similar to that of lithium?

A beryllium   **B** sodium   **C** magnesium   **D** hydrogen

12 The graph represents the variation of a property of the Group 2 elements.

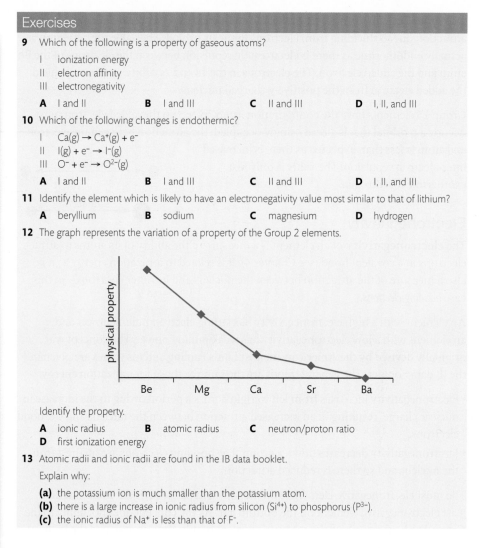

Identify the property.

A ionic radius   **B** atomic radius   **C** neutron/proton ratio
D first ionization energy

13 Atomic radii and ionic radii are found in the IB data booklet.

Explain why:

(a) the potassium ion is much smaller than the potassium atom.
(b) there is a large increase in ionic radius from silicon (Si^{4+}) to phosphorus (P^{3-}).
(c) the ionic radius of Na^+ is less than that of F^-.

Melting points

Comparisons between melting points of different elements are more complex as they depend on both the type of bonding and the structure (Chapter 4). Trends down Groups 1 and 17 can, however, be explained simply, as the elements within each group bond in similar ways. Trends in melting points down Group 1 and Group 17 are shown in the table below.

Element	Melting point (K)	Element	Melting point (K)
Li	454	F_2	54
Na	371	Cl_2	172
K	337	Br_2	266
Rb	312	I_2	387
Cs	302	At_2	575

Melting points decrease down Group 1. The elements have metallic structures which are held together by attractive forces between **delocalized** outer electrons and the positively charged ions. This attraction decreases with distance.

Melting points increase down Group 17. The elements have molecular structures which are held together by London (dispersion) forces. These increase with the number of electrons in the molecule. This is explained more fully in Chapter 4.

Melting points generally rise across a period and reach a maximum at Group 14. They then fall to reach a minimum at Group 18. In Period 3, for example, the bonding changes from metallic (Na, Mg, and Al) to giant covalent (Si) to weak van der Waals' attraction between simple molecules (P_4, S_8, Cl_2) and single atoms (Ar) (Figure 3.7). All the Period 3 elements are solids at room temperature except chlorine and argon.

▲
Figure 3.7 The melting points show a periodic pattern as the bonding changes from metallic, to giant covalent, to simple molecular.

Exercises

14 Explain why sulfur has a higher melting point than phosphorus.

15 Which physical property generally increases down a group but decreases from left to right across a period?

    A melting point   **B** electronegativity   **C** ionization energy   **D** atomic radius

16 The elements in the Periodic Table are arranged in order of increasing:

    A relative atomic mass
    B ionic radii
    C nuclear charge
    D ionization energy

17 What is the order of decreasing radii for the species Cl, Cl^+, and Cl^-?

18 Which one of the following elements has the highest electronegativity?

    A Be   **B** Cl   **C** Ca   **D** Br

19 Which properties of the Period 3 elements increase from sodium to argon:

    A nuclear charge and atomic radius
    B atomic radius and electronegativity
    C nuclear charge and electronegativity
    D nuclear charge, atomic radius, and electronegativity

20 The following graph shows the variation of a physical property, X, of the first 20 elements in the Periodic Table with the atomic number.

Identify the property X.

    A atomic radius   **B** first ionization energy
    C ionic radius   **D** melting point

TOK No one knows how high the atomic number of the elements will go, but it is expected that all new elements will fit into the current scheme. Could there ever be an 'end' to science? Could we reach a point where everything important in a scientific sense is known?

TOK

The structure of the Periodic Table was first discovered by observing patterns in the chemical and physical properties of the elements. We now realize that it is determined by the electron configuration of the elements. What roles did inductive and deductive reasoning play in the development of the Periodic Table? What role does inductive and deductive reasoning have in science in general?

Exercises

21 Identify the graph which shows the correct ionic radii for the isoelectronic ions Cl^-, K^+, and Ca^{2+}?

NATURE OF SCIENCE

Although Mendeleyev is given most of the credit for arranging the elements into a Periodic Table in 1869, the periodicity in the physical properties was independently demonstrated the same year by the German chemist Lothar Meyer. Meyer plotted a range of physical properties against relative atomic mass. The graph of density against relative atomic mass is shown in Figure 3.8. Elements in the same group occur at similar points on the curve. The noble gases, for example, are all near the minimum points in the curve. Many scientific laws and theories have been developed independently by different scientists working in different countries. This illustrates the objective nature of science.

Figure 3.8 The relationship between relative atomic mass and density.

Chemical properties

The chemical properties of an element are determined by the electron configuration of its atoms. Elements of the same group have similar chemical properties as they have the same number of valence electrons in their outer energy level. The alkali metals in Group 1, for example, all have one electron in their outer shell and the halogens in Group 17 have seven outer electrons. The trends in their chemical properties can be accounted for by the trends in their properties discussed earlier.

Group 18: the noble gases

To understand the reactivity of the elements it is instructive to consider Group 18, which contains the least reactive elements – the noble gases. This chemically aloof family of elements was only discovered at the end of the 19th century after Mendeleyev first published his table.

- They are colourless gases.
- They are monatomic: they exist as single atoms.
- They are very unreactive.

Their lack of reactivity can be explained by the inability of their atoms to lose or gain electrons. They do not generally form positive ions as they have the highest ionization energies. They do not form negative ions as extra electrons would have to be added to an empty outer energy level shell where they would experience a negligible effective nuclear force, with the protons shielded by an equal number of inner electrons. With the exception of helium, they have complete valence energy levels with eight electrons; a **stable octet**. Helium has a complete principal first energy level with two electrons.

The reactivity of elements in other groups can be explained by their unstable incomplete electron energy levels. They lose or gain electrons so as to achieve the electron configuration of their nearest noble gas.

- Elements in Groups 1, 2, and 13 lose electrons to adopt the arrangement of the nearest noble gas with a lower atomic number. They are generally metals.
- Elements in Groups 15 to 17 gain electrons to adopt the electron configuration of the nearest noble gas on their right in the Periodic Table. They are generally non-metals.
- The metalloids in the middle of the table show intermediate properties.

Group 1: the alkali metals

All the elements are silvery metals and are too reactive to be found in nature. They are usually stored in oil to prevent contact with air and water. The properties of the first three elements are summarized in the table below.

Physical properties	Chemical properties
<ul><li>They are good conductors of electricity and heat.</li><li>They have low densities.</li><li>They have grey shiny surfaces when freshly cut with a knife.</li></ul>	<ul><li>They are very reactive metals.</li><li>They form ionic compounds with non-metals.</li></ul>

Chemical properties of an element are largely determined by the number of valence electrons in the outer energy level.

TOK

What characteristics must an explanation possess to be considered 'good' within the natural sciences? What is the difference between explanations in the different areas of knowledge?

Group 18 used to be called the 'inert gases' as it was thought that they were completely unreactive. No compounds of helium or neon have ever been found. The first compound of xenon was made in 1962 and compounds of krypton and argon have now been prepared. The most reactive element in the group has the lowest ionization energy as reactions involve the withdrawal of electrons from the parent atom.

Lithium is a soft reactive metal. When freshly cut, it has a metallic lustre. However, it rapidly reacts with oxygen in the air, giving it a dark oxide coat.

It has been estimated that at any one time there are only 17 francium atoms on the Earth.

Sodium is softer and more reactive than lithium.

Potassium is softer and more reactive than sodium.

Potassium reacting with water. The heat generated causes the hydrogen to ignite.

Note that the metal hydroxide is produced when Group 1 elements are added to water. A common mistake is to give the oxide as the product.

Observations must be something that can be observed. You cannot usually identify chemicals by simple observations. If you are asked to describe what you would see, saying 'a gas was produced' would gain more marks than 'hydrogen was produced'.

They form single charged ions, M^+, with the stable octet of the noble gases when they react. Their low ionization energies give an indication of the ease with which the outer electron is lost. Reactivity increases down the group as the elements with higher atomic number have the lowest ionization energies. Their ability to conduct electricity and heat is also due to the mobility of their outer electron.

Reaction with water

The alkali metals react with water to produce hydrogen and the metal hydroxide. When you drop a piece of one of the first three elements into a small beaker containing distilled water, the following happens.

• Lithium floats and reacts slowly. It releases hydrogen but keeps its shape.
• Sodium reacts with a vigorous release of hydrogen. The heat produced is sufficient to melt the unreacted metal, which forms a small ball that moves around on the water surface.
• Potassium reacts even more vigorously to produce sufficient heat to ignite the hydrogen produced. It produces a lilac coloured flame and moves excitedly on the water surface.

The metals are called alkali metals because the resulting solution is alkaline owing to the presence of the hydroxide ion formed.

For example, with potassium:

$$2K(s) + 2H_2O(l) \rightarrow 2KOH(aq) + H_2(g)$$

As KOH is an ionic compound (Chapter 4) which dissociates in water, it is more appropriate to write the equation as:

$$2K(s) + 2H_2O(l) \rightarrow 2K^+(aq) + 2OH^-(aq) + H_2(g)$$

The reaction becomes more vigorous as the group is descended. The most reactive element, caesium, has the lowest ionization energy and so forms positive ions most readily.

Exercises

22 State two observations you could make during the reaction between sodium and water. Give an equation for the reaction.

23 Which property increases down Group 1 from lithium to caesium?

    A   electronegativity   **B**   first ionization energy   **C**   melting point

    D   chemical reactivity

Group 17: the halogens

The Group 17 elements exist as diatomic molecules, X_2. Their physical and chemical properties are summarized in the table below.

Physical properties	Chemical properties
• They are coloured. • They show a gradual change from gases (F_2 and Cl_2), to liquid (Br_2), and solids (I_2 and At_2).	• They are very reactive non-metals. Reactivity decreases down the group. • They form ionic compounds with metals and covalent compounds with other non-metals.

The trend in reactivity can be explained by their readiness to accept electrons, as illustrated by their very exothermic electron affinities discussed earlier. The nuclei have a high effective charge, of approximately +7, and so exert a strong pull on any electron from other atoms. This electron can then occupy the outer energy level of the halogen atom and complete a stable octet. The attraction is greatest for the smallest atom fluorine, which is the most reactive non-metal in the Periodic Table. Reactivity decreases down the group as the atomic radius increases and the attraction for outer electrons decreases.

Reaction with Group 1 metals

The halogens react with the Group 1 metals to form ionic **halides**. The halogen atom gains one electron from the Group 1 elements to form a halide ion X^-. The resulting ions both have the stable octet of the noble gases. For example:

$$2Na(s) + Cl_2(g) \rightarrow 2NaCl(s)$$

The electrostatic force of attraction between the oppositely charged Na^+ and Cl^- ions bonds the ions together. The outer electron moves like a harpoon from the sodium to the chlorine. Once the transfer is complete the ions are pulled together by the mutual attraction of their opposite charges (Figure 3.9).

 The names of diatomic elements all end in *-ine* or *-gen*.

 Group 1 and Group 17 are on opposite sides of the Periodic Table and show opposite trends in their reactivities and melting points.

From left to right: chlorine (Cl_2), bromine (Br_2), and iodine (I_2). These are toxic and reactive non-metals. Chlorine is a green gas at room temperature. Bromine is a dark liquid, although it readily produces a brown vapour. Iodine is a crystalline solid.

 Two halogens are named by their colours: *chloros* means 'yellowish green' and *ioeides* is 'violet' in Greek. One is named by its smell: '*bromos*' is the Greek word for 'stench'.

 TOK Chlorine was used as a chemical weapon during World War I. Should scientists be held morally responsible for the applications of their discoveries?

 TOK The electron involved in the bonding of sodium is described as a harpoon. How useful are similes and metaphors in the sciences? Does the language we use in the sciences have a descriptive or interpretive function?

Na   Cl   Na⁺   Cl⁻

Figure 3.9 The high effective charge of the chlorine nucleus pulls the outer electron from the sodium atom. Once the transfer is complete the ions are pulled together by electrostatic attraction.

Sodium reacting with chlorine to form sodium chloride (NaCl, table salt). The violent reaction is exothermic and releases much heat.

When chlorine water is added to the colourless potassium bromide solution, bromine (yellow/orange) is formed. Bromine is displaced from solution by the more reactive chlorine.

The more reactive halogen displaces the ions of the less reactive halogen from its compounds.

The most vigorous reaction occurs between the elements which are furthest apart in the Periodic Table: the most reactive alkali metal, francium, at the bottom of Group 1, with the most reactive halogen, fluorine, at the top of Group 17.

Displacement reactions

The relative reactivity of the elements can also be seen by placing them in direct competition for an extra electron. When chlorine is bubbled through a solution of potassium bromide the solution changes from colourless to orange owing to the production of bromine:

$$2KBr(aq) + Cl_2(aq) \rightarrow 2KCl(aq) + Br_2(aq)$$

$$2Br^-(aq) + Cl_2(aq) \rightarrow 2Cl^-(aq) + Br_2(aq)$$

A chlorine nucleus has a stronger attraction for an electron than a bromine nucleus because of its smaller atomic radius and so takes the electron from the bromide ion. The chlorine has gained an electron and so forms the chloride ion, Cl^-. The bromide ion loses an electron to form bromine.

Other reactions are:

$$2I^-(aq) + Cl_2(aq) \rightarrow 2Cl^-(aq) + I_2(aq)$$

The colour changes from colourless to dark orange/brown owing to the formation of iodine.

$$2I^-(aq) + Br_2(aq) \rightarrow 2Br^-(aq) + I_2(aq)$$

The colour darkens owing to the formation of iodine. To distinguish between bromine and iodine more effectively, the final solution can be shaken with a hydrocarbon solvent. Iodine forms a violet solution and bromine a dark orange solution as shown in the photo.

Solutions of chlorine (left), bromine (middle) and iodine (right) in water (lower part) and cyclohexane (upper part). Chlorine dissolves in water, but the halogens are generally more soluble in non-polar solvents like cyclohexane.

The halides

The halogens form insoluble salts with silver. Adding a solution containing the halide to a solution containing silver ions produces a **precipitate** that is useful in identifying the halide ion.

$$Ag^+(aq) + X^-(aq) \rightarrow AgX(s)$$

This is shown in this photo.

Silver halide precipitates formed by reacting silver nitrate ($AgNO_3$) with solutions of the halides. From left to right, these are silver chloride (AgCl), silver bromide (AgBr), and silver iodide (AgI).

Exercises

24 How do the reactivities of the alkali metals and the halogens vary down the group?

25 Which property of the halogens increases from fluorine to iodine?

  A ionic charge   **C** melting point of the element

  B electronegativity   **D** chemical reactivity with metals.

26 Which pair of elements reacts most readily?

  A $Li + Br_2$ **B** $Li + Cl_2$ **C** $K + Br_2$ **D** $K + Cl_2$

27 Chlorine is a greenish-yellow gas, bromine is a dark red liquid, and iodine is a dark grey solid. Identify the property which most directly causes these differences in volatility.

  A the halogen–halogen bond energy

  B the number of neutrons in the nucleus of the halogen atom

  C the number of outer electrons in the halogen atom

  D the number of electrons in the halogen molecule

28 A paper published in April 2010 by Yu. Ts. Oganessian and others claims the synthesis of isotopes of a new element with atomic number 117. One of the isotopes is $^{293}_{117}Uus$. Which of the following statements is correct?

  A the nucleus of the atom has a relative charge of +117

  B $^{293}_{117}Uus$ has a mass number of 117

  C there are 262 neutrons in $^{293}_{117}Uus$

  D the atomic number is 293 – 117

NATURE OF SCIENCE

Element 117 would be a new halogen. Whereas the discovery of the early elements involved the practical steps of extraction and isolation often performed by one individual, later elements are made by teams of scientists working together. New elements are as much invented as discovered, but their existence provides further knowledge about the natural world. The first synthetic elements were the transuranics. They are radioactive elements which are heavier than uranium, the heaviest natural element.

Claims that a new halogen, element 117, has been made were first made in April 2010 but these findings have yet to be confirmed. Scientists publish their own results in scientific journals after their work has been reviewed by several experts working in the same field. This process is called peer review. If the element turns out to have the properties predicted of a halogen below astatine, it will provide more evidence to support our model of the atom and the Periodic Table.

Glenn Seaborg (1912–1999) pointing to the element seaborgium (Sg). Seaborg discovered the transuranic element plutonium (Pu) in 1940. Seaborg also discovered americium (Am) and seven other transuranics. He won the 1951 Nobel Prize in Chemistry.

 TOK How can the production of artificial elements give us more knowledge of the natural world?

Bonding of the Period 3 oxides

The transition from metallic to non-metallic character is illustrated by the bonding of the Period 3 oxides. Ionic compounds are generally formed between metal and non-metal elements and so the oxides of elements Na to Al have **giant ionic** structures. Covalent compounds are formed between non-metals, so the oxides of phosphorus, sulfur, and chlorine are **molecular covalent**. The oxide of silicon, which is a metalloid, has a **giant covalent** structure.

The ionic character of a compound depends on the *difference* in electronegativity between its elements. Oxygen has an electronegativity of 3.4, so the ionic character of the oxides decreases from left to right, as the electronegativity values of the Period 3 elements approach this value (Figure 3.10).

Cut and polished slices of agate. Agate is a variety of quartz (silicon dioxide). The colours are formed by impurities and the concentric bands are formed as successive layers of the oxide precipitate out of solution during formation of the agate.

Figure 3.10 Electronegativities increase across the period and approach 3.4, the value for oxygen.

The oxides become more ionic down a group as the electronegativity decreases.

The conductivity of the molten oxides gives an experimental measure of their ionic character, as is shown in the table below. They only conduct electricity in the liquid state, when the ions are free to move.

Note that the maximum oxidation state of a Period 3 element is related to the group number. It is +1 for elements in Group 1, +2 for elements in Group 2, +3 for elements in Group 13, +4 for elements in Group 14, and so on. Oxidation states are discussed in Chapter 9.

Formula of oxide	$Na_2O(s)$	$MgO(s)$	$Al_2O_3(s)$	$SiO_2(s)$	$P_4O_{10}(s)$/ $P_4O_6(s)$	$SO_3(l)$/ $SO_2(g)$	$Cl_2O_7(l)$/ $Cl_2O(g)$
Oxidation state	+1	+2	+3	+4	+5/+3	+6/+4	+7/+1
Electrical conductivity in molten state	high	high	high	very low	none	none	none
Structure	giant ionic			giant covalent	molecular covalent		

Acid–base character of the Period 3 oxides

The acid–base properties of the oxides are closely linked to their bonding and structure. Metallic elements, which form ionic oxides, are basic; non-metal oxides, which are covalent, are acidic. Aluminium oxide, which can be considered as an ionic oxide with some covalent character, shows amphoteric properties – reacting with both acids and bases. The acid–base properties of Period 3 oxides are shown in the table below.

Formula of oxide	$Na_2O(s)$	$MgO(s)$	$Al_2O_3(s)$	$SiO_2(s)$	$P_4O_{10}(s)/$ $P_4O_6(s)$	$SO_3(l)/$ $SO_2(g)$	$Cl_2O_7(l)/$ $Cl_2O(g)$
Acid–base character	basic	basic	amphoteric	acidic	acidic	acidic	acidic

Aqueous solutions of the oxides of some elements with universal indicator. Sulfur trioxide forms sulfuric acid in water, which is highly acidic. Sodium oxide forms sodium hydroxide, which is a strong alkali. Non-metal oxides have low pH and metal oxides have high pH.

Oxides of metals are ionic and basic. Oxides of the non-metals are covalent and acidic. Aluminium oxide is amphoteric.

Amphoteric oxides show both acidic and basic properties.

Alkalis are bases which are soluble in water. They form hydroxide ions in aqueous solution.

Basic oxides

Sodium oxide and magnesium oxide dissolve in water to form alkaline solutions owing to the presence of hydroxide ions:

$$Na_2O(s) + H_2O(l) \rightarrow 2NaOH(aq)$$

$$MgO(s) + H_2O(l) \rightarrow Mg(OH)_2(aq)$$

A basic oxide reacts with an acid to form a salt and water. The oxide ion combines with two H^+ ions to form water:

$$O^{2-}(s) + 2H^+(aq) \rightarrow H_2O(l)$$

$$Li_2O(s) + 2HCl(aq) \rightarrow 2LiCl(aq) + H_2O(l)$$

$$MgO(s) + 2HCl(aq) \rightarrow MgCl_2(aq) + H_2O(l)$$

When an element forms a number of different oxides it is useful to use the oxidation number of the element to distinguish between them. The oxidation number is shown by a Roman numeral. Oxidation numbers are discussed in more detail in Chapter 9. It is worth noting here that the oxidation numbers of sulfur, phosphorus, and chlorine remain unchanged as their oxides are added to water, in the examples shown. This is not always the case. The oxidation number of one of the chlorine atoms increases, and the other decreases, when the gas is added to water.

$$Cl_2(g) + H_2O(l) \rightleftharpoons HOCl(aq) + HCl(aq)$$
$$0 \qquad\qquad\qquad +1 \qquad -1 \text{ oxidation state of Cl}$$

Acidic oxides

The non-metallic oxides react readily with water to produce acidic solutions. Phosphorus(V) oxide reacts with water to produce phosphoric(V) acid:

$$P_4O_{10}(s) + 6H_2O(l) \rightarrow 4H_3PO_4(aq)$$

Phosphorus(III) oxide reacts with water to produce phosphoric(III) acid:

$$P_4O_6(s) + 6H_2O(l) \rightarrow 4H_3PO_3(aq)$$

Non-metal oxides are responsible for Acid Rain. This is discussed in more detail in Chapter 8.

Sulfur trioxide reacts with water to produce sulfuric(VI) acid:

$$SO_3(l) + H_2O(l) \rightarrow H_2SO_4(aq)$$

Sulfur dioxide reacts with water to produce sulfuric(IV) acid:

$$SO_2(g) + H_2O(l) \rightarrow H_2SO_3(aq)$$

Dichlorine heptoxide (Cl_2O_7) reacts with water to produce chloric(VII) acid ($HClO_4$):

$$Cl_2O_7(l) + H_2O(l) \rightarrow 2HClO_4(aq)$$

Dichlorine monoxide (Cl_2O) reacts with water to produce chloric(I) acid ($HClO$):

$$Cl_2O(l) + H_2O(l) \rightarrow 2HClO(aq)$$

Silicon dioxide does not react with water, but reacts with concentrated alkalis to form silicates:

$$SiO_2(s) + 2OH^-(aq) \rightarrow SiO_3{}^{2-}(aq) + H_2O(l)$$

The Periodic Table has been called the most elegant classification chart ever devised. Is it a description or an explanation of periodic trends? Do other unifying systems exist in other areas of knowledge? To what extent do the classification systems we use affect the knowledge we obtain?

Amphoteric oxides

Aluminium oxide does not affect the pH when it is added to water as it is essentially insoluble. It has amphoteric properties, however, as it shows both acid and base behaviour. For example, it behaves as a base as it reacts with sulfuric acid:

$$Al_2O_3(s) + 6H^+ \rightarrow 2Al^{3+}(aq) + 3H_2O(l)$$

$$Al_2O_3(s) + 3H_2SO_4(aq) \rightarrow Al_2(SO_4)_3(aq) + 3H_2O(l)$$

and behaves as an acid when it reacts with alkalis such as sodium hydroxide:

$$Al_2O_3(s) + 3H_2O(l) + 2OH^-(aq) \rightarrow 2Al(OH)_4(aq)$$

Exercises

29 An oxide of a Period 3 element is solid at room temperature and forms a basic oxide. Identify the element.

    A Mg   **B** Al   **C** P   **D** S

30 Which pair of elements has the most similar chemical properties?

    A N and S   **B** N and P   **C** P and Cl   **D** N and Cl

31 Identify the oxide which forms an acidic solution when added to water.

    A $Na_2O(s)$ **B** $MgO(s)$ **C** $SiO_2(s)$ **D** $SO_3(g)$

32 (a) Use the data below to identify the state of the four oxides listed under standard conditions.

Oxides	Melting point / K	Boiling point / K
MgO	3125	3873
SiO_2(quartz)	1883	2503
P_4O_{10}	297	448
SO_2	200	263

(b) Explain the difference in melting points by referring to the bonding and structure in each case.

(c) The oxides are added to separate samples of pure water. State whether the resulting liquid is acidic, neutral, or alkaline. Describe all chemical reactions by giving chemical equations.

(d) Use chemical equations to describe the reactions of aluminium oxide with:

    (i) hydrochloric acid

    (ii) sodium hydroxide

33 Describe the acid–base character of the oxides of the Period 3 elements Na to Ar. For sodium oxide and sulfur trioxide, write balanced equations to illustrate their acid–base character.

High melting points are associated with ionic or covalent giant structures, low melting points with molecular covalent structures.

Make sure that you understand all the chemical equations presented in this topic. You could be expected to reproduce them under exam conditions.

Practice questions

1 Which property generally decreases across Period 3?

    A atomic number   **B** electronegativity   **C** atomic radius

    D first ionization energy

2 Which statements about Period 3 are correct?

    I   The electronegativity of the elements increases across Period 3.

    II   The atomic radii of the elements decreases across Period 3.

    III The oxides of the elements change from acidic to basic across Period 3.

    A I and II only   **B** I and III only   **C** II and III only   **D** I, II, and III

3 Which property decreases down Group 17 in the Periodic Table?

    A melting point   **B** electronegativity   **C** atomic radius   **D** ionic radius

4 Which oxides produce an acidic solution when added to water?

    I P_4O_{10}

    II MgO

    III SO_3

    A I and II only   **B** I and III only   **C** II and III only   **D** I, II, and III

5 The *x*-axis of the graph on the right represents the atomic number of the elements in Period 3. Which variable could represent the *y*-axis?

    A melting point   **B** electronegativity   **C** ionic radius   **D** atomic radius

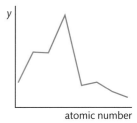

atomic number

6 Which is the best definition of *electronegativity*?

    A Electronegativity is the energy required for a gaseous atom to gain an electron.

    B Electronegativity is the attraction of an atom for a bonding pair of electrons.

    C Electronegativity is the attraction between the nucleus and the valence electrons of an atom.

    D Electronegativity is the ability of an atom to attract electrons from another atom.

7 What are the products of the reaction between chlorine and water?

    A O_2, H_2, and HCl   **B** H_2 and OCl_2 **C** HCl and HOCl   **D** HOCl, H_2, and Cl_2

8 (a) Define the term *first ionization energy*.   (2)

    (b) Explain why the first ionization energy of magnesium is higher than that of sodium.   (2)

    (Total 4 marks)

9 Samples of sodium oxide and sulfur trioxide are added to separate beakers of water. Deduce the equation for each reaction and identify each oxide as acidic, basic, or neutral.

    (3)

10 (a) Outline two reasons why a sodium ion has a smaller radius than a sodium atom.   (2)

    (b) Explain why the ionic radius of P^{3-} is greater than the ionic radius of Si^{4+}.   (2)

    (Total 4 marks)

11 Sodium oxide, Na_2O, is a white solid with a high melting point.

    (a) Explain why solid sodium oxide is a non-conductor of electricity.   (1)

    (b) Molten sodium oxide is a good conductor of electricity. State the half-equation for the reaction occurring at the positive electrode during the electrolysis of molten sodium oxide.   (1)

    (c) (i) State the acid/base nature of sodium oxide.   (1)

         (ii) State the equation for the reaction of sodium oxide with water.   (1)

    (Total 4 marks)

To access weblinks on the topics covered in this chapter, please go to www.pearsonhotlinks.com and enter the ISBN or title of this book.

04 Chemical bonding and structure

Essential ideas

4.1 Ionic compounds consist of ions held together in lattice structures by ionic bonds.

4.2 Covalent compounds form by the sharing of electrons.

4.3 Lewis (electron dot) structures show the electron domains in the valence shell and are used to predict molecular shape.

4.4 The physical properties of molecular substances result from different types of forces between their molecules.

4.5 Metallic bonds involve a lattice of cations with delocalized electrons.

Scanning electron micrograph of graphite shows its layered structure. Graphite is a form of pure carbon, in which the bonding of atoms within a layer is much stronger than the forces between the layers. An understanding of bonding enables scientists to explain and predict many of the properties of materials.

We learned in Chapter 2 that all elements are made of atoms but that there are only about 100 chemically different types of atom. Yet we know that we live in a world made up of literally millions of different substances: somehow these must all be formed from just these 100 atomic building blocks. The extraordinary variety arises from the fact that atoms readily combine with each other and they do so in a myriad of different ways. They come together in small numbers or large, with similar atoms or very different atoms, but always the result of the combination is a stable association known as a **chemical bond**. Atoms linked together by bonds therefore have very different properties from their parent atoms.

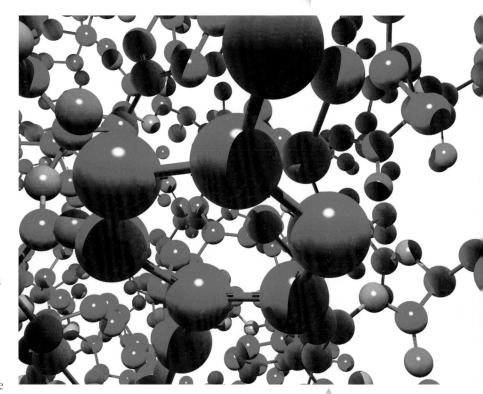

A molecule of insulin, the hormone essential for the regulation of glucose in the body. The ball-and-stick model shows all the atoms and bonds within the protein molecule. Insulin was the first protein to have its entire structure elucidated.

In this chapter we will study the main types of chemical bonds – the ionic bond, the covalent bond, and the metallic bond – and also consider other forces that help to hold substances together. Our study of the covalent bond at this level will use some of the concepts from quantum mechanical theory developed in Chapter 2 to explain the shapes and properties of molecules in more detail. As electrons are the key to the formation of all these bonds, a good understanding of electron configurations in atoms will help you.

Chemical reactions take place when some bonds break and others re-form. Being able to predict and understand the nature of the bonds within a substance is therefore central to explaining its chemical reactivity.

4.1 Ionic bonding and structure

Understandings:
- Positive ions (cations) form by metals losing valence electrons.
- Negative ions (anions) form by non-metals gaining electrons.
- The number of electrons lost or gained is determined by the electron configuration of the atom.
- The ionic bond is due to electrostatic attraction between oppositely charged ions.
- Under normal conditions, ionic compounds are usually solids with lattice structures.

Applications and skills:
- Deduction of the formula and name of an ionic compound from its component ions, including polyatomic ions.

  Guidance
  Students should be familiar with the names of these polyatomic ions: NH_4^+, OH^-, NO_3^-, HCO_3^-, CO_3^{2-}, SO_4^{2-}, and PO_4^{3-}.
- Explanation of the physical properties of ionic compounds (volatility, electrical conductivity, and solubility) in terms of their structure.

Ions form when electrons are transferred

All atoms are electrically neutral, even though they contain charged particles known as protons and electrons. This is because the number of protons (+) is equal to the number of electrons (–), and so their charges cancel each other out. The positively charged protons, located within the nucleus of the atom, are not transferred during chemical reactions. Electrons, however, positioned outside the nucleus, are less tightly held and outer electrons, known as **valence electrons**, can be transferred when atoms react together. When this happens the atom is no longer neutral, but instead carries an electric charge and is called an **ion**. The charge on the ion which forms is therefore determined by how many electrons are lost or gained.

We learned in Chapter 3 that the group number in the Periodic Table relates to the number of electrons in the outer shell of the atoms of all the elements in that group. We also learned that Group 18 elements, known as the **noble gases,** where the atoms all have full outer shells of electrons, are especially stable and have almost no tendency to react at all. This full outer shell behaves in a sense like the 'ultimate goal' for other atoms: they react to gain the stability associated with this by losing or gaining the appropriate number of electrons, whichever is the easiest (in energetic terms).

An ion is a charged particle. Ions form from atoms or from groups of atoms by loss or gain of one or more electrons.

It may help you to remember: CATion is PUSSYtive and aNion is Negative.

An energy-efficient light bulb. A compact fluorescent lamp has a gas-filled glass tube which contains a small amount of mercury vapour mixed with argon under low pressure. As argon is a noble gas, it is very unreactive owing to its stable electron arrangement, so it helps to provide an inert environment.

- Elements that have a small number of electrons in their outer shells (Groups 1, 2, and 3) will lose those electrons and form positive ions called **cations.** These elements are the **metals**.
- Elements that have higher numbers of electrons in their outer shells (Groups 15, 16, and 17) will gain electrons and form negative ions called **anions**. These elements are the **non-metals**.

We are now able to summarize how the position of an element in the Periodic Table enables us to predict the type of ion that it will form.

Group number	Example	Number of valence electrons	Electrons lost or gained	Number of electrons transferred	Charge on ion formed	Type of element
1	sodium	1	lost	1	1+	metal
2	calcium	2	lost	2	2+	metal
13	aluminium	3	lost	3	3+	metal
14	carbon	4	–	–	–	non-metal
15	phosphorus	5	gained	3	3–	non-metal
16	oxygen	6	gained	2	2–	non-metal
17	bromine	7	gained	1	1–	non-metal

Note that elements in Group 14, having four electrons in their outer shell, do not have a tendency to gain or to lose electrons, and so they generally do not form ions. This is because the energy involved in transferring four electrons would simply be too large to be favourable. These elements therefore react to form a different type of bond, which we will discuss later in this chapter.

Worked example

Refer to the Periodic Table to deduce the charge on the ion formed when the following elements react:

(i) lithium

(ii) sulfur

(iii) argon

Solution

(i) lithium is in Group 1 so forms Li^+

(ii) sulfur is in Group 16 so forms S^{2-}

(iii) argon is in Group 18 so does not form ions

For some elements though, it is difficult to predict the ion that will form from its position in the Periodic Table. For example, as we learned in Chapter 3, the metals occurring in the middle of the Periodic Table, known as the **transition elements**, have an electron configuration that allows them to lose different numbers of electrons from their d sub-shell and so form stable ions with different charges. The transition element iron, Fe, for example, can form Fe^{2+} by losing two electrons or Fe^{3+} by losing three electrons, depending on the reacting conditions. The two ions have distinct properties, such as forming compounds with different colours.

When an atom loses electrons it forms a positive ion, called a cation. When an atom gains electrons it forms a negative ion, called an anion. The number of charges on the ion formed is equal to the number of electrons lost or gained.

Metals form cations by losing valence electrons. Non-metals form anions by gaining electrons.

Do we have direct or indirect evidence for the existence of ions? Is there an important difference between the two types of evidence?

Compounds containing different ions of iron can be distinguished by colour: the left beaker contains $Fe^{2+}(aq)$ and the right beaker $Fe^{3+}(aq)$. Similar colour changes occur when iron rusts as it reacts with oxygen to form these different ions.

Fehling's reagent uses the different colours of the copper ions to test for simple sugars. The left tube containing the blue Cu^{2+} ion changes to the red Cu^+ ion seen on the right when warmed with glucose and other 'reducing sugars'.

Likewise, the element copper can exist as Cu^{2+} and Cu^+ and again these ions can be distinguished by colour.

Other examples of elements that form ions that are not obvious from their group number are:

- lead, Pb, despite being in Group 14, forms a stable ion Pb^{2+};
- tin, Sn, also in Group 14, can form Sn^{4+} and Sn^{2+};
- silver, Ag, forms the ion Ag^+;
- hydrogen, H, can form H^- (hydride) as well as the more common H^+.

When the charge on an ion needs to be specified, the oxidation number is given in Roman numerals in brackets after the name of the element. For example, the red Cu^+ ion shown above can be written as copper(I) oxide. Oxidation numbers are explained fully in Chapter 9.

Finally, there are some ions that are made up of more than one atom which together have experienced a loss or gain of electrons and so carry a charge. These species are called **polyatomic ions**, and many of them are found in commonly occurring compounds. It will help you to become familiar with the examples in the table below, as you will often use them when writing formulas and equations. (Note that this information is not supplied in the IB data booklet.)

(!) When writing the symbol for ions, note the charge is written as a superscript with the number first and the charge next, e.g. N^{3-}. When an ion X carries a charge of 1+ or 1– it is written just as X^+ or X^-.

(!) Note the common names of some compounds give a clue to their composition. Here you can see that the ending '-ate' refers to ions that contain oxygen bonded to another element.

Polyatomic ion name	Charge on ion	Symbol	Example of compound containing this ion
nitrate	1–	NO_3^-	lead nitrate
hydroxide	1–	OH^-	barium hydroxide
hydrogencarbonate	1–	HCO_3^-	potassium hydrogencarbonate
carbonate	2–	CO_3^{2-}	magnesium carbonate
sulfate	2–	SO_4^{2-}	copper sulfate
phosphate	3–	PO_4^{3-}	calcium phosphate
ammonium	1+	NH_4^+	ammonium chloride

We will learn how to write the formulas for these compounds in the next section.

Ionic compounds form when oppositely charged ions attract

Ions do not form in isolation. Rather the process of **ionization** – where electrons are transferred between atoms – occurs when an atom that loses electrons passes them directly to an atom that gains them. Typically, this means electrons are transferred from a metal element to a non-metal element. For example, sodium (metal) passes an electron to chlorine (non-metal) when they react together.

$$\text{Na} \cdot \quad + \quad \overset{\times\times}{\underset{\times\times}{\times\text{Cl}\times}} \quad \longrightarrow \quad [\text{Na}]^+ \quad [\overset{\times\times}{\underset{\times\times}{\,:\text{Cl}\,:}}]^-$$

$1s^22s^22p^63s^1$	$1s^22s^22p^63s^23p^5$		$1s^22s^22p^6$	$1s^22s^22p^63s^23p^6$
sodium	chlorine		sodium	chloride
atom	atom		ion	ion

Note that both ion products, Na^+ and Cl^-, have the electron configuration of a noble gas.

Now the oppositely charged ions resulting from this electron transfer are attracted to each other and are held together by electrostatic forces. These forces are known as an **ionic bond**, and ions held together in this way are known as **ionic compounds**.

Remember that in forming the ionic compound there is no net loss or gain of electrons, and so the ionic compound, like the atoms that formed it, must be electrically neutral. Writing the formula for the ionic compound therefore involves *balancing the total number of positive and negative charges*, taking into account the different charges on each ion.

For example, magnesium oxide is made up of magnesium ions Mg^{2+} and oxide ions O^{2-}. Here each magnesium atom has transferred *two* electrons to each oxygen atom and so the compound contains equal numbers of each ion. Its formula, $Mg^{2+}O^{2-}$, is usually written as MgO. But when magnesium reacts with fluorine, each Mg loses *two* electrons, whereas each F gains only *one* electron. So it will take two fluorine atoms to combine with each magnesium atom, and the compound that results will therefore have the ratio $Mg:F = 1:2$. This is written as $Mg^{2+}F^-_2$ or MgF_2.

Worked example

Write the formula for the compound that forms between aluminium and oxygen.

Solution

1   Check the Periodic Table for the ions that each element will form.
    aluminium in Group 13 will form Al^{3+}; oxygen in Group 16 will form O^{2-}

2   Write the number of the charge above the ion: **3**   **2**
                                                      Al   O

    Cross-multiply these numbers

    $$\overset{\textbf{3}}{\text{Al}} \underset{\text{O}}{\searrow\swarrow} \overset{\textbf{2}}{}$$

    Or you can directly balance the charges: here you need 6 of each charge
    $$2 \times Al^{3+} = 6+ \quad \text{and} \quad 3 \times O^{2-} = 6-$$

3   Write the final formula using subscripts to show the number of ions: Al_2O_3

Coloured scanning electron micrograph of crystals of table salt, sodium chloride, NaCl. The very reactive elements sodium and chlorine have combined together to form this stable compound containing Na^+ and Cl^- ions.

The ionic bond is due to electrostatic attraction between oppositely charged ions.

Note that in many non-metal elements the ending of the name changes to '-ide' when ions are present. For example, *chlorine* (the element) becomes *chloride* (the ion), *oxygen* becomes *oxide*, *nitrogen* becomes *nitride*, etc.

Note the convention in naming ionic compounds that the positive ion is written first and the negative ion second.

Note that the formula of the compound shows the *simplest ratio* of the ions it contains. So, for example, magnesium oxide is not Mg_2O_2 but MgO.

It is common practice to leave the charges out when showing the final formula. If the formula contains more than one polyatomic ion, brackets are used around the ion before the subscript.

Worked example

Write the formula for ammonium phosphate.

Solution

The compound contains two polyatomic ions, and you need to know these:

$$NH_4^+ \text{ and } PO_4^{3-}$$

Balancing the charges: $3 \times NH_4^+ = 3+$ and $1 \times PO_4^{3-} = 3-$ or:

Following the steps above:

$$\begin{array}{ccc} 1 & \diagdown\diagup & 3 \\ NH_4^+ & & PO_4^{3-} \end{array}$$

So the formula is $(NH_4)_3PO_4$.

Exercises

1 Write the formula for each of the compounds in the table on page 116.

2 Write the formula for each of the following compounds:

   (a) potassium bromide   **(d)** copper(II) bromide
   (b) zinc oxide   **(e)** chromium(III) sulfate
   (c) sodium sulfate   **(f)** aluminium hydride

3 Name the following compounds:

   (a) $Sn_3(PO_4)_2$ **(d)** $BaSO_4$
   (b) $Ti(SO_4)_2$ **(e)** Hg_2S
   (c) $Mn(HCO_3)_2$

4 What are the charges on the positive ions in each of the compounds in Q3 above?

5 What is the formula of the compound that forms from element A in Group 2 and element B in Group 5?

6 Explain what happens to the electron configurations of Mg and Br when they react to form the compound magnesium bromide.

Ionic compounds have a lattice structure

The forces of electrostatic attraction between ions in a compound cause them to surround themselves with ions of opposite charge. As a result, the ionic compound takes on a predictable three-dimensional crystalline structure known as an **ionic lattice.** The details of the lattice's geometry vary in different compounds, depending mainly on the sizes of the ions, but it always involves this fixed arrangement of ions based on a repeating unit. The term **coordination number** is used to express the number of ions that surround a given ion in the lattice. For example, in the sodium chloride lattice, the coordination number is six because each Na^+ ion is surrounded by six Cl^- ions and each Cl^- ion is surrounded by six Na^+ ions.

Note that the lattice consists of a very large number of ions and it can grow indefinitely. As ionic compounds do not therefore exist as units with a fixed number of ions, their formulas are simply an expression of the *ratio* of ions present. The simplest ratio is known as the **formula unit**, which is an empirical formula, as described in Chapter 1.

Cl^- ion

Na^+ ion

Figure 4.1 The NaCl lattice is built up from oppositely charged sodium and chloride ions.

 Make sure that you avoid the term 'molecular formula' when describing ionic compounds, but instead use the term formula unit.

We will learn in Chapter 5 that **lattice energy** is a measure of the strength of attraction between the ions within the lattice. This is greater for ions that are small and highly charged, as they have a larger charge density.

The physical properties of ionic compounds reflect their lattice structure

Physical properties are those that can be examined without chemically altering the substance. Our knowledge of ionic bonds and lattice structure helps us to interpret and explain some of these properties for ionic compounds.

Melting points and boiling points

Ionic compounds tend to have high melting and boiling points as the forces of electrostatic attraction between the ions in the lattice are strong and so require large amounts of heat energy to break. These compounds are therefore solids at room temperature, and will only melt at very high temperatures. Sodium chloride, for example, remains solid until about 800 °C.

The melting and boiling points are generally higher when the charge on the ions is greater, due to the increased attraction between the ions. For example, the table below compares the melting points of sodium oxide and magnesium oxide.

Ionic compound	Charge on metal ion	Melting point
Na_2O	1+	1132 °C
MgO	2+	2800 °C

The high melting points of ionic compounds become an economic consideration in many industrial processes, such as the electrolysis of molten ionic compounds discussed in Chapter 9. It can be very expensive to maintain such high temperatures, and this is an important factor in considering suitable methods to extract a reactive metal such as aluminium from its ore.

Volatility is a term used to describe the tendency of a substance to vaporize. In summary, ionic compounds can be described as having a low volatility or being non-volatile. Our everyday encounter with them as crystalline solids with low odour is consistent with this.

Solubility

Solubility refers to the ease with which a solid (the solute) becomes dispersed through a liquid (the solvent) to form a solution. You probably know from common observations that common salt, sodium chloride, readily dissolves in water but does not dissolve in oil. Why is this? There are several factors involved, but in general, solubility is determined by the degree to which the separated particles of solute are able to form bonds or attractive forces with the solvent.

Computer graphic of crystallized common salt, NaCl. Small spheres represent Na^+ ions and larger spheres Cl^-. The lattice is arranged so each Na^+ ion has six oppositely charged nearest neighbours and vice versa.

 Ionic liquids are efficient solvents with low volatility and are being used increasingly as solvents in Green Chemistry for energy applications and industrial processes. They are usually made of organic salts.

CHALLENGE YOURSELF

1 The melting point of aluminium oxide, Al_2O_3, is slightly lower than that of magnesium oxide, despite the 3+ charge on the aluminium ion. What factors might help to explain this?

 Ionic compounds have low volatility.

119

Consider an ionic compound being placed in water. As we will learn in the next section, water molecules are polar, which means they have some separation of charge in their structure. At the contact surface, the partial charges in the water molecules are attracted to ions of opposite charge in the lattice, which may cause the ions to dislodge from their position. As these ions separate from the lattice, they become surrounded by water molecules and are said to be **hydrated**. When this happens the solid is dissolved. State symbols are used to show this change as follows.

$$+H_2O$$
$$NaCl(s) \rightarrow NaCl(aq)$$

or

$$+H_2O$$
$$NaCl(s) \rightarrow Na^+(aq) + Cl^-(aq)$$

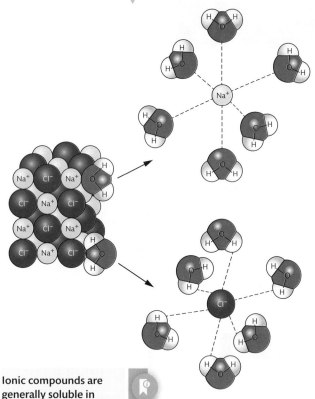

If a liquid other than water is able to dissolve the solid, the ions are said to be **solvated** and an appropriate state symbol to denote the solvent is used.

In the case of solvents like oil or hexane, C_6H_{14}, which are non-polar and so have no charge separation, there is no attraction between the liquid and the ions. So here the ions remain tightly bound to each other in the lattice, and the solid is insoluble.

This suggests that solubility trends are based on the similar chemical nature of the solute and solvent, as this is most likely to lead to successful interactions between them. The expression *'like dissolves like'* is often used to capture this notion. Note though that this is a generalized statement and somewhat over-simplified as there are some important exceptions.

Ionic compounds are generally soluble in ionic or polar solvents but not soluble in non-polar solvents.

Condom conductivity test. Condoms are tested for holes by being filled with water and placed in a solution of NaCl, and then attached to electrodes. The current will not be conducted across the insulating material of the condom, but if there is a hole the current will be conducted into the salty water, triggering an alarm. All condoms are conductivity tested in this way.

Ionic compounds do not conduct electricity in the solid state, but conduct when molten or in aqueous solution.

Electrical conductivity

The ability of a compound to conduct electricity depends on whether it contains ions that are able to move and carry a charge. Ionic compounds are not able to conduct electricity in the solid state as the ions are firmly held within the lattice and so cannot move. However, when the ionic compound is either present in the liquid state (molten), or dissolved in water (aqueous solution), the ions *will* be able to move. Therefore ionic compounds as liquids or aqueous solutions do show electrical conductivity.

Brittleness

Ionic compounds are usually brittle, which means the crystal tends to shatter when force is applied. This is because movement of the ions within the lattice places ions of the same charge alongside each other, so the repulsive forces cause it to split.

Different ionic compounds have a different extent of ionic character

A **binary** compound is one that contains only two elements. We have seen that in order for any two elements to react to form an ionic compound, they must have *very different tendencies to lose or gain electrons*. A relatively simple assessment of this can be made by looking at their positions on the Periodic Table. Metals on the left lose electrons most easily, while non-metals on the right gain electrons most easily. Also, we learned in Chapter 3 that the tendency to lose electrons and form positive ions increases *down* a group, whereas the tendency to gain electrons and form negative ions increases *up* a group. So the highest tendency to react together and form ionic compounds will be between metals on the *bottom left* and non-metals on the *top right* of the Periodic Table.

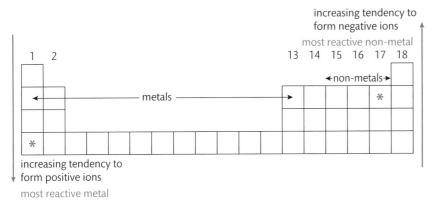

Another way to judge the tendency of two elements to form an ionic compound is by looking at **electronegativity values**. As explained in Chapter 3 on page 99, electronegativity is a measure of the ability of an atom to attract electrons in a covalent bond, and is described using the Pauling scale of values. These are given in section 8 of the IB data booklet and are summarized here.

NATURE OF SCIENCE

The theory that ionic compounds have a lattice structure of discrete ions leads to some predictions about their physical properties. The fact that these predictions can be tested by observation and experiment is central to the scientific process, and helps develop the theory. In general, data on the volatility, solubility, and conductivity of ionic compounds as discussed here support the lattice model. Yet there are some exceptions too, which need to be explained. The fact that aluminium oxide's melting point is not as high as would be expected from a model based purely on Al^{3+} and O^{2-} ions opens the question of what other types of bonding might be present, and why.

Figure 4.3 The pairs of elements that react most easily to form ionic compounds are metals on the bottom left of the Periodic Table and non-metals on the top right, indicated here by asterisks.

Figure 4.4 Periodic trends in electronegativity values show an increase along a period and up a group.

1 H 2.2																	
3 Li 1.0	4 Be 1.6											5 B 2.0	6 C 2.6	7 N 3.0	8 O 3.4	9 F 4.0	
11 Na 0.9	12 Mg 1.3											13 Al 1.6	14 Si 1.9	15 P 2.2	16 S 2.6	17 Cl 3.2	
19 K 0.8	20 Ca 1.0	21 Sc 1.4	22 Ti 1.5	23 V 1.6	24 Cr 1.7	25 Mn 1.6	26 Fe 1.8	27 Co 1.9	28 Ni 1.9	29 Cu 1.9	30 Zn 1.7	31 Ga 1.8	32 Ge 2.0	33 As 2.2	34 Se 2.6	35 Br 3.0	
37 Rb 0.8	38 Sr 1.0	39 Y 1.2	40 Zr 1.3	41 Nb 1.6	42 Mo 2.2	43 Tc 2.1	44 Ru 2.2	45 Rh 2.3	46 Pd 2.2	47 Ag 1.9	48 Cd 1.7	49 In 1.8	50 Sn 2.0	51 Sb 2.1	52 Te 2.1	53 I 2.7	
55 Cs 0.8	56 Ba 0.9	57 La* 1.1	72 Hf 1.3	73 Ta 1.5	74 W 1.7	75 Re 1.9	76 Os 2.2	77 Ir 2.2	78 Pt 2.2	79 Au 2.4	80 Hg 1.9	81 Tl 1.8	82 Pb 1.8	83 Bi 1.9	84 Po 2.0	85 At 2.2	
87 Fr 0.7	88 Ra 0.9	89 Ac* 1.1															

Pauling electronegativity values

<1.0		2.0 – 2.4
1.0 – 1.4		2.5 – 2.9
1.5 – 1.9		3.0 – 4.0

The determining factor in ionic bond formation is the *difference* in electronegativity values. It is generally recognized that a difference of 1.8 units or more on the Pauling scale will give a compound that is predominantly ionic.

Worked example

Explain which of the following pairs will be most likely to form an ionic bond.

A Be and F   **B** Si and O   **C** N and Cl   **D** K and S

Solution

Consider the difference in electronegativity of each pair:

A 1.6 and 4.0   **B** 1.9 and 3.4   **C** 3.0 and 3.2   **D** 0.8 and 2.6

D has the greatest difference, so the compound K_2S will be the most ionic.

Exercises

7 Which fluoride is the most ionic?

    A NaF   **B** CsF   **C** MgF_2 **D** BaF_2

8 Which pair of elements reacts most readily?

    A $Li + Br_2$ **B** $Li + Cl_2$ **C** $K + Br_2$ **D** $K + Cl_2$

9 You are given two white solids and told that only one of them is an ionic compound. Describe three tests you could carry out to determine which it is.

The fact that compounds differ in their extent of ionic character suggests that other types of bonding are involved, and we will consider these in the next section. We will see that the distinction between ionic and covalent bonds is not black and white, but is best described as a **bonding continuum** with all intermediate types possible.

ionic compounds	**covalent compounds**
reactive metal + reactive non-metal	two non-metals
electronegativity difference > 1.8	electronegativity difference << 1.8

polar covalent compounds
0 < electronegativity difference < 1.8

4.2 Covalent bonding

Understandings:

- A covalent bond is formed by the electrostatic attraction between a shared pair of electrons and the positively charged nuclei.
- Single, double, and triple covalent bonds involve one, two, and three shared pairs of electrons respectively.
- Bond length decreases and bond strength increases as the number of shared electrons increases.
- Bond polarity results from the difference in electronegativities of the bonded atoms.

Guidance

Bond polarity can be shown either with partial charges, dipoles, or vectors.

Applications and skills:

● Deduction of the polar nature of a covalent bond from electronegativity values.

Guidance
Electronegativity values are given in the section 8 of the IB data booklet.

A covalent bond forms by atoms sharing electrons

When atoms of two non-metals react together, each is seeking to gain electrons in order to achieve the stable electron structure of a noble gas. By sharing an electron pair they are effectively each able to achieve this. The shared pair of electrons is concentrated in the region between the two nuclei and is attracted to them both. It therefore holds the atoms together by electrostatic attraction and is known as a **covalent bond**. A group of atoms held together by covalent bonds forms a **molecule**.

For example, two hydrogen atoms form a covalent bond as follows.

$$H^{\times} + {\cdot}H \longrightarrow H{\overset{\times}{\cdot}}H$$

two hydrogen
atoms (2H)

a molecule of
hydrogen (H_2)

Note that in the molecule H_2 each hydrogen atom has a share of two electrons so it has gained the stability of the electron arrangement of the noble gas helium, He.

The formation of the covalent bond stabilizes the atoms so energy is released as the bond forms. The forces of attraction between the nuclei and shared electrons are balanced by the forces of repulsion between the two nuclei, and this holds the atoms at a fixed distance apart. Figure 4.6 shows how the bond forms at this point of lowest energy as two hydrogen atoms approach each other and their electron density shifts.

Figure 4.5 In a covalent bond the shared electrons are attracted to the nuclei of both atoms.

Computer artwork of hydrogen molecules. Each molecule consists of two hydrogen atoms bonded covalently.

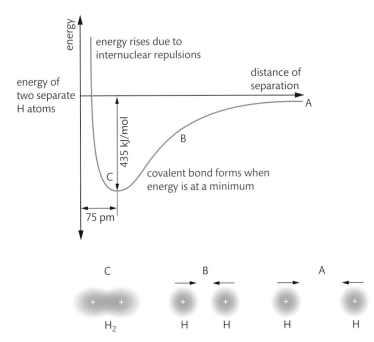

Figure 4.6 When two hydrogen atoms form a covalent bond, the distance between them corresponds to the lowest energy. The letters A, B, and C show the correspondence between shifts in electron density and the distance apart of the atoms.

A covalent bond is the electrostatic attraction between a pair of electrons and positively charged nuclei. A molecule is a group of atoms held together by covalent bonds.

Similarly, two chlorine atoms react together to form a chlorine molecule in which both atoms have gained a share of eight electrons in their outer shells (the electron arrangement of argon, Ar). This tendency of atoms to form a stable arrangement of eight electrons in their outer shell is referred to as the **octet rule**. The diagrams below only show the outer electrons, not the inner full shells, as these are the only electrons that take part in bonding.

two chlorine   a molecule of
atoms (2Cl)   chlorine (Cl_2)

Note that in the chlorine molecule, each atom has three pairs of electrons that are not involved in forming the bond. These are known as **non-bonding pairs**, or **lone pairs,** and they play an important role in determining the shape of more complex molecules, as we will see later.

Hydrogen and chlorine also react together to form a molecule of hydrogen chloride, HCl, which has the structure shown below. Note that the formation of the covalent bond enables both H and Cl to gain a stable outer shell.

Atoms can share more than one pair of electrons to form multiple bonds

Sometimes it seems there are not enough electrons to achieve octets on all the atoms in the molecule. In these cases, the atoms will have to share more than one electron pair, in other words form a multiple bond. A **double bond** forms when two electron pairs, a total of four electrons, are shared; a **triple bond** forms when three electron pairs, a total of six electrons, are shared.

For example the two most abundant gases in the air, oxygen and nitrogen, both exist as diatomic molecules containing multiple bonds:

As shown above, it is often convenient to use a line to represent a shared pair of electrons, two lines to represent a double bond and three lines a triple bond. In fact, the multiple bonds in double and triple bonds are not the same as each other, which is why a double bond is not twice as strong as a single bond between the same atoms. We can see this in the bond enthalpy data in section 11 of the IB data booklet.

Short bonds are strong bonds

Every covalent bond is characterized by two values.

- **Bond length**: a measure of the distance between the two bonded nuclei.
- **Bond strength**: usually described in terms of **bond enthalpy**, which will be discussed in Chapter 5, and is effectively a measure of the energy required to break the bond.

Data on both these values are given in sections 10 and 11 of the IB data booklet.

As atomic radius increases as we go down a group, we would expect the atoms to form molecules with longer bonds. For example:

Cl$_2$ bond length 199 pm   Br$_2$ bond length 228 pm

As a result, the shared electron pair is further from the pull of the nuclei in the larger molecules, and so the bond would be expected to be weaker. Data on Group 17 elements, which exist as diatomic molecules, mostly confirm these trends.

(F$_2$ F–F)
Cl$_2$ Cl–Cl
Br$_2$ Br–Br   bond length increases
I$_2$ I–I   bond enthalpy decreases

Multiple bonds have a greater number of shared electrons and so have a stronger force of electrostatic attraction between the bonded nuclei. This means there is a greater pulling power on the nuclei, bringing them closer together, resulting in bonds that are shorter and stronger than single bonds. We can see this by comparing different bonds involving the same atoms, such as in the hydrocarbons.

Hydrocarbon	C_2H_6	C_2H_4	C_2H_2
Structural formula	H–C–C–H (with H atoms above and below each C)	C=C (with H atoms on each C)	H–C≡C–H
Bond between carbon atoms	single	double	triple
Bond length / pm	154	134	120
Bond enthalpy / kJ mol^{-1}	346	614	839

These data confirm that triple bonds are stronger and shorter than double bonds, which are shorter and stronger than single bonds. Note though that the double bond is not twice as strong as the single bond, due to the fact that it is made up of two different bonds. (These are known as a sigma bond and a pi bond that is weaker.)

CHALLENGE YOURSELF

2 Fluorine, F$_2$, is shown in brackets opposite, as a close look at its bond enthalpy data shows that it is an outlier in the trends described here. What explanation might account for this?

Also, we can compare two different carbon–oxygen bonds within the molecule ethanoic acid, CH_3COOH.

	C—O	C=O
Bond length / pm	143	122
Bond enthalpy / kJ mol^{-1}	358	804

single bonds	double bonds	triple bonds

decreasing length, increasing strength

Polar bonds result from unequal sharing of electrons

Not all sharing is equal. It may be the case that you share this textbook with a class mate, but if you have it for more than half the time, it clearly belongs more to you than to your friend. So it is with electron pairs. In simple terms, if they spend more time with one atom than the other, they are not equally shared. This occurs when there is a difference in the electronegativities of the bonded atoms as the more electronegative atom exerts a greater pulling power on the shared electrons and so gains more 'possession' of the electron pair. The bond is now unsymmetrical with respect to electron distribution and is said to be **polar**.

The term **dipole** is often used to indicate the fact that this type of bond has two separated opposite electric charges. The more electronegative atom with the greater share of the electrons, has become partially negative or **δ–**, and the less electronegative atom has become partially positive or **δ+**.

For example, in HCl the shared electron pair is pulled more strongly by the Cl atom than the H atom, resulting in a polar molecule.

Figure 4.7 The distribution of electrons in the H—Cl bond is unsymmetrical, with a greater electron density over the Cl atom.

Note that the symbol **δ** (Greek letter, pronounced 'delta') is used to represent a partial charge. This has no fixed value, but is always less than the unit charge associated with an ion such as X$^+$ or X$^-$.

H   Cl
δ$^+$ δ$^-$

δ+   δ−
H ——×• Cl
partially partially
positive negative

In water, the electronegativity difference results in polar O–H bonds with the electron density greater on the oxygen.

The extent of polarity in a covalent bond varies, depending on how big a difference exists in the electronegativity values of the two bonded atoms. We can estimate this from knowledge of the periodic trends in electronegativity, discussed in Chapter 3 and summarized here.

electronegativity increases across a period →

electronegativity increases up a group

As fluorine is in the top right of the Periodic Table, it is clearly the most electronegative atom, so we can predict it will have the greater electron density whenever it is bonded to another element. Fluorine has a value of 4.0 on the Pauling scale of electronegativity given on page 121, and all other elements have lower values. This scale can be used to assess the relative polarity of a bond. For example, the table below compares the polarities of the hydrogen halides.

	Electronegativity values of atoms		Difference in electronegativity
H—F	2.2	4.0	1.8
H—Cl	2.2	3.2	1.0
H—Br	2.2	3.0	0.8
H—I	2.2	2.7	0.5

↑ increasing bond polarity

Worked example

Use the electronegativity values on page 121 to put the following bonds in order of decreasing polarity.

N—O in NO_2 N—F in NF_3 H—O in H_2O N—H in NH_3

Solution

Bond polarity: H—O > N—F > N—H > N—O

Difference in electronegativity values: 1.2   1.0   0.8   0.4

A microwave oven generates microwaves that have lower frequencies and longer wavelengths than visible light. Microwaves are used for cooking because certain wavelengths are absorbed by polar molecules, notably water, and also by sugar and fat. The absorption causes the water to heat up and cook the food, leaving the oven surface and containers of glass, plastic, or ceramic unaffected.

The only bonds that are truly non-polar are bonds between the same atoms such as F_2, H_2, and O_2, because clearly here the *difference* in electronegativity is zero. These are sometimes referred to as **pure covalent** to express this. All other bonds have some degree of polarity, although it may be very slight. The C–H bond, ubiquitous in organic chemistry, is often considered to be largely non-polar, although in fact carbon

There are several ways to denote the polar nature of a bond in a structure. One is to write the partial charges δ+ and δ− over the less electronegative and more electronegative atom respectively. Another is to represent the direction of electron pull as a vector with an arrow on the bond indicating the pull on the electrons by the more electronegative atoms. The dipole notation +⟶ is also useful. As you can see in the diagram of water here, it is quite acceptable to show more than one way together.

CHALLENGE YOURSELF

3 Oxygen is a very electronegative element with a value of 3.4 on the Pauling scale. Can you determine the formula of a compound in which oxygen would have a partial positive charge?

In a covalent bond, the greater the difference in the electronegativity values of the atoms, the more polar the bond.

is slightly more electronegative than hydrogen. As we will see in Chapter 10, the low polarity of the C–H bond is an important factor in determining the properties of organic compounds.

The presence of polar bonds in a molecule has a significant effect on its properties. Effectively, the partial separation of charges introduces some ionic nature into covalent bonds, so the more polar the bond, the more like an ionic compound the molecule behaves. Polar bonds are therefore considered to be intermediates in relation to pure covalent bonds and ionic bonds, part of the bonding continuum that was mentioned on page 122. We now see why the boundaries between ionic and covalent bonds are somewhat 'fuzzy', and why it is often appropriate to describe substances using terms such as 'predominantly' covalent or ionic, or of being 'strongly' polar.

The idea of the bonding continuum is summarized below.

Ionic	Polar covalent	Pure covalent
complete transfer of electrons	partial transfer of electrons unequal sharing of electrons	equal sharing of electrons
Na^+Cl^-	HF, HCl, HBr, HI	Cl_2
ionic lattice		discrete molecules

NATURE OF SCIENCE

Scientists observe the natural world where variations in structure or properties are often continuous rather than discontinuous. In other words, a spectrum of intermediates exists and this can make classification difficult. At the same time, the properties of such intermediates can strengthen our understanding. For example, we have seen here that the existence of polar covalent molecules in the bonding continuum adds to our interpretation of electron behaviour in bond formation.

Exercises

10 Which substance contains only ionic bonds?

    A $NaNO_3$ **B** H_3PO_4 **C** NH_4Cl **D** $CaCl_2$

11 Which of the following molecules contains the shortest bond between carbon and oxygen?

    A CO_2 **B** H_3COCH_3 **C** CO   **D** CH_3COOH

12 For each of these molecules, identify any polar bonds and label them using δ+ and δ– appropriately.

    (a) HBr   **(b)** CO_2 **(c)** ClF
    (d) O_2 **(e)** NH_3

13 Use the electronegativity values in section 8 of the IB data booklet to predict which bond in each of the following pairs is more polar:

    (a) C–H or C–Cl   **(b)** Si–Li or Si–Cl   **(c)** N–Cl or N–Mg

Understandings:

- Lewis (electron dot) structures show all the valence electrons in a covalently bonded species.

  Guidance
  - *The term 'electron domain' should be used in place of 'negative charge centre'.*
  - *Electron pairs in a Lewis (electron dot) structure can be shown as dots, crosses, a dash, or any combination.*
  - *Coordinate covalent bonds should be covered.*

- The 'octet rule' refers to the tendency of atoms to gain a valence shell with a total of 8 electrons.
- Some atoms, like Be and B, might form stable compounds with incomplete octets of electrons.
- Resonance structures occur when there is more than one possible position for a double bond in a molecule.
- Shapes of species are determined by the repulsion of electron pairs according to VSEPR theory.
- Carbon and silicon form giant covalent/network covalent/macromolecular structures.

  Guidance
  Allotropes of carbon (diamond, graphite, graphene, C_{60} buckminsterfullerene) and SiO_2 should be covered.

Applications and skills:

- Deduction of Lewis (electron dot) structure of molecules and ions showing all valence electrons for up to four electron pairs on each atom.
- The use of VSEPR theory to predict the electron domain geometry and the molecular geometry for species with two, three, and four electron domains.
- Prediction of bond angles from molecular geometry and presence of non-bonding pairs of electrons.
- Prediction of molecular polarity from bond polarity and molecular geometry.
- Deduction of resonance structures, including C_6H_6, CO_3^{2-} and O_3.
- Explanation of the properties of giant covalent compounds in terms of their structures.

Lewis diagrams are used to show the arrangement of electrons in covalent molecules

When describing the structure of covalent molecules, the most convenient method is known as a **Lewis structure**. This uses a simple notation of dots and crosses to represent the outer energy level, or valence shell, electrons of all the atoms in the molecule. It can be derived as follows.

Gilbert Newton Lewis (1875–1946) was one of the greatest and most influential American chemists of the last century. He formulated the idea that the covalent bond consists of a shared pair of electrons, proposed the electron pair theory of acid/base reactions, and was the first person to produce a pure sample of deuterium oxide (heavy water). He also published important theories on chemical thermodynamics and first coined the term 'photon' for the smallest unit of radiant energy. Since 1916 his dot diagrams for covalent structures have been used almost universally.

Steps to follow in drawing a Lewis structure.

1 Calculate the total number of valence electrons in the molecule by multiplying the number of valence electrons of each element by the number of atoms of the element in the formula and totalling these.

2 Draw the skeletal structure of the molecule to show how the atoms are linked to each other.

4 Add more electron pairs to complete the octets (8 electrons) around the atoms (other than hydrogen which must have 2 electrons and the exceptions noted below).

3 Use a pair of crosses, a pair of dots, or a single line to show one electron pair and put a pair in each bond between atoms.

5 If there are not enough electrons to complete the octets, form double bonds and if necessary triple bonds.

6 Check that the total number of electrons in your finished structure is equal to your calculation in the first step.

Electron pairs can be represented by dots, crosses, a combination of dots and crosses, or by a line. Use whichever notation you prefer, but be prepared to recognize all versions. The important thing is to be clear, consistent, and to avoid vague and scattered dots.

Worked example

Draw the Lewis structure for the molecule CCl_4.

Solution

Note that in Lewis structures, as in the examples on page 131, only the valence electrons are shown, as these are the only ones that take part in bonding.

1 Total number of valence electrons = $4 + (7 \times 4) = 32$

2 Skeletal structure   **3** Bonded pairs   **4** Completed Lewis structure

There are several different ways of drawing Lewis structures, and some alternative acceptable forms are shown below.

The table on page 131 shows some examples of molecules with their Lewis structures.

Molecule	Total number of valence electrons	Lewis structure
CH_4	$4 + (1 \times 4) = 8$	H : C : H (with H above and below) H—C—H (with H above and below)
NH_3	$5 + (1 \times 3) = 8$	H : N : H (with H below) H—N—H (with H below)
H_2O	$(1 \times 2) + 6 = 8$	H : O : H H—O—H
CO_2	$4 + (6 \times 2) = 16$	: O : C : O : O=C=O
HCN	$1 + 4 + 5 = 10$	H : C : N : H—C≡N

When drawing the Lewis structure of ions, note that you must:

- calculate valence electrons as above and then add one electron for each negative charge and subtract one electron for each positive charge;
- put the Lewis structure in a square bracket with the charge shown outside.

Worked example

Draw the Lewis structures for:

(i) OH^-

(ii) SO_4^{2-}

Solution

(i) valence electrons $= 6 + 1 + 1 = 8$

$$\left[\; O \; H \; \right]^-$$

(ii) valence electrons $= 6 + (6 \times 4) + 2 = 32$

$$\left[\begin{array}{c} O \\ O \; S \; O \\ O \end{array} \right]^{2-}$$

When drawing the Lewis structure of an ion, make sure you remember to put a square bracket around the structure with the charge shown clearly outside the bracket.

In coordinate bonds both shared electrons come from one atom

The examples so far involve covalent bonds where each bonded atom contributes one electron to the shared pair. However, sometimes the bond forms by *both* the electrons in the pair originating from the same atom. This means that the other atom accepts and gains a share in a donated electron pair. Such bonds are called **coordinate covalent bonds**. An arrow on the head of the bond is sometimes used to show a coordinate bond, with the direction indicating the origin of the electrons.

For example:

H_3O^+

$$\left[H \overset{\times\times}{\underset{\underset{H}{\bullet\times}}{\cdot}} O \cdot H \right]^+ \qquad \left[H - \overset{\times\times}{\underset{\underset{H}{|}}{O}} \rightarrow H \right]^+$$

NH_4^+

$$\left[H \overset{\overset{H}{\times\bullet}}{\underset{\underset{H}{\bullet\times}}{\cdot}} N \overset{\times}{\cdot} H \right]^+ \qquad \left[H - \overset{\overset{H}{|}}{\underset{\underset{H}{|}}{N}} \rightarrow H \right]^+$$

CO $\qquad :C \overset{\times}{\underset{\times\times}{\bullet\times}} O \overset{\times}{}$ $\qquad\qquad :C \Equiv O \overset{\times}{}$

Note that in CO the triple bond consists of two bonds that involve sharing an electron from each atom, and the third bond is a coordinate bond where both electrons come from the oxygen. The three bonds are nonetheless identical to each other. This illustrates an important point about coordinate bonds: once they are formed, they are no different from other covalent bonds. Understanding the origin of bonding electrons can be important, however, in interpreting some reaction mechanisms.

> **A coordinate bond is a covalent bond in which both the shared electrons are provided by one of the atoms.**

The octet rule is not always followed

There are a few molecules that are exceptions to the octet rule. Small atoms such as beryllium (Be) and boron (B) form stable molecules in which the central atom has fewer than eight electrons in its valence shell. This is known as an **incomplete octet**. For example, the structures of $BeCl_2$ and BF_3 are shown below.

$BeCl_2$ valence electrons $= 2 + (7 \times 2) = 16$ $\qquad \overset{\times\times}{\underset{\times\times}{\times}}Cl \overset{\times}{\underset{\times\times}{\cdot}} Be \overset{\cdot}{\underset{\times\times}{\times}}Cl \overset{\times}{}$

BF_3 valence electrons $= 3 + (7 \times 3) = 24$ $\qquad \overset{\times\times}{\underset{\times\times}{\times}}F \overset{\cdot}{\cdot} B \overset{\cdot}{\cdot} F \overset{\times\times}{\underset{\times\times}{\times}}$

$\qquad\qquad\qquad\qquad\qquad\qquad\qquad \overset{\times}{\underset{\times\times}{\times}}F \overset{\times}{}$

Molecules with incomplete octets are said to be **electron deficient**, and have a tendency to accept an electron pair from a molecule with a lone pair, such as NH_3 or H_2O. This leads to the formation of a coordinate compound in which the central atom has now gained an octet.

$$H - \overset{\overset{H}{|}}{\underset{\underset{H}{|}}{N}} \rightarrow \overset{\overset{F}{|}}{\underset{\underset{F}{|}}{B}} - F$$

> Remember to include *all lone pairs* in your Lewis structures. Structures which show only bonded pairs, e.g. H–Cl, are structural formulas, not Lewis structures.

BCl_3 is an important catalyst in several synthetic reactions as a result of this tendency to accept electrons.

Exercises

14 Draw the Lewis structures of :

(a) HF
(b) CF_3Cl
(c) C_2H_6
(d) PCl_3
(e) C_2H_4
(f) C_2H_2

15 How many valence electrons are in the following molecules?

(a) $BeCl_2$
(b) BCl_3
(c) CCl_4
(d) PH_3
(e) NCl_3

16 Use Lewis structures to show the formation of a coordinate bond between H_2O and H^+.

17 Draw the Lewis structures of:

   (a) NO_3^- **(b)** NO^+ **(c)** NO_2^- **(d)** O_3
   (e) N_2H_4

Molecules that have an expanded octet have central atoms that are larger and are found in Period 3 (and beyond), where the valence shell can hold 18 electrons.

VSEPR theory: The shape of a molecule is determined by repulsion between electron domains

Once we know the Lewis structure of a molecule, we can predict exactly how the bonds will be orientated with respect to each other in space – in other words, the three-dimensional shape of the molecule. This is often a crucial feature of a substance in determining its reactivity. For example, biochemical reactions depend on a precise 'fit' between the enzyme, which controls the rate of the reaction, and the reacting molecule, known as the substrate. Anything that changes the shape of either of these may therefore alter the reaction dramatically; many drugs work in this way.

Predictions of molecular shape are based on the **Valence Shell Electron Pair Repulsion (VSEPR) theory**. As its name suggests, this theory is based on the simple notion that *because electron pairs in the same valence shell carry the same charge, they repel each other and so spread themselves as far apart as possible.*

Before applying this theory, it is useful to clarify some of the language involved because the term VS**EP**R, evidently referring to <u>E</u>lectron <u>P</u>airs, is actually an over-simplification. As we have seen, molecules frequently contain multiple pairs of shared electrons, and these behave as a single unit in terms of repulsion because they are orientated together. So a better, more inclusive, term than electron pair is **electron domain**. This includes all electron locations in the valence shell, be they occupied by lone pairs, single, double, or triple bonded pairs. What matters in determining shape is the *total number of electron domains*, and this can be determined from the Lewis structure.

Worked example

How many electron domains exist in the central atom of the following molecules whose Lewis structures are shown?

(i)   (ii)   (iii)

H—N—H   O=C=O   O=O—O
     |
     H

Solution

Each electron domain is ringed in red.

(i)   (ii)   (iii)

H—N—H   O=C=O   O=O—O
     |
     H

(i) 4 electron domains: 3 bonding and 1 non-bonding

(ii) 2 electron domains: 2 bonding and 0 non-bonding

(iii) 3 electron domains: 2 bonding and 1 non-bonding

Technically then, VSEPR theory should be called Valence Shell Electron Domain Repulsion. It can be summarized as follows:

- The repulsion applies to electron domains, which can be single, double, or triple bonding electron pairs, or non-bonding pairs of electrons.
- The total number of electron domains around the central atom determines the geometrical arrangement of the electron domains.
- The shape of the molecule is determined by the angles between the bonded atoms.
- Non-bonding pairs (lone pairs) have a higher concentration of charge than a bonding pair because they are not shared between two atoms, and so cause slightly more repulsion than bonding pairs. The repulsion decreases in the following order:

    lone pair–lone pair > lone pair–bonding pair > bonding pair–bonding pair

As a result, molecules with lone pairs on the central atom have some distortions in their structure that reduce the angle between the bonded atoms.

Note that in the diagrams in this section, non-bonding electrons on the surrounding atoms have been omitted for clarity – these are therefore *not* Lewis structures.

Note that when you are asked to draw a Lewis structure, you must show all the non-bonding pairs on all the atoms.

The repulsion between electron pairs varies as follows:

strongest repulsion	lone pair–lone pair
weakest repulsion	lone pair–bonding pair
	bonding pair–bonding pair

Species with two electron domains

Molecules with two electron domains will position them at **180°** to each other, giving a **linear** shape to the molecule.

$BeCl_2$ Cl — Be — Cl

CO_2 O = C = O   } linear 180°

C_2H_2 H — C ≡ C — H

Species with three electron domains

Molecules with three electron domains will position them at **120°** to each other, giving a **triangular planar** shape to the electron domain geometry. If all three electron domains are bonding, the shape of the molecule will also be triangular planar.

triangular planar 120°

The electron domain geometry is determined by the positions of *all* the electron domains, but the molecular geometry depends only on the positions of the *bonded* atoms.

However, if one of the electron domains is a lone pair, this will not be 'seen' in the overall shape of the molecule, as it is part of the central atom. The molecular shape is determined by the positions of the atoms fixed by the bonding pairs only. A further consideration is that, as described above, lone pairs cause slightly more repulsion than bonding pairs, so in their presence the angles are slightly altered.

For example, as shown on page 133, the Lewis structure of ozone, O_3, has three electron domains. Therefore the electron domain geometry of the molecule is triangular planar. But, as only two of the three electron domains are bonding electrons, the molecular geometry will not be triangular planar. The red outline below shows the positions of the bonding electrons that determine the shape. The molecule is described as **bent** or **V-shaped**. The lone pair of electrons distorts the shape slightly, so the angle is slightly less than 120°; it is approximately 117°.

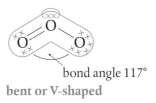

bond angle 117°

bent or V-shaped

If there are lone pairs on the central atom, the electron domain geometry and the molecular geometry will not be the same as each other.

Species with four electron domains

Molecules with four electron domains will position them at **109.5°** to each other, giving a **tetrahedral** shape to the electron domains. If all four electron domains are bonding, the shape of the molecule will also be tetrahedral.

CH_4 NH_4^+

tetrahedral
109.5°

However, if one or more of the electron domains is a lone pair, we must again focus on the number of bonded pairs to determine the shape of the molecule. The table on page 136 compares molecules with 0, 1, and 2 lone pairs respectively.

Models of H_2O, NH_3, and CH_4, showing the different molecular geometry due to the different numbers of lone pairs on the central atom.

	CH$_4$	NH$_3$	H$_2$O
Lewis structure	H–C–H with H top and bottom	H–N–H with H below and lone pair	H–O–H with two lone pairs
Number of electron domains	4	4	4
Electron domain geometry	tetrahedral	tetrahedral	tetrahedral
Number of lone pairs	0	1	2
Number of bonded electron domains	4	3	2
Molecular geometry	tetrahedral	trigonal pyramidal	bent or V-shaped
Bond angles	109.5°	approximately 107°	approximately 105°

With 4 electron domains on the central atom: 0 lone pairs → tetrahedral, 1 lone pair → trigonal pyramidal, 2 lone pairs → V-shaped.

Always draw the Lewis structure before attempting to predict the shape of a molecule, as you have to know the total number of bonding and lone pairs around the central atom.

Note that the presence of two lone pairs in H$_2$O causes more repulsion than the single lone pair in NH$_3$. This is why the bond angle is reduced further in H$_2$O from the 109.5° of the symmetrical tetrahedron.

Here is a summary of the steps used in determining the shape of a molecule.

1 Draw the Lewis structure, following the steps on page 130.
2 Count the total number of electron domains on the central atom.
3 Determine the electron domain geometry as follows:
   2 electron domains → linear
   3 electron domains → triangular planar
   4 electron domains → tetrahedral.
4 Determine the molecular geometry from the number of bonding electron domains.
5 Consider the extra repulsion caused by the lone pairs and adjust the bond angles accordingly.

Exercises

18 Predict the shape and bond angles of the following molecules:
   (a) H$_2$S (b) CF$_4$ (c) HCN (d) NF$_3$
   (e) BCl$_3$ (f) NH$_2$Cl (g) OF$_2$

19 Predict the shape and bond angles of the following ions:
   (a) CO$_3^{2-}$ (b) NO$_3^-$ (c) NO$_2^+$ (d) NO$_2^-$
   (e) ClF$_2^+$ (f) SnCl$_3^-$

20 How many electron domains are there around the central atom in molecules that have the following shapes?
   (a) tetrahedral (b) bent (c) linear
   (d) trigonal pyramidal (e) triangular planar

Summary of shapes of molecules predicted from VSEPR theory

The shapes of molecules for two, three, and four electron domains are summarized below.

Number of electron domains	Electron domain geometry	Number of bonding electron domains	Number of non-bonding pairs of electrons	Molecular geometry	Example	
2	linear	2	0	linear	CO_2	O=C=O
3	planar triangular	3	0	planar triangular	BF_3	F F B F
3	planar triangular	2	1	V-shaped	SO_2	
4	tetrahedral	4	0	tetrahedral	CH_4	H C H H H
4	tetrahedral	3	1	pyramidal	NH_3	H N H H
4	tetrahedral	2	2	V-shaped	H_2O	H O H

Molecules with polar bonds are not always polar

We have learned that the polarity of a *bond* depends on the charge separation between its two bonded atoms, which is a result of differences in their electronegativities. The polarity of a *molecule*, however, depends on:

• the polar bonds that it contains;
• the way in which such polar bonds are orientated with respect to each other, in other words, on the shape of the molecule.

If the bonds are of equal polarity (i.e. involving the same elements) *and* are arranged symmetrically with respect to each other, their charge separations will oppose each other and so will effectively cancel each other out. In these cases the molecule will be non-polar, despite the fact that it contains polar

VSEPR theory in nature. Different numbers of snowberries growing together spontaneously adopt the geometry of maximal repulsion. Clockwise from the top: four berries form a tetrahedral shape bond angle 109.5°, three berries form a triangular planar shape bond angle 120°, and two berries are linear bond angle 180°. What other examples of VSEPR shapes can you find in nature?

Figure 4.8 Equal and opposite pulls cancel each other out.

Figure 4.9 When the pulls are not equal and opposite there is a net pull.

Bond dipoles can be thought of as vectors, so the polarity of a molecule is the resultant force. This approach may help you to predict the overall polarity from considering the sum of the bond dipoles.

bonds. It is a bit like a game of tug-of-war between players who are equally strong and symmetrically arranged, as shown in Figure 4.8.

The molecules below are all non-polar because the dipoles cancel out. The arrows, shown here in blue, are the notation for a dipole that results from the pull of electrons in the bond towards the more electronegative atom.

$$CO_2 \qquad BF_3 \qquad CCl_4$$

However, if *either* the molecule contains bonds of different polarity, *or* its bonds are not symmetrically arranged, then the dipoles will not cancel out, and the molecule will be polar. Another way of describing this is to say that it has a net **dipole moment,** which refers to its turning force in an electric field. This is what would happen in a game of tug-of-war if the players were not equally strong or were not pulling in exactly opposite directions, as shown in Figure 4.9.

These molecules are all polar because the dipoles do not cancel out.

$$CH_3Cl \qquad NH_3 \qquad H_2O$$

Exercises

21 Predict whether the following will be polar or non-polar molecules:

(a) PH_3 (b) CF_4 (c) HCN
(d) $BeCl_2$ (e) C_2H_4 (f) ClF
(g) F_2 (h) BF_3

22 The molecule $C_2H_2Cl_2$ can exist as two forms known as *cis–trans* isomers, which are shown below.

trans   *cis*

Determine whether either of these has a net dipole moment.

CHALLENGE YOURSELF

4 If you were given two solutions and told one contained a polar substance and the other a non-polar substance, suggest experiments that might enable you to identify which is which.

Electrons in multiple bonds can sometimes spread themselves between more than one bonding position

Our account of covalent bonding so far describes a bond as a pair of electrons held in a specific position within a molecule. However, in some molecules bonding electrons are less restricted than this. Instead of being confined to one location they show a tendency to be shared between more than one bonding position, and are said to be **delocalized**. Free from the constraints of a single bonding position, delocalized electrons spread themselves out, giving greater stability to the molecule or ion.

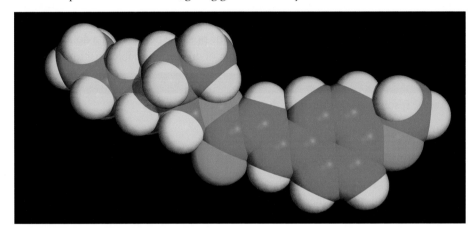

Computer graphic of a molecule of the sunscreen $C_{18}H_{26}O_3$. Carbon atoms are shown in green, hydrogen atoms in yellow, and oxygen atoms in blue. Note the benzene ring and carbon–carbon double bonds in the molecule. Sunscreens help to protect the skin from sun damage by absorbing UV radiation and releasing it as heat. They are able to do this due to the many double bonds and delocalized electrons in their structure.

Delocalization is a characteristic of electrons in multiple bonds when there is more than one possible position for a double bond within a molecule. For example, let us look again at the Lewis structure of ozone, O_3, from page 133,

$$\overset{\times\times}{\underset{\times\times}{O}} = \overset{\times\times}{O} - \overset{\times\times}{\underset{\times\times}{O}}^{\times}$$

We can see that a different Lewis structure would be equally valid:

$$\overset{\times\times}{\underset{\times\times}{O}}^{\times} - \overset{\times\times}{O} = \overset{\times\times}{\underset{\times\times}{O}}$$

These structures suggest that the molecule should contain one oxygen–oxygen double bond and one oxygen–oxygen single bond, which we would expect to be different in bond length and bond strength. However, experimental data reveal that ozone actually contains two *equal* oxygen–oxygen bonds, intermediate in length and strength between single and double bonds.

	O–O single bond	O=O double bond	Oxygen–oxygen bonds in O_3
Bond length / pm	148	121	127
Bond enthalpy / kJ mol^{-1}	144	498	364

We can explain this by considering that the electrons from the double bond have delocalized and spread themselves equally between both possible bonding positions. The true structure for ozone is a blend or hybrid of the Lewis structures shown above.

$$O \cdots O \cdots O$$

This cannot be accurately represented by a single Lewis structure, so a concept known as **resonance** is introduced. The Lewis structures that can be drawn are known as

resonance structures, depicted as shown below, while it is recognized that neither of these is the correct structure. The true structure is an intermediate form, known as the **resonance hybrid**.

It is as if you were trying to explain to someone what a mule (a cross between a horse and a donkey) looks like: you might draw a horse and a donkey and a double-headed arrow between them implying the mule is an intermediate. You wouldn't mean that the animal is a horse one minute and a donkey the next! Likewise, resonance structures do not represent forms that flip from one to the other. Resonance structures can be drawn for any molecule in which there is more than one possible position for a double bond; the number of structures will equal the number of different possible positions.

> Resonance occurs when more than one valid Lewis structure can be drawn for a particular molecule. The true structure is an average of these, known as a resonance hybrid.

> You can deduce how many resonance structures exist for a molecule or ion by looking at the number of possible positions for its double bond.

Worked example

Draw the resonance structures for the carbonate ion CO_3^{2-}.

Solution

Count the number of valence electrons: $4 + (6 \times 3) + 2 = 24$

Draw the Lewis structure, noting that there are three possible positions for the double bond. This means there will be three resonance structures, as follows:

Some other ions and molecules that have delocalized electrons and so can be represented by resonance structures are shown in the table below.

Species name and formula	Number of valence electrons	Resonance structures
nitrate(V), NO_3^-	24	
nitrate(III), NO_2^-	18	
methanoate, $HCOO^-$	18	

Computer artwork of the structure of benzene showing carbon atoms in orange, hydrogen atoms in white, and the delocalized bonds as purple grids above and below the plane of the molecule. The alternating single and double bonds shown in the model could be misleading – you should understand why when you have read this section.

Benzene, C_6H_6, is a particularly interesting case of a molecule with delocalized electrons. The six carbon atoms are arranged in a hexagonal ring, each also bonded to a hydrogen atom in a triangular planar arrangement with 120° bond angles. A possible Lewis structure is:

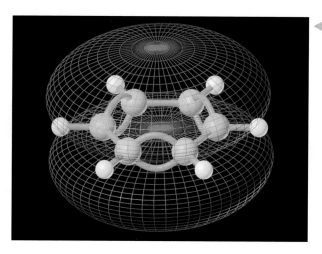

But we can see there are other possible positions for the double bonds, indicating the existence of resonance structures.

In Chapter 10 we will discuss evidence that indicates that benzene's properties cannot be explained by either of these Lewis structures. The true form is the resonance hybrid:

[hexagon with dashed circle], which is most commonly represented by: [hexagon with circle]

The circle inside the hexagon represents delocalized electrons, which are spread equally through the ring, rather than being in confined double bonds. As we would expect, this results in carbon–carbon bonds that are equal in length and strength, and intermediate between those of single and double bonds.

141

The current model of benzene with a symmetrical ring of delocalized electrons developed when predictions based on the so-called Kekulé model with alternating double bonds failed to match observations. Differences between the calculated and measured values of bond energy, bond length, and the ability to undergo addition reactions all indicated that the Kekulé model was not correct. Progress in science sometimes depends on the need to abandon a model or an interpretation if it cannot explain valid experimental results.

Bond order is a measure of the number of electrons involved in bonds between two atoms. Values for bond order are: single bonds = 1, double bonds = 2, triple bonds = 3. Resonance hybrids have fractional values of bond order. The carbon–carbon bonds in benzene have a bond order of 1.5.

	C–C single bond	C=C double bond	Carbon–carbon bonds in benzene
Bond length / pm	154	134	140
Bond enthalpy / kJ mol^{-1}	346	614	507

Resonance gives great stability to the benzene molecule, making it chemically quite unreactive. In our study of organic chemistry we will learn that this is unusual given its high ratio of carbon to hydrogen (unsaturation).

Worked example

Compare the structures of CH_3COOH and CH_3COO^- with reference to their possible resonance structures.

Solution

Draw the Lewis structure of each, and note if there is more than one possible position for a double bond to be placed.

$$CH_3COOH \qquad \begin{array}{c} H \quad\; O \\ | \quad\;\; \| \\ H-C-C \\ | \qquad\; \\ H \quad O-H \end{array}$$

There is only one possible Lewis structure, so the molecule has one carbon–oxygen double bond and one carbon–oxygen single bond.

$$CH_3COO^- \qquad \left[\begin{array}{c} H \quad\; O \\ | \quad\;\; \| \\ H-C-C \\ | \qquad\; \\ H \qquad O \end{array}\right]^- \longleftrightarrow \left[\begin{array}{c} H \quad\; O \\ | \quad\;\; \\ H-C-C \\ | \qquad\; \| \\ H \qquad O \end{array}\right]^-$$

Two resonance structures exist, so the ion exists as a hybrid with two equal carbon–oxygen bonds, intermediate in length and strength between the two carbon–oxygen bonds in CH_3COOH.

$$\left[\begin{array}{c} H \quad\; O \\ | \quad\;\; \ddots \\ H-C-C \\ | \qquad\; \ddots \\ H \qquad O \end{array}\right]^-$$

Resonance is an important concept that gives special properties to the structures where it occurs. We have seen its influence on bond lengths and strengths, which in turn can influence reactivity. The different strengths of organic acids and bases, for example, can often be explained by resonance.

23 Put the following species in order of increasing carbon–oxygen bond length:

$$CO \qquad CO_2 \qquad CO_3^{2-} \qquad CH_3OH$$

24 By reference to their resonance structures, compare the nitrogen–oxygen bond lengths in nitrate(V) (NO_3^-) and nitric(V) acid (HNO_3).

Some covalent substances form giant molecular crystalline solids

Most covalent substances exist as discrete molecules with a finite number of atoms. However, there are some that have a very different structure, a crystalline lattice in which the atoms are linked together by covalent bonds. Effectively, the crystal is a single molecule with a regular repeating pattern of covalent bonds, so has no finite size. It is referred to as a **giant molecular** or **network covalent** structure or **macromolecular structure**. As we might expect, such crystalline structures have very different properties from other smaller covalent molecules. A few examples are considered here.

Allotropes of carbon

Allotropes are different forms of an element in the same physical state, such as oxygen (O_2) and ozone (O_3) which both exist as gases. Different bonding within these structures gives rise to distinct forms with different properties.

Carbon has several allotropes and these are described and compared in the table on page 144.

▲ Coloured scanning electron micrograph of layers making up the core of a graphite pencil. Because graphite is a soft form of carbon, the tip of the pencil disintegrates under pressure to leave marks on the paper.

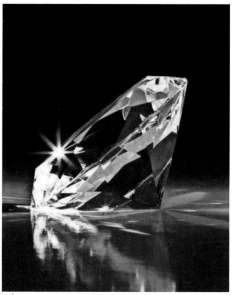

▲ Cut and polished diamond. Diamond is a naturally occurring form of carbon that has crystallized under great pressure. It is the hardest known mineral. Beautiful crystals are found in South Africa, Russia, Brazil, and Sierra Leone.

CHALLENGE YOURSELF

5 For the most part, good electrical conductors are also good thermal conductors, but this is not the case with diamond. Can you think why this might be, and whether there are other substances that are not electrical conductors but good thermal conductors?

	Graphite	Diamond	Fullerene C_{60}	Graphene
Structure	Each C atom is covalently bonded to 3 others, forming hexagons in parallel layers with bond angles of 120°. The layers are held only by weak London dispersion forces so they can slide over each other.	Each C atom is covalently bonded to 4 others tetrahedrally arranged in a regular repetitive pattern with bond angles of 109.5°.	Each C atom is bonded in a sphere of 60 carbon atoms, consisting of 12 pentagons and 20 hexagons. Structure is a closed spherical cage in which each carbon is bonded to 3 others. (Note it is not a giant molecule as it has a fixed formula).	Each C atom is covalently bonded to 3 others, as in graphite, forming hexagons with bond angles of 120°. But it is a single layer, so exists as a two-dimensional material only. It is often described as a honeycomb or chicken wire structure.
Electrical conductivity	Good electrical conductor; contains one non-bonded, delocalized electron per atom that gives electron mobility.	Non-conductor of electricity; all electrons are bonded and so non-mobile.	A semiconductor at normal temperature and pressure due to some electron mobility; easily accepts electrons to form negative ions.	Very good electrical conductor; one delocalized electron per atom gives electron mobility across the layers.
Thermal conductivity	Not a good conductor, unless the heat can be forced to conduct in a direction parallel to the crystal layers.	Very efficient thermal conductor, better than metals.	Very low thermal conductivity.	Best thermal conductivity known, even better than diamond.
Appearance	Non-lustrous, grey crystalline solid.	Highly transparent, lustrous crystal.	Yellow crystalline solid, soluble in benzene.	Almost completely transparent.
Special properties	Soft and slippery due to slippage of layers over each other; brittle, very high melting point; the most stable allotrope of carbon.	The hardest known natural substance; it cannot be scratched by anything; brittle; very high melting point.	Very light and strong; reacts with K to make superconducting crystalline material; low melting point.	The thickness of just one atom so the thinnest material ever to exist; but also the strongest – 100 times stronger than steel; very flexible; very high melting point.
Uses	A dry lubricant, in pencils, electrode rods in electrolysis.	Polished for jewellery and ornamentation; tools and machinery for grinding and cutting glass.	Lubricants, medical, and industrial devices for binding specific target molecules; related forms are used to make nanotubes and nanobuds used as capacitors in electronics industry, and catalysts.	TEM (transmission electron microscopy) grids, photo-voltaic cells, touch screens, high performance electronic devices; many applications are still being developed.

Graphene is a planar sheet of carbon atoms arranged in a hexagonal pattern.

Figure 4.10 Graphite occurs naturally, and a single separated layer is graphene. A rolled up layer of graphene is a nanotube, and a closed cage is fullerene.

graphite

graphene

nanotube

fullerene

Graphene is a relatively new form of carbon, isolated for the first time in 2004. Given its hardness, strength, lightness, flexibility, conductivity and chemical inertness, it has enormous potential applications. Currently though, many of these are only in the development stage as they are dependent on the production of large sheets of pure graphene, which is difficult to achieve economically. But this is an intense field of research and breakthroughs are common. Some of the potential applications and advantages of graphene are as follows:

• new conductive materials could be made by mixing graphene with plastics;
• transistors of graphene are predicted to be faster and smaller than silicon transistors in electronics;
• touch screens of graphene printed on thin plastic instead of coatings layered onto glass would be light, flexible, and almost unbreakable;
• supercapacitors for storing charge could replace batteries and more efficiently power mobile devices and electric cars;
• solar panels in which photovoltaic cells (that generate electricity from sunlight) contain graphene would be light and flexible, and so could be wrapped around any surface such as clothing, furniture, or vehicles.

Whether graphene will realize its potential and lead to innovative materials and applications remains an open question. What is the role of imagination in helping to direct the research focus of scientists?

Computer artwork of spherical and cylindrical fullerenes – buckyballs and carbon nanotubes. These substances are being investigated for a wide range of technical and medical uses. Here the carbon nanotubes have been engineered to have a diameter just large enough to allow buckyballs to pass through them.

The name 'fullerene' was given to the newly discovered spheres C_{60} in honour of the American architect R. Buckminster Fuller. He had designed the World Exhibition building in Montreal, Canada, on the same concept of hexagons and a small number of pentagons to create a curved surface known as a geodesic dome. The dome of the Epcot Centre in Disney World, Florida, is similarly designed. Perhaps more familiarly it is also the structure of a European soccer ball. The term 'buckyballs' has slipped into common usage, derived from the full name of the structure 'buckminsterfullerene'.

NATURE OF SCIENCE

The discoveries of the allotropes of carbon – buckminsterfullerene and graphene – illustrate the importance of collaboration between scientists.

The discovery of fullerenes in 1985 was the result of teamwork between scientists with different experience and research objectives. Harold Kroto from the UK was interested in red giant stars and how carbon might polymerize near them. Robert Curl and Richard Smalley working in Texas, USA, had developed a technique using a laser beam for evaporating and analysing different substances. When they worked together and applied this technique to graphite, clusters of stable C_{60} and C_{70} spheres were formed. The three scientists shared the Nobel Prize in Chemistry for 1996.

The isolation of graphene was announced by Kostya Novoselov and Andre Geim in 2004, both working at the University of Manchester, UK. It led to their shared award of the Nobel Prize in Physics in 2010. Novoselov and Geim were research collaborators over many years in different countries, originally as research student and supervisor respectively. Their work involved the use of adhesive tape to rip successively thinner flakes off graphite and analyse them by attachment to a layer of silicon oxide. Many scientists over many years had attempted to isolate graphene, and through their successes and failures indirectly contributed to the later discovery.

The development of structures such as nanotubes, nanobuds, and graphene is part of the growing science of **nanotechnology** (Chapter 12), which deals with the atomic scale manipulation of matter. An interesting development is a new material called **graphone,** which is made by adding hydrogen to graphene. Controlling the amount of hydrogen coverage gives variable magnetic properties, which may in turn lead to wider graphene applications. A further development is fluorographene, which has one fluorine atom attached to each carbon atom giving a rippled rather than a flat structure. As all the electrons are held in bonds, it is an insulator.

CHALLENGE YOURSELF

6 Graphite is thermodynamically more stable than diamond. The reaction

$$C(diamond) \rightarrow C(graphite)$$

is accompanied by a loss of energy, $\Delta H = -2$ kJ mol^{-1}.

But we commonly hear that 'diamonds are forever'. Are they?

The structure of fullerene has the same arrangements of hexagons and pentagons as a soccer ball.

Silicon and silicon dioxide

Coloured scanning electron micrograph of the surface of a microprocessor computer chip. Silicon chips are tiny pieces of silicon as small as 1 mm² made to carry minute electrical circuits used in computers and transistors. Silicon is the most widely used semiconductor.

Silicon is the most abundant element in the Earth's crust after oxygen, occurring as silica (SiO_2) in sand and in the silicate minerals. Since silicon is just below carbon in Group 14, the possibility of silicon-based life has been proposed. But unlike carbon, silicon is not able to form long chains, multiple bonds, or rings so cannot compete with the diversity possible in organic chemistry, based on carbon. However, there is some evidence that the first forms of life were forms of clay minerals that were probably based on the silicon atom.

Like carbon, silicon is a Group 14 element and so its atoms have four valence shell electrons. In the elemental state, each silicon atom is covalently bonded to four others in a tetrahedral arrangement. This results in a giant lattice structure much like diamond.

Silicon dioxide, SiO_2, commonly known as silica or quartz, also forms a giant covalent structure based on a tetrahedral arrangement. But here the bonds are between silicon and oxygen atoms, where each Si atom is covalently bonded to four O atoms, and each O to two Si atoms. You can think of the oxygen atoms as forming bridges between the tetrahedrally bonded carbon atoms.

The silicon crystal structure and the arrangement of bonds around a central silicon atom.

Quartz crystals shown in a coloured scanning electron micrograph. Quartz is a form of silica (SiO_2) and the most abundant mineral in the Earth's crust. Quartz is used in optical and scientific instruments and in electronics such as quartz watches.

147

silicon atoms
oxygen atoms

Figure 4.11 The structure of quartz SiO_2.

Note here the formula SiO_2 refers to the *ratio* of atoms within the giant molecule – it is an empirical formula and the actual number of atoms present will be a very large multiple of this. As the atoms are strongly held in tetrahedral positions that involve all four silicon valence electrons, the structure has the following properties:

- strong;
- insoluble in water;
- high melting point;
- non-conductor of electricity.

These are all properties we associate with glass and sand – different forms of silica.

Exercises

25 Describe the similarities and differences you would expect in the properties of silicon and diamond.

26 Explain why graphite and graphene are good conductors of electricity whereas diamond is not.

4.4 Intermolecular forces

Understandings:

- Intermolecular forces include London (dispersion) forces, dipole–dipole forces, and hydrogen bonding.

Guidance
The term 'London (dispersion) forces' refers to instantaneous dipole-induced dipole forces that exist between any atoms or groups of atoms and should be used for non-polar entities. The term 'van der Waals' is an inclusive term, which includes dipole–dipole, dipole-induced dipole, and London (dispersion) forces.

- The relative strengths of these interactions are London (dispersion) forces < dipole–dipole forces < hydrogen bonds.

Applications and skills:

- Deduction of the types of intermolecular force present in substances, based on their structure and chemical formula.
- Explanation of the physical properties of covalent compounds (volatility, electrical conductivity, and solubility) in terms of their structure and intermolecular forces.

Note that the prefix *intra-* refers to *within*, whereas the prefix *inter-* refers to *between*. For example, the Internet gives communication between many different places, while an intranet works within an organization.

Covalent bonds hold atoms together *within* molecules, but of course molecules do not exist in isolation. A gas jar full of chlorine, Cl_2, for example, will contain millions of molecules of chlorine. So what are the forces that exist *between* these molecules, the so-called **intermolecular forces**? The answer depends on the polarity and size of the molecules involved, and so the intermolecular forces will vary for different molecules. We will consider three types of intermolecular force here, and see how they differ from each other in origin and in strength.

The strength of intermolecular forces determines the physical properties of a substance. Volatility, solubility, and conductivity can all be predicted and explained from knowledge of the nature of the forces between molecules.

London (dispersion) forces

Non-polar molecules such as chlorine, Cl_2, have no permanent separation of charge within their bonds because the shared electrons are pulled equally by the two chlorine atoms. In other words, they do not have a permanent dipole. Likewise, atoms of a noble gas such as argon exist as non-polar particles.

However, because electrons behave somewhat like mobile clouds of negative charge, the density of this cloud may at any one moment be greater over one region of a molecule or atom than over another region. When this occurs, a weak dipole known as a temporary or instantaneous dipole is formed. This will not last for more than an instant as the electron density is constantly changing, but it may influence the electron distribution in a neighbouring atom or molecule, causing an **induced dipole.**

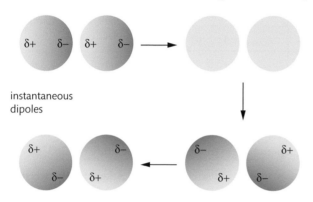

instantaneous
dipoles

As a result, weak forces of attraction, known as **London (dispersion) forces**, will occur between opposite ends of these two temporary dipoles in the molecules. These are the weakest form of intermolecular force. Their strength increases with increasing molecular size; this is because the greater number of electrons within a molecule increases the probability of temporary dipoles developing.

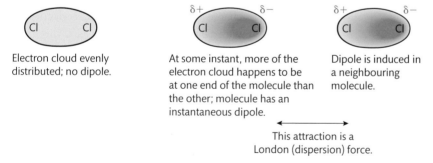

Electron cloud evenly distributed; no dipole.

At some instant, more of the electron cloud happens to be at one end of the molecule than the other; molecule has an instantaneous dipole.

Dipole is induced in a neighbouring molecule.

This attraction is a London (dispersion) force.

London (dispersion) forces are the *only* forces that exist between non-polar molecules. Such molecules generally have low melting and boiling points, because relatively little energy is required to break the weak London (dispersion) forces and separate the molecules from each other. This is why many non-polar elements and compounds are gases at room temperature, for example O_2, Cl_2, and CH_4. Boiling point data also indicate how the strength of London (dispersion forces) increases with increasing molecular size. This is shown in the tables on page 150 that compare the boiling points of the halogens (Group 17 elements) and of the family of hydrocarbons known as the alkanes.

Fritz London (1900–1954) was a German physicist who pioneered the interpretation of covalent bond formation and intermolecular forces in the emerging field of quantum mechanics. As he was of Jewish descent, he had to leave his university post in Germany during the Nazi regime before World War II, and completed most of his research in Duke University, USA.

Figure 4.12 A series of instantaneous views of electron density in an atom. Each image is like a snap-shot of a possible electron distribution at a moment in time. Although the instantaneous dipole varies it always leads to an attractive force with its neighbour.

Figure 4.13 Instantaneous dipole-induced dipole causes London (dispersion) forces between molecules of Cl_2.

Element	M_r	Boiling point / °C	State at room temperature
F_2	38	−188	gas
Cl_2	71	−34	gas
Br_2	160	59	liquid
I_2	254	185	solid

boiling point increases with increasing number of electrons

Alkane	M_r	Boiling point / °C
CH_4	16	−164
C_2H_6	30	−89
C_3H_8	44	−42
C_4H_{10}	58	−0.5

boiling point increases with increasing number of electrons

Although London (dispersion) forces are weak, they are responsible for the fact that non-polar substances can be condensed to form liquids and sometimes solids at low temperatures. For example, nitrogen gas, N_2, liquefies below −196 °C, and even helium gas has been liquefied at the extremely low temperature of −269 °C.

London (dispersion) forces are also components of the forces between polar molecules, but often get somewhat overlooked because of the presence of stronger forces.

> When asked to name forces between molecules, London (dispersion) forces should be given in all cases, regardless of what additional forces may be present.

Dipole–dipole attraction

Polar molecules such as hydrogen chloride, HCl, have a permanent separation of charge within their bonds as a result of the difference in electronegativity between the bonded atoms. One end of the molecule is electron deficient with a partial positive charge (δ+), while the other end is electron rich with a partial negative charge (δ−). This is known as a **permanent dipole**. It results in opposite charges on neighbouring molecules attracting each other, generating a force known as a **dipole–dipole attraction.**

Figure 4.14 Permanent dipoles cause forces of dipole–dipole attraction between molecules of HCl.

The strength of this intermolecular force will vary depending on the distance and relative orientation of the dipoles. But dipole–dipole forces are generally stronger than London (dispersion) forces, as we might expect from their origin in permanent rather than instantaneous dipoles. These forces cause the melting and boiling points of polar compounds to be higher than those of non-polar substances of comparable molecular mass.

> When examining the boiling points of different substances to see the effect of different intermolecular forces, it is important to compare substances with similar molecular mass. Otherwise the difference could be attributed solely to stronger London (dispersion) forces in the molecules with more electrons.

	C_3H_8	CH_3OCH_3
Molar mass / g mol^{-1}	44	46
Intermolecular attraction	London dispersion forces	London dispersion forces and dipole–dipole attraction
Boiling point / K	229	249

Note that dipole–dipole attractions can occur between any combinations of polar molecules, such as between PCl_3 and $CHCl_3$, and generally lead to the solubility of polar solutes in polar solvents.

The umbrella term **van der Waals' forces** is used to include both London (dispersion) forces and dipole–dipole attractions. It also covers a less common type of attraction known as dipole-induced dipole. In other words, van der Waals' forces refers to all forces between molecules that do not involve electrostatic attractions between ions or bond formation. We can summarize this as follows:

London dispersion force, e.g. Cl_2----Cl_2
dipole–dipole attraction HCl----HCl $\Big\}$ **van der Waals' forces**
dipole–induced dipole HCl----Cl_2

In some cases, van der Waals' forces may occur within a molecule (intramolecularly) if the different groups can position themselves appropriately. This is an important feature of proteins, for example, which is discussed in detail in Chapter 13.

Hydrogen bonding

When a molecule contains hydrogen covalently bonded to a very electronegative atom (fluorine, nitrogen, or oxygen), these molecules are attracted to each other by a particularly strong type of intermolecular force called a **hydrogen bond**. The hydrogen bond is in essence a particular case of dipole–dipole attraction. The large electronegativity difference between hydrogen and the bonded fluorine, oxygen, or nitrogen results in the electron pair being pulled away from the hydrogen. Given its small size and the fact that it has no other electrons to shield the nucleus, the hydrogen now exerts a strong attractive force on a lone pair in the electronegative atom of a neighbouring molecule. This is the hydrogen bond.

Hydrogen bonds are the strongest form of intermolecular attraction. Consequently, they cause the boiling points of substances that contain them to be significantly higher than would be predicted from their molar mass. We can see this in Figure 4.16, in which boiling points of the hydrides from Groups 14 to 17 are compared down the Periodic Table.

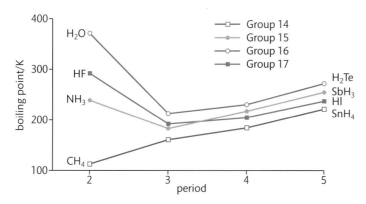

In all four groups there is a general trend that boiling point increases down the group as molar mass increases. The anomalies are NH_3, HF, and H_2O, which all have significantly higher boiling points than would be expected from their molar mass. This can only be explained by the presence of hydrogen bonding in these molecules. If it wasn't for the fact that it is hydrogen bonded, H_2O would be a gas not a liquid at room temperature.

Likewise, when we compare the boiling points of some organic molecules that have similar or equal values of molar mass, we find a higher value where hydrogen bonding occurs between the molecules. For example, the following table compares two different forms of C_2H_6O, known as isomers, both with a molar mass of 46.

CH_3–O–CH_3	CH_3CH_2–O–H
methoxymethane	ethanol
M = 46 g mol^{-1}	M = 46 g mol^{-1}
does not form hydrogen bonds	forms hydrogen bonds
boiling point = −23 °C	boiling point = +79 °C

Water makes a particularly interesting case for the study of hydrogen bonding. Here, because of the two hydrogen atoms in each molecule and the two lone pairs on the oxygen atom, each H_2O can form up to *four* hydrogen bonds with neighbouring molecules. Liquid water contains fewer than this number, but in the solid form, ice, each H_2O is maximally hydrogen bonded in this way. The result is a tetrahedral arrangement that holds the molecules a fixed distance apart, forming a fairly open structure, which is actually *less* dense than the liquid. This is a remarkable fact – in nearly all other substances the solid form with closer packed particles is *more* dense than its liquid. The fact that ice floats on water is evidence of the power of hydrogen bonds in holding the molecules together in ice. This density change means that water expands on freezing, which can lead to all kinds of problems in cold climates such as burst pipes and cracked machinery. The same force of expansion is at work in the Earth's crust, fragmenting and splitting rocks, ultimately forming sand and soil particles. The humble hydrogen bond is truly responsible for massive geological changes!

Figure 4.17 The arrangement of water molecules in ice. Each molecule is held by hydrogen bonds to four other molecules in a tetrahedral arrangement.

Icebergs float on water. Hydrogen bonds create a very open structure in ice which is less dense than liquid water.

Make sure you realize that although hydrogen bonds are strong in relation to other types of intermolecular force, they are very much weaker (about 15–20 times) than covalent bonds and ionic bonds. Photographed in Baffin Island, Canada.

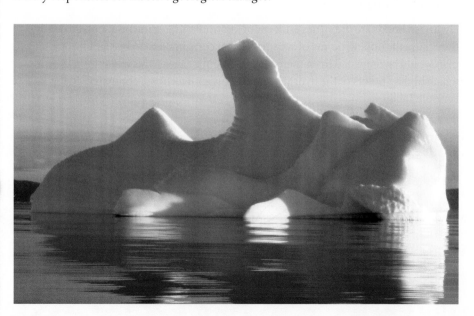

In these examples we have looked at hydrogen bonds as an intermolecular force, that is, *between* molecules, but like van der Waals' forces, they can occur *within* large molecules where they play a key role in determining properties. Proteins, for example, are fundamentally influenced by hydrogen bonding – you can read about this in Chapter 13, Option B: Biochemistry. Another fascinating example is DNA (deoxyribonucleic acid) which, as the chemical responsible for storing the genetic information in cells, is able to replicate itself exactly, a feat only possible because of its use of hydrogen bonding.

We can now summarize the intermolecular forces we have discussed in this section.

Computer artwork of a DNA molecule replicating. DNA is composed of two strands, held together by hydrogen bonds and twisted into a double helix. Before replication the strands separate from each other by breaking the hydrogen bonds and each strand then acts as a template for the synthesis of a new molecule of DNA.

	Non-polar molecules	Polar molecules	Molecules which contain H–O, H–N, or H–F
London dispersion forces	✓	✓	✓
Dipole–dipole attractions		✓	✓
Hydrogen bonding			✓

London dispersion forces and Dipole–dipole attractions are grouped as van der Waals' forces.

increasing strength of intermolecular force →

The physical properties of covalent compounds are largely a result of their intermolecular forces

If we know the type of intermolecular force in a substance, we are in a good position to predict its physical properties.

Melting and boiling points

Changing state by melting or boiling both involve separating particles by overcoming the forces between them. So the stronger the intermolecular forces, the more energy will be required to do this, and the higher will be the substance's melting and boiling points.

Covalent substances generally have lower melting and boiling points than ionic compounds. The forces to be overcome to separate the molecules are the relatively weak intermolecular forces, which are significantly easier to break than the electrostatic attractions in the ionic lattice. This is why many covalent substances are liquids or gases at room temperature.

Make sure you realize that when a covalent substance melts or boils, it is the bonds *between* the molecules that break, not the covalent bonds *within* the molecules. When you boil a kettle of water, you do not fill the kitchen with separated oxygen and hydrogen atoms.

As discussed on page 150, the strength of the intermolecular forces increases with increasing molecular size and with an increase in the extent of polarity within the molecule, and so these features help us to predict relative melting and boiling points.

Worked example

Put the following molecules in order of increasing boiling point and explain your choice:

$$CH_3CHO \qquad CH_3CH_2OH \qquad CH_3CH_2CH_3$$

Solution

First check the value of M for each molecule:

$CH_3CHO = 44$

$CH_3CH_2OH = 46$

$CH_3CH_2CH_3 = 44$, so they are all very similar.

Now consider the type of bonding and intermolecular attractions:

CH_3CHO	CH_3CH_2OH	$CH_3CH_2CH_3$
polar bonds $\Rightarrow$ dipole–dipole	O–H bond $\Rightarrow$ H bonding	non-polar bonds $\Rightarrow$ London (dispersion) forces

So the order, starting with the lowest boiling point, will be:

$$CH_3CH_2CH_3 < CH_3CHO < CH_3CH_2OH$$

By contrast, macromolecular or giant covalent structures have high melting and boiling points, often at least as high as those of ionic compounds. This is because covalent bonds must be broken for the change of state to occur. Diamond, for example, remains solid until about 4000 °C.

Solubility

Non-polar substances are generally able to dissolve in non-polar solvents by the formation of London (dispersion) forces between solute and solvent. For example, the halogens, all of which are non-polar molecules (e.g. Br_2), are readily soluble in the non-polar solvent paraffin oil. It is another example of *like dissolves like*, which is a useful guiding principle here.

Likewise, polar covalent compounds are generally soluble in water, a highly polar solvent. Here the solute and solvent interact through dipole interactions and hydrogen bonding. Common examples include the aqueous solubility of HCl, glucose ($C_6H_{12}O_6$), and ethanol (C_2H_5OH). Biological systems are mostly based on polar covalent molecules in aqueous solution.

The aqueous solubility of polar compounds is, however, reduced in larger molecules where the polar bond is only a small part of the total structure. The non-polar parts of the molecule, unable to associate with water, reduce its solubility. For example, while ethanol (C_2H_5OH) is readily soluble in water, the larger alcohol heptanol ($C_7H_{15}OH$) is not.

Figure 4.18 Water and ethanol form hydrogen bonds and mix readily, as we know from the homogeneous nature of alcoholic drinks.

The difference in solubility is due to the size of the non-polar hydrocarbon group.

It follows from this that non-polar covalent substances do not dissolve well in water. Nitrogen, N_2, for example, has very low solubility in water at normal pressure, as do hydrocarbons such as candle wax and large covalent molecules like chlorophyll. If you think about the substances that mark clothes and are not easily removed with water – grease, red wine, grass stains, and gravy are good examples – they are all relatively large insoluble non-polar molecules.

Likewise, polar substances have low solubility in non-polar solvents as they will remain held to each other by their dipole–dipole attractions and cannot interact well with the solvent. You can observe this by putting some sugar into cooking oil, and noticing that it does not dissolve.

Giant molecular substances are generally insoluble in all solvents, as too much energy would be required to break the strong covalent bonds in their structure. Beaches made primarily of sand, SiO_2, do not dissolve when the tide comes in and a diamond ring can safely be immersed in water.

Electrical conductivity

Covalent compounds do not contain ions, and so are not able to conduct electricity in the solid or liquid state. Some polar covalent molecules, however, in conditions where they can ionize will conduct electricity. For example, HCl dissolved in water (hydrochloric acid) is an electrical conductor as it dissociates into $H^+(aq) + Cl^-(aq)$.

As discussed on page 144, the giant covalent molecules graphite and graphene are electrical conductors due to mobile electrons. In addition, fullerene and silicon have semiconductivity properties. Diamond is a non-conductor of electricity.

Summary of physical properties

We can now summarize the physical properties of ionic and covalent compounds, though it should be recognized that the table below gives only general trends and does not apply universally.

The moss plant *Philonotis fontana* has a waxy substance on its surface which repels water. The wax is a large non-polar covalent molecule that is unable to form hydrogen bonds with water.

Dry-cleaning is a process where clothes are washed without water. Instead, a less polar organic liquid is used which may be a better solvent for stains caused by large non-polar molecules such as grass and grease.

Non-polar covalent substances dissolve best in non-polar solvents; polar substances dissolve best in polar solvents.

	Ionic compounds	Polar covalent compounds	Non-polar covalent compounds	Giant covalent
Volatility	low	higher	highest	low
Solubility in polar solvent, e.g. water	soluble	solubility increases as polarity increases	non-soluble	non-soluble
Solubility in non-polar solvent, e.g. hexane	non-soluble	solubility increases as polarity decreases	soluble	non-soluble
Electrical conductivity	conduct when molten (l) or dissolved in water (aq)	non-conductors	non-conductors	non-conductors except graphite, graphene and semi-conductivity of Si and fullerene

Investigation of the physical properties of a variety of substances

Full details of how to carry out this experiment with a worksheet are available on your eBook.

Exercises

27 The physical properties of five solids labelled A, B, C, D, and E are summarized below. The substances are: an ionic compound, a non-polar molecular solid, a metal, a polar molecular solid, and a giant molecular substance. Classify each correctly.

Sample	Solubility in water	Conductivity of solution	Conductivity of solid	Relative melting point
A	insoluble	–	yes	third to melt
B	insoluble	–	no	highest
C	soluble	no	no	second to melt
D	insoluble	–	no	lowest
E	soluble	yes	no	fourth to melt

28 Which substance is the most soluble in water?

    A CH_3OH **B** CH_4 **C** C_2H_6 **D** C_2H_5OH

29 State the intermolecular forces that exist between molecules of each of the following:

    (a) dry ice, $CO_2(s)$ **(b)** $NH_3(l)$ **(c)** $N_2(l)$ **(d)** CH_3OCH_3

30 Which of each pair has the lower boiling point?

    (a) C_2H_6 and C_3H_8 **(b)** H_2O and H_2S **(c)** Cl_2 and Br_2 **(d)** HF and HCl

4.5 Metallic bonding

Understandings:
- A metallic bond is the electrostatic attraction between a lattice of positive ions and delocalized electrons.
- The strength of a metallic bond depends on the charge of the ions and the radius of the metal ion.
- Alloys usually contain more than one metal and have enhanced properties.

    Guidance
    Examples of various alloys should be covered.

Applications and skills:
- Explanation of electrical conductivity and malleability in metals.
- Explanation of trends in melting points of metals.

    Guidance
    Trends should be limited to s- and p-block elements.

- Explanation of the properties of alloys in terms of non-directional bonding.

Metals are found on the left of the Periodic Table and have a small number of electrons in their outer shell. These are atoms with low ionization energies, and typically react with other elements by losing their valence electrons and forming positive ions. So these elements are characterized by having a loose control over their outer shell electrons.

In the elemental state, when there is no other element present to accept the electrons and form an ionic compound, the outer electrons are held only loosely by the metal atom's nucleus and so tend to 'wander off' or, more correctly, become **delocalized**. As we saw in Section 4.3, delocalized electrons are not fixed in one position. This means that in metals they are no longer associated closely with any one metal nucleus but instead can spread themselves through the metal structure. The metal atoms without these electrons have become positively charged ions and form a regular lattice structure through which these electrons can move freely.

You can think of it like a close neighbourhood of families where the children do not belong specifically to any one set of parents but are free to wander between the homes. This arrangement causes a close association between the families. Likewise in metals there is a force of electrostatic attraction between the lattice of cations and the delocalized electrons, and this is known as **metallic bonding**.

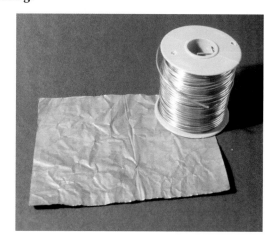

The strength of the metallic bond is determined by:

• the number of delocalized electrons;
• the charge on the cation;
• the radius of the cation.

The greater the number of delocalized electrons and the smaller the cation, the greater the binding force between them. For example, if we compare:

• sodium, Na, Group 1, electron configuration $1s^2 2s^2 2p^6 3s^1$ and
• magnesium, Mg, Group 2, electron configuration $1s^2 2s^2 2p^6 3s^2$

we can deduce that Na will have one delocalized electron per atom and the Na^+ ion, whereas Mg will have two delocalized electrons per atom and the Mg^{2+} ion. In addition, the radius of Mg^{2+} is slightly smaller than that of Na^+. These factors all indicate that Mg has stronger metallic bonding than Na, which can be confirmed by a comparison of their melting points.

	Na	Mg
Melting point / °C	98	650

The strength of metallic bonding tends to decrease down a group as the size of the cation increases, reducing the attraction between the delocalized electrons and the positive charges. Again melting points confirm this.

	Na	K	Rb
Melting point / °C	98	63	39

The transition elements tend to have very strong metallic bonds due to the large number of electrons that can become delocalized, from both 3d and 4s sub-shells.

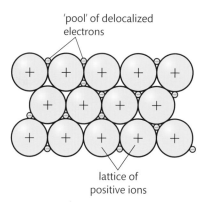

'pool' of delocalized electrons

lattice of positive ions

Figure 4.19 A model of metallic bonding. It is often described as a lattice of cations surrounded by a sea of electrons.

Copper is one of the oldest metals ever used. It is malleable, ductile, and a good conductor of heat and electricity. Brass and bronze are copper alloys.

Metallic bonds are the strong forces of attraction between delocalized electrons and positive ions.

The extraction of metals from their ores is a major part of industry and development in many countries, but is associated with some complex environmental issues. These include the destruction of landscapes by strip mining, the 'tailings' or waste material that accumulate in spoil tips, and the release of toxic materials that leach out of waste and pollute the environment. An important step to reduce the impact of these effects is to maximize the reuse and recycling of all metal objects, and avoid metal dumping. Despite their apparent abundance, metals are a precious resource, available only at considerable cost.

Metals share characteristic physical properties, which can be explained through this model of metallic bonding. They are summarized below.

Metallic property	Explanation	Application
good electrical conductivity	delocalized electrons are highly mobile, and so can move through the metal structure in response to an applied voltage	electrical circuits use copper
good thermal conductivity	delocalized electrons and close packed ions enable efficient transfer of heat energy	cooking utensils
malleable, can be shaped under pressure	movement of delocalized electrons is non-directional and essentially random through the cation lattice, so the metallic bond remains intact while the conformation changes under applied pressure	moulded into many forms including machinery and structural components of buildings and vehicles
ductile, can be drawn out into threads		electric wires and cables
high melting points	a lot of energy is required to break the strong metallic bonds and separate the atoms	high speed tools and turbine engines; tungsten has the highest melting point
shiny, lustrous appearance	delocalized electrons in metal crystal structure reflect light	ornamental structures

NATURE OF SCIENCE

Atomic theory enables scientists to explain the distinct properties of metals. This is applied in research in the development of new materials such as alloys that combine the characteristics of different metals. The ability to explain natural phenomena such as metallic properties through the application of theory is an important feature of science.

Figure 4.20 Alloys consist of different metal ions and a sea of delocalized electrons . The smaller ions are able to fit in the spaces between the larger ions in the lattice structure.

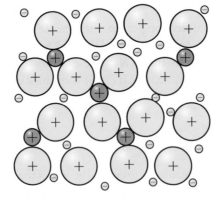

Alloys are solid solutions usually containing more than one metal, and held together by metallic bonding.

Alloys are solutions of metals with enhanced properties

Alloys are produced by adding one metal element to another metal (or carbon) in the molten state, so that the different atoms can mix. As the mixture solidifies, ions of the different metals are scattered through the lattice and bound by the delocalized electrons, so they contain metallic bonds. The production of alloys is possible because of the non-directional nature of the delocalized electrons, and the fact that the lattice can accommodate ions of different size.

Alloys have properties that are distinct from their component elements due to the different packing of the cations in the lattice. The alloy is often more chemically stable, and also often stronger and more resistant to corrosion.

Name of alloy	Component metals	Properties and uses
steel	iron with carbon and other elements	high tensile strength but corrodes, used as structural material
stainless steel	iron with other elements such as nickel and chromium	widely used in domestic and industrial appliances due to strength and corrosion resistance
brass	copper and zinc	variety of plumbing fittings
bronze	copper and tin	coins, medals, tools, heavy gears
pewter	tin and antimony and copper	decorative objects
duralumin	aluminium, copper, and manganese	aircraft, boats, and machinery due to high strength and resistance to corrosion
nichrome	nickel and copper	heating elements in toasters, electric heaters
solder	lead and tin	low melting point, used in joining two metals together, especially in electric circuitry
sterling silver	silver and copper	jewellery, art objects

You do not need to learn all these examples, but you should be able to use the examples you choose to explain why the structure of alloys gives them enhanced properties compared with their component metals.

Steel manufacture is one of the world's largest industries and is sometimes used as a measure of a country's development and economic progress. Many countries are investing in technologies to become self-sufficient in steel making. Production has increased steadily in Asia, which in 2013 accounted for about 65% of global steel production, with China and India the major contributors. Steel is the most recycled material in the world and, in developed countries, recycling accounts for almost half of the steel produced.

Naturally occurring alloys have been used by humans since ancient times, and civilizations learned to make alloys by smelting, largely influenced by the availability of native metals. The Bronze Age in Europe dates from about 2500 BCE, while in the Middle East, brass was produced from about 400 BCE. The availability of these alloys played a major part in establishing cultures and trading relationships.

Exercises

31 Which is the best definition of metallic bonding?

    A the attraction between cations and anions
    B the attraction between cations and delocalized electrons
    C the attraction between nuclei and electron pairs
    D the attraction between nuclei and anions

32 Aluminium is a widely used metal. What properties make it suitable for the following applications?

    (a) baking foil
    (b) aircraft bodywork
    (c) cooking pans
    (d) tent frames

33 Suggest two ways in which some of the properties of aluminium can be enhanced.

Nichrome wire is used in carrying out flame tests in the laboratory. It is a convenient material because it is resistant to oxidation at high temperatures.

Practice questions

1 Which bonds are arranged in order of increasing polarity?

    A   H–F < H–Cl < H–Br < H–I

    B   H–I < H–Br < H–F < H–Cl

    C   H–I < H–Br < H–Cl < H–F

    D   H–Br < H–I < H–Cl < H–F

2 Which row correctly describes the bonding type and melting point of carbon and carbon dioxide?

	Carbon		Carbon dioxide	
A	covalent bonding	high melting point	covalent bonding	low melting point
B	ionic bonding	low melting point	ionic bonding	high melting point
C	ionic bonding	high melting point	ionic bonding	low melting point
D	covalent bonding	low melting point	covalent bonding	high melting point

3 What is the correct order of increasing boiling points?

    A $CH_3CH_3 < CH_3CH_2Cl < CH_3CH_2Br < CH_3CH_2I$

    B $CH_3CH_2Cl < CH_3CH_2Br < CH_3CH_3 < CH_3CH_2I$

    C $CH_3CH_2I < CH_3CH_2Br < CH_3CH_2Cl < CH_3CH_3$

    D $CH_3CH_2Br < CH_3CH_2Cl < CH_3CH_2I < CH_3CH_3$

4 Which compound forms hydrogen bonds in the liquid state?

    A C_2H_5OH **B** $CHCl_3$

    C CH_3CHO **D** $(CH_3CH_2)_3N$

5 Which species contain a coordinate covalent bond?

    I   HCHO

    II   CO

    III H_3O^+

    A   I and II only   **B**   I and III only

    C   II and III only   **D**   I, II, and III

6 A Group 2 element, A, forms a compound with a Group 17 element, B. Which is the most likely formula and type of bonding in this compound?

A	A_2B	ionic
B	AB_2	ionic
C	A_2B	covalent
D	AB_2	covalent

7 Which structure below contains at least one double bond?

    I N_2

    II O_2

    III CO_2

    A   I only   **B**   III only   **C**   II and III only   **D**   I, II, and III

8 Which molecule, according to VSEPR theory, would be expected to have the smallest bond angle?

A H_2O **B** PH_3 **C** CCl_4 **D** H_2CO

9 Which compound is most ionic?

A HF **B** KF **C** CF_4 **D** LiF

10 Which of the following molecules is polar?

A Cl_2 **B** BCl_3 **C** NCl_3 **D** CCl_4

11 Which is the best description of the carbonate ion, CO_3^{2-}?

A	pyramidal	bond angle 107°
B	tetrahedral	bond angle 109°
C	planar triangular	bond angle 120°
D	V-shaped	bond angle 105°

12 Which molecule contains polar bonds but is non-polar?

A O_3 **B** CCl_4 **C** NH_3 **D** N_2

13 Which substance would be expected to have the lowest electrical conductivity?

A Al(s) **B** Al_2O_3(l) **C** $MgCl_2$(aq) **D** HCl(g)

14 Which substance can form intermolecular hydrogen bonds in the liquid state?

A CH_3OCH_3 **B** CH_3CH_2OH
C CH_3CHO **D** $CH_3CH_2CH_3$

15 Carbon and silicon belong to the same group of the Periodic Table.

(a) Describe and compare three features of the structure and bonding in the three allotropes of carbon: diamond, graphite, and C_{60} fullerene. (6)

(b) Both silicon and carbon form oxides.

   (i) Describe the structure and bonding in SiO_2. (2)

   (ii) Explain why silicon dioxide is a solid and carbon dioxide is a gas at room temperature. (2)

(c) Describe the bonding within the carbon monoxide molecule. (2)

(Total 12 marks)

16 Methoxymethane, CH_3OCH_3, and ethanol, C_2H_5OH, have the same relative molecular mass. Explain why methoxymethane has a much lower boiling point than ethanol. (3)

17 CCl_2F_2 was used as a coolant in refrigerators, but this use has been discontinued due to concerns about destruction of the ozone layer.

(a) Draw the Lewis (electron dot) structure of CCl_2F_2. (2)

(b) Predict the shape of the molecule and state the bond angles in CCl_2F_2. (2)

(c) State, giving your reasons, whether CCl_2F_2 is a polar or a non-polar molecule. (2)

(d) Explain what is meant by resonance with reference to Lewis (electron dot) structures of ozone, O_3. (3)

(e) Contrast and compare the bonds in oxygen, O_2, and ozone, O_3, and suggest why ozone may be more easily broken down in the stratosphere. (3)

(Total 12 marks)

18 VSEPR theory can be used to predict the shapes of molecules.

   (a) Explain the application of VSEPR theory in the following, including in your answers full Lewis (electron dot) structures, the name of the shape of the molecule and bond angles present.

      (i) PH_3

      (ii) H_2O

      (iii) C_2H_6

      (iv) CH_3CHO (12)

   (b) Only one of the molecules in (a) is able to form intermolecular hydrogen bonding. State which molecule this is, and describe the features it possesses which make it possible for it to form hydrogen bonds. (2)

(Total 14 marks)

19 The properties of elements and compounds can often be predicted from knowledge of their bonding, deduced from their positions in the Periodic Table.

   (a) (i) Describe the bonding in potassium metal. (3)

      (ii) State three properties of potassium, and explain each in terms of the bonding described. (6)

   (b) (i) Describe the bonding in fluorine gas. (3)

      (ii) Name and describe the forces present between molecules of fluorine in the liquid state. (3)

   (c) With reference to their electron configurations, describe how atoms of potassium and fluorine combine to form potassium fluoride. (4)

   (d) Explain why sodium fluoride does not conduct electricity in the solid state, but is a conductor in its molten form or in aqueous solution. (2)

(Total 21 marks)

20 (a) Sketch and state the names of the shapes of the following molecules.

      (i) SiH_4

      (ii) PH_3 (4)

   (b) State the bond angle in SiH_4 and explain why it is greater than that in PH_3. (2)

(Total 6 marks)

21 Ammonia, NH_3, reacts with hydrogen ions, H^+, to form ammonium ions, NH_4^+.

   (a) Draw a Lewis (electron dot) structure of ammonia and state its shape and bond angle. (3)

   (b) Predict and explain whether the ammonia molecule is polar. (2)

   (c) Draw a Lewis (electron dot) structure of the ammonium ion and state its shape and bond angle. (3)

   (d) State the name of the bond that forms between ammonia and the hydrogen ion, and explain its formation. (2)

   (e) Explain why the bond angle in ammonia is different from the bond angle in the ammonium ion. (3)

(Total 13 marks)

22 The structure of ethanoic acid is shown below.

(a) Comment on whether or not this representation is a Lewis (electron dot) structure.　(3)

(b) Predict the bond angles around each of the two carbon atoms labelled 1 and 2

C1 bond angle: _____　　C2 bond angle: _____　(2)

(c) Compare and contrast the bonds between the carbon atom and the two oxygen atoms in the molecule.　(2)

(d) When ethanoic acid ionizes it loses a hydrogen ion and forms the ethanoate ion CH_3COO^-.

Explain why in this structure, the carbon-oxygen bonds are different from either of the carbon-oxygen bonds in ethanoic acid.　(3)

(Total 10 marks)

NATURE OF SCIENCE

A model of the lattice structure of NaCl, with sodium ions shown in green and chloride ions shown in black. Can you suggest in what ways this model may not be an accurate representation of the real structure of sodium chloride? Compare it with the models pictured on page 119, and consider which you think may be the better model.

To access weblinks on the topics covered in this chapter, please go to www.pearsonhotlinks.com and enter the ISBN or title of this book.

05 Energetics and thermochemistry

Essential ideas

5.1 The enthalpy changes from chemical reactions can be calculated from their effect on the temperature of their surroundings.

5.2 In chemical transformations energy can neither be created nor destroyed (the first law of thermodynamics).

5.3 Energy is absorbed when bonds are broken and is released when bonds are formed.

All chemical reactions are accompanied by energy changes. Energy changes are vital. Our body's processes are dependent on the energy changes which occur during respiration, when glucose reacts with oxygen. Modern lifestyles are dependent on the transfer of energy that occurs when fuels burn. As we explore the source of these energy changes, we will deepen our understanding of why bonds are broken and formed during a chemical reaction, and why electron transfer can lead to the formation of stable ionic compounds. The questions of why things change will lead to the development of the concept of entropy. We will see that this concept allows us to give the same explanation for a variety of physical and chemical changes: the universe is becoming more disordered. This provides us with a signpost for the direction of all change. The distinction between the quantity and quality of energy will lead to the development of the concept of free energy, a useful accounting tool for chemists to predict the feasibility of any hypothetical reaction.

We will see how creative thinking, accurate calculations, and careful observations and measurement can work together to lead to a deeper understanding of the relationship between heat and chemical change.

The burning of a firework increases the disorder in the universe, as both energy and matter become dispersed. This is the natural direction of change.

▲
James Prescott Joule (1818–89) was devoted to making accurate measurements of heat. The SI unit of energy is named after him.

5.1 Measuring energy changes

Understandings:
- Heat is a form of energy.
- Temperature is a measure of the average kinetic energy of the particles.
- Total energy is conserved in chemical reactions.
- Chemical reactions that involve transfer of heat between the system and the surroundings are described as endothermic or exothermic.
- The enthalpy change (ΔH) for chemical reactions is indicated in kJ mol^{-1}.
- ΔH values are usually expressed under standard conditions, known as $\Delta H^{\ominus}$, including standard states.

Guidance
Enthalpy changes of combustion ($\Delta H_c^{\ominus}$) and formation ($\Delta H_f^{\ominus}$) should be covered.

Applications and skills:
- Calculation of the heat change when the temperature of a pure substance is changed using $q = mc\Delta T$.

Guidance
The specific heat capacity of water is provided in the IB data booklet in section 2.

- A calorimetry experiment for an enthalpy of reaction should be covered and the results evaluated.

Guidance

- *Consider reactions in aqueous solution and combustion reactions.*
- *Standard state refers to the normal, most pure stable state of a substance measured at 100 kPa.*
- *Temperature is not a part of the definition of standard state, but 298 K is commonly given as the temperature of interest.*
- *Students can assume the density and specific heat capacities of aqueous solutions are equal to those of water, but should be aware of this limitation.*
- *Heat losses to the environment and the heat capacity of the calorimeter in experiments should be considered, but the use of a bomb calorimeter is not required.*

The joule is the unit of energy and work. You do 1 J of work when you exert a force of 1 N over a distance of 1 m. 1 J of energy is expended every time the human heart beats.

Energy is conserved in chemical reactions.

surroundings

system

Figure 5.1 The system is the sample or reaction vessel of interest. The surroundings are the rest of the universe.

Enthalpy (*H*) is a measure of the amount of heat energy contained in a substance. It is stored in the chemical bonds and intermolecular forces as potential energy. When substances react, the difference in the enthalpy between the reactants and products (at constant pressure) results in a heat change which can be observed.

Work and heat transfer energy

Energy is a measure of the ability to do **work**, that is to move an object against an opposing force. It comes in many forms and includes heat, light, sound, electricity, and chemical energy – the energy released or absorbed during chemical reactions. This chapter will focus on reactions which involve heat changes. Heat is a mode of energy transfer which occurs as a result of a temperature difference and produces an increase in disorder in how the particles behave. Heat increases the average kinetic energy of the molecules in a disordered fashion. This is to be contrasted with work, which is a more ordered process of transferring energy. When you do work on a beaker of water, by lifting it from a table, for example, you raise all the molecules above the table in the same way.

System and surroundings

Chemical and physical changes take place in many different environments such as test tubes, polystyrene cups, industrial plants and living cells. It is useful in these cases to distinguish between the **system** – the area of interest and the **surroundings** – in theory everything else in the universe (Figure 5.1). Most chemical reactions take place in an **open system** which can exchange energy and matter with the surroundings. A **closed system** can exchange energy but not matter with the surroundings. Although energy can be exchanged between a system and the surroundings, the total energy cannot change during the process; any energy lost by the system is gained by the surroundings and vice versa.

The heat content of a system is its enthalpy

Although, according to the conservation of energy, the total energy of the system and surroundings cannot change during a process, heat can be transferred between a system and its surroundings. The heat content of a system is called its **enthalpy**, a name which comes from the Greek word for 'heat inside'. A system acts like a reservoir of heat. When heat is added to a system from the surroundings its enthalpy increases. Changes in enthalpy are denoted by ΔH. ΔH is positive when heat is added to the system.

When heat is released from the system to the surroundings the enthalpy of the system decreases and ΔH is negative.

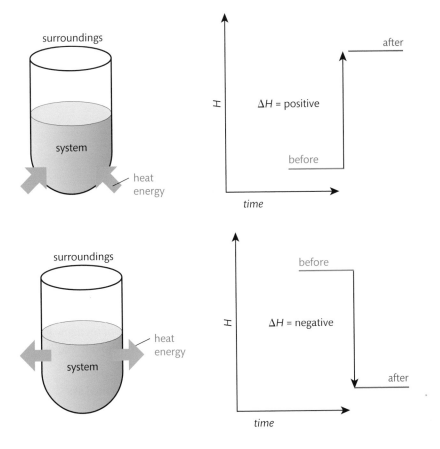

Figure 5.2 When heat is gained by the system from the surroundings, the enthalpy of the system increases and ΔH is positive.

Figure 5.3 When heat is lost from the system to the surroundings the enthalpy of the system decreases and ΔH is negative.

TOK How important are technical terms such as *enthalpy* in different areas of knowledge? Is their correct use a necessary or sufficient indicator of understanding?

Exothermic and endothermic reactions

The enthalpy (*H*) of the system is stored in the chemical bonds and intermolecular forces as potential energy. When substances react, the difference in the enthalpy between the reactants and products produces an enthalpy change which can be observed. Most chemical reactions, including most combustion and all neutralization reactions, are exothermic. They give out heat and result in a transfer of enthalpy from the chemicals to the surroundings and $\Delta H_{reaction}$ is negative.

A few reactions are **endothermic** as they result in an energy transfer from the surroundings to the system. In this case the products have more enthalpy than the reactants and ΔH is positive.

For exothermic reactions heat is given out by the system and ΔH is negative.

For endothermic reactions heat is absorbed by the system and ΔH is positive.

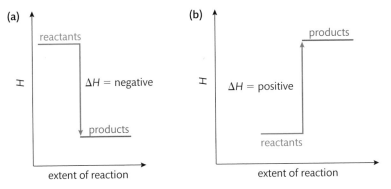

Figure 5.4 (a) An exothermic reaction. The enthalpy of the products is less than the enthalpy of the reactants. (b) An endothermic reaction. The enthalpy of the products is greater than the enthalpy of the reactants.

Standard enthalpy changes

As the enthalpy of a system also depends on the intermolecular forces of the reactants and products, the enthalpy change for a reaction depends on the conditions under which the reaction occurs. The **standard enthalpy changes**, $\Delta H^{\ominus}$, given in the literature are measured under the following conditions:

- a pressure of 100 kPa;
- concentration of 1 mol dm^{-3} for all solutions;
- all substances in their standard states.

Temperature is not part of the definition of standard state, but 298 K is usually given as the specified temperature.

> The standard conditions for enthalpy changes are:
> - a pressure of 100 kPa
> - concentrations of 1 mol dm^{-3} for all solutions
> - all the substances in their standard states.

Thermochemical equations

The combustion of methane can be described by the thermochemical equation:

$$CH_4(g) + 2O_2(g) \rightarrow CO_2(g) + 2H_2O(l) \qquad \Delta H^{\ominus} = -890 \text{ kJ mol}^{-1}$$

This is a shorthand way of expressing information that *one mole* of methane gas reacts with *two moles* of oxygen gas to give *one mole* of gaseous carbon dioxide and *two moles* of liquid water and *releases* 890 kJ of heat energy.

The thermochemical equation for photosynthesis can be represented as:

$$6CO_2(g) + 6H_2O(l) \rightarrow C_6H_{12}O_6(aq) + 6O_2(g) \qquad \Delta H^{\ominus}_{reaction} = +2802.5 \text{ kJ mol}^{-1}$$

which means that 2802.5 kJ of energy is absorbed when one mole of glucose is formed under standard conditions from gaseous carbon dioxide and liquid water.

> The standard state of a substance is the pure form of the substance under standard conditions.

> It is important to give the state symbols in thermochemical equations as the enthalpy changes depend on the state of the reactants and the products.

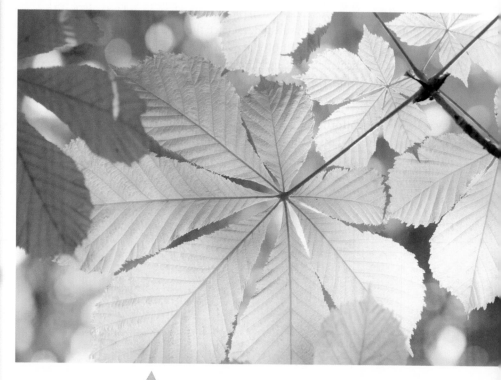

Photosynthesis is an endothermic reaction which occurs in green leaves.

Scientists share their knowledge using a precise language. In everyday language heat and work are both nouns and verbs, whereas in science they are nouns which describe energy transfer processes. Heat is often said to flow from high temperature to low temperature. This image originates from the incorrect outdated view that heat was a liquid, *calorique*, which was included in Lavoisier's list of chemical elements. Heat is now more correctly characterized as a process of energy transfer.

Enthalpy is a word rarely used in non-scientific discourse; it is an abstract entity with a precise mathematical definition. At this level we need not concern ourselves with absolute enthalpy values but only enthalpy changes which can be determined from temperature changes at constant pressure which can be measured.

The use of appropriate terminology is a key issue with scientific literacy and the public understanding of science and scientists need to take this into account when communicating with the public.

Noms nouveaux.	Noms anciens correspondans.
Lumière........	Lumière.
Calorique........	Chaleur. Principe de la chaleur. Fluide igné. Feu. Matière du feu & de la chaleur.
Oxygène........	Air déphlogistiqué. Air empiréal. Air vital. Base de l'air vital.
Azote........	Gaz phlogistiqué. Mofete. Base de la mofete.
Hydrogène........	Gaz inflammable. Base du gaz inflammable.
Soufre........	Soufre.
Phosphore........	Phosphore.
Carbone........	Charbon pur.
Radical muriatique.	Inconnu.
Radical fluorique .	Inconnu.
Radical boracique.	Inconnu.
Antimoine........	Antimoine.
Argent........	Argent.
Arsenic........	Arsenic.
Bismuth........	Bismuth.
Cobolt........	Cobolt.
Cuivre........	Cuivre.
Etain........	Etain.
Fer........	Fer.
Manganèse........	Manganèse.
Mercure........	Mercure.
Molybdène........	Molybdène.
Nickel........	Nickel.
Or........	Or.
Platine........	Platine.
Plomb........	Plomb.
Tungstène........	Tungstène.
Zinc........	Zinc.
Chaux........	Terre calcaire, chaux.
Magnésie........	Magnésie, base du sel d'Epsom.
Baryte........	Barote, terre pesante.
Alumine........	Argile, terre de l'alun, base de l'alun.
Silice........	Terre siliceuse, terre vitrifiable.

Substances simples qui appartiennent aux trois règnes & qu'on peut regarder comme les élémens des corps.

Substances simples non métalliques oxidables & acidifiables.

Substances simples métalliques oxidables & acidifiables.

Substances simples salifiables terreuses.

CHALLENGE YOURSELF

1 Most combustion reactions are exothermic but there are exceptions. Find an element in the second period which has a positive enthalpy of combustion.

Lavoisier's list of chemical elements includes heat (*calorique*) which was thought to be a liquid.

Temperature is a measure of average kinetic energy

The movement or kinetic energy of the particles of a substance depends on the temperature. If the temperature of a substance is decreased, the average kinetic energy of the particles also decreases. **Absolute zero** (−273 °C) is the lowest possible temperature attainable as this is the temperature at which all movement has stopped. The **Kelvin scale** emphasizes this relationship between average kinetic energy and temperature. The absolute temperature, measured in kelvin, is directly proportional to the average kinetic energy of its particles.

The SI unit of temperature is the kelvin (K), but the Celsius scale (°C), which has the same incremental scaling, is commonly used in most countries. The USA, however, continues to use the Fahrenheit (°F) scale for all non-scientific communication.

Heat changes can be calculated from temperature changes

If the same amount of heat is added to two different objects, the temperature change will not be the same, as the average kinetic energy of the particles will not increase by the same amount. The object with the smaller number of particles will experience the larger temperature increase, as the same energy is shared amongst a smaller collection of particles.

In general, the increase in temperature when an object is heated depends on:

• the mass of the object;
• the heat added;
• the nature of the substance.

The specific heat capacity is the property of a substance which gives the heat needed to increase the temperature of unit mass by 1 K. The specific heat capacity depends on the number of particles present in a unit mass sample, which in turn will depend on the mass of the individual particles.

heat change (q) = mass (m) × specific heat capacity (c) × temperature change (ΔT)

heat change = $m \times c \times \Delta T$

heat change (J) = m (g) × c (J g^{-1} K^{-1}) × ΔT (K)

When the heat is absorbed by water, $c = 4.18$ J g^{-1} K^{-1}

This value is given in the IB data booklet.

This relationship allows the heat change in a material to be calculated from the temperature change.

The water in the kettle has a higher temperature but the water in the swimming pool has more heat energy. Temperature is a measure of the average kinetic energy of the molecules.

When considering the relationship between different objects the **heat capacity** is often a more convenient property. The heat capacity (C) is defined as the heat needed to increase the temperature of an object by 1 K.

$$\text{heat capacity } (C) = \frac{\text{heat change } (q)}{\text{temperature change } (\Delta T)}$$

A swimming pool has a larger heat capacity than a kettle.

A temperature rise of 1 K is the same as a temperature rise of 1 °C.

- **The specific heat capacity (c) is defined as the heat needed to increase the temperature of unit mass of material by 1 K.**

$$\text{specific heat capacity } (c) = \frac{\text{heat change } (q)}{\text{mass } (m) \times \text{temperature change } (\Delta T)}$$

- **The heat capacity (C) is defined as the heat needed to increase the temperature of an object by 1 K.**

$$\text{heat capacity } (C) = \frac{\text{heat change } (q)}{\text{temperature change } (\Delta T)}$$

Our shared knowledge is passed on from one generation to the next by language. The language we use today is often based on the shared knowledge of the past which can sometimes be incorrect. What do such phrases as "keep the heat in and the cold out" tell us about previous concepts of heat and cold? How does the use of language hinder the pursuit of knowledge?

NATURE OF SCIENCE

Although heat is a concept that is familiar to us all – we need it to cook our food and to keep us warm – it is a subject that has proved to be difficult for science to understand. We are equipped by our sense of touch to distinguish between high and low temperature but heat has proved challenging on a more fundamental level. The development of different temperature scales was an important technological and scientific step as it recognized the need for objectivity in scientific measurement, and the need to calibrate the instruments to one or more one fixed points. However, scientific understanding in this area was still confused at the time. The original Celsius scale, for example, had the boiling point of water at a lower temperature than its melting point, so it was not clear what it was quantifying and other scales used arbitrary fixed points such as the melting points of butter, or the temperatures of the Paris wine cellars.

The observation that heat can be added to melting ice or boiling water without changing its temperature was a significant observation in the distinction between the heat and temperature.

Our modern distinction is based on our particulate theory of matter. Temperature is a measure of the individual particle's kinetic energy and heat, a process by which energy is transferred.

Worked example

How much heat is released when 10.0 g of copper with a specific heat capacity of 0.385 J g^{-1} °C^{-1} is cooled from 85.0 °C to 25.0 °C?

Solution

$$\text{heat change} = m \times c \times \Delta T$$
$$= 10.0 \text{ g} \times 0.385 \text{ J g}^{-1}\,^{\circ}\text{C}^{-1} \times -60.0\,^{\circ}\text{C} \text{ (the value is negative as}$$
$$\text{the Cu has lost heat)}$$
$$= -231 \text{ J}$$

Exercises

1 When a sample of NH_4SCN is mixed with solid $Ba(OH)_2.8H_2O$ in a glass beaker, the mixture changes to a liquid and the temperature drops sufficiently to freeze the beaker to the table. Which statement is true about the reaction?

   A The process is endothermic and ΔH is –
   B The process is endothermic and ΔH is +
   C The process is exothermic and ΔH is –
   D The process is exothermic and ΔH is +

2 Which one of the following statements is *true* of all exothermic reactions?

   A They produce gases.
   B They give out heat.
   C They occur quickly.
   D They involve combustion.

3 If 500 J of heat is added to 100.0 g samples of each of the substances below, which will have the largest temperature increase?

	Substance	Specific heat capacity / J g^{-1} K^{-1}
A	gold	0.129
B	silver	0.237
C	copper	0.385
D	water	4.18

4 The temperature of a 5.0 g sample of copper increases from 27 °C to 29 °C. Calculate how much heat has been added to the system. (Specific heat capacity of Cu = 0.385 J g^{-1}K^{-1})

   A 0.770 J　　　　**B** 1.50 J　　　　**C** 3.00 J　　　　**D** 3.85 J

5 Consider the specific heat capacity of the following metals.

Metal	Specific heat capacity / J g^{-1} K^{-1}
Al	0.897
Be	1.82
Cd	0.231
Cr	0.449

   1 kg samples of the metals at room temperature are heated by the same electrical heater for 10 min. Identify the metal which has the highest final temperature.

   A Al　　　　**B** Be　　　　**C** Cd　　　　**D** Cr

6 The specific heat of metallic mercury is 0.138 J g^{-1} °C^{-1}. If 100.0 J of heat is added to a 100.0 g sample of mercury at 25.0 °C, what is the final temperature of the mercury?

CHALLENGE YOURSELF

2 Suggest an explanation for the pattern in specific heat capacities of the metals in Exercise 3.

Enthalpy changes and the direction of change

There is a natural direction for change. When we slip on a ladder, we go down, not up. The direction of change is in the direction of lower stored energy. In a similar way, we expect methane to burn when we strike a match and form carbon dioxide and water. The chemicals are changing in a way which reduces their enthalpy (Figure 5.5).

Figure 5.5 An exothermic reaction can be compared to a person falling off a ladder. Both changes lead to a decrease in stored energy. The state of lower energy is more stable. The mixture of carbon dioxide and water is more stable than a mixture of methane and oxygen.

Diamonds are not forever as they are unstable relative to graphite.

$C(diamond) \rightarrow C(graphite)$

$\Delta H = -1.9$ kJ mol^{-1}

However, the change is very slow.

Diamond is a naturally occurring form of carbon that has crystallized under great pressure. It is unstable relative to graphite.

There are many examples of exothermic reactions and we generally expect a reaction to occur if it leads to a reduction in enthalpy. In the same way that a ball is more stable on the ground than in mid-air, we can say that the products in an exothermic reaction are more stable than the reactants. It is important to realize that stability is a relative term. Hydrogen peroxide, for example, is stable with respect to its elements but unstable relative to its decomposition to water and oxygen (Figure 5.6).

The sign of ΔH is a guide for the likely direction of change but it is not completely reliable. We do not expect a person to fall up a ladder but some endothermic reactions can occur. For example, the reaction:

$$6SOCl_2(l) + FeCl_3.6H_2O(s) \rightarrow FeCl_3(s) + 6SO_2(g) + 12HCl(g) \qquad \Delta H = +11\,271 \text{ kJ mol}^{-1}$$

is extremely endothermic. Endothermic reactions are less common and occur when there is an increase in disorder of the system, for example owing to the production of gas. This is discussed in more detail later in the chapter.

Figure 5.6 Hydrogen peroxide is stable relative to the hydrogen and oxygen but unstable relative to water.

Measuring enthalpy changes of combustion

For liquids such as ethanol, the enthalpy change of combustion can be determined using the simple apparatus shown in Figure 5.7.

The standard enthalpy change of combustion ($\Delta H_c^\ominus$) is the enthalpy change for the complete combustion of one mole of a substance in its standard state in excess oxygen under standard conditions.

Sherbet contains sodium hydrogencarbonate and tartaric acid. When sherbet comes into contact with water on the tongue an endothermic reaction takes place. The sherbet absorbs heat energy from the water on the tongue creating a cold sensation.

The temperature of the water increases as it has increased its heat content, owing to the heat released by the combustion reaction. There is a decrease of enthalpy during the reaction.

Calculating enthalpies of reaction in solution from temperature changes

When the heat released by an exothermic reaction is absorbed by water, the temperature of the water increases. The heat produced by the reaction can be calculated if it is assumed that all the heat is absorbed by the water.

$$\Delta H_{\text{reaction}} = -\Delta H(\text{water}) = -m(H_2O) \times c(H_2O) \times \Delta T(H_2O)$$

As the water has gained the heat produced by the reaction, the enthalpy change of reaction is negative when the temperature of the water increases.

When an endothermic reaction is carried out in solution, the heat absorbed by the reaction is taken from the water so the temperature of the water decreases. As the reaction has taken in the heat lost by the water, the enthalpy change of reaction is positive.

As the heat change observed depends on the amount of reaction, for example the number of moles of fuel burned, enthalpy changes are usually expressed in kJ mol^{-1}.

Worked example

Calculate the enthalpy of combustion of ethanol from the following data. Assume all the heat from the reaction is absorbed by the water. Compare your value with the IB data booklet value and suggest reasons for any differences.

Mass of water in copper calorimeter / g	200.00
Temperature increase in water / °C	13.00
Mass of ethanol burned / g	0.45

It is important to state all assumptions when processing data. Simple treatments of heat of combustion reactions assume that all the heat is absorbed by the water, but the heat absorbed by the copper calorimeter can also be calculated.

The energy content of different foods and fuels could also be investigated.

173

It is important that you record qualitative as well as quantitative data when measuring enthalpy changes – for example, evidence of incomplete combustion in an enthalpy of combustion determination. When asked to evaluate experiments and suggest improvements, avoid giving trivial answers such as incorrect measurement. Incomplete combustion, for example, can be reduced by burning the fuel in oxygen. Heat loss can be reduced by insulating the apparatus.

Combustion reactions are generally exothermic, so ΔH_c values are generally negative.

Solution

$$\text{number of moles of ethanol} = \frac{m(C_2H_5OH)}{M(C_2H_5OH)} \text{ mol}$$

$$M(C_2H_5OH) = (12.01 \times 2) + (6 \times 1.01) + 16.00 = 46.08 \text{ g mol}^{-1}$$

$$\Delta H_{reaction} = -m(H_2O) \times c(H_2O) \times \Delta T(H_2O)$$

$$\Delta H_c = \Delta H_{reaction} \text{ (for one mole of ethanol)}$$

$$= \frac{-m(H_2O) \times c(H_2O) \times \Delta T(H_2O)}{m(C_2H_5OH)/M(C_2H_5OH)} \text{ J mol}^{-1}$$

$$= \frac{-200 \text{ g} \times 4.18 \text{ J g}^{-1}\,°C^{-1} \times 13.00°C}{0.45 \text{g} / 46.08 \text{ g mol}^{-1}} \text{ J mol}^{-1}$$

$$= -1112\,883 \text{ J mol}^{-1}$$

$$= -1112.883 \text{ kJ mol}^{-1}$$

$$= -1100 \text{ kJ mol}^{-1}$$

The precision of the final answer is limited by the precision of the mass of the ethanol (Chapter 11).

The IB data booklet value is -1367 kJ mol^{-1}. The difference between the values can be accounted for by any of the following factors:

- Not all the heat produced by the combustion reaction is transferred to the water. Some is needed to heat the copper calorimeter and some has passed to the surroundings.
- The combustion of the ethanol is unlikely to be complete owing to the limited oxygen available, as assumed by the literature value.
- The experiment was not performed under standard conditions.

Exercises

7   The mass of the burner and its content is measured before and after the experiment. The thermometer is read before and after the experiment. What are the expected results?

	Mass of burner and contents	Reading on thermometer
A	decreases	increases
B	decreases	stays the same
C	increases	increases
D	increases	stays the same

8   The experimental arrangement in Figure 5.7 is used to determine the enthalpy of combustion of an alcohol. Which of the following would lead to an experimental result which is **less** exothermic than the literature value?

I   Heat loss from the sides of the copper calorimeter.
II   Evaporation of alcohol during the experiment.
III The thermometer touches the bottom of the calorimeter.

A   I and II only   B   I and III only   C   II and III only   D   I, II, and III

9 A copper calorimeter was used to determine the enthalpy of combustion of butan-1-ol. The experimental value obtained was −2100 ± 200 kJ mol⁻¹ and the data booklet value is −2676 kJ mol⁻¹. Which of the following accounts for the difference between the two values?

I   random measurement errors
II   incomplete combustion
III heat loss to the surroundings

   A I and II only   **B** I and III only   **C** II and III only   **D** I, II, and III

10 1.10 g of glucose was completely burnt in a copper calorimeter. The temperature of the water increased from 25.85 °C to 36.50 °C.

   (a) Calculate the enthalpy of combustion of glucose from the data below.

Mass of water / g	200.00
Specific heat capacity of water / g⁻¹ K⁻¹	4.18
Mass of copper / g	120.00
Specific heat capacity of copper / g⁻¹ K⁻¹	0.385

   (b) Draw an enthalpy level diagram to represent this reaction.

11 The heat released from the combustion of 0.0500 g of white phosphorus increases the temperature of 150.00 g of water from 25.0 °C to 31.5 °C. Calculate a value for the enthalpy change of combustion of phosphorus. Discuss possible sources of error in the experiment.

A common error when calculating heat changes is using the incorrect mass of substance heated.

NATURE OF SCIENCE

Qualitative and quantitative experimental data are the lifeblood of science. The best data for making accurate and precise descriptions and predictions are often quantitative data that are amenable to mathematical analysis but qualitative observations always have a role in chemistry: the lower than expected exothermic value for a heat of combustion of a hydrocarbon for example is often as a result of incomplete combustion. The evidence for this comes from any black soot and residue observed during the experiment.

The combustion of fossil fuel, which meets many of our energy needs, produces carbon dioxide which is a greenhouse gas. It is important we are aware of how our lifestyle contributes to global warming. It is a global problem but we need to act locally to solve it. Global warming is discussed in more detail in Chapter 12.

Figure 5.8 A simple calorimeter. The polystyrene is a very good thermal insulator with a low heat capacity.

Enthalpy changes of reaction in solution

The enthalpy changes of reaction in solution can be calculated by carrying out the reaction in an insulated system, for example, a polystyrene cup (Figure 5.8). The heat released or absorbed by the reaction can be measured from the temperature change of the water.

reaction occurs in solution– temperature increases or decreases

insulating polystyrene cup traps heat or keeps out heat from the surroundings

Figure 5.9 A known volume of copper sulfate solution is added to the calorimeter and its temperature measured every 25 s. Excess zinc powder is added after 100 s and the temperature starts to rise until a maximum after which it falls in an approximately linear fashion.

In the previous calculation, we assumed that all the heat produced in the reaction is absorbed by water. One of the largest sources of error in experiments conducted in a polystyrene cup is heat loss to the environment. Consider, for example, the exothermic reaction between zinc and aqueous copper sulfate (Figure 5.9):

$$Cu^{2+}(aq) + Zn(s) \rightarrow Cu(s) + Zn^{2+}(aq)$$

Heat is lost from the system as soon as the temperature rises above the temperature of the surroundings, in this case 20 °C, and so the maximum recorded temperature is lower than the true value obtained in a perfectly insulated system. We can make some allowance for heat loss by extrapolating the cooling section of the graph to the time when the reaction started (100 s).

To proceed we can make the following assumptions:

1 no heat loss from the system;
2 all the heat goes from the reaction to the water;
3 the solution is dilute: $V(CuSO_4) = V(H_2O)$;
4 water has a density of 1.00 g cm^{-3}.

$$\Delta H(\text{system}) = 0 \text{ (assumption 1)}$$

$$\Delta H(\text{system}) = \Delta H(\text{water}) + \Delta H_{\text{reaction}} \text{ (assumption 2)}$$

$$\Delta H_{\text{reaction}} = -\Delta H(\text{water})$$

For an exothermic reaction, $\Delta H_{\text{reaction}}$ is negative as heat has passed from the reaction into the water.

$$\Delta H(\text{water}) = m(H_2O) \times c(H_2O) \times \Delta T(H_2O)$$

The limiting reactant must be identified in order to determine the molar enthalpy change of reaction.

$$\Delta H_{\text{reaction}} = \frac{-m(H_2O) \times c(H_2O) \times \Delta T(H_2O)}{\text{moles of limiting reactant}}$$

As the zinc was added in excess, the copper sulfate is the limiting reactant. From Chapter 1 (page 30):

$$\text{number of moles } (n) = \text{concentration (mol dm}^{-3}) \times \text{volume } (V \text{ cm}^3)$$

There are 1000 cm³ in 1 dm³

$$\text{volume } (V \text{ dm}^3) = \text{volume } (V \text{ cm}^3) / 1000 \text{ (cm}^3 \text{ dm}^{-3})$$

$$\text{number of moles of CuSO}_4 \ (n(CuSO_4)) = [CuSO_4] \times \frac{V(CuSO_4)}{1000} \text{ mol}$$

$$\Delta H_{\text{reaction}} = \frac{-m(H_2O) \times c(H_2O) \times \Delta T(H_2O)}{n(CuSO_4)} \text{ J mol}^{-1}$$

$$= \frac{-m(H_2O) \times c(H_2O) \times \Delta T(H_2O)}{[CuSO_4] \times V(CuSO_4)/1000} \text{ J mol}^{-1}$$

$$\Delta H_{reaction} = \frac{-m(H_2O) \times c(H_2O) \times \Delta T(H_2O)}{[CuSO_4] \times V(CuSO_4)/1000} \text{ J (assumption 3)}$$

$$\Delta H_{reaction} = \frac{c(H_2O) \times \Delta T(H_2O)}{[CuSO_4]/1000} \text{ (assumption 4)}$$

$$\Delta H_{reaction} = \frac{c(H_2O) \times \Delta T(H_2O)}{[CuSO_4]} \text{ kJ mol}^{-1}$$

Worked example

The neutralization reaction between solutions of sodium hydroxide and sulfuric acid was studied by measuring the temperature changes when different volumes of the two solutions were mixed. The total volume was kept constant at 120.0 cm^3 and the concentrations of the two solutions were both 1.00 mol dm^{-3} (Figure 5.10).

Key

■ Volume of NaOH added
▪ Volume of H$_2$SO$_4$ added

Figure 5.10 Temperature changes produced when different volumes of sodium hydroxide and sulfuric acid are mixed.

(a) Determine the volumes of the solutions which produce the largest increase in temperature.

(b) Calculate the heat produced by the reaction when the maximum temperature was produced.

(c) Calculate the heat produced for one mole of sodium hydroxide.

(d) The literature value for the enthalpy of neutralization is $= -57.5$ kJ mol^{-1}.

Calculate the percentage error value and suggest a reason for the discrepancy between the experimental and literature values.

Solution

(a) From the graph: $V(NaOH) = 80.0$ cm^3
$\qquad\qquad\quad V(H_2SO_4) = 40.0$ cm^3

(b) Assuming 120.0 cm^3 of the solution contains 120.0 g of water and all the heat produced by the neutralization reaction passes into the water.

$$\Delta H_{reaction} = -m(H_2O) \times c(H_2O) \times \Delta T(H_2O) \text{ J}$$

$$= -120.0 \text{ g} \times 4.18 \text{ J g}^{-1} \text{ K}^{-1} \times (33.5 - 25.0) \text{ K}$$

$$= -4264 \text{ J}$$

177

(c) $\Delta H_{\text{reaction}} = \dfrac{-4264}{n(\text{NaOH})}\ \text{J mol}^{-1}$

$$= \dfrac{-4264}{1.00 \times 80.0 / 1000}\ \text{J mol}^{-1}$$

$$= \dfrac{-4264}{80.0}\ \text{kJ mol}^{-1}$$

$$= -53.3\ \text{kJ mol}^{-1}$$

(d) % error $= \dfrac{-57.5 - -53.3}{-57.5} \times 100\% = 7\%$

The calculated value assumes:

- no heat loss from the system
- all heat is transferred to the water
- the solutions contain 120 g of water.
- There are also uncertainties in the temperature, volume, and concentration measurements.

The literature value assumes standard conditions.

NATURE OF SCIENCE

The accurate determination of enthalpy changes involves making careful observations and measurements, which inevitably have experimental uncertainties. The calculated enthalpy values are also dependent on the assumptions made. All these elements should be considered when reporting and evaluating experimental enthalpy values.

Mathematics is a powerful tool in the sciences, but scientific systems are often too complex to treat rigorously. These underlying assumptions, made to make a problem solvable, should not be ignored when evaluating quantitative data generated by a mathematical model.

TOK

What criteria do we use in judging whether discrepancies between experimental and theoretical values are due to experimental limitations or theoretical assumptions?

Being courageous is one element of the IB Learner Profile. When is a scientist justified in rejecting the literature value in favour of their experimentally determined value?

A common error is to miss out or incorrectly state the units and to miss out the negative sign for ΔH.

CHALLENGE YOURSELF

3 A piece of brass is held in the flame of a Bunsen burner for several minutes. The brass is then quickly transferred into an aluminium calorimeter which contains 200.00 g of water. Determine the temperature of the Bunsen flame from the following data.

m(brass) / g	21.20
m(aluminium calorimeter) / g	80.00
c(brass) / J g^{-1} K^{-1}	0.400
c(Al) / J g^{-1} K^{-1}	0.900
Initial temperature of water / °C	24.50
Final temperature of water / °C	77.50

The temperature of the Bunsen flame and the enthalpy of fusion can be investigated.

Exercises

12 Calculate the molar enthalpy change from the data in Figure 5.9. The copper sulfate has a concentration of 1.00 mol dm^{-3} and a volume of 1.00 dm^3.

13 Calculate the enthalpy of neutralization based on the following data.

Initial temperature of solutions / °C	24.5
Concentration of KOH(aq) / mol dm^{-3}	0.950
Concentration of HNO$_3$(aq) / mol dm^{-3}	1.050
Volume of HCl(aq) / cm^3	50.00
Volume of NaOH(aq) / cm^3	50.00
Final temperature of mixture / °C	32.3

State the assumptions you have made in your calculation.

14 A student added 5.350 g of ammonium chloride to 100.00 cm^3 of water. The initial temperature of the water was 25.55 °C but it decreased to 21.79 °C. Calculate the enthalpy change that would occur when 1 mol of the solute is added to 1.000 dm^3 of water.

15 Explain the meaning of the term ΔH and describe how it is measured.

5.2 Hess's law

Understandings:
- The enthalpy change for a reaction that is carried out in a series of steps is equal to the sum of the enthalpy changes for the individual steps.

Applications and skills:
- Application of Hess's law to calculate enthalpy changes.
- Calculation of reactions using $\Delta H_f^{\ominus}$ data.

  ### Guidance
  - *Enthalpy of formation data can be found in the IB data booklet in section 12.*
  - *An application of Hess's law is*

  $$\Delta H_{reactions} = \sum(\Delta H_f^{\ominus}(products)) - \sum(\Delta H_f^{\ominus}(reactants))$$

- Determination of the enthalpy change of a reaction that is the sum of multiple reactions with known enthalpy changes.

Enthalpy cycles

As it is sometimes difficult to measure the enthalpy change of a reaction directly, chemists have developed a method which uses an indirect route. The enthalpy change for a particular reaction is calculated from the known enthalpy change of other reactions. Consider the **energy cycle** in Figure 5.11: in the clockwise route, the carbon and hydrogen are first combined to form ethanol and then ethanol is burned. In the anticlockwise route, the elements are burned separately. The experimentally determined enthalpy changes are included in the figure.

Consider the clockwise route:

$$\Delta H_1 + \Delta H_2 = -277 + -1367 = -1644 \text{ kJ mol}^{-1}$$

Consider the anticlockwise route:

$$\Delta H_3 = -1646 \text{ kJ mol}^{-1}$$

Given the uncertainty of the experimental values, we can conclude that:

$$\Delta H_3 = \Delta H_1 + \Delta H_2$$

The values are the same as both changes correspond to the combustion of two moles of carbon and three moles of hydrogen. The result is a consequence of the law of conservation of energy, otherwise it would be possible to devise cycles in which energy was created or destroyed (Figure 5.12). Consider a clockwise cycle in which carbon and hydrogen and oxygen are converted to ethanol and then carbon dioxide and water, which are then converted to the original elements.

Figure 5.11 In the clockwise route, the elements are first combined to form ethanol and then ethanol is burned. In the anticlockwise route, the elements are burned separately.

Figure 5.12 There is no net chemical change in a complete cycle as the starting reactants and final products are the same.

TOK

Hess's law is a natural consequence of the law of conservation of energy. If you know the law of conservation of energy, do you automatically know Hess's law?

Hess's law states that the enthalpy change for any chemical reaction is independent of the route, provided the starting conditions and final conditions, and reactants and products, are the same.

Figure 5.13 $\Delta H_1 + \Delta H_2 = \Delta H_3$, therefore $\Delta H_1 = \Delta H_3 - \Delta H_2$. Although ΔH_1 cannot be measured directly it can be calculated from the enthalpy of combustion of carbon, hydrogen, and propane.

Figure 5.14 Energy level diagram used to obtain the enthalpy of formation of propane indirectly.

Reversing the direction of a reaction reverses the sign of ΔH.

From the law of conservation of energy:

in Figure 5.12, the enthalpy change in a complete cycle = 0

$$= \Delta H_1 + \Delta H_2 - \Delta H_3$$

therefore $\Delta H_1 + \Delta H_2 = \Delta H_3$

This result can be generalized and is known as **Hess's law.**

Using Hess's law

Hess's law states that the enthalpy change for any chemical reaction is independent of the route provided the starting conditions and final conditions, and reactants and products, are the same.

The importance of Hess's law is that it allows us to calculate the enthalpy changes of reactions that we cannot measure directly in the laboratory. For example, although the elements carbon and hydrogen do not combine directly to form propane, C_3H_8, the enthalpy change for the reaction:

$$3C(\text{graphite}) + 4H_2(g) \rightarrow C_3H_8(g)$$

can be calculated from the enthalpy of combustion data of the elements and the compound (Figure 5.13).

The steps in an enthalpy cycle may be hypothetical and may refer to reactions that do not actually take place. The only requirement is that the individual chemical reactions in the sequence must balance. The relationship between the different reactions is clearly shown in an energy level diagram (Figure 5.14).

Worked example

$$S(s) + 1\tfrac{1}{2}O_2(g) \rightarrow SO_3(g) \qquad \Delta H^\ominus = -395\ \text{kJ} \qquad (1)$$

$$SO_2(g) + \tfrac{1}{2}O_2(g) \rightarrow SO_3(g) \qquad \Delta H^\ominus = -98\ \text{kJ} \qquad (2)$$

Calculate the standard enthalpy change, $\Delta H^\ominus$, for the reaction:

$$S(s) + O_2(g) \rightarrow SO_2(g)$$

Solution

We can think of the reaction as a journey from S(s) to $SO_2(g)$. As the standard enthalpy change cannot be measured directly, we must go by an alternative route suggested by the equations given.

Reaction 1 starts from the required starting point:

$$S(s) + 1\frac{1}{2}O_2(g) \rightarrow SO_3(g) \qquad \Delta H^\ominus = -395 \text{ kJ} \qquad (1)$$

Reaction 2 relates $SO_3(g)$ to $SO_2(g)$. To finish with the required product, we reverse the chemical change and the sign of enthalpy change:

$$SO_3(g) \rightarrow SO_2(g) + \frac{1}{2}O_2(g) \qquad \Delta H^\ominus = +98 \text{ kJ} \qquad (2)$$

We can now combine these equations:

$$S(s) + \frac{3}{2}O_2(g) + SO_3(g) \rightarrow SO_3(g) + SO_2(g) + \frac{1}{2}O_2(g) \qquad \Delta H^\ominus = -395 + 98 \text{ kJ}$$

Simplifying:

$$S(s) + \frac{2}{2}O_2(g) + \cancel{SO_3(g)} \rightarrow \cancel{SO_3(g)} + SO_2(g) + \cancel{\frac{1}{2}O_2(g)} \qquad \Delta H^\ominus = -297 \text{ kJ}$$

$$S(s) + O_2(g) \rightarrow SO_2(g) \qquad \Delta H^\ominus = -297 \text{ kJ}$$

> ! It is good practice always to give the sign (+ or −) for the values of ΔH. This includes giving endothermic reactions an explicitly positive value.

> The enthalpy change for the decomposition of metal carbonates can be determined by adding the metal carbonate and metal oxide to dilute acids using Hess's law.

Exercises

16 The diagram illustrates the enthalpy changes of a set of reactions.

Which of the following statements are correct?

I	P → S	$\Delta H = -10$ kJ
II	R → Q	$\Delta H = +90$ kJ
III	P → R	$\Delta H = +20$ kJ

  A I and II only   **B** I and III only   **C** II and III only   **D** I, II, and III

17 Calculate the enthalpy change, $\Delta H^\ominus$, for the reaction:

$$C(graphite) + \frac{1}{2}O_2(g) \rightarrow CO(g)$$

from the information below:

$$C(graphite) + O_2(g) \rightarrow CO_2(g) \qquad \Delta H^\ominus = -394 \text{ kJ}$$
$$CO(g) + \frac{1}{2}O_2(g) \rightarrow CO_2(g) \qquad \Delta H^\ominus = -283 \text{ kJ}$$

18 Calculate the enthalpy change, $\Delta H^\ominus$, for the reaction:

$$2NO(g) + O_2(g) \rightarrow 2NO_2(g)$$

from the information below:

$$N_2(g) + O_2(g) \rightarrow 2NO(g) \qquad \Delta H^\ominus = +180.5 \text{ kJ}$$
$$N_2(g) + 2O_2(g) \rightarrow 2NO_2(g) \qquad \Delta H^\ominus = +66.4 \text{ kJ}$$

19 Calculate the enthalpy change for the dimerization of nitrogen dioxide:

$$2NO_2(g) \rightarrow N_2O_4(g)$$

from the following data:

$$\tfrac{1}{2}N_2(g) + O_2(g) \rightarrow NO_2(g) \qquad \Delta H^\ominus = +33.2 \text{ kJ mol}^{-1}$$

$$N_2(g) + 2O_2(g) \rightarrow N_2O_4(g) \qquad \Delta H^\ominus = +9.16 \text{ kJ mol}^{-1}$$

20 The thermochemical equations for three related reactions are shown.

$$CO(g) + \tfrac{1}{2}O_2(g) \rightarrow CO_2(g) \qquad \Delta H_1 = -283 \text{ kJ mol}^{-1}$$

$$2H_2(g) + O_2(g) \rightarrow 2H_2O(l) \qquad \Delta H_2 = -572 \text{ kJ mol}^{-1}$$

$$CO_2(g) + H_2(g) \rightarrow CO(g) + H_2O(l) \qquad \Delta H_3$$

Determine ΔH_3

A $+289$ kJ mol^{-1} **B** -3 kJ mol^{-1} **C** -289 kJ mol^{-1} **D** -855 kJ mol^{-1}

Standard enthalpy changes of reaction

As discussed earlier, the enthalpy change of a reaction depends on the physical state of the reactants and the products and the conditions under which the reaction occurs. For this reason, **standard enthalpy changes**, $\Delta H^\ominus$, which are measured under standard conditions of 298 K (25 °C) and 1.00×10^5 Pa, are generally tabulated.

The **standard enthalpy change of formation**, $\Delta H_f^\ominus$, of a substance is the enthalpy change that occurs when one mole of the substance is formed from its elements in their standard states. These standard measurements are taken at a temperature of 298 K (25 °C) and a pressure of 1.00×10^5 Pa. They are important as they:

- give a measure of the stability of a substance relative to its elements;
- can be used to calculate the enthalpy changes of all reactions, either hypothetical or real.

Worked example

The enthalpy of formation of ethanol is given in section 12 of the IB data booklet. Give the thermochemical equation which represents the standard enthalpy of formation of ethanol.

Solution

The value from the IB data booklet = -278 kJ mol^{-1}

Ethanol (C_2H_5OH) is made from the elements carbon (C(graphite)) and hydrogen ($H_2(g)$) and oxygen ($O_2(g)$).

$$\_\_C(\text{graphite}) + \_\_H_2(g) + \_\_O_2(g) \rightarrow C_2H_5OH(l)$$

Balance the equation:

$$2C(\text{graphite}) + 3H_2(g) + \tfrac{1}{2}O_2(g) \rightarrow C_2H_5OH(l) \qquad \Delta H = -278 \text{ kJ mol}^{-1}$$

Note that as the enthalpy change of formation refers to one mole of product, there are fractional coefficients in the balanced equation.

Exercises

21 Which of the following does **not** have a standard heat of formation value of **zero** at 25 °C and 1.00×10^5 Pa?

A $Cl_2(g)$ **B** $I_2(s)$ **C** $Br_2(g)$ **D** $Na(s)$

22 Which of the following does **not** have a standard heat of formation value of **zero** at 25 °C and 1.00×10^5 Pa?

A $H(g)$ **B** $Hg(s)$ **C** $C(\text{diamond})$ **D** $Si(s)$

The standard enthalpy of formation of a substance is the enthalpy change that occurs when one mole of the substance is formed from its elements in their standard states under standard conditions of 298 K (25 °C) and 1.00×10^5 Pa.

Be careful with definitions of all key terms. Many students have difficulty defining standard enthalpy of formation – they refer to the energy required rather than enthalpy change and do not refer to the formation of one mole of substance in its standard state.

The standard enthalpy change of formation of an element in its most stable form is zero. There is no chemical change and so no enthalpy change when an element is formed from itself.

23 For which equation is the enthalpy change described as an enthalpy change of formation?

A $CuSO_4(aq) + Zn(s) \rightarrow ZnSO_4(aq) + Cu(s)$

B $Cu(s) + S(s) + 2O_2(g) \rightarrow CuSO_4(aq)$

C $5H_2O(l) + CuSO_4(s) \rightarrow CuSO_4.5H_2O(s)$

D $Cu(s) + S(s) + 2O_2(g) \rightarrow CuSO_4(s)$

24 (a) Write the thermochemical equation for the standard enthalpy of formation of propanone CH_3COCH_3.

(b) State the conditions under which standard enthalpy changes are measured.

Using standard enthalpy changes of formation

Standard enthalpy changes of formation can be used to calculate the standard enthalpy change of any reaction. Consider the general energy cycle in Figure 5.15.

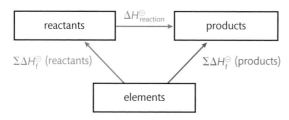

Figure 5.15 The chemical change elements → products can either occur directly or indirectly. The total enthalpy change must be the same for both routes. $\sum$ means 'the sum of'.

We have from the diagram:

$$\sum \Delta H_f^\ominus(\text{reactants}) + \Delta H_{\text{reaction}} = \sum \Delta H_f^\ominus(\text{products})$$

This gives the general expression for $\Delta H_{\text{reaction}}$ of any reaction

$$\Delta H_{\text{reaction}} = \sum \Delta H_f^\ominus(\text{products}) - \sum \Delta H_f^\ominus(\text{reactants})$$

Worked example

Calculate the enthalpy change for the reaction

$$C_3H_8(g) + 5O_2(g) \rightarrow 3CO_2(g) + 4H_2O(g)$$

from the following standard enthalpy changes of formation.

Substance	$\Delta H_f^\ominus$ / kJ mol^{-1}
$C_3H_8(g)$	−105
$CO_2(g)$	−394
$H_2O(l)$	−286

Solution

First, write down the equation with the corresponding enthalpies of formation underneath:

$$C_3H_8(g) \quad + \quad 5O_2(g) \quad \rightarrow \quad 3CO_2(g) \quad + \quad 4H_2O(g) \qquad \Delta H_f^\ominus / \text{kJ mol}^{-1}$$
$$-105 \qquad\qquad 0 \qquad\qquad 3(-394) \qquad 4(-286)$$

As the standard enthalpies of formation are given per mole they must be multiplied by the number of moles in the balanced equation, shown in red above.

Write down the general expression for the $\Delta H_{\text{reaction}}$

$$\Delta H_{\text{reaction}} = \sum \Delta H_f^\ominus(\text{products}) - \sum \Delta H_f^\ominus(\text{reactants})$$

$\Delta H_{\text{reaction}} =$
$\sum \Delta H_f^\ominus(\text{products}) -$
$\sum \Delta H_f^\ominus(\text{reactants})$

and express $\Delta H_{\text{reaction}}$ in terms of the data given:

$$\Delta H_{\text{reaction}}^{\ominus} = 3(-394) + 4(-286) - (-105)$$
$$= -2221 \text{ kJ mol}^{-1}$$

Exercises

25 Calculate $\Delta H^{\ominus}$ (in kJ mol^{-1}) for the reaction

$$Fe_3O_4(s) + 2C(graphite) \rightarrow 3Fe(s) + 2CO_2(g)$$

from the data below:

	$\Delta H_f^{\ominus}$ / kJ mol^{-1}
$Fe_3O_4(s)$	−1118
$CO_2(g)$	−394

26 Calculate $\Delta H^{\ominus}$ (in kJ mol^{-1}) for the reaction

$$2NO_2(g) \rightarrow N_2O_4(g)$$

from the data below:

	$\Delta H_f^{\ominus}$ / kJ mol^{-1}
$NO_2(g)$	+33.2
$N_2O_4(g)$	+9.2

27 Hydrogen peroxide slowly decomposes into water and oxygen:

$$2H_2O_2(l) \rightarrow 2H_2O(l) + O_2(g)$$

Calculate the enthalpy change of this reaction from the data table.

	$\Delta H_f^{\ominus}$ / kJ mol^{-1}
$H_2O_2(l)$	−188
$H_2O(l)$	−286

A +98 kJ mol^{-1} **B** −98 kJ mol^{-1} **C** +196 kJ mol^{-1} **D** −196 kJ mol^{-1}

28 Calculate the enthalpy change for the hypothetical reduction of magnesium oxide by carbon, according to the equation below from the data given. Comment on its feasibility.

$$2MgO(s) + C(s) \rightarrow CO_2(g) + 2Mg(s)$$

	$\Delta H_f^{\ominus}$ / kJ mol^{-1}
$CO_2(g)$	−394
$MgO(l)$	−602

5.3 Bond enthalpies

Understandings:

- Bond forming releases energy and bond breaking requires energy.
- Average bond enthalpy is the energy needed to break one mole of a bond in a gaseous molecule averaged over similar compounds.

Applications and skills:

- Calculation of the enthalpy changes from known bond enthalpy values and comparison of these to experimentally measured values.

Guidance
• *Bond enthalpy values are given in the IB data booklet in section 11.*
• *Average bond enthalpies are only valid for gases and calculations involving bond enthalpies may be inaccurate because they do not take into account intermolecular forces.*
• Sketching and evaluation of potential energy profiles in determining whether reactants or products are more stable and if the reaction is exothermic or endothermic.
• Discussion of the bond strength in ozone relative to oxygen in its importance to the atmosphere.

Chemical reactions involve the breaking and making of bonds. To understand the energy changes in a chemical reaction, we need to look at the energies needed to break the bonds that hold the atoms together in the reactants and the energy released when new bonds are formed in the products.

Breaking bonds is an endothermic process

A covalent bond is due to the electrostatic attraction between the shared pair of electrons and the positive nuclei of the bonded atoms. Energy is needed to separate the atoms in a bond.

The bond enthalpy is the energy needed to break one mole of bonds in gaseous molecules under standard conditions.

The energy change, for example, during the formation of two moles of chlorine atoms from one mole of chlorine molecules can be represented as:

$$Cl_2(g) \rightarrow 2Cl(g) \qquad \Delta H^\ominus = +242 \text{ kJ mol}^{-1}$$

The situation is complicated in molecules which contain more than two atoms. Breaking the first O—H bond in a water molecule requires more heat energy than breaking the second bond:

$$H_2O(g) \rightarrow H(g) + OH(g) \qquad \Delta H^\ominus = +502 \text{ kJ mol}^{-1}$$

$$OH(g) \rightarrow H(g) + O(g) \qquad \Delta H^\ominus = +427 \text{ kJ mol}^{-1}$$

Similarly the energy needed to break the O—H in other molecules such as ethanol, C_2H_5OH, is different. In order to compare bond enthalpies which exist in different environments, **average bond enthalpies** are tabulated.

Using Hess's law:

$$H_2O(g) \rightarrow H(g) + OH(g) \qquad \Delta H = +502 \text{ kJ mol}^{-1}$$

$$OH(g) \rightarrow H(g) + O(g) \qquad \Delta H = +427 \text{ kJ mol}^{-1}$$

Average bond enthalpy over numbers on right

$$H_2O(g) \rightarrow H(g) + OH(g) \qquad \Delta H = +502 + 427 \text{ kJ mol}^{-1}$$

$$\text{Average bond enthalpy } E(\text{O—H}) = \frac{+502 + 427}{2} \text{ kJ mol}^{-1}$$

$$= \frac{929}{2}$$

$$= 464.5 \text{ kJ mol}^{-1}$$

This value should be compared with the bond enthalpies given in the table on page 186 which are calculated from a wide range of molecules. Multiple bonds generally have higher bond enthalpies and shorter bond lengths than single bonds.

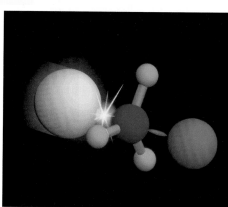

A chemical reaction involves the breaking and making of bonds. 500 to 1000 kJ of heat are typically needed to break one mole of chemical bonds. This image shows a change in the bond between the atoms represented by the yellow and the dark blue.

The average bond enthalpy is the energy needed to break one mole of bonds in gaseous molecules under standard conditions averaged over similar compounds.

Note carefully the definition of bond enthalpy. A common error is to fail to indicate that all the species have to be in the gaseous state.

Bond	E(X–Y) / kJ mol^{-1}	Bond length / 10^{-9} m
H—H	+436	0.074
C—C	+347	0.154
C=C	+614	0.134
C—H	+414	0.108
O=O	+498	0.121
O—H	+463	0.097
C=O	+804	0.122
Cl—Cl	+242	0.199

All bond enthalpies refer to reactions in the gaseous state so that the enthalpy changes caused by the formation and breaking of intermolecular forces can be ignored.

Making bonds is an exothermic process

The same amount of energy is absorbed when a bond is broken as is given out when a bond is made (Figure 5.16). For example:

$$H(g) + H(g) \rightarrow H_2(g)$$

$$\Delta H^\ominus = -436 \text{ kJ mol}^{-1}$$

Endothermic processes involve the separation of particles which are held together by a force of attraction.

Exothermic processes involve the bringing together of particles which have an attractive force between them.

Figure 5.16 The energy changes that occur when bonds are broken and bonds are formed.

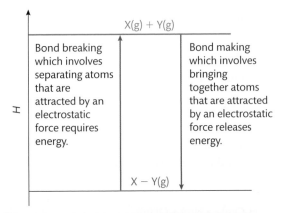

Worked example

Which of the following processes are endothermic?

A $2Cl(g) \rightarrow Cl_2(g)$

B $Na(g) \rightarrow Na^+(g) + e^-$

C $Na^+(g) + Cl^-(g) \rightarrow NaCl(s)$

D $Na(g) \rightarrow Na(s)$

Solution

Only one of the processes involves the separation of particles:

$$Na(g) \rightarrow Na^+(g) + e^-$$

In this case, a negatively charged electron is separated from a positive ion $Na^+(g)$.

Answer = B

29 Which of the following processes are endothermic?

I $H_2O(s) \rightarrow H_2O(g)$
II $CO_2(g) \rightarrow CO_2(s)$
III $O_2(g) \rightarrow 2O(g)$

  A I and II only   **B** I and III only   **C** II and III only   **D** I, II, and III

30 Identify the equation which represents the bond enthalpy for the H–Cl bond.

  A $HCl(g) \rightarrow H(g) + Cl(g)$
  B $HCl(g) \rightarrow \frac{1}{2}H_2(g) + \frac{1}{2}Cl_2(g)$
  C $HCl(g) \rightarrow H^+(g) + Cl^-(g)$
  D $HCl(aq) \rightarrow H^+(aq) + Cl^-(aq)$

31 Which of the following processes are endothermic?

I $CO_2(g) \rightarrow CO_2(s)$
II $H_2O(s) \rightarrow H_2O(g)$
III $O_2(g) \rightarrow 2O(g)$

  A I and II only   **B** I and III only   **C** II and III only   **D** I, II, and III

32 Identify the bonds which are broken in the following process.

$$C_2H_6(g) \rightarrow 2C(g) + 6H(g)$$

Using bond enthalpies to calculate the enthalpy changes of reaction

We are now in a position to understand how energy changes occur in chemical reactions. Consider, for example, the complete combustion of methane when we use a Bunsen burner:

$$\begin{array}{c} \quad\;\; H \\ \quad\;\; | \\ H\!-\!\!\overset{\displaystyle}{\underset{\displaystyle}{C}}\!-\!H + 2O\!=\!O \rightarrow O\!=\!C\!=\!O + 2H\!-\!O\!-\!H \\ \quad\;\; | \\ \quad\;\; H \end{array}$$

Energy is needed to break the C—H and O=O bonds in the reactants, but energy is given out when the C=O and O—H bonds are formed. The reaction is exothermic overall as the bonds which are formed are stronger than the bonds which are broken. A reaction is endothermic when the bonds broken are stronger than the bonds which are formed.

Worked example

Use bond enthalpies to calculate the heat of combustion of methane, the principal component of natural gas.

Solution

1 Write down the equation for the reaction showing all the bonds. This has already been done above.

2 Draw a table which shows the bonds which are broken and those that are formed during the reaction with the corresponding energy changes.

Bonds broken	ΔH / kJ mol^{-1} (endothermic)	Bonds formed	ΔH / kJ mol^{-1} (exothermic)
4 C—H	4 (+414)	2 C=O	2 (−804)
2 O=O	2 (+498)	4 O—H	4 (−463)
Total	= +2652		= −3460

$$\Delta H^{\ominus} = \sum E(\text{bonds broken}) - \sum E(\text{bonds formed})$$

$$\Delta H^{\ominus} = +2652 + (-3460) \text{ kJ mol}^{-1} = -808 \text{ kJ mol}^{-1}$$

The value calculated from the bond enthalpies should be compared with the experimental value of −891 kJ mol^{-1} measured under standard conditions given in section 13 of the IB data booklet. The values are different because the standard state of water is liquid and the bond enthalpy calculation assumes that the reaction occurs in the gaseous state. The use of average bond enthalpies is an additional approximation.

CHALLENGE YOURSELF

4 Compare the value of the enthalpy of combustion of methane obtained in the Worked example to that in section 13 of the IB data booklet and use Hess's law to estimate the strength of a hydrogen bond.

> Make sure that you select the correct values for the bond enthalpies. For example don't confuse C=C with C—C, and use the correct coefficients for the number of bonds broken and formed.

Exercises

33 Which of the following is equivalent to the bond enthalpy of the carbon–oxygen bond in carbon monoxide?

    A   CO(g) → C(s) + O(g)
    B   CO(g) → C(g) + O(g)
    C   CO(g) → C(s) + ½O$_2$(g)
    D   CO(g) → C(g) + ½O$_2$(g)

34 Use the bond enthalpies below to calculate $\Delta H^{\ominus}$ for the reaction:

$$H_2C=CH_2 + H_2 \rightarrow H_3C-CH_3$$

Bond	Bond enthalpy / kJ mol^{-1}
C—C	+347
C=C	+612
H—H	+436
C—H	+413

35 Use the bond enthalpies below to calculate $\Delta H^{\ominus}$ for the reaction:

$$2H_2(g) + O_2(g) \rightarrow 2H_2O(g)$$

Bond	Bond enthalpy / kJ mol^{-1}
O=O	+498
H—H	+436
O—H	+464

36 The hydrogenation of the alkene double bond in unsaturated oils is an important reaction in margarine production. Calculate the enthalpy change when one mole of C=C bonds is hydrogenated from the bond energy data shown.

Bond	Bond enthalpy / kJ mol^{-1}
H—H	436
C—C	347
C—H	412
C=C	612

    A −224 kJ mol^{-1} **B** −123 kJ mol^{-1} **C** +123 kJ mol^{-1} **D** +224 kJ mol^{-1}

37 Use the bond enthalpy data given to calculate the enthalpy change of reaction between methane and fluorine:

$$C_2H_4(g) + F_2(g) \rightarrow CH_2FCH_2F(g)$$

Bond	Bond enthalpy / kJ mol⁻¹
C—C	347
C=C	612
F—F	158
H—F	568
C—F	467

A +776   **B** +164   **C** −511   **D** −776

38 Use the bond enthalpies given in section 11 of the IB data booklet to estimate the enthalpy of combustion of ethanol and comment on the reliability of your result.

CHALLENGE YOURSELF

5 Suggest, based on the discussion of bonding and structure in Chapter 4, why graphite is more stable than diamond.

Ozone depletion

The Earth is unique among the planets in having an atmosphere that is chemically active and rich in oxygen. Oxygen is present in two forms, normal oxygen (O_2) and ozone (O_3), and both forms play a key role in protecting life on the Earth's surface from harmful ultraviolet (UV) radiation. They form a protective screen which ensures that radiation that reaches the surface of the Earth is different from that emitted by the Sun. O_2 and O_3 differ in their bonding as follows:

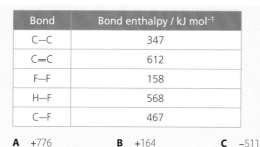

O_2; double bonds	O_3; the oxygen to oxygen bond is between a single bond and a double bond

Don't confuse the different methods of calculating enthalpy changes. A common error when using bond enthalpies is the reversal of the sign.

The correct expression is:

$\Delta H = \sum E(\text{bonds broken}) - \sum E(\text{bonds formed})$

This should be contrasted with the expression using standard enthalpies of formation:

$\Delta H_{\text{reaction}} = \sum \Delta H_f^{\ominus}(\text{products}) - \sum \Delta H_f^{\ominus}(\text{reactants})$

The bonds in oxygen and ozone are broken by UV of different wavelengths

The bonds in oxygen and ozone are both broken when they absorb UV radiation of sufficient energy. The double bond in O_2 is stronger than the 1.5 bond in ozone and so is broken by radiation of higher energy and shorter wavelengths.

The energy E_{photon} of a photon of light is related to its frequency v by Planck's equation (see Chapter 2):

$$E_{\text{photon}} = hv$$

The wavelength λ is related to the frequency: $v = c/\lambda$ where c is the speed of light. Substituting for v in Planck's equation:

$$E_{\text{photon}} = \frac{h \times c}{\lambda}$$

As oxygen has the strongest bond, shorter wavelength radiation is needed to break its bonds. The wavelengths of light needed to break the bonds in ozone are calculated in the following example.

Worked example

The bond energy in ozone is 363 kJ mol⁻¹. Calculate the wavelength of UV radiation needed to break the bond.

The depletion of the ozone layer is an important transdisciplinary topic.

Solution

One mole of photons are needed to break one mole of bonds. The energy of a mole of photons is the energy of one photon multiplied by Avogadro's number (L).

$$L \times E_{photon} = 363 \text{ kJ} = 363\,000 \text{ J}$$

$$E_{photon} = \frac{363\,000}{6.02 \times 10^{23}} \text{ J}$$

$$\lambda = \frac{hc}{E_{photon}}$$

$$= 6.63 \times 10^{-34} \text{ Js} \times 3.00 \times 10^{8} \text{ ms}^{-1} \times \frac{6.02 \times 10^{23}}{363\,000} \text{ J}^{-1}$$

$$= 3.30 \times 10^{-7} \text{ m}$$

$$= 330 \text{ nm}$$

Any radiation in the UV region with a wavelength smaller than 330 nm breaks the bond in ozone.

The natural formation and depletion of ozone

The temperature of the atmosphere generally decreases with height but at 12 km above the Earth's surface the temperature starts to rise because ultraviolet radiation is absorbed in a number of photochemical reactions.

In the stratosphere, the strong covalent double bond in normal oxygen O_2 is broken by high-energy UV radiation with a wavelength shorter than 242 nm to form two oxygen atoms:

$$O_2(g) \xrightarrow{\text{UV light, } \lambda < 242 \text{ nm}} O\bullet(g) + O\bullet(g) \text{(atomic oxygen)}$$

The oxygen atoms have unpaired electrons. They are reactive **free radicals** and so react with another oxygen molecule to form ozone.

$$O\bullet(g) + O_2(g) \rightarrow O_3(g)$$

This second step is *exothermic*; bonds are formed and the energy given out raises the temperature of the stratosphere.

As the bonds in ozone are weaker than the double bond in oxygen, ultraviolet light of lower energy is needed to break them:

$$O_3(g) \xrightarrow{\text{UV light, } \lambda < 330 \text{ nm}} O\bullet(g) + O_2(g)$$

The oxygen atoms then react with another ozone molecule to form two oxygen molecules.

$$O_3(g) + O\bullet(g) \rightarrow 2O_2(g)$$

As bonds are formed this is another exothermic reaction which produces heat that maintains the relatively high temperature of the stratosphere. The level of ozone in the stratosphere – less than 10 ppm – stays at a constant level if the rate of formation of ozone is balanced by its rate of removal. This is known as a **steady state**. The whole process is described by the Chapman Cycle.

A free radical is a species with an unpaired electron.

CHALLENGE YOURSELF

6 Explain why oxygen behaves as a free radical despite having an even number of electrons.

$$O_2 \xrightarrow[\substack{\text{high}\\\text{energy}\\\text{UV } \lambda < 242\text{nm}}]{\text{Step 1}} 2\,O^{\bullet}$$

$$O^{\bullet} + O_2 \underset{\substack{\text{Step 3}\\\text{lower}\\\text{energy}}}{\overset{\text{Step 2}}{\rightleftharpoons}} O_3$$

$$O_3 + O^{\bullet} \xrightarrow[\text{(slow)}]{\text{Step 4}} 2\,O_2$$

This cycle of reactions is significant because dangerous ultraviolet light has been absorbed and the stratosphere has become warmer. Both these processes are essential for the survival of life on Earth.

Technician releasing a balloon to measure stratospheric ozone over the Arctic. This research was part of a joint project by NASA and the European Union to look at the amount and rate of stratospheric ozone depletion.

Exercises

39 The concentration of ozone in the upper atmosphere is maintained by the following reactions.

I $\quad O_2 \rightarrow 2O\bullet$
II $\quad O_2 + O\bullet \rightarrow O_3$
III $\quad O_3 \rightarrow O_2 + O\bullet$

The presence of chlorofluorocarbons (CFCs) in the upper atmosphere has led to a reduction in ozone concentration.

(a) Identify the step which is exothermic.
(b) Identify with reference to the bonding in O_2 and O_3, the most endothermic step.

40 Use section 11 of the IB data booklet to calculate the minimum wavelength of radiation needed to break the O=O double bond in O_2.

41 Explain why ozone can be decomposed by light with a longer wavelength than that required to decompose oxygen.

Ozone depletion is a global political issue. Consider the following quote from Maneka Gandhi, former Indian Minister of the Environment and delegate to the *Montreal Protocol*. 'India recognizes the threat to the environment and the necessity for a global burden sharing to control it. But is it fair that the industrialized countries who are responsible for the ozone depletion should arm-twist the poorer nations into bearing the cost of their mistakes?'

Stratospheric ozone depletion is a particular concern in the polar regions of the planet, although the pollution that causes it comes from a variety of regions and sources. International action and cooperation have helped to ameliorate the ozone depletion problem.

Practice questions

1 A pure aluminium block with a mass of 10 g is heated so that its temperature increases from 20 °C to 50 °C. The specific heat capacity of aluminium is 8.99×10^{-1} J g⁻¹ K⁻¹. Which expression gives the heat energy change in kJ?

A $\quad 10 \times 8.99 \times 10^{-1} \times 303$

B $\quad 10 \times 8.99 \times 10^{-1} \times 30$

C $\quad \dfrac{10 \times 8.99 \times 10^{-1} \times 303}{1000}$

D $\quad \dfrac{10 \times 8.99 \times 10^{-1} \times 30}{1000}$

2 Which processes have a negative enthalpy change?

I $2CH_3OH(l) + 3O_2(g) \rightarrow 2CO_2(g) + 4H_2O(l)$

II $HCl(aq) + NaOH(aq) \rightarrow NaCl(aq) + H_2O(l)$

III $H_2O(g) \rightarrow H_2O(l)$

A I and II only   **B** I and III only   **C** II and III only   **D** I, II, and III

3 Identical pieces of magnesium are added to two beakers, A and B, containing hydrochloric acid. Both acids have the same initial temperature but their volumes and concentrations differ.

beaker A   beaker B

100 cm^3
$1.0 \text{ mol dm}^{-3} \text{ HCl(aq)}$

200 cm^3
$0.50 \text{ mol dm}^{-3} \text{ HCl(aq)}$

0.05 g Mg   0.05 g Mg

Which statement is correct?

A The maximum temperature in A will be higher than in B.

B The maximum temperature in A and B will be equal.

C It is not possible to predict whether A or B will have the higher maximum temperature.

D The temperature in A and B will increase at the same rate.

4 Consider the following reactions.

$$Cu_2O(s) + \tfrac{1}{2}O_2(g) \rightarrow 2CuO(s) \qquad\qquad \Delta H^{\ominus} = -144 \text{ kJ}$$

$$Cu_2O(s) \rightarrow Cu(s) + CuO(s) \qquad\qquad \Delta H^{\ominus} = +11 \text{ kJ}$$

What is the value of $\Delta H^{\ominus}$, in kJ, for this reaction?

$$Cu(s) + \tfrac{1}{2}O_2(g) \rightarrow CuO(s)$$

A $-144 + 11$ **B** $+144 - 11$ **C** $-144 - 11$ **D** $+144 + 11$

5 Which equation best represents the bond enthalpy of HCl?

A $HCl(g) \rightarrow H^+(g) + Cl^-(g)$ **C** $HCl(g) \rightarrow \tfrac{1}{2}H_2(g) + \tfrac{1}{2}Cl_2(g)$

B $HCl(g) \rightarrow H(g) + Cl(g)$ **D** $2HCl(g) \rightarrow H_2(g) + Cl_2(g)$

6 Consider the equations below.

$$CH_4(g) + O_2(g) \rightarrow HCHO(l) + H_2O(l) \qquad\qquad \Delta H^{\ominus} = x$$

$$HCHO(l) + \tfrac{1}{2}O_2(g) \rightarrow HCOOH(l) \qquad\qquad \Delta H^{\ominus} = y$$

$$2HCOOH(l) + \tfrac{1}{2}O_2(g) \rightarrow (COOH)_2(s) + H_2O(l) \qquad\qquad \Delta H^{\ominus} = z$$

What is the enthalpy change of the reaction below?

$$2CH_4(g) + 3\tfrac{1}{2}O_2(g) \rightarrow (COOH)_2(s) + 3H_2O(l)$$

A $x + y + z$ **B** $2x + y + z$ **C** $2x + 2y + z$ **D** $2x + 2y + 2z$

7 Which process represents the C–Cl bond enthalpy in tetrachloromethane?

A $CCl_4(g) \rightarrow C(g) + 4Cl(g)$ **C** $CCl_4(l) \rightarrow C(g) + 4Cl(g)$

B $CCl_4(g) \rightarrow CCl_3(g) + Cl(g)$ **D** $CCl_4(l) \rightarrow C(s) + 2Cl_2(g)$

8   What is the energy, in kJ, released when 1.00 mol of carbon monoxide is burned according to the following equation?

$$2CO(g) + O_2(g) \rightarrow 2CO_2(g) \qquad\qquad \Delta H^\ominus = -564 \text{ kJ}$$

A 141   **B** 282   **C** 564   **D** 1128

9   Methanol is made in large quantities as it is used in the production of polymers and in fuels. The enthalpy of combustion of methanol can be determined theoretically or experimentally.

$$CH_3OH(l) + 1\tfrac{1}{2}O_2(g) \rightarrow CO_2(g) + 2H_2O(g)$$

(a) Using the information from section 10 of the IB data booklet, determine the theoretical enthalpy of combustion of methanol.   (3)

(b) The enthalpy of combustion of methanol can also be determined experimentally in a school laboratory. A burner containing methanol was weighed and used to heat water in a test tube, as illustrated below.

The following data were collected.

Initial mass of burner and methanol / g	80.557
Final mass of burner and methanol / g	80.034
Mass of water in test tube / g	20.000
Initial temperature of water / °C	21.5
Final temperature of water / °C	26.4

(i)   Calculate the amount, in mol, of methanol burned.   (2)
(ii) Calculate the heat absorbed, in kJ, by the water.   (3)
(iii) Determine the enthalpy change, in kJ mol^{-1}, for the combustion of 1 mole of methanol. (2)

(c) The data booklet value for the enthalpy of combustion of methanol is −726 kJ mol⁻¹. Suggest why this value differs from the values calculated in parts (a) and (b).

    (i) Part (a)   (1)

    (ii) Part (b)   (1)

(Total 12 marks)

10 The data below are from an experiment to measure the enthalpy change for the reaction of aqueous copper(II) sulfate, $CuSO_4(aq)$, and zinc, $Zn(s)$.

$$Cu^{2+}(aq) + Zn(s) \rightarrow Cu(s) + Zn^{2+}(aq)$$

50.0 cm³ of 1.00 mol dm⁻³ copper(II) sulfate solution was placed in a polystyrene cup and zinc powder was added after 100 seconds. The temperature–time data were taken from a data-logging software program. The table shows the initial 23 readings.

	A	B	C	D	E	F	G	H
1	time/s	temperature/°C						
2	0.0	24.8						
3	1.0	24.8						
4	2.0	24.8						
5	3.0	24.8						
6	4.0	24.8						
7	5.0	24.8						
8	6.0	24.8						
9	7.0	24.8						
10	8.0	24.8						
11	9.0	24.8						
12	10.0	24.8						
13	11.0	24.8						
14	12.0	24.8						
15	13.0	24.8						
16	14.0	24.8						
17	15.0	24.8						
18	16.0	24.8						
19	17.0	24.8						
20	18.0	24.8						
21								
22								
23								
24								

linear fit for selected data
$T = -0.050t + 78/0$
T temperature
t time

A straight line has been drawn through some of the data points. The equation for this line is given by the data-logging software as

$$T = -0.050t + 78.0$$

where T is the temperature at time t.

(a) The heat produced by the reaction can be calculated from the temperature change, ΔT, using the expression below.

        heat change = volume of $CuSO_4(aq)$ × specific heat capacity of H_2O × ΔT

Describe **two** assumptions made in using this expression to calculate heat changes.   (2)

(b) (i) Use the data presented by the data-logging software to deduce the temperature change, ΔT, which would have occurred if the reaction had taken place instantaneously with no heat loss.   (2)

    (ii) State the assumption made in part (b)(i).   (1)

    (iii) Calculate the heat, in kJ, produced during the reaction using the expression given in part (a).   (1)

(c) The colour of the solution changed from blue to colourless. Deduce the amount, in moles, of zinc which reacted in the polystyrene cup.   (1)

(d) Calculate the enthalpy change, in kJ mol^{-1}, for this reaction. (1)

(Total 8 marks)

11 Two students were asked to use information from the IB data booklet to calculate a value for the enthalpy of hydrogenation of ethene to form ethane.

$$C_2H_4(g) + H_2(g) \rightarrow C_2H_6(g)$$

John used the average bond enthalpies from section 10. Marit used the values of enthalpies of combustion from section 12.

(a) Calculate the value for the enthalpy of hydrogenation of ethene obtained using the average bond enthalpies given in section 10. (2)

(b) Marit arranged the values she found in section 12 into an energy cycle.

Calculate the value for the enthalpy of hydrogenation of ethene from the energy cycle. (1)

(c) Suggest **one** reason why John's answer is slightly less accurate than Marit's answer. (1)

(d) John then decided to determine the enthalpy of hydrogenation of cyclohexene to produce cyclohexane.

$$C_6H_{10}(l) + H_2(g) \rightarrow C_6H_{12}(l)$$

(i) Use the average bond enthalpies to deduce a value for the enthalpy of hydrogenation of cyclohexene. (1)

(ii) The percentage difference between these two methods (average bond enthalpies and enthalpies of combustion) is greater for cyclohexene than it was for ethene. John's hypothesis was that it would be the same. Determine why the use of average bond enthalpies is less accurate for the cyclohexene equation shown above, than it was for ethene. Deduce what extra information is needed to provide a more accurate answer. (2)

(Total 7 marks)

12 Hydrazine is a valuable rocket fuel. The equation for the reaction between hydrazine and oxygen is given below.

$$N_2H_4(g) + O_2(g) \rightarrow N_2(g) + 2H_2O(g)$$

Use the bond enthalpy values from section 10 of the IB data booklet to determine the enthalpy change for this reaction.

(3)

13 The following reactions take place in the ozone layer by the absorption of ultraviolet light.

I $O_3 \rightarrow O_2 + O\bullet$

II $O_2 \rightarrow O\bullet + O\bullet$

State and explain, by reference to the bonding, which of the reactions, I or II, requires a shorter wavelength. (2)

 To access weblinks on the topics covered in this chapter, please go to www.pearsonhotlinks.com and enter the ISBN or title of this book.

06 Chemical kinetics

Essential ideas

6.1 The greater the probability that molecules will collide with sufficient energy and proper orientation, the higher the rate of reaction.

Copper is commonly used in roofing due to its durability; however, over time it reacts with oxygen and turns green. Scientists have found ways to both accelerate and slow down this reaction in order to get the desired appearance of the metal.

The word **kinetics**, derived from the Greek word *kinesis*, refers to movement. The word 'cinema' (kine-ma) has the same origin and is used to describe 'the movies'. Movement in chemistry refers to the progress of a reaction, so kinetics is the study of how fast a reaction goes.

Imagine you are cooking in the kitchen. As you drop an egg into hot fat in the pan it immediately changes to a white solid; meanwhile a container of milk that was left out of the refrigerator is slowly turning sour. We observe a similar wide variation in the rate of reactions that we study in the laboratory, and these data can very useful. Kinetic studies are of prime importance in industry because they give information on how quickly products form and on the conditions that give the most efficient and economic yield. They can also be useful in situations where we want to slow reactions down – for example, those that cause the destruction of ozone in the stratosphere, or the reactions where pollutants in the air combine to produce smog. At other times, it is important to know for how long a certain reaction will continue – for example, the radioactive effect from radioactive waste. Knowledge of reaction kinetics also gives insights into how reactions happen at the molecular level by suggesting a sequence of bond breaking and bond making, known as the **reaction mechanism**.

This chapter begins with a study of reaction rates and a consideration of how these are measured in different cases. Through the postulates of the **collision theory**, we will come to understand why different factors affect the rate of reactions, and then go on to develop mathematical equations to explore these relationships.

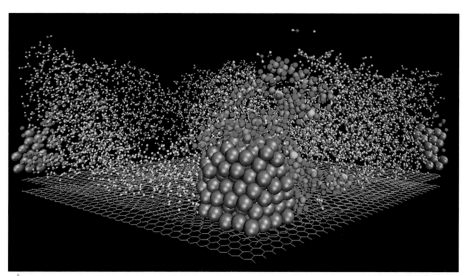

Computer simulation of fuel cell nanocatalysts. Platinum nanoparticles, shown in yellow, on a carbon substrate, shown as the green grid, are being investigated for their catalytic activity in fuel cell reactions. The red and white molecules are water, and the coloured chains are fragments of a polymer used in the proton exchange membranes. Research and development in fuel cell technology rely on an understanding of the factors that control reaction rates, including the action of catalysts.

Collision theory and rates of reaction

Understandings:

- Species react as a result of collisions of sufficient energy and proper orientation.
- The rate of reaction is expressed as the change in concentration of a particular reactant/product per unit time.
- Concentration changes in a reaction can be followed indirectly by monitoring changes in mass, volume, and colour.
- Activation energy (E_a) is the minimum energy that colliding molecules need in order to have successful collisions leading to a reaction.
- By decreasing E_a, a catalyst increases the rate of a chemical reaction, without itself being permanently chemically changed.

Applications and skills:

- Description of the kinetic theory in terms of the movement of particles whose average kinetic energy is proportional to temperature in kelvin.
- Analysis of graphical and numerical data from rate experiments.

  ### Guidance
  - *Calculation of reaction rates from tangents of graphs of concentration, volume, or mass vs time should be covered.*
  - *Students should be familiar with the interpretation of graphs of changes in concentration, volume, or mass against time.*

- Explanation of the effects of temperature, pressure/concentration, and particle size on rate of reaction.
- Construction of Maxwell–Boltzmann energy distribution curves to account for the probability of successful collisions and factors affecting these, including the effect of a catalyst.
- Investigation of rates of reaction experimentally and evaluation of the results.
- Sketching and explanation of energy profiles with and without catalysts.

Rate of reaction is defined as the rate of change in concentration

When we are interested in how quickly something happens, the factor that we usually measure is **time**. For example, in a sports race the competitors are judged by the time it takes them to reach the finishing line. However, if we want to compare their performance in different races over different distances, we would need to express this as a **rate** – in other words how they performed *per unit time*.

Rate takes the reciprocal value of time, so is expressed *per unit time* or in SI units *per second* (symbol = s^{-1}).

> Note that because time and rate are reciprocal values, as one increases, the other decreases. So in the example of a race, the racer with the *shortest time* wins the race because they had the *highest rate*.

$$\text{rate} = \frac{1}{\text{time}} = \frac{1}{s} = s^{-1}$$

In the study of chemical reactions we use the concept of **rate of reaction** to describe how quickly a reaction happens. As the reaction proceeds, reactants are converted into products, and so the concentration of reactants decreases as the concentration of products increases. The graphs in Figures 6.1 and 6.2 show sketches of typical data from reactions.

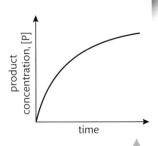

Figure 6.1 Concentration of product against time.

Figure 6.2 Concentration of reactant against time.

The rate of a reaction depends on how quickly the concentration of either reactant or product changes with respect to time. It can be defined as follows:

$$\text{rate of reaction} = \frac{\text{increase in product conc.}}{\text{time taken}} \quad \text{or} \quad \frac{\text{decrease in reactant conc.}}{\text{time taken}}$$

Using Δ to represent 'change in', $[R]$ for concentration of reactant and $[P]$ for concentration of product, we can express this as

$$\text{rate of reaction} = \frac{\Delta[P]}{\Delta t} \quad \text{or} \quad -\frac{\Delta[R]}{\Delta t}$$

The negative sign in the reactant expression indicates that reaction concentration is decreasing, but, by convention, rate is expressed as a positive value.

As rate = change in concentration per time, its units are **mol dm^{-3} s^{-1}**.

Figure 6.3 represents graphs of two different reactions showing the change in concentration of reactant against time. We can see that the concentration of reactants is decreasing more quickly in reaction A than in reaction B – the curve is steeper. The steepness, or gradient, of the curve is a measure of the change in concentration per unit time, in other words, the rate of the reaction.

Because the graphs are curves and not straight lines, the gradient is not constant and so can only be given for a particular value of time. We can measure this by drawing a tangent to the curve at the specified time point and measuring its gradient. This is shown in Figure 6.4 for the time point 120 seconds. Note that the gradient of this graph is negative as the reactant concentration is decreasing, but rate is expressed as a positive value.

The rate of a chemical reaction is the increase in concentration of products or the decrease in concentration of reactants per unit time.

Figure 6.3 Reactant concentration against time for two different reactions A and B.

Figure 6.4 Measuring the gradient of the tangent to the curve at an interval of time $t = 120$ seconds. The measured rate of the reaction is 8.48×10^{-3} mol dm^{-3} s^{-1} at this time.

Note the difference between the two instructions 'draw a graph' and 'sketch a graph'. *Drawing* is based on actual data so scales must be chosen appropriately and data points and units clearly marked; *sketching* is a way of showing a trend in the variables, without reference to specific data. Note that in both cases the axes must be clearly labelled with the dependent variable on the y-axis and the independent variable on the x-axis.

The shape of the curve indicates that the rate of the reaction is not constant during the reaction, but is greatest at the start and slows down as the reaction proceeds. This is illustrated in Figure 6.5, which shows the calculation of reaction rate at two different times during a reaction.

• $t = 0$ s rate $= 2.9 \times 10^{-2}$ mol dm^{-3} s^{-1}
• $t = 90$ s rate $= 7.2 \times 10^{-3}$ mol dm^{-3} s^{-1}

Figure 6.5 Measuring the gradient of the tangent to the curve at two different times during a reaction. The rate decreases as the reaction proceeds.

You will get a more accurate value for the slope of the tangent if you draw it as long as you reasonably can so that the 'y' value (concentration) and the 'x' value (time) are as large as possible.

The rate of a reaction is not constant during a reaction, but is greatest at the start and decreases as the reaction proceeds.

The rate is greatest at the start because this is when the reactant concentration is highest. The effect of concentration on reaction rate is discussed later in this chapter. Because of this variation in rate as a reaction proceeds, in order to compare the rates of reactions under different conditions it is common to compare the **initial rate** of each reaction by taking the tangent to the curve at $t = 0$. As we will see later in this chapter, initial rates data are very useful in analysing the effect of concentration on rate.

Measuring rates of reaction uses different techniques depending on the reaction

Choosing whether to measure the change in concentration of reactants or products, and the technique with which to measure that change really depends on what is the most convenient for a particular reaction. This is different for different reactions. In most cases the concentration is not measured directly, but is measured by means of a signal which is related to the changing concentration. If, for example, a reaction produces a coloured precipitate as product, the change in colour could be measured; if a reaction gives off a gas, then the change in volume or change in mass could be measured. The raw data collected using these 'signals' will be in a variety of units, rather than as concentrations measured in mol dm^{-3} directly. This is generally not a problem, as it still enables us to determine the rate of the reaction. Many of the experiments used here can be carried out using data-logging devices. Some examples of common techniques in relation to specific reactions are discussed in the following text.

TOK Note that the balanced equation of a reaction gives us no information about its rate. We can obtain this information only from experimental (empirical) data. Is there a fundamental difference between knowledge claims based on conclusions from theoretical data and those based on experimental data?

1 Change in volume of gas produced

This is a convenient method if one of the products is a gas. Collecting the gas and measuring the change in volume at regular time intervals enables a graph to be plotted of volume against time. A **gas syringe** can be used for this purpose. It consists of a ground glass barrel and plunger, which moves outwards as the gas collects and is calibrated to record the volume directly. Alternatively, the gas can be collected by displacement of water from an inverted burette. Note though that the displacement method can only be used if the gas collected has low solubility in water. Data loggers are also available for continuous monitoring of volume change against time. The rate of reaction of a metal with dilute acid to release hydrogen gas can be followed in this way.

$$Mg(s) + 2HCl(aq) \rightarrow MgCl_2(aq) + H_2(g)$$

Figure 6.6 Experiments to measure rate of reaction by following change in volume against time.

2 Change in mass

Many reactions involve a change in mass, and it may be convenient to measure this directly. If the reaction is giving off a gas, the corresponding decrease in mass can be measured by standing the reaction mixture directly on a balance. This method is unlikely to work well where the evolved gas is hydrogen, as it is too light to give significant changes in mass. The method allows for continuous readings, so a graph can be plotted directly of mass against time. For example, the release of carbon dioxide from the reaction between a carbonate and dilute acid can be followed in this way.

$$CaCO_3(s) + 2HCl(aq) \rightarrow CaCl_2(aq) + CO_2(g) + H_2O(l)$$

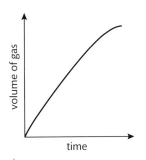

Figure 6.7 Volume of gas against time.

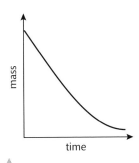

Figure 6.9 Mass against time.

Figure 6.8 Experiment to measure rate of reaction by following change in mass against time.

3 Change in transmission of light: colorimetry/spectrophotometry

This technique can be used if one of the reactants or products is coloured and so gives characteristic absorption in the visible region (wavelengths about 320–800 nm). Sometimes an indicator can be added to generate a coloured compound that can then be followed in the reaction. A colorimeter or spectrophotometer works by passing light of a selected wavelength through the solution being studied and measures the intensity of the light transmitted by the reaction components. As the concentration of the coloured compound increases, it absorbs proportionally more light, so less is transmitted. A photocell generates an electric current according to the amount of light transmitted and this is recorded on a meter or connected to a computer.

Figure 6.10 A spectrophotometer measures absorbance, which directly relates to concentration. Light of a specific wavelength is selected from an internal source and passes through the solution placed in the cuvette. The transmitted light passes through a diffraction grating, then the diffracted light is collected and changed into a digital signal by the CCD (charge-coupled device) detector.

The method allows for continuous readings to be made, so a graph of absorbance against time can be plotted directly. It is possible to convert the absorbance values into concentrations using a standard curve based on readings of known concentration. Often, however, it is sufficient to record absorbance itself (or transmittance, which is inversely proportional) as a function against time.

For example, the reaction between the dye crystal violet and sodium hydroxide solution can be written in an abbreviated form as follows.

$$CV^+ + OH^- \rightarrow CVOH$$

The initial crystal violet solution (CV^+) is coloured but this slowly changes to a colourless solution as the product (CVOH) is formed. So we can determine the rate of product formation by measuring the *decrease in absorbance* that occurs as the coloured reactant is depleted. The screen shot below shows data from this reaction, with absorbance at 591 nm measured against time.

Results of an experiment to determine the rate of reaction by following change in absorbance against time using a digital spectrophotometer.

4 Change in concentration measured using titration

In some reactions it may be possible to measure the concentration of one of the reactants or products by titrating it against a known 'standard' (see Chapter 1). However, because this technique involves chemically changing the reaction mixture, it cannot be done continuously as the reaction proceeds. Instead, samples must be withdrawn from the reaction mixture at regular time intervals and then analysed by titration. A problem here is that the process of titration takes time, during which the reaction mixture in the sample will continue to react. To overcome this, a technique known as **quenching** can be used, where a substance is introduced which effectively stops the reaction in the sample at the moment it is withdrawn. It is rather like obtaining a 'freeze frame' shot of the reaction at a particular interval of time. In order to see how concentration changes as the reaction proceeds, it is necessary to repeat this process at several intervals of time.

For example, the reaction between H_2O_2 and acidified KI yields I_2, which can be titrated against sodium thiosulfate, $Na_2S_2O_3$, to determine its concentration. Sodium carbonate, Na_2CO_3, is used to quench the reaction by neutralizing the added acid.

$$H_2O_2(aq) + 2H^+(aq) + 2I^-(aq) \rightarrow I_2(aq) + 2H_2O(l)$$

5 Change in concentration measured using conductivity

The total electrical conductivity of a solution depends on the total concentration of its ions and on their charges. If this changes when reactants are converted to products, it can provide a convenient method to follow the progress of the reaction. Conductivity can be measured directly using a conductivity meter which involves immersing inert electrodes in the solution. As with colorimetry, the apparatus can be calibrated using solutions of known concentration so that readings can be converted into the concentrations of the ions present.

For example, in the reaction:

$$BrO_3^-(aq) + 5Br^-(aq) + 6H^+(aq) \rightarrow 3Br_2(aq) + 3H_2O(l)$$

the sharp decrease in the concentration of ions (12 on the reactants side and 0 on the products side) will give a corresponding decrease in the electrical conductivity of the solution as the reaction proceeds.

6 Non-continuous methods of detecting change during a reaction: 'clock reactions'

Sometimes it is difficult to record the continuous change in the rate of a reaction. In these cases, it may be more convenient to measure the time it takes for a reaction to reach a certain chosen fixed point – that is, something observable which can be used as an arbitary 'end point' by which to stop the clock. The time taken to reach this point for the same reaction under different conditions can then be compared and used as a means of judging the different rates of the reaction. Note though the limitation of this method is that the data obtained give only an average rate over the time interval.

For example, the following can be measured:

• the time taken for a certain size of magnesium ribbon to react completely with dilute acid, until it is no longer visible

$$Mg(s) + 2HCl(aq) \rightarrow MgCl_2(aq) + H_2(g)$$

In all these reactions the goal is to measure change in concentration against time. This allows a comparison of reaction rates under different conditions. But because the rate is dependent on temperature, it is essential to control the temperature throughout these experiments. It is sometimes suitable to carry out the reactions in a thermostatically controlled water bath.

Experiments can be done to investigate the rate of reaction with changing reactant concentration, termperature, particle size, and catalyst. Full details of how to carry out an experiment on the effect of concentration, with a worksheet are available on your eBook.

Recording the increase in opaqueness during a reaction. Sodium thiosulfate (left) is a clear liquid, which reacts with hydrochloric acid (upper centre) to form an opaque solution (right). A cross (left) drawn onto paper is placed under the reaction beaker to allow the end point to be confirmed. The experiment is timed from when the reactants are mixed until the cross disappears from sight.

- the time taken for a solution of sodium thiosulfate with dilute acid to become opaque by the precipitation of sulfur, so that a cross viewed through the solution is no longer visible

$$Na_2S_2O_3(aq) + 2HCl(aq) \rightarrow$$
$$2NaCl(aq) + SO_2(aq) + H_2O(l) + S(s)$$

Exercises

1 Consider the following reaction:

$$2MnO_4^-(aq) + 5C_2O_4^{2-}(aq) + 16H^+(aq) \rightarrow 2Mn^{2+}(aq) + 10CO_2(g) + 8H_2O(l)$$

Describe three different ways in which you could measure the rate of this reaction.

2 Which units are used to express the rate of a reaction?

   A mol dm^{-3} time   **B** mol^{-1} dm^3 time^{-1} **C** mol dm^{-3} time^{-1} **D** mol time^{-1}

3 The reaction between calcium carbonate and hydrochloric acid is carried out in an open flask. Measurements are made to determine the rate of the reaction.

$$CaCO_3(s) + 2HCl(aq) \rightarrow CaCl_2(aq) + H_2O(l) + CO_2(g)$$

  (a) Suggest three different types of data that could be collected to measure the rate of this reaction.
  (b) Explain how you would expect the rate of the reaction to change with time and why.

4 The following data were collected for the reaction

$$2H_2O_2(aq) \rightarrow 2H_2O(l) + O_2(g) \text{ at } 390\ °C$$

[H$_2$O$_2$] / mol dm^{-3}	Time / s	[H$_2$O$_2$] / mol dm^{-3}	Time / s
0.200	0	0.070	120
0.153	20	0.063	140
0.124	40	0.058	160
0.104	60	0.053	180
0.090	80	0.049	200
0.079	100		

Draw a graph of concentration against time and determine the reaction rate after 60 s and after 120 s.

TOK

The Kelvin scale of temperature gives a natural measure of the kinetic energy of gas, whereas the Celsius scale is based on the properties of water. Are physical properties such as temperature invented or discovered?

Collision theory

Kinetic energy and temperature

Since the early 18th century, theories have been developed to explain the fact that gases exert a pressure. These theories developed alongside a growing understanding of the atomic and molecular nature of matter, and were extended to include the behaviour of particles in all states of matter. Today they are summarized as the **kinetic-molecular theory of matter** (see Chapter 1).

The essence of kinetic molecular theory is that particles in a substance move randomly as a result of the **kinetic energy** that they possess. Because of the random nature of these movements and collisions, not all particles in a substance at any one time have the same values of kinetic energy, but will have instead a range of values. A convenient way to describe the kinetic energy of a substance is therefore to take the *average* of these values, and this is directly related to its **absolute temperature** – that is, its temperature measured in kelvin.

Increasing temperature therefore means an increase in the average kinetic energy of the particles of a substance. As we supply a substance with extra energy through heating it, we raise the average kinetic energy of the particles and so also raise its temperature. When we compare the behaviour of the particles in the three states of matter from solid, through liquid, to gas, the differences are a result of this increase in the average kinetic energy of the particles, as described on page 9.

For a given substance this can be summarized as follows:

Solid   Liquid   Gas

→ increasing kinetic energy

→ increasing temperature

Temperature in kelvin (K) is proportional to the average kinetic energy of the particles in a substance.

There is more heat in an iceberg than in a cup of boiling coffee.

As heat is a form of energy, the total heat in the iceberg will be the sum of all the energy of all its particles. The iceberg's *temperature* is of course much lower than that of the cup of coffee, which means its particles have, on average, much lower kinetic energy. But because there are vastly more particles in the iceberg than the cup of coffee, its *total* energy is greater.

The Maxwell–Boltzmann distribution curve

The fact that particles in a gas at a particular temperature show a range in their values of kinetic energy is expressed by the **Maxwell–Boltzmann distribution curve**.

Like other distribution curves, this shows the number having a particular value, in this case of particles with a particular value of kinetic energy (or the probability of that value occurring) plotted against the values for kinetic energy. The area under the curve represents the total number of particles in the sample.

Figure 6.11 The Maxwell–Boltzmann distribution curve.

Figure 6.12 Particles react by colliding.

Although their names are linked in the famous energy distribution curve discussed here, James Clerk Maxwell and Ludwig Boltzmann were two people with very different outlooks on life. Maxwell was a Scottish physicist, known for his insatiable curiosity and overflowing humour. His wife worked alongside him in many of his experiments. Boltzmann, an Austrian, was prone to depression and eventually took his own life while on a family holiday, seemingly believing that his work was not valued. Nonetheless as peers during the 19th century, both seeking to explain the observed properties of gases, they refined and developed each other's ideas, culminating in the distribution curve that bears their two names.

How reactions happen

When reactants are placed together, the kinetic energy that their particles possess causes them to collide with each other. The energy of these collisions may result in some bonds between the reactants being broken, and some new bonds forming. As a result, products form and the reaction 'happens'.

It follows that the rate of the reaction will depend on the number of collisions between particles which are 'successful', that is, which lead to the formation of products. But a very important point is that *not all collisions will be successful*. There are two main factors that influence this:

• energy of collision; and
• geometry of collision.

i Energy of collision

In order for a collision to lead to reaction, the particles must have a certain minimum value for their kinetic energy, known as the **activation energy**, E_a. This energy is necessary for overcoming repulsion between molecules, and often for breaking some bonds in the reactants before they can react. When this energy is supplied, the reactants achieve the **transition state** from which products can form. The activation energy therefore represents an energy barrier for the reaction, and it has a different value in different reactions.

> Activation energy (E_a) is defined as the minimum value of kinetic energy which particles must have before they are able to react.

Figure 6.13 Energy path of a reaction with the activation energy for (a) endothermic and (b) exothermic reactions. ✱ represents the transition state.

We can think of the activation energy as a 'threshold value' – a bit like a pass mark in an examination: values greater than this mark achieve a pass, lower values do not achieve a pass. The activation energy threshold similarly determines which particles react and which do not. So only particles that have a kinetic energy value greater than the activation energy will have successful collisions. Note that particles with lower values of kinetic energy may still collide, but these collisions will not be 'successful' in the sense of causing a reaction.

It therefore follows that the rate of the reaction depends on the proportion of particles that have values for kinetic energy greater than the activation energy.

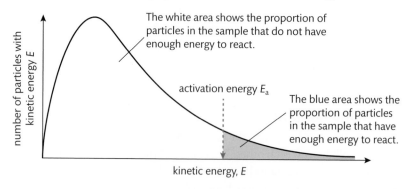

Figure 6.14 Maxwell–Bolzmann distribution showing how the activation energy, E_a, distinguishes between particles which have greater or lesser values of kinetic energy.

The magnitude of the activation energy varies greatly fom one reaction to another, and is an important factor in determining the overall rate of the reaction. In general, reactions with high activation energy proceed more slowly than those with low activation energy.

ii Geometry of collision

Because collisions between particles are random, they are likely to occur with the particles in many different orientations. In some reactions this can be crucial in determining whether or not the collisions will be successful, and therefore what proportion of collisions will lead to a reaction.

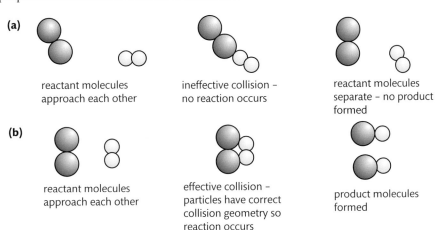

(a)

reactant molecules
approach each other

ineffective collision –
no reaction occurs

reactant molecules
separate – no product
formed

(b)

reactant molecules
approach each other

effective collision –
particles have correct
collision geometry so
reaction occurs

product molecules
formed

Figure 6.15 The effect of collision geometry. In (a) the particles do not have the correct collision geometry and no reaction occurs. In (b) the particles collide with the correct geometry, enabling products to form.

Summary

The rate of a reaction depends on the frequency of collisions which occur between particles possessing both:

• values of kinetic energy greater than the activation energy; and
• appropriate collision geometry.

Understanding this theory will help us to investigate and explain the factors that influence the rate of reaction.

In order to react, particles must collide with kinetic energy greater than the activation energy and have the correct collision geometry.

Exercises

5 Which statement is correct for a collison between reactant particles that leads to reaction?

    A Colliding particles must have different energy.
    B Colliding particles must have the same energy.
    C Colliding particles must have kinetic energy greater than the average kinetic energy.
    D Colliding particles must have kinetic energy greater than the activation energy.

6 Which of the following determine whether a reaction will occur?

    I   the orientation of the molecules
    II the energy of the molecules
    III the volume of the container

    A I and II   **B** I and III   **C** II only   **D** I, II, and III

7 If we compare two reactions, one which requires the simultaneous collision of three molecules and the other which requires a collision between two molecules, which reaction would you expect to be faster? Explain why.

The collision between a small number of reacting species resulting in chemical change has not been observed directly. Instead, collision theory is based on an application of kinetic molecular theory and theory of how chemical reactions occur through bond breaking and bond making. In science, theories generally accommodate the assumptions and premises of other theories in this way. The fact that collision theory helps to explain the observed effects of factors influencing the rate of reactions adds to its validity. The theory enables chemists to make predictions about the impact of different factors on the rates of specific reactions, which has important applications in many branches of chemistry such as industry, biochemistry, and environmental chemistry.

Be careful not to confuse the question of 'how fast?' a reaction goes with the question of 'how far?' it goes. We are discussing only the first question here. The question of how far a reaction goes, which influences the *yield* of the reaction, will be discussed in Chapter 7, Equilibrium.

Factors affecting rate of reaction

From the collision theory we know that any factor which increases the number of successful collisions will increase the rate of the reaction. We will investigate five such factors here.

1 Temperature

Increasing the temperature causes an increase in the average kinetic energy of the particles. We can see this by comparing Maxwell–Boltzmann distribution curves of the same sample of particles at two different temperatures.

Figure 6.16 Maxwell–Boltzmann distribution curves for a sample of gas at 300 K and 310 K. At the higher temperature the curve has shifted to the right and become broader, showing a larger number of particles with higher values for kinetic energy.

The area under the two curves is equal as this represents the total number of particles in the sample. But at the higher temperature, more of the particles have higher values for kinetic energy and the peak of the curve shifts to the right. In Figure 6.17, we can see how this shift increases the proportion of particles that have values for kinetic energy greater than that of the activation energy.

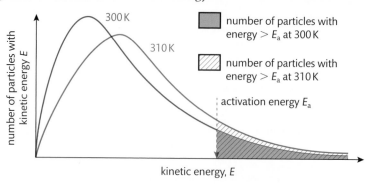

Figure 6.17 Maxwell–Boltzmann distribution curves for a sample of gas at two different temperatures, showing the higher proportion of particles with kinetic energy greater than the activation energy at the higher temperature.

So, as temperature increases, there is an increase in collision frequency due to the higher kinetic energy, but more importantly there is an increase in the frequency of collisions involving particles with the necessary activation energy to overcome the activation energy barrier. Consequently, there is an increase in the frequency of *successful* collisions

Specimens of the extinct mammal the mammoth, dated as 10 000 years old, have been found perfectly preserved in the Arctic ice, whereas individual specimens of a similar age found in California, have only bones that remain. This is an illustration of the effect of the low temperature in the Arctic decreasing the rate of the reactions of decay. The same concept is used in the process of refrigerating or freezing food to preserve it.

Figure 6.18 Effect of concentration on collision frequency.

and so an increase in the rate of reaction. Many reactions double their reaction rate for every 10 °C increase in temperature.

2 Concentration

Increasing the concentration of reactants increases the rate of reaction. This is because as concentration increases, the frequency of collisions between reactant particles increases, as shown in Figure 6.18. The frequency of successful collisions therefore increases too.

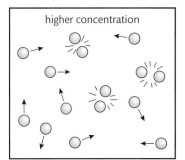

| low concentration | higher concentration |

When particles are closer together they have a greater chance of reacting.

We can see the effect of concentration by following the rate of a reaction as it progresses. As reactants are used up, their concentration falls and the rate of the reaction decreases, giving the typical rate curve we saw in Figure 6.2.

3 Particle size

Decreasing the particle size increases the rate of reaction. This is important in heterogeneous reactions where the reactants are in different phases, such as a solid reacting with a solution. Subdividing a large particle into smaller parts increases the total surface area and therefore allows more contact and a higher probability of collisions between the reactants. You know, for example, how much easier it is to start a fire using small pieces of wood, rather than a large log – it's because with the small pieces there is more contact between the wood and the oxygen with which it is reacting. In reactions involving dispersions, stirring may help to decrease particle size and so increase the rate.

The effect of particle size can be demonstrated in the reaction between marble ($CaCO_3$) and hydrochloric acid. When marble chips are replaced with powder, the effervescence caused by carbon dioxide release is much more vigorous.

This effect of particle size on reaction rate can be quite dramatic. It has been responsible for many industrial accidents involving explosions of flammable dust powders – for example coal dust in mines and flour in mills.

The effect of concentration on the rate of reaction between zinc and sulfuric acid. The tube on the left has a more concentrated solution of the acid, the one on the right a more dilute solution. The product, hydrogen gas, is seen collecting much more quickly in the presence of the more concentrated acid.

Milk powder dropped on a flame. As milk powder is dropped onto a flame the fine particles expose a huge surface area to the flame, leading to very fast burning.

4 Pressure

For reactions involving gases, increasing pressure increases the rate of reaction. This is because the higher pressure compresses the gas, effectively increasing its concentration. This will increase the frequency of collisions.

5 Catalyst

A catalyst is a substance that increases the rate of a chemical reaction without itself undergoing permanent chemical change. Most catalysts work by providing an alternate route for the reaction that has a lower activation energy.

Figure 6.19 Effect of a catalyst on lowering the activation energy of a reaction.

This means that without increasing the temperature, a larger number of particles will now have values of kinetic energy greater than the activation energy, and so will be able to undergo successful collisions. Think again of activation energy as being like the pass mark in an examination: the effect of the catalyst is like lowering the pass mark. This means that with the same work in the tests, a higher number of people would be able to achieve a pass!

Figure 6.20 uses the Maxwell–Boltzmann distribution to show how a catalyst increases the proportion of particles having values of kinetic energy greater than the activation energy.

Figure 6.20 Effect of catalyst on increasing the proportion of particles able to react.

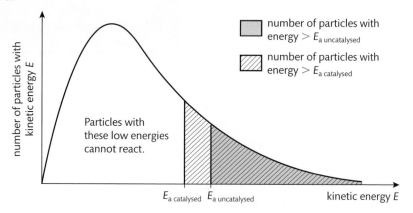

Catalysts bring about an equal reduction in the activation energy of both the forward and the reverse reactions, so they do not change the position of equilibrium or the yield (Chapter 7). However, because of their ability to increase the rate of reactions, they influence the rate of formation of product and so play an essential role in the efficiency of many industrial processes. Without catalysts, many reactions would proceed too slowly, or would have to be conducted at such high temperatures that they would simply not be worthwhile. This is why the discovery of the 'best' catalyst for a particular reaction is a very active area of research, and often the exact specification of a catalyst used in an industrial process is a matter of secrecy.

A catalyst is a substance that increases the rate of a chemical reaction without itself undergoing permanent chemical change.

Every biological reaction is controlled by a catalyst, known as an **enzyme**. Thousands of different enzymes exist as they are each specific for a particular biochemical reaction. Enzymes are finding increasingly widespread uses in many domestic and industrial processes, from biological detergents to acting as 'biosensors' in medical studies. Some of these applications, like cheese making, are centuries old, but others are developing rapidly, constituting the field known as **biotechnology**. Enzyme kinetics is discussed further in Chapter 13, Option B: Biochemistry.

Catalysis is also an important aspect of Green Chemistry, which seeks to reduce the negative impact of chemical processes on the environment. Catalysts can replace stoichiometric reagents, and can greatly enhance the selectivity of processes. As they are effective in very small quantities and can frequently be reused, catalysts do not contribute to the chemical waste, and so they increase the atom economy.

Exercises

8 Which of the following statements is correct?

  A A catalyst increases the rate of the forward reaction only.
  B A catalyst increases the rate of the forward and backward reactions.
  C A catalyst increases the yield of product formed.
  D A catalyst increases the activation energy of a reaction.

9 Which statements are correct for the effects of catalyst and temperature on the rate of reaction?

	Adding a catalyst	Increasing the temperature
A	collision frequency increases	collision frequency increases
B	activation energy decreases	collision frequency increases
C	collision frequency increases	activation energy increases
D	activation energy increases	activation energy decreases

10 In the reaction between marble (calcium carbonate) and hydrochloric acid, which set of conditions would give the highest rate of reaction?

$$CaCO_3(s) + 2HCl \rightarrow CaCl_2(aq) + CO_2(g) + H_2O(l)$$

  A marble chips and 1.0 mol dm^{-3} HCl
  B marble powder and 1.0 mol dm^{-3} HCl
  C marble chips and 0.1 mol dm^{-3} HCl
  D marble powder and 0.1 mol dm^{-3} HCl

11 A sugar cube cannot be ignited with a match, but a sugar cube coated in ashes will ignite. Suggest a reason for this observation.

12 Catalytic converters are now used in most cars to convert some components of exhaust gases into less environmentally damaging molecules. One of these reactions converts carbon monoxide and nitrogen monoxide into carbon dioxide and nitrogen. The catalyst usually consists of metals such as platinum or rhodium.

(a) Write an equation for this reaction.

(b) Explain why it is important to reduce the concentrations of carbon monoxide and nitrogen monoxide released into the atmosphere.

(c) Why do you think the converter sometimes consists of small ceramic beads coated with the catalyst?

(d) Suggest why the converter usually does not work effectively until the car engine has warmed up.

(e) Discuss whether the use of catalytic converters in cars solves the problem of car pollution.

Practice questions

1 Curve X on the graph below shows the volume of oxygen formed during the catalytic decomposition of a 1.0 mol dm^{-3} solution of hydrogen peroxide:

$$2H_2O_2(aq) \rightarrow O_2(g) + 2H_2O(l)$$

Which change would produce the curve Y?

A adding water

B adding some 0.1 mol dm^{-3} hydrogen peroxide solution

C using a different catalyst

D lowering the temperature

2 Which changes increase the rate of the reaction below?

$$C_4H_{10}(g) + Cl_2(g) \rightarrow C_4H_9Cl(l) + HCl(g)$$

I   increase of pressure

II   increase of temperature

III removal of HCl(g)

A I and II only   **B** I and III only   **C** II and III only   **D** I, II, and III

3 Which experimental procedure could be used to determine the rate of reaction for the reaction between a solution of cobalt chloride, CoCl$_2$(aq), and concentrated hydrochloric acid, HCl(aq)?

$$Co(H_2O)_6^{2+}(aq) + 4Cl^-(aq) \rightleftharpoons CoCl_4^{2-}(aq) + 6H_2O(l)$$

A measure the change in pH in a given time

B measure the change in mass in a given time

C use a colorimeter to measure the change in colour in a given time

D measure the change in volume of the solution in a given time

4 Powdered manganese(IV) oxide, MnO$_2$(s), increases the rate of the decomposition reaction of hydrogen peroxide, H$_2$O$_2$(aq). Which statements about MnO$_2$ are correct?

I   The rate is independent of the particle size of MnO$_2$.

II MnO$_2$ provides an alternative reaction pathway for the decomposition with a lower activation energy.

III All the MnO$_2$ is present after the decomposition of the hydrogen peroxide is complete.

A I and II only   **B** I and III only   **C** II and III only   **D** I, II, and III

5 Which of the following statements is **incorrect**?

    A The rate of a chemical reaction depends on the temperature.

    B Rate and time are directly proportional.

    C The rate of most chemical reactions decreases with time.

    D A catalyst for a reaction increases the rate of both its forward and backward reactions.

6 A student measures the rate of a reaction by timing the appearance of a precipitate that forms in aqueous solution. Which of the following factors would increase the time required for the precipitate to form?

    A raising the temperature

    B adding a catalyst

    C diluting the solution

    D stirring the reaction mixture

Questions 7–9 refer to the reaction between magnesium carbonate and hydrochloric acid, which is as follows:

$$MgCO_3(s) + 2HCl(aq) \rightarrow MgCl_2(aq) + H_2O(l) + CO_2(g)$$

7 Which of the conditions described below will produce the fastest rate of reaction?

    A 2.0 mol dm^{-3} HCl and MgCO$_3$ lumps

    B 1.0 mol dm^{-3} HCl and MgCO$_3$ powder

    C 2.0 mol dm^{-3} HCl and MgCO$_3$ powder

    D 1.0 mol dm^{-3} HCl and MgCO$_3$ lumps

8 Which of the following measurements would **not** be a suitable means to follow the rate of this reaction?

    A increase in mass

    B increase in volume at constant pressure

    C decrease in pH

    D increase in pressure at constant volume

9 The sketch graph below represents the result of an experiment to measure the rate of this reaction.

Which of the following is the best explanation for the shape of the graph?

    A The rate of the reaction increases with time because the acid becomes more dilute.

    B The rate of the reaction increases with time because the calcium carbonate pieces become smaller.

C The rate of the reaction decreases with time because the acid becomes more dilute.

D The rate of the reaction decreases with time because the calcium carbonate pieces become smaller.

10 Collision theory states that collisions between reactant molecules do not always lead to the formation of product. Which of the following is the best explanation for this statement?

A The reactant molecules are at too low a concentration.

B The reaction is at equilibrium.

C The reaction needs a catalyst in order to occur.

D The reactant molecules do not have sufficient energy.

11 It is found that in the reaction:

$$NO_2(g) + CO(g) \rightarrow NO(g) + CO_2(g)$$

an increase in temperature increases the rate of the reaction. Which of the statements below is the **main** reason for this?

A The molecules collide more frequently.

B The proportion of molecules with energy greater than the activation energy increases.

C The pressure exerted by the molecules increases.

D The proportion of the molecules with the correct collision geometry increases.

12 Zinc metal reacts with copper(II) sulfate solution as follows:

$$Zn(s) + CuSO_4(aq) \rightarrow Cu(s) + ZnSO_4(aq)$$

Which of the following factors will increase the rate of this reaction?

I increasing the concentration of $CuSO_4(aq)$

II decreasing the size of the zinc pieces

III carrying out the reaction at a higher temperature

A I and II   **B** I and III   **C** II only   **D** I, II, and III

13 Which of the following units could **not** be used to express the rate of a reaction?

A $mol\ dm^{-3}\ s$ **B** $g\ cm^{-3}\ s^{-1}$ **C** $mol\ dm^{-3}\ s^{-1}$ **C** $g\ dm^{-3}\ s^{-1}$

14 The atmosphere consists mostly of nitrogen, N_2 gas and oxygen, O_2 gas. Under normal conditions these two gases react together to form nitrogen oxide, NO, extremely slowly.

$$N_2(g) + O_2(g) \rightarrow 2NO(g)$$

Which statement below is the best explanation for the low rate of this reaction?

A The atmosphere does not contain a catalyst for this reaction.

B The reaction between nitrogen and oxygen has a very high activation energy.

C Oxygen molecules are more likely to collide with themselves than with nitrogen molecules.

D The simultaneous collision of three molecules is unlikely.

15 The graph below was obtained when zinc carbonate reacted with dilute hydrochloric acid under two different conditions, denoted as experiments A and B.

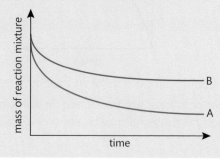

(a) Write an equation including state symbols for the reaction occurring. (2)

(b) Explain why the mass of the reaction mixture decreases in both cases. (1)

(c) Make reference to collision theory to explain the shape of curve A. (3)

(d) Describe the measurements that could be made from the graph to compare the initial rates of the reactions in A and B. Comment on the results expected. (3)

(e) The concentration of hydrochloric acid used in experiments A and B was the same. Suggest three possible differences in the conditions of experiments A and B. (3)

(f) For each of the conditions given in (d), explain why it would affect the rate of the reaction. (6)

(g) The experiment was repeated using zinc metal in place of zinc carbonate.

$$Zn(s) + 2HCl(aq) \rightarrow ZnCl_2(aq) + H_2(g)$$

Describe the differences you would expect in the results, and evaluate whether this is likely to be a satisfactory method for following the rate of the reaction. (2)

(Total 20 marks)

16 The figure below shows a Maxwell–Boltzmann distribution curve for a sample of a gas at two different temperatures, T1 and T2.

(a) Deduce the relative values of T1 and T2. (1)

(b) Make reference to your answer to (a) to explain the differences in the shape of the two graphs. (2)

(c) 'A catalyst provides a reaction route with a lower activation energy, and so increases the rate of reaction.'

Justify this statement by means of a suitably labelled Maxwell–Boltzmann distribution curve, showing the proportion of reacting particles with and without a catalyst. (4)

(d) Explain why catalysts increase the rate of a reaction but have no effect on:
(i) the enthalpy change
(ii) the stoichiometric yield of product (4)

(Total 11 marks)

To access weblinks on the topics covered in this chapter, please go to www.pearsonhotlinks.com and enter the ISBN or title of this book.

07

Equilibrium

Essential ideas

Many reactions are reversible. These reactions will reach a state of equilibrium when the rates of the forward reaction and reverse reaction are equal. The position of equilibrium can be controlled by changing the conditions.

Electron micrograph of a section through human lung tissue, showing air spaces called alveoli. Equilibrium considerations help us to understand how oxygen and carbon dioxide are exchanged between the blood and the air in these spaces.

Imagine that you are part way along an escalator (a moving staircase) that is moving up and you decide to run down. If you can run down at exactly the same speed as the escalator is moving up, you will have no *net* movement. So, if someone were to take a picture of you at regular time intervals, it would seem as if you were not moving at all. Of course, in reality both you and the escalator *are* moving, but because there is no net change neither movement is observable. In chemical reactions a similar phenomenon occurs when a reaction takes place at the same rate as its reverse reaction, so no net change is observed. This is known as the **equilibrium state**.

In this chapter, we explore some of the features of the equilibrium state and learn how to derive and use the equilibrium constant expression. Application of the **equilibrium law** enables us to quantify reaction components and to predict how far reactions will proceed under different conditions. Industrial processes rely significantly on this type of study to determine the conditions that will maximise the yield of product. Equilibrium studies are also important in many biochemical and environmental processes, such as predicting the solubility of gases in the blood and knowing how certain chemicals in the atmosphere may react together to form pollutants that contribute to climate change. By the end of this chapter, you will be ready to tackle some of these applications in subsequent chapters.

Snow and ice-covered peak in the Cordillera Huayhuash, Peru. Equilibrium considerations help explain the relationship between water vapour in the clouds and precipitations in the form of liquid (rain) and solid (snow) at different temperatures and pressures.

7.1 Equilibrium

Understandings:

- A state of equilibrium is reached in a closed system when the rates of the forward and reverse reactions are equal.

Guidance
Physical and chemical systems should be covered.

- The equilibrium law describes how the equilibrium constant (K_c) can be determined for a particular chemical equation.
- The magnitude of the equilibrium constant indicates the extent of a reaction at equilibrium and is temperature dependent.
- The reaction quotient (Q) measures the relative amount of products and reactants present during a reaction at a particular point in time. Q is the equilibrium expression with non-equilibrium concentrations. The position of the equilibrium changes with changes in concentration, pressure, and temperature.
- A catalyst has no effect on the position of equilibrium or the equilibrium constant.

Bromine stored in a sealed jar. The system is in dynamic equilibrium, so the concentrations of liquid and vapour do not change at constant temperature.

Bromine is the only non-metallic element that is liquid at room temperature. It is extremely toxic and takes its name from a Greek word meaning stench.

Figure 7.1 Establishing dynamic equilibrium in the evaporation of bromine. Equilibrium is established when the rate of evaporation equals the rate of condensation.

Figure 7.2 The rates of evaporation and condensation as liquid–vapour equilibrium are established in a closed system. The rate of evaporation is constant, while the rate of condensation increases with increasing concentration of vapour. Equilibrium is established when the two rates are equal.

Applications and skills:

- The characteristics of chemical and physical systems in a state of equilibrium.
- Deduction of the equilibrium constant expression (K_c) from an equation for a homogeneous reaction.
- Determination of the relationship between different equilibrium constants (K_c) for the same reaction at the same temperature.

Guidance
Relationship between K_c values for reactions that are multiples or inverses of one another should be covered.

- Application of Le Chatelier's principle to predict the qualitative effects of changes of temperature, pressure, and concentration on the position of equilibrium and on the value of the equilibrium constant.

Guidance
Specific details of any industrial process are not required.

Physical systems

Consider what happens when some bromine, Br_2, is placed in a sealed container at room temperature.

As bromine is a **volatile** liquid, with a boiling point close to room temperature, a significant number of particles (molecules of Br_2) will have enough energy to escape from the liquid state and form vapour in the process known as **evaporation**. As the container is sealed, the bromine vapour cannot escape and so its concentration will increase. Some of these vapour molecules will collide with the surface of the liquid, lose energy, and become liquid in the process known as **condensation**.

$$Br_2(l) \underset{\text{condensation}}{\overset{\text{evaporation}}{\rightleftharpoons}} Br_2(g)$$

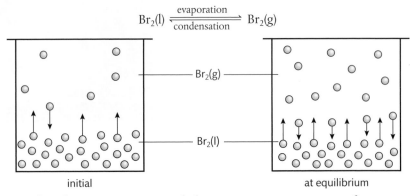

initial   at equilibrium

The rate of condensation increases with the increase in concentration of vapour, as more vapour particles collide with the surface of the liquid. Eventually, the rate of condensation is *equal* to the rate of evaporation, and at this point there will be no net change in the amounts of liquid and gas present (Figure 7.2). We say that the system has reached **equilibrium**. This will only occur in a closed system, where the $Br_2(g)$ cannot escape as vapour but may condense back into the liquid.

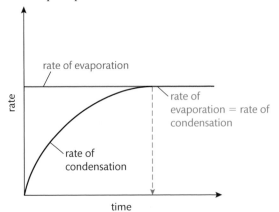

Chemical systems

Consider the reaction of dissociation between hydrogen iodide (HI) and its elements hydrogen (H_2) and iodine (I_2). Hydrogen and hydrogen iodide are both colourless, whereas iodine is released as a purple gas, so this helps us to see what is happening.

$$2HI(g) \quad \rightleftharpoons \quad H_2(g) \quad + \quad I_2(g)$$
colourless gas   colourless gas   purple gas

If we carry out this reaction starting with hydrogen iodide in a sealed container, there will at first be an increase in the purple colour owing to the production of iodine gas. But after a while this increase in colour will stop, and it may appear that the reaction too has stopped. In fact, what has happened is that the rate of the dissociation of HI is fastest at the start when the concentration of HI is greatest and falls as the reaction proceeds. Meanwhile, the reverse reaction, which initially has a zero rate because there is no H_2 and I_2 present, starts slowly and increases in rate as the concentrations of H_2 and I_2 increase. Eventually, the rate of dissociation of HI has become equal to the rate of the reverse reaction of association between H_2 and I_2, so the concentrations remain constant. This is why the colour in the flask remains the same. At this point, equilibrium has been reached. It is described as **dynamic** because both forward and backward reactions are still occurring.

If we were to analyse the contents of the flask at this point, we would find that HI, H_2, and I_2 would all be present and that if there were no change in conditions, their concentrations would remain constant over time. We refer to this as the **equilibrium mixture**.

If we reversed the experiment and started with H_2 and I_2 instead of HI, we would find that eventually an equilibrium mixture would again be achieved in which the concentrations of H_2, I_2, and HI would remain constant. These relationships are shown in Figure 7.3.

Iodine gas in a stoppered flask. Iodine is a crystalline solid at room temperature, but sublimes on heating to form a purple gas.

TOK The study of chemical change often involves both the macroscopic and microscopic scales. Which ways of knowing do we use in moving from the macroscopic to the microscopic?

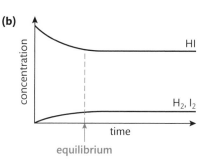

Figure 7.3 Equilibrium is reached when the concentrations of reactants and products become constant. Note the same equilibrium mixture is reached starting from (a) a mixture of H_2 and I_2 or (b) from pure HI.

The equilibrium state has specific characteristics

In studies of equilibria we are dealing with reversible reactions – those that occur in both directions. The convention is to describe the reaction from left to right (reactants to products) as the **forward reaction**, and the reaction from right to left (products to reactants) as the **backward** or **reverse reaction**. The symbol $\rightleftharpoons$ is used to show that the reaction is an equilibrium reaction.

The examples of physical and chemical systems discussed have shown that *at equilibrium the rate of the forward reaction is equal to the rate of the backward reaction.*

These reactions have also shown some of the main features of the equilibrium state, and these can now be summarized as they apply to *all* reactions at equilibrium.

forward
reaction
reactants $\rightleftharpoons$ products
backward
reaction

Strictly speaking, all reactions can be considered as equilibrium reactions. However, in many cases the equilibrium mixture consists almost entirely of products – that is, it is considered to have gone virtually to completion. By convention we use the symbol → rather than the equilibrium symbol in these cases. In other reactions there may be so little product formed that it is undetectable and the reaction is considered to have effectively not happened.

Make sure that you use the equilibrium symbol ⇌ when writing equations for reactions where the reverse reactions are significant. For example, it must be used when explaining the behaviour of weak acids and bases (Chapter 8).

At equilibrium the rate of the forward reaction is equal to the rate of the backward reaction.

What are the differences between theories and analogies as forms of explanation?

	Feature of equilibrium state	Explanation
1	Equilibrium is dynamic	The reaction has not stopped but both forward and backward reactions are still occurring at the same rate.
2	Equilibrium is achieved in a closed system	A closed system has no exchange of matter with the surroundings, so equilibrium is achieved where both reactants and products can react and recombine with each other.
3	The concentrations of reactants and products remain constant at equilibrium	They are being produced and destroyed at an equal rate.
4	At equilibrium there is no change in macroscopic properties	Macroscopic properties are observable properties such as colour and density. These do not change as they depend on the concentrations of the components of the mixture.
5	Equilibrium can be reached from either direction	The same equilibrium mixture will result under the same conditions, no matter whether the reaction is started with all reactants, all products, or a mixture of both.

It is important to understand that even though the concentrations of reactant and product are *constant* at equilibrium, this in no way implies that they are *equal*. In fact, most commonly there will be a much higher concentration of either reactant or product in the equilibrium mixture, depending both on the reaction and on the conditions. We can see, for example, in Figure 7.3 that when the dissociation of HI reaches equilibrium, there is a higher concentration of HI than of H_2 and I_2.

Thinking back to the analogy in the introduction to this chapter, of you running in the opposite direction on a moving staircase where the top and bottom represent reactants and products respectively, it would be possible for you to be 'at equilibrium' near the top of the staircase, near the bottom, or anywhere in between. As long as you were moving at the same speed as the staircase you would still have no net change in position.

The proportion of reactant and product in the equilibrium mixture is referred to as its **equilibrium position**. Reactions where the mixture contains predominantly products are said to 'lie to the right', reactions with predominantly reactants are said to 'lie to the left'. It is, however, often useful to be able to capture this information mathematically to compare the equilibrium mixtures of different reactions and the effect of different conditions. In the next section we will look at how this is done.

NATURE OF SCIENCE

At equilibrium no change is observed on the macroscopic level, although particles are reacting at the microscopic level. These changes can be deduced using techniques such as isotopic labelling, which allow the progress of a specific reactant to be followed. Our power of understanding is enhanced by contributions from instrumentation and sensors that may gather information beyond human sense perception.

Exercises

1 Which statements are correct for a reaction at equilibrium?

    I   The forward and reverse reactions both continue.
    II   The rates of the forward and reverse reactions are equal.
    III   The concentrations of reactants and products are equal.

    A I and II only   **B** I and III only   **C** II and III only   **D** I, II, and III

2 Which statement is always true for a chemical reaction that has reached equilibrium at constant temperature?

    A The yield of product(s) is greater than 50%.
    B The rate of the reverse reaction is lower than that of the forward reaction.
    C The amounts of reactants and products do not change.
    D Both forward and reverse reactions have stopped.

3 Which statement is *not* true for a mixture of ice and water at equilibrium at constant temperature?

    A The rates of melting and freezing are equal.
    B The amounts of ice and water are equal.
    C The same position of equilibrium can be reached by cooling water and by heating ice.
    D There is no observable change in the system.

The equilibrium constant K_c can be predicted from a reaction's stoichiometry

Consider now the reaction

$$H_2(g) + I_2(g) \rightleftharpoons 2HI(g)$$

If we were to carry out a series of experiments on this reaction with different starting concentrations of H_2, I_2, and HI, we could wait until each reaction reached equilibrium and then measure the composition of each equilibrium mixture. Here are some typical results obtained at 440 °C.

	Initial concentration / mol dm⁻³	Equilibrium concentration / mol dm⁻³
H_2	0.100	0.0222
I_2	0.100	0.0222
HI	0.000	0.156

Experiment I

	Initial concentration / mol dm⁻³	Equilibrium concentration / mol dm⁻³
H_2	0.000	0.0350
I_2	0.0100	0.0450
HI	0.350	0.280

Experiment II

	Initial concentration / mol dm⁻³	Equilibrium concentration / mol dm⁻³
H_2	0.0150	0.0150
I_2	0.000	0.0135
HI	0.127	0.100

Experiment III

At a glance these data may not appear to show any pattern. However, there is a predictable relationship among the different compositions of these equilibrium mixtures, and the key to discovering it is in the stoichiometry of the reaction equation.

Sometimes you may see the equilibrium sign written with unequal arrows such as $\rightleftharpoons$. This is used to represent the reaction that lies in favour of products. Likewise, $\rightleftharpoons$ is used to represent a reaction that lies in favour of reactants.

CHALLENGE YOURSELF

1 A closed system is defined differently in different disciplines. In thermodynamics it means that no matter can be exchanged with the surroundings, but energy can flow freely. To what extent can the Earth be considered a closed system?

$$H_2(g) + I_2(g) \rightleftharpoons 2HI(g)$$

If we take the *equilibrium* concentrations and process them in the following way:

$$\frac{[HI]^2_{eqm}}{[H_2]^1_{eqm}[I_2]^1_{eqm}}$$

2 = coefficient of HI in the reaction equation

1 = coefficient of H_2 in the reaction equation

1 = coefficient of I_2 in the reaction equation

we find the following results:

Experiment I	Experiment II	Experiment III
$\dfrac{(0.156)^2}{0.0222 \times 0.0222} = 49.4$	$\dfrac{(0.280)^2}{0.035 \times 0.0450} = 49.8$	$\dfrac{(0.100)^2}{0.0150 \times 0.0135} = 49.4$

Clearly this way of processing the equilibrium data produces a constant value within the limits of experimental accuracy. This constant is known as the **equilibrium constant, K_c**. It has a fixed value for this reaction *at a specified temperature*.

In fact, every reaction has its own particular value of K_c which can be derived in a similar way. First we use the balanced reaction equation to write the **equilibrium constant expression**.

For the reaction:

$$aA + bB \rightleftharpoons cC + dD$$

the equilibrium constant expression is

$$\frac{[C]^c_{eqm}[D]^d_{eqm}}{[A]^a_{eqm}[B]^b_{eqm}} = K_c$$

The value for K_c can then be determined by substituting the equilibrium concentrations of all reactants and products into this equation.

Note:

• The equilibrium constant expression has the concentrations of products in the numerator and the concentrations of reactants in the denominator.

• Each concentration is raised to the power of its coefficient in the balanced equation. (Where it is equal to one it does not have to be given.)

• Where there is more than one reactant or product the terms are multiplied together.

Worked example

Write the equilibrium expression for the following reactions.

(i) $2H_2(g) + O_2(g) \rightleftharpoons 2H_2O(g)$

(ii) $Cu^{2+}(aq) + 4NH_3(aq) \rightleftharpoons [Cu(NH_3)_4]^{2+}$

Solution

(i) $K_c = \dfrac{[H_2O]^2}{[H_2]^2[O_2]}$

(ii) $K_c = \dfrac{[[Cu(NH_3)_4]^{2+}]}{[Cu^{2+}][NH_3]^4}$

Remember square brackets [ ] are commonly used to show concentration in mol dm^{-3}.

Many sources give units for K_c which are a multiple of mol dm^{-3}, depending on the stoichiometry of the reaction. In fact this is not fully correct, as the terms in the equilibrium expression are really a thermodynamic quality known as 'activity' that has no units. For this reason, we are omitting them in the values of K_c here, and you will not be required to include them in IB examination answers.

The equilibrium constant K_c has a fixed value for a particular reaction at a specified temperature. The only thing that changes the value of K_c for a reaction is the temperature.

The equilibrium constant expression will only give the value K_c when the concentrations used in the equation are the *equilibrium* concentrations for all reactants and products. Strictly speaking, the subscript 'eqm' should always be used in the equation, but by convention this is generally left out. However, make completely sure that the only values you substitute into an equation to calculate K_c are the equilibrium concentrations.

Exercises

4 Write the equilibrium constant expression for the following reactions:

(a) $2NO(g) + O_2(g) \rightleftharpoons 2NO_2(g)$

(b) $4NH_3(g) + 7O_2(g) \rightleftharpoons 4NO_2(g) + 6H_2O(g)$

(c) $CH_3Cl(aq) + OH^-(aq) \rightleftharpoons CH_3OH(aq) + Cl^-(aq)$

5 Write the equations for the reactions represented by the following equilibrium constant expressions:

(a) $K_c = \dfrac{[NO_2]^2}{[N_2O_4]}$

(b) $K_c = \dfrac{[CO][H_2]^3}{[CH_4][H_2O]}$

6 Write the equilibrium constant expressions for the following chemical reactions:

(a) fluorine gas and chlorine gas combine to form $ClF_3(g)$

(b) NO dissociates into its elements

(c) methane, CH_4, and steam react to form carbon monoxide and hydrogen

> The equilibrium constant expressions described here apply to homogeneous reactions, that is reactions where reactants and products are in the same phase, as gases, liquids, or in solution. It is good practice always to include state symbols in your equations to ensure this is being applied correctly.

The magnitude of K_c gives information on the extent of reaction

Different reactions have different values of K_c. What does this value tell us about a particular reaction?

As the equilibrium constant expression puts products on the numerator and reactants on the denominator, a high value of K_c will mean that at equilibrium there are proportionately more products than reactants. In other words, such an equilibrium mixture lies to the right and the reaction goes almost to completion. By contrast, a low value of K_c must mean that there are proportionately less products with respect to reactants, so the equilibrium mixture lies to the left and the reaction has barely taken place.

Consider the following three reactions and their K_c values measured at 550 K.

$H_2(g) + I_2(g) \rightleftharpoons 2HI(g)$ $K_c = 2$

$H_2(g) + Br_2(g) \rightleftharpoons 2HBr(g)$ $K_c = 10^{10}$

$H_2(g) + Cl_2(g) \rightleftharpoons 2HCl(g)$ $K_c = 10^{18}$

The large range in their K_c values tells us about the differing extents of these reactions. We can deduce that the reaction between H_2 and Cl_2 has taken place the most fully at this temperature, while H_2 and I_2 have reacted the least.

A good rule of thumb to apply to these situations is that if $K_c \gg 1$, the reaction is considered to go almost to completion (very high conversion of reactants into products), and if $K_c \ll 1$, the reaction hardly proceeds.

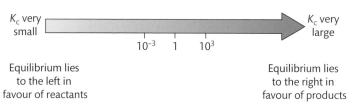

Note that the magnitude of K_c does not give us any information on the *rate* of the reaction. It informs us of the nature of the equilibrium mixture, but not on how quickly the equilibrium state will be achieved.

> The magnitude of the equilibrium constant K_c gives information about how far a reaction goes at a particular temperature, but not about how fast it will achieve the equilibrium state.

Figure 7.4 The larger the value of K_c, the further the equilibrium mixture lies to the right.

The reaction quotient, Q, enables us to predict the direction of reaction

Remember that the value of K_c is calculated from substituting the *equilibrium* concentrations of all reactants and products into the equilibrium constant expression. Any other values used will not give the equilibrium value K_c for that reaction at that temperature.

This in itself can be useful. If we take the concentrations of the reactants and products at the same moment in time when the reaction is not at equilibrium, and substitute these into the equilibrium constant expression, we obtain a value known as the **reaction quotient, Q**. As time passes and the reaction continues, the concentrations of all reaction components change and eventually reach the equilibrium concentrations. In other words, the value of Q changes in the direction of K_c. This enables us to predict the direction in which the reaction will proceed.

For example, if we again consider the reaction:

$$H_2(g) + I_2(g) \rightleftharpoons 2HI(g)$$

for which $K_c = 49.5$ at 440 °C, as we saw on page 222.

The table below shows experimental data for the concentrations of the reaction components from experiments I and II at a time when the reaction mixture was not at equilibrium.

	Experiment I: concentration at time t / mol dm^{-3}	Experiment II: concentration at time t / mol dm^{-3}
H_2	0.0500	0.0250
I_2	0.0500	0.0350
HI	0.100	0.300

The equilibrium constant expression $= \dfrac{[HI]^2}{[H_2][I_2]}$

Experiment I, time t $\qquad Q = \dfrac{(0.100)^2}{(0.0500)(0.0500)} = 4.00$

Experiment II, time t $\qquad Q = \dfrac{(0.300)^2}{(0.0250)(0.0350)} = 103$

In experiment I, $Q < K_c$ and so Q must increase as the reaction moves towards equilibrium. This means that the net reaction must be to the right, in favour of products.

In experiment II, $Q > K_c$ and so Q must decrease as the reaction moves towards equilibrium. This means that the net reaction must be to the left, in favour of reactants.

We can summarize the use of the reaction quotient, Q, in determining the direction of reaction as follows:

• if $Q = K_c$, reaction is at equilibrium, no net reaction occurs;
• if $Q < K_c$, reaction proceeds to the right in favour of products;
• if $Q > K_c$, reaction proceeds to the left in favour of reactants.

The reaction quotient, Q, is a measure of the relative amounts of reactants and products present in a reaction at a particular time. Its value is determined from substituting concentrations of reaction components, all measured at the same time, into the equilibrium expression.

Note that the value of Q for a reaction does not have a fixed value as it can be measured at any interval of time, whereas the value of K_c for a reaction is a constant at a specified temperature.

Comparison of the value of the reaction quotient, Q, at a specific time in a reaction with the value of K_c for the reaction, enables us to predict the direction of change.

Worked example

The equilibrium constant K_c for the reaction

$$N_2(g) + 3H_2(g) \rightleftharpoons 2NH_3(g)$$

is 1.7×10^2 at 500 K.

Determine whether the reaction mixture is at equilibrium when the concentrations of the components at this temperature are as follows:

$[N_2] = 1.50$

$[H_2] = 1.00$

$[NH_3] = 8.00$.

If it is not at equilibrium, state and explain in which direction the reaction will proceed.

Solution

First write the equilibrium constant expression.

$$\frac{[NH_3]^2}{[N_2][H_2]^3}$$

Calculate the value of Q at these conditions by substituting the given concentration values into the equilibrium expression.

$$Q = \frac{(8.00)^2}{(1.50)(1.00)^3} = 42.7$$

Compare the value of Q at the given conditions with K_c.

$$42.7 < 1.7 \times 10^2$$

Therefore the reaction is not at equilibrium. It will proceed to the right in favour of products, as the value of Q must increase to be equal to K_c at equilibrium.

Relationships between K_c for different equations of a reaction

As K_c is defined with products on the numerator and reactants on the denominator, each raised to the power of their stoichiometric coefficients in the balanced equation, we can manipulate its value according to changes made to these terms. For this discussion we will consider the generic reaction:

$$aA + bB \rightleftharpoons cC + dD$$

for which the equilibrium constant is:

$$K_c = \frac{[C]^c[D]^d}{[A]^a[B]^b}$$

1 K_c for the inverse reaction

The inverse reaction

$$cC + dD \rightleftharpoons aA + bB$$

defines the products as reactants and vice versa. We will denote its equilibrium constant as $K_c{}'$.

$$K_c{}' = \frac{[A]^a[B]^b}{[C]^c[D]^d}$$

We can see that $K_c{}' = \dfrac{1}{K_c}$ or $K_c{}' = K_c^{-1}$.

In other words the equilibrium constant for a reaction is the reciprocal of the equilibrium constant for its inverse reaction.

2 K_c for a multiple of a reaction

Consider now the reaction

$$2aA + 2bB \rightleftharpoons 2cC + 2dD$$

We will denote its equilibrium constant as K_c^x.

$$K_c^x = \frac{[C]^{2c}[D]^{2d}}{[A]^{2a}[B]^{2b}}$$

We can see that each term has been squared in K_c^x relative to its value in K_c.

So $K_c^x = K_c^2$.

By similar thinking, we can conclude that tripling of the stoichiometric coefficients would lead to a cubing of the value of K_c, halving of the stoichiometric coefficents would lead to a square rooting of the value of K_c, and so on.

These manipulations of the value of K_c are summarized below.

	Effect on equilibrium expression	Effect on K_c
inversing the reaction	inverts the expression	$\dfrac{1}{K_c}$ or K_c^{-1}
doubling the reaction coefficients	squares the expression	K_c^2
tripling the reaction coefficients	cubes the expression	K_c^3
halving the reaction coefficients	square roots the expression	$\sqrt{K_c}$
adding together two reactions	multiplies the two expressions	$K_c^i \times K_c^{ii}$

CHALLENGE YOURSELF

3 In heterogeneous equilibrium, the terms for pure solids or liquids are not shown in the equilibrium expression. Suggest why this is the case.

Worked example

The equilibrium constant for the reaction

$$2HI(g) \rightleftharpoons H_2(g) + I_2(g)$$

is 0.04 at a certain temperature. What would be the value of the equilibrium constant, K_c', for the following reaction at the same temperature?

$$\tfrac{1}{2}H_2(g) + \tfrac{1}{2}I_2(g) \rightleftharpoons HI(g)$$

Solution

$$K_c = \frac{[H_2][I_2]}{[HI]^2}$$

$$K_c' = \frac{[HI]}{[H_2]^{1/2}[I_2]^{1/2}}$$

Note that the reaction is reversed and the coefficients in the equation are halved. Overall, the value of K_c' is the square root of the value of K_c.

So $K_c' = \dfrac{1}{\sqrt{K_c}}$ or $\sqrt{(K_c)^{-1}}$.

$$\therefore K_c' = \sqrt{\frac{1}{0.04}} = 5.0$$

Exercises

7   When the following reactions reach equilibrium, does the equilibrium mixture contain mostly reactants or mostly products at the specified temperature? Assume that the value for K_c given corresponds to the temperature of the reaction mixture.

   (a) $N_2(g) + 2H_2(g) \rightleftharpoons N_2H_4(g)$ $K_c = 7.4 \times 10^{-26}$
   (b) $N_2(g) + O_2(g) \rightleftharpoons 2NO(g)$ $K_c = 2.7 \times 10^{-18}$
   (c) $2NO(g) + O_2(g) \rightleftharpoons 2NO_2(g)$ $K_c = 6.0 \times 10^{13}$

8   The equilibrium constant for the reaction

$$H_2O(g) + Cl_2O(g) \rightleftharpoons 2HOCl(g)$$

   is 0.0900 at 298 K.

   Determine whether the following sets of conditions represent an equilibrium mixture for the reaction at this temperature. For those not at equilibrium, determine in which direction the reaction will proceed.

	[H₂O]	[Cl₂O]	[HOCl]
(a)	0.100	0.100	1.00
(b)	0.49	0.040	0.042
(c)	0.19	0.00033	0.083

9   At a given temperature, the reaction

$$2SO_2 + O_2(g) \rightleftharpoons 2SO_3(g)$$

   has a value of $K_c = 278$. Determine values of K_c for the following reactions at this temperature.

   (a) $4SO_2 + 2O_2(g) \rightleftharpoons 4SO_3(g)$
   (b) $2SO_3(g) \rightleftharpoons 2SO_2 + O_2(g)$
   (c) $SO_3(g) \rightleftharpoons SO_2 + \tfrac{1}{2}O_2(g)$

When equilibrium is disrupted

A system remains at equilibrium so long as the rate of the forward reaction equals the rate of the backward reaction. But as soon as this balance is disrupted by any change

Henri-Louis Le Chatelier was a French chemist who published his equilibria principle in 1884. Amongst other research, he also investigated the possibility of ammonia synthesis, but abandoned his efforts after suffering a devastating explosion in his laboratory. After Haber's later elucidation of the conditions required in the reaction, Le Chatelier realized that he had been very close to the discovery himself. Late in his life he wrote 'I let the discovery of the ammonia synthesis slip through my hands. It was the greatest blunder of my career.' We can only speculate on how history might have been re-written if this discovery had in fact been made in France rather than in Germany before World War I.

When a system at equilibrium is subjected to a change, it will respond in such a way as to minimize the effect of the change.

in conditions that unequally affects the rates of these reactions, the equilibrium condition will no longer be met. It has been shown, however, that equilibria respond in a predictable way to such a situation, based on a principle known as **Le Chatelier's principle**. This states that *a system at equilibrium when subjected to a change will respond in such a way as to minimize the effect of the change.* Simply put, this means that whatever we do to a system at equilibrium, the system will respond in the opposite way. Add something and the system will react to remove it, remove something and the system will react to replace it. After a while, a new equilibrium will be established and this will have a different composition from the earlier equilibrium mixture. Applying the principle therefore enables us to predict the qualitative effect of typical changes that occur to systems at equilibrium.

Changes in concentration

Suppose an equilibrium is disrupted by an increase in the concentration of one of the reactants. This will cause the rate of the forward reaction to increase while the backward reaction will not be affected, so the reaction rates will no longer be equal. When equilibrium re-establishes itself, the mixture will have new concentrations of all reactants and products, and the equilibrium will have shifted in favour of products. The value of K_c will be unchanged. This is in keeping with the prediction from Le Chatelier's principle: addition of reactant causes the system to respond by removing reactant – this favours the forward reaction and so shifts the equilibrium to the right.

Similarly, the equilibrium could be disrupted by a decrease in the concentration of product by removing it from the equilibrium mixture. As the rate of the backward reaction is now decreased, there will be a shift in the equilibrium in favour of the products. A different equilibrium position will be achieved, but the value of K_c will be unchanged. Again this confirms the prediction from Le Chatelier's principle: removal of product causes the system to respond by making more product – this favours the forward reaction and so shifts the equilibrium to the right.

The graph in Figure 7.5 illustrates these disruptions to equilibrium for the reaction

$$N_2(g) + 3H_2(g) \rightleftharpoons 2NH_3(g)$$

Experiment to show the effect of changing the concentration of chloride ions on the cobalt chloride equilibrium reaction:

$[Co(H_2O)_6]^{2+}(aq) + 4Cl^-(aq) \rightleftharpoons CoCl_4^{2-}(aq) + 6H_2O(l)$

The flask on the left has a low concentration of chloride ions, giving the pink colour of the compex ion with water. As the concentration of chloride ions is increased, the equilibrium shifts to the right, changing the colour from pink to blue. Adding water would shift the equilibrium in the opposite direction. Cobalt chloride is often used to test for the presence of water because of this colour change.

Figure 7.5 Effects of the addition of reactant and removal of product on the equilibrium $N_2(g) + 3H_2(g) \rightleftharpoons 2NH_3(g)$. When H_2 is added some N_2 reacts and more NH_3 is formed as the equilibrium shifts to the right. When NH_3 is removed, more N_2 reacts with H_2 as the equilibrium again shifts to the right. After each change a new equilibrium mixture is achieved.

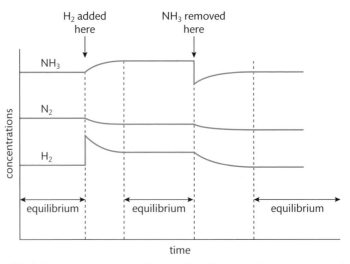

After H_2 is added, the concentrations of N_2 and H_2 decrease (in a 1:3 ratio in keeping with their reaction stoichiometry), while the concentration of NH_3 rises (in a 2:1 ratio relative to N_2) as the rate of the forward reaction increases and the equilibrium shifts to the right. The new equilibrium mixture has a higher proportion of products. In the second part of the graph, removal of NH_3 from the equilibrium mixture causes a decrease in the concentrations of N_2 and H_2 as they react to form more NH_3.

Often in an industrial process the product will be removed as it forms. This ensures that the equilibrium is continuously pulled to the right, so increasing the yield of product.

Applying Le Chatelier's principle, can you think what concentration changes would cause an equilibrium to shift to the left? The answer is either an increase in concentration of product or a decrease in concentration of reactant.

Changes in pressure

Equilibria involving gases will be affected by a change in pressure if the reaction involves a change in the number of molecules. This is because there is a direct relationship between the number of gas molecules and the pressure exerted by a gas in a fixed volume. So if such a reaction at equilibrium is subject to an increase in pressure, the system responds to decrease this pressure by favouring the side with the smaller number of molecules. Conversely, a decrease in pressure will cause a shift in the equilibrium position to the side with the larger number of molecules of gas. A different equilibrium position will be achieved but the value of K_c will be unchanged, so long as the temperature remains the same.

For example, consider the reaction used in the production of methanol:

$$CO(g) + 2H_2(g) \rightleftharpoons CH_3OH(g)$$

In total there are three molecules of gas on the left side and one molecule of gas on the right side. So here high pressure will shift the equilibrium to the right, in favour of the smaller number of gas molecules, which increases the yield of CH_3OH.

Note that many common equilibrium reactions do not involve a change in the number of gas molecules and so are not affected by changes in pressure. For example, the reaction

$$H_2(g) + I_2(g) \rightleftharpoons 2HI(g)$$

has two molecules of gas on both sides of the equation. Changing pressure for this reaction will affect the rate of the reaction but not the position of equilibrium or the value of K_c.

Changes in temperature

We have noted that K_c is temperature dependent, so changing the temperature will change K_c. However, in order to predict *how* it will change we must examine the enthalpy changes (see Chapter 5) of the forward and backward reactions. Remember that an exothermic reaction releases energy (ΔH negative), whereas an endothermic reaction absorbs energy (ΔH positive). The enthalpy changes of the forward and backward reactions are equal and opposite to each other.

So if we apply Le Chatelier's principle, including the energy change in the chemical reaction, we can predict how the reaction will respond to a change in temperature.

Consider the reaction:

$$2NO_2(g) \rightleftharpoons N_2O_4(g) \qquad \Delta H = -57 \text{ kJ mol}^{-1}$$
$$\text{brown} \qquad \text{colourless}$$

Changes in the concentration of reactants or products alter the equilibrium position and so change the composition of the equilibrium mixture. But the value of K_c stays the same.

Changes in pressure or volume will affect the position of equilibrium of a reaction if it involves a change in the number of gas molecules. The value of K_c remains unchanged.

When describing the effects of volume or pressure on equilibrium reactions, you must state it depends on the relative number of *gas* molecules on both sides of the equation. Solids and liquids are hardly affected by changes in pressure.

An increase in pressure favours the side of an equilibrium reaction that has the smaller number of gas molecules.

When ΔH is given for an equilibrium reaction, by convention its sign refers to the forward reaction. So a negative sign for ΔH means that the forward reaction is exothermic, and the backward reaction is endothermic.

CHALLENGE YOURSELF

4 Use information from this section to explain why there is very little NO in the atmosphere under ordinary conditions, and why severe air pollution is often characterized by a brownish haze.

The negative sign of ΔH tells us that the forward reaction is exothermic and so releases heat. If this reaction at equilibrium is subjected to a decrease in temperature, the system will respond by producing heat and it does this by favouring the forward exothermic reaction. This means that the equilibrium will shift to the right, in favour of the product N_2O_4. A new equilibrium mixture will be achieved and the value of K_c will increase. So here we can see that the reaction will give a higher yield of products at a *lower temperature*.

Conversely, increasing the temperature favours the backward endothermic reaction, and so shifts the equilibrium to the left, decreasing the value of K_c. The reaction mixture becomes a darker colour as the concentration of NO_2 increases.

The table below illustrates the effect of temperature on the value of K_c for this reaction.

Temperature / K	K_c for $2NO_2(g) \rightleftharpoons N_2O_4(g)$
273	1300
298	170

Even though in this case a lower temperature will produce an equilibrium mixture with a higher proportion of products, remember from Chapter 6 that low temperature also causes a lower rate of reaction. And so, although a higher yield will be produced eventually, it may simply take too long to achieve this from practical and economic considerations if this was an industrial-scale reaction. We will come back to this point later in this chapter.

Now consider the following reaction:

$$N_2(g) + O_2(g) \rightleftharpoons 2NO(g) \qquad\qquad \Delta H = +181 \text{ kJ mol}^{-1}$$

In this case we can see that the forward reaction is endothermic and so absorbs heat. So here the effect of a decreased temperature will be to favour the backward exothermic reaction. Therefore the equilibrium will shift to the left, in favour of reactants, and K_c will decrease. At higher temperatures, the forward endothermic reaction is favoured, so the equilibrium shifts to the right and K_c will increase.

The table below illustrates the effect of temperature on the value of K_c for this reaction.

Temperature / K	K_c for $N_2(g) + O_2(g) \rightleftharpoons 2NO(g)$
298	4.5×10^{-31}
900	6.7×10^{-10}
2300	1.7×10^{-3}

The reaction

$$N_2(g) + O_2(g) \rightleftharpoons 2NO(g)$$

takes place in motor vehicles where the heat released by the combustion of the fuel is sufficient to cause the nitrogen and oxygen gases from the air to combine together in this way. Unfortunately, the product NO is toxic, and, worse still, quickly becomes converted into other toxins that form the components of acid rain and smog. It is therefore of great interest to vehicle manufacturers to find ways of lowering the temperature during combustion in order to reduce the production of NO in the reaction above.

These examples illustrate that, unlike changes in concentration and pressure, changes in temperature *do* cause the value of K_c to change. An increase in temperature increases the value of K_c for an endothermic reaction and decreases the value of K_c for an exothermic reaction. This is because changes in temperature have a different effect

Experiment to show the effect of temperature on the reaction that converts NO_2 (brown) to N_2O_4 (colourless). As the temperature is increased, more NO_2 is produced and the gas becomes darker, as seen in the tube on the left.

TOK

Combustion reactions are generally described as exothermic, but the reaction

$N_2(g) + O_2(g) \rightleftharpoons 2NO(g)$

is endothermic. When is it appropriate to refer to an 'exception to a rule', and when does the rule need to be reconsidered?

Increasing the temperature causes an increase in the value of K_c for an endothermic reaction and a decrease in the value of K_c for an exothermic reaction.

on the rates of the forward and backward reactions, due to their different activation energies, as discussed in Chapter 6. In the next chapter, we will use this fact to explain why the pH of pure water is temperature dependent.

Addition of a catalyst

As we learned in Chapter 6, a catalyst speeds up the rate of a reaction by providing an alternate reaction pathway that has a transition state with a lower activation energy, E_a. This increases the number of particles that have sufficient energy to react without raising the temperature.

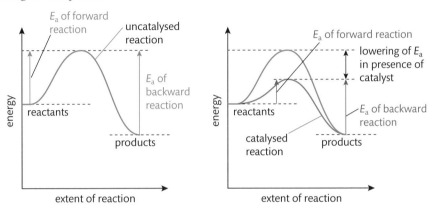

Figure 7.6 The effect of a catalyst in lowering the activation energy of both forward and backward reactions.

Because the forward and backward reactions pass through the same transition state, a catalyst lowers the activation energy by the same amount for the forward and backward reactions. So the rate of both these reactions will be increased by the same factor, as shown in Figure 7.6. The catalyst will therefore have no effect on the position of equilibrium, or on the value of K_c. In other words the catalyst will not increase the equilibrium yield of product in a reaction. It will, however, speed up the attainment of the equilibrium state and so cause products to form more quickly. Catalysts are generally not shown in the reaction equation or in the equilibrium constant expression as they are not chemically changed at the end of the reaction, and have no effect on the equilibrium concentrations.

Catalysts are widely used in industrial processes to increase the rate of product formation, and are involved in every single biochemical reaction. One of the key principles of Green Chemistry is that catalytic reagents, chosen to be as selective as possible, are superior to stoichiometric reagents as they are not consumed in the reaction. Catalysts, including the differences between homogeneous and heterogeneous catalysts, are discussed in more detail in Option A: Materials, topic A.3.

Summary

We can now summarize the effects of changes in concentration, pressure, temperature, and catalyst on the position of equilibrium and on the value of K_c.

	Effect of ...	Change in position of equilibrium	Change in value of K_c
1	concentration	changes	no change
2	pressure	changes if reaction involves a change in the number of gas molecules	no change
3	temperature	changes	changes
4	catalyst	no change	no change

Observations of shifts in the position of chemical equilibria

Full details of how to carry out this experiment with a worksheet are available on your eBook.

Catalysts do not change the position of equilibrium or the yield of a single reaction, but they enable the equilibrium mixture to be achieved more quickly. Catalysts do not change the value of K_c.

A particular reaction at a specified temperature can have many different possible equilibrium positions, but only one value for the equilibrium constant K_c.

231

NATURE OF SCIENCE

Knowledge of how systems at equilibrium respond to change has many applications, as we will see in the next section. Le Chatelier's principle is a useful predictive tool for this purpose, and has the advantage of being relatively simple to apply and effective. But it has some disadvantages too. Firstly, it leads only to qualitative predictions of the system's response. In some cases, such as investigations of when a precipitate will form in aqueous solution, this is insufficient. Secondly, Le Chatelier's principle offers no *explanation* for the response – it predicts what will happen, but not why. It can even be misleading in that it can suggest a false sense of purpose to systems' responses if the language used is such as 'the system tries to...'.

On the other hand, use of the reaction quotient, Q, to predict the consequence of change can often provide an effective explanation. As disturbances in concentration or pressure change the value of Q, the system responds as Q progresses towards K_c. But changes in temperature are different because they change the value of K_c – in this case the system responds as Q progresses towards the new value of K_c. The response of K_c to temperature can be explained through thermodynamics and the fact that the forward and backward reactions respond differently to temperature changes due to their different activation energies. Increased temperature favours the endothermic reaction as it has the higher activation energy. Scientific explanations often draw on different approaches and theories in this way. So long as the approaches do not contradict each other, together they can clarify and strengthen the understanding.

Note that you are not expected to learn specific conditions for any reaction, so there is no need to focus on the names of catalysts, specific temperature used, etc. But you should be able to apply an understanding of equilibria to any given example, and predict the conditions likely to be effective.

Fritz Haber 1886–1934.

Exercises

10 The manufacture of sulfur trioxide can be represented by the equation below:

$$2SO_2(g) + O_2(g) \rightleftharpoons 2SO_3(g) \qquad \Delta H^\ominus = -197 \text{ kJ mol}^{-1}$$

What happens when a catalyst is added to an equilibrium mixture from this reaction?

A The rate of the forward reaction increases and that of the reverse reaction decreases.
B The rates of both forward and reverse reactions increase.
C The value of $\Delta H^\ominus$ increases.
D The yield of sulfur trioxide increases.

11 What will happen to the position of equilibrium and the value of the equilibrium constant when the temperature is increased in the following reaction?

$$Br_2(g) + Cl_2(g) \rightleftharpoons 2BrCl(g) \qquad \Delta H^\ominus = +14 \text{ kJ}$$

	Position of equilibrium	Value of equilibrium constant
A	shifts towards the reactants	decreases
B	shifts towards the reactants	increases
C	shifts towards the products	decreases
D	shifts towards the products	increases

12 Which changes will shift the position of equilibrium to the right in the following reaction?

$$2CO_2(g) \rightleftharpoons 2CO(g) + O_2(g)$$

I   adding a catalyst
II decreasing the oxygen concentration
III increasing the volume of the container

A I and II only **B** I and III only **C** II and III only **D** I, II, and III

13 For each of the following reactions, predict in which direction the equilibrium will shift in response to an increase in pressure:

(a) $2CO_2(g) \rightleftharpoons 2CO(g) + O_2(g)$
(b) $CO(g) + 2H_2 \rightleftharpoons CH_3OH(g)$
(c) $H_2(g) + Cl_2(g) \rightleftharpoons 2HCl(g)$

14 How will the equilibrium:

$$CH_4(g) + 2H_2S(g) \rightleftharpoons CS_2(g) + 4H_2(g) \qquad \Delta H = +ve$$

respond to the following changes?

(a) addition of $H_2(g)$
(b) addition of $CH_4(g)$
(c) a decrease in the volume of the container
(d) removal of $CS_2(g)$
(e) increase in temperature

15 The reaction

$$2CO(g) + O_2(g) \rightleftharpoons 2CO_2(g) \qquad \Delta H = -566 \text{ kJ mol}^{-1}$$

takes place in catalytic converters in cars. If this reaction is at equilibrium, will the amount of CO increase, decrease, or stay the same when:

(a) the pressure is increased by decreasing the volume?
(b) the pressure is increased by adding $O_2(g)$?
(c) the temperature is increased?
(d) a platinum catalyst is added?

Equilibrium theory is applied in many industrial processes

In reactions involving the manufacture of a chemical it is obviously a goal to obtain as high a conversion of reactant to product as possible. Application of Le Chatelier's principle enables chemists to choose conditions that will cause the equilibrium to lie to the right, and so help to achieve this. But the *yield* of a reaction is only part of the consideration. The *rate* is also clearly of great significance as it would be of limited value if a process were able to claim a high equilibium yield of product, but took several years to achieve this. The economics of the process will depend on considerations of both the equilibrium and the kinetics of the reaction – in other words on how far and how fast the reaction will proceed. Sometimes these two criteria work against each other, and so the best compromise must be reached. A few case studies of industrial processes are discussed here.

The Haber process: the production of ammonia, NH₃

Fritz Haber was born in what is now Poland but moved to Germany early in his career. Together with Carl Bosch, also of Germany, he developed the process for the industrial synthesis of ammonia from its elements, and the first factory for ammonia production opened in Germany in 1913, just before World War I. This development had enormous significance for the country at war: it enabled the continued production of explosives despite the fact that imports of nitrate from Chile, used for producing nitric acid and explosives such as TNT, were barred through the blockaded ports. This effectively enabled Germany to continue its war efforts for another 4 years. Haber was awarded the Nobel Prize in Chemistry in 1918. In many ways history has recorded this as a controversial choice – not only had Haber's work helped to prolong the war, he had also been responsible for the development and use of chlorine as the first poison gas. Ironically, despite his evident patriotism towards Germany, he was expelled from the country in 1933 when the rising tide of anti-Semitism conflicted with his Jewish ancestry.

The book *The alchemy of air: a Jewish genius, a doomed tycoon, and the scientific discovery that fed the world but fueled the rise of Hitler* is written by Thomas Hager. It is a fascinating account of the historic discovery of the process to synthesize ammonia, and its continuing mixed consequences – these include the revolution in global food production, the death of millions through wars, and growing concerns of nitrate pollution and obesity.

The Haber process is based on the reaction

$$N_2(g) + 3H_2(g) \rightleftharpoons 2NH_3(g) \qquad \Delta H = -93 \text{ kJ mol}^{-1}$$

The following information can be derived from this equation:

• all reactants and products are gases;
• there is a change in the number of gas molecules as the reaction proceeds: four gas molecules on the left and two on the right;

It is estimated that as much as 130 million tonnes of ammonia, NH_3, are produced worldwide every year. China is responsible for nearly one-third of this, and India, Russia, and the USA also produce significant amounts. Approximately 80% of the ammonia is used to make fertilizers, notably ammonium nitrate, NH_4NO_3. Other uses include synthesis of textiles such as nylon and powerful explosives. In April 2013, a major explosion occurred in a fertiliser factory in Texas, USA, killing and injuring hundreds of people. It was caused by a fire in a stock of 250,000 kilograms of ammonium nitrate. Accidents such as this in industrial plants raise many questions regarding health and safety, storage, and handling of chemicals and the balance of reponsibility between companies, governments, and individuals.

Tractor applying a chemical solution of fertilizer to the soil. Ammonium salts such as ammonium nitrate and sulfate are particularly effective fertilizers as they supply nitrogen needed by plants and are readily soluble. It is estimated that without the use of ammonium fertilizers, two billion people would starve.

- the forward reaction is exothermic so releases heat; the backward reaction is endothermic so absorbs heat.

Application of Le Chatelier's principle to this reaction enables us to consider the optimum conditions.

- Concentration: the reactants nitrogen and hydrogen are supplied in the molar ratio 1:3 in accordance with their stoichiometry in the equation. The product ammonia is removed as it forms, thus helping to pull the equilibrium to the right and increasing the yield.
- Pressure: as the forward reaction involves a decrease in the number of gas molecules, it will be favoured by a *high pressure*. The usual pressure used in the Haber process is about 2×10^7 Pa.
- Temperature: as the forward reaction is exothermic, it will be favoured by a lower temperature. However, too low a temperature would cause the reaction to be uneconomically slow, and so a *moderate temperature* of about 450 °C is used.
- Catalyst: a catalyst will speed up the rate of production and so help to compensate for the moderate temperature used. A catalyst of finely divided iron is used, with small amounts of aluminium and magnesium oxides added to improve its activity. More recently, ruthenium has become the catalyst of choice, and this has helped reduce the energy requirement.

In fact, the Haber process achieves a conversion of H_2 and N_2 into NH_3 of only about 10–20% per pass through the reactor. After separation of the NH_3 product, the unconverted reactants are recycled to the reactor to obtain an overall yield of about 95%. This recycling of unconverted reactants is commonly used in industrial processes, and allows processes with low equilibrium yield to be made commercially viable.

The Contact process: the production of sulfuric acid, H_2SO_4

The Contact process involves a series of three simple reactions.

(i) the combustion of sulfur to form sulfur dioxide;

(ii) the oxidation of sulfur dioxide to sulfur trioxide:

$$2SO_2(g) + O_2(g) \rightleftharpoons 2SO_3(g) \qquad \Delta H = -196 \text{ kJ mol}^{-1}$$

(iii) the combination of sulfur trioxide with water to produce sulfuric acid.

It has been shown that the overall rate of the process depends on step (ii), the oxidation of sulfur dioxide. So applying Le Chatelier's principle to this step, we can predict the conditions that will most favour the formation of product. These are summarized in the table below.

	Influence on reaction	Condition used
pressure	forward reaction involves reduction in the number of molecules of gas from three molecules reactant to two molecules product: high pressure will favour product	2×10^5 Pa (this gives a very high equilibrium yield, so still higher pressure is not needed)
temperature	forward reaction is exothermic: low temperature will increase the equilibrium yield, but decrease the rate	450 °C
catalyst	increases the rate of reaction	vanadium(V) oxide

car batteries, electroplating, pulp, and paper

dyes, pigments, and paints

soaps, detergents, and plastics

agricultural: both phosphate and ammonium sulfate fertilizers

Figure 7.7 The uses of sulfuric acid.

More sulfuric acid by mass is produced worldwide than any other chemical. It has been found that the production of sulfuric acid closely mirrors historical events such as major wars that affect a country's economy. For this reason some economists use sulfuric acid production as a measure of a country's industrial strength. Sulfuric acid is used directly or indirectly in nearly all industrial processes, including the production of fertilizers, detergents, and paints and in ore processing, steel production, and water treatment. Approximately 250 million tonnes are produced annually across all continents.

The process gets its name the *Contact process* from the fact that molecules of the gases O_2 and SO_2 react in *contact* with the surface of the solid catalyst V_2O_5.

The production of methanol

$$CO(g) + 2H_2(g) \rightleftharpoons CH_3OH(g) \qquad \Delta H = -90 \text{ kJ mol}^{-1}$$

Again, Le Chatelier's principle can be used to consider the conditions that will optimize the production.

	Influence on reaction	Condition used
pressure	forward reaction involves reduction in the number of molecules of gas from three molecules reactant to one molecule product: high pressure will favour product	5–10×10^6 Pa
temperature	forward reaction is exothermic: low temperature will increase the yield, but decrease the rate	250 °C
catalyst	increases the rate of reaction	Cu–ZnO–Al_2O_3

NATURE OF SCIENCE

Scientific research is largely influenced by the social context, which helps to determine funding and set priorities. A good example is Haber's work on ammonia synthesis, which became pressing in Germany in the early years of the 20th century. Scientific discoveries often have significant economic, ethical, and political implications. Some of these may be unintended consequences of the discovery, such as the environmental degradation caused by the excess use of nitrate fertilizers as an outcome of the Haber process. This raises the question of who must take moral responsibility for the applications of scientific discoveries. The process of science includes risk benefit analyses, risk assessment, and ethical considerations, but sometimes the full consequences cannot be predicted and do not become known until much later.

Exercises

16 In the Haber process for the synthesis of ammonia, what effects does the catalyst have?

	Rate of formation of $NH_3(g)$	Amount of $NH_3(g)$ formed
A	increases	increases
B	increases	decreases
C	increases	no change
D	no change	increases

17 $2SO_2(g) + O_2(g) \rightleftharpoons 2SO_3(g) \quad \Delta H^\ominus = -200$ kJ

According to the above information, what temperature and pressure conditions produce the greatest amount of SO_3?

	Temperature	Pressure
A	low	low
B	low	high
C	high	high
D	high	low

18 Predict how you would expect the value for K_c for the Haber process to change as the temperature is increased. Explain the significance of this in terms of the reaction yield.

CHALLENGE YOURSELF

5 Consider the atom economy of the reactions described here using the formula

$$\text{atom economy} = \frac{\text{mass of desired product}}{\text{total mass of reactants}} \times 100$$

Explain how this is different from the reaction yield.

▲ Land contaminated by waste impurities from an old sulfuric acid plant close to a residential area in Bilbao, Spain. The waste largely derives from smelting and combustion processes. The full consideration of any industrial process must include an assessment of its impact on the environment, both locally and globally.

Methanol is used as a **chemical feedstock**, that is it is used to make other chemicals. A high proportion is converted into methanal, HCHO, which is then converted into plastics, paints, explosives, and plywood. Methanol is used as a laboratory solvent, an antifreeze agent, and in the process of producing biodiesel fuel from fats. Interest has also focused on the potential of methanol as an energy storage molecule in the so-called 'methanol economy'. In ongoing efforts to reduce dependence on imported fossil fuels, China has greatly increased production capacity and consumption of methanol for its transportation sector, and plans to produce five million alternative-energy vehicles a year by 2020.

Practice questions

1 Which statement about chemical equilibria implies they are dynamic?

  A The position of equilibrium constantly changes.
  B The rates of forward and backward reactions change.
  C The reactants and products continue to react.
  D The concentrations of the reactants and products continue to change.

2 The reaction below represents the Haber process for the industrial production of ammonia.

$$N_2(g) + 3H_2(g) \rightleftharpoons 2NH_3(g) \qquad \Delta H^\ominus = -92 \text{ kJ}$$

The optimum conditions of temperature and pressure are chosen as a compromise between those that favour a high yield of ammonia and those that favour a fast rate of production. Economic considerations are also important. Which statement is correct?

  A A higher temperature would ensure a higher yield and a faster rate.
  B A lower pressure would ensure a higher yield at a lower cost.
  C A lower temperature would ensure a higher yield and a faster rate.
  D A higher pressure would ensure a higher yield at a higher cost.

3 What is the effect of an increase of temperature on the yield and the equilibrium constant for the following reaction?

$$2H_2(g) + CO(g) \rightleftharpoons CH_3OH(l) \qquad \Delta H^\ominus = -128 \text{ kJ}$$

	Yield	Equilibrium constant
A	increases	increases
B	increases	decreases
C	decreases	increases
D	decreases	decreases

4 Consider the equilibrium between methanol, $CH_3OH(l)$, and methanol vapour, $CH_3OH(g)$.

$$CH_3OH(l) \rightleftharpoons CH_3OH(g)$$

What happens to the position of equilibrium and the value of K_c as the temperature decreases?

	Position of equilibrium	Value of K_c
A	shifts to the left	decreases
B	shifts to the left	increases
C	shifts to the right	decreases
D	shifts to the right	increases

5 An increase in temperature increases the amount of chlorine present in the following equilibrium.

$$PCl_5(s) \rightleftharpoons PCl_3(l) + Cl_2(g)$$

What is the best explanation for this?

  A The higher temperature increases the rate of the forward reaction only.
  B The higher temperature increases the rate of the reverse reaction only.
  C The higher temperature increases the rate of both reactions but the forward reaction is affected more than the reverse.
  D The higher temperature increases the rate of both reactions but the reverse reaction is affected more than the forward.

6 Consider the following reversible reaction.

$$Cr_2O_7^{2-}(aq) + H_2O(l) \rightleftharpoons 2CrO_4^{2-}(aq) + 2H^+(aq)$$

What will happen to the position of equilibrium and the value of K_c when more H^+ ions are added at constant temperature?

	Position of equilibrium	Value of K_c
A	shifts to the left	decreases
B	shifts to the right	increases
C	shifts to the right	does not change
D	shifts to the left	does not change

7 Consider this equilibrium reaction in a sealed container.

$$H_2O(g) \rightleftharpoons H_2O(l)$$

What will be the effect on the equilibrium of increasing the temperature from 20 °C to 30 °C?

A More of the water will be in the gaseous state at equilibrium.

B More of the water will be in the liquid state at equilibrium.

C At equilibrium the rate of condensation will be greater than the rate of evaporation.

D At equilibrium the rate of evaporation will be greater than the rate of condensation.

8 Which statement is correct for the equilibrium

$$H_2O(l) \rightleftharpoons H_2O(g)$$

in a closed system at 100 °C?

A All the $H_2O(l)$ molecules have been converted to $H_2O(g)$.

B The rate of the forward reaction is greater than the rate of the reverse reaction.

C The rate of the forward reaction is less than the rate of the reverse reaction.

D The pressure remains constant.

9 Consider the following equilibrium.

$$2SO_2(g) + O_2(g) \rightleftharpoons 2SO_3(g) \qquad \Delta H^\ominus = -198 \text{ kJ mol}^{-1}$$

(a) Deduce the equilibrium constant expression, K_c, for the reaction. (1)

(b) State and explain the effect of increasing the pressure on the yield of sulfur trioxide. (2)

(c) State and explain the effect of increasing the temperature on the yield of sulfur trioxide. (2)

(d) State the effects of a catalyst on the forward and reverse reactions, on the position of equilibrium, and on the value of K_c. (3)

(Total 8 marks)

10 An example of a homogeneous reversible reaction is the reaction between hydrogen and iodine.

$$H_2(g) + I_2(g) \rightleftharpoons 2HI(g)$$

(a) Outline the characteristics of a homogeneous chemical system that is in a state of equilibrium. (2)

(b) Deduce the expression for the equilibrium constant, K_c. (1)

(c) Predict what would happen to the position of equilibrium if the pressure is increased from 1 atm to 2 atm. (1)

(d) The value of K_c at 500 K is 160 and the value of K_c at 700 K is 54. Deduce what this information tells us about the enthalpy change of the forward reaction. (1)

(e) The reaction can be catalysed by adding platinum metal. State and explain what effect the addition of platinum would have on the value of the equilibrium constant. (2)

(Total 7 marks)

 To access weblinks on the topics covered in this chapter, please go to www.pearsonhotlinks.com and enter the ISBN or title of this book.

08 Acids and bases

Essential ideas

8.1 Many reactions involve the transfer of a proton from an acid to a base.

8.2 The characterization of an acid depends on empirical evidence such as the production of gases in reactions with metals, the colour changes of indicators, or the release of heat in reactions with metal oxides and hydroxides.

8.3 The pH scale is an artificial scale used to distinguish between acid, neutral, and basic/alkaline solutions.

8.4 The pH depends on the concentration of the solution. The strength of acids or bases depends on the extent to which they dissociate in aqueous solution.

8.5 Increased industrialization has led to greater production of nitrogen and sulfur oxides leading to acid rain, which is damaging our environment. These problems can be reduced through collaboration with national and intergovernmental organizations.

Acid–base theory informs much of our research into rainwater pollution and other aspects of environmental change.

The burning feeling of acid indigestion, the sour taste of grapefruit, and the vinegary smell of wine that has been exposed to the air are just some of the everyday encounters we have with acids. Likewise alkalis, or bases, are familiar substances – for example in baking soda, in household cleaners that contain ammonia, and in medication against indigestion. So what are the defining properties of these two groups of substances?

This question has intrigued chemists for centuries. The word 'acid' is derived from the Latin word *acetum* meaning sour – early tests to determine whether a substance was acidic were based on tasting! But it was learned that acids had other properties in common too: for example they changed the colour of the dye litmus from blue to red and they corroded metals. Similarly, alkalis were known to have distinctive properties such as being slippery to the touch, being able to remove fats and oils from fabrics, and turning litmus from red to blue. The name alkali comes from the Arabic word for plant ash, *alkalja*, where they were first identified. Early theories about acids and alkalis focused only on how they reacted together – it was actually suggested that the sourness of acids came from their possession of sharp angular spikes which became embedded in soft, rounded particles of alkali!

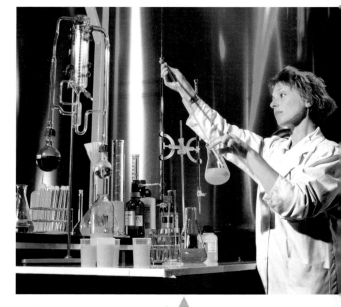

A food scientist testing a sample of a batch of orange juice in a factory in France. pH measurements are an important part of the quality control of the product.

Over the last 120 years, our interpretation of acid–base behaviour has evolved alongside an increasing knowledge of atomic structure and bonding. In this chapter, we explore the modern definitions of acids and bases and learn how these help us to interpret and predict their interactions. Acid–base theory is central to topics such as air and water pollution, how global warming may affect the chemistry of the oceans,

239

the action of drugs in the body, and many other aspects of cutting-edge research. As most acid–base reactions involve equilibria, much of the approach and mathematical content is based on work covered in Chapter 7. It is strongly recommended that you are familiar with this work before starting this chapter.

8.1 Theories of acids and bases

Understandings:
- A Brønsted–Lowry acid is a proton/H⁺ donor and a Brønsted–Lowry base is a proton/H⁺ acceptor.
  - *Guidance*
  - *Students should know the representation of a proton in aqueous solution as both $H^+(aq)$ and $H_3O^+(aq)$.*
- Amphiprotic species can act as both Brønsted–Lowry acids and bases.
- A pair of species differing by a single proton is called a conjugate acid–base pair.

Applications and skills:
- Deduction of the Brønsted–Lowry acid and base in a chemical reaction.
  - *Guidance*
  - *The location of the proton transferred should be clearly indicated. For example, CH_3COOH/CH_3COO- rather than $C_2H_4O_2/C_2H_3O_2^-$.*
- Deduction of the conjugate acid or conjugate base in a chemical reaction.
  - *Guidance*
  - *Lewis theory is not required here.*

Early theories

The famous French chemist Lavoisier proposed in 1777 that oxygen was the 'universal acidifying principle'. He believed that an acid could be defined as a compound of oxygen and a non-metal. In fact, the name he gave to the newly discovered gas *oxygen* means 'acid-former'. This theory, however, had to be dismissed when the acid HCl was proven to be made of hydrogen and chlorine only – no oxygen. To hold true, of course, any definition of an acid has to be valid for *all* acids.

A big step forward came in 1887 when the Swedish chemist Arrhenius suggested that an acid could be defined as a substance that dissociates in water to form hydrogen ions (H⁺) and anions, while a base dissociates into hydroxide (OH⁻) ions and cations. He also recognized that the hydrogen and hydroxide ions could form water, and the cations and anions form a salt. In a sense, Arrhenius was very close to the theory that is widely used to explain acid and base properties today, but his focus was only on aqueous systems. A broader theory was needed to account for reactions occurring without water, and especially for the fact that some insoluble substances show base properties.

Svante August Arrhenius (1859–1927) wrote up his ideas on acids dissociating into ions in water as part of his doctoral thesis while a student at Stockholm University. But his theory was not well received and he was awarded the lowest possible class of degree. Later, his work gradually gained recognition and he received one of the earliest Nobel Prizes in Chemistry in 1903.

Arrhenius may be less well known as the first person documented to predict the possibility of global warming as a result of human activity. In 1896, aware of the rising levels of CO_2 caused by increased industrialization, he calculated the likely effect of this on the temperature of the Earth. Today, over 100 years later, the significance of this relationship between increasing CO_2 and global temperatures has become a subject of major international concern.

Brønsted–Lowry: a theory of proton transfer

In 1923 two chemists, Martin Lowry of Cambridge, England, and Johannes Brønsted of Copenhagen, Denmark, working independently, published similar conclusions regarding the definitions of acids and bases. Their findings overcame the limitations of Arrhenius' work and have become established as the **Brønsted–Lowry theory**.

This theory focuses on the transfer of H^+ ions during an acid–base reaction: acids donate H^+ while bases accept H^+. For example, in the reaction between HCl and NH_3:

$$HCl + NH_3 \rightleftharpoons NH_4^+ + Cl^-$$

HCl transfers H^+ to NH_3 and so acts as an acid, NH_3 accepts the H^+ and so acts as a base.

H^+ transferred

Reaction between vapours of HCl and NH_3 forming the white smoke of ammonium chloride NH_4Cl.

$$HCl(aq) + NH_3(aq) \rightarrow NH_4Cl(s)$$

◀ **Figure 8.1** HCl transfers H^+ to NH_3.

Hydrogen atoms contain just one proton and one electron, so when they ionize by losing the electron, all that is left is the proton. Therefore *H^+ is equivalent to a proton*, and we will use the two terms interchangeably here.

The Brønsted–Lowry theory can therefore be stated as:

- a Brønsted–Lowry acid is a proton (H^+) donor;
- a Brønsted–Lowry base is a proton (H^+) acceptor.

> **A Brønsted–Lowry acid is a proton (H^+) donor.**
>
> **A Brønsted–Lowry base is a proton (H^+) acceptor.**

NATURE OF SCIENCE

Brønsted and Lowry's work on acid–base theory may be a good example of what is sometimes referred to as 'multiple independent discovery'. This refers to cases where similar discoveries are made by scientists at almost the same time, even though they have worked independently from each other. Examples include the independent discovery of the calculus by Newton and Leibniz, the formulation of the mechanism for biological evolution by Darwin and Wallace, and derivation of the pressure–volume relationships of gases by Boyle and Mariotte. Nobel Prizes in Chemistry are commonly awarded to more than one person working in the same field, who may have made the same discovery independently. Multiple independent discoveries are likely increasing as a result of communication technology, which enables scientists who may be widely separated geographically to have access to a common body of knowledge as the basis for their research.

When a discovery is made by more than one scientist at about the same time, ethical questions can arise, such as whether the credit belongs to one individual or should be shared, and whether there are issues regarding intellectual property and patent rights. Historically, these issues have been settled in very different ways in different cases. Nonetheless, the peer review process in science aims to ensure that credit is correctly awarded to the scientist or scientists responsible for a discovery, and that published work represents a new contribution to work in that field.

Conjugate pairs

The act of donating cannot happen in isolation – there must always be something present to play the role of acceptor. In Brønsted–Lowry theory, an acid can therefore only behave as a proton donor if there is also a base present to accept the proton.

Let's consider the acid–base reaction between a generic acid HA and base B:

$$HA + B \rightleftharpoons A^- + BH^+$$

We can see that HA acts as an acid, donating a proton to B while B acts as a base, accepting the proton from HA. But if we look also at the reverse reaction, we can pick out another acid–base reaction: here BH^+ is acting as an acid, donating its proton to A^- while A^- acts as a base accepting the proton from BH^+. In other words acid HA has reacted to form the base A^-, while base B has reacted to form acid BH^+.

$$\overbrace{HA + B}^{\text{conjugate acid–base pair}} \rightleftharpoons A^- + \underbrace{BH^+}_{}$$

conjugate acid–base pair

Acids react to form bases and vice versa. The acid–base pairs related to each other in this way are called **conjugate acid–base pairs**, and you can see that they *differ by just one proton*. It is important to be able to recognize these pairs in a Brønsted–Lowry acid–base reaction.

One example of a conjugate pair is H_2O and H_3O^+, which is found in all acid–base reactions in aqueous solution. The reaction

$$H_2O(l) + H^+(aq) \rightleftharpoons H_3O^+(aq)$$

occurs when a proton released from an acid readily associates with H_2O molecules forming H_3O^+. In other words, protons become hydrated. H_3O^+ is variously called the hydroxonium ion, the oxonium ion, or the hydronium ion and is always the form of hydrogen ions in aqueous solution. However, for most reactions it is convenient simply to write it as $H^+(aq)$. Note that in this pair H_3O^+ is the conjugate acid and H_2O its conjugate base.

> Note that $H_3O^+(aq)$ and $H^+(aq)$ are both used to represent a proton in aqueous solution.

> (i) Lowry described the ready hydration of the proton as 'the extreme reluctance of the hydrogen nucleus to lead an isolated existence'.

Worked example

Label the conjugate acid–base pairs in the following reaction:

$$CH_3COOH(aq) + H_2O(l) \rightleftharpoons CH_3COO^-(aq) + H_3O^+(aq)$$

Solution

$$\underbrace{CH_3COOH / CH_3COO^-}_{\text{conjugate pair}}$$
$$\text{acid} \qquad \text{base}$$

$$\underbrace{H_2O / H_3O^+}_{\text{conjugate pair}}$$
$$\text{base} \quad \text{acid}$$

The fact that in a conjugate pair the acid always has one proton more than its conjugate base, makes it easy to predict the formula of the corresponding conjugate for any given acid or base.

Worked example

1 Write the conjugate base for each of the following.

    (a) H_3O^+ (b) NH_3 (c) H_2CO_3

2 Write the conjugate acid for each of the following.

    (a) NO_2^- (b) OH^- (c) CO_3^{2-}

Solution

1 To form the base from these species, remove one H^+

    (a) H_2O (b) NH_2^- (c) HCO_3^-

2 To form the acid from these species, add one H^+

    (a) HNO_2 (b) H_2O (c) HCO_3^-

> (!) When writing the conjugate acid of a base, add one H^+; when writing the conjugate base of an acid, remove one H^+. Remember to adjust the charge by the 1+ removed or added.

Some species can act as acids and as bases

You may be surprised to see water described in the answers to the Worked examples on page 242 as a base (Q1, part a), and as an acid (Q2, part b), as you are probably not used to thinking of water as an acid, or as a base, but rather as a neutral substance. The point is that Brønsted–Lowry theory describes acids and bases in terms of how they react together, so it all depends on what water is reacting with. Consider the following:

$$CH_3COOH + H_2O \rightleftharpoons CH_3COO^- + H_3O^+$$
$$\text{acid} \qquad \text{base} \qquad \text{base} \qquad \text{acid}$$

$$NH_3 + H_2O \rightleftharpoons NH_4^+ + OH^-$$
$$\text{base} \quad \text{acid} \qquad \text{acid} \quad \text{base}$$

So with CH_3COOH, water acts as a Brønsted–Lowry base, but with NH_3 it acts as a Brønsted–Lowry acid.

Notice that water is not the only species that can act as both an acid and a base – for example, we see in the Worked example below that HCO_3^- behaves similarly. Substances which can act as Brønsted–Lowry acids and bases in this way are said to be **amphiprotic**. What are the features that enable these species to have this 'double identity'?

To act as a Brønsted–Lowry acid, they must be able to dissociate and release H^+.

To act as a Brønsted–Lowry base, they must be able to accept H^+, which means they must have a lone pair of electrons.

So substances that are amphiprotic according to Brønsted–Lowry theory must possess both a lone pair of electrons and hydrogen that can be released as H^+.

Worked example

Write equations to show HCO_3^- acting (a) as a Brønsted–Lowry acid and (b) as a Brønsted–Lowry base.

Solution

(a) to act as an acid, it donates H^+
$$HCO_3^-(aq) + H_2O(l) \rightleftharpoons CO_3^{2-}(aq) + H_3O^+(l)$$

(b) to act as a base, it accepts H^+
$$HCO_3^-(aq) + H_2O(l) \rightleftharpoons H_2CO_3(aq) + OH^-(aq)$$

Exercises

1 Deduce the formula of the conjugate acid of the following:
   (a) SO_3^{2-} (c) $C_2H_5COO^-$ (e) F^-
   (b) CH_3NH_2 (d) NO_3^- (f) HSO_4^-

2 Deduce the formula of the conjugate base of the following:
   (a) H_3PO_4 (c) H_2SO_3 (e) OH^-
   (b) CH_3COOH (d) HSO_4^- (f) HBr

3 For each of the following reactions, identify the Brønsted-Lowry acids and bases and the conjugate acid–base pairs:
   (a) $CH_3COOH + NH_3 \rightleftharpoons NH_4^+ + CH_3COO^-$
   (b) $CO_3^{2-} + H_3O^+ \rightleftharpoons H_2O + HCO_3^-$
   (c) $NH_4^+ + NO_2^- \rightleftharpoons HNO_2 + NH_3$

4 Show by means of equations how the anion in K_2HPO_4 is amphiprotic.

The acid and base in a conjugate acid–base pair differ by just one proton.

Amphoteros is a Greek word meaning 'both'. For example amphibians are adapted both to water and to land.

An amphiprotic substance is one which can act as both a proton donor and a proton acceptor.

NATURE OF SCIENCE

Terminology in science has to be used appropriately according to the context. *Amphiprotic* specifically relates to Brønsted–Lowry acid–base theory, where the emphasis is on the transfer of a proton. The term *amphoteric*, on the other hand, has a broader meaning as it is used to describe a substance which can act as an acid and as a base, including reactions that do not involve the transfer of a proton. For example, as described in Chapter 3, aluminium oxide is an amphoteric oxide as it reacts with both dilute acids and alkalis. Note that all amphiprotic substances are also amphoteric, but the converse is not true. The fact that the two terms exist reflects the fact that different theories are used to describe acid–base reactions.

Properties of acids and bases

Understandings:

- Most acids have observable characteristic chemical reactions with reactive metals, metal oxides, metal hydroxides, hydrogencarbonates, and carbonates.

  Guidance
  Bases which are not hydroxides, such as ammonia, soluble carbonates, and hydrogencarbonates should be covered.
- Salt and water are produced in exothermic neutralization reactions.

Applications and skills:

- Balancing chemical equations for the reaction of acids.
- Identification of the acid and base needed to make different salts.
- Candidates should have experience of acid–base titrations with different indicators.

  Guidance
  The colour changes of different indicators are given in the data IB booklet in section 22.

While we have commented that ideas regarding the defining nature of acids and bases have been long debated, the recognition of what these substances *do* has been known for centuries.

We will look here at some typical reactions of acids and bases in aqueous solutions where H^+ is the ion common to all acids. The bases considered here are those that neutralize acids to produce water, which include:

- metal oxides and hydroxides;
- ammonia;
- soluble carbonates (Na_2CO_3 and K_2CO_3) and hydrogencarbonates ($NaHCO_3$ and $KHCO_3$).

The soluble bases are known as **alkalis**. When dissolved in water they all release the hydroxide ion OH^-. For example:

$$K_2O(s) + H_2O(l) \rightarrow 2K^+(aq) + 2OH^-(aq)$$

$$NH_3(aq) + H_2O(l) \rightleftharpoons NH_4^+(aq) + OH^-(aq)$$

$$CO_3^{2-}(aq) + H_2O(l) \rightleftharpoons HCO_3^-(aq) + OH^-(aq)$$

$$HCO_3^-(aq) \rightleftharpoons CO_2(g) + OH^-(aq)$$

Figure 8.2 The relationship between alkalis and bases.

Alkalis are bases that dissolve in water to form the hydroxide ion OH^-.

In acid–base theory the words ionization and dissociation are often used interchangeably as acid dissociation always leads to ion formation.

Acids react with metals, bases, and carbonates to form salts

The term **salt** refers to the ionic compound formed when the hydrogen of an acid is replaced by a metal or another positive ion. Salts form by reaction of acids with metals or bases. The familiar example, sodium chloride, NaCl, known as common salt, is derived from the acid HCl by reaction with a base that contains Na, such as NaOH. The terms **parent acid** and **parent base** are sometimes used to describe this relationship between an acid, a base, and their salt.

parent base   parent acid

NaOH   HCl

H_2O

NaCl

salt

There are three main types of reaction by which acids react to form salts.

1 Acid + metal → salt + hydrogen

$$2HCl(aq) + Zn(s) \rightarrow ZnCl_2(aq) + H_2(g)$$

$$H_2SO_4(aq) + Fe(s) \rightarrow FeSO_4(aq) + H_2(g)$$

$$2CH_3COOH(aq) + Mg(s) \rightarrow Mg(CH_3COO)_2(aq) + H_2(g)$$

We can also write these as ionic equations. For example:

$$2H^+(aq) + 2Cl^-(aq) + Zn(s) \rightarrow Zn^{2+}(aq) + 2Cl^-(aq) + H_2(g)$$

Species which do not change during a reaction, like Cl^- here, are called **spectator ions** and can be cancelled out. So the net reaction is:

$$2H^+(aq) + Zn(s) \rightarrow Zn^{2+}(aq) + H_2(g)$$

These reactions of metals with acids are the reason why acids have corrosive properties on most metals, and why, for example, it is important to keep car battery acid well away from the metal bodywork of the car.

You can demonstrate the release of hydrogen from acids in simple experiments by adding a small piece of metal to a dilute solution of the acid. There is a big range, however, in the reactivity of metals in these reactions. More reactive metals such as sodium and potassium in Group 1 would react much too violently, while copper and other less reactive metals such as silver and gold will usually not react at all. This is partly why these less reactive metals are so valuable – they are much more resistant to corrosion. We will consider this differing reactivity in Chapter 9. Another point to note is that although the common acid nitric acid, HNO_3, does react with metals, it usually does not release hydrogen owing to its oxidizing properties (Chapter 9).

2 Acid + base → salt + water

$$HCl(aq) + NaOH(aq) \rightarrow NaCl(aq) + H_2O(l)$$

$$HNO_3(aq) + NH_4OH(aq) \rightarrow NH_4NO_3(aq) + H_2O(l)$$

$$2CH_3COOH(aq) + CuO(s) \rightarrow Cu(CH_3COO)_2(aq) + H_2O(l)$$

These reactions between acids and bases are known as **neutralization** reactions. They can all be represented by one common ionic equation that shows the net reaction clearly:

$$H^+(aq) + OH^-(aq) \rightarrow H_2O(l)$$

Neutralization reactions of acids with bases are exothermic – heat is released. The **enthalpy of neutralization** is defined as the enthalpy change that occurs when an acid and a base react together to form one mole of water. For reactions between all strong acids and strong bases, the enthalpy change is very similar with $\Delta H = -57$ kJ mol^{-1} approximately. This is because the net reaction is the same, involving the formation of water from its ions.

Magnesium reacting with HCl.

$$Mg(s) + 2HCl(aq) \rightarrow$$
$$MgCl_2(aq) + H_2(g)$$

The tiny bubbles are hydrogen gas being liberated.

Acid + reactive metal → salt + hydrogen

Acid + carbonate → salt + water + carbon dioxide

Neutralization reactions occur when an acid and base react together to form a salt and water. They are exothermic reactions.

There are times when neutralization reactions are useful to help reduce the effect of an acid or a base. For example, treatment for acid indigestion often involves using 'antacids' which contain a mixture of weak alkalis such as magnesium hydroxide and aluminium hydroxide. As we will learn in section 8.5, in places where the soil has become too acidic, the growth of many plants will be restricted. Adding a weak alkali such as lime, CaO, can help to reduce the acidity and so increase the fertility of the soil.

3 Acid + carbonate → salt + water + carbon dioxide

$$2HCl(aq) + CaCO_3(s) \rightarrow CaCl_2(aq) + H_2O(l) + CO_2(g)$$

$$H_2SO_4(aq) + Na_2CO_3(aq) \rightarrow Na_2SO_4(aq) + H_2O(l) + CO_2(g)$$

$$CH_3COOH(aq) + KHCO_3(aq) \rightarrow KCH_3COO(aq) + H_2O(l) + CO_2(g)$$

These reactions can also be represented as an ionic equation:

$$2H^+(aq) + CO_3^{2-}(aq) \rightarrow H_2O(l) + CO_2(g)$$

The reactions, like the reaction of acids with metals, involve a gas being given off so they visibly produce bubbles, known as **effervescence**.

Rainwater dissolves some carbon dioxide from the air to form a weak solution of carbonic acid, H_2CO_3.

$$H_2O(l) + CO_2(g) \rightleftharpoons H_2CO_3(aq)$$

Greater pressure, such as that found in capillary beds of limestone (CaCO₃) rocks, increases the tendency of CO_2 to dissolve, giving rise to a more acidified solution. This then reacts on the limestone as follows:

$$H_2CO_3(aq) + CaCO_3(s) \rightleftharpoons Ca(HCO_3)_2(aq)$$

CaCO₃, limestone, is virtually insoluble whereas the product calcium hydrogencarbonate, $Ca(HCO_3)_2$, is soluble and washes away, leading to erosion of the rocks. This is why caves commonly form in limestone regions. Inside the cave where the pressure is lower, the reaction above may be reversed, as less CO_2 dissolves. In this case CaCO₃ comes out of solution and precipitates, giving rise to the formations known as stalagtites and stalagmites.

Similar reactions of rainwater dissolving CaCO₃ rocks can give rise to water supplies with elevated levels of Ca^{2+} ions, known as 'hard water'.

Kitchen chemistry. Baking soda (NaHCO₃) and vinegar (CH₃COOH) react together in a powerful acid–base reaction, releasing carbon dioxide gas.

$$NaHCO_3(s) + CH_3COOH(aq) \rightarrow NaCH_3COO(aq) + H_2O(l) + CO_2$$

Limestone rock shaped by natural chemical erosion in Switzerland. Rainwater, a weak solution of H₂CO₃, reacts with the calcium carbonate, slowly dissolving it.

In section 8.5, these reactions between acids and metals and metal carbonates are discussed in the context of the environmental problem known as acid deposition.

Acids and bases can be distinguished using indicators

Indicators act as chemical detectors, giving information about a change in the environment. The most widely used in chemistry are **acid–base indicators** that change colour reversibly according to the concentration of H^+ ions in the solution. This happens because they are weak acids and bases whose conjugates have different colours. The colour change means that they can be used to identify the pH of a substance. Indicators are generally used either as aqueous solutions or absorbed onto 'test paper'.

Probably the best known acid–base indicator is **litmus**, which is a dye derived from lichens, and which turns pink in the presence of acid and blue in the presence of alkalis. It is widely used to test for acids or alkalis, but is not so useful in distinguishing between different strengths of acid or alkali.

Other indicators give different colours in different solutions of acid and alkali. Some common examples are given in the table here, and there are more in section 22 of your IB data booklet.

Litmus indicator compared in acid and alkali solutions.

Be careful not to assume that indicator tests always show acids as pink and alkalis as blue. This is true with litmus, but other indicators give many different colours including pink in alkali.

Indicator	Colour in acid	Colour in alkali
litmus	pink	blue
methyl orange	red	yellow
phenolphthalein	colourless	pink

Many of these indicators are derived from natural substances such as extracts from flower petals and berries. A common indicator in the laboratory is **universal indicator**, which is formed by mixing together several indicators. It changes colour many times across a range of different acids and alkalis and so can be used to measure the concentration of H^+ on the pH scale. We will discuss this later in the chapter.

Acid–base titrations are based on neutralization reactions

Neutralization reactions are often used in the laboratory to calculate the exact concentration of an acid or an alkali when the other concentration is known. As we learned in Chapter 1, the solution of known concentration is known as the standard solution. The technique known as **acid–base titration** involves reacting together a carefully measured volume of one of the solutions, and adding the

Figure 8.3 Simple titration apparatus.

- burette records volume of acid added
- pipette
- fixed volume of alkali measured and placed in flask
- conical flask
- white tile
- neutralization reaction happens here

other solution gradually until the so-called **equivalence point** is reached where they exactly neutralize each other. A convenient way to determine when the equivalence point has been reached is to use an indicator, chosen to change colour as the acid and base exactly neutralize each other.

For example, titration can be used in the following experiments:

• to calculate the concentration of ethanoic acid in vinegar by titration with a standard solution of aqueous sodium hydroxide, using phenolphthalein indicator;
• to calculate the concentration of sodium hydroxide by titration with a standard solution of hydrochloric acid, using methyl orange indicator.

A good indicator is one that gives a distinct or sharp colour change at the equivalence point.

Acid–base titration to calculate the concentration of ethanoic acid in vinegar

Full details of how to carry out this experiment with a worksheet are available on your eBook.

When you need to choose a base in solution to make a specific salt, it is useful to know some simple solubility rules.

• The only soluble carbonates and hydrogencarbonates are $(NH_4)_2CO_3$, Na_2CO_3, K_2CO_3, $NaHCO_3$, $KHCO_3$, and $Ca(HCO_3)_2$.
• The only soluble hydroxides are NH_4OH, $LiOH$, $NaOH$, and KOH.

Exercises

5 Write equations for the following reactions:

   (a) sulfuric acid and copper oxide
   (b) nitric acid and sodium hydrogencarbonate
   (c) phosphoric acid and potassium hydroxide
   (d) ethanoic acid and aluminium

6 An aqueous solution of which of the following reacts with calcium metal?

   A ammonia   **C** potassium hydroxide
   B hydrogen chloride   **D** sodium hydrogencarbonate

7 Which of the following is/are formed when a metal oxide reacts with a dilute acid?

   I   a metal salt
   II   water
   III carbon dioxide gas

   A I only   **B** I and II only   **C** II and III only   **D** I, II, and III

8 Suggest by name a parent acid and parent base that could be used to make the following salts. Write equations for each reaction.

   (a) sodium nitrate   **(c)** copper(II) sulfate
   (b) ammonium chloride   **(d)** potassium methanoate

8.3 The pH scale

Understandings:

• $pH = -\log[H^+(aq)]$ and $[H^+] = 10^{-pH}$.
• A change of one pH unit represents a 10-fold change in the hydrogen ion concentration $[H^+]$.

   Guidance
   Knowing the temperature dependence of K_w is not required.

• pH values distinguish between acidic, neutral, and alkaline solutions.
• The ionic product constant, $K_w = [H^+][OH^-] = 10^{-14}$ at 298 K.

Applications and skills:

• Solving problems involving pH, $[H^+]$, and $[OH^-]$.

   Guidance
   • *Students should be concerned only with strong acids and bases in this sub-topic.*
   • *Students will not be assessed on pOH values.*

• Students should be familiar with the use of a pH meter and universal indicator.

pH is a logarithmic expression of [H⁺]

Chemists realized a long time ago that it would be useful to have a quantitative scale of acid strength based on the concentration of hydrogen ions. As the majority of acids encountered are weak, the hydrogen ion concentration expressed directly as $mol\ dm^{-3}$ produces numbers with large negative exponents; for example the H^+ concentration in our blood is $4.6 \times 10^{-8}\ mol\ dm^{-3}$. Such numbers are not very user-friendly when it comes to describing and comparing acids. The introduction of the pH scale in 1909 by Sørensen led to wide acceptance owing to its ease of use. It is defined as follows:

$$pH = -\log_{10}[H^+]$$

In other words, pH is the negative number to which the base 10 is raised to give the [H⁺]. This can also be expressed as:

$$[H^+] = 10^{-pH}$$

- A solution that has $[H^+] = 0.1\ mol\ dm^{-3} \Rightarrow [H^+] = 10^{-1}\ mol\ dm^{-3} \Rightarrow pH = 1$.
- A solution that has $[H^+] = 0.01\ mol\ dm^{-3} \Rightarrow [H^+] = 10^{-2}\ mol\ dm^{-3} \Rightarrow pH = 2$.

Now we can explore some of the features of the pH scale that help to make it so convenient.

pH numbers are usually positive and have no units

Although the pH scale is theoretically an infinite scale (and can even extend into negative numbers), most acids and bases encountered will have positive pH values and fall within the range 0–14, corresponding to [H⁺] from $1\ mol\ dm^{-3}$ to $10^{-14}\ mol\ dm^{-3}$.

The pH number is inversely related to the [H⁺]

Solutions with a higher [H⁺] have a lower pH and vice versa. So stronger and more concentrated acids have a lower pH, weaker and more dilute acids have a higher pH.

A change of one pH unit represents a 10-fold change in [H⁺]

This means increasing the pH by one unit represents a decrease in [H⁺] by 10 times; decreasing by one pH unit represents an increase in [H⁺] by 10 times.

The Danish chemist Søren Peder Lauritz Sørensen (1868–1939) developed the pH concept in 1909, originally proposing that it be formulated as p_H. He did not account for his choice of the letter 'p' though it has been suggested to originate from the German word *potenz* for power. It could equally well derive from the Latin, Danish, or French terms for the same word.

TOK The pH scale can be considered to be an artificial or an arbitrary scale. To what extent is this true of all scales used in measuring?

$$pH = -\log_{10}[H^+];$$
$$[H^+] = 10^{-pH}$$

Figure 8.4 The inverse relationship between pH and H⁺.

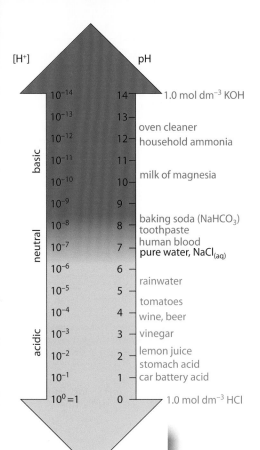

[H⁺] pH

[H⁺]	pH	
10^{-14}	14	1.0 mol dm⁻³ KOH
10^{-13}	13	
10^{-12}	12	oven cleaner
		household ammonia
10^{-11}	11	
10^{-10}	10	milk of magnesia
10^{-9}	9	
10^{-8}	8	baking soda (NaHCO₃)
		toothpaste
10^{-7}	7	human blood
		pure water, NaCl(aq)
10^{-6}	6	
10^{-5}	5	rainwater
10^{-4}	4	tomatoes
		wine, beer
10^{-3}	3	vinegar
10^{-2}	2	lemon juice
		stomach acid
10^{-1}	1	car battery acid
$10^{0} = 1$	0	1.0 mol dm⁻³ HCl

basic / neutral / acidic

Figure 8.5 The pH scale at 298 K and pH values of some common substances.

Logarithmic scales are used in other disciplines where they can help in the presentation of data. In medicine, the logarithmic decay of levels of drugs in the blood against time is used. In seismic studies, the Richter scale is a logarithmic expression of the relative energy released during earthquakes. In sense perception the decibel scale of sound intensity and the scale for measuring the visible brightness of stars (their magnitude) are also logarithmic scales.

Worked example

If the pH of a solution is changed from 3 to 5, deduce how the hydrogen ion concentration changes.

Solution

$pH = 3 \Rightarrow [H^+] = 10^{-3}$ mol dm⁻³; $pH = 5 \Rightarrow [H^+] = 10^{-5}$ mol dm⁻³

So [H⁺] has changed by 10^{-2} or decreased by 100.

In the last 40 years, researchers have developed so-called 'super acids' by mixing together various substances. These are several orders of magnitude more acidic than conventional acids, and one example known as 'magic acid' is even able to dissolve candle wax.

The pH scale is a measure of [H⁺] and so at first glance may appear to be more suited for the measurement of acids than of bases. But we can in fact use the same scale to describe the alkalinity of a solution. As will be explained on page 252, this is because the relationship between [H⁺] and [OH⁻] is inverse in aqueous solutions, and so lower [H⁺] (higher pH) means higher [OH⁻] and vice versa. Therefore the scale of pH numbers represents a range of values from strongly acidic through to strongly alkaline.

pH 0	**pH 7**	**pH 14**
increasing [H⁺]	neutral	increasing [OH⁻]
increasing acidity		increasing alkalinity

pH calculations

From the definition of pH we can:

(i) calculate the value of pH from a known concentration of H⁺;

(ii) calculate the concentration of H⁺ from a given pH.

In pH calculations you will need to be able to work out logarithms to base 10 and anti-logarithms. Make sure that you are familiar with these operations on your calculator.

Note that the logarithms used in all the work on acids and bases are logarithms to base 10 (log). Do not confuse these with natural logarithms, to base e, (ln).

Worked example

A sample of lake water was analysed at 298 K and found to have [H⁺] = 3.2 × 10⁻⁵ mol dm⁻³. Calculate the pH of this water and comment on its value.

Solution

$$pH = -\log_{10}[H^+]$$
$$= -\log_{10}(3.2 \times 10^{-5}) = -(-4.49485)$$
$$pH = 4.49$$

At 298 K this pH < 7, and the lake water is therefore acidic.

Worked example

Human blood has a pH of 7.40. Calculate the concentration of hydrogen ions present.

Solution

$$[H^+] = 10^{-pH}$$

$$= 10^{-7.40} = 4.0 \times 10^{-8}$$

$$[H^+] = 4.0 \times 10^{-8} \text{ mol dm}^{-3}$$

Measuring pH

An easy way to measure pH is with universal indicator paper or solution. The substance tested will give a characteristic colour, which can then be compared with a colour chart supplied with the indicator. Narrower range indicators give a more accurate reading than broad range, but they always depend on the ability of the user's eyes to interpret the colour.

A more objective and usually more accurate means is by using a **pH meter** or probe that directly reads the [H⁺] concentration

A digital probe showing a pH of 3.20 for the solution in the beaker. The temperature dial is adjusted to the room temperature, allowing the pH meter to compensate for the temperature.

through a special electrode. pH meters can record to an accuracy of several decimal points. They must, however, be calibrated before each use with a buffer solution, and standardized for the temperature, as pH is a temperature-dependent measurement.

The rule to follow for significant figures in logarithms is that *the number of decimal places in the logarithm should equal the number of significant figures in the number.* In other words, the number to the left of the decimal place in the logarithm is not counted as a significant figure (this is because it is derived from the exponential part of the number). In the last example on page 250, the number given has two significant figures (3.2) and so the answer is given to two decimal places (.49).

Use of a pH meter and universal indicator in measuring pH

Full details of how to carry out this experiment with a worksheet are available on your eBook.

The pH scale and universal indicator. The tubes contain universal indicator added to solutions of pH 0–14 from left to right.

The ionization of water

As the majority of acid–base reactions involve ionization in aqueous solution, it is useful to consider the role of water in more detail. Water itself does ionize, albeit only very slightly at normal temperatures and pressures, so we can write an equilibrium expression for this reaction.

$$H_2O(l) \rightleftharpoons H^+(aq) + OH^-(aq)$$

Therefore $K_c = \dfrac{[H^+][OH^-]}{[H_2O]}$

Water is a pure liquid so its concentration is just a function of its density, which is 1 g cm^{-3}.

From $n = \dfrac{m}{M}$, this gives

$n(H_2O) = \dfrac{1000}{18}$ in 1 dm^3

so concentration $(H_2O) =$ 55 mol dm^{-3}.

The concentration of water can be considered to be constant due to the fact that so little of it ionizes, and it can therefore be combined with K_c to produce a modified equilibrium constant known as K_w.

$K_c[H_2O] = [H^+][OH^-]$

Therefore $K_w = [H^+][OH^-]$

K_w is known as the **ionic product constant of water** and has a fixed value at a specified temperature. At 298 K, $K_w = 1.00 \times 10^{-14}$.

The value $K_w = 1.00 \times 10^{-14}$ at 298 K is given in section 2 of the IB data booklet so does not have to be learned.

In pure water because $[H^+] = [OH^-]$, it follows that $[H^+] = \sqrt{K_w}$

So at 298 K, $[H^+] = 1.00 \times 10^{-7}$ which gives pH = 7.00

This is consistent with the widely known value for the pH of water at room temperature.

$K_w = [H^+][OH^-]$

The relationship between H$^+$ and OH$^-$ is inverse

Because the product $[H^+] \times [OH^-]$ gives a constant value, it follows that the concentrations of these ions must have an inverse relationship. In other words, in aqueous solutions the higher the concentration of H$^+$ the lower the concentration of OH$^-$. Solutions are defined as acidic, neutral, or basic according to their relative concentrations of these ions as shown on page 253.

		at 298 K
Acidic solutions are defined as those in which	$[H^+] > [OH^-]$	pH < 7
Neutral solutions are defined as those in which	$[H^+] = [OH^-]$	pH = 7
Alkaline solutions are defined as those in which	$[H^+] < [OH^-]$	pH > 7

So if we know the concentration of either H^+ or OH^-, we can calculate the other from the value of K_w.

$$[H]^+ = \frac{K_w}{[OH]^-} \quad \text{and} \quad [OH]^- = \frac{K_w}{[H]^+}$$

The concentrations of H^+ and OH^- are inversely proportional in an aqueous solution.

Worked example

A sample of blood at 298 K has $[H^+] = 4.60 \times 10^{-8}$ mol dm^{-3}.

Calculate the concentration of OH^- and state whether the blood is acidic, neutral, or basic.

Solution

At 298 K, $K_w = 1.00 \times 10^{-14} = [H^+][OH^-]$

$$[OH]^- = \frac{1.00 \times 10^{-14}}{4.60 \times 10^{-8}} = 2.17 \times 10^{-7} \text{ mol dm}^{-3}$$

As $[OH^-] > [H^+]$ the solution is basic.

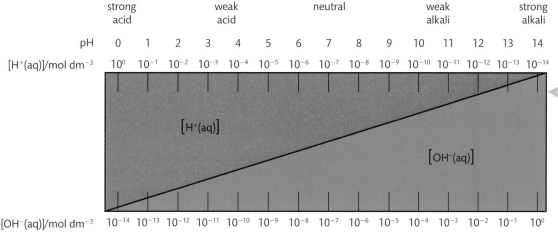

Figure 8.6 Relationship between $[H^+]$, $[OH^-]$ and pH.

Summary of steps in calculations of H^+, OH^- and pH

$[H^+] = 10^{-pH}$ $[OH^-] = \dfrac{K_w}{[H^+]}$

pH ⟶ H$^+$(aq) ⟶ OH$^-$(aq)

$pH = -\log_{10}[H^+]$ $[H^+] = \dfrac{K_w}{[OH^-]}$

Exercises

9 What happens to the pH of an acid when 10 cm^3 of it is added to 90 cm^3 of water?

10 Beer has a hydrogen ion concentration of 1.9×10^{-5} mol dm^{-3}. What is its pH?

11 An aqueous solution has a pH of 9 at 25 °C. What are its concentrations for H$^+$ and OH$^-$?

12 For each of the following solutions, calculate [OH$^-$] from [H$^+$] or [H$^+$] from [OH$^-$]. Classify each solution as acidic, basic, or neutral at 298 K.

   (a) [H$^+$] = 3.4×10^{-9} mol dm^{-3}
   (b) [OH$^-$] = 0.010 mol dm^{-3}
   (c) [OH$^-$] = 1.0×10^{-10} mol dm^{-3}
   (d) [H$^+$] = 8.6×10^{-5} mol dm^{-3}

13 What is the pH of a 0.01 mol dm^{-3} solution of HCl which dissociates fully?

$$HCl(aq) \rightarrow H^+(aq) + Cl^-(aq)$$

14 For each of the following biological fluids, calculate the pH from the given concentration of H$^+$ or OH$^-$ ions.

   (a) bile: [OH$^-$] = 8×10^{-8} mol dm^{-3}
   (b) gastric juice: [H$^+$] = 10^{-2} mol dm^{-3}
   (c) urine: [OH$^-$] = 6×10^{-10} mol dm^{-3}

15 A solution of sodium hydroxide is prepared by adding distilled water to 6.0 g NaOH to make 1.0 dm^3 of solution. What is the pH of this solution? Assume that NaOH dissociates completely in solution:

$$NaOH(aq) \rightarrow Na^+(aq) + OH^-(aq)$$

8.4 Strong and weak acids and bases

Understandings:

- Strong and weak acids and bases differ in the extent of ionization.

   ### Guidance
   The terms ionization and dissociation can be used interchangeably.

- Strong acids and bases of equal concentrations have higher conductivities than weak acids and bases.

   ### Guidance
   See section 21 in the IB data booklet for a list of weak acids and bases.

- A strong acid is a good proton donor and has a weak conjugate base.
- A strong base is a good proton acceptor and has a weak conjugate acid.

Applications and skills:

- Distinction between strong and weak acids and bases in terms of the rates of their reactions with metals, metal oxides, metal hydroxides, metal hydrogencarbonates, and metal carbonates and their electrical conductivities for solutions of equal concentrations.

The strength of an acid or base depends on its extent of ionization

We have seen that the reactions of acids and bases are dependent on the fact that they dissociate in solution, acids to produce H$^+$ ions and bases to produce OH$^-$ ions. As we will see here, the extent of this dissociation is what defines the strength of an acid or a base.

Consider the acid dissociation reaction:

$$HA(aq) + H_2O(l) \rightleftharpoons A^-(aq) + H_3O^+(aq)$$

If this acid dissociates fully, it will exist entirely as ions in solution. It is said to be a **strong acid**. For example, hydrochloric acid, HCl, is a strong acid.

The reaction is written without the equilibrium sign.

$$HCl(aq) + H_2O(l) \rightarrow H_3O^+(aq) + Cl^-(aq)$$

If, on the other hand, the acid dissociates only partially, it produces an equilibrium mixture in which the undissociated form dominates. It is said to be a **weak acid**. For example, ethanoic acid, CH_3COOH, is a weak acid.

$$CH_3COOH(aq) + H_2O(l) \rightleftharpoons H_3O^+(aq) + CH_3COO^-(aq)$$

Here it is essential to use the equilibrium sign for its dissociation reaction.

Strong acids are good proton donors. As their dissociation reactions go to completion, their conjugate bases are not readily able to accept a proton. For example, HCl reacts to form the conjugate base Cl^-, which shows virtually no basic properties.

$$\begin{array}{ccccccc} HCl(aq) & + & H_2O(l) & \rightarrow & H_3O^+(aq) & + & Cl^-(aq) \\ \text{strong acid} & & \text{base} & & \text{conjugate acid} & & \text{conjugate base} \end{array}$$

Weak acids are poor proton donors. As their dissociation reactions are equilibria which lie to the left, in favour of reactants, their conjugate bases are readily able to accept a proton. For example, CH_3COOH reacts to form the conjugate base CH_3COO^-, which is a stronger base than Cl^-.

$$\begin{array}{ccccccc} CH_3COOH(aq) & + & H_2O(l) & \rightleftharpoons & H_3O^+(aq) & + & CH_3COO^-(aq) \\ \text{weak acid} & & \text{base} & & \text{conjugate acid} & & \text{conjugate base} \end{array}$$

So acid dissociation reactions favour the production of the weaker conjugate.

In a similar way, bases can be described as strong or weak on the basis of the extent of their ionization. For example, NaOH is a **strong base** because it ionizes fully.

$$NaOH(aq) \rightarrow Na^+(aq) + OH^-(aq)$$

Its dissociation is written without equilibrium signs.

(Note that it is the OH^- ions that show Brønsted–Lowry base behaviour by accepting protons.)

On the other hand, NH_3 is a **weak base** as it ionizes only partially, so its equilibrium lies to the left and the concentration of ions is low.

$$NH_3(aq) + H_2O(l) \rightleftharpoons NH_4^+(aq) + OH^-(aq)$$

Strong bases are good proton acceptors; they react to form conjugates that do not show acidic properties. Weak bases are poor proton acceptors; they react to form conjugates with stronger acidic properties than the conjugates of strong bases. Base ionization reactions favour the production of the weaker conjugate.

The strength of an acid or base is therefore a measure of how readily it dissociates in aqueous solution. This is an inherent property of a particular acid or base, dependent on its bonding. Do not confuse acid or basic *strength* with its *concentration,* which is a variable depending on the number of moles per unit volume, according to how much solute has been added to the water. Note, for example, that it is possible for an acid or base to be strong but present in a dilute solution, or weak and present in a concentrated solution.

Strong acids and strong bases ionize almost completely in solution; weak acids and weak bases ionize only partially in solution.

In writing the ionization reactions of weak acids and bases, it is essential to use the equilibrium sign.

Be careful not to confuse two different pairs of opposites:

- strong and weak acids or bases refer to their extent of dissociation;
- concentrated and dilute refer to the ratio of solute and water in the solution.

NATURE OF SCIENCE

The use of advanced analytical techniques has allowed the strengths of different acids and bases to be quantified and compared. Experimental evidence has been obtained from accurate pH and concentration measurements. Sometimes the results may seem surprising, and this has led to a fuller exploration of the factors involved at the molecular level. For example, the relative acidic strengths of the hydrogen halides (HF, HCl, HBr, and HI) are found to increase down the group, despite the decreasing polarity of the molecules. This is explained by the decreasing bond strength of H–halogen as the halogen atom increases in size. In other cases, such as the organic acids, factors such as electronegativity, ion stability, and inductive effects are used to explain the patterns in acid strength. Theories must explain experimental evidence and be subject to testable predictions.

Weak acids and bases are much more common than strong acids and bases

It is often useful to know which of the acids and bases we come across are strong and which are weak. Fortunately this is quite easy as there are very few common examples of strong acids and bases, so this short list can be committed to memory. You will then know that any other acids and bases you come across are likely to be weak.

	Acid		Base	
common examples of **strong** forms	HCl	hydrochloric acid	LiOH	lithium hydroxide
	HNO_3	nitric acid	NaOH	sodium hydroxide
	H_2SO_4	sulfuric acid	KOH	potassium hydroxide
			$Ba(OH)_2$	barium hydroxide
some examples of **weak** forms	CH_3COOH and other organic acids	ethanoic acid	NH_3	ammonia
	H_2CO_3	carbonic acid	$C_2H_5NH_2$ and other amines	ethylamine
	H_3PO_4	phosphoric acid		

Note that amines such as ethylamine, $C_2H_5NH_2$, can be considered as organic derivatives of NH_3 in which one of the hydrogen atoms has been replaced by an alkyl (hydrocarbon) group. There are literally hundreds of acids and bases in organic chemistry (Chapter 10), nearly all of which are weak in comparison with the strong inorganic acids listed here. Many of these are listed in section 21 of the IB data booklet. Amino acids, the building blocks of proteins, as their name implies contain both the basic –NH_2 amino group and the –COOH acid group. The 'A' in DNA, the store of genetic material, stands for 'acid', in this case the acid present is phosphoric acid.

Distinguishing between strong and weak acids and bases

Due to their greater ionization in solution, strong acids and strong bases will contain *a higher concentration of ions* than weak acids and weak bases. This then can be used as a means of distinguishing between them. Note though that such comparisons will only be valid when solutions of the same concentration (mol dm^{-3}) are compared at the same temperature. We will consider here three properties that depend on the concentration of ions and so can be used for this purpose.

1 Electrical conductivity

Electrical conductivity of a solution depends on the concentration of mobile ions. Strong acids and strong bases will therefore show higher conductivity than weak acids and bases – so long as solutions of the same concentration are compared. This can be measured using a conductivity meter or probe, or by using the conductivity setting on a pH meter.

2 Rate of reaction

The reactions of acids described in section 8.2 depend on the concentration of H$^+$ ions. They will therefore happen at a greater rate with stronger acids.

These different rates of reactions may be an important consideration, for example, regarding safety in the laboratory, but they usually do not provide an easy means of quantifying data to distinguish between weak and strong acids.

3 pH

Because it is a measure of the H$^+$ concentration, the pH scale can be used directly to compare the strengths of acids (providing they are of equal molar concentration.) Remember the higher the H$^+$ concentration, the lower the pH value. Universal indicator or a pH meter can be used to measure pH.

▲
The different rates of reaction between magnesium metal and hydrochloric acid and ethanoic acid. The mass and surface area of the magnesium added and the concentrations and volumes of the acids are equal in both tubes. The higher rate with the strong acid HCl is shown on the left, where large bubbles of hydrogen form. The slower reaction with CH$_3$COOH, shown on the right, causes smaller bubbles of hydrogen gas, which gives the milky appearance.

Exercises

16 Which of the following 1 mol dm^{-3} solutions will be the poorest conductor of electricity?

   A   HCl   **B**   CH$_3$COOH   **C**   NaOH   **D**   NaCl

17 Which methods will distinguish between equimolar solutions of a strong base and a strong acid?

   I   Add magnesium to each solution and look for the formation of gas bubbles.
   II   Add aqueous sodium hydroxide to each solution and measure the temperature change.
   III   Use each solution in a circuit with a battery and lamp and see how brightly the lamp glows.

   A   I and II only   **B**   I and III only   **C**   II and III only   **D**   I, II, and III

18 Which acid in each of the following pairs has the stronger conjugate base?

   (a) H$_2$CO$_3$ or H$_2$SO$_4$
   (b) HCl or HCOOH

8.5   Acid deposition

Understandings:

- Rain is naturally acidic because of dissolved CO$_2$ and has a pH of 5.6. Acid deposition has a pH below 5.6.
- Acid deposition is formed when nitrogen or sulfur oxides dissolve in water to form HNO$_3$, HNO$_2$, H$_2$SO$_4$, and H$_2$SO$_3$.
- Sources of the oxides of sulfur and nitrogen and the effects of acid deposition should be covered.

Applications and skills:

- Balancing the equations that describe the combustion of sulfur and nitrogen to their oxides and the subsequent formation of H_2SO_3, H_2SO_4, HNO_2, and HNO_3.
- Distinction between the pre-combustion and post-combustion methods of reducing sulfur oxide emissions.
- Deduction of acid deposition equations for acid deposition with reactive metals and carbonates.

Causes of acid deposition

All rainwater is naturally acidic owing to the presence of dissolved carbon dioxide, which dissolves in water to form the weak acid carbonic acid, H_2CO_3.

$$H_2O(l) + CO_2(g) \rightleftharpoons H_2CO_3(aq)$$

Carbonic acid ionizes to form the following equilibrium:

$$H_2CO_3(aq) \rightleftharpoons H^+(aq) + HCO_3^-(aq)$$

This gives a solution with a minimum pH of 5.6. **Acid rain** refers to solutions with a pH below 5.6, and which therefore contain additional acids. The main contributors to acid rain are the oxides of sulfur and nitrogen, which are primary pollutants. Acid rain is a secondary pollutant produced when these acidic gases dissolve in water.

Acid deposition is a broader term than acid rain and includes all processes by which acidic components as precipitates or gases leave the atmosphere. There are two main types of acid deposition:

- wet acid deposition: rain, snow, sleet, hail, fog, mist, dew fall to ground as aqueous precipitates;
- dry acid deposition: acidifying particles, gases fall to ground as dust and smoke, later dissolve in water to form acids.

TOK

Although all rainwater is acidic, the term 'acid rain' only applies to some rainwater. How does language as a way of knowing influence communication in science?

Test tubes containing normal rainwater (left) and acid rain (right) with universal indicator solution added to show acidity. The normal rainwater has a pH of above 5.6, while the acid rain has a lower pH. In this example the pH = 4.0.

Rainwater is naturally acidic due to dissolved CO_2. Rainwater with a pH < 5.6 is known as acid rain.

Sulfur oxides

Sulfur dioxide, SO_2, is produced from the burning of fossil fuels, particularly coal and heavy oil in power plants used to generate electricity. It is also released in industrial processes of smelting where metals are extracted from their ores. It is estimated that about 50% of annual global emissions of sulfur dioxide come from coal.

$$S(s) + O_2(g) \rightarrow SO_2(g)$$

Sulfur dioxide is a colourless gas with a sharp smell. It dissolves in water to form sulfurous acid, $H_2SO_3(aq)$.

$$H_2O(l) + SO_2(g) \rightarrow H_2SO_3(aq)$$

Sulfur dioxide can also be oxidized to sulfur trioxide, SO_3, which then dissolves in water to form sulfuric acid, H_2SO_4.

$$2SO_2(g) + O_2(g) \rightarrow 2SO_3(g)$$

$$H_2O(l) + SO_3(g) \rightarrow H_2SO_4(aq)$$

There are several mechanisms that might occur in these reactions, and the chemistry is complex given the wide range of conditions and other chemicals found in the atmosphere. During sunlight hours photo-oxidation may occur, and oxidation may also be catalysed by tiny particles of metal present in the clouds, such as iron or manganese. Ozone (O_3) or hydrogen peroxide (H_2O_2) present as pollutants in the atmosphere, can be involved. A more detailed study involves hydroxyl free radicals, •HO, which form by reactions between water and atomic oxygen or ozone. A free radical possesses an unpaired electron and so is a short-lived and reactive species. It is shown with the symbol •.

$$•HO + SO_2 \rightarrow •HOSO_2$$

$$•HOSO_2 + O_2 \rightarrow •HO_2 + SO_3$$

Nitrogen oxides

Nitrogen monoxide, NO, is produced mainly from internal combustion engines, where the burning of the fuel releases heat energy that causes nitrogen and oxygen from the air to combine.

$$N_2(g) + O_2(g) \rightarrow 2NO(g) \qquad \Delta H = +181 \text{ kJ mol}^{-1}$$

A similar reaction gives rise directly to the brown gas, nitrogen dioxide, NO_2.

$$N_2(g) + 2O_2(g) \rightarrow 2NO_2(g)$$

Nitrogen dioxide also forms from the oxidation of nitrogen monoxide:

$$2NO(g) + O_2(g) \rightarrow 2NO_2(g)$$

Nitrogen dioxide dissolves in water to form a mixture of nitrous acid (HNO_2) and nitric acid (HNO_3).

$$H_2O(l) + 2NO_2(g) \rightarrow HNO_2(aq) + HNO_3(aq)$$

Alternatively, nitrogen dioxide can be oxidized to form nitric acid.

$$2H_2O(l) + 4NO_2(g) + O_2(g) \rightarrow 4HNO_3(aq)$$

CHALLENGE YOURSELF

1 What is the source of sulfur in fossil fuels? Consider why some fuels such as coal contain higher amounts of sulfur.

 Free radicals are discussed in more detail in Chapters 4 and 10.

CHALLENGE YOURSELF

2 How can you explain the fact that the reaction of nitrogen and oxygen is endothermic, whereas other combustion reactions are exothermic?

CHALLENGE YOURSELF

3 By reference to Chapter 9, deduce the oxidation states of S and N in each of the species given here, and suggest names using oxidation numbers for HNO_2, HNO_3, H_2SO_3, and H_2SO_4.

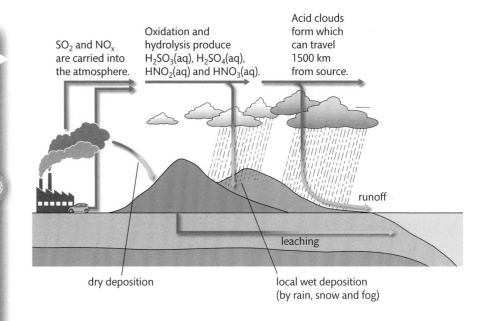

Figure 8.7 The formation of acid deposition.

SO$_2$ and NO$_x$ are carried into the atmosphere.

Oxidation and hydrolysis produce H$_2$SO$_3$(aq), H$_2$SO$_4$(aq), HNO$_2$(aq) and HNO$_3$(aq).

Acid clouds form which can travel 1500 km from source.

runoff

leaching

dry deposition

local wet deposition (by rain, snow and fog)

Several other oxides of nitrogen exist, and the term NO$_x$ is used somewhat variably. But in atmospheric chemistry it refers specifically to the total of the two oxides of nitrogen NO and NO$_2$ present.

One of the most controversial aspects of acid deposition is that its effects often occur far from the source of the pollutants, due to atmospheric weather patterns. In many cases, this means countries are suffering the impact of other countries' industrial processes. Legislation to reduce the impact of acid deposition has therefore been the subject of intense political debate, and several international protocols have developed. These have led to significant reductions in sulfur emissions in many countries, but reduction in nitrogen oxide emissions has been less effective.

These reactions also proceed via different mechanisms, depending on the conditions and chemical cocktail in the atmosphere. Photo-oxidation, the presence of ozone, and hydroxyl free-radicals (•HO) all contribute to the production of nitrous acid and nitric acid.

$$\bullet HO + NO \rightarrow HNO_2$$

$$\bullet HO + NO_2 \rightarrow HNO_3$$

In summary, a complex set of reactions in the atmosphere converts the primary pollutants SO$_2$ and NO into acid rain. The main active components of acid rain are H$_2$SO$_3$(aq), H$_2$SO$_4$(aq), HNO$_2$(aq), and HNO$_3$(aq).

Effects of acid deposition

Impact on materials

The building materials marble and limestone are both forms of calcium carbonate, CaCO$_3$. Both sulfur dioxide (in dry deposition) and sulfuric acid (in acid rain) react with this, forming the calcium salt, CaSO$_4$:

$$2CaCO_3(s) + 2SO_2(g) + O_2(g) \rightarrow 2CaSO_4(aq) + 2CO_2(g)$$

$$CaCO_3(s) + H_2SO_4(aq) \rightarrow CaSO_4(aq) + H_2O(l) + CO_2(g)$$

As calcium sulfate is somewhat more soluble than calcium carbonate, it washes out of the limestone or flakes off. Calcium sulfate has a greater molar volume than calcium carbonate, so its formation causes expansion and stress in the stonework. A similar reaction occurs with nitric acid, forming the soluble nitrate salt:

$$CaCO_3(s) + 2HNO_3(aq) \rightarrow Ca(NO_3)_2(aq) + H_2O(l) + CO_2(g)$$

These reactions all lead to erosion of structures, and many historic buildings and statues have suffered in this way.

Acid deposition also affects metals, causing corrosion. Again components of both dry deposition and acid rain react with metals such as iron, forming the salt. This enables ionic conductivity to occur, which leads to an increase in the rate of electrochemical corrosion reactions such as rusting:

$$Fe(s) + SO_2(g) + O_2(g) \rightarrow FeSO_4(s)$$

$$Fe(s) + H_2SO_4(aq) \rightarrow FeSO_4(aq) + H_2(g)$$

In addition, acid rain is able to react with and so remove the protective oxide layer on the surface of metals such as aluminium:

$$Al_2O_3(s) + 6HNO_3(aq) \rightarrow 2Al(NO_3)_3(aq) + 3H_2O(l)$$

As a result, acid rain causes significant damage to metallic structures such as bridges, rail road tracks, and vehicles.

> You should be able to write equations for the reactions between the different components of acid rain and reactive metals and metal carbonates, similar to those developed in section 8.2. Note though that nitric acid, HNO_3, does not react as a typical acid releasing hydrogen from metals, as it is an oxidizing agent and releases NO instead. (So in fact this reaction releases more pollutant into the air to form more acid rain.)

Marble statue damaged by acid rain.

Impact on plant life

Acid rain has been shown to be a direct cause of slower growth, injury, or death of plants. One of its effects is to cause important minerals such as Mg^{2+}, Ca^{2+}, and K^+ held in the soil to become soluble and so wash away in a process called **leaching**, before they can be absorbed by plants. Without sufficient Mg^{2+} ions, for example, a plant cannot synthesize chlorophyll and so cannot make its food through photosynthesis. At the same time, acid rain causes the release of substances that are toxic to plants, such as Al^{3+}, which damage plant roots. In addition, dry deposition can directly affect plants by blocking the pores for gas exchange, known as stomata. Forests in hilly regions seem to be particularly vulnerable because they tend to be surrounded by acidic clouds and mists. Some of the worst effects on forests have been in Europe, though the impact is seen worldwide.

Impact on water

Acid rain has caused a number of lakes to become 'dead' – unable to support life. Many fish including trout and perch cannot survive at pH values below 5. Below pH 4, rivers are effectively dead as toxic Al^{3+} ions normally trapped in the rock as insoluble aluminium hydroxide leach out under acid conditions:

$$Al(OH)_3(s) + 3H^+(aq) \rightarrow Al^{3+}(aq) + 3H_2O(l)$$

Aluminium ions interfere with the operation of the fish's gills and reduce their ability to take in oxygen.

Acid rain also contributes to an additional problem known as **eutrophication**. This is over-fertilization of bodies of water, and can be caused by nitrates present in acid rain. It results in algal blooms leading to oxygen depletion, and sometimes the death of the lake or stream.

Woodland devastated by the effects of acid rain in the Czech Republic, near the border with Germany. This is one of the most affected areas in Europe.

Impact on human health

Acid rain does not directly affect human health but its components can react to form fine sulfate and nitrate particles that can travel long distances and be present in inhaled air. These particles irritate the respiratory tract and increase the risk of illnesses such as asthma, bronchitis, and emphysema. They can also cause irritation to the eyes. The release of toxic metal ions such as Al^{3+}, Pb^{2+}, and Cu^{2+} by the reaction of acid rain on metal structures such as pipes is also a potential health risk.

Responses to acid deposition

The link between increasing industrialization causing atmospheric pollution and acid rain was first described in Manchester, England, in 1852. However, the phenomenon did not gain widespread attention until the 1970s when some of the impacts described above became evident in several countries. As a result, many governments responded with measures aimed to reduce the emissions of nitrogen and sulfur oxides. Some of these are summarized below.

Reduction of SO_2 emissions

i) Pre-combustion methods

These are processes that reduce or remove the sulfur present in coal or oil before combustion. Where the sulfur is present as a metal sulfide, it can be removed by crushing the coal and washing with water. The high density metal sulfide sinks to the bottom and so separates from the clean coal. **Hydrodesulfurization** (HDS) is a catalytic process that removes sulfur from refined petroleum products by reacting it with hydrogen to form hydrogen sulfide, H_2S. This is a highly toxic gas, so it is captured and later converted into elemental sulfur for use in the manufacture of sulfuric acid, H_2SO_4.

ii) Post-combustion methods

Flue-gas desulfurization can remove up to 90% of SO_2 from flue gas in the smoke stacks of coal-fired power stations before it is released into the atmosphere. The process uses a wet slurry of CaO and $CaCO_3$ which reacts with SO_2 to form the neutral product calcium sulfate, $CaSO_4$.

$$CaO(s) + SO_2(g) \rightarrow CaSO_3(s)$$

$$CaCO_3(s) + SO_2(g) \rightarrow CaSO_3(s) + CO_2(g)$$

$$2CaSO_3(s) + O_2(g) \rightarrow 2CaSO_4(s)$$

The calcium sulfate has industrial uses such as making plasterboard.

Reduction of NO_x emissions

i) Catalytic converters in vehicles

Exhaust gases can be controlled by the use of catalytic converters in which the hot gases are mixed with air and passed over a platinum- or palladium-based catalyst. The reaction converts toxic emissions into relatively harmless products. For example:

$$2CO(g) + 2NO(g) \rightarrow 2CO_2(g) + N_2(g)$$

ii) Lower temperature combustion

As mentioned in Chapter 7, the formation of nitrogen monoxide is reduced at lower temperature. Recirculating the exhaust gases back into the engine lowers the temperature to reduce the nitrogen oxide in the emissions.

Other options

In addition to finding ways to reduce the emission of the primary pollutants when fossil fuels are burnt, other solutions to the problem of acid deposition include lowering the demand for fossil fuels. More efficient energy transfer systems, greater use of public transport, and switching to renewable energy sources are all part of this.

The restoration of ecosystems damaged by acid rain is a long-term process. One method is to use calcium oxide (CaO), known as lime, or calcium hydroxide (Ca(OH)₂) to neutralize the acid.

$$CaO(s) + H_2SO_4(aq) \rightarrow CaSO_4(s) + H_2O(l)$$

$$Ca(OH)_2(s) + H_2SO_4(aq) \rightarrow CaSO_4(s) + 2H_2O(l)$$

Response to acid rain in Sweden. The dosing column is adding $Ca(OH)_2$ to the stream, to help neutralize the acidity of the water.

NATURE OF SCIENCE

Acid deposition has been recognized as a problem for over a century, but it was not until there was convincing evidence for the long-range transport of pollutants that it became a subject of international concern in the 1970s. Intense scientific research into the formation and impacts of acidic rainfall then led to policy responses at the national and local level. Environmental issues like this are almost always global in nature, but the responses must be tackled at source locally. Scientists need to make the public aware of their findings so that corrective actions are understood, and individuals can make informed lifestyle choices.

Exercises

19 (a) Explain why natural rain has a pH of around 5.6. Give a chemical equation to support your answer.

(b) Acid rain may be 50 times more acidic than natural rain. One of the major acids present in acid rain originates mainly from burning coal. State the name of the acid and give equations to show how it is formed.

(c) The second major acid responsible for acid rain originates mainly from internal combustion engines. State the name of this acid and state two different ways in which its production can be reduced.

(d) Acid rain has caused considerable damage to buildings and statues made of marble ($CaCO_3$). Write an equation to represent the reaction of acid rain with marble.

(e) State three consequences of acid rain.

(f) Suggest a method of controlling acid rain, not involving a chemical reaction, for reducing sulfur dioxide emissions from power stations.

20 The table gives some substances found in air.

Name	Formula
sulfur dioxide	SO_2
nitrogen monoxide	NO
particulates	–

(a) Identify the pollutant(s) which contribute(s) to acid rain.

(b) Identify the pollutant(s) which come(s) mainly from power stations.

(c) The presence of one of these pollutants makes the ill effects of the others worse. Identify the pollutant and explain why it has this effect.

(d) Emissions of one of these pollutants have been controlled by reaction with calcium oxide. Identify this pollutant and write an equation for the reaction with calcium oxide.

(e) Identify the pollutants that come primarily from motor vehicles and describe the basis for their production.

21 (a) Describe the difference in dispersion between dry acid deposition and wet acid deposition.

(b) Explain the physical and chemical processes involved in the development of wet acid deposition.

22 Identify the free radical involved in the formation of sulfuric acid and nitric acid in acid rain and explain how it is formed.

Practice questions

1 When the pH of solutions of each of the following liquids with a concentration of 0.10 mol dm^{-3} are compared, which has the highest value?

   A $C_2H_5NH_2$　　　　**B** HNO_3　　　　**C** $Ba(OH)_2$　　　　**D** C_2H_5COOH

2 All of the following would be described as typical of an acid except

   A produces bubbles when it reacts with calcium carbonate
   B conducts electricity
   C releases heat when it reacts with sodium hydroxide
   D has a soapy feel

3 What is the conjugate base of HSO_3^-?

   A H_2SO_3　　　　**B** SO_3^{2-}　　　　**C** H_2O　　　　**D** $H_2SO_3^-$

4 Which of the following can be described as amphiprotic?

   A OH^-　　　　**B** NH_4^+　　　　**C** $BeCl_2$　　　　**D** SO_4^{2-}

5 When equal concentrations of a strong and a weak acid are compared, which of the following measurements will be the same?

   I   the volume of base used to neutralize the acid
   II the electrical conductivity
   III the rate of the reaction with calcium carbonate

   A I only　　　　**B** I and II only　　　　**C** I, II, and III　　　　**D** None of I, II, or III

6 CH_3OH is a very weak Brønsted–Lowry acid. What is true of the ion CH_3O^-?

   A It is a good proton donor.
   B It will be present in high concentration in CH_3OH at equilibrium.
   C It is a strong Brønsted–Lowry base.
   D It is a stronger Brønsted–Lowry acid than CH_3OH.

7 In the reaction $CH_3OH + NH_2^- \rightleftharpoons CH_3O^- + NH_3$ the two Brønsted–Lowry acids are:

   A NH_2^- and CH_3OH　　　　　　　　**B** NH_2^- and CH_3O^-
   C CH_3O^- and NH_3　　　　　　　　　**D** CH_3OH and NH_3

8 Which of these reduces the production of acid rain?

   I   removing SO_2 from power station emissions
   II neutralizing acidified lakes with lime
   III switching to renewable energy sources

   A I and II　　　　**B** I and III　　　　**C** II and III　　　　**D** I, II, and III

9 Which of the following occurs as a result of acid deposition?

   I Ca^{2+} ions are washed out of the soil.
   II Thermal expansion of oceans.
   III Fish are killed due to high levels of aluminium in the water.

   A I and II　　　　**B** I and III　　　　**C** II and III　　　　**D** I, II, and III

10 Which of the following are conjugate acid–base pairs?

   I HNO_3/NO_3^-
   II H_2O/OH^-
   III H_2/H^+

   A I only　　　　**B** I and II　　　　**C** I and III　　　　**D** I, II, and III

11 Two acids, X and Y, both of concentration 0.20 mol dm^{-3} have pH values of 2 and 4, respectively. Which of the following statements is true?

A X is a stronger acid than Y.

B Y is more dilute than X.

C X contains more undissociated molecules than Y.

D Y contains a higher concentration of H$^+$ ions than X.

12 Which of the following statements is the defining property of a Brønsted–Lowry base?

A donates protons

B produces OH$^-$ ions

C conducts electricity

D accepts H$^+$ ions

13 The pH scale can be used to distinguish between different acids and bases in the laboratory.

You are provided with five unlabelled bottles which are known to contain 0.10 mol dm^{-3} solutions of each of the following:

$$HCOOH(aq), \ KCl(aq), \ HNO_3(aq), \ Ba(OH)_2(aq), \ NH_3(aq)$$

(a) Describe **two** ways in which you could measure the pH of the solutions. (2)

(b) Suggest expected pH values for each solution. (3)

(c) (i) In the laboratory, some solid sodium hydrogencarbonate was added to an aqueous solution of hydrochloric acid. Formulate an equation for this reaction including state symbols, and predict what you would expect to observe during the reaction. (5)

(ii) The hydrogencarbonate can be described as amphiprotic. Explain this statement with reference to the Brønsted–Lowry theory of acids and bases. (4)

(d) Another method to distinguish between a weak and a strong acid of the same concentration is to observe their reactions with magnesium metal. Explain the expected results of this experiment, including equations for a weak and a strong acid of your choice. (4)

(e) Conductivity can also be used for the purpose of distinguishing between strong and weak acids of the same concentration. Justify the claim that use of a conductivity meter is a more scientifically acceptable approach than the method described in (b). (2)

(Total 20 marks)

14 (a) Define the terms *acid* and *base* according to the Brønsted–Lowry theory. Distinguish between a weak base and a strong base. State **one** example of a weak base. (3)

(b) Weak acids in the environment may cause damage. Identify a weak acid in the environment **and** outline **one** of its effects. (2)

(Total 5 marks)

To access weblinks on the topics covered in this chapter, please go to www.pearsonhotlinks.com and enter the ISBN or title of this book.

09 Redox processes

Essential ideas

9.1 Redox (reduction–oxidation) reactions play a key role in many chemical and biochemical processes.

9.2 Voltaic cells convert chemical energy to electrical energy and electrolytic cells convert electrical energy to chemical energy. Energy conversions between electrical and chemical energy lie at the core of electrochemical cells.

The vigorous reaction here shows the redox change that occurs when magnesium metal and copper oxide are heated together, forming magnesium oxide and copper. $Mg(s) + CuO(s) \rightarrow MgO(s) + Cu(s)$
Redox reactions occur when electrons are transferred between species, and are the basis of electrochemistry.

Oxygen makes up only about 20% by volume of the air, yet it is the essential component for so many reactions. Without it fuels would not burn, iron would not rust, and we would be unable to obtain energy from our food molecules through respiration. Indeed, animal life on the planet did not evolve until a certain concentration of oxygen had built up in the atmosphere over 600 million years ago. The term **oxidation** has been in use for a long time to describe these and other reactions where oxygen is involved in chemical change. Oxidation, though, is only half of the story, as it is always accompanied by the opposite process **reduction**, which was originally thought of in terms of loss of oxygen.

Later, however, the terms widened to include a much broader range of reactions. We now define these two processes, oxidation and reduction, as occurring whenever electrons are transferred from one reactant to another – and many of these reactions do not use oxygen. For example, photosynthesis, the process by which plants store chemical energy from light energy, involves oxidation and reduction reactions, although oxygen itself is not a reactant. Transferring electrons from one substance to another leads to a flow of electrons, in other words an electric current. So, chemical reactions can be used to generate electricity – a simple **voltaic cell** or **battery** works in this way. By reversing the process and using an electric current to drive reactions of oxidation and reduction, stable compounds can be broken down into their elements. This is the process known as **electrolysis**. These applications of oxidation and reduction, collectively known as **electrochemical cells**, have truly revolutionized our world. For example, it would be hard to imagine life without the many battery-powered mobile devices we use every day, or without metals such as aluminium that are only available from electrolysis. An understanding of oxidation and reduction is therefore at the heart of the study of a large branch of chemistry both in the laboratory and beyond.

Coloured X-ray of a smart phone, showing its rechargeable battery. Mobile devices such as this are powered by electrical energy generated from the reactions of oxidation and reduction occurring within the battery.

9.1 Oxidation and reduction

Understandings:

- Oxidation and reduction can be considered in terms of oxygen gain/hydrogen loss, electron transfer, or change in oxidation number.
- An oxidizing agent is reduced and a reducing agent is oxidized.

Guidance
Oxidation states should be represented with the sign given before the number, e.g. +2 not 2+.

- Variable oxidation numbers exist for transition metals and for most main-group non-metals.

Guidance
The oxidation state of hydrogen in metal hydrides (–1) and oxygen in peroxides (–1) should be covered.

- The activity series ranks metals according to the ease with which they undergo oxidation.

Guidance
A simple activity series is given in the IB data booklet in section 25.

- The Winkler method can be used to measure biochemical oxygen demand (BOD), used as a measure of the degree of pollution in a water sample.

Applications and skills:

- Deduction of the oxidation state of an atom in an ion or a compound.
- Deduction of the name of a transition metal compound from a given formula, applying oxidation numbers represented by Roman numerals.

Guidance
Oxidation number and oxidation state are often used interchangeably, though IUPAC does formally distinguish between the two terms. Oxidation numbers are represented by Roman numerals according to IUPAC.

- Identification of the species oxidized and reduced and the oxidizing and reducing agents, in redox reactions.
- Deduction of redox reactions using half-equations in acidic or neutral solutions.
- Deduction of the feasibility of a redox reaction from the activity series or reaction data.
- Solution of a range of redox titration problems.
- Application of the Winkler method to calculate BOD.

Introduction to oxidation and reduction

Early attempts to define oxidation and reduction were based on observations of the gain and loss of oxygen and hydrogen during chemical change. They can be summarized as follows.

Oxidation	Reduction
gain of oxygen	loss of oxygen
loss of hydrogen	gain of hydrogen

These definitions are still useful in some cases, particularly in organic chemistry, but they have largely been replaced by a more inclusive approach. It is now recognized that oxidation and reduction occur during chemical change whenever there is a shift in electron density from one atom to another. In other words, the focus has become the transfer of electrons, whether complete or partial, and whether oxygen and hydrogen are involved or not. Some examples will help to explain this.

When magnesium is burned in air, it gives a bright white flame with the production of a white powder, magnesium oxide:

$$2Mg(s) + O_2(g) \rightarrow 2MgO(s)$$

The fact that magnesium gains oxygen in this reaction makes it easy to see why we say it is an **oxidation** reaction and that magnesium has been oxidized. However, during the same reaction a small amount of the magnesium combines with the nitrogen of the air too, forming magnesium nitride. It may be less obvious that this is also an oxidation reaction and that again magnesium is oxidized.

$$3Mg(s) + N_2(g) \rightarrow Mg_3N_2(s)$$

What do these two reactions have in common which means they can both be defined in this way? If we divide them into so-called **half-equations**, each showing what happens to one reactant, we can examine what is happening in terms of electrons.

$$2Mg(s) \rightarrow 2Mg^{2+}(s) + 4e^-$$
$$\underline{O_2(g) + 4e^- \rightarrow 2O^{2-}(s)}$$
$$2Mg(s) + O_2(g) \rightarrow 2MgO(s)$$

$$3Mg(s) \rightarrow 3Mg^{2+}(s) + 6e^-$$
$$\underline{N_2(g) + 6e^- \rightarrow 2N^{3-}(s)}$$
$$3Mg(s) + N_2(g) \rightarrow Mg_3N_2(s)$$

In both reactions Mg is forming Mg^{2+} by losing electrons, while O and N are forming O^{2-} and N^{3-} respectively by gaining electrons. It is this transfer of electrons that now defines oxidation, and its opposite reaction, reduction. *Oxidation is the loss of electrons, reduction is the gain of electrons.*

So in the reactions above, magnesium is oxidized while oxygen and nitrogen are reduced. Clearly each process is dependent on the other, so oxidation and reduction will always occur together and reactions of this type are known as **redox reactions**.

Magnesium ribbon burning in air. It forms mostly magnesium oxide with small amounts of magnesium nitride.

It may help you to remember OILRIG: Oxidation Is Loss (of electrons), Reduction Is Gain (of electrons).

Fresh fruits and vegetables are good sources of anti-oxidants, which may help prevent damaging oxidative reactions in cells.

The free-radical theory of ageing suggests that the physiological changes associated with ageing are the result of oxidative reactions in cells causing damage to membranes and large molecules such as DNA. These changes accumulate with time and may explain the increase in degenerative diseases, such as cancer, with age. The theory suggests that supplying cells with anti-oxidants will help to slow down the damaging oxidative reactions. Anti-oxidants are particularly abundant in fresh fruit and vegetables, as well as in red wine, tea, and cocoa. Although there is strong evidence that anti-oxidant supplementation may help protect against certain diseases, it has not yet been shown to produce a demonstrated increase in the human life span.

Oxidation is the loss of electrons, reduction is the gain of electrons.

Oxidation numbers enable us to track redox change

In reactions involving ions, such as the examples above, it is easy to identify the electron transfers occurring. But what about reactions where electrons are not transferred but instead are shared in a covalent bond, such as the combination of hydrogen and oxygen to produce water? Can oxidation and reduction be identified here too?

$$2H_2(g) + O_2(g) \rightarrow 2H_2O(l)$$

The answer is 'yes', through the introduction of the concept of **oxidation state**. This is a value we assign to each atom in a compound that is a measure of the electron control or possession it has relative to the atom in the pure element. Oxidation state can be defined as the apparent charge that an atom has in a molecule or ion. It is as if we exaggerate the unequal sharing in a covalent bond, based on electronegativity differences, to the point where each atom has complete gain or loss of the electrons shared – in other words, has formed ions. This enables us to keep track of the relative electron density in a compound and how it changes during a reaction. There are two parts to the oxidation state:

- the sign: '+' means the atom has lost electron control , '–' means it has gained electron control;
- its value: this refers to the number of electrons over which control has changed.

The oxidation state is written with the sign first, followed by the number, e.g. +2 or –3.

Strategy for assigning oxidation states

There are a few simple rules to follow which help in determining the oxidation state of an atom in any species. We will use blue to show oxidation states throughout this text.

1   Atoms in the free (uncombined) element have an oxidation state of zero: for example,

2   In simple ions, the oxidation state is the same as the charge on the ion: for example,

3   The oxidation states of all the atoms in a neutral (uncharged) compound must add up to zero:

   for example, in H_2SO_4 the sum of oxidation states = 0.

4   The oxidation states of all the atoms in a polyatomic ion must add up to the charge on the ion:

   for example, in SO_4^{2-} the sum of oxidation states = –2.

5   The usual oxidation state for an element is the same as the charge on its most common ion:

   for example, Group 1 elements have oxidation state = +1, H is usually +1, O is usually –2.

6   Most main group non-metals, the elements at the bottom of Group 14, and transition elements have oxidation states that vary in different compounds – depending on the conditions and other elements present. So for N, P, S, Sn, Pb, and all transition elements, the oxidation state of the element in a particular species needs to be determined on a case-by-case basis.

The table on page 271 summarizes some useful information about oxidation states.

Note that the charge on an ion X is written with the number first then the charge: e.g. X^{2+}. The oxidation state is written with the charge first then the number: e.g. +2.

What ways of knowing can we use to distinguish between the charge on an ion and the oxidation state?

TOK

Element	Usual oxidation state	Exceptions	Explanation
Li, Na, K	+1		
Mg, Ca	+2		
F	−1		there are no exceptions because F is the most electronegative element
O	−2	peroxides such as H_2O_2, where it is −1; OF_2, where it is +2	
H	+1	metal hydrides such as NaH, where it is −1	H is more electronegative than Na and so gains electron control
Cl	−1	when it is combined with O or F	Cl is less electronegative than O and F, and so loses electron control

When working out the oxidation states of atoms in compounds, it is usually best to assign the oxidation state to the atoms that are easy to predict first, then use Rules 3 and 4 above to find the more unpredictable elements by subtraction.

Assign oxidation states to all the elements in (a) H_2SO_4 and (b) SO_3^{2-}.

Solution

(a) We can assign H and O as follows:

Note that the oxidation states apply to each atom and that here the sum of all the oxidation states must be zero as H_2SO_4 is electrically neutral.

Therefore, $2(+1) + S + 4(-2) = 0 \Rightarrow S = +6$

(b) Here we start by assigning O:

Note that here the oxidation states must add up to −2, the charge on the ion.

Therefore, $S + 3(-2) = -2 \Rightarrow S = +4$

Interpreting oxidation states

We can see that an element like sulfur can have a wide range of oxidation states in different compounds.

increasing oxidation state

What is the significance of these different values? Because the oxidation state is a measure of the electron control that an atom has, it follows that the higher the positive number, the more the atom has lost control over electrons, in other words the more oxidized it is. Likewise, the greater the negative number, the more it has gained electron control, so the more reduced it is. Therefore H_2S represents sulfur in its most reduced form (lowest oxidation number), and SO_3 and H_2SO_4 represent sulfur in its most oxidized form (highest oxidation number).

It follows that any change in oxidation states during a reaction is an indication that redox processes are occurring: increase in oxidation number represents oxidation, and a decrease in oxidation number represents reduction.

So, going back to the reaction between hydrogen and oxygen discussed earlier, we can now clearly follow the redox process

$$2H_2(g) + O_2(g) \rightarrow 2H_2O(l)$$
$$\quad 0 \qquad\quad 0 \qquad\quad +1 \;\; -2$$

Hydrogen has been oxidized (oxidation state increased from 0 to +1) and oxygen has been reduced (oxidation state decreased from 0 to −2).

> **A redox reaction is a chemical reaction in which changes in the oxidation states occur.**

> **Oxidation occurs when there is an increase in oxidation state of an element, reduction occurs when there is a decrease in oxidation state of an element.**

Worked example

Use oxidation states to deduce which species is oxidized and which is reduced in the following reactions:

(a) $Ca(s) + Sn^{2+}(aq) \rightarrow Ca^{2+}(aq) + Sn(s)$

(b) $4NH_3(g) + 5O_2(g) \rightarrow 4NO(g) + 6H_2O(l)$

Solution

(a) $Ca(s) + Sn^{2+}(aq) \rightarrow Ca^{2+}(aq) + Sn(s)$
$\quad\; 0 \qquad +2 \qquad\quad +2 \qquad\quad 0$

Ca is oxidized because its oxidation state increases from 0 to + 2; Sn^{2+} is reduced because its oxidation state decreases from +2 to 0.

(b) $4NH_3(g) + 5O_2(g) \rightarrow 4NO(g) + 6H_2O(l)$
$\quad\; -3 +1 \qquad\; 0 \qquad +2\; -2 \quad +1\; -2$

NH_3 is oxidized because the oxidation state of N increases from −3 to +2; O_2 is reduced because its oxidation state decreases from 0 to −2.

Coloured scanning electron micrograph (SEM) of rust on painted sheet metal. Rust is hydrated iron oxide resulting from electrochemical reactions between iron and atmospheric water vapour and oxygen. Rusting spontaneously causes iron to revert to its more stable oxidized state, unless this is prevented by protecting the iron. Rust flakes off the surface of the iron, causing it to be degraded and weakened.

Systematic names of compounds use oxidation numbers

We have seen that elements such as sulfur exhibit different oxidation states in different compounds. In these cases it is useful to include information about the oxidation state in the name. Traditional names used descriptive language that became associated with a particular oxidation state. For example, ferrous and ferric iron oxides referred to FeO and Fe_2O_3, in which Fe has oxidation states $+2$ and $+3$ respectively.

The IUPAC system, founded in 1919, introduced a nomenclature using **oxidation numbers** to make the names more recognizable and unambiguous. This uses a Roman numeral corresponding to the oxidation state which is inserted in brackets after the name of the element. For example copper(I) oxide contains copper in the oxidation state $+1$. Different compounds in which the same elements have different oxidation states are then shown with different oxidation numbers, such as copper(I) oxide and copper(II) oxide.

The table shows some common examples.

Formula of compound	Oxidation state	Name using oxidation number	Formula of compound	Oxidation state	Name using oxidation number
FeO	Fe $+2$	iron(II) oxide	MnO_4^-	Mn $+7$	manganate(VII) ion
Fe_2O_3	Fe $+3$	iron(III) oxide	$K_2Cr_2O_7$	Cr $+6$	potassium dichromate(VI)
Cu_2O	Cu $+1$	copper(I) oxide	Cr_2O_3	Cr $+3$	chromium(III) oxide
CuO	Cu $+2$	copper(II) oxide	NO	N $+2$	nitrogen(II) oxide
MnO_2	Mn $+4$	manganese(IV) oxide	NO_2	N $+4$	nitrogen(IV) oxide

Worked example

Deduce the name of the following compounds using oxidation numbers.

(a) V_2O_5 (b) $Ni(OH)_2$ (c) $TiCl_4$

Solution

1. First deduce the oxidation state:
   (a) V_2O_5 V is $+5$
   (b) $Ni(OH)_2$ Ni is $+2$
   (c) $TiCl_4$ Ti is $+4$

2. Then the corresponding Roman numeral is inserted after the name of the element. There is no space between the name and the number, and the number is placed in brackets.
   (a) vanadium(V) oxide
   (b) nickel(II) hydroxide
   (c) titanium(IV) chloride

Although this nomenclature can theoretically be used in the naming of all compounds, it is really only worthwhile when an element has more than one common oxidation state. For example Na_2O could be called sodium(I) oxide, but as we know Na always has oxidation state $+1$, it is perfectly adequate to call it simply sodium oxide.

Oxidation state is shown with a '+' or '−' sign and an Arabic numeral, e.g $+2$.

Oxidation number is shown by inserting a Roman numeral in brackets after the name or symbol of the element, e.g. copper(II) oxide.

Although we have made the distinction here between oxidation number and oxidation state according to IUPAC guidelines, in reality this is not the main point of this discussion. In fact many sources use oxidation number and oxidation state interchangeably, so it is not too important. What does matter though, is the information represented in these values in terms of the electron density associated with an atom in a compound.

The IUPAC system aims to help chemists communicate more easily in all languages by introducing systematic names into compounds. However, its success in achieving this will be determined by how readily it is adopted. What do you think might prevent chemists using exclusively the 'new names'?

Photochromic lenses darken in response to increasing light intensity and become lighter in dim light. The change is brought about by a redox reaction between silver chloride and copper(I) chloride, which are both embedded in the lens. In bright light, Ag^+ ions oxidize Cu^+ forming Ag and Cu^{2+}:

$$Ag^+(s) + Cu^+(s) \rightarrow Ag(s) + Cu^{2+}$$

The silver metal produced creates a film over the lens, cutting out glare. In dim light the reaction reverses as Cu^{2+} oxidizes Ag, and the lens clears.

Redox equations

Writing half-equations

Although we have seen that oxidation cannot take place without reduction and vice versa, it is sometimes useful to separate out the two processes from a redox equation and write separate equations for the oxidation and reduction processes. These are therefore called **half-equations**. Electrons are added on one side of each equation to balance the charges.

Worked example

Deduce the two half-equations for the following reaction

$$Zn(s) + Cu^{2+}(aq) \rightarrow Zn^{2+}(aq) + Cu(s)$$

Solution

Assign oxidation states so we can see what is being oxidized and what is reduced.

$$Zn(s) + Cu^{2+}(aq) \rightarrow Zn^{2+}(aq) + Cu(s)$$
$$\quad 0 \qquad +2 \qquad\quad +2 \qquad\quad 0$$

Here we can see that Zn is being oxidized and Cu^{2+} is being reduced.

oxidation:	$Zn(s) \rightarrow Zn^{2+}(aq) + 2e^-$	electrons are lost
reduction:	$Cu^{2+}(aq) + 2e^- \rightarrow Cu(s)$	electrons are gained

Note there must be equal numbers of electrons in the two half-equations, so that when they are added together the electrons cancel out.

Writing redox equations using half-equations

Sometimes we may know the species involved in a redox reaction, but not the overall equation so we need to work this out, making sure it is balanced for both atoms and charge. A good way to do this is to write half-equations for the oxidation and reduction processes separately, and then add these two together to give the overall reaction. Many of these reactions take place in acidified solutions and we therefore use H_2O and/ or H^+ ions to balance the half-equations. The process is best broken down into a series of steps, as shown in the example below.

Worked example

Write an equation for the reaction in which NO_3^- and Cu react together in acidic solution to produce NO and Cu^{2+}.

Solution

1. Assign oxidation states to determine which atoms are being oxidized and which are being reduced:

$$NO_3^-(aq) + Cu(s) \rightarrow NO(g) + Cu^{2+}(aq) \qquad \text{equation is unbalanced}$$
$$+5 \; -2 \qquad\quad 0 \qquad +2-2 \qquad +2$$

Therefore Cu is being oxidized ($0 \rightarrow +2$) and N is being reduced ($+5 \rightarrow +2$).

2. Write half-equations for oxidation and reduction.

   (a) Balance the atoms other than H and O:

   oxidation: $\quad Cu(s) \rightarrow Cu^{2+}(aq)$

   reduction: $\quad NO_3^-(aq) \rightarrow NO(g)$

   In this example the Cu and N are already balanced.

(b) Balance each half-equation for O by adding H_2O as needed.

Here the reduction equation needs two more O atoms on the right-hand side:

reduction: $NO_3^-(aq) \rightarrow NO(g) + 2H_2O(l)$

(c) Balance each half-equation for H by adding H^+ as needed.

Here the reduction equation needs four H atoms on the left-hand side:

reduction: $NO_3^-(aq) + 4H^+(aq) \rightarrow NO(g) + 2H_2O(l)$

(d) Balance each half-equation for charge by adding electrons to the side with the more positive charge. (Electrons will be products in the oxidation equation and reactants in the reduction equation.)

oxidation: $Cu(s) \rightarrow Cu^{2+}(aq) + 2e^-$

reduction: $NO_3^-(aq) + 4H^+(aq) + 3e^- \rightarrow NO(g) + 2H_2O(l)$

(e) Now check that each half-equation is balanced for atoms and for charge.

3 Equalize the number of electrons in the two half-equations by multiplying each appropriately.

Here the equation of oxidation must be multiplied by 3, and the equation of reduction by 2, to give six electrons in both equations:

oxidation: $3Cu(s) \rightarrow 3Cu^{2+}(aq) + 6e^-$

reduction: $2NO_3^-(aq) + 8H^+(aq) + 6e^- \rightarrow 2NO(g) + 4H_2O(l)$

4 Add the two half-equations together, cancelling out anything that is the same on both sides, which includes the electrons.

$$3Cu(s) + 2NO_3^-(aq) + 8H^+(aq) \rightarrow 3Cu^{2+}(aq) + 2NO(g) + 4H_2O(l)$$

The final equation should be balanced for atoms and charge and have no electrons.

Summary of steps in writing redox equations.

1 Assign oxidation states to determine which atoms are being oxidized and which are being reduced.

2 Write half-equations for oxidation and reduction as follows:

(a) balance the atoms other than H and O;

(b) balance each half-equation for O by adding H_2O as needed;

(c) balance each half-equation for H by adding H^+ as needed;

(d) balance each half-equation for charge by adding electrons to the sides with the more positive charge;

(e) check that each half-equation is balanced for atoms and for charge.

3 Equalize the number of electrons in the two half-equations by multiplying each appropriately.

4 Add the two half-equations together, cancelling out anything that is the same on both sides.

Exercises

1 Assign oxidation states to all elements in the following compounds:

(a) NH_4^+

(b) $CuCl_2$

(c) H_2O

(d) SO_2

(e) Fe_2O_3

(f) NO_3^-

(g) MnO_2

(h) PO_4^{3-}

(i) $K_2Cr_2O_7$

(j) MnO_4^-

2 Use oxidation states to deduce which species is oxidized and which is reduced in the following reactions:

(a) $Sn^{2+}(aq) + 2Fe^{3+}(aq) \rightarrow Sn^{4+}(aq) + 2Fe^{2+}(aq)$

(b) $Cl_2(aq) + 2NaBr(aq) \rightarrow Br_2(aq) + 2NaCl(aq)$

(c) $2FeCl_2(aq) + Cl_2(aq) \rightarrow 2FeCl_3(aq)$

(d) $2H_2O(l) + 2F_2(g) \rightarrow 4HF(aq) + O_2(g)$

(e) $I_2(aq) + SO_3^{2-}(aq) + H_2O(l) \rightarrow 2I^-(aq) + SO_4^{2-}(aq) + 2H^+(aq)$

3 Deduce the half-equations of oxidation and reduction for the following reactions:

(a) $Ca(s) + 2H^+(aq) \rightarrow Ca^{2+}(aq) + H_2(g)$

(b) $2Fe^{2+}(aq) + Cl_2(aq) \rightarrow 2Fe^{3+}(aq) + 2Cl^-(aq)$

(c) $Sn^{2+}(aq) + 2Fe^{3+}(aq) \rightarrow Sn^{4+}(aq) + 2Fe^{2+}(aq)$

(d) $Cl_2(aq) + 2Br^-(aq) \rightarrow 2Cl^-(aq) + Br_2(aq)$

4 Write balanced equations for the following reactions that occur in acidic solutions:

(a) $Zn(s) + SO_4^{2-}(aq) \rightarrow Zn^{2+}(aq) + SO_2(g)$

(b) $I^-(aq) + HSO_4^-(aq) \rightarrow I_2(aq) + SO_2(g)$

(c) $NO_3^-(aq) + Zn(s) \rightarrow NH_4^+(aq) + Zn^{2+}(aq)$

(d) $I_2(aq) + OCl^-(aq) \rightarrow IO_3^-(aq) + Cl^-(aq)$

(e) $MnO_4^-(aq) + H_2SO_3(aq) \rightarrow SO_4^{2-}(aq) + Mn^{2+}(aq)$

5 Which equation represents a redox reaction?

A $NaOH(aq) + HNO_3(aq) \rightarrow NaNO_3(aq) + H_2O(l)$

B $Zn(s) + 2HCl(aq) \rightarrow ZnCl_2(aq) + H_2(g)$

C $CuO(s) + 2HCl(aq) \rightarrow CuCl_2(aq) + H_2O(l)$

D $MgCO_3(s) + 2HNO_3(aq) \rightarrow Mg(NO_3)_2(aq) + H_2O(l) + CO_2(g)$

6 The oxidation state of chromium is the same in all the following compounds except:

A $CrCl_3$ **B** Cr_2O_3 **C** $Cr_2(CO_3)_3$ **D** CrO_3

7 Deduce the names of the following compounds, using their oxidation numbers:

(a) Cr_2O_3 **(c)** HNO_3 **(e)** PbO_2

(b) $CuCl$ **(d)** HNO_2

NATURE OF SCIENCE

We have seen that oxidation states have several important uses as they enable us to:

- track redox changes in reactions;
- apply systematic names to compounds;
- determine reacting ratios in redox reactions.

At the same time, because they do not have a structural basis, oxidation states can raise some potential misunderstandings or ambiguities.

- Oxidation states do not distinguish between partial and complete transfer of electrons: +4 for C in CO_2 or +7 for Mn in $KMnO_4$ do not represent losses of 4 and 7 electrons respectively.
- In some cases, especially in organic chemistry, oxidation states have fractional values: in propane, C_3H_8, the oxidation state of C is $-2\frac{2}{3}$.
- Oxidation states and Lewis (electron dot) structures sometimes suggest conflicting information: CH_4, C_2H_6, and C_3H_8 are all similarly bonded molecules, but their C atoms have different oxidation states, -4, -3, and $-2\frac{2}{3}$ respectively.

In $S_2O_3^{2-}$, the rules would suggest oxidation states of +2 on each S atom, but from the Lewis

structure, , values of +2 and +6 seem more appropriate.

Overall, oxidation states are best considered as a very useful tool that chemists use widely, while also keeping an eye on their limitations.

Oxidizing and reducing agents

We have seen that redox reactions *always* involve the simultaneous oxidation of one reactant with the reduction of another as electrons are transferred between them. The reactant that accepts electrons is called the **oxidizing agent** as it brings about oxidation of the other reactant. In the process it becomes reduced. Likewise the reactant that supplies the electrons is known as the **reducing agent**, because it brings about reduction and itself becomes oxidized. Sometimes the terms **reductant** and **oxidant** are used in place of reducing agent and oxidizing agent respectively.

For example, in the reaction where iron (Fe) is extracted from its ore (Fe_2O_3):

$$\begin{array}{cccc} \text{oxidizing} & \text{reducing} & & \\ \text{agent} & \text{agent} & & \\ Fe_2O_3(s) & + \quad 3C(s) & \rightarrow \quad 2Fe(s) & + \quad 3CO(g) \\ +3 & 0 & 0 & +2 \end{array}$$

(The oxidation state of O is not shown as it does not change during the reaction.)

The reducing agent C brings about the reduction of Fe ($+2 \rightarrow 0$), while it is oxidized to CO ($0 \rightarrow +2$). The oxidizing agent Fe_2O_3 brings about the oxidation of C, while itself is reduced to Fe.

Some examples of useful oxidizing and reducing agents are given below.

- oxidizing agent: O_2, O_3, H^+/MnO_4^-, $H^+/Cr_2O_7^{2-}$, F_2, Cl_2, conc. HNO_3, H_2O_2
- reducing agent: H_2, C, CO, SO_2, reactive metals

Note that whether a species acts as an oxidizing or as a reducing agent actually depends on what it is reacting with. For example, water can act as an oxidizing agent and be reduced to hydrogen, for example by sodium, or act as a reducing agent and be oxidized to oxygen, for example by fluorine.

- H_2O acting as an oxidizing agent:

$$\begin{array}{cc} 2H_2O(l) + 2Na(s) \rightarrow 2NaOH(aq) + H_2(g) \\ +1 \qquad\qquad\qquad\qquad\qquad 0 \end{array}$$

- H_2O acting as a reducing agent:

$$\begin{array}{cc} 2H_2O(l) + 2F_2(g) \rightarrow 4HF(aq) + O_2(g) \\ -2 \qquad\qquad\qquad\qquad\qquad 0 \end{array}$$

In fact, water is weak both as an oxidizing agent and as a reducing agent, which is why it is such a useful solvent for many redox reactions.

CHALLENGE YOURSELF

1 Hydrogen peroxide, H_2O_2, can also act as an oxidizing agent and as a reducing agent. With reference to the oxidation states of its atoms, suggest why this is so and which behaviour is more likely.

Treatment of drinking water to kill pathogens commonly uses oxidizing agents such as chlorine and ozone. The process is effective and relatively cheap, yet millions of people worldwide lack access to clean drinking water. 'Access to safe water is a fundamental human need and therefore a human right.' Kofi Annan, United Nations Secretary General. In 2010 this human right was passed into international law, but this does not yet make it a reality for millions of people in developing countries.

More reactive metals are stronger reducing agents

Of course not all oxidizing and reducing agents are of equal strength. Some will be stronger than others, depending on their relative tendencies to lose or gain electrons. We learned in Chapter 4 that metals have a tendency to lose electrons and form positive ions, so they will act as reducing agents, pushing their electrons on to another substance. More reactive metals lose their electrons more readily and so we might expect that they will be stronger reducing agents than less reactive metals.

We can check this out by seeing if one metal is able to reduce the ions of another metal in solution. If we immerse zinc in a solution of copper sulfate, a reaction occurs. The blue colour of the solution fades, the pinkish-brown colour of copper metal appears and there is a rise in temperature. What is happening is that the Cu^{2+} ions are being displaced from solution as they are reduced by Zn. At the same time Zn dissolves as it is oxidized to Zn^{2+}.

$$Zn(s) + CuSO_4(aq) \rightarrow ZnSO_4(aq) + Cu(s)$$

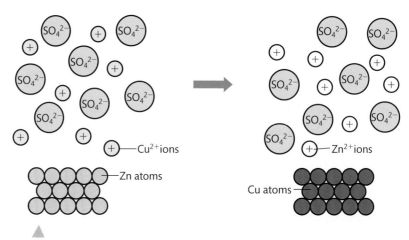

Figure 9.1 The reaction of zinc with copper(II) sulfate solution.

We can write this as an ionic equation without showing the sulfate ions as these act as spectator ions and are not changed during the reaction.

$$Zn(s) + Cu^{2+}(aq) \rightarrow Zn^{2+}(aq) + Cu(s)$$

So zinc has acted as the reducing agent – it is therefore the more reactive metal. We can think of it as having the reducing strength to 'force' copper ions to accept the electrons.

We could confirm this by trying the reaction the other way round, with copper metal immersed in a solution of zinc ions. Can you predict what will happen? The answer is there will be no reaction, because Cu is not a strong enough reducing agent to reduce Zn^{2+}. This is another way of saying that it is a less reactive metal, less able to push the electrons onto Zn^{2+}.

Single replacement reactions involving metals with metal ions

Full details of how to carry out this experiment with a worksheet are available on your eBook.

A strip of zinc metal half submerged in a solution of $CuSO_4$. Solid copper that appears brown is deposited and the blue colour fades as the copper ions are reduced by the zinc. Zinc is shown to be the stronger reducing agent.

More reactive metals are stronger reducing agents than less reactive metals.

By comparing **displacement** reactions like these between different combinations of metals and their ions, we can build up a list of relative strengths of the metals as reducing agents. This is called the **activity series** and it enables us to predict whether a particular redox reaction between a metal and the ions of another metal will be feasible. Later in this chapter we will learn how to quantify these differences in metal reactivity, which is of great importance in many industrial processes. For example, the extraction of a metal from its ore often involves choosing a suitable reducing agent by reference to these data.

Here is a small part of the activity series of metals:

Mg   strongest reducing agent, most readily becomes oxidized

Al

Zn

Fe

Pb

Cu

Ag   weakest reducing agent, least readily becomes oxidized

A simple activity series is given in section 25 of the IB data booklet and is not something that needs to be learned. The important thing is that you are able to interpret it and to deduce it from given data.

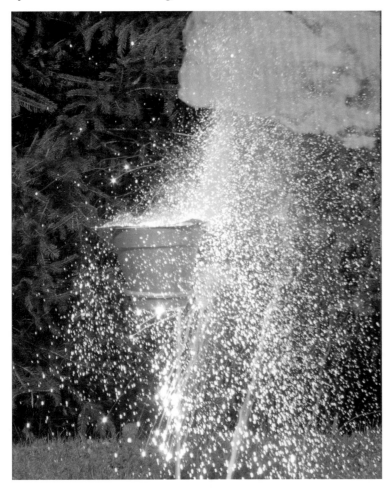

A more reactive metal is able to reduce the ions of a less reactive metal.

Redox reactions between a metal and the oxide of a less reactive metal can also confirm the activity series. Here powdered aluminium reduces iron oxide, forming aluminium oxide and iron.
$2Al(s) + Fe_2O_3(s) \rightarrow Al_2O_3(s) + 2Fe(s)$. This shows that aluminium is a stronger reducing agent than iron. The reaction is exothermic, creating short bursts of extremely high temperatures.

Worked example

Refer to the activity series given on page 279 to predict whether the following reactions will occur:

(a) $ZnCl_2(aq) + 2Ag(s) \rightarrow 2AgCl(s) + Zn(s)$

(b) $2FeCl_3(aq) + 3Mg(s) \rightarrow 3MgCl_2(aq) + 2Fe(s)$

Solution

(a) This reaction would involve Ag reducing Zn^{2+} in $ZnCl_2$. But Ag is a weaker reducing agent than Zn, so this will not occur.

(b) This reaction involves Mg reducing Fe^{3+} in $FeCl_3$. Mg is a stronger reducing agent than Fe so this will occur.

We can investigate how some non-metals such as carbon and hydrogen would fit into this activity series of metals by similar types of displacement reactions. Carbon is able to reduce the oxides of iron and metals below it in the series, which provides one of the most effective means for the extraction of these metals.

More reactive non-metals are stronger oxidizing agents

In a similar way, the different strengths of non-metals as oxidizing agents can be compared. For example, the halogens (Group 17 elements) react by gaining electrons and forming negative ions, so act as oxidizing agents by removing electrons from other substances. We learned in Chapter 3 that their tendency to do this decreases down the group, so we would expect the following trend.

F   strongest oxidizing agent, most readily becomes reduced

Cl

Br

I   weakest oxidizing agent, least readily becomes reduced

More reactive non-metals are stronger oxidizing agents than less reactive non-metals.

Chlorine gas bubbling through a clear solution of potassium iodide KI. The solution is turning brown due to the formation of iodine in solution, as chlorine oxidizes the iodide ions and forms chloride ions.

Again this can be verified by reacting one halogen with solutions containing the ions of another halogen (known as halide ions). For example

$$Cl_2(aq) + 2KI(aq) \rightarrow 2KCl(aq) + I_2(aq)$$

Here the Na^+ ions are spectator ions so we can write the ionic equation without showing them:

$$Cl_2(aq) + 2I^-(aq) \rightarrow 2Cl^-(aq) + I_2(aq)$$

The reaction occurs because Cl is a stronger oxidizing agent than I so is able to remove electrons from it. In simple terms, you can think of it as a competition for electrons where the stronger oxidizing agent, in this case chlorine, will always 'win'.

A more reactive non-metal is able to oxidize the ions of a less reactive non-metal.

Exercises

8 Identify the oxidizing agents and the reducing agents in the following reactions:

  (a) $H_2(g) + Cl_2(g) \rightarrow 2HCl(g)$
  (b) $2Al(s) + 3PbCl_2(s) \rightarrow 2AlCl_3(s) + 3Pb(s)$
  (c) $Cl_2(aq) + 2KI(aq) \rightarrow 2KCl(aq) + I_2(aq)$
  (d) $CH_4(g) + 2O_2(g) \rightarrow CO_2(g) + 2H_2O(l)$

9 Use the two reactivity series given to predict whether reactions will occur between the following reactants, and write equations where relevant.

  (a) $CuCl_2 + Ag$ **(b)** $Fe(NO_3)_2 + Al$ **(c)** $NaI + Br_2$ **(d)** $KCl + I_2$

10 (a) Use the following reactions to deduce the order of activity of the elements W, X, Y, Z, putting the most reactive first.

$$W + X^+ \rightarrow W^+ + X \qquad\qquad X + Z^+ \rightarrow X^+ + Z$$
$$Y^+ + z \rightarrow \text{no reaction} \qquad\qquad X + Y^+ \rightarrow X^+ + Y$$

  (b) Which of the following reactions would you expect to occur according to the reactivity series you established in part (a)?

  (i) $W^+ + Y \rightarrow W + Y^+$

  (ii) $W^+ + Z \rightarrow W + Z^+$

Redox titrations

As with acid–base titrations (discussed in Chapter 8), redox titrations are used to determine the unknown concentration of a substance in solution. But in this case, the technique is based on a redox reaction between the two reactants, and finds the equivalence point where they have reacted stoichiometrically by transferring electrons. The two types of titration are compared below.

Acid–base titration	Redox titration
neutralization reaction between acid and base	redox reaction between oxidizing agent and reducing agent
protons are transferred from acid to base	electrons are transferred from reducing agent to oxidizing agent

Redox titrations are carried out in much the same way as acid–base titrations, using a burette and pipette to measure volumes accurately, and a standard solution of one reactant. An indicator is usually used to signal the equivalence point, although some redox changes are accompanied by a colour change and may not need an external indicator. From the volume of the solution added from the burette to reach equivalence, which is known as the **titre**, the concentration of the other reactant can be determined. The calculations are based on the redox equation, which is typically developed from the half-equations.

Redox titrations are commonly used in the food and beverages industry, in the pharmaceutical industry, and in water and environmental analysis. For example, wines

CHALLENGE YOURSELF

2 Reactions in which the same element is simultaneously oxidized and reduced is known as **disproportionation**. Show how this happens in the reaction when Cl_2 and NaOH react to produce NaCl, NaClO, and H_2O.

The browning of fruit when it is exposed to the air is an oxidation reaction. It occurs when phenols released in damaged cells are oxidized with molecular oxygen at alkaline pH. The brown products are tannins. Food chemists are often interested in slowing down these reactions using reducing agents such as SO_2 or vitamin C, for example in lemon juice.

Redox titrations

Full details of how to carry out this experiment with a worksheet are available on your eBook.

can be analysed for the presence of sulfur dioxide, and the vitamin C content of foods can be determined in this way. Some examples of common redox titrations that can be carried out in the laboratory are given below, and more details on how to carry out these experiments can be found on your eBook.

1 Analysis of iron with manganate(VII)

This redox titration uses $KMnO_4$ in an acidic solution as the oxidizing agent, which oxidizes Fe^{2+} ions to Fe^{3+}. During the reaction MnO_4^- is reduced to Mn^{2+}, so the overall equation is:

$$5Fe^{2+} + MnO_4^- + 8H^+ \rightarrow 5Fe^{3+} + Mn^{2+} + 4H_2O$$
$$\text{purple} \qquad\qquad\qquad \text{colourless}$$

The reaction is accompanied by a colour change from deep purple to colourless, so the reaction acts as its own indicator, signalling the equivalence point.

Worked example

All the iron in a 2.000 g tablet was dissolved in an acidic solution and converted to Fe^{2+}. This was then titrated with $KMnO_4$. The titration required 27.50 cm^3 of 0.100 mol dm^{-3} $KMnO_4$. Calculate the total mass of iron in the tablet and its percentage by mass. Describe what would be observed during the reaction, and how the equivalence point can be detected.

Solution

First we need the balanced equation for the reaction, which is solved by the half-equation method described earlier.

> oxidation: $Fe^{2+} \rightarrow Fe^{3+} + e^-$
>
> reduction: $MnO_4^- + 8H^+ + 5e^- \rightarrow Mn^{2+} + 4H_2O$
>
> overall: $5Fe^{2+} + MnO_4^- + 8H^+ \rightarrow 5Fe^{3+} + Mn^{2+} + 4H_2O$

Next we need to know the amounts of reactants used to reach equivalence. We start with $KMnO_4$ as we know both its concentration and its volume.

$$n = cV$$

$$n(MnO_4^-) = 0.100 \text{ mol dm}^{-3} \times \frac{27.50}{1000} \text{ dm}^3 = 0.00275 \text{ mol } MnO_4^-$$

From the equation for the reaction we know the reacting ratio:

$MnO_4^- : Fe^{2+} = 1 : 5$

$\therefore$ mol $Fe^{2+} = 0.00275$ mol $MnO_4^- \times 5 = 0.01375$ mol

$M(Fe) = 55.85$ g mol^{-1}

$$n = \frac{m}{M}$$

$\therefore m(Fe) = 0.01375$ mol $\times 55.85$ g mol$^{-1} = 0.7679$ g

% Fe in tablet $= \dfrac{0.768 \text{ g}}{2.000 \text{ g}} \times 100 = 38.39\%$

$\therefore$ Fe in tablet: 0.768 g, 38.4 %

MnO_4^- in the burette is purple, but forms a nearly colourless solution in the flask as it reacts to form Mn^{2+}. But when the reducing agent Fe^{2+} in the flask has been used up at equivalence, MnO_4^- ions will not react and the purple colour will persist.

2 Iodine–thiosulfate reaction

Several different redox titrations use an oxidizing agent to react with excess iodide ions to form iodine.

$$2I^-(aq) + \text{oxidizing agent} \rightarrow I_2(aq) + \text{reduced product}$$

Examples of oxidizing agents used in this way include $KMnO_4$, KIO_3, $K_2Cr_2O_7$, and NaOCl.

The liberated iodine, I_2, is then titrated with sodium thiosulfate, $Na_2S_2O_3$, using starch as an indicator.

Redox equations:

oxidation: $2S_2O_3^{2-} \rightarrow S_4O_6^{2-} + 2e^-$

reduction: $I_2 + 2e^- \rightarrow 2I^-$

The overall equation is:

$$2S_2O_3^{2-}(aq) + I_2(aq) \rightarrow 2I^-(aq) + S_4O_6^{2-}(aq)$$

deep blue in
presence of starch

The starch indicator is added during the titration (not at the start) and forms a deep blue colour by forming a complex with free I_2. As the I_2 is reduced to I^- during the reaction, the blue colour disappears, marking the equivalence point.

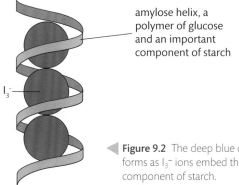

amylose helix, a polymer of glucose and an important component of starch

I_3^-

Figure 9.2 The deep blue complex between iodine solution and starch forms as I_3^- ions embed themselves within the helix of amylose, a component of starch.

> Because iodine, I_2, has a very low solubility in water, it is used instead in the form of 'iodine solution', which is made by dissolving I_2 in iodide ions, forming the complex ion $I_3^-(aq)$. It is the I_3^- ion that gives the deep blue complex with starch. Even though I_3^- is the reactant, it is still valid to use I_2 in the equations, as this is the 'active ingredient'. Technically, starch is not a redox indicator as such, as it responds to the disappearance of I_2, rather than to a change in the redox potential of the solution.

CHALLENGE YOURSELF

3 Find out about the structure of I_3^-, and consider why it forms a stable complex in the hydrophobic interior of the amylose helix.

Worked example

Household bleach is an oxidizing agent that contains sodium hypochlorite, NaOCl, as the active ingredient. It reacts with iodide ions in acidic solution as follows:

$$OCl^-(aq) + 2I^-(aq) + 2H^+(aq) \rightarrow I_2(aq) + Cl^-(aq) + H_2O(l)$$

A 10.00 cm³ sample of bleach was reacted with a solution of excess iodide ions, and the liberated iodine was then titrated with $Na_2S_2O_3$. The titration required 38.65 cm³ of 0.0200 mol dm⁻³ $Na_2S_2O_3$. Determine the concentration of OCl^- in the bleach.

Solution

First we need the balanced equation for the titration, which is solved by the half-equation method on page 274.

$$2Na_2S_2O_3(aq) + I_2(aq) \rightarrow 2NaI(aq) + Na_2S_4O_6(aq)$$

Next we calculate the number of moles of $Na_2S_2O_3$ as we know both its concentration and its volume.

In titration calculations, always look first for the reactant where you know both its reacting volume *and* its concentration. Start by using these data to calculate the number of moles. Then use the reacting ratio in the equation to deduce the moles of the other reactant.

$$n = cV$$

$$n(S_2O_3^{2-}) = 0.0200 \text{ mol dm}^{-3} \times \frac{38.65}{1000} \text{ dm}^3 = 7.73 \times 10^{-4} \text{ mol } S_2O_3^{2-}$$

From the equation for the reaction we know the reacting ratio:

$$S_2O_3^{2-} : I_2 = 2 : 1$$

$$\therefore \text{mol } I_2 = 7.73 \times 10^{-4} \times 0.5 = 3.865 \times 10^{-4}$$

This is a back-titration as the I_2 was liberated by the reaction of I^- with OCl^-, as given in the question. The reacting ratio is:

$$OCl^-(aq) : I_2(aq) = 1 : 1$$

$$\therefore \text{mol } OCl^- = \text{mol } I_2 = 3.865 \times 10^{-4}$$

The concentration of the OCl^- in the bleach can now be calculated.

$$n(OCl^-) = cV$$

$$\therefore 3.865 \times 10^{-4} \text{ mol} = c \times \frac{10.00}{1000} \text{ dm}^3$$

$$[OCl^-] = 0.0387 \text{ mol dm}^{-3}$$

A canal in England covered in a bloom of duckweed. This is an aquatic weed that thrives in water that contains pollutants such as phosphates. This is known as eutrophication. The bloom blocks out sunlight to deeper layers of the water ecosystem, and so lowers the level of dissolved oxygen.

3 Winkler method for calculating dissolved oxygen

The **dissolved oxygen** content of water is one of the most important indicators of its quality, as oxygen is essential to the survival of aquatic life. As the level of pollution in water increases, the dissolved oxygen content generally decreases, as the oxygen is used by bacteria in decomposition reactions. The **biological oxygen demand** (BOD) is therefore used as a means of measuring the degree of pollution. BOD is defined as the amount of oxygen used to decompose the organic matter in a sample of water over a specified time period, usually five days at a specified temperature. A high BOD indicates a greater quantity of degradable organic waste in the water, which means a lower level of dissolved oxygen.

BOD is the quantity of oxygen needed to oxidize organic matter in a sample of water over a five-day period at a specified temperature.

The BOD of a body of water increases with the addition of nitrates and phosphates in the run-off from soil, resulting from the excess use of inorganic fertilizers and detergents. These ions promote the growth of plants resulting in **blooms** of algae and aquatic weeds, which lead to a decrease in the dissolved oxygen content of the water. This is known as **eutrophication**, and significantly impacts the ability of lakes to support biodiversity. According to a United Nations report, eutrophication has increased significantly in most major lakes worldwide since the 1970s, and is a particular problem in Europe, Japan, China, and the Great Lakes of North America. Remedial action involves better treatment of waste-water and diversions of agricultural run-offs, but nitrates and phosphates continue to be released from the high concentrations stored in soil sediments. As is the case with some other environmental problems, the impact of damaging practices often persists long after corrective actions have been taken.

Redox titrations can be used to measure the dissolved oxygen in water, and from this calculate the BOD in a process known as the **Winkler method**. The principle is based on a sequence of redox reactions as follows.

1   The dissolved oxygen, $O_2(g)$, in the water is 'fixed' by the addition of a manganese(II) salt such as $MnSO_4$. Reaction of this salt with O_2 in basic solution causes oxidation of Mn(II) to higher oxidation states, such as Mn(IV):

$$2Mn^{2+}(aq) + O_2(g) + 4OH^-(aq) \rightarrow 2MnO_2(s) + 2H_2O(l)$$
$$\phantom{2Mn^{2+}}_{+2} _{+4}$$

2   Acidified iodide ions, I^-, are added to the solution, and are oxidized by the Mn(IV) to I_2:

$$MnO_2(s) + 2I^-(aq) + 4H^+(aq) \rightarrow Mn^{2+}(aq) + I_2(aq) + 2H_2O(l)$$
$$_{+4} \phantom{O_2(s) + 2I^-(aq) + 4H^+(aq) \rightarrow Mn^{2+}(aq) + I}_{+2}$$

3   The iodine produced is then titrated with sodium thiosulfate, as described earlier:

$$2S_2O_3^{2-}(aq) + I_2(aq) \rightarrow 2I^-(aq) + S_4O_6^{2-}(aq)$$

So we can see that in the overall sequence, for every 1 mole of O_2 in the water, 4 mol of $S_2O_3^{2-}$ are used.

CHALLENGE YOURSELF

4   How would you expect the dissolved oxygen content of a lake to be affected by discharge of hot water from an industrial site? Explain why this effect occurs.

Worked example

A 500 cm^3 sample of water was collected and tested for dissolved oxygen by the addition of $MnSO_4$ in basic solution, followed by the addition of acidified KI. It was found that 12.50 cm^3 of 0.0500 mol dm^{-3} $Na_2S_2O_3(aq)$ was required to react with the iodine produced. Calculate the dissolved oxygen content of the water in g dm^{-3}, using the equations given above.

Solution

Start with calculating the amount of $S_2O_3^{2-}$, as we are given both its volume and its concentration.

$$n = cV$$

$$n(S_2O_3^{2-}) = 0.0500 \text{ mol dm}^{-3} \times \frac{12.50}{1000} \text{ dm}^3 = 6.25 \times 10^{-4} \text{ mol}$$

From the reacting ratio in step 3, $S_2O_3^{2-} : I_2 = 2 : 1$

$\therefore n(I_2) = 0.5 \times 6.25 \times 10^{-4} = 3.175 \times 10^{-4}$ mol

From the reacting ratio in step 2, $I_2 : MnO_2 = 1 : 1$

$\therefore n(MnO_2) = 3.175 \times 10^{-4}$ mol

From the reacting ratio in step 1, $MnO_2 : O_2(g) = 2 : 1$

$\therefore n(O_2) = 0.5 \times 3.175 \times 10^{-4}$ mol $= 1.5875 \times 10^{-4}$ mol

(We could also go directly from a ratio of $O_2 : S_2O_3^{2-} = 1 : 4$)

Finally express the amount of $O_2(g)$ as g dm^{-3}

$m(O_2) = n \times M = 1.5875 \times 10^{-4}$ mol $\times 32.00$ g mol^{-1} $= 5.080 \times 10^{-3}$ g in 500 cm^3

$\therefore$ dissolved oxygen $= 0.0102$ g dm^{-3}

NATURE OF SCIENCE

We have seen that oxidation and reduction can be defined in different ways, and that these different definitions do not contradict but are consistent with each other. Which definition we choose to apply will be determined by the particular example, and by which approach gives the simplest, most useful interpretation of the type of reaction occurring.

Oxidation	Reduction
gain of oxygen	loss of oxygen
loss of hydrogen	gain of hydrogen
loss of electrons	gain of electrons
increase in oxidation state	decrease in oxidation state
brought about by an oxidizing agent that becomes reduced	brought about by a reducing agent that becomes oxidized

We have seen similar situations earlier in this text where different theories used to describe the same phenomenon persist. Sometimes the theories are distinct, such as the particle-wave theories of electron behaviour. At other times, one theory represents a broader generalization of the other, such as the Brønsted–Lowry theory and a broader theory of acid–base behaviour known as Lewis theory. As long as a theory leads to testable predictions and can be supported by experimental data, it has validity and contributes to the understanding of the phenomenon.

Exercises

11 A bag of 'road salt', used to melt ice and snow from roads, contains a mixture of calcium chloride, $CaCl_2$, and sodium chloride, NaCl. A 2.765 g sample of the mixture was analysed by first converting all the calcium into calcium oxalate, CaC_2O_4. This was then dissolved in H_2SO_4, and titrated with 0.100 mol dm^{-3} $KMnO_4$ solution. The titration required 24.65 cm^3 of $KMnO_4(aq)$ and produced $Mn^{2+}(aq)$, $CO_2(g)$, and $H_2O(l)$.

(a) What would be observed at the equivalence point of the titration?
(b) Write the half-equation for the oxidation reaction, starting with $C_2O_4^{2-}$.
(c) Write the half-equation for the reduction reaction, starting with MnO_4^-.
(d) Write the overall equation for the redox reaction.
(e) Determine the number of moles of $C_2O_4^{2-}$.
(f) Deduce the number of moles of Ca^{2+} in the original sample.
(g) What was the percentage by mass of $CaCl_2$ in the road salt?

12 Alcohol levels in blood can be determined by a redox titration with potassium dichromate, $K_2Cr_2O_7$, according to the following equation.

$$C_2H_5OH(aq) + 2Cr_2O_7^{2-}(aq) + 16H^+(aq) \rightarrow 2CO_2(g) + 4Cr^{3+}(aq) + 11H_2O(l)$$

(a) Determine the alcohol percentage in the blood by mass if a 10.000 g sample of blood requires 9.25 cm^3 of 0.0550 mol dm^{-3} $K_2Cr_2O_7$ solution to reach equivalence.
(b) Describe the change in colour that would be observed during the titration.

Electrochemical cells

Understandings:

Voltaic (Galvanic) cells
- Voltaic cells convert energy from spontaneous, exothermic chemical processes to electrical energy.
- Oxidation occurs at the anode (negative electrode) and reduction occurs at the cathode (positive electrode) in a voltaic cell.

Electrolytic cells
- Electrolytic cells convert electrical energy to chemical energy, by bringing about non-spontaneous processes.
- Oxidation occurs at the anode (positive electrode) and reduction occurs at the cathode (negative electrode) in an electrolytic cell.

Applications and skills:

- Construction and annotation of both types of electrochemical cells.

  Guidance
  For voltaic cells, a cell diagram convention should be covered.
- Explanation of how a redox reaction is used to produce electricity in a voltaic cell and how current is conducted in an electrolytic cell.
- Distinction between electron and ion flow in both electrochemical cells.
- Performance of laboratory experiments involving a typical voltaic cell using two metal/metal-ion half-cells.
- Deduction of the products of the electrolysis of a molten salt.

The fact that redox reactions involve transfers of electrons immediately suggests a link between this type of chemical reactivity and electricity. The main applications of this are collectively known as **electrochemical cells**, of which there are two main types.

electrochemical cells

voltaic (galvanic) cells
generate electricity from chemical reactions

electrolytic cells
drive chemical reactions using electrical energy

We will consider each of these types of cell in turn.

Voltaic cells

Voltaic cells generate electricity from spontaneous redox reactions

Let us consider again the reaction we discussed on page 278 in which zinc reduced copper ions. Remember that here zinc was the reducing agent and became oxidized while copper ions were reduced. When the reaction is carried out in a single test tube, as shown in the photo on page 278, the electrons flow spontaneously from the zinc to the copper ions in the solution, and as we noted, energy is released in the form of heat as it is an exothermic reaction. There is, however, a different way of organizing this reaction so that the energy released in the redox reaction, instead of being lost as heat, is available as electrical energy. It is really just a case of separating the two half-reactions

Building voltaic cells with different combinations of metals/metal ion electrodes will help in the understanding of this topic. Full details with a worksheet are available on your eBook.

oxidation $Zn(s) \rightarrow Zn^{2+}(aq) + 2e^-$ and

reduction $Cu^{2+}(aq) + 2e^- \rightarrow Cu(s)$

into so-called **half-cells**, and allowing the electrons to flow between them only through an external circuit. This is known as a **voltaic** or a **galvanic cell,** and we will see how it is constructed in the next section.

Half-cells generate electrode potentials

There are many types of half-cell but probably the simplest is made by putting a strip of metal into a solution of its ions.

Figure 9.3 Copper and zinc half-cells.

A copper half-cell consisting of a piece of copper metal dipping into a solution of a copper salt. An equilibrium is set up between the Cu metal and its ions:
$Cu^{2+}(aq) + 2e^- \rightleftharpoons Cu(s)$

In the zinc half-cell, zinc atoms will form ions by releasing electrons that will make the surface of the metal negatively charged with respect to the solution.

Figure 9.4 Zinc atoms form zinc ions by releasing electrons. An equilibrium is set up between the metal and its solution of ions.

There will therefore be a charge separation, known as an **electrode potential**, between the metal and its ions in solution. At the same time, ions in the solution gain electrons to form Zn atoms, so an equilibrium exists as follows:

$$Zn^{2+}(aq) + 2e^- \rightleftharpoons Zn(s)$$

The position of this equilibrium determines the size of the electrode potential in the half-cell, and depends on the reactivity of the metal.

Because copper is the less reactive metal, in its half-cell the equilibrium position for the equivalent reaction:

$$Cu^{2+}(aq) + 2e^- \rightleftharpoons Cu(s)$$

lies further to the right. In other words, copper has less of a tendency to lose electrons than zinc. Consequently, there are fewer electrons on the copper metal strip, so it will develop a higher (or less negative) electrode potential than the zinc half-cell.

zinc metal strip

zinc sulfate solution

$$Zn^{2+}(aq) + 2e^- \rightleftharpoons Zn(s)$$

Some zinc atoms from the metal strip release electrons, giving it a negative charge.

copper metal strip

copper sulfate solution

$$Cu^{2+}(aq) + 2e^- \rightleftharpoons Cu(s)$$

Some copper ions in the solution accept electrons from the copper rod giving it a positive charge.

Figure 9.5 The zinc half-cell develops a negative potential with respect to the copper half-cell.

The equilibrium as written for the copper half-cell lies further to the right than the equilibrium in the zinc half-cell.

In general the more reactive a metal, the more negative its electrode potential in its half-cell.

Two connected half-cells make a voltaic cell

If we now connect these two half-cells by an external wire, electrons will have a tendency to flow spontaneously from the zinc half-cell to the copper half-cell because of their different electrode potentials. The half-cells connected in this way are often called **electrodes**, and their name gives us information about the type of reaction that occurs there. The electrode where oxidation occurs is called the **anode**, in this case it is the zinc electrode and it has a negative charge:

$$Zn(s) \rightarrow Zn^{2+}(aq) + 2e^-$$

The electrode where reduction occurs is called the **cathode**, in this case it is the copper electrode and it has a positive charge:

$$Cu^{2+}(aq) + 2e^- \rightarrow Cu(s)$$

A potential difference will, however, only be generated between the electrodes when the circuit is complete.

Oxidation always occurs at the anode; reduction always occurs at the cathode. In the voltaic cell, the anode has a negative charge and the cathode has a positive charge.

voltmeter

0.00 V

Zn

Cu

$ZnSO_4(aq)$

$CuSO_4(aq)$

Figure 9.6 This cell has an incomplete circuit – no voltage is generated. A salt bridge must be added to allow ions to flow between the two electrodes.

The voltaic cell therefore must have the following connections between the half-cells.

- An external electronic circuit, connected to the metal electrode in each half-cell. A voltmeter can also be attached to this external circuit to record the voltage generated. Electrons will flow from the anode to the cathode through the wire.
- A salt bridge completes the circuit. The salt bridge is a glass tube or strip of absorptive paper that contains an aqueous solution of ions. Movement of these ions neutralizes any build-up of charge and maintains the potential difference. Anions move in the salt bridge from the cathode to the anode, which opposes the flow of electrons in the external circuit. Cations move in the salt bridge from the anode to the cathode. The solution chosen is often aqueous $NaNO_3$ or KNO_3 as these ions will not interfere with the reactions at the electrodes. Without a salt bridge, no voltage is generated.

Zinc–copper voltaic cell showing a copper half-cell and a zinc half-cell connected by a salt bridge that appears white. Electrons flow from the zinc electrode to the copper electrode through the electrical wires, while ions flow through the salt bridge to complete the circuit. The voltmeter is showing 1.10 V, the potential difference of this cell.

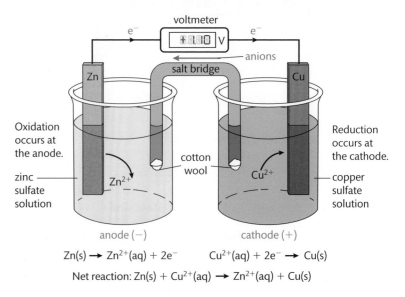

Figure 9.7 A copper–zinc voltaic cell.

Oxidation occurs at the anode.

zinc sulfate solution

Zn^{2+}

cotton wool

Cu^{2+}

Reduction occurs at the cathode.

copper sulfate solution

anode (−)

cathode (+)

$Zn(s) \rightarrow Zn^{2+}(aq) + 2e^-$ $Cu^{2+}(aq) + 2e^- \rightarrow Cu(s)$

Net reaction: $Zn(s) + Cu^{2+}(aq) \rightarrow Zn^{2+}(aq) + Cu(s)$

A voltaic cell converts the energy released from a spontaneous, exothermic reaction into electrical energy.

You may be familiar with the sensation of a mild electric shock when you happen to bite some aluminium foil on a tooth that has a filling. The filling is made of an amalgam of mercury and either tin or silver, and creates a voltaic cell when it touches the foil. Aluminium is the anode, the filling is the cathode, and the saliva is the electrolyte 'salt bridge'. A weak current flows between the electrodes and is detected by the sensitive nerves in the teeth.

Cell diagram convention

Rather than always drawing out all the components of a voltaic cell, a shorthand version known as a **cell diagram convention** can be used. This has the following features:

- a single vertical line represents a phase boundary such as that between a solid electrode and an aqueous solution within a half-cell;
- a double vertical line represents the salt bridge;
- the aqueous solutions of each electrode are placed next to the salt bridge;
- the anode is generally put on the left and the cathode on the right, so electrons flow from left to right;
- spectator ions are usually omitted from the diagram;
- if a half-cell includes two ions, they are separated by a comma because they are in the same phase.

The cell diagram convention is shown below for the copper–zinc cell.

The placing of the anode and cathode on the left and right is not universally used. The important thing is that the diagram is clearly labelled and leads to the correct interpretation of the direction of electron flow.

Fuel cells generate electricity from a redox reaction, most commonly hydrogen combining with oxygen to make water. Unlike other voltaic cells, they require a constant source of fuel and oxygen in order to produce electricity continuously. The first commercial use of fuel cells was in the NASA spacecraft launched by the USA, and many countries are now investing in fuel cell technologies as alternatives to fossil fuels. Fuel cells are discussed in more detail in Chapter 14, Option C: Energy.

Different half-cells make voltaic cells with different voltages

Any two half-cells can be connected together similarly to make a voltaic cell. For any such cell the direction of electron flow and the voltage generated will be determined by the *difference* in reducing strength of the two metals. In most cases this can be judged by the relative position of the metals in the reactivity series. For example if we changed the copper half-cell in the example above to a silver half-cell, a larger voltage would be produced because the difference in electrode potentials of zinc and silver is greater than between that of zinc and copper. Electrons would flow from zinc (anode) to silver (cathode), as shown in Figure 9.8.

Figure 9.8 A silver–zinc voltaic cell.

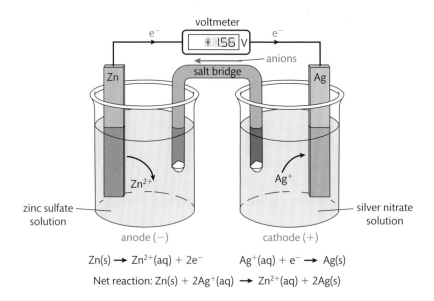

$$Zn(s) \rightarrow Zn^{2+}(aq) + 2e^-$$ $$Ag^+(aq) + e^- \rightarrow Ag(s)$$

Net reaction: $Zn(s) + 2Ag^+(aq) \rightarrow Zn^{2+}(aq) + 2Ag(s)$

Electrons always flow in the external circuit from anode to cathode.

If we now make a voltaic cell with one copper electrode and one silver electrode, the direction of electron flow would be *away* from copper towards silver. In other words, copper will be the anode and silver the cathode. This is due to the greater reducing power of copper – it has the lower electrode potential.

Figure 9.9 A silver–copper voltaic cell.

$$Cu(s) \rightarrow Cu^{2+}(aq) + 2e^-$$ $$Ag^+(aq) + e^- \rightarrow Ag(s)$$

Net reaction: $Cu(s) + 2Ag^+(aq) \rightarrow Cu^{2+}(aq) + 2Ag(s)$

We can now summarize the parts of a voltaic cell and the direction of movement of electrons and ions:

• electrons flow from anode to cathode through the external circuit;
• anions migrate from cathode to anode through the salt bridge;
• cations migrate from anode to cathode through the salt bridge.

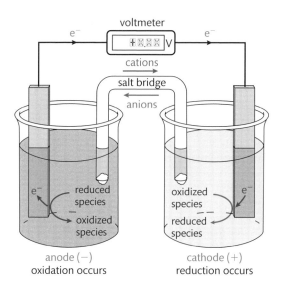

voltmeter

cations →

salt bridge

← anions

e⁻

reduced
species

oxidized
species

oxidized
species

reduced
species

e⁻

anode (−)
oxidation occurs

cathode (+)
reduction occurs

Figure 9.10 Summary of the components of a voltaic cell showing the ion and electron movements.

Batteries are an application of a voltaic cell, making electrical energy available as a source of power. Our reliance on batteries increases as global demand for mobile electronic devices such as smart phones, laptops, and tablets continues to grow. China is the largest market, while India and South Korea are growing the fastest. The largest growth is in the area of rechargeable batteries, with estimates placing the global market up to 100 billion US dollars. While demand for batteries looks set to continue, concern over toxicity and environmental damage from battery disposal has meant that mercury and cadmium batteries are being phased out in many places. The different types of batteries and their relative advantages are explained more fully in Chapter 14, Option C: Energy.

USB batteries. These rechargeable batteries are charged by plugging them into the USB port of a computer.

Exercises

13 Use the metal reactivity series in section 25 of the IB data booklet to predict which electrode will be the anode and which will be the cathode when the following half-cells are connected. Write half-equations for the reactions occurring at each electrode.

  (a) Zn/Zn^{2+} and Fe/Fe^{2+}
  (b) Fe/Fe^{2+} and Mg/Mg^{2+}
  (c) Mg/Mg^{2+} and Cu/Cu^{2+}

14 (a) Draw a voltaic cell with one half-cell consisting of Mg and a solution of Mg^{2+} ions and the other consisting of Zn and a solution of Zn^{2+} ions. Label the electrodes with name and charge, the direction of electron and ion movement, and write equations for the reactions occurring at each electrode.

  (b) Draw a cell diagram to represent the above voltaic cell.

15 Predict what would happen if an iron spatula was left in a solution of copper sulfate overnight.

Italian physicist Count Alessandro Volta (1745–1827) demonstrates his newly invented battery or 'voltaic pile' to Napoleon Bonaparte in 1801. Constructed from alternating discs of zinc and copper with pieces of cardboard soaked in brine between the metals, his voltaic pile was the first battery that produced a reliable, steady current of electricity.

The first observations of the link between electricity and chemical change are usually credited to the Italian scientist Luigi Galvani in 1791. He discovered what he called 'animal electricity' by accident, when he noticed twitching in the leg muscles of a dead frog when it was in contact with two different metals. After many experiments, he concluded that the contractions were caused by an electrical fluid that was carried to the muscles in the nerves. His contemporary and fellow countryman Alessandro Volta, however, had an intuition that the source of the electricity was not biological, but originated instead from the interaction between two metals. He set out to prove it by building a 'voltaic pile' from pairs of metals separated by a conducting solution, and demonstrated that this generated an electric current. The fact that the terms galvanic cell and voltaic cell are still both used reflects the recognition given to both men in the discovery.

The invention of the battery shows how a chance observation, followed by experimentation, debate, and the testing of hypotheses led to the development of theory with testable predictions which is then supported by evidence.

Electrolytic cells

An external source of electricity drives non-spontaneous redox reactions

Worker siphoning off molten aluminium in an aluminium processing plant. Electrolysis of a solution of alumina (Al_2O_3) dissolved in cryolite is used to reduce the Al^{3+} ions at the cathode. The molten aluminium is siphoned off and cooled before any further processing.

As we have seen, a voltaic cell takes the energy of a spontaneous redox reaction and harnesses it to generate electrical energy. An **electrolytic cell** does the reverse: it uses an external source of electrical energy to bring about a redox reaction that would otherwise be non-spontaneous. You can think of it in terms of an external power supply pumping electrons into the electrolytic cell, driving reactions of oxidation and reduction. As the word *electro-lysis* suggests, it is the process where electricity is used to bring about reactions of chemical breakdown.

The reactant in the process of electrolysis is present in the **electrolyte**. This is a liquid, usually a molten ionic compound or a solution of an ionic compound. As the electric current passes through the electrolyte, redox reactions occur at the **electrodes**, removing the charges on the ions and forming products that are electrically neutral. The ions are therefore said to be **discharged** during this process.

Reactive metals, including aluminium, lithium, magnesium, sodium, and potassium, are found naturally in compounds such as Al_2O_3 and NaCl where they exist as positive ions. Extraction of the metal therefore involves reduction of these ions. But this is a problem because there are no good reducing agents able to do this. In these cases, the only effective source of reduction is directly with electrons, using electrolysis. This means that electrolysis is the *only* means of extracting these metals from their ores. As we will see, it is also the process used in the production of many non-metal elements of industrial importance, and in the related procedures of electroplating and anodization.

The components of an electrolytic cell are shown in Figure 9.11 and described below.

Electrodes are electronically conducting, electrolytes are ionically conducting.

Figure 9.11 Components of an electrolytic cell.

- The source of electric power is a battery or a DC power source. This is shown in diagrams as where the longer line represents the positive terminal and the shorter line the negative terminal.
- The electrodes are immersed in the electrolyte and connected to the power supply. They must not touch each other! Electrodes are made from a conducting substance – generally a metal or graphite. They are described as **inert** when they do not take part in the redox reactions.
- Electric wires connect the electrodes to the power supply.

The power source pushes electrons towards the negative electrode where they enter the electrolyte. This is the cathode. Electrons are released at the positive terminal, the anode, and returned to the source. The current is passed through the electrolyte, not by electrons but by the ions as they are mobile and migrate to the electrodes. The chemical reactions occurring at each electrode remove the ions from the solution and so enable the process to continue.

Redox reactions occur at the electrodes

The ions in the electrolyte migrate to the electrodes by attraction of opposite charges. So positive ions (cations) are attracted to the negative electrode, the cathode, while negative ions (anions) are attracted to the positive electrode, the anode. At the electrodes, redox reactions occur, oxidation at the anode and reduction at the cathode, which result in the ions being discharged. In aqueous solutions, water can be oxidized to oxygen at the anode and reduced to hydrogen at the cathode.

- At the negative electrode (cathode): $M^+ + e^- \rightarrow M$
  cations gain electrons so are reduced.
- At the positive electrode (anode): $A^- \rightarrow A + e^-$
  anions lose electrons so are oxidized.

Michael Faraday, the English physicist and chemist (1791–1867), first defined and introduced the names electrolyte, electrode, anode, cathode, ion, anion, and cation, all of which are derived from Greek, into scientific language in 1834. He recognized the need to clarify the terminology, seeing the electrodes as surfaces where the current enters (anode) and leaves (cathode) the 'decomposing body' (electrolyte). He was referring to the established convention that current direction is always stated in reverse direction to electron flow. Faraday rather modestly suggested his names would be used only when necessary to avoid confusion, saying '*I am fully aware that names are one thing and science another*'.

At the anode negative ions lose electrons; at the cathode positive ions gain electrons.

The anode is the electrode where oxidation occurs, the cathode is the electrode where reduction occurs. In an electrolytic cell, the anode is positive and the cathode is negative.

Terminology of electrodes – a reminder

You will notice that the charges on the electrodes are inverted in an electrolytic cell compared with a voltaic cell. This is because it is the nature of the redox reaction, not the electrical charge, which defines the electrode: oxidation *always* occurs at the anode and reduction at the cathode, so electrons flow from anode to cathode. This never changes.

	Voltaic cell		Electrolytic cell	
Anode	oxidation occurs here	negative	oxidation occurs here	positive
Cathode	reduction occurs here	positive	reduction occurs here	negative

The electrolysis of molten salts

We can apply our knowledge of redox chemistry to electrolytic cells, determining the reactions that occur at the electrodes, and so predicting the products released. The following steps are a useful summary.

> **1** Identify all the ions present in the electrolyte and determine which will migrate to which electrode: anions to anode, and cations to cathode.

> **2** Write the half-equation for the reaction at each electrode, showing electrons released at the anode in oxidation and taken up at the cathode in reduction.

> **3** Balance the electrons lost and gained at the anode and the cathode, then add the two half-equations to write the equation for the net reaction.

> **4** Consider what changes would be observed in the cell as a result of the redox processes occurring. These may include colour changes in the electrolyte, precipitation of solid, gas discharge, or pH changes.

To help with this topic, you might find it useful to review the structure of ionic compounds, and particularly why they conduct when molten or in aqueous solution, but not when solid. See page 120.

Worked example

Describe the reactions that occur at the two electrodes during the electrolysis of molten lead(II) bromide. Write an equation for the overall reaction and comment on any likely changes that would be observed.

Solution

1   Deduce the ions present in the electrolyte and to which electrode they will be attracted:

$$PbBr_2(l) \quad \rightarrow \quad Pb^{2+}(l) \quad + \quad 2Br^-(l)$$

to cathode   to anode

2   Half-equations at the electrodes are:

anode: Br⁻ is oxidized:

$$2Br^-(l) \rightarrow Br_2(l) + 2e^-$$

cathode: Pb²⁺ is reduced:

$$Pb^{2+}(l) + 2e^- \rightarrow Pb(l)$$

3   Overall reaction: $Pb^{2+}(l) + 2Br^-(l) \rightarrow Pb(l) + Br_2(l)$

4   The observable changes will be a brown liquid with a strong smell (Br_2) at the anode and the appearance of a grey metal (Pb) at the cathode. The bright blue colour of the solution will fade.

Lead(II) bromide has a relatively low melting point of 373 °C, so this electrolysis experiment can be carried out in a school laboratory. Unfortunately though, as the two products lead and bromine are both toxic, it may not be practical to do this.

Most other ionic compounds have very high melting points, so electrolysis of their molten salts involves working at a high temperature, which can only be generated and maintained under industrial conditions.

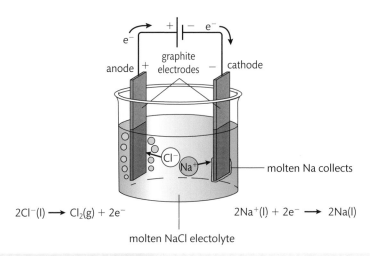

$$2Cl^-(l) \longrightarrow Cl_2(g) + 2e^-$$ $$2Na^+(l) + 2e^- \longrightarrow 2Na(l)$$

molten NaCl electolyte

Figure 9.12 Electrolysis of molten sodium chloride. Chloride ions are oxidized at the anode and sodium ions are reduced at the cathode. The overall equation is $2NaCl(l) \rightarrow 2Na(l) + Cl_2(g)$.

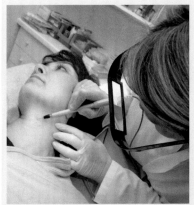

Electrolysis is used to remove unwanted hairs permanently. The needle is inserted into the hair shaft and passes an electric current through the follicle. Electrolytic reactions result in the production of NaOH, which destroys the hair follicle.

Worked example

Describe what you would expect to observe during the electrolysis of molten copper(II) chloride. Explain your answer in terms of the redox reactions occurring at the electrodes, including equations in your answer.

Solution

1
$$CuCl_2(l) \rightarrow Cu^{2+}(l) + 2Cl^-(l)$$

to cathode   to anode

2   Half-equations at the electrodes are:

anode, Cl^- is oxidized:
$$2Cl^-(l) \rightarrow Cl_2(l) + 2e^-$$

cathode, Cu^{2+} is reduced:
$$Cu^{2+}(l) + 2e^- \rightarrow Cu(l)$$

3   Overall reaction: $Cu^{2+}(l) + 2Cl^-(l) \rightarrow Cu(l) + Cl_2(g)$

4   The observable changes will be a pale green gas with a pungent smell (Cl_2) around the anode, and a pinkish metallic solid (Cu) at the cathode.

Aluminium is a unique metal: strong, flexible, lightweight, corrosion-resistant and 100% recyclable. Its commercial manufacture began in the 1880s when electrolysis made it possible to extract it from its ore bauxite, Al_2O_3. It is therefore a young metal in contrast to tin, lead, and iron, which have been in use for thousands of years, but in this short time it has become the world's second most used metal after steel. Aluminium production is, however, very energy intensive and also is associated with the production of perfluorocarbons (PFCs), strong greenhouse gases. A major emphasis must therefore be placed on recycling the metal as this uses only 5% of the energy and has only 5% of the greenhouse gas emissions compared with production. Countries vary in the success of their recycling programmes; in the recycling of aluminium beverage cans Japan and Brazil are world leaders with over 95% cans recycled.

The aluminium drink can is the world's most recycled container, with approximately 70% of all cans being recycled worldwide.

Metal-coated beetles. The metal has been added by electroplating.

Electroplating is a process of using electrolysis to deposit a layer of one metal on top of another metal. This is done to cover a metal with a decorative, more expensive or corrosion-resistant layer of another metal. For example silver plating a spoon uses a silver anode and an iron spoon cathode. Galvanizing iron involves depositing a layer of zinc on top of the iron to help protect it from corrosion as the zinc will preferentially be oxidized. This is sometimes called sacrificial protection.

Exercises

16 Write half-equations for the electrode reactions occurring during the electrolysis of the following molten salts using graphite electrodes.

   (a) KBr   **(b)** MgF_2 **(c)** ZnS

17 Magnesium metal is produced by the electrolysis of molten magnesium chloride using inert electrodes.

   (a) Make a fully labelled drawing of the electrolytic cell, including the charges on the electrodes and the direction of electron and ion migration.

   (b) Write equations for the reactions occurring at each electrode and the overall cell reaction.

18 Which statement is *not* correct for the electrolysis of molten copper(II) chloride?

   A   Copper ions and chloride ions move through the electrolyte.

   B   Oxidation of chloride takes place at the anode.

   C   Electrons move through the external circuit.

   D   Oxidation of chlorine takes place at the cathode.

NATURE OF SCIENCE

The applications of electrochemical cells are so widespread in society that it is not surprising they have also raised some difficult questions. The global demand for energy and metals drives research and development in this field, and leads to significant economic and environmental impacts. Some of these have been discussed here, such as the problems of disposal of batteries and the significant release of greenhouse gases in many electrolytic processes. Others include the release of toxic by-products such as mercury and the continuing use of asbestos in some electrolytic cells despite the fact that it is banned from many other applications. In addition, there are high energy costs of maintaining the required conditions in electrolytic cells. Innovations in science often involve both benefit and burden, and so place responsibilities on scientists, industries, and governments to monitor.

Practice questions

1 Which species could be reduced to form NO_2?

   A N_2O **B** NO_3^- **C** HNO_2 **D** NO

2 Consider the following reaction.

$$MnO_4^-(aq) + 8H^+(aq) + 5Fe^{2+}(aq) \rightarrow Mn^{2+}(aq) + 5Fe^{3+}(aq) + 4H_2O(l)$$

Which statement is correct?

   A MnO_4^- is the oxidizing agent and it loses electrons.

   B MnO_4^- is the reducing agent and it loses electrons.

   C MnO_4^- is the oxidizing agent and it gains electrons.

   D MnO_4^- is the reducing agent and it gains electrons.

3 What is the reducing agent in the reaction below?

$$2MnO_4^-(aq) + Br^-(aq) + H_2O(l) \rightarrow 2MnO_2(s) + BrO_3^-(aq) + 2OH^-(aq)$$

   A Br^- **B** BrO_3^- **C** MnO_4^- **D** MnO_2

4 Which changes could take place at the positive electrode (cathode) in the voltaic cell?

   I $Zn^{2+}(aq)$ to $Zn(s)$

   II $Cl_2(g)$ to $Cl^-(aq)$

   III $Mg(s)$ to $Mg^{2+}(aq)$

   A I and II only   **B** I and III only   **C** II and III only   **D** I, II, and III

5 What happens at the negative electrode in a voltaic cell and in an electrolytic cell?

	Voltaic cell	Electrolytic cell
A	oxidation	reduction
B	reduction	oxidation
C	oxidation	oxidation
D	reduction	reduction

6 In the reaction of NH_4^+ to form NO_2^-, what is the correct description of the change in oxidation state of nitrogen?

   A increased by 5   **B** decreased by 3   **C** increased by 6   **D** not changed

7 When the following half-reaction

$$P_4 \rightarrow H_2PO_4^-$$

is correctly balanced for a reaction in acidic solution, which statement is correct?

   A There are 20 electrons on the right.

   B There are $8H_2O$ on the right.

   C There are $4H_2O$ on the left.

   D There are 5 electrons on the right.

8 All the following statements are true about the electrolysis of a molten salt **except:**

   A The current is carried through the electrolyte by mobile ions.

   B Negative ions are oxidized at the anode.

   C Positive ions are attracted to the cathode which carries a negative charge.

   D The ions only move when an electric current flows.

9 Copper metal can reduce silver ions and zinc metal can reduce copper ions. Which of the following can be deduced from this?

    A In an electrochemical cell with half-cells of zinc and silver, the silver half-cell will be the cathode and the zinc half-cell will be the anode.

    B In an electrochemical cell with half-cells of copper and silver, electrons will flow from the silver half-cell to the copper half-cell.

    C A greater voltage will be generated in a copper/silver half-cell than in a zinc/ silver half-cell.

    D Copper ions are stronger oxidizing agents than silver ions.

10 In which of the conversions below is chlorine oxidized?

    I $Cl_2 \rightarrow OCl^-$

    II $Cl_2 + I_2 \rightarrow 2ICl$

    III $OCl^- \rightarrow ClO_3^-$

    A I only   **B** II only   **C** I, II, and III   **D** I and III

11 What is the function of a salt bridge in a voltaic cell?

    A It permits electrons to flow through the solution.

    B It acts as a catalyst.

    C It allows anions to flow into the anode.

    D It allows cations to flow into the anode.

12 How many moles of electrons are needed to oxidize 0.20 mol of Mn^{2+} to MnO_4^- during electrolysis?

    A 0.20 mol   **B** 3.0 mol   **C** 0.40 mol   **D** 1.0 mol

13 What is produced at the anode when molten $Cu(II)Cl_2$ is electrolyzed using carbon electrodes?

    A $Cu(s)$ **B** $Cu^{2+}(aq)$ **C** $Cl_2(g)$ **D** $Cl^-(aq)$

14 In which of the following redox changes does the substance on the left function as an oxidizing agent?

    A $NO_3^- \rightarrow NO_2$ **B** $N_2O_3 \rightarrow NO_2$ **C** $SO_2 \rightarrow SO_3$ **D** $Cu \rightarrow Cu^{2+}$

15 Deduce the oxidation number of cobalt in the following species.

    (a) $[Co(H_2O)_6]^{2+}$ (1)

    (b) $Co_2(SO_4)_3$ (1)

    (c) $[CoCl_4]^{2-}$ (1)

                                                              (Total 3 marks)

16 (a) Outline two differences between an electrolytic cell and a voltaic cell.   (2)

    (b) Explain why solid sodium chloride does not conduct electricity but molten sodium chloride does.   (2)

    (c) Molten sodium chloride undergoes electrolysis in an electrolytic cell. For each electrode deduce the half-equation and state whether oxidation or reduction takes place. Deduce the equation of the overall cell reaction including state symbols.   (5)

    (d) Electrolysis has made it possible to obtain reactive metals such as aluminium from their ores, which has resulted in significant developments in engineering and technology. State one reason why aluminium is preferred to iron in many uses.   (1)

                                                             (Total 10 marks)

17 Brass is a copper-containing alloy with many uses. An analysis is carried out to determine the percentage of copper present in three identical samples of brass. The reactions involved in this analysis are shown below.

Step 1: $Cu(s) + 2HNO_3(aq) + 2H^+(aq) \rightarrow Cu^{2+}(aq) + 2NO_2(g) + 2H_2O(l)$

Step 2: $4I^-(aq) + 2Cu^{2+}(aq) \rightarrow 2CuI(s) + I_2(aq)$

Step 3: $I_2(aq) + 2S_2O_3^{2-}(aq) \rightarrow 2I^-(aq) + S_4O_6^{2-}(aq)$

(a) (i) Deduce the change in the oxidation numbers of copper and nitrogen in step 1. (2)

(ii) Identify the oxidizing agent in step 1. (1)

(b) A student carried out this experiment three times, with three identical small brass nails, and obtained the following results.

mass of brass = 0.456 g ± 0.001 g

Titre	1	2	3
Initial volume of 0.100 mol dm^{-3} S$_2$O$_3^{2-}$(±0.05 cm^3)	0.00	0.00	0.00
Final volume of 0.100 mol dm^{-3} S$_2$O$_3^{2-}$(±0.05 cm^3)	28.50	28.60	28.40
Volume added of 0.100 mol dm^{-3} S$_2$O$_3^{2-}$(±0.10 cm^3)	28.50	28.60	28.40
Average volume added of 0.100 mol dm^{-3} S$_2$O$_3^{2-}$(±0.10 cm^3)	28.50		

(i) Calculate the average amount, in mol, of $S_2O_3^{2-}$ added in step 3. (2)

(ii) Calculate the amount, in mol, of copper present in the brass. (1)

(iii) Calculate the mass of copper in the brass. (1)

(iv) Calculate the percentage by mass of copper in the brass. (1)

(v) The manufacturers claim that the sample of brass contains 44.2% copper by mass. Determine the percentage error in the result. (1)

(Total 9 marks)

18 Hydrogen sulfide, H_2S, is a poisonous gas, found in low concentrations in natural gas. It can be removed by trapping it in an organic solvent and then reacting it with oxygen. The different reactions involved are shown below.

(i) $2H_2S(g) + O_2(g) \rightarrow 2S(s) + 2H_2O(l)$

(ii) $2H_2S(g) + 3O_2(g) \rightarrow 2SO_2(g) + 2H_2O(l)$

(iii) $2H_2S(g) + SO_2(g) \rightarrow 3S(s) + 2H_2O(l)$

(a) For equation (i), state which species have been oxidized and which have been reduced. Justify your answer using oxidation states. (4)

(b) For equation (iii), state and explain what is the reducing agent. (2)

(c) Predict and explain the change in pH you would expect to observe during reaction iii). (2)

(d) Removing hydrogen sulfide may help to reduce the problems associated with its toxicity, but the process used here may lead to a different environmental problem. Outline why this may be the case. (2)

(Total 10 marks)

19 The photograph below shows blocks of zinc metal bolted on to iron posts to help protect the iron from corrosion.

   (a) Write a half equation for the reaction in which zinc is oxidized. (2)

   (b) Suggest why this is described as 'sacrificial protection' of the iron. (2)

   (c) Predict what might be observed on the posts over time if the zinc blocks are removed. (2)

   (Total 6 marks)

20 A student writes the following as a balanced equation for a reaction

$$MnO_4^-(aq) + Sn^{2+}(aq) \rightarrow SnO_2(s) + MnO_2(s)$$

   (a) Comment on this, including what is not correct with the equation given. (2)

   (b) Write a corrected fully balanced equation for this reaction. (3)

   (Total 5 marks)

To access weblinks on the topics covered in this chapter, please go to www.pearsonhotlinks.com and enter the ISBN or title of this book.

10

Organic chemistry

Essential ideas

10.1 Organic chemistry focuses on the chemistry of compounds containing carbon.

10.2 Structure, bonding and chemical reactions involving functional group interconversions are key strands in organic chemistry.

The skier's clothing and equipment such as backpack and goggles, are made almost entirely of organic compounds which have been artificially synthesized. Organic chemists use knowledge of the functional groups in molecules to design compounds with the required properties such as weatherproofing, breathability, strength, flexibility, and insulation.

Organic chemistry is one of the major branches of chemistry. It includes the study of:

• all biological molecules – from simple sugars to complex nucleic acids;

• all fossil fuels – including oil, coal, and natural gas;

• nearly all synthetic materials – such as nylon, Lycra®, and Gore-Tex®;

• many domestic and industrial products – such as paints, detergents, and refrigerants.

So what defines an organic compound? Simply, it is a compound that contains carbon and, in nearly all cases, also contains hydrogen in a covalently bonded structure. Other elements such as oxygen, nitrogen, chlorine, and sulfur are often also present, but it is carbon that is the key. Amazingly, this single element carbon is able to form a larger number of compounds than all the other elements put together. This is because carbon forms four strong covalent bonds with other carbon atoms or with other elements, especially hydrogen. Carbon's ability to link to itself to form chains and rings, known as **catenation**, is one of the main reasons for the vast number of organic compounds that exist.

In this chapter, we will start with a study of the classification of organic compounds and learn how each compound can be described specifically by name and formula. The presence of specific **functional groups** in organic molecules brings order to the almost overwhelming diversity of structures, and enables organic chemists to predict and explain characteristic reactions and mechanisms. Examples of reactions and synthetic pathways discussed here give insights into the applications of organic chemistry used in medicine, agriculture, and the food and petro-chemicals industries, which are developed further in the chapters on the Option topics.

False-colour scanning electron micrograph (SEM) of a Velcro® hook. Velcro® is a nylon material manufactured in two separate pieces – one with a hooked surface and the other with a smooth surface made up of loops. When the two surfaces are brought together they form a strong bond, allowing for quick closure on clothing, etc. Velcro® is an example of a product of research and development in organic chemistry.

Definitions and conventions used in organic chemistry

The study of organic chemistry involves recognizing several different types of reactant and reaction. You should find the following summary a useful reference as you work through the chapter.

Types of reactant

Saturated	Unsaturated
• compounds which contain only single bonds • for example: alkanes	• compounds which contain double or triple bonds • for example: alkenes, arenes

Aliphatics	Arenes
• compounds which do not contain a benzene ring; may be saturated or unsaturated • for example: alkanes, alkenes	• compounds which contain a benzene ring; they are all unsaturated compounds • for example: benzene, phenol

Electrophile (electron-seeking)	Nucleophile (nucleus-seeking)
• an electron-deficient species which is therefore attracted to parts of molecules which are electron rich • electrophiles are positive ions or have a partial positive charge • for example: NO_2^+, H^+, $Br^{\delta+}$	• an electron-rich species which is therefore attracted to parts of molecules which are electron deficient • nucleophiles have a lone pair of electrons and may also have a negative charge • for example: Cl^-, OH^-, NH_3

Types of reaction

Addition	• occurs when two reactants combine to form a single product • characteristic of unsaturated compounds • for example $$C_2H_4 + Br_2 \rightarrow C_2H_4Br_2$$
Substitution	• occurs when one atom or group of atoms in a compound is replaced by a different atom or group • characteristic of saturated compounds and aromatic compounds • for example $$CH_4 + Cl_2 \rightarrow CH_3Cl + HCl$$

Addition–elimination	<ul><li>occurs when two reactants join together (addition) and in the process a small molecule such as H_2O, HCl, or NH_3 is lost (elimination)</li><li>reaction occurs between a functional group in each reactant</li><li>also called **condensation** reaction</li><li>for example</li></ul>

$$ROH + R'COOH \rightarrow R'COOR + H_2O$$

$$R\!-\!OH \;+\; \overset{\displaystyle O}{\underset{\displaystyle HO}{\overset{\|}{C}}}\!-\!R' \;\rightarrow\; R\!-\!O\!-\!\overset{\displaystyle O}{\overset{\|}{C}}\!-\!R' \;+\; \mathbf{H_2O}$$

alcohol   acid   ester

Types of bond breaking (bond fission)

Homolytic fission	Heterolytic fission
<ul><li>is when a covalent bond breaks by splitting the shared pair of electrons between the two products</li><li>produces two free radicals, each with an unpaired electron</li></ul> $$X\!:\!X \rightarrow X^{\bullet} + X^{\bullet}$$	<ul><li>is when a covalent bond breaks with both the shared electrons going to one of the products</li><li>produces two oppositely charged ions</li></ul> $$X\!:\!X \rightarrow X\!:^{-} + X^{+}$$

Convention for depicting organic reaction mechanisms

Describing organic reaction mechanisms often involves showing the movement of electrons within bonds and between reactants. The convention adopted for this is a **curly arrow**, drawn from the site of electron availability, such as a pair of non-bonding electrons, to the site of electron deficiency, such as an atom with a partial positive charge.

For example:

$X \overset{\frown}{} Y$	represents the electron pair being pulled towards Y so Y becomes δ– and X becomes δ+
$X\!:\!\rightleftharpoons \overset{\displaystyle \mid}{\underset{\displaystyle \mid}{C}}\!\!-\!\!\!-\, {}^{\delta+}$	the nucleophile X: is attracted to the electron-deficient C (δ+)

A 'normal' double-barbed arrow (⌒➤) represents the motion of an electron pair (as above). Often the mechanism involves several steps. The electrons are transferred ultimately to an atom or group of atoms that then detaches itself and is known as the **leaving group**. We will use blue throughout this chapter to show curly arrows and the pull of electrons.

Note that a single-barbed arrow (⌒↘), known as a **fish-hook**, represents the movement of a single electron. These single arrows are often used in reactions involving radicals.

10.1 Fundamentals of organic chemistry

Understandings:

- A homologous series is a series of compounds of the same family, with the same general formula, which differ from each other by a common structural unit.
- Structural formulas can be represented in full and condensed format.
- Structural isomers are compounds with the same molecular formula but different arrangements of atoms.
- Functional groups are the reactive parts of molecules.
- Saturated compounds contain single bonds only and unsaturated compounds contain double or triple bonds.
- Benzene is an aromatic, unsaturated hydrocarbon.

Guidance
The general formulas (e.g. C_nH_{2n+2}) of alkanes, alkenes, alkynes, ketones, alcohols, aldehydes, and carboxylic acids should be known.

Applications and skills:

- Explanation of the trends in boiling points of members of a homologous series.
- Distinction between empirical, molecular, and structural formulas.
- Identification of different classes: alkenes, alkynes, halogenoalkanes, alcohols, ethers, aldehydes, ketones, esters, carboxylic acids, amines, amides, nitriles, and arenes.
- Identification of typical functional groups in molecules, e.g. phenyl, hydroxyl, carbonyl, carboxyl, carboxamide, aldehyde, ester, ether, amine, nitrile, alkyl, alkenyl, and alkynyl.
- Construction of 3D models (real or virtual) of organic molecules.
- Application of IUPAC rules in the nomenclature of straight-chain and branched-chain isomers.
- Identification of primary, secondary, and tertiary carbon atoms in halogenoalkanes and alcohols and primary, secondary, and tertiary nitrogen atoms in amines.
- Discussion of the structure of benzene using physical and chemical evidence

Guidance
- *Skeletal formulas should be discussed in the course.*
- *The distinction between class names and functional group names needs to be made, e.g. for OH, hydroxyl is the functional group whereas alcohol is the class name.*
- *The following nomenclature should be covered:*
  - *non-cyclic alkanes and halogenoalkanes up to halohexanes*
  - *alkenes up to hexene and alkynes up to hexyne*
  - *compounds up to six carbon atoms (in the basic chain for nomenclature purposes) containing only one of the classes of functional groups: alcohols, ethers, aldehydes, halogenoalkanes, ketones, esters, and carboxylic acids.*

The total number of organic compounds that exists on Earth is so large that it is impossible to estimate with any accuracy. In any case, it is increasing all the time as new materials are synthesized. But we do know that there are at least ten million different organic molecules currently on the planet and every one of them is unique in its chemical structure and specific properties. Of course it is not possible or necessary to study the features of all of the compounds in this large branch of chemistry, but it is useful instead to introduce some system of classification.

Homologous series

Organic compounds are classified into 'families' of compounds known as **homologous series.** The members of each such series possess certain common features, as described in the following text.

For a long time it was believed that organic molecules were unique to living things, and could not therefore be synthesized outside a living organism. However, in 1828, the German chemist Friedrich Wöhler synthesized urea from inorganic reactants, commenting in a letter to Berzelius: 'I must tell you that I can make urea without the use of kidneys, either man or dog. Ammonium cyanate is urea'. This discovery, which like many great scientific discoveries was actually made by accident, destroyed the former belief in 'vitalism', and opened the door to the exploration of organic synthesis reactions. The development of new organic compounds is responsible for many of the innovations in our world today.

Successive members of a homologous series differ by a —CH₂— group

Consider the following compounds of carbon and hydrogen where the carbons are all bonded by single covalent bonds.

CH_4

H
|
H—C—H
|
H

methane

C_2H_6

H   H
| |
H—C—C—H
| |
H   H

ethane

C_3H_8

H   H   H
| | |
H—C—C—C—H
| | |
H   H   H

propane

C_4H_{10}

H   H   H   H
| | | |
H—C—C—C—C—H
| | | |
H   H   H   H

butane

These are members of a homologous series known as the **alkanes.** It can be seen that neighbouring members differ from each other by — CH_2 —. This same increment applies to successive members of each homologous series, and means that the molecular mass increases by a fixed amount as we go up a series.

Members of a homologous series can be represented by the same general formula

The four alkanes shown above can all be represented by the general formula C_nH_{2n+2}.

Other homologous series are characterized by the presence of a particular **functional group**, and this will be shown in the general formula for the series. For example, the homologous series known as the **alcohols** possess the functional group — OH as shown below.

CH_3OH

H
|
H—C—O—H
|
H

methanol

C_2H_5OH

H   H
| |
H—C—C—O—H
| |
H   H

ethanol

C_3H_7OH

H   H   H
| | |
H—C—C—C—O—H
| | |
H   H   H

propanol

C_4H_9OH

H   H   H   H
| | | |
H—C—C—C—C—O—H
| | | |
H   H   H   H

butanol

These compounds can be represented by the general formula $C_nH_{2n+1}OH$.

The functional group is usually a small group of atoms attached to a carbon atom in a molecule, and it gives the characteristic properties to the compound.

Members of a homologous series show a gradation in physical properties

As successive members of a homologous series differ by a — CH_2 — group, they have successively longer carbon chains. This is reflected in a gradual trend in the physical properties of the members of the series. For example, the effect of the length of the carbon chain on the boiling point of the alkanes is shown in the table on page 310.

TOK

The word 'organic' is now used in several different contexts beyond the chemistry of carbon compounds. Examples include organic food, organic growth, and organic degeneration. To what extent does this common vocabulary represent a common origin in meaning? Does it confuse or enhance communication?

Alkane		Boiling point / °C
methane	CH_4	−164
ethane	C_2H_6	−89
propane	C_3H_8	−42
butane	C_4H_{10}	−0.5
pentane	C_5H_{12}	36
hexane	C_6H_{14}	69
heptane	C_7H_{16}	98
octane	C_8H_{18}	125

gases at room temperature

liquids at room temperature

increasing boiling point

The data show that the boiling point increases with increasing carbon number. This is because of the increased instantaneous induced dipoles causing stronger London (dispersion) forces between the molecules as their molecular size increases. Note, though, that the increase is not linear, but steeper near the beginning as the influence of the increased chain length is proportionally greater for small molecules.

Other physical properties that show this predictable trend with increasing carbon number are density and viscosity.

Oil products. Containers of crude oil and various fractions obtained from it, on a background of a silhouetted oil refinery. The fractions are arranged here in order of increasing boiling point from left to right.

It is estimated that the top ten oil-producing countries of the world produce about two-thirds of the world's oil. This geo-political leverage of the major oil-exporting nations is an ongoing challenge to countries that are dependent on imported oil.

Members of a homologous series show similar chemical properties

As they have the same functional group, members of the same homologous series show similar chemical reactivity. For example:

- the alcohols have the —OH functional group, which can be oxidized to form organic acids
- the —COOH functional group, present in the homologous series of the **carboxylic acids**, is responsible for the acidic properties of these compounds.

It follows that if we know the characteristic reactions of a functional group, we will be able to predict the properties of all members of a series.

The main features of a homologous series are as follows:
- **Successive members of a homologous series differ by a —CH₂— group.**
- **Members of a homologous series can be represented by the same general formula.**
- **The members of a homologous series show a gradation in their physical properties.**
- **The members of a series have similar chemical properties.**

The study of organic chemistry is in some ways like the study of a language where rules have developed to enable communication to be clear and consistent. In order to describe an organic molecule in this way, there are two aspects to consider:

- the formula used to represent the molecule;
- the specific name given to the molecule, known as its **nomenclature**.

We will discuss each of these in turn and learn the rules that will enable us to communicate effectively in this study.

TOK To what extent is chemistry a separate language? What are the main differences between the language of chemistry and your mother tongue?

Formulas for organic compounds: empirical, molecular, and structural

The **empirical formula** of a compound is the simplest whole number ratio of the atoms it contains (see Chapter 1). For example, the empirical formula of ethane, C_2H_6, is CH_3. This formula can be derived from percentage composition data obtained from combustion analysis. It is, however, of rather limited use on its own, as it does not tell us the actual number of atoms in the molecule.

The **molecular formula** of a compound is the actual number of atoms of each element present in a molecule. For example, the molecular formula of ethane is C_2H_6. It is therefore a multiple of the empirical formula, and so can be deduced if we know both the empirical formula and the molar mass M. The relationship can be expressed as:

$$M = (\text{molar mass of empirical formula})_n$$

where n is an integer.

So, for example, if we know that the empirical formula of ethane is CH_3, and its molar mass $M = 30 \text{ g mol}^{-1}$, using the formula above:

$$30 \text{ g mol}^{-1} = (\text{mass of } CH_3)_n \text{ so } 30 = (12 + (3 \times 1))_n, \text{ which gives } n = 2$$

Therefore the molecular formula is $(CH_3)_2$ or C_2H_6.

However, the molecular formula is also of quite limited value as the properties of a compound are determined not only by the atoms it contains, but also by how those atoms are arranged in relation to each other and in space.

The **structural formula** is a representation of the molecule showing how the atoms are bonded to each other. There are variations in the amount of detail this shows.

 Be careful to mark all the hydrogen atoms with –H when drawing structural formulas. Leaving these out gives what is called a **skeletal structure** and is not acceptable as a structural formula.

- A **full structural formula** (graphic formula or displayed formula) shows every bond and atom. Usually 90° and 180° (and 120°) angles are used to show the bonds because this is the clearest representation on a two-dimensional page, although in most cases this is not the true geometry of the molecule.

- A **condensed structural formula** often omits bonds where they can be assumed, and groups atoms together. It contains the minimum information needed to describe the molecule non-ambiguously – in other words there is only one possible structure that could be described by this formula.

- A **stereochemical formula** attempts to show the relative positions of atoms and groups around carbon in three dimensions. The convention is that a bond sticking forwards from the page is shown as a solid, enlarging wedge, whereas a bond sticking behind the page is shown as a hashed line. A bond in the plane of the paper is a solid line. When carbon forms four single bonds, the arrangement is tetrahedral with bond angles of 109.5°; when it forms a double bond, the arrangement is triangular planar with bonds at 120°.

goes back — in the plane of the paper

comes forward

For example: methanol, CH_3OH ethene, C_2H_4

The table below shows these different formulas applied to three compounds.

Compound	Ethane	Ethanoic acid	Glucose
Empirical formula	CH_3	CH_2O	CH_2O
Molecular formula	C_2H_6	$C_2H_4O_2$	$C_6H_{12}O_6$
Full structural formula			
Condensed structural formula	CH_3CH_3	CH_3COOH	$CHO(HCOH)_4CH_2OH$

Sometimes we do not need to show the exact details of the hydrocarbon, or **alkyl**, part of the molecule, so we can abbreviate this to **R**. For molecules which contain a benzene ring, C_6H_6, known as **aromatic compounds**, we use ⬡ to show the ring.

Nomenclature for organic compounds: the IUPAC system

For over a hundred years, chemists have recognized the need for a specific set of rules for the naming of organic compounds. IUPAC names are logically based on the chemistry of the compounds, and so give information about the functional groups present and the size of the molecules. Some guidelines for applying the IUPAC nomenclature are discussed below.

Rule 1: Identify the longest straight chain of carbon atoms

The longest chain of carbon atoms gives the **stem** of the name as follows.

Number of carbon atoms in longest chain	Stem in IUPAC name	Example of compound
1	meth-	CH_4, methane
2	eth-	C_2H_6, ethane
3	prop-	C_3H_8, propane
4	but-	C_4H_{10}, butane
5	pent-	C_5H_{12}, pentane
6	hex-	C_6H_{14}, hexane

Note that 'straight chain' refers to continuous or unbranched chains of carbon atoms – it does not mean angles of 180°. Be careful when identifying the longest straight chain not to be confused by the way the molecule may appear on paper, because of the free rotation around carbon–carbon single bonds. For example, in Figure 10.1, all three structures are the same molecule pentane C_5H_{12}, even though they may look different.

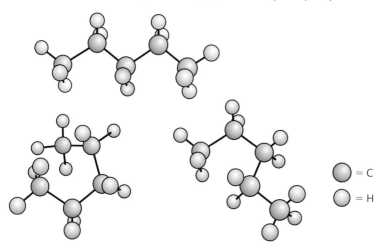

○ = C
○ = H

Figure 10.1 Different representations of the same molecule C_5H_{12}, pentane. These can all be interconverted by rotating the carbon–carbon bonds.

Rule 2: Identify the functional group

The functional group usually determines the specific ending or **suffix** to the name, which replaces the 'ane' ending in the parent alk*ane*. The suffixes used for some common functional groups are shown in the table below. Note the distinction between *class*, which refers to the type of compound, and *functional group*, which refers to the site of reactivity in the molecule.

Class	Functional group	Name of functional group	Suffix in IUPAC name	Example of compound	General formula
alkane			-ane	C_2H_6, ethane	C_nH_{2n+2}
alkene	$C=C$	alkenyl	-ene	$H_2C = CH_2$, ethene	C_nH_{2n}
alkyne	$-C \equiv C-$	alkynyl	-yne	$HC \equiv CH$, ethyne	C_nH_{2n-2}
alcohol	$-OH$	hydroxyl	-anol	C_2H_5OH, ethanol	$C_nH_{2n+1}OH$
ether	$R-O-R'$	ether	-oxyalkane	$H_3C-O-C_2H_5$, methoxyethane	$R-O-R'$
aldehyde	(structure)	aldehyde (carbonyl)	-anal	C_2H_5CHO, propanal	$R-CHO$
ketone	(structure)	carbonyl	-anone	CH_3COCH_3, propanone	$R-CO-R'$
carboxylic acid	(structure)	carboxyl	-anoic acid	C_2H_5COOH, propanoic acid	$C_nH_{2n+1}COOH$
ester*	(structure)	ester	-anoate	$C_2H_5COOCH_3$, methyl propanoate	$R-COO-R'$
amide	(structure)	carboxyamide	-anamide	$C_2H_5CONH_2$, propanamide	
amine	$-NH_2$	amine	-anamine	$C_2H_5NH_2$, ethanamine	
nitrile	$-C \equiv N$	nitrile	-anenitrile	C_2H_5CN, propanenitrile	
arene	C_6H_5-	phenyl	-benzene	$C_6H_5CH_3$, methyl benzene	

*Esters form when the alkyl group of an alcohol replaces the hydrogen of a carboxylic acid in a condensation reaction:

$$R-COOH + R'OH \rightarrow R-COO-R' + H_2O$$

They are named in a similar way to salts, which form when a metal has replaced the hydrogen of a carboxylic acid. Salts take the stem of the name from the parent acid. For example, C_2H_5COONa is sodium propanoate. In esters, the alkyl group of the alcohol is the prefix, so $C_2H_5COOCH_3$ is methyl propanoate.

The position of a functional group is shown by a number between dashes inserted before the functional group ending. The number refers to the carbon atom to which it is attached. The chain is numbered starting at the end that will give the smallest number to the group.

For example:

propan-2-ol

but-1-ene

here we number the carbon chain starting from the right-hand side so that the number of the group will be 1 and not 3

Sometimes a functional group can only be in one place, and in these cases we do not need to give a number to show its position.

For example:

butanoic acid

propanone

Rule 3: Identify the side chains or substituent groups

Side chains, or functional groups in addition to the one used as the suffix, are known as **substituents** and are given as the first part or **prefix** of the name. Some common examples are shown in the table.

Class	Functional group	Name of functional group	Prefix in IUPAC name	Example of compound
alkane			methyl, ethyl, propyl, etc.	$CH_3CH(CH_3)C_2H_5$, 2-methylbutane $CH(C_2H_5)_3$, 3-ethylpentane $CH(C_3H_7)_3$, 4-propylheptane
halogenoalkane	—F, —Cl, —Br, —I	halogeno	fluoro, chloro, bromo, iodo	C_2H_5Cl, chloroethane $CH_3CH_2BrCH_3$, 2-bromopropane
amine	—NH_2	amine	amino	$CH_2(NH_2)COOH$, 2-aminoethanoic acid

You will notice that —NH_2 appears as both a possible suffix and a prefix. Usually when it is the only functional group it will take the suffix, but if there are two or more functional groups in the molecule it will be a prefix, as for example in *amino* acids.

As shown above, the position of the substituent groups is given by a number followed by a dash in front of its name showing the carbon atom to which it is attached, again numbering the chain to give the smallest number to the group.

You are expected to be familiar with the nitrogen-containing functional groups at the bottom of the table (amine, amide, and nitrile), but nomenclature of these classes of compounds will not be assessed.

Remember that the name for the stem is derived from the *longest* carbon chain, which may include the carbon of the functional group. Look in the table and see how this applies to carboxylic acids and their derivatives (esters and amides) as well as to nitriles.

Make sure you don't confuse ethers and esters. Ethers are derived by replacing the H of an alcohol by an alkyl group, esters by replacing the H of an acid by an alkyl group.

For example:

2-methylbutane   2-methylpentane

If there is more than one substituent group of the same type, we use commas between the numbers and the prefixes di-, tri-, or tetra- before the name. Substituents are given in order of the number of the carbon atom to which they are attached; if there is more than one group on the same atom they are put in alphabetical order.

For example:

1,2-dichloropropane   1-chloro-2-methylpropane   2-bromo-2-chloropropane

For example:

3,3-dimethylbutanal

Summary

IUPAC nomenclature has three possible parts, which are usually written together as a single word.

Prefix ·········	**Stem** ·········	**Suffix**
position, number and name of substituents	number of carbon atoms in longest chain	class of compound determined by functional group

There is an H in aldeHyde but not in ketone.

When you are asked to name a compound from a condensed structural formula, it is a good idea to draw out the full structural formula first.

Exercises

1 For each of the following molecules give its class and its IUPAC name:

(a) $CH_3CH_2CH_2COOH$ (c) $CH_3CH_2COCH_3$ (e) $CH_3CH_2OCH_3$
(b) $CHCl_2CH_2CH_3$ (d) CH_3COOCH_3 (f) $CH_3CH_2CH_2CH_2COOCH_2CH_3$

2 Give the structural formulas of the following molecules (condensed form is acceptable):

(a) hexanoic acid   (d) 1-bromo-2-methylbutane   (f) methoxypropane
(b) butanal   (e) ethyl methanoate   (g) but-2-yne
(c) pent-1-ene

3 Which of the following is an amine?

A $CH_3CH_2NH_2$ B CH_3CONH_2 C CH_3CH_2CN D $C_2H_5CONH(CH_3)$

4 Which compound is a member of the same homologous series as 1-bromopropane?

A 1-iodopropane   C 1-bromopropene
B 1,2-dibromopropane   D 1-bromopentane

Structural isomers: different arrangements of the same atoms

The molecular formula of a compound shows the atoms that are present in the molecule, but gives no information on how they are arranged. Consider for example the formula C_4H_{10}. There are two possible arrangements for these atoms that correspond to different molecules with different properties.

butane,
boiling point −0.5 °C

2-methylpropane,
boiling point −11.7 °C

Such molecules, having the same molecular formula but different arrangements of the atoms, are known as **structural isomers**.

Construction of 3D models and working with virtual models online is important experience that helps in gaining an understanding of the structural concepts described here. Full details with worksheets are available on your eBook.

Structural isomers are molecules that have the same molecular formula but different arrangement of the atoms.

Molecular models of the two isomers of C_4H_{10}. On the left is butane (sometimes called n-butane to denote a straight chain), and on the right is 2-methylpropane.

Each isomer is a distinct compound, having unique physical and chemical properties. As we will see, the number of isomers that exists for a molecular formula increases with the size of the molecule. This is one of the reasons for the vast number of compounds that can be formed from carbon.

Deducing the structural formulas and names for all possible isomers from a given molecular formula gives us a good opportunity to practise the earlier work on IUPAC nomenclature. We will apply this to isomers in the first six members of the alkanes, the alkenes, and the alkynes.

Structural isomers in alkanes

- C_4H_{10} has two isomers, as shown on page 317.
- C_5H_{12} has the following isomers:

pentane

2-methylbutane

2,2-dimethylpropane

- C_6H_{14} has the following five isomers:

hexane

2-methylpentane

3-methylpentane

2,2-dimethylbutane

2,3-dimethylbutane

As we can see here, the number of isomers that exist for a molecular formula increases as the molecular size increases. In fact the increase is exponential; there are 75 possible isomers of $C_{10}H_{22}$ and 366319 of $C_{20}H_{42}$!

When drawing structural formulas, double check that you haven't drawn the same thing twice by drawing it the other way round.

Starting in 1923 a compound called tetraethyl lead – marketed as 'ethyl' from America – was added to petroleum in most parts of the world. It proved to be a very successful 'anti-knocking agent', allowing lower grades of fuel to be used in combustion engines without causing premature burning known as 'knocking'. Many decades and thousands of tonnes of lead emissions later, mounting concern about the effect of rising lead levels in the atmosphere led to the additive being banned in most countries from about 1986 onwards. Lead is a neurotoxin that is linked to many health effects, particularly brain damage. Since its phase-out from petroleum, blood levels of lead have fallen dramatically but still remain about 600 times higher than they were a century ago.

The person who researched and patented tetraethyl lead as a petroleum additive was the same person who later was responsible for the discovery and marketing of chlorofluorocarbons (CFCs) as refrigerants. Thomas Midgley of Ohio, USA, did not live to know the full extent that the long-term impact of his findings would have on the Earth's atmosphere. He died in 1944, aged 55, from accidental strangulation after becoming entangled in ropes and pulleys he had devised to get himself in and out of bed following loss of use of his legs caused by polio. Perhaps his epitaph should have been 'The solution becomes the problem'.

The existence of these different straight-chain and branched-chain isomers of the alkanes is of great significance in the petroleum industry. It has been found that branched-chain isomers generally burn more smoothly in internal combustion engines than straight-chain isomers, and so oil fractions with a higher proportion of these branched-chain isomers are considered to be of 'better grade'. This is often referred to as a higher 'octane number' and means that it fetches a higher price at the pump.

Structural isomers in alkenes

A different type of structural isomer occurs when the carbon–carbon double bond is found in different positions.

- C_4H_8 has the following straight chain isomers:

but-1-ene   but-2-ene

Note that the molecules are named using the smallest numbered carbon that is part of the double bond.

- C_5H_{10} has the following two straight chain isomers:

pent-1-ene   pent-2-ene

A good exercise when practising this work is to give the names that you give to isomers to one of your classmates, and see if they can correctly draw the structures. There should be only one possible structure for each name.

- C_6H_{12} has the following three straight-chain isomers:

hex-1-ene   hex-2-ene   hex-3-ene

Similarly, the structures and names of the isomers of the alkynes can be deduced from considering different possible positions for the triple bond.

There are many different types of isomers, including those in which the molecules have different functional groups and so are members of different classes of compounds with very different reactivities. For example, the molecular formula C_2H_6O describes both an alcohol and an ether.

Methoxymethane and ethanol are functional group isomers, both with the molecular formula C_2H_6O. Ethanol is widely used in alcoholic drinks while methoxymethane is a gas used in aerosol propellants.

Isomers are of great significance in biochemistry and the drugs industry, as discussed in more detail in Chapters 13 and 15.

Primary, secondary, and tertiary compounds

The activity of a functional group is often influenced by its position in the carbon chain, identified as follows.

A **primary carbon atom** is attached to the functional group and also to at least two hydrogen atoms. Molecules with this arrangement are known as primary molecules.

For example, ethanol, C_2H_5OH, is a primary alcohol and chloroethane, C_2H_5Cl, is a primary halogenoalkane.

A **secondary carbon atom** is attached to the functional group and also to one hydrogen atom and two alkyl groups. These molecules are known as secondary molecules. For example, propan-2-ol, $CH_3CH(OH)CH_3$, is a secondary alcohol, and 2-chloroethane, $CH_3CHClCH_3$, is a secondary halogenoalkane.

Butan-2-ol, a secondary alcohol. Carbon atoms are black, hydrogen atoms are white, and oxygen atoms are red. Note there is only one hydrogen atom on the carbon attached to the —OH group.

A **tertiary carbon atom** is attached to the functional group and is also bonded to three alkyl groups and so has no hydrogen atoms. These molecules are known as tertiary molecules. For example, 2-methylpropan-2-ol, $C(CH_3)_3OH$, is a tertiary alcohol, and 2-chloro-2-methylpropane, $C(CH_3)_3Cl$, is a tertiary halogenoalkane.

2-methylpropan-2-ol, a tertiary alcohol. Carbon atoms are black, hydrogen atoms are white, and oxygen atoms are red. Note there are no hydrogen atoms on the carbon attached to the —OH group.

In amines, a similar classification can be applied according to the number of alkyl groups and hydrogen atoms bonded to the nitrogen atom.

Arenes

Arenes are a class of compounds that are derived from **benzene**, C_6H_6. They form a special branch of organic compounds known as the **aromatics**, which have properties somewhat distinct from other organic compounds, known as **aliphatics**. Arenes contain the phenyl functional group:

C_6H_5-

The key to understanding their properties comes from a study of the parent arene molecule – benzene itself.

Amines and amides, including the substituted derivatives, are widely found in many medicinal compounds. The hormone adrenaline, well known as the 'emergency' hormone as well as a transmitter in the nervous system, is a secondary amine.

Benzene does not behave like other unsaturated molecules

The 1 : 1 ratio of carbon to hydrogen in benzene, C_6H_6, indicates a high degree of unsaturation, greater than that of alkenes or alkynes. Yet early observations on benzene indicated that it does not show the characteristic properties of possible structures such as:

For example, benzene has no isomers, and is reluctant to undergo addition reactions – both features that would be expected from these molecules.

In 1865 Kekulé suggested a cyclic arrangement of the carbon atoms with alternating single and double bonds. This is 1,3,5-cyclohexatriene:

which is usually drawn without the atoms marked as

The symmetry of this model explained some of the known properties of benzene, such as the fact that it has no isomers, but again fell short of explaining benzene's atypical reactivity for such an unsaturated molecule. Clearly, modifications to the Kekulé structure were needed. Advances in technology, such as X-ray diffraction, provided data that helped to develop the current model of benzene structure.

Benzene is an important industrial solvent and is used in the synthesis of drugs, dyes, and plastics such as polystyrene. Because of its frequent use, benzene has become widespread in the environment of developed countries. In the USA, petroleum contains up to 2% benzene by volume and it may be as high as 5% in other countries. But benzene is a toxic compound and a known carcinogen. Chronic exposure at low levels can lead to aplastic anaemia and leukaemia. Regulating bodies in many countries have set permissible exposure limits for benzene levels in drinking water, foods, and air in the workplace.

Friedrich August Kekulé von Stradonitz (1829–1896) was a German organic chemist who also spent parts of his working life in France, Switzerland, and England. He was a principal founder of the theory of chemical structure, establishing the tetravalence of carbon and the ability of carbon atoms to link to each other. He provided the first molecular formulas using lines to represent bonds between atoms, and most famously the ring structure of benzene. In addition, he was evidently an influential teacher as three of the first five Nobel Prizes in Chemistry were won by his students: van't Hoff in 1901, Fischer in 1902, and Baeyer in 1905.

Non-polar liquids like benzene can be separated from aqueous solutions using a separating funnel because they form a separate layer and the lower liquid can be drained. Here, the lower aqueous layer has been coloured purple to make the separation more visible.

Scale
0   0.1 nm

Figure 10.2 Electron density map for benzene at –3 °C. The blue lines join parts of the molecule with equal electron density, showing that all bonds between carbon atoms are equal and of length 0.139 nm.

The special stability of the benzene ring is the result of delocalized electrons

Benzene is a cyclic structure, in which a framework of single bonds attaches each carbon to one on either side and to a hydrogen atom. So each carbon forms three single bonds with bond angles of 120° forming the planar shape.

This leaves one electron on each carbon atom. But instead of pairing up to form alternating double bonds, they are delocalized through all six carbon atoms. Delocalization of electrons in benzene produces a symmetrical 'cloud' of electron charge above and below the plane of the ring. This is a very stable arrangement and lowers the internal energy of the molecule.

There is a well-established account that Kekulé visualized the ring structure of benzene after experiencing a dream about snakes biting each other's tails. To what extent can imagination and unconscious processes be important in scientific advancement?

Figure 10.3 The bonding in benzene. This is a symmetrical arrangement where all the p electrons are shared equally by all of the bonded carbon atoms. It is a very stable structure and lowers the internal energy of the molecule. (a) The single-bond framework. (b) The p orbitals before overlapping sideways. (c) The delocalized p electrons form regions of high electron density above and below the planar benzene ring.

Figure 10.4 A space-filling model of benzene, showing its planar shape.

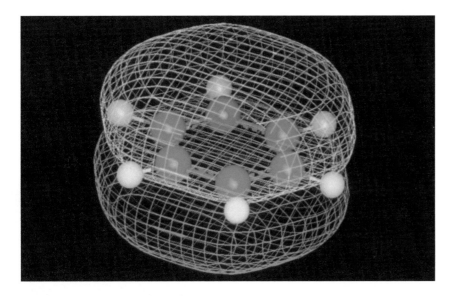

Computer graphics representation of the structure of benzene showing the delocalized electron clouds which confer great stability on the molecule. They appear as the blue and yellow cages above the flat plane of the molecule. Carbon atoms are shown in green and hydrogen atoms in white.

Make sure that when you are writing the structure of benzene you do not forget to include the ring inside the hexagon. If you do, and draw instead

[hexagon] , this denotes an

entirely different structure, cyclohexane C_6H_{12}.

The usual convention for depicting this structure of benzene uses a ring inside the hexagon to denote the delocalized electrons.

This model is supported by evidence, and provides explanations for most observed properties of benzene, as described below.

Property	Observation / evidence	Explanation
1 Bond lengths	All carbon–carbon bond lengths in benzene are equal and intermediate in length between single and double bonds.	Each bond contains a share of three electrons between the bonded atoms. X-ray bond length data / nm: alkane single bond C—C 0.154 nm; alkene double bond C==C 0.134 nm; benzene [hexagon] 0.139 nm
2 $\Delta H_{hydrogenation}$ for the reaction $C_6H_6 + 3H_2 \rightarrow C_6H_{12}$	Theoretical value based on adding H_2 across three C==C double bonds = -362 kJ mol^{-1}. Experimental value for benzene = -210 kJ mol^{-1}. Benzene is more stable than predicted from the Kekulé structure by approx. 152 kJ mol^{-1}.	Delocalization minimizes the repulsion between electrons and so gives benzene a more stable structure, lowering its internal energy by 152 kJ mol^{-1}. This is the amount of energy that would have to be supplied in order to overcome the special stability of the delocalized ring. It is called the **resonance energy** or the **stabilization energy** of benzene. See Figure 10.5.
3 Type of reactivity	Benzene is reluctant to undergo addition reactions and is more likely to undergo substitution reactions.	Addition reactions are energetically not favoured as they would involve disrupting the entire cloud of delocalized electrons. The resonance energy would have to be supplied and the product, without the delocalized ring of electrons, would be *less* stable. Benzene can instead undergo substitution reactions that preserve the stable ring structure.
4 Isomers	Only one isomer exists of compounds such as 1,2-dibromobenzene.	As benzene is a symmetrical molecule with no alternating single and double bonds, all adjacent positions in the ring are equal. For example 1,2-dibromobenzene, $C_6H_4Br_2$ [structure showing hexagon with two Br groups]

Figure 10.5 Enthalpy changes for the hydrogenation of benzene and related molecules. Note that the molecule 1,3,5-cyclohexatriene does not exist, so the value for its hydrogenation is theoretical only.

Trends in physical properties

We have seen that the structure of organic compounds can be thought of in two parts.

1 A framework consisting of carbon and hydrogen only, known as the **hydrocarbon skeleton**. This differs in size in different members of the same homologous series.

2 A functional group. This differs in identity in different homologous series.

Both of these components influence the physical properties of a compound. Most of these properties were discussed in relation to intermolecular forces in Chapter 4, pages 153–155, and a few additional points are made here.

The increase in boiling point with carbon number that we saw in the alkanes applies to other homologous series. In general, the lower members of a series are likely to be gases or liquids at room temperature, while the higher members are more likely to be solids. Branching of the hydrocarbon chain also has an effect on volatility as it influences the strength of the intermolecular forces. Think, for example, how tree logs with lots of branches sticking out cannot stack together as closely as a pile of logs which have no branches. In a similar way branched-chain isomers have less contact with each other than their straight-chain isomers, and so have weaker intermolecular forces and so lower boiling points. We saw earlier that the straight-chain molecule butane has a higher boiling point (−0.5 °C) than its branched-chain isomer, 2-methylpropane (boiling point −11.7 °C).

Owing to their different polarities and resulting differences in intermolecular forces, functional groups have a significant effect on volatility. This can be summarized as follows.

most volatile					least volatile
alkane > halogenoalkane > aldehyde > ketone > alcohol > carboxylic acid					
London (dispersion) force → dipole–dipole interaction → hydrogen bonding					
increasing strength of intermolecular attraction ⟶					
increasing boiling point ⟶					

 NATURE OF SCIENCE

The changing model of the structure of benzene has largely been a result of advances in technology and instrumentation. The Kekulé model seemed to explain many of the known properties of benzene at the time, but had to be reconsidered when quantitative data obtained through X-ray diffraction experimentation provided counter evidence, for example on bond lengths. The progress of science sometimes demands a refinement or abandonment of a model as new data are obtained, and the acceptance of this is dependent on the objectivity and openness of scientists.

5 Draw and name all the structural isomers of $C_3H_3Cl_5$.

6 Which formula is that of a secondary halogenoalkane?

    A $CH_3CH_2CH_2CH_2Br$ **B** $CH_3CHBrCH_2CH_3$ **C** $(CH_3)_2CHCH_2Br$ **D** $(CH_3)_3CBr$

7 Describe the bonding in a benzene molecule and use it to explain benzene's energetic stability.

8 **(a)** When comparing the boiling points of different classes of compound, why is it important to choose molecules that have similar molar mass?

    (b) Explain how you would expect the solubility of alcohols in hexane to change with increasing chain length.

10.2 Functional group chemistry

Understandings:

- **Alkanes:** have low reactivity and undergo free radical substitution reactions.
- **Alkenes:** are more reactive than alkanes and undergo addition reactions. Bromine water can be used to distinguish between alkenes and alkanes.
- **Alcohols:** undergo nucleophilic substitution reactions with acids (also called esterification or condensation) and some undergo oxidation reactions.
- **Halogenoalkanes:** are more reactive than alkanes. They can undergo (nucleophilic) substitution reactions. A nucleophile is an electron-rich species containing a lone pair that it donates to an electron-deficient carbon.
- **Polymers:** addition polymers consist of a wide range of monomers and form the basis of the plastics industry.
- **Benzene:** does not readily undergo addition reactions but does undergo electrophilic substitution reactions.

Applications and skills:

- **Alkanes**:
  - Writing equations for the complete and incomplete combustion of hydrocarbons.
  - Explanation of the reaction of methane and ethane with halogens in terms of a free radical substitution mechanism involving photochemical homolytic fission.
- **Alkenes**:
  - Writing equations for the reactions of alkenes with hydrogen and halogens and of symmetrical alkenes with hydrogen halides and water.
  - Outline of the addition polymerization of alkenes.
  - Relationship between the structure of the monomer to the polymer and repeating unit.
- **Alcohols**:
  - Writing equations for the complete combustion of alcohols.
  - Writing equations for the oxidation reactions of primary and secondary alcohols (using acidified potassium dichromate(VI) or potassium manganate(VII) as oxidizing agents). Explanation of distillation and reflux in the isolation of the aldehyde and carboxylic acid products.
  - Writing the equation for the condensation reaction of an alcohol with a carboxylic acid, in the presence of a catalyst (e.g. concentrated sulfuric acid) to form an ester.
- **Halogenoalkanes**:
  - Writing the equation for the substitution reactions of halogenoalkanes with aqueous sodium hydroxide.

  Guidance
  - *Reference should be made to initiation, propagation, and termination steps in free radical substitution reactions. Free radicals should be represented by a single dot.*
  - *The mechanisms of S_N1 and S_N2 and electrophilic substitution reactions are not required.*

Alkanes

- General formula is C_nH_{2n+2}
- Alkanes are **saturated hydrocarbons**.

The term hydrocarbons refers to compounds which contain carbon and hydrogen *only*. Alkanes are said to be saturated because they contain all single carbon–carbon bonds.

Alkanes contain only C—C and C—H bonds, which are both strong bonds: C—C = 348 kJ mol^{-1} and C—H = 412 kJ mol^{-1}. So these molecules will only react in the presence of a strong source of energy, strong enough to break these bonds. As a result, alkanes are stable under most conditions and can be stored, transported, and even compressed safely – which is one of the reasons why they are such useful compounds.

The C—C and C—H bonds are also characteristically non-polar, so these molecules are not susceptible to attack by most common reactants. These two factors taken together mean that alkanes are generally of very low reactivity.

There are, however, two reactions involving alkanes that we will consider here – combustion and substitution reactions.

Combustion: alkanes as fuels

Alkanes are widely used as fuels, in internal combustion engines and household heating for example, because they release significant amounts of energy when they burn. In other words, the reactions of combustion are highly exothermic. This is mainly because of the large amount of energy released in forming the double bonds in CO_2 and the bonds in H_2O.

Alkanes burn in the presence of excess oxygen to produce carbon dioxide and water. This is known as complete combustion because the products are fully oxidized.

For example:

$$C_3H_8(g) + 5O_2(g) \rightarrow 3CO_2(g) + 4H_2O(g)$$

However, when the oxygen supply is limited, incomplete combustion occurs giving rise to carbon monoxide and water. For example:

$$2C_3H_8(g) + 7O_2(g) \rightarrow 3CO(g) + H_2O(g)$$

Molecular models of the first three members of the alkane homologous series: methane (CH_4), ethane (C_2H_6), and propane (C_3H_8). Carbon atoms are shown in black and hydrogen atoms in white. There is free rotation around the carbon–carbon bonds in these saturated molecules.

When asked to define a hydrocarbon, make sure you include the word *only* after the fact that they contain carbon and hydrogen – as otherwise your description would apply to *all* organic compounds!

Methane, CH_4, is both a fuel and an atmospheric pollutant. As a greenhouse gas, it has a much higher potential for trapping infrared radiation than carbon dioxide. It is emitted from natural sources such as wetlands, but about 60% of CH_4 released is from human activities. The three main sources are the petroleum industry, domestic livestock, and landfill sites. Strategies to reduce CH_4 emission include its capture and use as a source of energy.

Aeroplane landing with exhaust behind. The burning of hydrocarbon fuels releases large amounts of carbon dioxide, as well as carbon monoxide and other pollutants, into the atmosphere.

In conditions of extreme oxygen limitation, carbon will also be produced. For example:

$$C_3H_8(g) + 2O_2(g) \rightarrow 3C(g) + 4H_2O(g)$$

Other hydrocarbons, the alkenes, alkynes, and arenes, similarly undergo complete or incomplete combustion depending on the availability of oxygen, with the release of large amounts of energy. As the C : H ratio increases with unsaturation, there is an increase in the smokiness of the flame, due to unburned carbon.

The products of all these reactions have serious impact on the environment, which is why the burning of these and other **fossil fuels** on a very large scale is widely recognized as a global problem.

• Carbon dioxide and water are both so-called **greenhouse gases**, which means that they absorb infrared radiation and so contribute to **global warming** and **climate change**. Rising levels of carbon dioxide are largely implicated in the increase in average world temperatures over the last century.

• Carbon monoxide is a toxin because it combines irreversibly with the haemoglobin in the blood and prevents it from carrying oxygen. Slow idling vehicle engines in regions of high traffic densities produce higher concentrations of carbon monoxide. It is essential to provide adequate ventilation when these fuels are being burned in a confined space to avoid carbon monoxide poisoning, which can be fatal.

• Unburned carbon is released into the air as particulates, which have a direct effect on human health, especially the respiratory system. In addition, these particulates act as catalysts in forming smog in polluted air, and have also been targeted as the source of another serious environmental problem known as **global dimming**.

Given all the negative environmental effects associated with the burning of fossil fuels, how can we make changes in our lifestyles to lessen these impacts?

CHALLENGE YOURSELF

1 Use oxidation numbers to show the differences in the extent of oxidation in reactions of complete and incomplete combustion of hydrocarbons.

Substitution reactions of alkanes: halogenation

As alkanes are saturated molecules, the main type of reaction that they can undergo is **substitution**. This occurs when another reactant, such as a halogen, takes the place of a hydrogen atom in the alkane. For example, methane, CH_4, reacts with chlorine producing chloromethane and hydrogen chloride.

$$CH_4(g) + Cl_2(g) \xrightarrow{\text{UV light}} CH_3Cl(g) + HCl(g)$$

The reaction does not take place in the dark as the energy of UV light is necessary to break the covalent bond in the chlorine molecule. This splits it into chlorine atoms, which each have an unpaired electron and are known as **free radicals**. Once formed, these radicals will start a chain reaction in which a mixture of products including the halogenoalkane is formed. We can describe the reaction as a sequence of steps, known as the **reaction mechanism**.

Initiation

$$Cl_2 \xrightarrow{\text{UV light}} 2\,Cl\bullet \text{ radicals}$$

$$\overset{\times\times}{\underset{\times\times}{\vdots}} Cl \overset{\times}{\underset{\times}{\vdots}} Cl \overset{\times\times}{\underset{\times\times}{\vdots}} \xrightarrow{\text{UV light}} \overset{\times\times}{\underset{\times\times}{\vdots}} Cl \overset{\times}{} \quad \overset{}{\times} Cl \overset{\times\times}{\underset{\times\times}{\vdots}}$$

2 chlorine radicals

This process occurs in the presence of ultra-violet light. It is known as **photochemical homolytic fission** because the bond between the chlorine atoms is broken, splitting the shared pair of electrons between the two atoms. *Homo-* means 'the same' and refers to the fact that the two products have an equal assignment of electrons from the bond.

Propagation

Propagation reactions both use and produce free radicals. For example:

$$Cl\bullet + CH_4 \rightarrow CH_3\bullet + HCl$$

$$CH_3\bullet + Cl_2 \rightarrow CH_3Cl + Cl\bullet$$

$$CH_3Cl + Cl\bullet \rightarrow CH_2Cl\bullet + HCl$$

$$CH_2Cl\bullet + Cl_2 \rightarrow CH_2Cl_2 + Cl\bullet$$

There are many possible propagation steps, which all allow the reaction to continue. This is why this type of reaction is often called a **chain reaction**.

Termination

Termination reactions remove free radicals from the mixture by causing them to react together and pair up their electrons. For example:

$$Cl\bullet + Cl\bullet \rightarrow Cl_2$$

$$CH_3\bullet + Cl\bullet \rightarrow CH_3Cl$$

$$CH_3\bullet + CH_3\bullet \rightarrow C_2H_6$$

Again there are many possible termination steps.

So the reaction mixture may contain mono- and di-substituted halogenoalkanes, as well as HCl and larger alkanes. A similar reaction occurs with other alkanes and with bromine. The change in colour from brown to colourless of bromine water when it reacts with an alkane occurs only in the presence of UV light, as shown in Figure 10.6. This is sometimes used to distinguish between alkanes and alkenes.

Side notes

A free radical contains an unpaired electron and so is very reactive.

Homolytic fission occurs when a bond breaks by splitting the shared pair of electrons between the two products. It produces two free radicals, each with an unpaired electron.

$$X : X \rightarrow X\cdot + X\cdot$$

Make sure that you understand the difference between a free radical and an ion. A free radical has an unpaired electron but no net charge; an ion carries a charge.

Figure 10.6 The reaction between hexane, C_6H_{14}, and bromine water takes place only in the presence of UV light.

Alkanes are saturated hydrocarbons and undergo substitution reactions.

Alkenes

A molecular model of propene, C_3H_6, showing the carbon–carbon double bond between two of the carbon atoms. The double bond is the site of reactivity of the alkenes, as one of the bonds can break enabling the molecule to undergo addition reactions. This is why the alkenes are described as being unsaturated.

CHALLENGE YOURSELF

2 The mechanism for the addition reactions of alkenes is completely different from the substitution reactions we discussed for alkanes; addition reactions involve **heterolytic fission**. Think about what this term suggests about the type of bond breaking involved. What might the mechanism for the addition reaction be, based on this?

• General formula C_nH_{2n}
• Alkenes are **unsaturated hydrocarbons** containing a carbon–carbon double bond.

$$\underset{H}{\overset{H}{\diagdown}}C = C\underset{H}{\overset{H}{\diagup}}$$

As we learned in Chapter 4, the carbon atoms that form the double bond have a trigonal planar shape with angles of 120°.

Alkenes are more reactive than alkanes as the double bond is the site of reactivity of the molecule. One of the bonds is relatively easily broken, which creates two new bonding positions on the carbon atoms. This enables alkenes to undergo **addition reactions** and so form a range of different saturated products. These are described in the following text.

Addition of hydrogen

Hydrogen reacts with alkenes to form alkanes in the presence of a nickel catalyst at about 150 °C.

$$H-\underset{\underset{H}{|}}{\overset{\overset{H}{|}}{C}}-\overset{\overset{H}{|}}{C}=\overset{\overset{H}{|}}{C}-H + H_2 \longrightarrow H-\underset{\underset{H}{|}}{\overset{\overset{H}{|}}{C}}-\underset{\underset{H}{|}}{\overset{\overset{H}{|}}{C}}-\underset{\underset{H}{|}}{\overset{\overset{H}{|}}{C}}-H$$

$$CH_3CHCH_2 + H_2 \xrightarrow[150\,°C]{\text{Ni catalyst}} CH_3CH_2CH_3$$
$$\text{propene} \qquad\qquad\qquad \text{propane}$$

This process, known as **hydrogenation**, is used in the margarine industry to convert oils containing many unsaturated hydrocarbon chains into more saturated compounds which have higher melting points. This is done so that margarine will be a solid at room temperature. However, there are now widespread concerns about the health effects of so-called **trans fats**, produced by partial hydrogenation.

Oct-1-ene, C_8H_{16}, an alkene, burning in a crucible. The flame is smoky due to unburned carbon, an indication of unsaturation.

Addition of halogens

Halogens react with alkenes to produce dihalogeno compounds. These reactions happen quickly at room temperature, and are accompanied by the loss of colour of the reacting halogen. Note that the name and structure of the product indicates that a halogen atom attaches to each of the two carbon atoms of the double bond.

$$CH_3CHCH_2 + Br_2 \longrightarrow CH_3CHBrCH_2Br$$
propene   1,2-dibromopropane

Addition of halogen halides

Hydrogen halides, such as HCl and HBr, react with alkenes to produce halogenoalkanes. These reactions take place rapidly in solution at room temperature.

$$CH_2CH_2 + HCl \longrightarrow CH_3CH_2Cl$$
ethene   chloroethane

All the hydrogen halides are able to react in this way, but the reactivity is in the order HI > HBr > HCl due to the decreasing strength of the hydrogen halide bond down Group 7. So HI, with the weakest bond, reacts the most readily.

Addition of water

The reaction with water is known as **hydration**, and converts the alkene into an alcohol. In the laboratory, it can be achieved using concentrated sulfuric acid as a catalyst. The reaction involves an intermediate in which both H^+ and HSO_4^- ions are added across the double bond, but this is quickly followed by hydrolysis with replacement of the HSO_4^- by OH^- and reformation of the H_2SO_4.

$$CH_2CH_2 \xrightarrow{H_2SO_4(conc.)} CH_3CH_2(HSO_4) \xrightarrow{H_2O} CH_3CH_2OH + H_2SO_4$$
ethene   ethyl   ethanol
hydrogensulfate

Conditions: heat with steam and catalyst of concentrated H_2SO_4

This reaction is of industrial significance because ethanol is a very important solvent, and so is manufactured on a large scale.

Alkenes are unsaturated hydrocarbons and undergo addition reactions.

Be careful not to confuse the terms *hydrogenation* (addition of hydrogen) with *hydration* (addition of water)

The modern process for ethanol synthesis is by direct catalytic hydration of ethane over a phosphoric acid catalyst absorbed on silica.

NATURE OF SCIENCE

Two observable differences in the reactions of alkanes and alkenes have been mentioned in this section.

- Alkenes decolorize bromine water rapidly at room temperature, whereas alkanes will only do this in the presence of UV light.
- Alkenes burn with a dirtier, smokier flame than alkanes.

Either of these tests might be considered as a way to distinguish between the two classes of compound, but both rely on qualitative data and are subjective, based on the eye of the observer. Wherever possible, experiments are designed to produce quantitative data that is more objective and able to be analysed. Consider what instrumentation and sensors could be used to develop these observations into more rigorous tests to distinguish between saturated and unsaturated hydrocarbons.

Use of bromine water to distinguish between an alkane (hexane) and an alkene (hex-1-ene). Without UV light, the brown colour is decolorized by the alkene but not by the alkane. This is due to the addition reaction that occurs with the unsaturated alkene that does not occur with the alkane.

Polymerization of alkenes

Because alkenes readily undergo addition reactions by breaking their double bond, they can be joined together to produce long chains known as **addition polymers**. The alkene used in this reaction is known as the **monomer**, and its chemical nature determines the properties of the polymer. Polymers, typically containing thousands of molecules of the monomer, are a major product of the organic chemical industry and many of our most familiar and useful plastics are polymers of alkenes.

Figure 10.7 People cannot form a chain until they unfold their arms to release their hands. Similarly, alkenes must break their double bonds in order to join together to form the polymer.

As polymers are such large molecules, their structures are shown using a **repeating unit**, which has open bonds at each end. It is put in a bracket with n as subscript to denote the number of repeating units. For example, ethene polymerizes to form poly(ethene), commonly known as **polythene**.

$$n \left(\begin{array}{cc} H & H \\ | & | \\ C = C \\ | & | \\ H & H \end{array} \right) \longrightarrow \left(\begin{array}{cc} H & H \\ | & | \\ -C - C- \\ | & | \\ H & H \end{array} \right)_n$$

ethene   the repeating unit

The disposal of plastics is a major global problem. The very features that make plastics so useful, such as their impermeability to water and low reactivity, mean they are often non-biodegradable and so remain in landfill sites for indefinite periods of time. It is estimated that about 10% of plastics produced end up in the ocean, causing widespread hazards to marine life. Measures to try to address this problem include developments of more efficient recycling processes, biodegradable plastics, and plastic-feeding microorganisms. A reduction in the quantities of plastic produced and used is also urgently needed – which is something for which every individual can share responsibility.

Waste plastic on a beach in Italy. Plastic waste from oceans is washed up on shores creating problems for wildlife and unsightly scenes such as this.

Coloured scanning electron micrograph of a section through a sheet of a biodegradable plastic. The orange spheres are granules of starch embedded in the plastic. When the plastic is buried in soil, the starch grains take up water and expand. This breaks the plastic into many small fragments, increasing the contact area with bacteria in the soil which digest the plastic. Such plastics help to address the major problem of waste plastic disposal.

Similarly, propene polymerizes to form poly(propene), often called polypropylene.

$$n\left(\begin{array}{cc} H & H \\ | & | \\ C = C \\ | & | \\ H & CH_3 \end{array}\right) \longrightarrow \left(\begin{array}{cc} H & H \\ | & | \\ -C - C- \\ | & | \\ H & CH_3 \end{array}\right)_n$$

propene   the repeating unit

Other common addition polymers include poly(chloroethene), also known as PVC, and PTFE, poly(tetrafluoroethene), often marketed as Teflon®. Their repeating units are given below.

$$\left(\begin{array}{cc} H & H \\ | & | \\ -C - C- \\ | & | \\ H & Cl \end{array}\right)_n \qquad \left(\begin{array}{cc} F & F \\ | & | \\ -C - C- \\ | & | \\ F & F \end{array}\right)_n$$

PVC   PTFE

The example with propene shows that it is helpful to draw the structure of the monomer with the double bond in the *middle* and the other groups off at 90°. Then it is easy to see how the monomers link together when the double bond breaks.

CHALLENGE YOURSELF

3 Draw the repeating unit in polystyrene, given that the formula of the monomer is $C_6H_5CHCH_2$.

Polymers are discussed further in Chapter 12, Option A: Materials.

In summary, alkenes:

- readily undergo addition reactions;
- are used as starting materials in the manufacture of many industrially important chemicals.

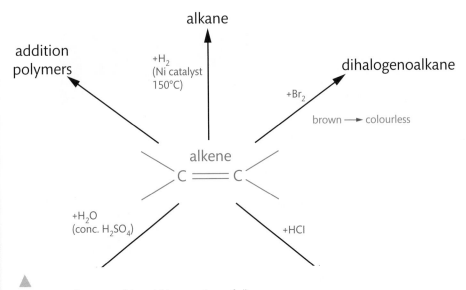

Figure 10.8 Summary of the addition reactions of alkenes.

Polythene has excellent insulating properties and is commonly used in household containers, carrier bags, water tanks, and piping. Polypropylene is used in the manufacture of clothing, especially thermal wear for outdoor activities. PVC is used in all forms of construction materials, packaging, electrical cable sheathing, etc. There is some controversy regarding its use, linked to health and environmental concerns, and some organizations are advocating its phase-out. PTFE has a very low surface friction so is widely used in non-stick pans. It also makes up one of the layers in waterproof, breathable fabrics such as GoreTex®. Its resistance to van der Waals' forces means that it is the only known surface to which a gecko cannot stick.

NATURE OF SCIENCE

It is hard to assess the scale of the impact that alkanes and alkenes have had on society. As fuels, alkanes have made energy widely available, and as chemical feedstock, alkenes have led to the synthesis of diverse plastics. Yet these innovations have come at significant cost to the environment, and the long-term consequences are still being determined. While scientific progress is responsible for both the intended and unintended consequences, it is scientists who must respond to the problems. The issues of climate change, air pollution, and plastic disposal are currently pressing areas of research and development.

Exercises

9 Write equations for the following reactions:

   (a) incomplete combustion of pentane, forming $CO(g)$
   (b) complete combustion of butane
   (c) incomplete combustion of propyne, forming $C(s)$.

10 Write equations showing possible steps leading to a mixture of products in the reaction between bromine and ethane reacting together in UV light.

11 Give the name and structure of the products of the following reactions:

   (a) $CH_3CH_2CH = CH_2 + H_2$ over Ni catalyst
   (b) $CH_3CH = CHCH_3 + $ conc. H_2SO_4
   (c) $CH_3CH = CHCH_3 + HBr$

12 What would you observe during the following experiments carried out in test tubes at room temperature?

   (a) some bromine water is added to cyclohexane in a test tube covered in aluminium foil
   (b) a few drops of methylbenzene are burned on a watch glass
   (c) some bromine water is added to propane in a test tube in UV light.

Alcohols

- General formula $C_nH_{2n+1}OH$
- Alcohols have —OH functional group.

The —OH group is polar, and so increases the solubility in water of the molecules, relative to alkanes of comparable molar mass. The most common alcohol, ethanol (C_2H_5OH), is soluble in water in all proportions, as we know from its presence in alcoholic drinks.

Combustion: alcohols as fuels

Like the hydrocarbons, alcohols burn in oxygen to form carbon dioxide and water, along with the release of significant amounts of energy. Alcohols are an important fuel, used in alcohol burners, etc. The amount of energy released per mole of alcohol increases as we go up the homologous series, chiefly due to the increasing number of carbon dioxide molecules produced.

For example, the burning of methanol:

$$2CH_3OH(l) + 3O_2(g) \rightarrow 2CO_2(g) + 4H_2O(g) \qquad \Delta H_c^\ominus = -726.1 \text{ kJ mol}^{-1}$$

$\Rightarrow 1:1$ ratio of alcohol:CO_2

By comparison, the burning of pentanol:

$$2C_5H_{11}OH(g) + 15O_2(g) \rightarrow 10CO_2(g) + 12H_2O(g) \qquad \Delta H_c^\ominus = -3330.9 \text{ kJ mol}^{-1}$$

$\Rightarrow 1:5$ ratio of alcohol:CO_2 and a corresponding increase in the molar enthalpy of combustion.

As is the case with the hydrocarbons, in the presence of a limited supply of oxygen, alcohols will produce carbon monoxide instead of carbon dioxide.

Oxidation of alcohols

Combustion involves the *complete* oxidation of the alcohol molecules, but it is also possible for them to react with oxidizing agents which selectively oxidize the carbon atom attached to the —OH group, keeping the carbon skeleton of the molecule intact. In this way, alcohols can be oxidized into other important organic compounds. The products of these reactions are determined by whether the alcohol is primary, secondary, or tertiary, as described on the following pages.

Various oxidizing agents can be used for these reactions, but commonly the laboratory process uses acidified potassium dichromate(VI). This is a bright orange solution owing to the presence of Cr(VI), which is reduced to green Cr(III) as the alcohol is oxidized on heating. When writing these reactions it is often easier to show the oxidizing agent simply as '+[O]'. The oxidation reactions of the different alcohols are as follows.

Primary alcohols are oxidized in a two-step reaction, first forming the **aldehyde**, which under prolonged conditions is oxidized further to the **carboxylic acid**. For example:

Alcohol burning in a beaker.

Methanol is considered to be a potential candidate to replace fuels based on crude oil. It can be burned directly as a fuel, or used in the production of hydrogen for fuel cells. It is synthesized on a large scale by the reduction of carbon dioxide and carbon monoxide.

Alcoholic drinks are widely consumed globally. However, as individuals' blood alcohol levels rise, they become impaired with loss of balance and judgement, and so most countries have set legal limits for activities such as driving. Analysis of ethanol concentration is based on samples of breath, blood, or urine. Common techniques use the oxidation reactions of ethanol in fuel cells or photocells (in which orange Cr(VI) is reduced to green Cr(III)) or infrared spectroscopy. Alcohol abuse is a major contributor to social and economic problems in some societies.

Distillation apparatus is used to separate liquids with different boiling points. In the oxidation of primary alcohols, the aldehyde has a lower boiling point than the alcohol or the acid, and so is collected as a gas and passes into the condensing tube, which is surrounded by cold flowing water. The gas condenses back into a liquid, which is collected in the beaker at the bottom. This prevents further oxidation of the aldehyde to the carboxylic acid.

ethanol
primary alcohol

$\xrightarrow{\text{+[O], heat}}$

ethanal
aldehyde

$\xrightarrow[\text{reflux}]{\text{+[O], heat}}$

ethanoic acid
carboxylic acid

ethanol $\xrightarrow{\text{+ [O], heat}}$ ethanal $\xrightarrow[\text{reflux}]{\text{+ [O], heat}}$ ethanoic acid
primary alcohol   aldehyde   carboxylic acid

$H^+/Cr(VI)$ ⟶ $Cr(III)$

This is why when we leave a bottle of wine exposed to the air, bacteria slowly oxidize the ethanol to ethanoic acid, giving the smell of vinegar.

It is possible to stop the reaction after the first step and obtain the aldehyde product by using **distillation** to remove it from the reaction mixture. This is possible because aldehydes have lower boiling points than either alcohols or carboxylic acids, because they do not have hydrogen bonding between their molecules.

If, on the other hand, we want to obtain the carboxylic acid as the product, then we must leave the aldehyde in contact with the oxidizing agent for a prolonged period of time. This will be achieved most efficiently using apparatus for **reflux**.

When you are asked for the conditions for the oxidation reactions, make sure that you specify acidified oxidizing agent and heat, as well as distillation or reflux.

Student heating a pear-shaped flask with a Bunsen burner and using a reflux condenser. This collects and condenses vapours that would otherwise escape from the reaction mixture, and so enables the volatile components to remain in the reaction for long enough to complete their reaction. In this case it is used to oxidize a primary alcohol to completion, to the carboxylic acid.

Secondary alcohols are oxidized to the **ketone** by a similar process of oxidation.

$$H-\underset{\underset{H}{|}}{\overset{\overset{H}{|}}{C}}-\underset{\underset{OH}{|}}{\overset{\overset{H}{|}}{C}}-\underset{\underset{H}{|}}{\overset{\overset{H}{|}}{C}}-H \xrightarrow[\text{reflux}]{+[O],\text{ heat}} H-\underset{\underset{H}{|}}{\overset{\overset{H}{|}}{C}}-\underset{\overset{||}{O}}{C}-\underset{\underset{H}{|}}{\overset{\overset{H}{|}}{C}}-H \;+\; H_2O$$

CH₃CHOHCH₃
propan-2-ol

(CH₃)₂CO
propanone

propan-2-ol $\xrightarrow[\text{reflux}]{+\,[O],\text{ heat}}$ propanone + H₂O
CH₃CHOHCH₃   (CH₃)₂CO

H⁺/Cr(VI) ⟶ Cr(III)

Tertiary alcohols are not readily oxidized under comparable conditions. This would involve breaking the carbon skeleton of the molecule, which requires significantly more energy. Therefore we will not see a colour change in the potassium dichromate(VI) oxidizing agent when it is reacted with a tertiary alcohol.

$$H-\underset{\underset{H}{|}}{\overset{\overset{H}{|}}{C}}-\underset{\underset{OH}{|}}{\overset{\overset{CH_3}{|}}{C}}-\underset{\underset{H}{|}}{\overset{\overset{H}{|}}{C}}-H \xrightarrow{+[O],\text{ heat}} \quad X$$

2-methylpropan-2-ol

no reaction

2-methylpropan-2-ol $\xrightarrow{+\,[O],\text{ heat}}$ no reaction
H⁺/Cr(VI) ⟶ no change in colour

Propan-1-ol (primary alchohol)   Propan-2-ol (secondary alchohol)   2-methyl-propan-2-ol (tertiary alchohol)

Summary of oxidation of alcohols

	Oxidation product	Colour change with acidified K₂Cr₂O₇(aq)
Primary alcohol	aldehyde → carboxylic acid	orange → green
Secondary alcohol	ketone	orange → green
Tertiary alcohol	not oxidized	no colour change

Reactions of alcohols
Full details of how to carry out this experiment with a worksheet are available on your eBook.

The colour of the solutions after oxidation with potassium dichromate(VI) solution, K₂Cr₂O₇, which is orange. Primary and secondary alcohols are oxidized, to carboxylic acids and ketones respectively, and the Cr(VI) is reduced to green Cr(III). Tertiary alcohols are not oxidized and do not react.

Esterification reaction

Alcohols react with carboxylic acids to form esters in a **condensation** reaction in which water is also produced.

$$\text{carboxylic acid} + \text{alcohol} \rightleftharpoons \text{ester} + \text{water}$$

For example, the reaction between ethanoic acid and ethanol is as follows.

ethyl ethanoate

$$CH_3COOH + C_2H_5OH \xrightleftharpoons{\text{conc. } H_2SO_4} CH_3COOC_2H_5 + H\text{-}O\text{-}H$$

The reaction is an equilibrium reaction, and is catalysed by concentrated sulfuric acid, H_2SO_4. The ester has the lowest boiling point of the components of the reaction mixture and so can be separated by distillation. Esters have distinct smells that can often be detected if the reaction mixture is poured into a beaker of water. Unlike their parent acid and alcohol, esters have no free –OH groups so they cannot form hydrogen bonds and so are mostly quite insoluble and form a layer on the surface.

Some other esterification reactions are given below.

$$HCOOH + C_2H_5OH \rightleftharpoons HCOOC_2H_5 + H_2O$$

methanoic   ethanol   ethyl
acid   methanoate

$$C_3H_7COOH + CH_3OH \rightleftharpoons C_3H_7COOCH_3 + H_2O$$

butanoic   methanol   methyl
acid   butanoate

Halogenoalkanes

- General formula is $C_nH_{2n+1}X$ (where X = halogen).
- Halogenoalkanes contain an atom of fluorine, chlorine, bromine, or iodine bonded to the carbon skeleton of the molecule.

Halogenoalkanes are saturated molecules so, like alkanes, their reactions involve substitution – that is the replacement of one atom by another atom or group. But, unlike the alkanes, the halogenoalkanes possess a polar bond and this makes them more reactive.

Nucleophilic substitution reactions of halogenoalkanes

The polarity in halogenoalkanes is due to the fact that the halogen atom is more electronegative than carbon and so exerts a stronger pull on the shared electrons in the carbon–halogen bond. As a result the halogen gains a partial negative charge ($\delta-$), and the carbon gains a partial positive charge ($\delta+$) and is said to be **electron deficient**. It is this electron-deficient carbon that defines much of the reactivity of the halogenoalkanes.

$$-\overset{|}{\underset{|}{C}}{}^{\delta+} \longrightarrow Cl^{\delta-}$$

Nucleophiles are reactants that are themselves electron rich, as they have a lone pair of electrons and may also carry a negative charge. These species are therefore attracted to the electron-deficient carbon atom in the halogenoalkane. This leads to reactions in which substitution of the halogen occurs, known as **nucleophilic substitution** reactions.

The hydroxide ion, OH^-, is a good nucleophile. For example, halogenoalkanes react with alkalis such as NaOH to form alcohols.

$$\underset{\text{chloromethane}}{CH_3Cl} + NaOH \rightarrow \underset{\text{methanol}}{CH_3OH} + NaCl$$

$$\underset{\text{bromopropane}}{C_3H_7Br} + NaOH \rightarrow \underset{\text{propanol}}{C_3H_7OH} + NaBr$$

These reactions, and others like them in which the halogen is substituted by another group, mean that halogenoalkanes can be converted into many other classes of compound and so are very useful intermediates in organic synthetic pathways.

A nucleophile is an electron-rich species that is attracted to parts of molecules that are electron deficient.

Halogenoalkanes known as CFCs (chlorofluorocarbons) have been associated with damage to the ozone layer in the stratosphere which protects the Earth from harmful radiation. The satellite image shows the ozone hole over Antarctica in 2010. Ozone layer thicknesses are colour coded from purple (lowest) through blue, cyan and green to yellow (highest). The ozone hole was at its annual maximum, covering an area of over 22 million square kilometres. Although CFCs responsible for much of the damage were phased out from the 1980s, damage to the ozone did not peak until 2006. Ozone depleting chemicals in the stratosphere persist at high concentrations.

Benzene

We saw on page 323 that the delocalized electrons in benzene give it a special stability. This means that addition reactions, which would lead to loss of the stable aromatic ring, are generally not favoured as the products would be of higher energy than the reactants. Instead, substitution reactions, in which one or more of the hydrogen atoms is replaced by an incoming group, occur more readily as these lead to products in which the aromatic ring is conserved. The delocalized ring of electrons, which represents an area of electron density, is the site of reactivity.

Figure 10.9 Electrophilic substitution reaction of benzene with a generic electrophile E⁺. Note that the product has the arene ring conserved.

Electrophilic substitution reactions of benzene

Electrophiles are reactants that are themselves electron deficient, as they have a positive charge or a partial positive charge. These species are therefore attracted to the electron-rich benzene ring, leading to **electrophilic substitution** reactions.

For example, benzene reacts with the nitronium ion, NO_2^+ (derived from nitric acid, HNO_3), as follows:

$$C_6H_6 + HNO_3 \xrightarrow[50\,°C]{\text{conc. } H_2SO_4} C_6H_5NO_2 + H_2O$$

The reaction of benzene with halogens is as follows:

$$C_6H_6 + Cl_2 \xrightarrow{\text{AlCl}_3 \text{ in dry ether}} C_6H_5Cl + HCl$$

An electrophile is an electron-deficient species that forms a bond by accepting an electron pair. Electrophiles are positive ions or have a partial positive charge.

The mechanisms of the substitution reactions with halogenoalkanes and benzene will not be assessed in IB examinations.

Exercises

13 Write equations for

   (a) the complete combustion of ethanol and propanol

   (b) the esterification reaction between propanoic acid and butanol.

14 Predict the products of heating the following alcohols with acidified potassium dichromate(VI) solution, and the colour changes that would be observed in the reaction mixture.

   (a) butan-2-ol

   (b) methanol (product collected by distillation immediately)

   (c) 2-methylbutan-2-ol

15 Explain what is meant by nucleophilic substitution, using the reaction between NaOH and chloroethane to illustrate your answer.

16 Discuss why benzene, which is highly unsaturated, tends to undergo substitution reactions rather than addition reactions.

Practice questions

1 Which reaction type is typical for halogenoalkanes?

  A electrophilic substitution   **C** nucleophilic substitution
  B electrophilic addition   **D** nucleophilic addition

2 From which monomer is this polymer made?

A
$$\begin{matrix} H & & Cl \\ & C=C & \\ H & & H \end{matrix}$$

C
$$\begin{matrix} Cl & H \\ H-C-C-H \\ H & H \end{matrix}$$

B
$$\begin{matrix} Cl & & H \\ & C=C & \\ H & & Cl \end{matrix}$$

D
$$\begin{matrix} H & & Cl \\ & C=C & \\ H & & Cl \end{matrix}$$

3 What is the correct order of reaction types in the following sequence?

$$C_3H_7Br \xrightarrow{\ I\ } C_3H_7OH \xrightarrow{\ II\ } C_2H_5COOH \xrightarrow{\ III\ } C_2H_5COOC_2H_5$$

	I	II	III
A	substitution	oxidation	condensation
B	addition	substitution	condensation
C	oxidation	substitution	condensation
D	substitution	oxidation	substitution

4 Which reactants could be used to form the compound below?

  A butanoic acid and ethanol   **C** ethanoic acid and propan-1-ol
  B propanoic acid and ethanol   **D** ethanoic acid and butan-1-ol

5 Which substances are possible products of the incomplete combustion of octane?

  A carbon dioxide and hydrogen gas   **C** carbon monoxide and hydrogen gas
  B carbon monoxide and water vapour   **D** methane and hydrogen gas

6 Which reaction occurs via a free-radical mechanism?

A $C_2H_6 + Br_2 \rightarrow C_2H_5Br + HBr$

B $C_2H_4 + Br_2 \rightarrow C_2H_4Br_2$

C $C_4H_9I + OH^- \rightarrow C_4H_9OH + I^-$

D $(CH_3)_3CI + H_2O \rightarrow (CH_3)_3COH + HI$

7 Which conditions are required to obtain a good yield of a carboxylic acid when ethanol is oxidized using potassium dichromate(VI), $K_2Cr_2O_7(aq)$?

I   add sulfuric acid

II   heat the reaction mixture under reflux

III distil the product as the oxidizing agent is added

A I and II only   **B** I and III only   **C** II and III only   **D** I, II, and III

8 What will be observed after hexane has reacted with bromine in the dark?

A No observable change.

B An acidic gas is released.

C The colour changes from brown to colourless.

D The two liquids have formed separate layers.

9 When propan-1-ol is heated with acidified potassium dichromate and refluxed, what is the final product of the reaction?

A C_2H_5CHO **B** $C_2H_5CH(OH)CH_3$ **C** C_2H_5COOH **D** C_3H_7COOH

10 What is the name of the following compound?

$$HCOOC_3H_7$$

A methyl propanoate   **B** propyl methanoate

C propyl methyl ether   **D** butanone

11 Which pair below contains two compounds that each possess a carbonyl group?

A ethanal and ethanol   **B** ethanoic acid and diethyl ether

C propanone and propanal   **D** ethyl ethanoate and ethanamine

12 Which of the following compounds has the highest boiling point?

A CH_3COOH **B** C_3H_7OH **C** $C_2H_5OCH_3$ **D** C_2H_5Cl

13 How many isomers can be drawn for C_5H_{12}?

A 2   **B** 3   **C** 4   **D** 5

14 Below are four structural isomers with molecular formula C_4H_9Br. State the name of each of the isomers A, B, C, and D.

A   B

C   D

Key:

● Bromine

● Carbon

○ Hydrogen

(4)

15 Alkenes are an economically and chemically important family of organic compounds.

(a) The reaction of alkenes with bromine water provides a test for unsaturation in the laboratory. Describe the colour change when bromine water is added to chloroethene. (1)

(b) Deduce the Lewis structure of chloroethene and identify the formula of the repeating unit of the polymer poly(chloroethene). (2)

(c) Besides polymerization, state **two** commercial uses of the reactions of alkenes. (2)

(Total 5 marks)

16 (a) Two compounds, **A** and **D**, each have the formula C_4H_9Cl.

Compound **A** is reacted with dilute aqueous sodium hydroxide to produce compound **B** with a formula of $C_4H_{10}O$. Compound **B** is then oxidized with acidified potassium manganate(VII) to produce compound **C** with a formula of C_4H_8O. Compound **C** resists further oxidation by acidified potassium manganate(VII).

Compound **D** is reacted with dilute aqueous sodium hydroxide to produce compound **E** with a formula of $C_4H_{10}O$. Compound **E** does not react with acidified potassium manganate(VII). Deduce the structural formulas for compounds **A**, **B**, **C**, **D**, and **E**. (5)

(b) Deduce an equation for the reaction between propanoic acid and methanol. Identify the catalyst and state the name of the organic compound, **X**, formed. (4)

(Total 9 marks)

17 (a) An acidified solution of potassium dichromate is often used as an oxidizing agent in organic chemistry. During the oxidation reaction of ethanol to ethanal the dichromate ion is reduced to chromium(III) ions according to the following **unbalanced** half-equation.

$$Cr_2O_7{}^{2-}(aq) + H^+(aq) + e^- \rightarrow Cr^{3+}(aq) + H_2O(l)$$

Describe the colour change that will be observed in the reaction. (1)

(b) Deduce the oxidation number of chromium in $Cr_2O_7{}^{2-}$. (1)

(c) State the balanced half-equation for the reduction of dichromate ions to chromium(III) ions. (1)

(d) Deduce the half-equation for the oxidation of ethanol to ethanal and hence the overall redox equation for the oxidation of ethanol to ethanal by acidified dichromate ions. (3)

(e) Explain why it is necessary to carry out the reaction under acidic conditions. (1)

(f) Identify the organic product formed if excess potassium dichromate is used and the reaction is carried out under reflux. (1)

(Total 8 marks)

To access weblinks on the topics covered here, please go to www.pearsonhotlinks.com and enter the ISBN or title of this book.

11 Measurement and data processing and analysis

Essential ideas

11.1	All measurement has a limit of precision and accuracy, and this must be taken into account when evaluating experimental results.
11.2	Graphs are a visual representation of trends in data.
11.3	Analytical techniques can be used to determine the structure of a compound, analyse the composition of a substance, or determine the purity of a compound. Spectroscopic techniques are used in the structural identification of organic and inorganic compounds.

Sample preparation for research. Experimental conclusions must take into account any systematic errors and random uncertainties that could have occurred, for example, when measuring.

Science is a communal activity and it is important that information is shared openly and honestly. An essential part of this process is the way the international scientific community subjects the findings of scientists to intense critical scrutiny through the repetition of experiments and the peer review of results in journals and at conferences. All measurements have uncertainties and it is important these are reported when data are exchanged, as these limit the conclusions that can be legitimately drawn. Science has progressed and is one of the most successful enterprises in our culture because these inherent uncertainties are recognized. Chemistry provides us with a deep understanding of the material world but it does not offer absolute certainty.

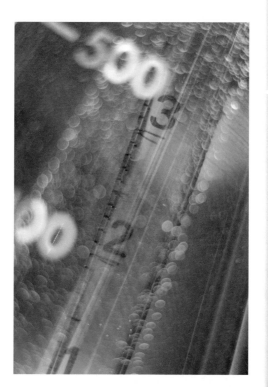

The scales on two pieces of measuring glassware. The white numbers (left) belong to a measuring cylinder, while the black numbers (centre) mark out much smaller volumes on the side of a graduated pipette. A greater degree of measuring precision can be obtained by using the pipette rather than the cylinder.

Analytical chemistry plays a significant role in today's society. It is used in forensic, medical, and industrial laboratories and helps us monitor our environment and check the quality of the food we eat and the materials we use. Early analysts relied on their senses to discover the identity of unknown substances, but we now have the ability to probe the structure of substances using electromagnetic radiation beyond the visible region. This has allowed us to discover how atoms are bonded in different molecules, and to detect

NMR is the basis of the diagnostic medical tool known as **magnetic resonance imaging** (MRI). This is a MRI scan of a normal brain. MRI is ideal for detecting brain tumours, infections in the brain, spine, and joints, and in diagnosing strokes and multiple sclerosis.

minute quantities of substances in mixtures down to levels of parts per billion. No one method supplies us with all the information we need, so a battery of tools and range of skills have been developed.

Data collected from investigations are often presented in graphical form. This provides a pictorial representation of how one quantity is related to another. A graph is also a useful tool to assess errors as it identifies data points which do not fit the general trend and so gives another measure of the reliability of the data.

11.1 Uncertainties and errors in measurement and results

Understandings:

- Qualitative data include all non-numerical information obtained from observations not from measurement.
- Quantitative data are obtained from measurements, and are always associated with random errors/uncertainties, determined by the apparatus, and by human limitations such as reaction times.
- Propagation of random errors in data processing shows the impact of the uncertainties on the final result.
- Experimental design and procedure usually lead to systematic errors in measurement, which cause a deviation in a particular direction.
- Repeat trials and measurements will reduce random errors but not systematic errors.

  Guidance
  SI units should be used throughout the programme.

Applications and skills:

- Distinction between random errors and systematic errors.
- Record uncertainties in all measurements as a range ($\pm$) to an appropriate precision.
- Discussion of ways to reduce uncertainties in an experiment.
- Propagation of uncertainties in processed data, including the use of percentage uncertainties.
- Discussion of systematic errors in all experimental work, their impact on the results, and how they can be reduced.
- Estimation of whether a particular source of error is likely to have a major or minor effect on the final result.
- Calculation of percentage error when the experimental result can be compared with a theoretical or accepted result.
- Distinction between accuracy and precision in evaluating results.

  Guidance
  - *Note that the data value must be recorded to the same precision as the random error.*
  - *The number of significant figures in a result is based on the figures given in the data. When adding or subtracting, the answer should be given to the least number of decimal places. When multiplying or dividing the final answer is given to the least number of significant figures.*

Uncertainty in measurement

Measurement is an important part of chemistry. In the laboratory, you will use different measuring apparatus and there will be times when you have to select the instrument that is most appropriate for your task from a range of possibilities. Suppose, for example, you wanted 25 cm³ of water. You could choose from measuring cylinders, pipettes, burettes, volumetric flasks of different sizes, or even an analytical balance if you know the density. All of these could be used to measure a volume of 25 cm³, but with different levels of uncertainty.

Uncertainty in analogue instruments

An uncertainty range applies to any experimental value. Some pieces of apparatus state the degree of uncertainty, in other cases you will have to make a judgement. Suppose you are asked to measure the volume of water in the measuring cylinder shown in Figure 11.1. The bottom of the meniscus of a liquid usually lies between two graduations and so the final figure of the reading has to be estimated. The smallest division in the measuring cylinder is 4 cm³ so we should report the volume as 62 (±) 2 cm³. The same considerations apply to other equipment such as burettes and alcohol thermometers that have analogue scales. The uncertainty of an analogue scale is half the smallest division.

Uncertainty in digital instruments

A top pan balance has a digital scale. The mass of the sample of water shown here is 100.00 g but the last digit is uncertain. The degree of uncertainty is (±) 0.01 g: the smallest scale division. The uncertainty of a digital scale is (±) the smallest scale division.

Other sources of uncertainty

Chemists are interested in measuring how properties change during a reaction and this can lead to additional sources of uncertainty. When time measurements are taken for example, the reaction time of the experimenter should be considered. Similarly there are uncertainties in judging, for example, the point that an indicator changes colour when measuring the equivalence point in a titration, or what is the temperature at a particular time during an exothermic reaction, or what is the voltage of an electrochemical cell. These extra uncertainties should be noted even if they are not actually quantified when data are collected in experimental work.

Significant figures in measurements

The digits in the measurement up to and including the first uncertain digit are the **significant figures** of the measurement. There are two significant figures, for example, in 62 cm³ and five in 100.00 g. The zeros are significant here as they signify that the uncertainty range is (±) 0.01 g. The number of significant figures may not always be clear. If a time measurement is 1000 s, for example, are there one, two, three, or four significant figures? As this is ambiguous, scientific notation is used to remove any confusion as the number is written with one non-zero digit on the left of the decimal point.

Figure 11.1 The volume reading should be taken from the bottom of the meniscus. You could report the volume as 62 cm³ but this is not an exact value.

> The uncertainty of a digital scale is (±) the smallest scale division.

The mass of the water is recorded as 100.00 (±) 0.01 g.

An analytical balance is one of the most precise instruments in a school laboratory. This is a digital instrument. Analytical balances are more precise than top pan balances as they have a shield to remove any fluctuations due to air currents.

Measurement	Significant figures	Measurement	Significant figures
1000 s	unspecified	0.45 mol dm^{-3}	2
1 × 10^3 s	1	4.5 × 10^{-1} mol dm^{-3}	2
1.0 × 10^3 s	2	4.50 × 10^{-1} mol dm^{-3}	3
1.00 × 10^3 s	3	4.500 × 10^{-1} mol dm^{-3}	4
1.000 × 10^3 s	4	4.5000 × 10^{-1} mol dm^{-3}	5

Exercises

1 What is the uncertainty range in the measuring cylinder in the close up photo here?

2 A reward is given for a missing diamond, which has a reported mass of 9.92 (±) 0.05 g. You find a diamond and measure its mass as 10.1 (±) 0.2 g. Could this be the missing diamond?

3 Express the following in standard notation:
   (a) 0.04 g   **(b)** 222 cm^3 **(c)** 0.030 g   **(d)** 30 °C

4 What is the number of significant figures in each of the following?
   (a) 15.50 cm^3 **(b)** 150 s   **(c)** 0.0123 g   **(d)** 150.0 g

Experimental errors

The experimental error in a result is the difference between the recorded value and the generally accepted or literature value. Errors can be categorized as **random** or **systematic**.

Random errors

When an experimenter approximates a reading, there is an equal probability of being too high or too low. This is a random error.

Random errors are caused by:

- the readability of the measuring instrument;
- the effects of changes in the surroundings such as temperature variations and air currents;
- insufficient data;
- the observer misinterpreting the reading.

You should compare your results to literature values where appropriate.

As they are random, the errors can be reduced through repeated measurements; the readings that are randomly too high will be balanced by those that are too low if sufficient readings are taken.

This is why it is good practice to duplicate experiments when designing experiments. If the same person duplicates the experiment with the same result the results are **repeatable**; if several experimenters duplicate the results they are **reproducible**.

Suppose the mass of a piece of magnesium ribbon is measured several times and the following results obtained:

$$0.1234 \text{ g} \quad 0.1232 \text{ g} \quad 0.1233 \text{ g} \quad 0.1234 \text{ g} \quad 0.1235 \text{ g} \quad 0.1236 \text{ g}$$

$$\text{average mass} = \frac{0.1234 + 0.1232 + 0.1233 + 0.1234 + 0.1235 + 0.1236}{6} \text{ g}$$

$$= 0.1234 \text{ g}$$

The mass is reported as 0.1234 (±) 0.0002 g as it is in the range 0.1232 to 0.1236 g.

Systematic errors

Systematic errors occur as a result of poor experimental design or procedure. They cannot be reduced by repeating the experiments. Suppose the top pan balance was incorrectly zeroed in the previous example and the following results were obtained:

$$0.1236 \text{ g} \quad 0.1234 \text{ g} \quad 0.1235 \text{ g} \quad 0.1236 \text{ g} \quad 0.1237 \text{ g} \quad 0.1238 \text{ g}$$

All the values are too high by 0.0002 g.

$$\text{average mass} = \frac{0.1236 + 0.1234 + 0.1235 + 0.1236 + 0.1237 + 0.1238}{6} \text{ g}$$

$$= 0.1236 \text{ g}$$

Examples of systematic errors include the following:

- measuring the volume of water from the top of the meniscus rather than the bottom will lead to volumes which are too high;
- overshooting the volume of a liquid delivered in a titration will lead to volumes which are too high;
- using an acid–base indicator whose end point does not correspond to the equivalence point of the titration;
- heat losses in an exothermic reaction will lead to smaller temperature changes.

Systematic errors can be reduced by careful experimental design.

Accuracy and precision

The smaller the systematic error, the greater is the **accuracy**. The smaller the random uncertainties, the greater the **precision**. The masses of magnesium in the earlier example are measured to the same precision but the first set of values is more accurate. Precise measurements have small random errors and are reproducible in repeated trials; accurate measurements have small systematic errors and give a result close to the accepted value (Figure 11.2).

TOK

Systematic errors cannot be reduced by simply repeating the measurement in the same way. If you were inaccurate the first time you will be inaccurate the second.

So, how do you know that you have a systematic error? Why do you trust one set of results more than another?

!

When evaluating investigations, distinguish between systematic and random errors.

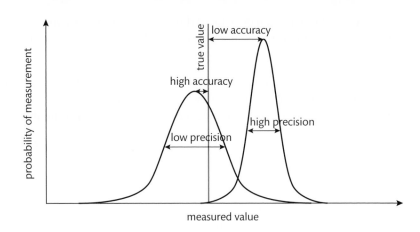

Figure 11.2 The set of readings on the left are of high accuracy and low precision. The readings on the right are of low accuracy and high precision.

Exercises

5 Repeated measurements of a quantity can reduce the effects of:

I   random errors
II systematic errors

A I only   **B** II only   **C** I and II   **D** neither I nor II

6 A student makes measurements from which she calculates the enthalpy of neutralization as 58.5357 kJ mol^{-1}. She estimates that her result is precise to $\pm2\%$.

Which of the following gives her result expressed to the appropriate number of significant figures?

A 59 kJ mol^{-1} **B** 58.5 kJ mol^{-1} **C** 58.54 kJ mol^{-1} **D** 58.536 kJ mol^{-1}

7 Using a measuring cylinder, a student measures the volume of water incorrectly by reading the top instead of the bottom of the meniscus. This error will affect:

A neither the precision nor the accuracy of the readings
B only the accuracy of the readings
C only the precision of the readings
D both the precision and the accuracy of the readings

8 A known volume of sodium hydroxide solution is added to a conical flask using a pipette. A burette is used to measure the volume of hydrochloric acid needed to neutralize the sodium hydroxide. Which of the following would lead to a systematic error in the results?

I   the use of a wet burette
II   the use of a wet pipette
III the use of a wet conical flask

A I and II only   **B** I and III only   **C** II and III only   **D** I, II, and III

9 Which type of errors can cancel when differences in quantities are calculated?

I random errors
II systematic errors

A I only   **B** II only   **C** I and II   **D** neither I nor II

10 Measurements are subject to both random errors and to systematic errors. Identify the **correct** statements.

I   Systematic errors can be reduced by modifying the experimental procedure.
II   A random error results in a different reading each time the same measurement is taken.
III Random errors can be reduced by taking the average of several measurements.

A I and II only   **B** I and III only   **C** II and III only   **D** I, II, and III

11 The volume of a water sample was repeatedly measured by a student and the following results were recorded.

	I	II	III	IV	V
Volume (± 0.1) / cm^3	38.2	38.1	38.2	38.3	38.2

The true volume of the sample is 38.5 cm^3.

Which is the correct description of the measurements?

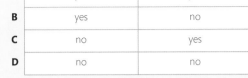

	Accuracy (± 0.1) / cm³	Precision (± 0.1) / cm³
A	yes	yes
B	yes	no
C	no	yes
D	no	no

12 The time for a 2.00 cm sample of magnesium ribbon to react completely with 20.0 cm³ of 1.00 mol dm⁻³ hydrochloric acid is measured four times. The readings are 48.8, 48.9, 49.0, 49.1, and 49.2 (±) 0.1 s.

State the value that should be quoted for the time measurement.

Percentage uncertainties and errors

An uncertainty of 1 s is more significant for time measurements of 10 s than it is for 100 s. It is helpful to express the uncertainty using absolute, fractional or percentage values.

$$\text{fractional uncertainty} = \frac{\text{absolute uncertainty}}{\text{measured value}}$$

This can be expressed as a percentage:

$$\text{percentage uncertainty} = \frac{\text{absolute uncertainty}}{\text{measured value}} \times 100\%$$

The percentage uncertainty should not be confused with **percentage error**. Percentage error is a measure of how close the **experimental value** is to the literature or accepted value.

$$\text{percentage error} = \frac{\text{accepted value} - \text{experimental value}}{\text{accepted value}} \times 100\%$$

Propagation of uncertainties in calculated results

Uncertainties in the raw data lead to uncertainties in processed data and it is important that these are propagated in a consistent way.

Addition and subtraction

Consider two burette readings:

- initial reading (±) 0.05 / cm³ = 15.05
- final reading (±) 0.05 / cm³ = 37.20

What value should be reported for the volume delivered?

The initial reading is in the range: 15.00 to 15.10 cm³.

The final reading is in the range: 37.15 to 37.25 cm³.

The maximum volume is formed by combining the maximum final reading with the minimum initial reading:

$$\text{vol}_{max} = 37.25 - 15.00 = 22.25 \text{ cm}^3$$

The minimum volume is formed by combining the minimum final volume with the maximum initial reading:

$$\text{vol}_{min} = 37.15 - 15.10 = 22.05 \text{ cm}^3$$

Precise measurements have small random errors and are reproducible in repeated trials. Accurate measurements have small systematic errors and give a result close to the accepted value.

percentage uncertainty
$$= \frac{\text{absolute uncertainty}}{\text{measured value}} \times 100\%$$

percentage error =
$$\frac{\text{accepted value} - \text{experimental value}}{\text{accepted value}} \times 100\%$$

When adding
or subtracting
measurements, the
uncertainty in the
calculated value is the
sum of the absolute
uncertainties.

therefore the volume = 22.15 (±) 0.1 cm^3

The volume depends on two measurements and the uncertainty is the sum of the two absolute uncertainties.

Multiplication and division

Working out the uncertainty in calculated values can be a time-consuming process. Consider the density calculation:

	Value	Absolute uncertainty	% Uncertainty
mass / g	24.0	(±) 0.5	$= \dfrac{0.5}{24.0} \times 100\% = 2\%$
volume / cm^3	2.0	(±) 0.1	$= \dfrac{0.1}{2.0} \times 100\% = 5\%$

	Value	Maximum value	Minimum value
density / g cm^{-3}	$= \dfrac{24.0}{2.0} = 12.0$	$= \dfrac{24.5}{1.9} = 12.89$	$= \dfrac{23.5}{2.1} = 11.19$

	Value	Absolute uncertainty	% Uncertainty
density / g cm^{-3}	12	$= 12.89 - 12.00 = (\pm) 0.89$	$= \dfrac{0.89}{12} \times 100\% = 7.4\%$

The density should only be given to two significant figures given the uncertainty in the mass and volume values, as discussed in the next section. The uncertainty in the calculated value of the density is 7% (given to one significant figure). This is equal to the sum of the uncertainties in the mass and volume values: (5% + 2% to the same level of accuracy). This approximate result provides us with a simple treatment of propagating uncertainties when multiplying and dividing measurements.

When multiplying or dividing measurements, the total percentage uncertainty is the sum of the individual percentage uncertainties. The absolute uncertainty can then be calculated from the percentage uncertainty.

Significant figures in calculations

Multiplication and division

Consider a sample of sodium chloride with a mass of 5.00 (±) 0.01 g and a volume of 2.3 (±) 0.1 cm^3. What is its density?

Using a calculator:

$$\text{density } (\rho) = \frac{\text{mass}}{\text{volume}} = \frac{5.00}{2.3} = 2.173913043 \text{ g cm}^{-3}$$

Can we claim to know the density to such precision when the value is based on less precise raw data?

The value is misleading as the mass lies in the range 4.99 to 5.01 g and the volume is between 2.2 and 2.4 cm^3. The best we can do is to give a range of values for the density.

The maximum value is obtained when the maximum value for the mass is combined with the minimum value of the volume:

$$\rho_{max} = \frac{\text{maximum mass}}{\text{minimum volume}} = \frac{5.01}{2.2} = 2.277\ 273\ \text{g cm}^{-3}$$

The minimum value is obtained by combining the minimum mass with a maximum value for the volume:

$$\rho_{min} = \frac{\text{minimum mass}}{\text{maximum volume}} = \frac{4.99}{2.4} = 2.079\ 167\ \text{g cm}^{-3}$$

The density falls in the range between the maximum and minimum value.

The second significant figure is uncertain and the reported value must be reported to this precision as 2.2 g cm^{-3}. The precision of the density is limited by the volume measurement as this is the least precise.

This leads to a simple rule. Whenever you multiply or divide data, the answer should be quoted to the same number of significant figures as the least precise data.

Addition and subtraction

When values are added or subtracted, the number of decimal places determines the precision of the calculated value.

Suppose we need the total mass of two pieces of zinc of mass 1.21 g and 0.56 g.

$$\text{total mass} = 1.77\ (\pm)\ 0.02\ \text{g}$$

This can be given to two decimal places as the balance was precise to ($\pm$) 0.01 in both cases.

Similarly, when calculating a temperature increase from 25.2 °C to 34.2 °C.

$$\text{temperature increase} = 34.2 - 25.2\ °C = 9.0\ (\pm)\ 0.2\ °C.$$

 Whenever you multiply or divide data, the answer should be quoted to the same number of significant figures as the least precise data.

 Whenever you add or subtract data, the answer should be quoted to the same number of decimal places as the least precise value.

When evaluating procedures you should discuss the precision and accuracy of the measurements. You should specifically look at the procedure and use of equipment.

Worked example

Report the total mass of solution prepared by adding 50 g of water to 1.00 g of sugar. Would the use of a more precise balance for the mass of sugar result in a more precise total mass?

Solution

total mass = 50 + 1.00 g = 51 g

The precision of the total is limited by the precision of the mass of the water. Using a more precise balance for the mass of sugar would not have improved the precision.

Worked example

The lengths of the sides of a wooden block are measured and the diagram on page 354 shows the measured values with their uncertainties.

What is the percentage and absolute uncertainty in the calculated area of the block?

Solution

area = 40.0×20.0 mm^2 = 800 mm^2 (area is given to three significant figures)

% uncertainty of area = % uncertainty of length + % uncertainty of breadth

% uncertainty of length = $\dfrac{0.5}{40.0} \times 100\%$ = 1.25%

% uncertainty of breadth = $\dfrac{0.5}{20.0} \times 100\%$ = 2.5%

% uncertainty of area = 1.25 + 2.5 = 3.75 ≈ 4%

absolute uncertainty = $\dfrac{3.75}{100} \times 800$ mm^2 = 30 mm^2

area = 800 (±) 30 mm^2

Discussing errors and uncertainties

An experimental conclusion must take into account any systematic errors and random uncertainties. You should recognize when the uncertainty of one of the measurements is much greater than the others as this will then have the major effect on the uncertainty of the final result. The approximate uncertainty can be taken as being due to that quantity alone. In thermometric experiments, for example, the thermometer often produces the most uncertain results, particularly for reactions which produce small temperature differences.

Can the difference between the experimental and literature value be explained in terms of the uncertainties of the measurements or were other systematic errors involved? This question needs to be answered when evaluating an experimental procedure. Heat loss to the surroundings, for example, accounts for experimental enthalpy changes for exothermic reactions being lower than literature values. Suggested modifications, such as improved insulation to reduce heat exchange between the system and the surroundings, should attempt to reduce these errors. This is discussed in more detail in Chapter 5.

NATURE OF SCIENCE

Lord Kelvin (1824–1907): 'When you can measure what you are speaking about and express it in numbers, you know something about it, but when you cannot measure it, when you cannot express it in numbers, your knowledge is of a meagre and unsatisfactory kind.'

Data are the lifeblood of scientists. They may be qualitative, obtained from observations, or quantitative, collected from measurements. Quantitative data are generally more reliable as they can be analysed mathematically but nonetheless will suffer from unavoidable uncertainties.

continued ...

continued ...

This analysis helps identify significant relationships and eliminate spurious outliers. Scientists look for relationships between the key factors in their investigations. The errors and uncertainties in the data must be considered when assessing the reliability of the data.

A key part of the training and skill of scientists is being able to decide which technique will produce the most precise and accurate results. Although many scientific results are very close to certainty, scientists can never claim 'absolute certainty' and the level of uncertainty should always be reported, With this in mind, scientists often speak of 'levels of confidence' when discussing experimental outcomes.

Science is a collaborative activity. Scientific papers are only published in journals after they have been anonymously peer reviewed by fellow scientists researching independently in the same field. The work must represent a new contribution to knowledge and be based on sound research methodologies.

Exercises

13 A block of ice was heated for 10 minutes. The diagram shows the scale of the thermometer with the initial and final temperatures.

What is the temperature change expressed to the appropriate precision?

A 1.40 ± 0.01 K   **B** 2.05 ± 0.01 K   **C** 2.050 ± 0.005 K   **D** 2.1 ± 0.1 K

14 A thermometer which can be read to a precision of ±0.5 °C is used to measure a temperature increase from 30.0 °C to 50.0 °C.

What is the percentage uncertainty in the measurement of the temperature increase?

A 1%   **B** 2.5%   **C** 3%   **D** 5%

15 What is the main source of error in experiments carried out to determine enthalpy changes in a school laboratory?

     A   uncertain volume measurements
     B   heat exchange with the surroundings
     C   uncertainties in the concentrations of the solutions
     D   impurities in the reagents

16 The mass of an object is measured as 1.652 g and its volume 1.1 cm^3. If the density (mass per unit volume) is calculated from these values, to how many significant figures should it be expressed?

     A   1   **B**   2   **C**   3   **D**   4

17 The number of significant figures that should be reported for the mass increase which is obtained by taking the difference between readings of 11.6235 g and 10.5805 g is:

     A   3   **B**   4   **C**   5   **D**   6

18 A 0.266 g sample of zinc is added to hydrochloric acid. 0.186 g of zinc is later recovered from the acid. What is the percentage mass loss of the zinc to the correct number of significant figures?

   A   30%   **B**   30.1%   **C**   30.07%   **D**   30.08%

19 A 0.020 ± 0.001 g piece of magnesium ribbon takes 20 ± 1 s to react in an acid solution.

The average rate can be calculated from these data:

$$\text{average rate} = \frac{\text{mass of Mg}}{\text{time taken to dissolve}}$$

Identify the average rate that should be recorded.

   A 0.001 ± 0.0001 g s^{-1} **C** 0.0010 ± 0.0001 g s^{-1}
   B 0.001 ± 0.001 g s^{-1} **D** 0.0010 ± 0.001 g s^{-1}

20 The concentration of a solution of hydrochloric acid = $1.00 \, (\pm) \, 0.05$ mol dm^{-3} and the volume = $10.0 \, (\pm) \, 0.1$ cm^3. Calculate the number of moles and give the absolute uncertainty.

21 The enthalpy change of the reaction:

$$CuSO_4(aq) + Zn(s) \rightarrow ZnSO_4(aq) + Cu(s)$$

was determined using the procedure outlined on page 176. Assume that:

- zinc is in excess;
- all the heat of reaction passes into the water.

The molar enthalpy change can be calculated from the temperature change of the solution using the expression:

$$\Delta H = \frac{-c(H_2O) \times (T_{final} - T_{initial})}{[CuSO_4]}$$

where $c(H_2O)$ is the specific heat capacity of water, $T_{initial}$ is the temperature of the copper sulfate before zinc was added, and T_{final} is the maximum temperature of the copper sulfate solution after the zinc was added.

The following results were recorded:

    $T_{initial} \, (\pm) \, 0.1/°C = 212$

    $T_{final} \, (\pm) \, 0.1/°C = 43.2$

    $[CuSO_4] = 0.500$ mol dm^{-3}

(a) Calculate the temperature change during the reaction and give the absolute uncertainty.
(b) Calculate the percentage uncertainty of this temperature change.
(c) Calculate the molar enthalpy change of reaction.
(d) Assuming the uncertainties in any other measurements are negligible, determine the percentage uncertainty in the experimental value of the enthalpy change.
(e) Calculate the absolute uncertainty of the calculated enthalpy change.
(f) The literature value for the standard enthalpy change of reaction = -217 kJ mol^{-1}. Comment on any differences between the experimental and literature values.

> **(!)** There should be no variation in the precision of raw data measured with the same instrument and the same number of decimal places should be used. For data derived from processing raw data (for example, averages), the level of precision should be consistent with that of the raw data.

11.2 Graphical techniques

Understandings:

- Graphical techniques are an effective means of communicating the effect of an independent variable on a dependent variable, and can lead to determination of physical quantities.
- Sketched graphs have labelled but unscaled axes, and are used to show qualitative trends, such as variables that are proportional or inversely proportional.
- Drawn graphs have labelled and scaled axes, and are used in quantitative measurements.

Applications and skills:

- Drawing graphs of experimental results, including the correct choice of axes and scale.
- Interpretation of graphs in terms of the relationships of dependent and independent variables.

- Production and interpretation of best-fit lines or curves through data points, including an assessment of when it can and cannot be considered as a linear function
- Calculation of quantities from graphs by measuring slope (gradient) and intercept, including appropriate units.

A graph is often the best method of presenting and analysing data. It shows the relationship between the **independent variable** plotted on the horizontal axis and the **dependent variable** on the vertical axis and gives an indication of the reliability of the measurements.

The independent variable is the *cause* and is plotted on the horizontal axis. The dependent variable is the *effect* and is plotted on the vertical axis.

Plotting graphs

When you draw a graph you should:

- Give the graph a title.
- Label the axes with both quantities and units.
- Use the available space as effectively as possible.
- Use sensible linear scales – there should be no uneven jumps.
- Plot all the points correctly.
- A line of best fit should be drawn smoothly and clearly. It does not have to go through all the points but should show the overall trend.
- Identify any points which do not agree with the general trend.
- Think carefully about the inclusion of the origin. The point (0, 0) can be the most accurate data point or it can be irrelevant.

The 'best-fit' straight line

In many cases the best procedure is to find a way of plotting the data to produce a straight line. The 'best-fit' line passes as near to as many of the points as possible. For example, a straight line through the origin is the most appropriate way to join the set of points in Figure 11.3.

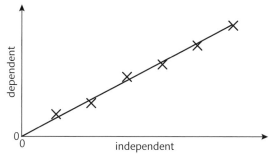

Figure 11.3 A straight-line graph which passes through the origin shows that the dependent variable is proportional to the independent variable.

The best-fit line does not necessarily pass through any of the points plotted. Sometimes a line has to be extended beyond the range of measurements of the graph. This is called **extrapolation**. Absolute zero, for example, can be found by extrapolating the volume/temperature graph for an ideal gas (Figure 11.4).

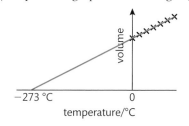

Figure 11.4 The straight line can be extrapolated to lower temperatures to find a value for absolute zero.

357

The process of assuming that the trend line applies between two points is called **interpolation**.

Two properties of a straight line are particularly useful: the gradient and the intercept.

Finding the gradient of a straight line or curve

The equation for a straight line is $y = mx + c$.

- x is the independent variable
- y is the dependent variable
- m is the gradient
- c is the intercept on the vertical axis.

The gradient of a straight line (m) is the increase in the dependent variable divided by the increase in the independent variable.

This can be expressed as

$$m = \frac{\Delta y}{\Delta x}$$

The triangle used to calculate the gradient should be as large as possible (Figure 11.5).

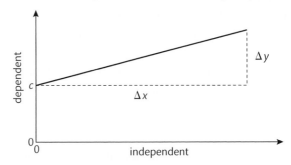

Figure 11.5 The gradient (m) can be calculated from the graph. $m = \Delta y/\Delta x$.

The gradient of a straight line has units; the units of the vertical axis divided by the units of the horizontal axis.

The gradient of a curve at any point is the gradient of the tangent to the curve at that point (Figure 11.6).

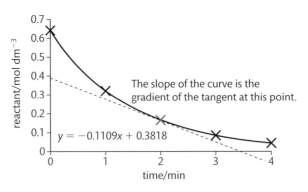

The slope of the curve is the gradient of the tangent at this point.

$y = -0.1109x + 0.3818$

Figure 11.6 This graph shows how the concentration of a reactant decreases with time. The gradient of a slope is given by the gradient of the tangent at that point. The equation of the tangent was calculated by computer software. The rate at the point shown is -0.11 mol dm^{-3} min^{-1}. The negative value shows that reactant concentration is decreasing with increasing time.

Errors and graphs

Systematic errors and random uncertainties can often be recognized from a graph (Figure 11.7). A graph combines the results of many measurements and so minimizes the effects of random uncertainties in the measurements.

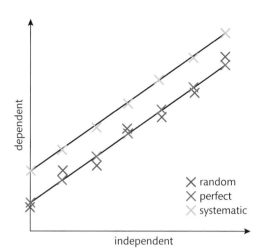

Figure 11.7 A systematic error produces a displaced straight line. Random uncertainties lead to points on both sides of the perfect straight line.

The presence of an outlier also suggests that some of the data are unreliable.

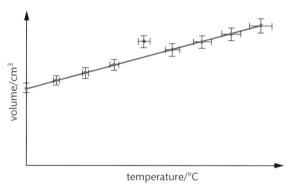

Figure 11.8 A graph showing an outlier which does not fit the line.

Choosing what to plot to produce a straight line

Sometimes the data need to be processed in order to produce a straight line.

For example, when the relationship between the pressure and volume of a gas is investigated, the ideal gas equation $PV = nRT$ can be rearranged to give a straight line graph when P is plotted against $1/V$:

$$P = nRT\frac{1}{V}$$

The pressure is **inversely proportional** to the volume. This relationship is clearly seen when a graph of $1/V$ against P gives a straight line passing through the origin at constant temperature (Figure 11.9).

 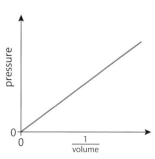

TOK We often dismiss results which don't fit the expected pattern because of experimental error. When are you justified in dismissing a data point which does not fit the general pattern?

TOK Data can be presented in a variety of graphical formats. How does the presentation of the data affect the way the data are interpreted?

Figure 11.9 The pressure of a gas is inversely proportional to the volume. A graph of P against $1/V$ produces a straight line through the origin.

Sketched graphs are used to show qualitative trends

Many of the graphs shown in this chapter, such as Figure 11.9, have labelled but unscaled axes. These are called sketched graphs, and are generally used to show qualitative trends, such as when variables are proportional or inversely proportional.

Drawn graphs used to present experimental data must have labelled and scaled axes if they are going to be used to display quantitative measurements.

Using spreadsheets to plot graphs

There are many software packages which allow graphs to be plotted and analysed; the equation of the best-fit line can be found, and other properties calculated. For example, the tangent to the curve in Figure 11.6 has the equation:

$$y = -0.1109x + 0.3818$$

so the gradient of the tangent at that point = -0.11 mol dm^{-3} min^{-1}

The closeness of the generated line to the data points is indicated by the R^2 value. An R^2 of 1 represents a perfect fit between the data and the line drawn through them, and a value of 0 shows there is no correlation.

Care should, however, be taken when using these packages, as is shown by Figure 11.10.

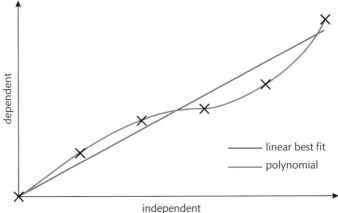

linear best fit

polynomial

Figure 11.10 An equation which produces a 'perfect fit' is not necessarily the best description of the relationship between the variables.

The set of data points in Figure 11.10 can either be joined by a best-fit straight line which does not pass through any point except the origin:

$$y = 1.6255x \ (R^2 = 0.9527)$$

or a polynomial which gives a perfect fit as indicated by the R^2 value of 1:

$$y = -0.0183x^5 + 0.2667x^4 - 1.2083x^3 + 1.7333x^2 + 1.4267x \ (R^2 = 1)$$

The polynomial equation is unlikely, however, to be physically significant. Any series of random points can fit a polynomial of sufficient length, just as any two points define a straight line.

An infinite number of patterns can be found to fit the same experimental data. What criteria do we use in selecting the correct pattern?

CHALLENGE YOURSELF

The closeness of the generated line to the data points is indicated by the R^2 value. R is a correlation function computed from the formula:

$$R = \frac{\Sigma(Y_1 n - Y_1^{av})(Y_2 n_{calc} - Y_2^{av})}{\sqrt{\Sigma(Y_1 n - Y_1^{av})^2\,\Sigma(Y_2 m_c - Y_2^{av})^2}}$$

with the sum over all the data points.

$Y_1 n$ is the vertical coordinate of an individual data point value, and $Y_2 n$ the value calculated from the x coordinate using the best-fit function. Y^{av} is the average of Y values.

R can be used to measure the correlation between two sets of data points.

1 Show that $R = 1$ for this set of data:

Y_1	1	2	3	4	5
Y_2	1	2	3	4	5

2 Show that $R = -1$ for this set of data:

Y_1	1	2	3	4	5
Y_2	5	4	3	2	1

3 Calculate R for this set of data:

Y_1	1	2	3	4	5
Y_2	1	5	3	4	2

NATURE OF SCIENCE

The ideas of correlation and causation are very important in science. A correlation, often displayed graphically, is a statistical link or association between one variable and another. It can be positive or negative and a correlation coefficient can be calculated that will have a value between +1, 0 and −1. A strong correlation (positive or negative) between one factor and another is a necessary but not sufficient condition for a causal relationship. More evidence is usually required. There needs to be a mechanism to explain the link between the variables. There is, for example, a negative correlation between the concentration of chlorine monoxide and the concentration of ozone in the atmosphere over the Antarctic (Figure 11.11). Ozone levels are high at latitudes with low chlorine monoxide levels and low at latitudes with high chlorine monoxide levels, but the causal relationship can only be confirmed if a mechanism is provided to explain the causal relationship.

One distinguishing factor between the 'harder' physical sciences and the 'softer' human sciences is that the former is concerned with simpler causal relationships. It is simpler to explain an increase in the rate of reaction than an increase in the annual rate of unemployment, as only a limited number of factors affect the former but many variables need to be considered when explaining the latter.

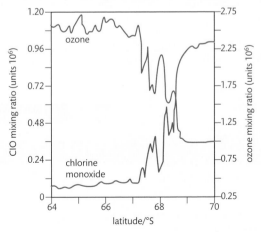

Figure 11.11 A plot of chlorine monoxide and ozone concentrations over the Antarctic.

Exercises

22 The volume V, pressure P, temperature T, and number of moles of an ideal gas n are related by the ideal gas equation: $PV = nRT$. If the relationship between pressure and volume at constant temperature of a fixed amount of gas is investigated experimentally, which one of the following plots would produce a linear graph?

A P against V

B P against $\dfrac{1}{V}$

C $\dfrac{1}{P}$ against $\dfrac{1}{V}$

D no plot can produce a straight line

23 The volume and mass of different objects made from the same element, X, are measured independently. A graph of mass against volume, with error bars, is displayed.

The literature values of the density of some elements are shown.

Element	Density / g cm⁻³
aluminium	2.70
iron	7.86
copper	8.92
zinc	7.14

These experimental results suggest:

	Identity of X	Systematic errors	Random errors
A	aluminium	significant	not significant
B	aluminium	not significant	significant
C	inconclusive	not significant	not significant
D	inconclusive	significant	significant

24 In an experiment to measure the pH of distilled water at 25 °C the following results were obtained.

Sample	pH
1	6.69
2	6.70
3	6.69
4	6.68
5	6.70

The results are

A accurate and precise
B inaccurate but precise
C accurate but imprecise
D inaccurate and imprecise

25 The amount of light absorbed by atoms at a characteristic wavelength can be used to measure the concentration of the element in a sample. A sample of sea water was analysed along with six standard solutions. Determine the concentration of chromium in the sea water by plotting a graph of the data.

Chromium concentration/ μg dm^{-3}	Absorbance at λ = 358 nm
1.00	0.062
2.00	0.121
3.00	0.193
4.00	0.275
5.00	0.323
6.00	0.376
sample	0.215

11.3 Spectroscopic identification of organic compounds

Understandings:

- The degree of unsaturation or index of hydrogen deficiency (IHD) can be used to determine from a molecular formula the number of rings or multiple bonds in a molecule.
- Mass spectrometry (MS), proton nuclear magnetic resonance spectroscopy (^{1}H NMR), and infrared spectroscopy (IR) are techniques that can be used to help identify and to determine the structure of compounds.

Guidance

- The electromagnetic spectrum (EMS) is given in the IB data booklet in section 3. The regions employed for each technique should be understood.
- The operating principles are not required for any of these methods.

Applications and skills:

- Determination of the IHD from a molecular formula.
- Deduction of information about the structural features of a compound from percentage composition data, MS, ^{1}H NMR, or IR.

Guidance

The IB data booklet contains characteristic ranges for IR absorptions (section 26), ^{1}H NMR data (section 27), specific MS fragments (section 28), and the formula to determine IHD. For ^{1}H NMR, only the ability to deduce the number of different hydrogen (proton) environments and the relative numbers of hydrogen atoms in each environment is required. Integration traces should be covered but splitting patterns are not required.

Analytical techniques

Chemical analysts identify and characterize unknown substances, determine the composition of a mixture, and identify impurities. Their work can be divided into three types of analysis:

- **qualitative analysis**: the detection of the *presence* but not the quantity of a substance in a mixture; for example, forbidden substances in an athlete's blood;
- **quantitative analysis**: the measurement of the *quantity* of a particular substance in a mixture; for example, the alcohol levels in a driver's breath;

Using spectra to confirm the structure of a compound

Full details of how to carry out this experiment with a worksheet are available on your eBook.

• **structural analysis**: a description of how the atoms are arranged in molecular structures; for example, the determination of the structure of a naturally occurring or artificial product.

Many instruments are available to provide structural analysis but they generally work by analysing the effect of different forms of energy on the substance analysed.

• **Infrared spectroscopy** is used to identify the bonds in a molecule.
• **Mass spectrometry** is used to determine relative atomic and molecular masses. The fragmentation pattern can be used as a fingerprint technique to identify unknown substances or for evidence for the arrangements of atoms in a molecule.
• **Nuclear magnetic resonance spectroscopy** is used to show the chemical environment of certain isotopes (hydrogen, carbon, phosphorus, and fluorine) in a molecule and so gives vital structural information.

No one method is definitive, but a combination of techniques can provide strong evidence for the structure.

A mass spectrometer. The molecules are ionized and accelerated towards a detector. The sensor array can be seen through the round window (lower left).

Mass spectrometry

Determining the molecular mass of a compound

The mass spectrometer was introduced in Chapter 2 where we saw it was used to find the mass of individual atoms and the relative abundances of different isotopes. The instrument can be used in a similar way to find the relative molecular mass of a compound. If the empirical formula is also known from compositional analysis, the molecular formula can be determined. The technique also provides useful clues about the molecular structure.

Fragmentation patterns

The ionization process in the mass spectrometer involves an electron from an electron gun hitting the incident species and removing an electron:

$$X(g) + e^- \rightarrow X^+(g) + 2e^-$$

The molecular ion or parent ion is formed when a molecule loses one electron but otherwise remains unchanged.

The collision can be so energetic that it causes the molecule to break up into different fragments. The largest mass peak in the mass spectrum corresponds to a parent ion passing through the instrument unscathed, but other ions, produced as a result of this break up, are also detected.

The **fragmentation pattern** can provide useful evidence for the structure of the compound. A chemist pieces together the fragments to form a picture of the complete molecule, in the same way that archaeologists find clues about the past from the pieces of artefacts discovered in the ground.

Consider Figure 11.12, which shows the mass spectrum of ethanol.

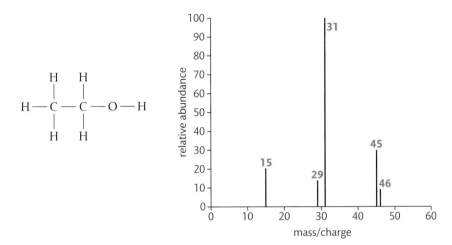

Figure 11.12 The structure of ethanol and its mass spectrum.

The molecular ion corresponds to the peak at 46. The ion that appears at a relative mass of 45, one less than the parent ion, corresponds to the loss of a hydrogen atom.

Figure 11.13 shows fragmentation paths that explain the rest of the spectrum.

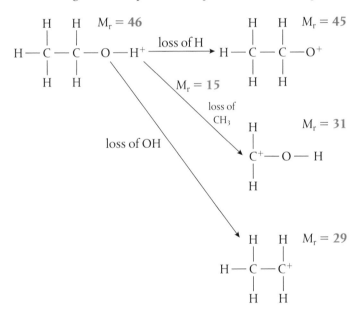

Figure 11.13 Possible fragmentation pattern produced when ethanol is bombarded with high energy electrons.

The parent ion can break up into smaller ions in a mass spectrometer. A compound is characterized by this fragmentation pattern.

For each fragmentation, one of the products keeps the positive charge. So, for example, if the C–C bond breaks in an ethanol molecule, two outcomes are possible, as seen in Figure 11.14.

$$C_2H_5OH^+ \nearrow CH_3 + CH_2OH^+ \quad 31$$
$$\searrow CH_3^+ + CH_2OH \quad 15$$

Figure 11.14 Two possible ways in which the C–C bond can break in ethanol. Only the charged species can be detected, as electric and magnetic fields have no effect on neutral fragments.

The fragmentation shown in Figure 11.14 explains the presence of peaks at both 15 and 31. Generally the fragment that gives the most stable ion is formed.

The cleavage of the C–O bond leads to the formation of the $C_2H_5^+$ ion in preference to the OH^+ ion in the example above, so there is an observed peak at 29 but not at 17.

Full analysis of a mass spectrum can be a complex process. We make use of the mass difference between the peaks to identify the pieces which have fallen off. You are expected to recognize the mass fragments shown below. You are not expected to memorize the details as the data are given in section 28 of the IB data booklet.

Mass lost	Fragment lost
15	$CH_3\cdot$
17	$OH\cdot$
18	H_2O
28	$CH_2{=}CH_2$, $C{=}O\cdot$
29	$CH_3CH_2\cdot$, $CHO\cdot$
31	$CH_3O\cdot$
45	$COOH\cdot$

Don't forget to include the positive charge on the ions detected by the mass spectrometer when identifying different fragments.

Worked example

A molecule with an empirical formula CH_2O has the simplified mass spectrum below. Deduce the molecular formula and possible structure of the compound.

Solution

empirical formula = CH_2O; molecular formula = $C_nH_{2n}O_n$

We can see that the parent ion has a relative mass of 60.

$M_r = n(12.01) + 2n(1.01) + n(16.00) = 30.03n$

$n = \dfrac{60}{30.03} = 2$

molecular formula = $C_2H_4O_2$

From the spectrum we can identify the following peaks:

Peaks	Explanation
15 (60 – 45)	presence of CH_3^+ loss of COOH from molecule
43 (60 – 17)	presence of $C_2H_3O^+$ loss of OH from molecule
45 (60 – 15)	presence of $COOH^+$ loss of CH_3 from molecule

The structure consistent with this fragmentation pattern is:

Exercises

26 The mass spectrum shown below was produced by a compound with the formula $C_nH_{2n}O$.

Which ions are detected in the mass spectrometer?

I $C_2H_3O^+$
II $C_3H_5O^+$
III $C_4H_8O^{2+}$

  A I and II only   **B** I and III only   **C** II and III only   **D** I, II, and III

27 While working on an organic synthesis, a student isolated a compound X, which they then analysed with a mass spectrometer.

Identify X from the mass spectrum shown.

  A $CH_3CH_2CH_3$ **B** $C_3H_7CO_2H$ **C** $C_2H_5CO_2CH_3$ **D** $(CH_3)_2CHCO_2H$

28 The mass spectra of two compounds are shown below. One is propanone (CH_3COCH_3) and the other is propanal (CH_3CH_2CHO). Identify the compound in each case and explain the similarities and differences between the two spectra.

29 The simplified mass spectrum of a compound with empirical formula C_2H_5 is shown below.

(a) Explain which ions give rise to the peaks shown.

(b) Deduce the molecular structure of the compound.

The degree of unsaturation/IHD

The **degree of unsaturation** or **index of hydrogen deficiency (IHD)** provides a useful clue to the structure of a molecule once its formula is known. It is a measure of how many molecules of H_2 would be needed in theory to convert the molecule to the corresponding saturated, non-cyclic molecule. Cyclohexane and hex-1-ene, for example, have the same molecular formula (C_6H_{12}) and so have the same degree of unsaturation and IHD. One molecule of hydrogen is needed to convert them to the saturated alkane hexane (C_6H_{14}). Similarly ethene, with a double bond, has an IHD of 1 whereas the more unsaturated ethyne, with a triple bond, has an IHD of 2.

The IHD values of a selection of molecules are tabulated below.

Molecule	Saturated non-cyclic target	Index of hydrogen deficiency (IHD)
C_2H_4	C_2H_6	1
C_2H_2	C_2H_6	2
cyclobutane and but-1-ene, C_4H_8	C_4H_{10}	1
C_2H_5OH	C_2H_5OH	0
C_2H_4O	C_2H_6O	1
C_2H_5Cl	C_2H_5Cl	0

Exercise

30 Deduce the IHD of the following by copying and completing the table below.

Molecule	Corresponding saturated non-cyclic molecule	IHD
C_6H_6		
CH_3COCH_3		
$C_7H_6O_2$		
C_2H_3Cl		
C_4H_9N		
$C_6H_{12}O_6$		

CHALLENGE YOURSELF

4 Show that the IHD of a molecule with the molecular formula $C_nH_pO_qN_rX_s$ is given by the general formula:

$$IHD = \frac{1}{2} \times [2n + 2 - p - s + r]$$

Explain why q, the number of oxygen atoms, doesn't appear in the general formula?

Different regions of the electromagnetic spectrum give different information about the structure of organic molecules

Spectroscopy is the main method we have of probing into the atom and the molecule. There is a type of spectroscopy for each of the main regions of the electromagnetic spectrum. As discussed in Chapter 2 (page 70), electromagnetic radiation is a form of energy transferred by waves and characterized by its:

- **wavelength** (λ): the distance between successive crests or troughs;
- **frequency** (ν): the number of waves which pass a point every second.

The electromagnetic spectrum can be found in section 3 of the IB data booklet. Typical wavelengths and frequencies for each region of the spectrum are summarized in the table below.

- The distance between two successive crests (or troughs) is called the wavelength.
- The frequency of the wave is the number of waves which pass a point in one second.

For electromagnetic waves, the wavelength and frequency are related by the equation

$$c = \nu\lambda$$

where c is the speed of light.

TOK The physical analytical techniques now available to us are due to advances in technology. How does technology extend and modify the capabilities of our senses? What are the knowledge implications of this?

Type of electromagnetic radiation	Typical frequency $(\nu)/s^{-1}$	Typical wavelength $(\lambda)/m$
radio waves (low energy)	3×10^6	10^2
microwaves	3×10^{10}	10^{-2}
infrared	3×10^{12}	10^{-4}
visible	3×10^{15}	10^{-7}
ultraviolet	3×10^{16}	10^{-8}
X rays	3×10^{18}	10^{-10}
gamma rays	greater than 3×10^{22}	less than 10^{-14}

It should be noted from the table that $\nu \times \lambda = 3.0 \times 10^8$ m s^{-1} = c, the speed of light. This gives $\nu = c/\lambda$.

In infrared spectroscopy, the frequency of radiation is often measured as number of waves per centimetre (cm^{-1}), also called the **wavenumber**.

Microwave cookers heat food very quickly as the radiation penetrates deep into the food. The frequency used corresponds to the energy needed to rotate water molecules, which are present in most food. The radiation absorbed by the water molecules makes them rotate faster. As they bump into other molecules the extra energy is spread throughout the food and the temperature rises.

As well as transferring energy, the electromagnetic radiation can also be viewed as a carrier of information. Different regions give different types of information, by interacting with substances in different ways.

- **Radio waves** can be absorbed by certain nuclei, causing them to reverse their spin. They are used in NMR and can give information about the environment of certain atoms.
- **Microwaves** cause molecules to increase their rotational energy. This can give information about bond lengths. It is not necessary to know the details at this level.
- **Infrared radiation** is absorbed by certain bonds causing them to stretch or bend. This gives information about the bonds in a molecule.
- **Visible light** and **ultraviolet light** can produce electronic transitions and give information about the electronic energy levels within the atom or molecule.

CHALLENGE YOURSELF

5 Calculate the energy of a photon of visible light with a frequency of 3.0×10^{14} s^{-1}. Express your answer in kJ mol^{-1}.

Infrared (IR) spectroscopy

The natural frequency of a chemical bond

A chemical bond can be thought of as a spring. Each bond vibrates and bends at a natural frequency which depends on the bond strength and the masses of the atoms. Light atoms, for example, vibrate at higher frequencies than heavier atoms and multiple bonds vibrate at higher frequencies than single bonds.

Simple diatomic molecules such as HCl, HBr, and HI, can only vibrate when the bond stretches (Figure 11.15a). The HCl bond has the highest frequency of these three as it has the largest bond energy and the halogen atom with the smallest relative atomic mass.

Figure 11.15 IR radiation can cause a bond to stretch or bend.

In more complex molecules, different types of vibration can occur, such as bending, so that a complex range of frequencies is present (Figure 11.15b).

Using infrared radiation to excite molecules

The energy needed to excite the bonds in a molecule and so make them vibrate with greater amplitude, occurs in the IR region (Figure 11.16). A bond will only interact with the electromagnetic infrared radiation, however, if it is polar. The presence of separate areas of partial positive and negative charge in a molecule allows the electric field component of the electromagnetic wave to excite the vibrational energy of the molecule. The change in the vibrational energy produces a corresponding change in the dipole moment of the molecule. The intensity of the absorptions depends on the polarity of the bond. Symmetrical non-polar bonds in N≡N and O=O do not absorb radiation, as they cannot interact with an electric field.

frequency ranges

| 1.20×10^{14} s^{-1} | 7.50×10^{13} s^{-1} | 5.70×10^{13} s^{-1} | 4.50×10^{13} s^{-1} | 1.95×10^{13} s^{-1} |

C—H O—H N—H single bond to H stretches	C≡C C≡N triple bond stretches	C=C C=O double bond stretches	fingerprint region (see page 372)

| 4000 cm^{-1} | 2500 cm^{-1} | 1900 cm^{-1} | 1500 cm^{-1} | 650 cm^{-1} |

wavenumber ranges

Stretching and bending in a polyatomic molecule

In a polyatomic molecule such as water, it is more correct to consider the molecule stretching and bending as a whole, rather than considering the individual bonds. Water, for example, can vibrate at three fundamental frequencies as shown in Figure 11.17. As each of the three modes of vibration results in a change in dipole of the molecule, they can be detected with IR spectroscopy.

symmetric stretch ≈ 3650 cm^{-1}	asymmetric stretch ≈ 3760 cm^{-1}	symmetric bend ≈ 1600 cm^{-1}

Figure 11.17 The three vibrational modes of the water molecule are all IR active as they each produce a change in the dipole moment of the molecule.

For a symmetrical linear molecule such as carbon dioxide, there are four modes of vibration (Figure 11.18). However, the symmetric stretch is IR inactive as it produces no change in dipole moment. The dipoles of both C=O bonds are equal and opposite throughout the vibration.

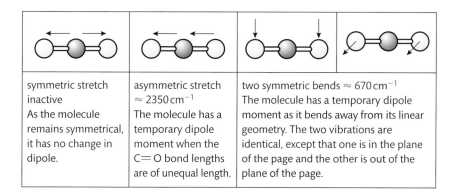

symmetric stretch inactive As the molecule remains symmetrical, it has no change in dipole.	asymmetric stretch ≈ 2350 cm^{-1} The molecule has a temporary dipole moment when the C=O bond lengths are of unequal length.	two symmetric bends ≈ 670 cm^{-1} The molecule has a temporary dipole moment as it bends away from its linear geometry. The two vibrations are identical, except that one is in the plane of the page and the other is out of the plane of the page.

Figure 11.18 Three of the vibrational modes of the carbon dioxide molecule are IR active. The symmetric stretch produces no change in dipole and so is IR inactive.

Matching wavenumbers with bonds

The absorption of particular wavenumbers of IR radiation helps the chemist identify the bonds in a molecule. The precise position of the absorption depends on the environment of the bond, so a range of wavenumbers is used to identify different bonds. Characteristic infrared absorption bands are shown in the table on page 372.

You are not expected to remember the characteristic wavenumbers. A more complete list is given in section 26 of the IB data booklet.

Bond	Wavenumber / cm⁻¹	Intensity
C–O	1050–1410	strong
C=C	1620–1680	medium–weak; multiple bands
C=O	1700–1750	strong
C≡C	2100–2260	variable
O–H, hydrogen bonded in carboxylic acids	2500–3000	strong, very broad
C–H	2850–3090	strong
O–H, hydrogen bonded in alcohols and phenols	3200–3600	strong
N–H	3300–3500	strong

Some bonds can also be identified by the distinctive shapes of their signals: for example, the O–H bond gives a broad signal and the C=O bond gives a sharp signal.

Exercises

31 Which of the following types of bond is expected to absorb IR radiation of the longest wavelength?

	Bond order	Mass of atoms bonded together
A	1	small
B	1	large
C	2	small
D	2	large

32 The infrared spectrum was obtained from a compound and showed absorptions at 2100 cm⁻¹, 1700 cm⁻¹, and 1200 cm⁻¹. Identify the compound.

A CH_3COOCH_3 **B** C_6H_5COOH **C** $CH_2 = CHCH_2OH$ **D** $CH \equiv CCH_2CO_2CH_3$

33 A molecule absorbs IR at a wavenumber of 1720 cm⁻¹. Which functional group could account for this absorption?

I   aldehydes
II   esters
III ethers

A I only   **B** I and II   **C** I, II, and III   **D** none of the above

34 An unknown compound has the following mass composition: C, 40.0%; H, 6.7%; O, 53.3%. The largest mass recorded on the mass spectrum of the compound corresponds to a relative molecular mass of 60.

(a) Determine the empirical and molecular formula of the compound.
(b) Deduce the IHD of the compound.
(c) The IR spectrum shows an absorption band at 1700 cm⁻¹ and a very broad band between 2500 and 3300 cm⁻¹. Deduce the molecular structure of the compound.

35 Draw the structure of a sulfur dioxide molecule and identify its possible modes of vibration. Predict which of these is likely to absorb IR radiation.

Hydrogen bonds can be detected by a broadening of the absorptions. For example, hydrogen bonding between hydroxyl groups changes the O–H vibration; it makes the absorption much broader and shifts it to a lower frequency.

Molecules with several bonds can vibrate in many different ways and with many different frequencies. The complex pattern can be used as a 'fingerprint' to be matched against the recorded spectra of known compounds in a database (Figure 11.19). A comparison of the spectrum of a sample with that of a pure compound can also be used as a test of purity.

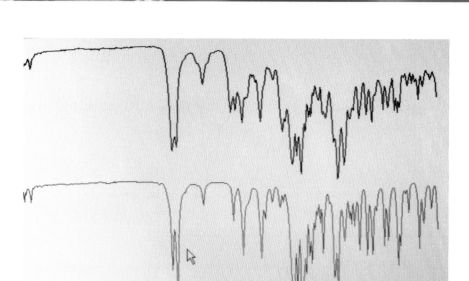

Figure 11.19 The IR spectrum of heroin (blue) compared with that of an unknown sample (black). The near-perfect match indicates that the sample contains a high percentage of heroin. Spectral analysis such as this can identify unknown compounds in mixtures or from samples taken from clothing or equipment. The technique is widely used in forensic science.

Consider the spectrum of propanone (Figure 11.20). The baseline at the top corresponds to 100% transmittance and the key features are the troughs which occur at the natural frequencies of the bonds present in the molecule.

Figure 11.20 The molecular structure and spectrum of propanone.

The absorption at just below 1800 cm^{-1} shows the presence of the C=O bond and the absorption near 3000 cm^{-1} is due to the presence of the C–H bond. The more polar C=O bond produces the more intense absorption.

The presence of the C–H bond can again be seen near 3000 cm^{-1} in the spectrum of ethanol (Figure 11.21). The broad peak at just below 3400 cm^{-1} shows the presence of hydrogen bonding which is due to the hydroxyl (OH) group.

NATURE OF SCIENCE

Scientists use models to clarify certain features and relationships that are not directly observable. These models can become more and more sophisticated but they can never become the real thing. Models are just a representation of reality. The IR spectra of organic molecules for example are based on the bond vibration model, in which the covalent bond between two atoms is compared to a spring, with its natural frequency depending on the bond strength and the masses of an atom in the same way that the natural frequency of a spring depends on its stiffness and mass. We often use our everyday experiences to help us construct models to understand processes that are occurring on a scale beyond our experience. This is the strength of such models as it helps understanding; the same mass/spring model can be used to explain a float bobbing up and down in water for example. However, models also have limitation.

Scientists often take a complex problem and reduce it to a simpler, more manageable one that can be treated mathematically. We should not forget that the bond vibration model is a simplification – albeit an effective one. It is molecules, and not individual bonds, that are vibrating, as we saw in the examples of water and carbon dioxide (page 371).

Exercises

36 Identify the bonds which will produce strong absorptions in the IR region of the electromagnetic spectrum.

I   C–O
II C=C
III C=O

A I and II only   **B** I and III only   **C** II and III only   **D** I, II, and III

37 State what occurs at the molecular level when infrared radiation is absorbed.

38 Cyclohexane and hex-1-ene are isomers. Suggest how you could use infrared spectroscopy to distinguish between the two compounds.

39 The intoximeter, used by the police to test the alcohol levels in the breath of drivers, measures the absorbance at 2900 cm^{-1}. Identify the bond which causes ethanol to absorb at this wavenumber.

40 A molecule has the molecular formula C_2H_6O. The infrared spectrum shows an absorption band at 1000–1300 cm^{-1}, but no absorption bands above 3000 cm^{-1}. Deduce its structure.

CHALLENGE YOURSELF

6 A bond has an IR absorption of 2100 cm^{-1}. Calculate the wavelength of the radiation and the natural frequency of the bond.

The Spectra Database for Organic Compounds was opened in 1997 and has given the public free access to the spectra of many organic compounds. The total accumulated number of visits reached 350 million at the end of February 2011, and the database has sent information from Japan to all over the world. The open exchange of information is a key element of scientific progress.

Nuclear magnetic resonance (NMR) spectroscopy

The principles of NMR

Nuclear magnetic resonance spectroscopy, a powerful technique for finding the structure and shape of molecules, depends on a combination of nuclear physics and chemistry. The nuclei of atoms with an odd number of protons such as ^1H, ^{13}C, ^{19}F, and ^{31}P, spin and behave like tiny bar magnets. If placed in an external magnetic field, some of these nuclei will line up with an applied field and, if they have sufficient energy, some will line up against it (Figure 11.22). This arrangement leads to two nuclear energy levels; the energy needed for the nuclei to reverse their spin and change their orientation in a magnetic field can be provided by radio waves.

Screen display of a nuclear magnetic resonance spectrum. In the background, a scientist is seen loading a sample into the NMR spectrometer's magnet.

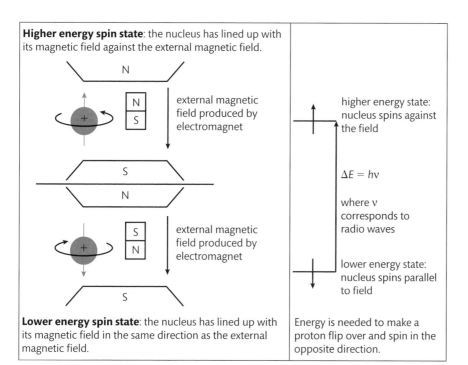

Higher energy spin state: the nucleus has lined up with its magnetic field against the external magnetic field.

external magnetic field produced by electromagnet

external magnetic field produced by electromagnet

Lower energy spin state: the nucleus has lined up with its magnetic field in the same direction as the external magnetic field.

higher energy state: nucleus spins against the field

$\Delta E = h\nu$

where ν corresponds to radio waves

lower energy state: nucleus spins parallel to field

Energy is needed to make a proton flip over and spin in the opposite direction.

Figure 11.22 A spinning nucleus can be thought of as a small bar magnet. The energy between the two states depends on the strength of the external magnetic field (applied by an electromagnet) and the chemical environment of the nucleus.

In practice, a sample is placed in an electromagnet. The field strength is varied until the radio waves have the exact frequency needed to make the nuclei flip over and spin in the opposite direction. This is called **resonance** and can be detected electronically and recorded in the form of a spectrum (Figure 11.23).

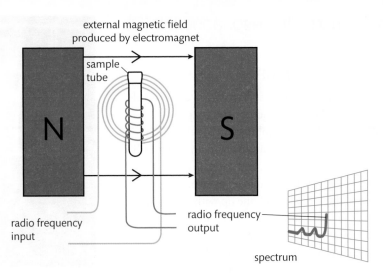

NMR spectroscopy is non-invasive as the small quantities of the sample are recovered unchanged after the experiment.

Hydrogen nuclei in different chemical environments have different chemical shifts

As electrons shield the nucleus from the full effects of the external magnetic field, differences in electron distribution produce different energy separations between the two spin energy levels. The technique is a very useful analytical tool, as nuclei in different **chemical environments** produce different signals in the spectrum. Proton or ^{1}H NMR is particularly useful. The hydrogen nuclei, present in all organic molecules, effectively act as spies and give information about their position in a molecule.

The signals are measured against the standard signal produced by the 12 hydrogen nuclei in tetramethylsilane (TMS), the structure of which is shown in Figure 11.24.

$$CH_3 - Si - CH_3$$
with CH_3 above and CH_3 below the Si

The position of the NMR signal relative to this standard is called the **chemical shift** of the proton. Hydrogen nuclei in particular environments have characteristic chemical shifts. Some examples are given in the table below. A more complete list is given in section 27 of the IB data booklet.

Type of proton	Chemical shift / ppm
TMS	0
$-CH_3$	0.9–1.0
$RO-C(=O)-CH_2-$	2.0–2.5

Type of proton	Chemical shift / ppm
(R—C(=O)—CH₂—)	2.2–2.7
—C≡C—H	1.8–3.1
R—O—CH₂—	3.3–3.7
(R—C(=O)—O—CH₂—)	3.7–4.8
(R—C(=O)—O—H)	9.0–13.0*
R—O—H	1.0–6.0*
—HC=CH₂	4.5–6.0
(aromatic ring)—OH	4.0–12.0*
(aromatic ring)—H	6.9–9.0
(R—C(=O)—H)	9.4–10.0

* Signals from the hydrogen atoms in the —OH groups are very variable owing to hydrogen bonding.

Interpreting ¹H NMR spectra

The ¹H NMR spectrum of ethanal is shown in Figure 11.25.

Figure 11.25 The ¹H NMR spectrum of ethanal shows two peaks because the hydrogen atoms are in two different environments. The **integrated trace** indicates the relative number of hydrogen atoms in the two environments.

The spectrum trace has a peak at 9.7, which corresponds to the CHO proton and a peak at 2.1 which corresponds to the three protons in the CH₃ group. The area under the CH_3 peak is three times larger than that under the CHO peak as it indicates the relative number of protons in each environment. The integrated trace gives this information more directly, as it goes up in steps which are proportional to the number of protons.

Worked example

The NMR spectrum of a compound which has the molecular formula C_3H_8O is shown here.

(a) Draw the full structural formulas and give the names of the three possible isomers of C_3H_8O.

(b) Identify the substance responsible for the peak at 0 ppm and state its purpose.

(c) Identify the unknown compound from the number of peaks in the spectrum.

(d) Identify the group responsible for the signal at 0.9 ppm.

Solution

(a) The structures and names are:

propan-1-ol

propan-2-ol

methoxyethane

(b) Tetramethylsilane is used as a reference standard.

(c) For each structure, I–IV identifies the different environments of the H atoms in the molecule. 1–3 represents the number of atoms in each environment. There are four peaks in the spectrum. Propan-1-ol has four peaks with the correct areas.

(d) The peak at 0.9 ppm corresponds to the CH_3 group.

Exercises

41 The ^1H NMR spectrum of a compound exhibits three major peaks and the splitting patterns below.

Chemical shift / ppm	Peak area
1.0	3
2.0	3
2.3	2

Identify the compound.

A $CH_3CH_2CH_3$ **B** CH_3CH_2CHO **C** $CH_3CH_2COCH_3$ **D** $CH_3CH_2CH_2CH_2CH_3$

42 The low resolution ^1H NMR spectrum of a fuel Y is shown.

chemical shift

Identify Y.

A CH_3OH **B** C_2H_6 **C** C_2H_5OH **D** CH_3OCH_3

43 How many peaks will the following compounds show in their ^1H NMR spectra?

(a) $CH_3-\overset{\overset{\displaystyle O}{\|}}{C}-O-CH_3$

(b) CH_3-O-CH_3

(c) $CH_3-\overset{\overset{\displaystyle CH_3}{|}}{\underset{\underset{\displaystyle CH_3}{|}}{C}}-CH_3$

(d) $CH_3-\overset{\overset{\displaystyle CH_3}{|}}{\underset{\underset{\displaystyle Cl}{|}}{C}}-H$

44 Describe and explain the ^1H NMR spectrum of CH_3CH_2OH.

NATURE OF SCIENCE

The use of IR and radio wave technology has allowed us to gain information about individual molecules which was previously thought to be unattainable. Technology originally emerged before science, but new technologies drive developments in science. Evidence can now be obtained using instrumentation which gathers information beyond the normal range of human sense perception. Improvement in mass spectrometry, nuclear magnetic resonance, and infrared spectroscopy have made identification and structural determination of compounds routine. We now understand what happens when a molecule vibrates and rotates and the flipping of a proton's spin can give us crucial information about what is happening within a human cell. In recent decades, the growth in computing power and sensor technology has allowed scientists to collect increasingly larger amounts of data which can be interpreted to give objective scientific evidence.

Analytical chemistry depends on combining information

The techniques discussed in this chapter provide the analytical chemist with different types of information. The skill of the analyst is to combine these methods to give a complete description of the structure of the substance being studied. For example, infrared spectroscopy gives some information about the bonds present in a molecule, but often this information needs to be supplemented with data from other sources to give a complete structure of the molecule.

Worked example

(a) An unknown compound is found to have the following composition:

	% composition by mass
C	85.6
H	14.4

Deduce the empirical formula of the compound.

(b) The mass spectrum of the compound is shown below. Deduce the molecular formula and the IHD of the compound.

(c) Is the molecule likely to contain a CH_3 group? Explain your answer.

(d) The infrared spectrum shows one absorption close to 2900 cm^{-1}, but there is no absorption close to 1600 cm^{-1}. State what can be deduced from this information.

(e) Deduce the molecular structure from the ^1H NMR spectrum shown.

Solution

(a) To find the empirical formula calculate the relative number of moles:

	C	H
mass / g	85.6	14.4
moles	$= \dfrac{85.6}{12.01}$ $= 7.13$	$= \dfrac{14.4}{1.01}$ $= 14.3$
simple ratio	$= \dfrac{7.13}{7.13}$ $= 1.00$	$= \dfrac{14.4}{7.13}$ $= 2.02$

The empirical formula is CH_2.

(b) The mass spectrum shows a parent ion at 84. The molecular formula is C_nH_{2n}.

$$n(12.01) + 2n(1.01) = 84$$
$$14.03n = 84$$
$$n = 84/14.03 = 5.99$$

The molecular formula is C_6H_{12}.

The saturated non-cyclic compound with six carbons is C_6H_{14}, so the IHD = 1. The molecule contains a C=C or a ring.

(c) The absence of peaks at 15 or 69 (84 − 15) suggests that the molecule probably does not contain a methyl group.

(d) The absorption close to 2900 cm^{-1} is due to the C–H bond.

The absence of an absorbance at 1600 cm^{-1} suggests that the molecule does not contain a C=C bond. It must, therefore, have a ring structure.

(e) The NMR spectra shows only one peak, so all the hydrogen atoms are in the same chemical environment. This confirms that the molecule has a ring structure. It is cyclohexane.

Practice questions

1 A burette reading is recorded as 27.70 ± 0.05 cm^3. Which of the following could be the actual value?

   I   27.68 cm^3

   II   27.78 cm^3

   III 27.74 cm^3

   A I and II only   **B** I and III only   **C** II and III only   **D** I, II, and III

2 A piece of metallic aluminium with a mass of 10.044 g was found to have a volume of 3.70 cm^3. A student carried out the following calculation to determine the density.

Density (g cm^{-3}) = $\dfrac{10.044}{3.70}$

What is the best value the student could report for the density of aluminium?

   A 2.715 g cm^{-3} **B** 2.7 g cm^{-3} **C** 2.71 g cm^{-3} **D** 2.7146 g cm^{-3}

3 Which experimental procedure is most likely to lead to a large systematic error?

   A Determining the concentration of an alkali by titration with a burette.

   B Measuring the volume of a solution using a volumetric pipette.

   C Determining the enthalpy change of neutralization in a beaker.

   D Measuring the volume of a gas produced with a gas syringe.

4 Which would be the best method to decrease the random uncertainty of a measurement in an acid–base titration?

   A repeat the titration

   B ensure your eye is at the same height as the meniscus when reading from the burette

C use a different burette

D use a different indicator for the titration

5 The ^{1}H NMR spectrum of X with molecular formula C_3H_6O is shown below.

^{1}H NMR spectrum for question 5.

(a) Deduce which of the following compounds is X and explain your answer.

A CH_3—CO—CH_3

B CH_3—CH_2—CHO

C CH_2=CH—CH_2OH (2)

(b) Deduce which one of the peaks in the ^{1}H NMR spectrum of X would also occur in the spectrum of one of the other isomers, giving your reasoning. (2)

(c) The infrared and mass spectra for X were also recorded.

  (i) Apart from absorptions due to C—C and C—H bonds, suggest one absorption, in wavenumbers, that would be present in the infrared spectrum. (1)

  (ii) Apart from absorptions due to C—C and C—H bonds, suggest one absorption, in wavenumbers, absent in this infrared spectrum but present in one of the other compounds shown in part (a). (1)

(d) Suggest the formulas and *m/z* values of two species that would be detected in the mass spectrum. (2)

(Total 8 marks)

6 Infrared spectroscopy is commonly used as an analytical technique by inorganic, physical, and organic chemists.

(a) Explain why hydrogen bromide is IR active whereas bromine is IR inactive. (1)

(b) The IR spectrum, mass spectrum, and ^{1}H NMR spectrum of an unknown compound, X, of molecular formula $C_5H_{10}O_2$, are as follows.

IR spectrum for question 6b.

Mass spectrum for question 6b.

¹H NMR spectrum for question 6b.

(i) In the IR spectrum, identify the bond responsible for each of the absorptions labelled I, II, and III. (3)

(ii) In the mass spectrum, deduce which fragments the m/z values at 102, 57, and 45 correspond to. (3)

(iii) Identify the peak at 11.5 ppm in the ^{1}H NMR spectrum. (1)

(iv) State what information can be obtained from the integration traces in the ^{1}H NMR spectrum about the hydrogen atoms responsible for the peak at 1.2 ppm. (1)

(v) Deduce the structure of X. (1)

(vi) $CH_3COOCH_2CH_2CH_3$ is an isomer of X. Deduce two differences between the ^{1}H NMR spectrum of this isomer and that of X. (2)

(*Total 12 marks*)

7 Infrared (IR) spectroscopy is widely used as a technique in analytical chemistry. Explain what happens at a molecular level during the absorption of IR radiation by carbon dioxide, CO_2. (3)

8 Compounds A and B are alcohols with the molecular formula C_3H_8O. The following information was obtained from a mass spectrum of each alcohol.

A: peaks at $m/z = 29, 31, 60$

B: peaks at $m/z = 45, 60$

(a) Deduce the formula of the species responsible for the peak at $m/z = 60$. (1)

(b) Deduce the formula of the species with $m/z = 31$. (1)

(c) Deduce the structure of each alcohol.

Structure of A

Structure of B (2)

(*Total 4 marks*)

9 The IR spectrum, mass spectrum, and ^1H NMR spectrum of an unknown compound, X, of molecular formula $C_3H_6O_2$ are as follows.

IR spectrum for question 9.

Mass spectrum for question 9.

^1H NMR spectrum for question 9.

(a) Identify the bonds responsible for the peaks A, B, and C in the IR spectrum of X. (2)

(b) In the mass spectrum of X, deduce which ions the m/z values at 74, 45, and 29 correspond to. (3)

(c) Identify the peak at 11.73 ppm in the ^1H NMR spectrum. (1)

(d) Deduce the structure of X. (1)

(Total 7 marks)

10 The infrared spectrum of a substance, X, with empirical formula C_3H_6O is given below.

IR spectrum for question 10.

(a) Explain why the structural formula of X cannot be:

(2)

(b) The ^{1}H NMR spectrum of X consists of three peaks. Deduce the structural formula of X and the relative areas under each peak. (2)

(Total 4 marks)

11 Butan-1-ol, butan-2-ol, 2-methylpropan-1-ol, and 2-methylpropan-2-ol are four structural isomers with the molecular formula $C_4H_{10}O$.

(a) Details of the ^{1}H NMR spectra of two of these alcohols are given below.

Spectrum 1

Two peaks: One at 1.3 ppm (relative to the TMS reference) with an integration trace of nine units, and the other at 2.0 ppm with an integration trace of one unit.

Spectrum 2

Four peaks: The first at 0.9 ppm with an integration trace of six units, the second at 1.7 ppm with an integration trace of one unit, the third at 2.1 ppm with an integration trace of one unit, and the fourth at 3.4 ppm with an integration trace of two units.

Consider the proton environments present in each of the alcohol molecules when answering the following questions.

(i) Identify which alcohol gives spectrum 1 and explain your answer by stating which hydrogen atoms in the molecule are responsible for each of the two peaks. (3)

(ii) Deduce which alcohol gives spectrum 2. Explain which particular hydrogen atoms in the molecule are responsible for the peaks at 0.9 ppm and 3.4 ppm. (3)

(b) The mass spectrum of one of the alcohols shows peaks at *m/z* values of 74, 59, and 45.

(i) Deduce which two of the alcohols could produce this spectrum and identify the species responsible for the three peaks. (4)

(ii) The spectrum also shows a significant peak at *m/z* = 31. Suggest which alcohol is responsible for this spectrum and deduce the species responsible for the peak at *m/z* = 31. (2)

(c) Explain why the infrared spectra of all four alcohols are very similar. (2)

(Total 14 marks)

 To access weblinks on the topics covered in this chapter, please go to www. pearsonhotlinks.com and enter the ISBN or title of this book.

12

Option A: Materials

Essential ideas

A.1 Materials science involves understanding the properties of a material, and then applying those properties to desired structures.

A.2 Metals can be extracted from their ores and alloyed for desired characteristics. ICP-MS/OES spectroscopy ionizes metals and uses mass and emission spectra for analysis.

A.3 Catalysts work by providing an alternate reaction pathway for the reaction. Catalysts always increase the rate of the reaction and are left unchanged at the end of the reaction.

A.4 Liquid crystals are fluids that have physical properties which are dependent on molecular orientation relative to some fixed axis in the material.

A.5 Polymers are made up of repeating monomer units which can be manipulated in various ways to give structures with desired properties.

A.6 Chemical techniques position atoms in molecules using chemical reactions whilst physical techniques allow atoms/molecules to be manipulated and positioned to specific requirements.

A.7 Although materials science generates many useful new products, there are challenges associated with recycling and high levels of toxicity of some of these materials.

Light micrograph of high carbon steel. It contains 0.65% carbon by mass alloyed with iron. It is very strong but brittle and is used for cutting tools, high-strength wires and springs.

One of the key roles of the chemist is to transform natural resources which are readily available into more useful materials. Civilizations are sometimes characterized by the technology they have developed to accomplish this. The Bronze Age, for example, marks the time when the ancients were able to produce copper from smelted ores. The extraction of iron from its ores in the blast furnace is probably one of the most significant developments in the Industrial Revolution of the 18th century. These technological advances, however, often came without a full understanding of the underlying scientific principles. Today chemists are able to use their understanding of the bonding and structure of materials to develop new substances with properties to serve modern needs. This chapter discusses the materials we have used to make our life more comfortable, and our understanding more complete. We outline the extraction and analysis of metals, the properties of different addition plastics and their impact on their environment, the use of catalysts in improving the effectiveness of our chemistry to bring about important changes more effectively and more selectively, and liquid crystals, superconductors, and nanoparticles, which are modern materials with interesting properties.

Computer graphic of a molecular tube. Nanotechnology, which has grown rapidly since the 1990s, involves the construction of such devices. It has been described as 'the science of the very small with big potential' and could revolutionize computing, medicine, and manufacturing. Each of the coloured spheres represents a single atom: carbon (blue), oxygen (red), and hydrogen (yellow).

Understandings:

- Materials are classified based on their uses, properties, or bonding and structure.
- The properties of a material based on the degree of covalent, ionic, or metallic character in a compound can be deduced from its position on a bonding triangle.
- Composites are mixtures in which materials are composed of two distinct phases, a reinforcing phase that is embedded in a matrix phase.

Guidance

- *Consider properties of metals, polymers, and ceramics in terms of metallic, covalent, and ionic bonding.*
- *See section 29 of the IB data booklet for a triangular bonding diagram.*

Applications and skills:

- Use of bond triangle diagrams for binary compounds from electronegativity data.
- Evaluation of various ways of classifying materials.
- Relating physical characteristics (melting point, permeability, conductivity, elasticity, brittleness) of a material to its bonding and structures (packing arrangements, electron mobility, ability of atoms to slide relative to one another).

Guidance

Permeability to moisture should be considered with respect to bonding and simple packing arrangements.

Materials are classified based on their uses, properties, or bonding and structure

Whereas most living things survive by adapting to their environment, human beings have been particularly effective at doing the opposite. We have adapted the material in our environment to meet our needs. Initially this was a trial and error process. We made buildings out of strong materials such as wood, stone, and iron, made windows and drinking implements from transparent glass, and attractive jewellery from shiny minerals or precious metals.

A more systematic scientific approach has led us to identify and measure the properties of different materials more precisely and classify them into groups accordingly. Metals are strong and malleable, glasses are transparent and brittle, and ceramics are generally excellent insulators (superconductors are notable exceptions). In recent times our chemical understanding has allowed us to make great advances in the synthesis and uses of materials as we understand the link between their properties and their structure and composition. If the focus is on understanding the properties of a material, a classification based on its bonding and structure is helpful, whereas if we are interested in its properties and possible uses a classification based on the material type, metal, ceramic, composite, or polymer is more appropriate.

The properties of a material based on the degree of covalent, ionic, or metallic character can be deduced from its position on a bonding triangle

The structure and bonding of the different substances was discussed in Chapter 4. Although we generally classify solids as metallic, ionic, molecular, or giant covalent, this is a simplification as many materials show intermediate properties. The bonding in a material is determined by the magnitude and difference of the electronegativities (χ) of the constituent elements. This is illustrated by the triangle of bonding shown in Figure 12.1.

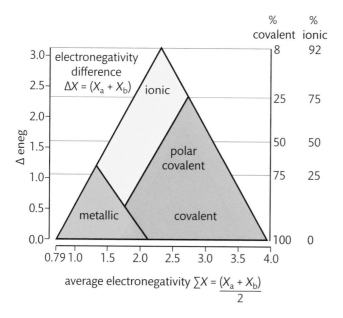

average electronegativity $\sum X = \dfrac{(X_a + X_b)}{2}$

Figure 12.1 Metals have low electronegativities and small electronegativity differences, which places them in the lower left corner. Ionic compounds are found at the top centre. Covalent structures are found in the lower right corner. They are made from non-metals that have high electronegativities.

To understand the triangle, consider the position of the elements caesium and fluorine and the binary compound they react to form.

Substance	$\chi_{average}$	$\Delta\chi$	Position in triangle
CsF	$\dfrac{4.0 + 0.8}{2} = 2.4$	$4.0 - 0.8 = 3.2$	Top of the triangle as 100% ionic compound. Made up from the most electropositive metal and most electronegative non-metal.
Cs	0.8	$0.8 - 0.8 = 0$	Bottom left as 100% metallic. Cs has the lowest absolute electronegativity.
F_2	4.0	$4.0 - 4.0 = 0.0$	Bottom right corner as 100% molecular covalent.

The percentage ionic character of a compound can be approximated using the formula:

$$\% \text{ ionic characacter} = \frac{\Delta\chi}{3.2} \times 100\,\%$$

According to this equation, sodium chloride is 72% ionic and hydrogen chloride is 32% ionic. We describe the bonding in NaCl as ionic and HCl as polar covalent.

Worked example

Locate the position of the following substances on the triangle of bonding:

(a) diamond

(b) silicon dioxide

(c) bronze (an alloy of copper and tin).

Solution

	Substance	$\chi_{average}$	$\Delta\chi$
(a)	diamond	2.6	0
(b)	silicon dioxide	$\frac{1.9+3.4}{2}=2.65$	$3.4-1.9=1.5$
(c)	Cu/Zn	$\frac{1.9+2.0}{2}=1.95$	$2.0-1.9=0.1$

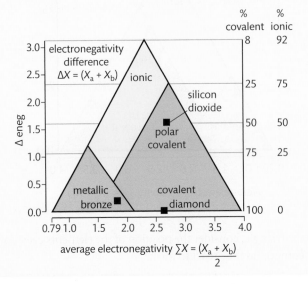

There are four distinct classes of materials

Materials fall into four distinct classes: metals, polymers, ceramics, and composites. We have discussed the properties of metals in Chapter 4 and polymers in Chapter 10. Details of thermoplastic plastics, thermoset plastics, and elastomers are given later in the chapter.

Ceramics are made by baking metal oxides and other minerals to high temperature

The term **ceramic** comes from the Greek word for pottery. This class of materials is so broad that it is often easier to define ceramics as all solid materials, except metals and their alloys, that are made by the high-temperature processing of inorganic raw materials. Their properties are generally the opposite of those found in the metals. Glasses and semiconductors can also be included in this class.

Ceramics can either form giant ionic or giant covalent structures, which explains why they are so hard. The presence of ions also explains their brittle properties. A shear force moves one layer of ions relative to another so that ions of the same charge are forced next to each other (Figure 12.2).

(a)   **(b)**

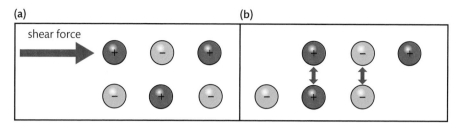

Ceramics can be porous materials as there are gaps in their structure that allow water molecules to pass.

Glasses have many properties in common with ceramics as they are made from giant covalent structures such as silicon dioxide fused with some metal oxide with an ionic structure. The key difference is that glasses are transparent and waterproof. They are made by cooling the molten mixture of silicon dioxide and metal oxide quickly so the solid formed retains some of the disorder of the liquid. They are hard and brittle like the ceramics.

Composites are mixtures composed of two distinct phases, a reinforcing phase that is embedded in a matrix phase

A **composite material** is a mixture of two materials. Generally a composite material is made up from fibres of a strong hard material embedded in a matrix of another material (Figure 12.3). The properties of the composite depend on the properties of its constituents.

fibre

matrix

Figure 12.3 A composite material has fibres of one material embedded in a matrix made from a different material.

If the composite is designed and fabricated correctly, it combines the strength of the fibre with the toughness of the matrix to achieve a combination of desirable properties not available in any single conventional material. Some composites also offer the advantage of being tailor-made so that properties, such as strength and stiffness, can easily be changed by changing the amount or orientation of the fibre.

The compositions of some common composites are shown below.

Composite	Fibre	Matrix
fibreglass	glass	plastic
carbon fibres	carbon	plastic
concrete	steel	cement
wood	cellulose	lignin
cermet	ceramic	metal

A technologist removing a sample of cermet from a furnace. Cermet is a composite material made from the ceramic boron carbide and the metal aluminium. The cermet is lighter than aluminium but stronger than steel.

TOK

We can classify materials according to their composition, their bonding and structure, or their properties. No single classification is 'perfect'. How do we evaluate the different classification systems we use in the different areas of knowledge? How does our need to categorize the world help and hinder the pursuit of knowledge?

Light micrograph of fibreglass. Fibreglass is a lightweight, extremely strong, and robust material. The plastic matrix may be a thermosetting plastic or thermoplastic.

Some physical properties of materials

All solid materials have a number of physical properties. Here are some which affect how different materials are used.

Property	Comments
Melting point	The temperature at which a solid begins to liquefy. Pure crystalline materials melt at constant temperature. Glasses have no defined melting point as they are generally mixtures. Thermosetting plastics do not melt when they are heated but burn. The carbon atoms combine with oxygen when the strong covalent bonds which hold the structure together are broken. Thermoplastics have molecular covalent structures and so have intermediate melting points as only intermolecular forces are broken when the plastic melts. The melting points of metals generally increase across a period as more delocalized electrons are used in bonding and decrease down a group as an increase in ionic radius leads to reduced attraction between the ions in the lattice and the bonding electrons. The melting points of the transition metals are generally high as the d electrons are involved in bonding.
Permeability	The facility with which a material allows the passage of liquid or gas. Some ceramics and composite are porous as there are gaps in their structure. For example, pores can form in the matrix structure of cement which allow water to pass through the material.
Electrical conductivity	A measure of the ability to conduct a current at a given potential difference. Metals and graphite are good conductors in the solid state as they have delocalized electrons which are free to move throughout their structures. Ionic compounds can conduct electricity in the liquid state or in aqueous solution where their ions are free to move. Composites made from metal or graphite can conduct.

Property	Comments
Elasticity	The ability of a material to return to its original shape once the stretching force has been removed. The physical reasons for elastic behaviour can be quite different for different materials. In metals, the atomic lattice changes size and shape when stretched. When the stretching force is removed, the lattice goes back to the original as the atoms are pulled back by the bonding electrons. Elastomers are elastic polymers, generally with double bonds in their structure. Their chains uncoil when a force is applied but return to a more stable coiled arrangement when the force is removed. More details are given later in the chapter (page 428).
Brittleness	A brittle material breaks into parts when it is stretched. Ionic and covalent bonds lead to brittle structures. Some ceramics and thermosetting plastics are brittle. This property is the opposite of toughness. Metals and thermoplastics are tough.
Ductility/ malleability	A ductile material can be stretched into long strands. Metals are ductile as their atoms can slide across each other without breaking their metallic bonds. The delocalized electrons adopt a new arrangement which ensures that the metallic bonding is maintained. A malleable material can be squeezed into any shape. Metals are malleable again because the delocalized electrons can accommodate any changes in structure without breaking the metallic bonding.

Damaged concrete. Scanning electron microscope of cracks that have formed around a trapped air bubble in a sample of concrete that has been damaged through chemical reactions.

The properties of the different materials are summarized on page 394. These are only general rules and there are many exceptions.

Property	Metal	Ceramic	Glass	Polymer	Composite
Melting point	Transition metals have the highest melting points as more electrons are involved in bonding. Group 1 metals have the lowest melting points. Pure metals have fixed melting points; alloys melt over a range of temperatures.	High: ionic and covalent bonds are strong.	High: covalent bonds are strong.	Thermoplastics have low melting points as intermolecular forces are weak. Thermosetting plastics don't melt but burn when heated to high temperature.	High: depends on the constituents.
Permeability	Low	Can be porous as there are gaps in the structure.	Low	No	Can be porous as there are gaps in the structure.
Electrical conductivity	High: there are delocalized electrons.	Low	Low, but some conductivity at very high temperature as ions are free to move.	Low, but some polymers with extended delocalized electrons have been synthesized which conduct electricity.	Generally low but can conduct if structure includes metal or graphite which have delocalized electrons.
Elasticity	Generally low: some metals show elastic properties; steel springs for example. The distance between the atoms increases when the metal is stretched but the atoms return to their original position due to the metallic bonding when the load is removed.	Low	Low	Low, but elastomers show elastic properties. Elastomers uncoil when a stretching force is applied but coil when force is removed.	Low, but carbon fibres show elastic properties.
Brittleness	Low	High: contain strong covalent or ionic bonds. When force is sufficiently strong to break these, the structure falls apart.	High: contain strong covalent or ionic bonds. When force is sufficiently strong to break these, the structure falls apart.	Some thermosetting plastics, which have a giant covalent structure, can be strong but brittle. Thermoplastics and elastomers are not brittle.	Generally low, but depends on composition.
Ductility	High: metal ions can be pulled apart without breaking the metallic bonds as the delocalized electrons can accommodate changes to the lattice structure.	Low	High	Low	Low

The use of materials has characterized the development of different civilizations in history. In the stone age, humans used materials which could be modified for use by simple physical processing but the iron age involved chemistry in which the element was extracted from available minerals. Scientific knowledge during this period was limited and these were essentially technological developments which relied on empirical knowledge gained through trial and error. More modern times have been characterized by the use of materials such as aluminium and plastic. This has relied on the application of available technology; the extraction of reactive metals such as aluminium relied on the use of electricity, but more importantly on our understanding of the link between the properties of a material and its structure. The evolution of science has made our environment more accommodating through technological developments and more understandable in terms of the models and theories we have developed. Both these motivations continue to drive materials science forward. It is a cross-disciplinary area of science which attracts scientists of different skills with different objectives. We are now more aware of the impact on our environment of our use of natural resources. This has made us more aware of our ethical responsibilities as scientists and brought new challenges.

Exercises

1 Identify which of the following statements refers to the composition of a composite material.

   A It is a mixture in which one material acts as the matrix or glue.
   B It contains at least three different materials, one of which is glue.
   C It must contain a metallic element.
   D It is a compound of two elements.

2 Use electronegativity values from section 8 of the data booklet to classify the bonding in the following materials: Cl_2O, $PbCl_2$, Al_2O_3, HBr, and NaBr.

3 Copper oxide can be added to give glass a blue or green colour. Deduce the position of copper oxide in the bonding triangle and describe the nature of its structure and bonding.

4 Explain why metals are ductile and ceramics are brittle.

5 Concrete is a composite of steel and cement. Outline its structure and suggest how the material could conduct electricity.

A.2 Metals and inductively coupled plasma (ICP) spectroscopy

Understandings:

- Reduction by coke (carbon), a more reactive metal, or electrolysis are means of obtaining some metals from their ores.
- The relationship between charge and the number of moles of electrons is given by Faraday's constant, F.
- Alloys are homogeneous mixtures of metals with other metals or non-metals.
- Diamagnetic and paramagnetic compounds differ in electron spin pairing and their behaviour in magnetic fields
- Trace amounts of metals can be identified and quantified by ionizing them with argon gas plasma in inductively coupled plasma (ICP) spectroscopy using mass spectroscopy ICP-MS and optical emission spectroscopy ICP-OES.

Guidance

- *Faraday's constant is given in the IB data booklet in section 2.*
- *Details of operating parts of ICP-MS and ICP-OES instruments will not be assessed.*

Applications and skills:

- Deduction of redox equations for the reduction of metals.
- Relating the method of extraction to the position of a metal on the activity series.
- Explanation of the production of aluminium by the electrolysis of alumina in molten cryolite.

- Explanation of how alloying alters properties of metals.
- Solving stoichiometric problems using Faraday's constant based on mass deposits in electrolysis.
- Discussion of paramagnetism and diamagnetism in relation to electron structure of metals.
- Explanation of the plasma state and its production in ICP-MS and ICP-OES.
- Identify metals and abundances from simple data and calibration curves provided from ICP-MS and ICP-OES.
- Explanation of the separation and quantification of metallic ions by ICP-MS and ICP-OES.
- Uses of ICP-MS and ICP-OES.

Guidance

- Only analysis of metals should be covered.
- The importance of calibration should be covered.

The method of extraction is related to its position in the activity series

The ability to extract metals was an important technological step in the development of our civilization. Some unreactive metals, such as gold and silver, occur in nature as the free element. More reactive metals are found in rocks or **ores** as compounds, combined with other elements present in the environment. These ores are usually oxides, sulfides, or carbonates of the metal mixed with impurities. The extraction of metals from these ores involves the reduction of the metal compounds (Chapter 9, page 278) and the removal of impurities.

The method of extraction is related to the position of the metal in the reactivity series.

Metal	Method of extraction
potassium	electrolysis of molten compounds
sodium	
magnesium	
aluminium	
carbon	
zinc	reduction of oxides with carbon/carbon monoxide
chromium	
iron	
tin	
hydrogen	
copper	occur native in the ground or produced by heating the ore
silver	
mercury	
gold	

(decreasing reactivity — arrow pointing downward alongside the table)

A more complete activity series is given in section 25 of the IB data booklet.

Reduction of compounds using more reactive metals

The more reactive elements, at the top of the series, will reduce the oxides of the less reactive elements at the bottom of the series. The practical use of this route depends on the relative cost of the two metals involved.

Magnesium could in theory reduce iron(III) oxide but is generally not used as the magnesium is too expensive to be wasted in this way:

$$3Mg(s) + Fe_2O_3(s) \rightarrow 3MgO(s) + 2Fe(s)$$

However, aluminium is used to extract the more expensive chromium from its ores:

$$2Al(s) + Cr_2O_3(s) \rightarrow Al_2O_3(s) + 2Cr(s)$$

Metals in the middle of the series are extracted from their oxides or sulfides with carbon

Coke, an impure form of carbon, formed by heating coal, is used as a relatively cheap reducing agent for metals in the middle of the activity series.

$$PbO(s) + C(s) \rightarrow Pb(s) + CO(g)$$

In the case of lead and zinc the sulfide is the most available ore. The sulfide is first roasted to produce the oxide, which is then reduced by carbon. Carbon monoxide is often the product of the reaction.

$$2ZnS(s) + 3O_2(g) \rightarrow 2ZnO(s) + 2SO_2(g)$$

$$ZnO(s) + C(s) \rightarrow CO(g) + Zn(s)$$

Metal oxides can be reduced with carbon monoxide

Iron oxide is reduced with carbon monoxide in a blast furnace (Figure 12.4).

Haematite is a form of iron oxide (Fe_2O_3), mined as one of the main ores of iron.

Figure 12.4 A blast furnace.

Iron ore, coke, and limestone ($CaCO_3$) are added at the top of the blast furnace and a blast of hot air is blown in from near the bottom.

The coke burns in the preheated air to form carbon dioxide:

$$C(s) + O_2(g) \rightarrow CO_2(g) \qquad\qquad \Delta H = -298 \text{ kJ mol}^{-1}$$

The carbon monoxide acts as the **reducing agent** and reduces the iron(III) oxide:

$$Fe_2O_3(s) + 3CO(g) \rightarrow 2Fe(l) + 3CO_2(g)$$

Less reactive metals can be produced by heating their ores

The less reactive metals at the bottom of the activity series can be extracted without carbon as the oxides are unstable at higher temperature. Mercury is produced when its sulfide ore, cinnabar, is heated in oxygen.

$$HgS(s) + O_2(g) \rightarrow Hg(l) + SO_2(g)$$

Cinnabar, an ore of mercury.

More reactive metals are extracted from their molten compounds by electrolysis

As discussed in Chapter 9, reducing agents are suppliers of electrons. The most direct way to supply electrons is via an electric circuit. The more reactive metals at the top of the series, which cannot be reduced by carbon, are extracted using electrolysis. The electrolysis of aqueous compounds of these metals cannot be used, as the less reactive element hydrogen, present in the water, would be produced in preference to the metal at the cathode.

The equations for the extraction can be deduced from changes in oxidation numbers

Worked example

Copper is extracted from its sulfide ore by a combination of two reactions:

1   copper(I) sulfide is heated in air to produce copper(I) oxide and sulfur dioxide;
2   the air supply is removed and copper(I) oxide is heated with excess copper(I) sulfide to produce sulfur dioxide and the metal.

Identify the element that is reduced in both redox reactions and deduce the equations.

1   Copper(I) sulfide has the formula $(Cu^+)_2S^{2-} = Cu_2S$

We can write an unbalanced equation that has the oxidation numbers below each element:

$$Cu_2S + O_2 \rightarrow Cu_2O + SO_2 \qquad \text{unbalanced}$$
$${+1\,-2}{0}{+1\,-2}{+4-2}\qquad \text{oxidation numbers (ON)}$$

• sulfur is oxidized: $(-2 \rightarrow +4)$: $\Delta(ON) = (+4) - (-2) = +6$
• oxygen is reduced: $(0 \rightarrow -2)$: $\Delta(ON) = (-2) - (0) = -2$

To balance these changes: three Os must be reduced for each S. The copper is unchanged.

$$Cu_2S + 3/2O_2 \rightarrow Cu_2O + SO_2 \qquad \text{balanced}$$
$${+1\,-2}{3/2(0)}{+1\,-2}{+4\,\,2(-2)}$$

multiplying by 2:

$$2Cu_2S + 3O_2 \rightarrow 2Cu_2O + 3SO_2 \qquad \text{balanced}$$

2   The unbalanced equation with oxidation numbers below each element:

$$Cu_2O + Cu_2S \rightarrow Cu + SO_2 \qquad \text{unbalanced}$$
$${+1\,-2}{+1\,\,0}{+4}{-2}\qquad \text{oxidation numbers (ON)}$$

• sulfur is oxidized $(-2 \rightarrow +4)$: $\Delta(ON) = (+4) - (-2) = +6$
• copper is reduced $(+1 \rightarrow 0)$: $\Delta(ON) = (0) - (+1) = -1$

To balance these changes: six Cu must be reduced for each S oxidized. The oxygen is unchanged.

$$2Cu_2O + Cu_2S \rightarrow 6Cu + SO_2 \qquad \text{balanced}$$

Aluminium is extracted from its ore (bauxite) by electrolysis

Aluminium is the most abundant metal in the Earth's crust and is found in the minerals **bauxite** and mica as well as in clay. It was, however, not discovered until 1825 by H.C. Oersted in Denmark. It is a reactive metal which means that its compounds are extremely difficult to break down by chemical reactions.

Nowadays, aluminium is a relatively cheap metal. The extraction of aluminium from the mineral bauxite involves three stages:

• **Purification**: the mineral is treated with aqueous sodium hydroxide. Bauxite is an impure form of hydrated aluminium oxide: $Al_2O_3.xH_2O$. The amphoteric nature of the oxide allows it to be separated from other metal oxides. Unlike most metal oxides, aluminium oxide dissolves in aqueous sodium hydroxide. The soluble aluminium oxide is separated by filtration from the insoluble metal oxides (iron(III) oxide) and sand.

$$Al_2O_3(s) + 2OH^-(aq) + 3H_2O(l) \rightarrow 2Al(OH)_4^-(aq)$$

The reaction can be reversed by passing carbon dioxide through the solution. Carbon dioxide forms the weak acid, carbonic acid, which neutralizes the solution.

▲ Bauxite is the primary ore from which aluminium is obtained.

Napoleon III, the Emperor of France from 1848 to 1870, owned an aluminium dinner service which was said to be more precious than gold. The high value reflects the difficulty of extracting the metal at the time.

An amphoteric oxide is an oxide that can act either as an acid or a base.

Figure 12.5 The electrolysis of molten aluminium oxide.

The top of the Washington Monument is a 2.8 kg pyramid of aluminium. Installed in 1884, it was as valuable as silver at the time.

In an electrolysis cell, the positive electrode is called the anode and the negative electrode is called the cathode.

The electrolytic extraction of aluminium was developed almost simultaneously by Charles Martin Hall and Paul Héroult, who worked independently on different sides of the Atlantic. They both discovered the process in the same year, 1886. Both were born in the same year (1863) and died in the same year (1914).

- **Solvation**: the purified aluminium oxide is dissolved in molten cryolite – a mineral form of Na_3AlF_6. This reduces the melting point of aluminium oxide and so reduces the energy requirements of the process. Pure aluminium oxide would not be a suitable electrolyte because it has a very high melting point and it is a poor electrical conductor even when molten. Its bonding is intermediate between ionic and polar covalent, as discussed earlier in the chapter.
- **Electrolysis**: the molten mixture is electrolysed (Figure 12.5). Graphite anodes are dipped into the molten electrolyte. The graphite-lined steel cell acts as the cathode.

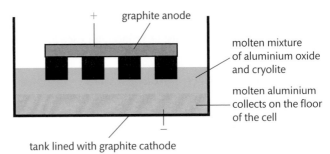

graphite anode

molten mixture of aluminium oxide and cryolite

molten aluminium collects on the floor of the cell

tank lined with graphite cathode

The negatively charged O^{2-} ions are attracted to the anode, where they lose electrons and are oxidized to oxygen gas:

$$2O^{2-}(l) \rightarrow O_2(g) + 4e^-$$

At the high temperature of the process, the oxygen reacts with the graphite anode to form carbon dioxide:

$$C(s) + O_2(g) \rightarrow CO_2(g)$$

As the graphite is burned away, the anode needs to be regularly replaced.

The positive aluminium ions, Al^{3+}, are attracted to the cathode, where they gain electrons and are reduced to molten aluminium:

$$Al^{3+}(l) + 3e^- \rightarrow Al(l)$$

The aluminium produced by this method is 99% pure with small amounts of silicon and iron impurities. As the electrolyte contains fluoride ions, fluorine gas is also produced in the process. This needs to be removed from the waste gases before they pass into the atmosphere as it would lead to environmental damage.

The need for high temperatures means that the process needs to be continuous to be economical. The cost of electricity is the most important factor to consider when

Worker controlling the pouring of molten aluminium from a crucible into an ingot casting vessel. This casting is taking place at one of the largest producers of aluminium in Russia.

deciding the location of an aluminium plant and they are often sited near hydroelectric power stations. The high energy demand emphasizes the importance of recycling. The energy requirements of recycling aluminium are less than 5% of that needed to extract the metal directly.

The amount of metal produced depends on the number of electrons supplied

The electric current (I) passing any point in an electric circuit is a measure of the amount of charge (Q) passing each point in a given time, t.

$$\text{current } (I) = \frac{\text{charge } (Q)}{\text{time } (t)}$$

This allows the amount of charge delivered to an electrolysis cell to be calculated from the current and the time:

$$\text{charge } (Q) = \text{current } (I) \times \text{time } (t)$$

If the time is measured in seconds and the current in amperes, the charge is given in coulombs.

To calculate the number of electrons, $N(e)$, passing any point any second we need to divide the total charge by the charge of one electron ($e^- = 1.602189 \times 10^{-19}$ C). This value is given in section 5 of the IB data booklet.

$$N(e^-) = \text{charge } (Q) \, / \, 1.602189 \times 10^{-19} \text{ C}$$

The amount of electrons, measured in moles, $n(e^-)$, can be obtained by dividing this number by Avogadro's constant (L).

$$n(e^-) = \text{charge } (Q) \, / \, 1.602189 \times 10^{-19} \text{ C} \times 6.02 \times 10^{23} \text{ mol}^{-1}$$

This expression can be simplified by combining the constants to give a new constant:

$$\text{Faraday's constant } (F) = 1.602189 \times 10^{-19} \text{ C} \times 6.02 \times 10^{23} \text{ mol}^{-1} = 96\,500 \text{ C mol}^{-1}$$

Faraday's constant is the charge of 1 mol of electrons.

The amount of product formed by an electric current is chemically equivalent to the amount of electrons supplied; a statement of **Faraday's law of electrolysis**. These relationships allow the amount of metal produced during electrolysis to be calculated from the current and time using the stoichiometric strategies developed in Chapter 1.

Worked example

Calculate the mass of aluminium that can be produced from an electrolytic cell in one year (365 days) operating with an average current of 1.20×10^5 A.

Solution

Equation at cathode:

$$Al^{3+}(l) + 3e^- \rightarrow Al(l)$$

$$\text{1 mol} \quad \text{3 mol} \quad \text{1 mol}$$

$$\frac{n(Al)}{n(e)} = \frac{1}{3}$$

$$n(Al) = \frac{1}{3} \times n(e)$$

charge (Q) = current (I) × time (t)

Faraday's constant is the charge of 1 mol of electrons.

Faraday's constant (F) = 96 500 C mol^{-1}

Faraday's law of electrolysis states that the amount of product formed by an electric current is chemically equivalent to the amount of electrons supplied.

The aluminium drink can is the world's most recycled container – more than 63% of all cans are recycled worldwide. You could watch three hours of television on the energy saved by recycling one aluminium can.

The number of moles of electrons can be calculated from the current:

$$n(e) = \frac{Q}{F} = \frac{I \times t}{F}$$

$$= \frac{1.20 \times 10^5 \text{ A} \times 365 \times 24 \times 60 \times 60 \text{ s}}{96\,500 \text{ C mol}^{-1}}$$

This gives

$$n(Al) = \frac{1}{3} \times \frac{1.20 \times 10^5 \times 365 \times 24 \times 60 \times 60}{96\,500} \text{ mol}$$

$$m(Al) = n(Al) \times M(Al)$$

$$m(Al) = 26.96 \text{ g mol}^{-1} \times \frac{1.20 \times 10^5 \times 365 \times 24 \times 60 \times 60}{3 \times 96\,500} \text{ mol}$$

$$= 352\,680\,323 \text{ g}$$

$$= 352\,680.32 \text{ kg}$$

$$= 3.53 \times 10^5 \text{ kg}$$

Exercises

6 **(a)** State the ore from which aluminium is extracted.
   (b) Explain why aluminium is not extracted from its oxide by carbon reduction in a blast furnace.
   (c) Describe and explain how aluminium atoms are formed during the extraction process.
   (d) Explain why aluminium cannot be obtained by electrolysis of an aqueous solution of an aluminium compound.
   (e) Explain the low conductivity of aluminium oxide.
   (f) Explain with chemical equations why the carbon anodes need to be replaced at regular intervals.

7 0.100 F of electric charge is passed through a saturated solution of copper(II) chloride. Calculate the mass of copper produced and the volume of chlorine gas produced, assuming the reaction is carried out under standard conditions of temperature and pressure.

8 A molten sample of titanium chloride was electrolysed using a current of 0.0965 A for 1000 s. 0.011 975 g of the metal was produced. Deduce the formula of the titanium chloride.

9 Methane is sometimes added to the preheated air in a blast furnace instead of coke. Deduce the equation for the complete reaction between methane and haematite ($Fe_2O_3(s)$), in the presence of air.

10 The extraction of titanium involves the conversion of titanium(IV) oxide to titanium(IV) chloride. Carbon is oxidized to carbon monoxide in the process.

   (a) Deduce the chemical equation for the reaction.
   (b) Titanium(IV) chloride is reduced to the metal by magnesium. Deduce the equation for this reaction.

Alloys are homogeneous mixtures of metals with other metals or non-metals

The iron produced by the blast furnace contains about 4% carbon. This high level of impurity makes the metal brittle and reduces its melting point. As this iron has limited uses, the majority is converted into an **alloy**: steel. An alloy is a homogeneous mixture containing at least one metal formed when liquid metals are added together and allowed to form a solid of *uniform* composition. Alloys are useful because they have a range of properties that are different from the pure metal. The presence of other elements in the metallic structure changes the regular arrangement of the metal atoms in the solid, making it more difficult for atoms to slip over each other, and so change the shape of the bulk material (Figure 12.6). Alloys are generally stronger than the pure metal. Alloying can also make materials more resistant to corrosion.

force ← force ←

pure metal
The shape of a pure metal can be changed as the atoms can easily slip over each other.

force ←

alloy
The presence of atoms of different sizes disrupts the regular structure and prevents the atoms from slipping across each other.

An alloy is a homogeneous mixture containing at least one metal formed when liquid metals are added together and allowed to form a solid of *uniform* composition.

Figure 12.6 An alloy is a stronger, harder, and less malleable metal than the pure metal.

There is no single material called 'steel'. Instead, steel is the general name for a mixture of iron and carbon and other metals. Small differences in the composition of the steel can produce a range of different properties. This makes steel a versatile material with properties that can be adjusted to suit its use.

Changing the composition of an alloy is not the only way to adjust its properties. Different forms of heat treatment can change the structure of the alloy. The atoms in a piece of metal are not all arranged in a regular way. This is shown by the different orientation of the squares in Figure 12.7. Areas of regular structure are called 'crystal grains'. The properties of an alloy depend on the size and orientations of the grain boundaries.

Light micrograph of high carbon steel. It contains 0.65% carbon by mass alloyed with iron. It is very strong but brittle and is used for cutting tools, high-strength wires, and springs.

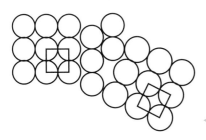

Figure 12.7 The atoms in a metal are not all perfectly arranged in a regular way. Areas of regular structure are called 'crystal grains'.

NATURE OF SCIENCE

The history of the extraction of the metals can be used to measure the evolution of civilization. Most of the elements are metals and the history of their extraction illustrates many features about the development of science and technology. Fire was the crucial agency which brought about the extraction of metals and the mixing of alloys. Fire was originally considered to be an element, but later came to be recognized as a form of energy. It breaks down ores like malachite to the soft metal copper and facilitates the reduction of the ore haematite to the hard metal iron. As there was limited scientific understanding as to the basis of these changes, many experimental procedures were based on ritual or mysticism. The need to repeat experimental procedure was recognized but as the underlying theory was not understood it was couched in ritual language; to heat steel to the correct temperature to make a Japanese sword it has to glow 'to the colour of the morning sun'. The metal gold has always held a special place in different cultures and became a focus for alchemy; gold is precious because it is incorruptible and hence eternal. Gold resists decay and thus prolongs life. The alchemist saw a sympathy between the metals of the earth and health of the human body. We now see these false analogies as naïve, but should appreciate that many scientific theories are also analogies which have turned out to be false. The scientific theories of today solve the problems of today but they are only provisional.

The grain structure of brass, an alloy of copper and zinc.

403

Paramagnetic and diamagnetic materials display different behaviour in magnetic fields because of their different electron spin pairings

Materials are classified as diamagnetic, paramagnetic, or ferromagnetic based on their behaviour when placed in an external magnetic field (Figure 12.8).

- **Diamagnetic materials** are repelled by an external magnetic field as the orbital motion of their electrons produces a very weak opposing magnetic field.
- **Paramagnetic materials** are attracted by an external magnetic field as they have unpaired electrons which behave like small magnets which align with the external field. The level of magnetization is proportional and in the same direction as the applied field. All atoms have orbiting electrons and so show diamagnetic behaviour but paramagnetic behaviour dominates in cases of single atoms or ions with unpaired electrons.

Substances with paired electrons are diamagnetic, as electrons with opposite spins behave like minute bar magnets with opposing orientation and so cancel each other out.

Many individual atoms and ions have unpaired electrons and display paramagnetic effects. Chemical bonding often involves the pairing of electrons and so most materials with ionic and covalent structures are diamagnetic. Free radicals and some transition metal ion complexes have unpaired electrons and so display paramagnetic effects. The interaction of electrons is more complex in metallic structures and some metals are paramagnetic.

Figure 12.8 The electrons in an atom have two types of motion which both lead to magnetic effects, equivalent to that of the bar magnet shown. (a) Orbital motion leads to diamagnetic behaviour. (b) Electrons lead to paramagnetic behaviour.

Ferromagnetism occurs when materials retain their magnetism after they have been removed from an external field. It occurs in materials containing iron, cobalt, and nickel where there is long-range ordering of the unpaired electrons, which remains in regions called **domains** after the external magnetic field is removed. Ferromagnetism is the largest effect, producing magnetizations sometimes orders of magnitude greater than the applied field.

(a)

(b)

nucleus

Paramagnetic materials are attracted by an external magnetic field as they have unpaired electrons. Diamagnetic materials are weakly repelled by an external magnetic field. They have no unpaired electrons.

A free radical is a species with an unpaired electron.

Worked example

Distinguish between the magnetic properties of H_2O and $[Fe(H_2O)_6]^{3+}$.

Solution

All the electrons are paired in the water molecule and so it is diamagnetic.

The Fe^{3+} in the complex ion has the electron configuration $[Ar]3d^5$ and so has 5 unpaired electrons. It is paramagnetic.

Exercises

11 Alloys of aluminium with nickel are used to make engine parts. Explain why this alloy is used rather than pure aluminium.

12 Classify the period 3 atoms as paramagnetic or diamagnetic and explain your answer. Identify the element which is likely to show the strongest paramagnetic properties.

13 Arrange the following atoms in order of increasing paramagnetism and explain your choice: K, Sc, V, Mn, Ga, As.

Inductively coupled plasma (ICP) spectroscopy determines the identity and concentration of metals

Inductively coupled plasma optical emission spectroscopy (ICP-OES)

Inductively coupled plasma (ICP) spectroscopy is one of the most powerful and popular analytical tools for the determination of metals and other elements in a variety of different samples. The technique is based upon an analysis of the element's emission spectra. We saw in Chapter 2 (page 71) that an emission spectrum is produced when the radiation from an excited sample is analysed. A line spectra is produced, with each line corresponding to an electron transition between different energy levels as electrons fall from a higher to lower energy levels. As each element has a unique set of energy levels it produces its own distinctive emission spectrum which can be used to identify the element (Figure 12.9).

The intensity of the lines depends on the concentration of the element in the sample. In ICP the sample is injected into a high-temperature **argon plasma** and the photons corresponding to the different frequencies are separated using a diffraction grating and counted using a photomultiplier which generates an electric signal.

SPECTRA OF THE METALS OF THE ALKALIES & ALKALINE EARTHS.
From the Drawings of BUNSEN & KIRCHHOFF.

Flame emission spectra of Group 1 and Group 2 metals, as recorded by Robert Bunsen (1811–1899) and Gustav Kirchhoff (1824–1887). They were the first to observe that heated elements emitted a light of characteristic wavelength.

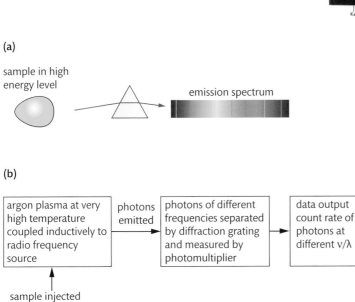

(a) sample in high energy level → emission spectrum

(b) argon plasma at very high temperature coupled inductively to radio frequency source → photons emitted → photons of different frequencies separated by diffraction grating and measured by photomultiplier → data output count rate of photons at different v/λ

sample injected

Figure 12.9 (a) An emission spectrum is produced from an excited atom when an electron drops from a higher to a lower energy. The different lines correspond to different transitions. (b) In ICP the sample is excited by injecting it into an argon plasma. The emitted photons are analysed using a diffraction grating and photomultiplier. The high temperature of the argon plasma is generated by coupling the argon to a high-energy radio frequency coil.

Plasma is a high energy state composed of isolated atoms, ions, and electrons

The plasma state occurs at very high temperatures when some or all of the gaseous atoms have been ionized. The interactions in the plasma are dominated by charge interactions between positive ions and electrons. The atoms and ions in the plasma are excited and emit photons at characteristic frequencies.

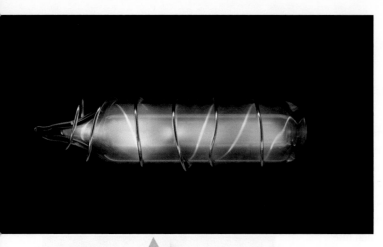

The plasma is a high-energy state composed of isolated atoms, ions, and electrons.

The plasma state is uncommon on Earth, but is the most common state for the visible matter in the universe.

ppm = one part in a million 10^6; ppb = one part in a billion 10^9: they are units of concentration.

The high temperature of the argon plasma is generated by inductively coupling the gas to a high-energy radio frequency source

The energy to form the argon plasma used in ICP is generated by a high-frequency radio frequency source, which is inductively coupled to the argon in a similar manner to the coils in an electric transformer. An electric discharge produces a 'seed' of ions and electrons in the argon which are then accelerated by the oscillating magnetic field of the radio waves, which results in further ionization as the excited electrons knock off electrons from other atoms. The processes continue until a high-temperature (10 000 K) plasma is formed. The induction coil controls the position of the plasma and keeps it away from the walls of the container, which would melt at such high temperatures.

Atoms from the sample are excited by colliding with the plasma particles and their emitted photons analysed

Sufficient energy is available to convert the atoms of the injected sample to ions and promote the electrons to excited states, which then fall to the lower energy levels with the emission of photons at characteristic energies. The wavelength of the photons can be used to identify the element and the total number of photons is directly proportional to the concentration of the element in the sample.

The concentration of an element can be determined from a calibration curve

The number of photons emitted by sample atoms at a characteristic wavelength is proportional to the concentration of the element in a sample. Unknown concentrations can be determined by comparing its photo emission rate with those of some standard solutions over a range of concentrations on a **calibration curve** (Figure 12.10). A calibration curve is necessary as there are possible variations in the intensity of the signals due to the operating conditions of the plasma such as the flow rate of the argon and temperature of the plasma. The intensity of each line is compared to the intensities of the same line from samples with known concentrations of the elements. The concentrations are then computed by interpolation along the calibration lines. As each element produces a number of characteristic lines, different calibration curves can be produced for different wavelengths. Standard calibration curves for most elements are linear. The solutions used in the calibration are generally made by successive dilution of a standard solution. An acid solvent is often used in the analysis of metal samples. The concentration of the unknown solution should fall inside of the calibrated region. Generally, the wavelengths of high intensity are selected for the analysis.

As the sample is vaporized and broken into atoms in the plasma, ICP determines the concentration of atoms irrespective of how they are combined together. It is an extremely sensitive method, allowing concentrations as low as 0.1 ppb (one part in 10^{10}) to be measured.

The amount of lead in alloys used in electrical and electronic equipment needs to be carefully monitored as it can pose risks to human health.

A range of solutions were made up with different lead concentrations. The resulting calibration curve is shown, with the intensity measured in 1000 counts per second.

Figure 12.10 A calibration curve for lead.

(a) Explain the number in the title of the graph.

(b) Suggest how the solutions used in the calibration were prepared, assuming the balance has a precision of (±) 0.0001 g and the concentrations need to be determined to three significant figures.

(c) Two alloy samples were tested using the same conditions.

Alloy sample	Intensity / kc s⁻¹
I	120
II	20

Determine the concentration of lead in the two samples and comment on the reliability of the results.

Solution

(a) 220 nm is the wavelength of the photons emitted.

(b) The smallest amount of Pb that can be accurately measured ≈ 0.0100 g.

To make most concentrated solution (1.50 mg dm^{-3}) needs 0.0150 g in 10 dm^3 of solution, which is 0.00150 g in 1 dm^3 of solution.

Concentrated acid (solvent) is added to dissolve the Pb metal. (A mixture of concentrated nitric acid and hydrochloric acid is actually used.)

The other solutions were prepared by successive dilution of this most concentrated solution.

(c)

Alloy sample	Intensity / kc s⁻¹	[Pb] /mg dm⁻³
I	120	0.469
II	20	≈ 0.078

The concentration of II is less reliable as it is outside the range of the concentrations used in the calibration.

NATURE OF SCIENCE

The development of ICP spectroscopy illustrates the fuzzy boundary between pure and applied science. It is based on atomic processes and makes use of state of matter not generally found on the Earth, but it is a very sensitive method of analysis which can show the presence of material which would be undetected by other methods, and has helped the production of improved materials. Improved instrumentation has allowed us to collect data beyond human sense perception.

Inductively coupled plasma (ICP) mass spectroscopy (ICP-MS)

Inductively coupled plasma (ICP) mass spectroscopy is capable of detecting metals and non-metals at concentrations of one part in 10^{12}. The sample is ionized with inductively coupled plasma and analysed using a mass spectrometer to separate and count the abundance of the ions. The technique is more effective with metals than non-metals. Metals have lower ionization energies and so form positive ions more readily. The ability to obtain isotopic information has made the method particularly effective in geochemistry.

Exercises

14 (a) Describe the plasma state used in ICP spectroscopy.
  (b) Identify one element that cannot be identified by ICP spectroscopy.
  (c) Which method is more sensitive to measuring lower concentrations: ICP-OES or ICP-MS?
  (d) Identify the ICP method which is more effective in determining non-metal concentrations. Explain your answer.

15 Levels of heavy metal ions in soil need to be carefully monitored as they can cause serious damage to the environment and human health.

A range of solutions were made up with different mercury concentrations. The resulting calibration curves are shown.

(a) Explain how three calibration curves could be produced for the same metal.
(b) One sample of soil was analysed in accordance with the methods for the red line (II). It produced 3.00×10^7 counts in one minute. Deduce the mercury concentration of the sample.
(c) Deduce the intensity of photons produced by the sample when it is analysed in accordance with the blue line (I).
(d) Which line will produce the most precise concentration determination?

16 The metallurgical properties of aluminium and its alloys are highly dependent on chemical composition. The presence of manganese increases the hardness of the alloy.

The manganese content in an alloy was determined by ICP-OES with alloys of known composition. The intensity signal = 120 kc s^{-1}. What is the manganese content in the alloy?

A.3 Catalysts

Understandings:
- Reactants adsorb onto heterogeneous catalysts at active sites and the products desorb.
- Homogeneous catalysts chemically combine with the reactants to form a temporary activated complex or a reaction intermediate.
- Transition metal catalytic properties depend on the adsorption/absorption properties of the metal and the variable oxidation states.
- Zeolites act as selective catalysts because of their cage structure.
- Catalytic particles are nearly always nanoparticles that have large surface areas per unit mass.

Applications and skills:
- Explanation of factors involved in choosing a catalyst for a process.
- Description of how metals work as heterogeneous catalysts.
- Description of the benefits of nanocatalysts in industry.

Guidance
- *Consider catalytic properties such as selectivity for only the desired product, efficiency, ability to work in mild/severe conditions, environmental impact, and impurities.*
- *The use of carbon nanocatalysts should be covered.*

Catalysts play an essential role in the chemical industry. Without them many chemical processes would go too slowly to be economical. Catalysts work by providing reactions with alternative reaction mechanisms that have lower activation energies.

A catalyst can't make more of a product than would eventually be produced without it. It can however act *selectively* when two or more competing reactions are possible with the same starting materials, producing more of the desired product by catalysing only that reaction.

Catalysts increase the rate of some reactions but they do not change the position of equilibrium. They are not chemically changed at the end of the reaction.

The word *catalyst* derives from the Chinese word for marriage broker.

In the Haber process, chemists can produce ammonia at an economical rate at temperatures of 525 °C and a pressure of 20 atm (2×10^6 Pa). To make one gram of ammonia at the same temperature and pressure but without a catalyst would require a reactor 10 times the size of the Solar System.

Homogeneous and heterogeneous catalysis

Chemists divide catalysts into two types: **homogeneous** and **heterogeneous**. Homogeneous catalysts are in the same state of matter as the reactants, whereas in heterogeneous catalysis, the catalyst and the reactants are in different states. For example, the catalyst may be a solid and the reactants gases or liquids (Figure 12.11).

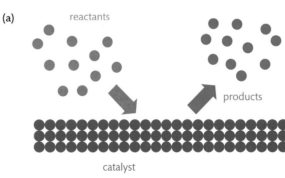

Figure 12.11 Diagram representing (a) heterogeneous catalysis and (b) homogeneous catalysis.

The area on the catalyst where the reaction takes place is called the **active site**. In heterogeneous catalysis the reactant molecules can only collide with the active sites on the *surface*. For the reactions to go significantly faster there must be a significant drop in activation energy to compensate for this. There are more active sites available in homogeneous catalysed reactions and a small drop in activation energy can lead to a dramatic increase in rate.

Heterogeneous catalysis is generally preferred in industrial processes as the catalyst can be easily removed by filtration from the reaction mixture. The use of iron in the Haber process and vanadium(v) oxide in the Contact process is discussed in Chapter 7 (page 234).

The use of homogeneous catalysis, which often requires expensive separation techniques, is generally reserved for the production of complex organic molecules. As they have greater activity, they work under milder conditions with greater selectivity. Enzyme-catalysed reactions in cells, which take place in aqueous solution, are examples of homogeneous catalysis.

> A substance is adsorbed when it is weakly attached to a surface. It is absorbed when it enters pores in the material.

Examples of catalysts: transition metals

Industrial process	Catalyst
Haber process: $N_2(g) + 3H_2(g) \rightleftharpoons 2NH_3(g)$	finely divided iron
Contact process: $2SO_2(g) + O_2(g) \rightleftharpoons 2SO_3(g)$	vanadium(v) oxide, platinum
hydrogenation of unsaturated oils to make margarine	nickel
reaction of CO and H_2 to make methanol: $CO(g) + 2H_2(g) \rightarrow CH_3OH(g)$	copper
catalytic cracking, e.g. $C_{10}H_{22}(g) \rightarrow C_4H_8(g) + C_6H_{14}(g)$	Al_2O_3/SiO_2, zeolites
polymerization of ethene to poly(ethene)	Ziegler–Natta catalyst, $AlR_3 + TiCl_4$

Many catalysts are either transition metals or their compounds. Transition metals show two properties that make them particularly effective as catalysts.

- They have variable oxidation states. They are particularly effective catalysts in redox reactions.
- They adsorb small molecules onto their surface. Transition metals are often good heterogeneous catalysts as they provide a surface for the reactant molecules to come together with the correct orientation. The products desorb from the surface once the reaction is complete.

Catalyst having variable oxidation state	Catalyst allowing adsorption onto surface
Vanadium(V) oxide as a catalyst: $V_2O_5(s) + SO_2(g) \rightarrow V_2O_4(s) + SO_3(g)$ $V_2O_4(s) + \frac{1}{2}O_2(g) \rightarrow V_2O_5(s)$ Overall reaction $SO_2(g) + \frac{1}{2}O_2(g) \rightarrow SO_3(g)$ Vanadium shows variable oxidation states. It is reduced from the +5 state to the +4 state and then oxidized back to the +5 state.	 The reactants are both gases. The reactants are both adsorbed on the Ni surface. Bonds are broken and formed on the surface. The product moves away from the surface.
	Nickel, shown in blue, adsorbs both C_2H_4 and H_2 and provides a surface for reaction. It brings the reactants together with the correct orientation for a successful addition reaction. C_2H_6 is the product.

Activated complexes and intermediates

An **activated complex** is an unstable combination of reactant molecules that can go on to form products or fall apart to form reactants as it corresponds to a state with partial bonds of maximum energy in the reaction profile. A heterogeneous catalyst decreases the activation energy by stabilizing the activated complex (Figure 12.12).

An activated complex is an unstable combination of reactant molecules that can go on to form products or fall apart to form reactants.

(a)

(b)

Figure 12.12 Heterogeneous catalysis stabilizes the activated complex. (a) The activated complex has more energy than either the reactants or products. It is an unstable state with partial bonds as they are partially broken and partially formed. (b) Heterogeneous catalysis allows the formation of a stabilized activated complex.

The V_2O_4 formed with vanadium in the +4 oxidation state in the homogeneous reaction above is a **reaction intermediate** (Figure 12.13). This is a species that occurs at a local minimum on the reaction profile that allows the reaction to follow a mechanism where all steps have lower activation energies than the uncatalysed reaction.

A reaction intermediate is a species that is produced and consumed during a reaction but does not occur in the overall equation.

411

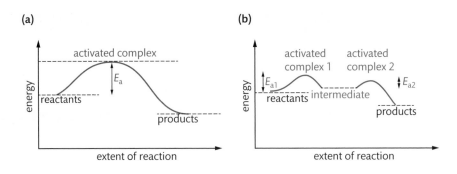

(a)

(b)

Figure 12.13 Homogeneous catalysis can involve the formation of reaction intermediates. (a) A reaction of one step which involves no intermediate step. (b) A reaction of two steps in which an intermediate is formed. An intermediate is more stable than an activated complex as it corresponds to a local minimum on the reaction energy profile.

Computer graphic representation of the structure of zeolite-Y, a mineral used in the catalytic cracking process in which large alkane molecules break down into smaller alkanes and alkenes. In this image, silicon and aluminium atoms are shown in yellow and oxygen atoms in red.

The word *zeolite* derives from the Greek words *zein* meaning to boil and *lithos* meaning stone. The first zeolite to be discovered released water when it was heated.

The open structure of zeolites is illustrated by the fact that a teaspoon of zeolite has a surface area of two tennis courts.

Zeolites act as selective catalysts because of their cage structures

Zeolites are a family of naturally occurring minerals of aluminium silicates.

The open caged structure of zeolites gives them excellent catalytic properties.

- They offer a huge surface for reactants to be adsorbed. Almost every atom in the solid is at a surface and is therefore available as an active site.
- The shape and size of the channels makes them *shape-selective* catalysts. Only reactants with the appropriate geometry can interact effectively with the active sites, and only smaller molecules can escape so the products can be controlled.

Nanoparticles are effective heterogeneous catalysts as they have large surface areas per unit mass

Nanoparticles with very small particle size are particularly effective **heterogeneous catalysts** as they have a large number of active sites on the surface relative to their mass. The surface structure and electronic properties of the particles can also be modified to improve their

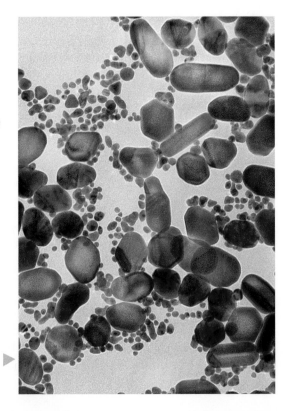

A coloured scanning electron micrograph (SEM) of gold nanoparticles.

catalytic performance. The benefits of nanoparticles are illustrated by the catalytic action of gold. Gold is relatively chemically inert, but in 1 nm clusters, which contain about 20 atoms, it becomes a very effective catalyst for a range of reactions which include the oxidation of carbon monoxide to form carbon dioxide in catalytic converters. The performance of a catalyst can be affected by local differences in composition, size, shape, and surface structure.

The hollow structures of carbon nanotubes discussed on page 435 also makes them very good candidates for shape-selective heterogeneous catalysis. They have large surface areas per unit mass, excellent electron conductivity, and are generally chemical stable. The catalytic properties can be varied by lining the tubes with different elements.

NATURE OF SCIENCE

Think about how models are used in science. Catalysts were used to increase reaction rates before the development of an understanding of how they work. This led to models that are constantly being tested and improved.

Supercomputer model of the structure of a gold nanoparticle (gold-coloured lattice) as it adsorbs carbon monoxide (CO, top). There are several hundred gold atoms in the lattice.

Catalytic activity can be modified with the use of promoters and inhibitors or inactivated by poisons

Catalytic activity can be deliberately modified with the use of **promoters** and **inhibitors**. The addition of promoters in small concentrations increases catalytic activity whereas inhibitors reduce the activity as they react with and remove the reaction intermediates.

Some catalysts have a limited working life as they can be **poisoned** or inactivated. Catalytic poisons block the active sites because they are adsorbed on the surface more strongly than reactant molecules. The iron catalysts in the Haber process work for between 5 and 10 years. Sulfur from traces of hydrogen sulfide in the natural gas used as the source of hydrogen presents the greatest problems. Similarly, the use of platinum as an effective catalyst for the Contact process is affected by even the smallest amounts of arsenic.

Other catalytic poisons include mercury(II) salts, carbon monoxide, and hydrogen cyanide.

Catalyst choice depends on selectivity for only the desired product and environmental impact

The choice of catalyst will depend on a number of factors.

• Selectivity: does the catalyst give a high yield of the desired product?
• Efficiency: how much faster is the reaction with the catalyst?
• Life expectancy: for how long does it work before it is poisoned?

• Environmental impact.
• Ability to work under a range of conditions of temperature and pressure. A heterogeneous catalyst may melt and or become less effective if its operating temperatures are too high or its surface becomes coated with unwanted products.

Although some catalysts, such as the transition metals platinum and palladium, are very expensive, their use is economical. They reduce the energy costs of the process, increase yields, and can be reused as they are not chemically changed.

NATURE OF SCIENCE

Catalysts are widely used in industry and it has been estimated that they contribute about one-sixth of the value of all manufactured goods in the industrialized world. Our understanding of the mechanisms of catalytic action has greatly improved recently because of the use of improved analytical spectroscopic and X-ray diffraction techniques. However, catalysis is a complex subject and there are still many areas where our understanding is incomplete. The growth in computing power has made modelling catalytic action much more powerful. These models can then be tested against the experimental results and modified accordingly.

▲ Platinum catalyst molecular modelling. Supercomputer model of the geometric and electronic structure of a platinum–carbon monoxide complex. A platinum cluster (seven yellow spheres) has adsorbed a carbon monoxide (CO) molecule (red and green spheres, bottom). The energetics of the bonding shown here is being studied because carbon monoxide can act to poison catalysts by adsorption on the surface of the metals used.

17 Explain why transition elements and their compounds are effective heterogeneous and homogeneous catalysts.

18 (a) Although many catalysts are very expensive, their use does allow the chemical industry to operate economically. Outline the advantages of using catalysts in industrial processes.

(b) Sulfur in crude oil must be removed before the crude oil is refined as the sulfur can poison the catalyst. Explain how the sulfur impurities poison the catalyst.

19 (a) Distinguish between a reaction intermediate and an activated complex. Which species can, in theory, be isolated?

(b) Explain why heterogeneous catalysts are generally used in industrial processes.

(c) Suggest two reasons why gold nanotubes are effective catalysts.

(d) Suggest a reason why it is difficult to regulate for the toxicity of nanoparticles.

A.4 Liquid crystals

Understandings:

- Liquid crystals are fluids that have physical properties (electrical, optical, and elasticity) that are dependent on molecular orientation to some fixed axis in the material.
- Thermotropic liquid crystal materials are pure substances that show liquid crystal behaviour over a temperature range.
- Lyotropic liquid crystals are solutions that show the liquid crystal state over a (certain) range of concentrations.
- The nematic liquid crystal phase is characterized by rod-shaped molecules which are randomly distributed but on average align in the same direction.

Guidance

- Soap and water are examples of lyotropic liquid crystals and biphenyl nitriles are examples of thermotropic liquid crystals.
- Smectics and other liquid crystal types need not be discussed.
- Liquid crystal behaviour should be limited to the biphenyl nitrates.

Applications and skills:

- Discussion of the properties needed for a substance to be used in liquid crystal displays (LCD).
- Explanation of liquid crystal behaviour on a molecular level.

Guidance

Properties needed for liquid crystals include: chemically stable, a phase which is stable over a suitable temperature range, polar so they can change orientation when an electric field is applied, and rapid switching speed.

The solid and liquid states are discussed in Chapter 1 (page 9). When a solid crystal melts, the ordered arrangement of the particles breaks down, to be replaced by the disordered state of the liquid. Some crystals, however, melt to give a state which retains some of the order of the solid state. This intermediate state of matter with properties between the solid and liquid state is called the **liquid crystal** state. Liquid crystals have many of the physical properties of solid crystals; however, these properties can be easily modified. In digital watches, for example, a small electric field can alter optical properties by changing the orientation of some of the molecules. Some areas of the display go dark and others remain light, allowing the shape of different digits to be displayed. Over the past 40 years liquid crystals have gone from being an academic curiosity to the basis of big business.

Liquid crystals typically all contain long, thin, rigid, polar organic molecules. Imagine a large number of pencils put into a rectangular box and shaken. When you open the box, the pencils will be facing in approximately the same direction, but will have no definite spatial organization. They are free to move, but generally line up almost parallel. This gives a simple model for the **nematic** type of a liquid phase liquid state. The molecules are randomly distributed as in a liquid, but the intermolecular forces are sufficiently strong to hold the molecule in one orientation in some regions or domains. These domains can be observed by viewing the liquid under a microscope with polarized light.

Although liquid crystals flow like a fluid, there is some order in their molecular arrangement. When viewed under a microscope using a polarized light, different regions, which have the molecules in different orientations, can be identified.

Thermotropic liquid crystals show liquid crystal behaviour over a temperature range

The liquid crystal phase is only stable over a small range of temperatures. The directional order is lost and the liquid state is formed when the molecules have too much kinetic energy to be constrained in the same orientation by the intermolecular forces (Figure 12.14).

Thermotropic liquid crystal materials are pure substances that show liquid crystal behaviour over a temperature range.

Figure 12.14 Thermotropic liquid crystals are formed in a temperature range between the solid and liquid state.

temperature increasing

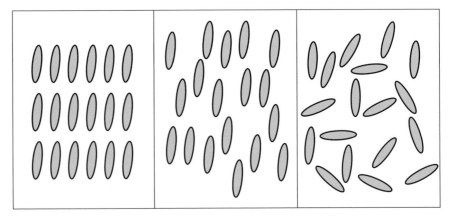

Solid The molecules have a regular arrangement and orientation.

Liquid crystal The molecules have an irregular arrangement and a regular orientation.

Liquid The molecules have an irregular arrangement and orientation.

Making a liquid crystal

Full details of how to carry out this experiment with a worksheet are available on your eBook.

Lyotropic liquid crystals are solutions

Some substances can form a different type of liquid crystal state in solution. Consider a solution containing some rod-like molecules as the solute. At low concentrations, the molecules generally have a disordered orientation and an irregular arrangement. If the concentration is increased sufficiently the molecules will adopt an ordered structure and solid crystals will form. At intermediate concentrations a **lyotropic** liquid crystal state may be possible where the molecules have an irregular arrangement with a regular orientation (Figure 12.15).

concentration decreasing →

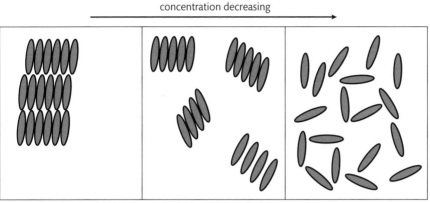

Solid The molecules have a regular arrangement and orientation.

Liquid crystal The molecules have an irregular arrangement and a regular orientation.

Liquid The molecules have an irregular arrangement and orientation.

Figure 12.15 The phase transitions of lyotropic liquid crystals depend on both temperature and concentration.

> The phase transitions of thermotropic liquid crystals depend on temperature, while those of lyotropic liquid crystals depend on both temperature and concentration.

Liquid crystal properties may play a central role in the processing of silk. The water-soluble silk molecules are stored in aqueous solution, but they can be assembled into rod-like units which form a lyotropic liquid crystal state.

The molecules that make up lyotropic liquid crystals generally consist of two distinct parts: a polar, often ionic, **head** and a non-polar, often hydrocarbon, **tail**. When dissolved in high enough concentrations in aqueous solutions, the molecules arrange themselves so that the polar heads are in contact with a polar solvent in an arrangement called a **micelle** (Figure 12.16).

hydrophobic hydrocarbon chain

hydrophobic non-polar tail   hydrophilic polar head

A micelle is formed when the molecules group together to form a spherical arrangement. The hydrophilic heads are exposed to water, shielding the non-polar tails.

Figure 12.16 The formation of a micelle.

Lyotropic liquid crystals are found in many everyday situations. Soaps and detergents, for example, form lyotropic liquid crystals when they combine with water. Many biological membranes also display lyotropic liquid crystalline behaviour.

Kevlar® can show lyotropic properties in solution as it is a rigid rod-shaped molecule due to its linked benzene rings. Although it is very resistant to most chemicals, Kevlar® is soluble in concentrated sulfuric acid as the hydrogen bonds between the chains are broken (Figure 12.17). At high concentrations a lyotropic liquid crystal state is formed. Some hydrogen bonding is present which forces the molecules into a parallel arrangement in localized regions like logs floating down a river.

Figure 12.17 The structure of Kevlar®. There are hydrogen bonds between the chains which can be broken when it is added to concentrated sulfuric acid.

The elasticity and electrical and optical properties depend on the orientation of the molecule to some fixed axis in the material

The practical application of liquid crystals makes use of the dependence of their physical properties, such as their elasticity, and their electrical and optical behaviour on their molecular orientation to some fixed axis in the material.

To understand the optical properties of liquid crystals, we need to consider the behaviour of **polarized** light when it passes through a polarizing filter. We saw in Chapter 2 (page 69) that light is an electromagnetic wave. It is said to be polarized when the electric field vector vibrates in one plane only. A polarizing filter will only transmit light when it is aligned with the electric field. This is illustrated by the arrangement in Figure 12.18.

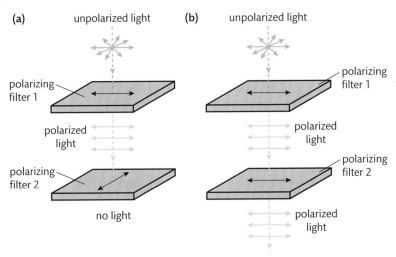

Figure 12.18 (a) When the polarizing filters are crossed so that their planes of polarization are at right angles to one another, no light is transmitted. (b) When the polarizing filters are parallel, all of the light passing through the first filter also passes through the second.

The two polarizing filters used together transmit light differently depending on their relative orientations. The second polarizing filter is sometimes called the **analyser**.

The ability of liquid crystals to transmit light depends on their relative orientation to the plane of polarization.

NATURE OF SCIENCE

Liquid crystals, like many scientific discoveries, were found by accident. In 1888 the Austrian botanist Friedrich Reinitzer was investigating the behaviour of derivatives of cholesterol at different temperatures when he observed that cholesteryl benzoate appeared to have two melting points. The crystals form a cloudy liquid at 145.5 °C which clears at 178.5 °C. It takes more than being in the right place, at the right time, to make a serendipitous discovery. Scientific research may be unpredictable but it is based on highly focused and creative thinking. 'Dans les champs de l'observation le hazard ne favorise que les esprits préparés.' 'In the field of observation, fortune only favours the prepared mind.' (Louis Pasteur 1822–1895). Reinitzer's experience had taught him the importance of careful observation and his background knowledge made him appreciate the significance of what he had observed. His inquisitive mind led him to ask a physics colleague, Otto Lehmann, for an explanation of the crystal's behaviour. Lehmann had the right tools for the task: his own research involved studying the properties of materials with polarized light. It was Lehmann who first used the term *fliessende Kristalle*, or liquid crystals.

TOK

What attributes of the IB learner profile help scientists turn a lucky break into a scientific breakthrough?

CHALLENGE YOURSELF

1 The molecular structure of cholesteryl benzoate is shown here.

(a) Identify a feature of its molecular structure that allows it to form a liquid crystal state.
(b) Classify cholesteryl benzoate as a thermotropic or lyotropic liquid.

Biphenyl nitriles show liquid crystal behaviour

The first liquid crystal molecules with suitable properties to be synthesized were the biphenyl nitriles (Figure 12.19).

The molecule is polar as nitrogen has a greater electronegativity than carbon.

Figure 12.19 The biphenyl nitriles are liquid crystals. They are polar rigid rod-shaped molecules.

These molecules have three key features.

- Long alkyl chain: this limits the ability of the molecules to pack together and so lowers the melting point and helps maintain the liquid crystal state. The melting range can be varied by changing the size and shape of the hydrocarbon chain.
- Biphenyl groups: the two planar benzene rings make the molecule rigid and rod-shaped.
- Nitrile group: the high electronegativity of nitrogen makes the functional group polar. This increases the intermolecular interactions between the molecules and allows the orientation of the molecule to be controlled by an electric field.

The presence of the unreactive alkyl groups and the two stable benzene rings increases the chemical stability of the molecule.

A number of rod-shaped molecules with thermotropic properties have been developed. Some examples are shown in Figure 12.20.

Figure 12.20 Rod-shaped molecules that show thermotropic liquid crystal behaviour.

The use of biphenyl nitriles in liquid crystal display devices

The ability of the rod-shaped biphenyl nitrile molecule to transmit light depends on its relative orientation to the plane of polarization. As the molecule is polar, this orientation can be controlled by the application of an electric field. When there is no applied voltage, light can be transmitted and the display appears light. When a small voltage is applied, the orientation of the molecules changes and light can no longer be transmitted through the film and the display appears dark. The areas of the display that are light and dark can thus be controlled, enabling different shapes to be displayed.

As discussed earlier, the nematic state for a thermotropic liquid crystal only exists within a small range of temperatures, which can limit the operating temperatures of LCDs.

Pentylcyanophenyl is suitable for liquid crystal displays (LCDs) as it has the following properties.

- It is chemically stable.
- It has a liquid crystal phase stable over a suitable range of temperatures.
- It is polar, making it able to change its orientation when an electric field is applied.
- It responds to changes of voltage quickly, i.e. it has a fast switching speed.

The dark areas of the display correspond to areas where a small voltage changes the orientation of the liquid crystal molecules, preventing light from passing through the film.

In general, no single compound can fulfil all the properties required for LCD applications, so complex mixtures are used. They contain 10–20 components, each one used to modify specific display properties, such as threshold voltage, switching speed, and temperature range

Twisted nematic LCDs

In a twisted nematic display, the liquid crystal material is located between two glass plates, all between two polarizing filters at right angles to each other. The surface of the glass plates is coated with a thin polymer layer with scratches in one direction. The molecules in contact with the glass line up with the scratches, like matches in the grooves of a piece of corrugated paper. Intermolecular bonds allow the molecules between the plates to form a twisted arrangement with the alignment varying smoothly across the cell (Figure 12.21).

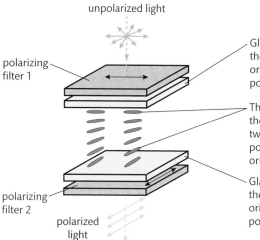

Glass plate is treated to ensure that the liquid crystal molecules are orientated parallel to the first polarizing filter.

The liquid crystal molecules between the glass plates twist between the two orientations. The plane of polarization of the light follows the orientation of the molecules.

Glass plate is treated to ensure that the liquid crystal molecules are orientated parallel to the second polarizing filter.

Figure 12.21 Light passes through the LCD despite the orientation of the polarizing filters because the plane of polarization of light rotates with the orientation of the molecules.

In the 'off' state, the light passes through the second polarizing filter as the plane of polarization rotates with the molecular orientation as the light passes through the cell.

However, when a small threshold voltage is applied across the cell (the 'on' state), the situation changes. The polar liquid crystal molecules now align with the field and so the twisted structure is lost. The plane-polarized light is no longer rotated, and so no light is transmitted and the cell appears dark (Figure 12.22).

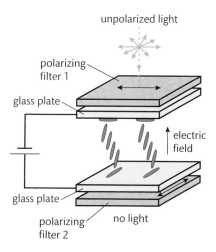

Figure 12.22 The liquid crystal molecules align themselves parallel to the electric field when the threshold voltage is applied.

CHALLENGE YOURSELF

2 The diagram below is a representation of a liquid crystal display. A liquid crystal has the property of being able to rotate the plane of polarization of light.

polarizer | glass plate with circular electrode | liquid crystal | glass plate with circular electrode | analyser crossed with polarizing filter | mirror

    (a) State, and explain, what the observer would see if the liquid crystal were not present.

    (b) State, and explain, what the observer would see if the liquid crystal were present.

    (c) Outline how the application of a potential difference between the circular electrodes allows the observer to see the circle on the second glass plate.

Exercises

20 (a) Distinguish between the liquid state and the liquid crystal state.

    (b) Distinguish between a lyotropic liquid crystal and a thermotropic liquid crystal.

    (c) Outline how a micelle forms in a soap solution.

21 Distinguish between thermotropic liquid crystals and lyotropic liquid crystals and state the name of one example of each.

22 The molecule below has liquid crystal properties.

$$C_5H_{11} - \text{(structure with rings)} - F, F$$

    (a) Explain how the hydrocarbon chain adds to the chemical stability of the molecule.

    (b) How does the presence of two fluorine atoms improve the liquid crystal properties?

23 The structure of a terphenyl molecule is shown below:

$$C_5H_{11} - \text{(three rings)} - C \equiv N \quad \delta^+ \quad \delta^-$$

    (a) State the molecular formula of the molecule.

    (b) Suggest why the molecule can show liquid crystal behaviour at higher temperatures than the biphenyl molecules.

A.5 Polymers

Understandings:

- Thermoplastics soften when heated and harden when cooled.
- A thermosetting polymer is a prepolymer in a soft solid or viscous state that changes irreversibly into a hardened thermoset by curing.

- Elastomers are flexible and can be deformed under force but will return to nearly their original shape once the stress is released.
- High-density poly(ethene) (HDPE) has no branching, allowing chains to be packed together.
- Low-density poly(ethene) (LDPE) has some branching and is more flexible.
- Plasticizers added to a polymer increase the flexibility by weakening the intermolecular forces between the polymer chains.
- Atom economy is a measure of efficiency applied in Green Chemistry.
- Isotactic addition polymers have substituents on the same side.
- Atactic addition polymers have the substituents randomly placed.

Guidance
The equation for percent atom economy is provided in the IB data booklet in section 1.

Applications and skills:
- Description of the use of plasticizers in poly(vinyl chloride) and volatile hydrocarbons in the formation of expanded polystyrene.
- Solving problems and evaluating atom economy in synthesis reactions.
- Description of how the properties of polymers depend on their structural features.
- Description of ways of modifying the properties of polymers including LDPE and HDPE.
- Deduction of structures of polymers formed from polymerizing 2-methylpropene.
- Consider only polystyrene foams as examples of polymer property manipulation.

An addition polymer is formed when the double bonds of many monomer molecules open up to form a long continuous chain.

In the 1930s some British scientists were investigating the reactions of ethene with other carbon compounds under high pressure. In some of the experiments, a hard waxy solid was produced, which was found to consist of only carbon and hydrogen atoms in the ratio 1 : 2. This accidental discovery has had a profound effect on all our lives. They had made poly(ethene). Plastics such as poly(ethene) are now the basis of many everyday materials. The addition polymerization reaction of ethene, in which many ethene molecules join together like a chain of paper clips, is outlined in Chapter 10 (page 332).

$$n \left(\begin{array}{c} H \quad\quad H \\ \backslash \quad\quad / \\ C = C \\ / \quad\quad \backslash \\ H \quad\quad H \end{array} \right) \longrightarrow \left(\begin{array}{c} H \quad\quad H \\ | \quad\quad | \\ -C - C - \\ | \quad\quad | \\ H \quad\quad H \end{array} \right)_n$$

monomer   polymer
ethene   poly(ethene)

Computer graphic representation of the packed chains of the poly(ethene) molecule, a long-chain hydrocarbon with a high molecular mass. Poly(ethene) is made by the polymerization of C_2H_4, by heating under pressure in the presence of oxygen. It may be essentially considered to be a very long chain alkane.

The double bond in ethene breaks open and allows many molecules to link together to form a chain. The value of n varies with the reaction conditions but it is generally in the thousands. The strength and melting points of the polymers increase with chain length, as the intermolecular forces increase with molecular size.

Polymers with different chemical compositions can be formed by changing the **monomer**: the formation of poly(ethene), poly(chloroethene), poly(propene), and poly(styrene) follow the same reaction scheme:

$$n \left(\begin{array}{c} H \quad\quad H \\ \backslash \quad\quad / \\ C = C \\ / \quad\quad \backslash \\ H \quad\quad X \end{array} \right) \longrightarrow \left(\begin{array}{c} H \quad\quad H \\ | \quad\quad | \\ -C - C - \\ | \quad\quad | \\ H \quad\quad X \end{array} \right)_n$$

monomer   polymer with a long straight
              chain of carbon atoms

423

Monomer	Polymer	Monomer	Polymer
ethene	polyethene	propene	polypropene
chloroethene (vinyl chloride)	polychloroethene (PVC)	styrene	polystyrene

Hermann Staudinger was the first polymer chemist to be awarded the Nobel Prize in 1953 'for his discoveries in the field of macromolecular chemistry'.

What role do disagreements play in the pursuit of knowledge?

TOK

NATURE OF SCIENCE

Although plastics were one of the key materials of the last century the notion of very large molecules was not widely accepted by the scientific community until 1929. The story of the acceptance of the theory of large molecules is the story of Hermann Staudinger's determination to push forward an idea despite widespread resistance from his academic peers. The academic chemistry community at the beginning of the 20th century thought that the newly invented plastics and natural materials such as rubber, starch, and cellulose had structures in which bundles of small molecules were held together by unknown intermolecular forces. Staudinger's idea that there was a covalent bond between the units had little support. He was told by one of his colleagues to 'drop the idea of large molecules'. The eventual acceptance of Staudinger's theory was a key step in our scientific understanding that led to the practical development of polymer chemistry. Science is a human activity and disputes of this sort are common. They are constructive if they focus on the science and do not degenerate into personal squabbles.

Worked example

Deduce the structure of the addition polymer formed from methylpropene. You should include three repeating units in the structure.

Solution

1   Draw three structures with the alkene double bond in the middle:

2   Open the double bond in each molecule so that single bonds extend in both directions:

Many students have difficulty drawing the structure of poly(propene). It is important to note that it follows the general scheme with the methyl group as a side chain. Practise drawing structures for polymers with side groups (formed from monomers such as propene and chloroethene).

Changing the chemical composition of the monomer and the chain length is not the only strategy used to change the properties of a polymer. The description of a polymer as one straight chain is an oversimplification as branching can occur along the main chain. The relative orientation of all the groups along the chain can also affect the properties of the polymer.

The density of poly(ethene) depends on the branching in the structure

The poly(ethene) used to make plastic bags has very different properties from the poly(ethene) used to make plastic buckets and toys. The carbon and hydrogen atoms are in the same ratio 1 : 2 but the molecules have different molecular structures. If poly(ethene) is polymerized at very high pressures, the reaction proceeds by a free radical mechanism and branched carbon chains are produced (Figure 12.23). This branching limits the interaction and alignment between neighbouring chains and the intermolecular forces are relatively weak. The resulting low-density polymer has a low melting point and quite flexible carbon chains.

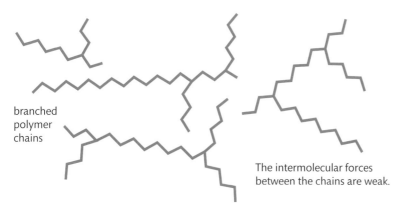

branched polymer chains

The intermolecular forces between the chains are weak.

Figure 12.23 Low-density poly(ethene) (LDPE). Branching limits the ability of the chains to pack closely. In this amorphous (non-crystalline) form, the intermolecular interactions between the chains are weak.

When ethene is polymerized at a lower temperature in the presence of a catalyst (a Ziegler catalyst with metal–carbon bonds) the reaction occurs by an ionic mechanism and a more crystalline structure is produced (Figure 12.24). In this high-density form the molecules have straight chains. It is more rigid, as the molecules are more closely packed with stronger intermolecular forces, and has a higher melting point.

A range of poly(ethene)s with varying properties can be produced by modifying the extent and location of branching in the low-density form.

The plastic used to make this bag was LDPE, low-density poly(ethene).

intermolecular forces between the straight chains are relatively strong

Figure 12.24 High-density poly(ethene) (HDPE). In this crystalline form the parallel chains are closely packed with relatively strong intermolecular bonds.

Different orientations of side groups lead to isotactic and atactic forms

The presence of a methyl group in propene introduces a structural feature into the polymer chain not found in poly(ethene). Methyl groups can be arranged with different orientations relative to the carbon backbone. The **isotactic** form of the polymer, with methyl groups arranged on one side, is an example of a **stereoregular** polymer (Figure 12.25). It is crystalline and tough and can be moulded into different shapes. It is used to make car bumpers and plastic toys and can be drawn into fibres to make clothes and carpets.

Figure 12.25 Isotactic poly(propene) has a regular structure with the methyl groups pointing in the same direction, making it crystalline and tough.

The **atactic** form, produced when the methyl groups are randomly orientated, is softer and more flexible (Figure 12.26). It is useful as a sealant and in other waterproof coatings.

Figure 12.26 Atactic poly(propene) has an irregular structure, which prevents the chains from packing together. It is soft and flexible.

The product of the polymerization reaction of propene can be controlled by using catalysts, allowing chemists to tailor-make polymers with precise properties. A free-radical catalyst will produce the atactic polymer; a **Ziegler–Natta** catalyst, which leads to an ionic mechanism, will produce the more ordered isotactic form. The monomer binds to the catalyst surface with the correct orientation to produce the more ordered polymer. Other polymers with side chains, such as PVC, can also exist in isotactic and atactic forms.

Catalysts used to make stereoregular polymers are called Ziegler–Natta catalysts. The German chemist Karl Ziegler and Italian Guillio Natta shared the 1963 Nobel Prize for their work in this field.

The properties of polyvinyl chloride are modified by using plasticizers

The non-systematic name for chloroethene is vinyl chloride and so the polymer of this monomer is more commonly known as poly(vinyl chloride) or PVC. The presence of the polar $C^{\delta+}$—$Cl^{\delta-}$ bond in PVC gives it very different properties from both poly(ethene) and poly(propene). The molecule has a permanent dipole, allowing a strong dipole–dipole intermolecular interaction to occur between neighbouring chains. The presence of the relatively large Cl atom also limits the ability of the chains to move across each other. The pure polymer is hard and brittle and has few uses. Its properties are radically improved, however, when **plasticizers**, such as di-(2-ethylhexyl)hexanedioate are added (Figures 12.27 and 12.28). The plasticizer molecules fit in between and separate the polymer chains. This allows the chains to slip across each other more easily. The most common plasticisers are di-esters such as the phthalates. The resulting plastic is softer and more flexible and is used, for example, to make credit cards. PVC with varying degrees of flexibility can be produced by varying the amount of plasticizer. The possible environmental impact of using plasticizers is discussed later (see page 439).

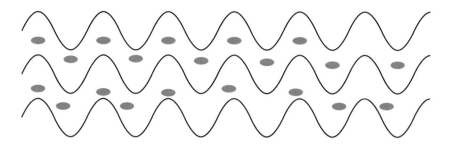

Figure 12.27 The plasticizer molecules shown here in red separate the polymer chains. This allows them to move freely past each other.

(a)

$$\begin{array}{c} O \\ \| \\ C \end{array} - O - CH_2 - \underset{\underset{(CH_2)_4}{|}}{CH} - CH_2 - CH_2 - CH_2 - CH_3$$

$$\begin{array}{c} \overset{|}{C} \\ \| \\ O \end{array} - O - CH_2 - \underset{\underset{CH_2CH_3}{|}}{CH} - CH_2 - CH_2 - CH_2 - CH_3$$

(b)

Figure 12.28 (a) Di-(2-ethylhexyl)hexanedioate and the (b) phthalates are common plasticizers. Note the presence of the two ester functional groups in both structures.

Light micrograph of fibres of PVC. PVC is a tough, white material, which softens with the application of a plasticizer.

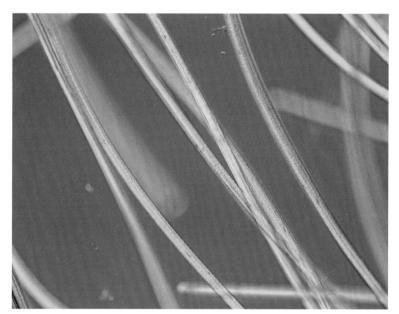

Expanded polystyrene is widely used as a thermally insulating and protective packaging material.

Expanded polystyrene is made by adding volatile hydrocarbons

Expanded polystyrene is made by **expansion moulding**. Polystyrene beads containing about 5% of a volatile hydrocarbon such as pentane are placed in a mould and heated. The heat causes the pentane to evaporate and bubbles of gas to form. The expansion of the gas causes the polymer to expand into the shape of the mould. The resulting plastic has a low density, is white, opaque, and an excellent thermal insulator. These properties should be contrasted with the polystyrene made without a foaming agent, which is colourless, transparent, and brittle.

Polymers can be classified based on their response to heat and applied forces

Thermoplastics soften when heated and harden when cooled

The plastics we have discussed are all examples of **thermosoftening** or **thermoplastic** polymers (Figure 12.29). They are made from polymer chains which interact only weakly via intermolecular forces. When they are heated one chain can slip across another making the polymer soften. They can be reheated and remoulded many times.

The intermolecular forces are strongest in crystalline regions, where the molecules are aligned. These areas increase the hardness of the bulk material. The molecules can slide across each other in amorphous regions which make the bulk material less brittle.

A **fibre** has a special crystalline structure in which all the molecules are aligned along the same direction. Isotactic poly(propene) can be made into such a strong fibre.

(a)   (b)

More generally the crystalline regions are not aligned in the same direction. This can be increased if the polymer is stretched. This increases the strength of the polymer in the direction of the force, but may weaken it in other directions (Figure 12.30).

(a)   (b)

stretching force

Figure 12.29 Schematic of thermosoftening plastics. (a) They are made from polymer chains which interact only weakly via intermolecular forces. (b) If the chains are allowed to line up, the intermolecular forces increase and a strong fibre with a crystalline structure is produced.

Figure 12.30 Stretching a thermoplastic increases the alignment between the crystalline regions of the polymer. The amorphous regions have been omitted for clarity. (a) Different crystalline regions of a thermoplastic where the molecules are aligned. (b) Stretching a thermoplastic increases the alignment between the different crystalline regions and increases the strength in this direction.

Elastomer polymers show elastic properties when stretched

Elastomers are flexible and can be deformed under force but will return to nearly their original shape once the force is removed. Rubber, for example, is a natural hydrocarbon polymer which can be reversibly extended to over six times its natural length without losing its natural shape – which returns when the stretching force is removed. Although we have generally represented the polymer chains as relatively straight, this, as already discussed, is a simplification. Free rotation about the C–C bonds allows some polymer chains to be coiled into many different arrangements. These coils are straightened when the material is stretched but can return if the force applied to stretch the material is removed.

The elastic behaviour of a plastic can be modified with the addition of a small number of covalent bonds which allow some cross-links to form between the chains (Figure 12.31). This limited cross-linking restricts the overall movement of the molecules but allows some local movement.

Figure 12.31 Two polymer chains ∿ linked by a covalent bond ∫. The chains can be uncoiled when the polymer is stretched but return once the force is removed. The cross-link between the chains keeps the chains knotted together which increases the elasticity of the polymer.

The elastic properties of rubber can be linked to the presence of double bonds in the rubber structure ($-[CH_2-C(CH_3)=CH-CH_2]_n-$), which react with sulfur when the polymer is heated in the vulcanization process. The sulfur atoms form $-S-S-$ bridges between neighbouring chains which keeps the molecule knotted together. The molecules are free to unwind under stress but the cross-links restrict the relative movement between the chains.

Poly(2-chlorobuta-1,3-diene) ($-[CH_2-CH=CCl-CH_2]_n-$), which also has an alkene double bond in the polymer chain, is an elastomer known as Neoprene.

A thermosetting polymer is hardened by heating

There is more extensive cross-linking in the thermosetting polymers. A soft solid or viscous **prepolymer** state, made up from molecules of intermediate size, is first formed which then changes irreversibly into a hardened thermoset by curing. Covalent bonds are formed between adjacent chains of the polymers. These strong covalent cross-linkages give the material increased strength and rigidity. The extensive cross-links prevent the plastic from melting when it is reheated and so they cannot be softened or remoulded (Figure 12.32).

Figure 12.32 Schematic of thermosetting plastics. The polymer chains ∿ are linked by cross-links of covalent bonds ∫.

One of the first thermosetting plastics was Bakelite, formed from the co-monomers phenol and methanol (Figure 12.33). Bakelite has a hard rigid structure which does not melt once it has been heated and set. Modern resins are made in a similar way to Bakelite but melamine is used instead of phenol (see Exercise 27).

Figure 12.33 The structure of Bakelite, a thermosetting plastic. Methanal (CH$_2$O) provides the CH$_2$ cross-links (shown in blue) between the benzene rings of phenol.

Atom economy is a measure of efficiency applied in Green Chemistry

Green Chemistry is the sustainable design of chemical products and chemical processes. It aims to minimize the use and generation of chemical substances that are hazardous to human health and the environment. Traditionally, the efficiency of a reaction has been measured by calculating the percentage yield (the proportion of the desired product obtained compared to the theoretical maximum), but this is only a limited measure as it gives no indication of the quantity of waste produced. A synthetic route should maximize the atom economy by incorporating as many of the atoms of the reactants as possible into the desired product.

The **atom economy** of a reaction can be calculated from the equation provided in section 1 of the IB data booklet:

$$\% \text{ atom economy} = \frac{\text{molar mass of desired product}}{\text{molar mass of all reactants}} \times 100\%$$

Efficient processes have high atom economies, and are important for sustainable development, as they use fewer natural resources and create less waste. Addition polymerization reactions, for example, have an atom economy of 100% as all the reacting atoms end up in the polymer and there are no side products. Many real-world processes in drug synthesis, for example, use deliberate excess of reactants to increase the yield but have low atom economies.

Catalysts have a crucial role in improving atom economy.

% atom economy =
molar mass of desired product
 molar mass of all reactants
× 100%

Worked example

Chloroethene is the monomer used in the manufacture of PVC. It can be produced from 1,2-dichloroethane by the following reaction.

$$CH_2ClCH_2Cl \rightarrow CH_2{=}CHCl + HCl$$

Calculate the atom economy for the reaction.

Solution

molar mass of reactant $= (2 \times 12.01) + (4 \times 1.01) + (2 \times 35.45) = 98.96$

molar mass desired product $= (2 \times 12.01) + (3 \times 1.01) + (1 \times 35.45) = 62.50$

$$\% \text{ atom economy} = \frac{62.50}{98.96} \times 100\% = 63.2\%$$

Exercises

24 Identify which of the options below best describes a thermoplastic material.

	Interaction within chains	Interaction between chains
A	strong covalent	strong van der Waals' forces
B	strong covalent	weak van der Waals' forces
C	strong van der Waals' forces	weak covalent
D	weak covalent	weak covalent

Explain your answer.

25 (a) Draw a full structural formula showing the repeating unit in isotactic poly(propene).

(b) Poly(propene) can exist in isotactic and atactic forms. Sketch the structure and name the stereoregular polymer.

(c) Explain why the more crystalline form can be used to make strong fibres for carpets.

(d) Deduce how many monomer units of propene could be joined together to make a polymer with an average relative molecular mass of 2.1×10^6.

(e) Explain why only an *average* value can be given for the relative molecular mass.

26 The properties of polystyrene and PVC can be modified during the manufacturing process.

(a) Distinguish between two forms of PVC and explain their difference in properties.

(b) Distinguish between two forms of polystyrene and explain their difference in properties.

27 Melamine has the following structure.

(a) It can be produced from urea in the following reaction.

$$6(NH_2)_2CO \rightarrow C_3H_6N_6 + 6NH_3 + 3CO_2$$

Calculate the atom economy for the reaction.

(b) Melamine combines with a co-monomer methanol to form a resin. Suggest a structure for this thermosetting plastic.

(c) Explain why thermoplastics such as poly(ethene) melt whereas thermosetting plastics such as the melamine resin do not.

(d) Discuss the role of cross-linking in the structures of thermosetting plastics and elastomers.

28 (a) Explain the use of expanded polystyrene as a packaging material.

(b) Describe how the expanded form is produced.

A.6 **Nanotechnology**

Understandings:

- Molecular self-assembly is the bottom-up assembly of nanoparticles and can occur by selectively attaching molecules to specific surfaces. Self-assembly can also occur spontaneously in solution.
- Possible methods of producing nanotubes are arc discharge, chemical vapour deposition (CVD), and high-pressure carbon monoxide (HIPCO).
- Arc discharge involves either vaporizing the surface of one of the carbon electrodes, or discharging an arc through metal electrodes submersed in a hydrocarbon solvent, which forms a small rod-shaped deposit on the anode.

Applications and skills:

- Distinguishing between physical and chemical techniques in manipulating atoms to form molecules.
- Description of the structure and properties of carbon nanotubes.
- Explanation of why an inert gas, and not oxygen, is necessary for CVD preparation of carbon nanotubes.
- Explanation of the production of carbon from hydrocarbon solvents in arc discharge by oxidation at the anode.
- Deduction of equations for the production of carbon atoms from HIPCO.
- Discussion of some implications and applications of nanotechnology.
- Explanation of why nanotubes are strong and good conductors of electricity.

Guidance

- *Possible implications of nanotechnology include uncertainty as to toxicity levels on a nanoscale, unknown health risks with new materials, concern that human defence systems are not effective against particles on the nanoscale, responsibilities of the industries and governments involved in this research.*
- *Conductivity of graphene and fullerenes can be explained in terms of delocalization of electrons. An explanation based on hybridization is not required.*

In 1959 the Nobel Prize winning physicist Richard Feynman gave a ground-breaking talk about the physical possibility of making, manipulating, and visualizing things on a small scale and arranging atoms 'the way we want'. Feynman challenged scientists to develop a new field where devices and machines could be built from tens or hundreds of atoms. This field is now called **nanotechnology**, which has been described as 'the science of the very small with big potential'.

Richard Feynman (1918–1988). His article 'There's plenty of room at the bottom' made predictions about nanotechnology before it was practically possible.

Individual silicon atoms (yellow) can be positioned to store data. These data can be written and read using a scanning tunnelling microscope.

Nanoscience research has rapidly grown internationally since the 1990s and it is now widely accepted that it will play an important role in the development of future technologies.

Nanotechnology involves structures in the 1–100 nm range

Nanotechnology is defined as the research and technology development in the 1–100 nm range. Nanotechnology creates and uses structures that have novel properties because of their small size. It builds on the ability to control or manipulate matter on the atomic scale.

Nanotechnology is an interdisciplinary subject which covers chemistry, physics, biology, and material science. To the chemist, who is familiar with the world of molecules and atoms, 1 nm (10^{-9} m) is relatively large, whereas 1 mm (10^{-6} m) is considered small on an engineering scale. There are two general ways that are available to produce nanomaterials. The **top-down** approach starts with a bulk material and breaks it into smaller pieces. The **bottom-up** approach builds the material from atomic or molecular species. It is important to understand that, on the nanoscale, materials behave very differently to their bulk properties. The rules are very different from those that apply to our everyday world. The electron, for example, behaves more like a wave on the nanoscale scale and is less localized in space and can tunnel through what should be impenetrable barriers. Substances that are insulators in bulk form might become semiconductors when reduced to the nanoscale. Melting points can change due to an increase in surface area. These quantum effects and the large surface-area-to-volume ratios can lead to the same material having a range of size-dependent properties. The colour of a material, for example, can depend on its size.

NATURE OF SCIENCE

Science is an exciting and challenging adventure involving much creativity and imagination as well as exacting and detailed thinking and application. Richard Feynman was well known for flashes of intuition and the pleasure he took 'in finding things out'. He likened the scientific endeavour to understand the natural world to someone trying to understand the rules of chess by observation alone. 'You might discover after a bit, for example, that when there's only one bishop around on the board that the bishop maintains its colour. Later on you might discover the law for the bishop as it moves on the diagonal which would explain the law that you understood before – that it maintained its colour – and that would be analogous to discovering one law and then later finding a deeper understanding of it. Then things can happen, everything's going good, and then all of a sudden some strange phenomenon occurs in some corner, so you begin to investigate that – it's castling, something you didn't expect.' It is things we don't understand that are the most interesting. The direct influence of Feynman on nanotechnology is open to debate, but it is notable that Feynman's vision of atomically precise fabrication was cited by Bill Clinton during his presidential address when he proposed financial backing for scientific research in nanotechnology in January 2000. All science has to be funded, and political and economic factors are important factors in determining where the money goes. Science is a human activity and Nobel laureates have more political influence than their less experienced colleagues.

Individual atoms can be visualized and manipulated using the scanning tunnelling and atomic force microscopes

One significant step in the bottom-up approach to the subject was the development of the scanning tunnelling microscope (STM) and the atomic force microscope (AFM),

It is theoretically possible to store the information in all the books of the world in a cube of material the size of the 'barest piece of dust that can be made out by the human eye'.

TOK

'Before you become too entranced with gorgeous gadgets ... let me remind you that information is not knowledge, knowledge is not wisdom ...' (Arthur C Clarke)

What is the difference between knowledge and information?

Nanotechnology involves research and technology development in the 1–100 nm range. It creates and uses structures that have novel properties because of their small size and builds on the ability to control or manipulate on the atomic scale. One nanometre is 0.000 000 001 m. It can be written as 1 nm or 1×10^{-9} m.

which can visualize and manipulate individual atoms in a physical way due to the interactions between the atoms of the probe and the atoms of the material under scrutiny.

Coloured atomic force micrograph (AFM) of molecules of yttrium oxide (Y_2O_3) on a thin film of yttrium. A thin probe is moved across the surface and its movements as it follows the contours of the surface are translated into an image.

Self-assembly can occur spontaneously in solution due to intermolecular interactions

Although ionic crystals naturally grow in solution as the opposite charged ions organize themselves into a lattice structure, the self-assembly of covalent structures is more complex.

Simple molecules such as water and glucose, for example, are just below 1 nm in size. The synthesis of nanoscale materials, which are 10–100 times larger, from such molecules is difficult using conventional chemical methods. It would involve large numbers of molecules spontaneously self-assembling. The process does, however, occur in nature where highly complex molecular structures such as proteins are built from the simple building blocks of 20 amino acids. This is possible as the amino molecules *recognize* and bind to each other by intermolecular interactions such as **hydrogen bonding** and **van der Waals'** forces. DNA-assisted assembly methods can be used in a similar way to make nanoscale materials. Strands of the molecule act as an 'intelligent sticky tape' allowing only certain base pairings to occur. Molecules can only bind to bases of the DNA when specific hydrogen bonding interactions occur. The field has developed in many directions, with chemists synthesizing ever more complex and finely tuned super-molecules.

NATURE OF SCIENCE

The top-down perspective of Richard Feynman contrasts with the bottom-up approach first advocated by Eric Drexler, who envisaged molecular machines 'manoeuvring things atom by atom'. Drexler's views are controversial and have been criticized by Nobel laureate Rick Smalley who has argued that fundamental physical principles would prevent them from ever being possible. Smalley believes that Drexler's speculations of molecular assemblers have threatened public support for the development of nanotechnology as some are concerned that these molecular assemblers could somehow get out of control. An understanding of science is vital when society needs to make decisions involving scientific issues but how do the public judge such issues? As experts in their particular fields scientists have a role in answering such questions responsibly.

Nanowires are used in electronic devices

Two examples of nanotechnology which are of interest are nanowires and nanotubes. Scientists hope to build tiny transistors from nanowires which can be as small as 1 nm in diameter, for use in computer chips and other electronic devices. These are generally constructed in a bottom-up approach in which atoms are organized on a surface by growing the nanowires on a donor substrate.

Coloured scanning tunnelling micrograph of nanowires. Just 10 atoms wide, these wires could be used in computers operating at the limits of miniaturization.

Carbon nanotubes are made from pentagons and hexagons of carbon atoms

The structure of buckminsterfullerene, C_{60}, was discussed in Chapter 4. The inclusion of pentagons into the hexagonal structure of graphite allows the carbon atoms to form a closed spherical cage (Figure 12.34). The discovery of C_{60} was one of the key developments in nanochemistry.

Figure 12.34 C_{60} has a structure consisting of interlinking hexagonal and pentagonal rings that form a hollow spherical shape similar to a soccer ball.

The discovery of C_{60} led to the discovery of a whole family of structurally related carbon nanotubes. These resemble a rolled-up sheet of graphite, with the carbon molecules arranged in repeating hexagons. The tubes, which have a diameter of 1 nm, can be closed if pentagons are present in the structure (Figure 12.35).

Figure 12.35 The carbon nanotube is capped owing to the presence of pentagons at the ends of the structure.

Single-walled carbon nanotubes (SWNTs) and multi-walled carbon nanotubes (MWNTs) can be made

A whole series of molecules, including structures with multiple walls of concentric tubes, have been produced. Carbon nanotubes have proved to have very useful properties.

Bundles of carbon nanotubes have tensile strengths between 50 and 100 times that of iron, as there is strong covalent bonding within the walls of the nanotube.

Different tubes have different electrical properties because, at the nanoscale, the behaviour of electrons is very sensitive to the dimensions of the tube. The electron behaves more like a wave than a particle at these dimensions, and its electrical properties are determined by the relationship between the wavelength of the electron and the tube length. Some tubes are conductors and some are semiconductors.

Their properties can also be altered by trapping different atoms inside the tubes. Silver chloride, for example, can be inserted into a tube and then decomposed to form an inner coat of silver. The resulting tube is a thin metallic electrical conductor.

As tubes have large surface areas and specific dimensions, they have the potential to be very efficient and size-selective heterogeneous catalysts. Their mechanical (stiffness, strength, toughness), thermal, and electrical properties allow a wide variety of applications, from batteries and fuel cells, to fibres and cables, to pharmaceuticals and biomedical materials.

Graphene is a single atomic plane of graphite

The 2010 Nobel Prize for Physics was awarded to Andre Geim and Konstantin Novoselov for their *groundbreaking experiments regarding the two-dimensional material graphene*.

Graphene is the thinnest material known and yet it is also one of the strongest. It conducts electricity as efficiently as copper as there is extensive delocalization of electrons throughout the structure and it outperforms all other materials as a conductor of heat. Graphene is almost completely transparent, yet so dense that even the smallest atom, helium, cannot pass through it. All these properties are quantum effects related to the single atom thickness of its structure.

Carbon nanotubes are made by arc discharge, chemical vapour deposition (CVD), and high-pressure carbon monoxide (HIPCO)

Open carbon nanotubes are generally formed when gaseous carbon atoms aggregate to form hexagonal arrangements with the same chicken wire structure as graphite. Closed tubes are formed if the conditions allow for the additional formation of carbon pentagons. The techniques used differ in the source of the carbon atoms, the method used to vaporize the carbon atoms, and the type of tubes generated. The carbon atoms need to be produced in an oxygen-free atmosphere so as to prevent combustion to carbon dioxide.

MWNTs are easier to produce in high volume quantities than SWNTs.

In 1996 scientists at the IBM Research Laboratory in Zurich built the world's smallest abacus. Individual C_{60} molecules could be pushed back and forth by the ultra-fine tip of a scanning tunnelling microscope.

The world's smallest test tube has been made from a carbon nanotube. One end of the tube is closed by a fullerene cap that contains both pentagons and hexagons. The tube has a volume of 10^{-24} dm^3.

Graphene is composed of hexagonally arranged carbon atoms (spheres) linked by strong covalent bonds. It transports electrons highly efficiently and may one day replace silicon in computer chips and other technology applications.

Method	Source of carbon	Details	Product
Arc discharge	Graphite	A large electric discharge is passed between two graphite electrodes in an inert atmosphere of low pressure helium or liquid nitrogen. The carbon atoms condense at the cathode and form carbon nanotubes. This was the method used to first make C_{60}.	A complex mixture is produced which requires further purification to separate the CNTs from the soot and the residual catalytic metals present in the crude product.
	Hydrocarbon solvent	An electric arc is discharged between metal electrodes submersed in a hydrocarbon solvent. A small rod-shaped deposit is formed on the anode.	
Laser ablation	Graphite	A high-powered laser atomizes a high-temperature graphite target in an inert atmosphere.	SWNTs are produced.
Chemical vapour deposition (CVD)	Hydrocarbon gas	A hydrocarbon gas is passed over heterogeneous metal catalysts in a silica or zeolite support. Nanotubes form on the catalyst's surface as the carbon atoms condense from the atomized hydrocarbon.	Both MWNTs and SWNTs can be made depending on the temperature.
High-pressure carbon monoxide (HIPCO) process	Carbon monoxide	An iron/carbon monoxide complex $Fe(CO)_5$ breaks up to produce iron nanoparticles, which act as a catalyst for the disproportionation of carbon monoxide: $$CO(g) + CO(g) \rightarrow C(s) + CO_2(g)$$ This allows the carbon nanotubes to form on the surface of the iron particles.	SWNT tubes are produced.

Implications of nanotechnology

Nanotechnology has the potential to provide significant advances over the next 50 years. Applications will be broad, including healthcare, medicine, security, electronics, communications, and computing.

Area	Current and potential uses
agriculture	nanoporous zeolites for slow release of water and fertilizers
healthcare/medicine	biological nanosensors as diagnostic tools
energy	nanoscale catalyst-enhanced fuels for better efficiency; nanomaterials for fuel cells/batteries/solar cells
electronics	carbon nanotube electronic components
ICT	flat panel flexible displays using nanotechnology; high-density data storage using nanomagnetic effects; faster processing using quantum computers
water treatment	nanomembranes for water treatment

 Nanotechnology will have an impact on the ethical, legal, and political issues that face the international community in the near future. It is important that international bodies such as UNESCO promote a dialogue between the public and the scientific communities.

Quantum dot nanoparticle probes, used to target and image tumours through the incorporation of antibodies that bind to the target cancer cells.

While scientists are very excited about the potential of nanotechnology, there are some concerns about the problems that the new technologies might cause. New technologies always carry new risks and concerns. There are unknown health effects

Environmental impact: plastics

Understandings:

- Plastics do not degrade easily because of their strong covalent bonds.
- Burning of poly(vinyl chloride) releases dioxins, HCl gas, and incomplete hydrocarbon combustion products.
- Dioxins contain unsaturated six-membered heterocyclic rings with two oxygen atoms, usually in positions 1 and 4.
- Chlorinated dioxins are hormone disrupting, leading to cellular and genetic damage.
- Plastics require more processing to be recycled than other materials.
- Plastics are recycled based on different resin types.

Guidance

- *Dioxins do not decompose in the environment and can be passed on in the food chain.*
- *Consider polychlorinated dibenzodioxins (PCCD) and PCBs as examples of carcinogenic chlorinated dioxins or dioxin like substances.*

Applications and skills:

- Deduction of the equation for any given combustion reaction.
- Discussion of why the recycling of polymers is an energy intensive process.
- Discussion of the environmental impact of the use of plastics.
- Comparison of the structures of polychlorinated biphenyls (PCBs) and dioxins.
- Discussion of the health concerns of using volatile plasticizers in polymer production.
- Distinguish possible resin identification codes (RICs) of plastics from an IR spectrum.

Guidance

- *House fires can release many toxins due to plastics (shower curtains, etc). Low smoke zero halogen cabling is often used in wiring to prevent these hazards.*
- *Consider phthalate esters as examples of plasticizers.*
- *Resin identification codes (RICs) are in the IB data booklet in section 30.*
- *Structures of various materials molecules are in the IB data booklet in section 31.*

Health concerns of using volatile plasticizer in polymer production

Plasticizer molecules have molecular covalent structures and so are generally volatile. Although they are trapped within the polymer structure, they are not chemically bonded to it and so can easily be released into the environment when a plastic ages and breaks down. There is some concern about the health effects of human exposure to the phthalate plasticizers. Many different phthalates exist with different properties, uses, and health effects. There is some evidence that phthalates affect the development of the male reproductive system in laboratory animals and phthalates are often classified as 'endocrine disruptors' or 'hormonally active agents' because of their ability to interfere with the endocrine system in the body. Experiments on laboratory animals have shown that they are potential carcinogens. The relatively high exposure of children to phthalates is of particular concern as PVC is present in many toys and childcare items. Levels are controlled in some countries to below 0.1% by mass. The evidence of adverse effects on human health is limited and more research is needed in this area.

Plastic waste is not biodegradable and persists for a long time, causing environmental problems.

Landfill sites are used to dispose of about 90% of the world's domestic waste.

Biodegradable plastics are produced using plant-based starch. These bioplastics break down much faster than petroleum plastics and also produce little, if any, toxic by-products when burned.

Plastics do not degrade easily because of their strong covalent bonds

As most plastic products have a short life cycle plastic accounts for about 10% by mass of our total waste and about 25% by volume. This leads to two problems:

- plastics are produced from crude oil which is non-renewable;
- most plastics are not biodegradable and waste placed in landfill does not degrade for hundreds of years.

Polymers are not broken down naturally as bacteria do not have the enzymes needed to break down the strong covalent C–C bond found in synthetic polymers.

Much of our plastic waste has been used to **landfill** disused quarries. However, suitable sites are becoming harder to find and reducing the amount of plastic dumped into landfills is a high priority.

Some poly(ethene) plastic bags, with added natural polymers such as starch, cellulose, or protein, however, can be made to biodegrade. The bacteria in the soil decompose the natural polymer and so the bag is broken down into smaller pieces. The synthetic polymer chains that remain have an increased surface area which speeds up the rate of decay further. One problem with biodegradability is that conditions in a landfill are often not suitable. The need to make sites watertight to prevent soluble products leaking into the environment also limits the supply of oxygen, preventing the bacteria from acting.

Incineration of plastics reduces bulk, releases energy but produces air pollution

As the addition polymers are made up from mainly carbon and hydrogen, they are a concentrated energy source. Waste plastic can be burned and used as a fuel – but there are problems.

- Carbon dioxide is a greenhouse gas.
- Carbon monoxide produced during incomplete combustion is poisonous.
- The combustion of PVC poses a particular problem as the hydrogen chloride produced causes acid rain. It must be removed from the fumes before they are released into the atmosphere.

Worked example

Complete combustion of PVC produces water, carbon dioxide, and hydrogen chloride (HCl).

Deduce an equation for the reaction using $(CH_2CHCl)_n$ as the molecular formula of the polymer.

Solution

The unbalanced equation:

$$(CH_2CHCl)_n + O_2 \rightarrow CO_2 + H_2O + HCl$$

1   Balancing carbon and chlorine: there are $2nC$ and nCl on the left – use this information on the right:

$$(CH_2CHCl)_n + O_2 \rightarrow 2nCO_2 + H_2O + nHCl$$

2   Balancing the hydrogens: there are $3nH$ on the left – again, use this information on the right:

$$(CH_2CHCl)_n + O_2 \rightarrow 2nCO_2 + nH_2O + nHCl$$

3   Balancing the oxygens: there are $5nO$ on the right – use this information on the left:

$$(CH_2CHCl)_n + \frac{5n}{2} O_2 \rightarrow 2nCO_2 + nH_2O + nHCl$$

Chemical waste incinerator, where toxic chemicals are broken down by high temperatures into harmless or non-toxic products.

Incomplete combustion of PVC produces dioxins

The complete combustion of plastics is rarely possible in reality, and dioxins can be unintentionally generated as by-products, depending on the incineration conditions. Dioxins contain unsaturated six-member heterocyclic rings with two oxygen atoms, usually in positions 1 and 4.

1.4-dioxin

polychlorinated dibenzo-*p*-dioxin

Each benzene ring can have up to four chlorine atoms. They are 10000 times more poisonous than the cyanide ion and disrupt the action of hormones and can cause cellular and genetic damage. The molecules do not readily decompose in the environment and so can be passed on in the food chain. Dioxins persist in fat and liver cells. Symptoms of dioxin poisoning are cirrhosis of the liver, damage to heart and memory, concentration problems, and depression. The skin disease chloracne is a result of the body attempting to remove the poison through the skin. Dioxin can cause malfunctions in fetuses. It was one of the herbicides present in the defoliant called Agent Orange used during the Vietnam War.

Environmentalists investigating dioxin contamination of soil at Times Beach, Missouri.

Polychlorinated biphenyls (PCBs) and polychlorinated dibenzofurans are dioxin-like substances and are also carcinogenic

The polychlorinated biphenyls have a high electrical resistance and are used in electrical transformers and capacitors. The structure is shown below. They contain a number of chlorine atoms attached to two connected benzene rings (biphenyl).

They are released into the environment from poorly maintained hazardous waste sites and the incomplete burning of waste from industrial incinerators. PCBs can accumulate in the leaves and above-ground parts of plants and food crops. They are also taken up into the bodies of small organisms and fish. As a result, people who ingest fish may be exposed to PCBs that have bioaccumulated in the fish they are ingesting. The polychlorinated dibenzofurans, shown below, are a group of toxic compounds associated with PCBs. They are produced in incinerators and are also carcinogenic.

House fires can release many toxins when plastic objects burn

The combustion products of plastics are a serious concern in the event of a house fire. Although PVC is often used for its fire-retarding properties, we have seen that it produces a nasty cocktail of dangerous gases, including the dioxins and hydrogen chloride, when it does burn. The hydrogen chloride reacts with any water present to form hydrochloric acid.

One possible solution to this problem is to use low-smoke zero-halogen cabling made from plastics such as poly(propene). These give off only limited amounts of smoke and no hydrogen chloride. They are particularly used in underground areas where smoke levels can build up. These materials also have a reduced environment impact if they are incinerated after use.

NATURE OF SCIENCE

There is some dispute over the carcinogenic properties of the phthalates. Testing the chemicals on animals raises many ethical issues and the only data available are based on tests on rats and mice. It may be true that what causes cancer in humans also causes cancer in rodents, but the reverse is not necessarily true. The IB has a strict animal experimentation policy.

Plastics require more processing to be recycled than other materials

Ideally materials should be reused so that no waste is produced. If this is not possible, the best alternative is recycling as it reduces:

• the use of raw materials;
• energy costs;
• the level of pollutants;
• the need of land for waste disposal.

One challenge is the separation and purification of the materials. Although methods of mechanical separation have been developed, ideally the plastics should be collected separately to reduce costs. Plastics are recycled based on different resin types and the **resin identification codes** are listed in section 30 of the IB data booklet. Recycled materials tend to be of a lower grade quality than new materials due to the problems of purification.

As thermoplastics can be melted down and remoulded they can be recycled mechanically. This is the simplest and cheapest method: the used plastics are cut into small pieces, separated according to their relative density in a floating tank, and heated and extruded to form new shapes.

Chemical methods involve **depolymerization**. The used plastics are heated in the absence of air and split up into their monomers in a process known as **pyrolysis**. The products are separated by fractional distillation and used as chemical feedstock by the petrochemical industry to make other products including plastics. There are energy costs in both processes.

For recycling to be successful and self-sustainable, the costs of recycling must be less than those needed to produce new materials.

TOK

Do animals have the same rights as human beings? Is experimenting on rats more acceptable than experimenting with monkeys? What criteria have you used to justify your answer?

The recycling symbol on the bottom of a bleach bottle indicates that the plastic is high-density poly(ethene). Different plastics can be identified by different numbers. This assists in sorting plastics before they are recycled.

Brooms made from recycled plastic.

Unfortunately, plastics require more processing to be recycled than other materials. There are costs in collecting and sorting the different used plastics. There are often lots of additives in plastic products, such as reinforcements, fillers, and colorants and mixtures of plastics are much weaker than the individual plastics so the recycled product is often of lower quality than the original with only a limited range of uses.

Plastics can be identified from their IR spectrum

As recycling companies don't usually know exactly what it is they are getting, it is important that they are able to identify plastics and process them appropriately. The plastics are first ground into little pellets and then passed on a conveyer belt where they are identified by a spectrometer which triggers the sorting process.

As discussed in Chapter 11, the positions of absorption bands in the IR spectrum give information about the presence or absence of specific functional groups in a molecule. The whole spectrum constitutes a 'fingerprint' that can be used to identify the plastic. Although the IR spectra for poly(ethene) and poly(propene) are very similar (as they are both made up from C—C and C—H bonds), they are not identical. As discussed in Chapter 11, the vibrations of the individual bonds are not independent as it is the whole molecule that vibrates. These differences are sufficient to distinguish between the two isomers.

The IR spectrum of PVC is shown in Figure 12.36. The absorption band between 600 and 700 cm^{-1} due to the presence of the C—Cl bond is a key feature of the spectrum.

IR spectroscopy can also be used to test the quality of the materials during all stages of the manufacturing process.

Figure 12.36 The IR spectrum of PVC. Note the absorption band at 600–700 cm^{-1}.

Worked example

The infrared spectrum of a compound shows a strong absorption at 1000–1400 cm^{-1} but no absorption between 2850 and 3090 cm^{-1}. Deduce the structure of the polymer using information in section 26 of the IB data booklet.

Solution

Absorption 1000–1400 cm^{-1} : C—F present

No absorption 2850–3050 cm^{-1}: no C—H present

It has the structure

$$\left(\!\!\begin{array}{cc} F & F \\ | & | \\ -C-C- \\ | & | \\ F & F \end{array}\!\!\right)_n$$

The polymer is called poly(tetrafluoroethene) or Teflon®.

It is said that the American space programme would have floundered without Teflon because the material was used to make so many things, from space suits to the bags used to hold samples of moon rock. It is now used to make non-stick pans, Gore-Tex® fabric, and hip joint replacements. Science has been used to solve many problems and improve human life, but it can also inadvertently cause environmental problems. Risk benefit analyses, risk assessments, and the precautionary principle are all parts of the scientific way of addressing the common good.

The discovery of the addition polymers poly(ethene) and Teflon both included some elements of luck. The significance of serendipity in scientific discovery was discussed on page 419.

Different countries have different recycling policies. For recycling to be successful, economic and political factors need to be considered. If it is not economical to recycle plastic at the moment perhaps we should bury the plastics separately so that future generations could recover them later. Plastic disposal is a global problem with local solutions.

CHALLENGE YOURSELF

3 Explain why the absorption of C—X bonds for the halogens occurs at such wavenumbers, compared to the C—H stretch.

TOK

One aspect of 'caring' in the IB Learner profile is to show a personal commitment to service and act to make a positive difference to the environment. What impact do your actions make on your local environment? Are there ethical obligations for humanity to treat the natural environment in a certain way?

Exercises

32 (a) Plastics have replaced many traditional materials. Suggest two properties which make plastic more suitable than wood for making children's toys.

(b) Increased use of polymers has led to problems of waste disposal. State one method of waste disposal and discuss issues other than cost associated with its use.

(c) Explain why synthetic polyalkenes are not generally biodegradable.

(d) Explain how a poly(ethene) bag can be made more biodegradable.

33 Discuss the advantages and disadvantages of incineration as a method of disposal compared with landfill sites.

34 Discuss the advantages and challenges of recycling plastics.

35 The general structure of some pollutants is given in section 31 of the IB data booklet.

(a) State the range of permissible values for n and m for the polychlorinated biphenyls.

(b) State the range of permissible values for n and m for the polychlorinated dibenzofurans.

36 Compare the IR spectra of ethene and its polymer.

Practice questions

1 Aluminium and its alloys are widely used in industry.

(a) Aluminium metal is obtained by the electrolysis of alumina dissolved in molten cryolite.

(i) Explain the function of the molten cryolite. (1)

(ii) State the half-equations for the reactions that take place at each electrode. (2)

(b) Outline two different ways that carbon dioxide may be produced during the production of aluminium. (2)

(Total 5 marks)

2 (a) Explain why iron is obtained from its ores using chemical reducing agents but aluminium is obtained from its ores using electrolysis. (2)

(b) Both carbon monoxide and hydrogen can be used to reduce iron ores. State the equations for the reduction of magnetite, Fe_3O_4, with

(i) carbon monoxide (1)

(ii) hydrogen. (1)

(Total 4 marks)

3 Alloys are important substances in industries that use metals.

(a) Describe an alloy. (1)

(b) Explain how alloying can modify the structure and properties of metals. (2)

(Total 3 marks)

4 Compare the modes of action of homogeneous and heterogeneous catalysts. State **one** example of each type of catalysis using a chemical equation **and** include state symbols.

(4)

5 (a) Name a thermotropic liquid crystal. (1)

   (b) Explain the liquid crystal behaviour of the thermotropic liquid crystal named in part (a), on the molecular level. (4)

(Total 5 marks)

6 Poly(vinyl chloride) (PVC) and poly(ethene) are both polymers made from crude oil.

   (a) Explain why PVC is less flexible than poly(ethene). (2)

   (b) State how PVC can be made more flexible during its manufacture and explain the increase in flexibility on a molecular level. (2)

   (c) PVC can exist in isotactic and atactic forms. Draw the structure of the isotactic form showing a chain of at least six carbon atoms. (1)

(Total 5 marks)

7 During the formation of poly(styrene), a volatile hydrocarbon such as pentane is often added. Describe how this affects the properties of the polymer and **one** use for this product.

(2)

8 Nanotechnology creates and uses structures that have novel properties because of their size.

   (a) State the size range of structures which are involved in nanotechnology. (1)

   (b) Distinguish between physical and chemical techniques in manipulating atoms to form molecules. (2)

   (c) Discuss **two** implications of nanotechnology. (2)

(Total 5 marks)

9 The disposal of all types of waste is an increasing problem. One method of removing waste is incineration. State **one** advantage and **one** disadvantage of incinerating waste.

(2)

10 Landfill sites are used to dispose of about 90% of the world's domestic waste, but incineration is being increasingly used in some countries.

   (a) State one advantage of each method. (2)

   (b) Suggest why some biodegradable plastics do not decompose in landfill sites. (1)

(Total 3 marks)

11 (a) State the materials used for the positive and negative electrodes in the production of aluminium by electrolysis. (2)

   (b) Aluminium is one of the most abundant elements found on Earth. Discuss why it is important to recycle aluminium. (2)

(Total 4 marks)

12 Nano-sized 'test-tubes' with one open end, can be formed from carbon structures.

   (a) Describe these 'test-tubes' with reference to the structures of carbon allotropes. (2)

   (b) These tubes are believed to be stronger than steel. Explain the strength of these 'test-tubes' on a molecular level. (1)

   (c) Carbon nanotubes can be used as catalysts.

      (i) Suggest two reasons why they are effective heterogeneous catalysts. (2)

      (ii) State **one** potential concern associated with the use of carbon nanotubes. (1)

(Total 6 marks)

13 The structure of 4-pentyl-4-cyanobiphenyl, a commercially available nematic crystalline material used in electrical display devices, is shown below.

(a) Explain how the three different parts of the molecule contribute to the properties of the compound used in electrical display devices.

(i) CN

(ii) C_5H_{11}

(iii) (3)

(b) Describe and explain in molecular terms the workings of a twisted nematic liquid crystal. (4)

(Total 7 marks)

14 Liquid crystal displays are used in digital watches, calculators, and laptops.
Describe the liquid crystal state, in terms of molecular arrangement, and explain what happens as temperature increases.

(3)

15 Poly(ethene) is the most commonly used synthetic polymer. It is produced in low-density and high-density forms. Identify which form has the higher melting point. Explain by reference to its structure and bonding.

(4)

16 (a) The properties of poly(vinyl chloride), PVC, may be modified to suit a particular use. State the main method of modifying PVC and the effect this has on its properties. (2)

(b) Outline two disadvantages of using polymers such as poly(propene) and PVC, and give one disadvantage that is specific to PVC. (3)

(Total 5 marks)

17 The diagram below represents a section of a polymer.

$$
\begin{array}{cccccccc}
\text{H} & \text{CH}_3 & \text{H} & \text{CH}_3 & \text{H} & \text{CH}_3 & \text{H} & \text{CH}_3 \\
| & | & | & | & | & | & | & | \\
-\text{C}-&\text{C}-&\text{C}-&\text{C}-&\text{C}-&\text{C}-&\text{C}-&\text{C}- \\
| & | & | & | & | & | & | & | \\
\text{H} & \text{H} & \text{H} & \text{H} & \text{H} & \text{H} & \text{H} & \text{H}
\end{array}
$$

(a) Draw the structure of the monomer from which this polymer is manufactured. (1)

(b) Polymers A and B both have the structure shown above, but the average chain length is much greater in A than in B. Suggest two physical properties that would be different for A and B. (2)

(c) Polymers A and B both have isotactic structures. Polymer C is manufactured from the same monomer but is not isotactic. State the name used to describe this different structure and outline how the structure differs. (2)

(Total 5 marks)

To access weblinks on the topics covered here, please go to www.pearsonhotlinks.com and enter the ISBN or title of this book.

13

Option B: Biochemistry

Essential ideas

B.1 Metabolic reactions involve a complex interplay between many different components in highly controlled environments.

B.2 Proteins are the most diverse of the biopolymers responsible for metabolism and structural integrity of living organisms.

B.3 Lipids are a broad group of biomolecules that are largely non-polar and are therefore insoluble in water.

B.4 Carbohydrates are oxygen-rich biomolecules that play a central role in metabolic reactions of energy transfer.

B.5 Vitamins are organic micronutrients with diverse functions and which must be obtained from the diet.

B.6 Our increasing knowledge of biochemistry has led to several environmental problems, while also helping to solve others.

Calcium carbonate ($CaCO_3$) plates on the surface of a marine organism, shown in blue in this coloured scanning electron micrograph. These plates are shed and sink to the ocean floor, forming an important part of deep-sea sediments and rocks such as chalk and limestone. Metabolic processes, controlled by enzymes, synthesize the structural components of organisms, which are later returned to the environment.

Living things show unique properties. They extract and transform energy from their environment to build complex structures, and have the ability to self-regulate and self-replicate. Yet all living organisms are made of molecules that individually are no different from any other molecules found in non-living matter. Somehow the interactions between component molecules in living things must explain the complex processes that we associate with life. Biochemistry is the subject that seeks to find such molecular level explanations for biological phenomena.

Although biochemistry is a relatively young discipline, it is a rapidly advancing area of knowledge, and applications of research are found in the fields of health, diet, and medicine as well as in new technologies. In recent years many of the Nobel Prizes in chemistry – generally considered to be the most prestigious recognition of leading research in chemistry – have been given to scientists working in this field. Prizes have been awarded for major advances made in our understanding of proteins, of chemical interactions at receptors, and of the detailed action of DNA.

Computer model of the enzyme glutamine synthetase. Enzymes are proteins that catalyse all biochemical reactions. Their activity depends on their specific three-dimensional structure, which is determined by their chemical composition. In turn this is controlled by the exact molecular sequence in the nucleic acid DNA. Glutamine synthetase is a complex protein, having a quaternary structure made of six different polypeptide subunits – shown in different colours here. It catalyses the reaction for the synthesis of the amino acid glutamine.

Biochemical molecules are an excellent example of the relationship between molecular structure and function, a theme that will be carried through this chapter. As biomolecules are all organic in nature, it is recommended that you are first familiar with the work in Chapter 10, Organic Chemistry. After studying the features of the major groups of biomolecules, this chapter ends with a consideration of some of the impacts and possible solutions to environmental problems related to biochemistry.

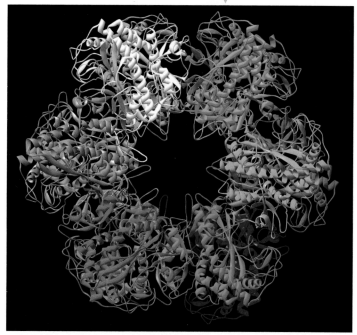

B.1 Introduction to biochemistry

Understandings:
- The diverse functions of biological molecules depend on their structures and shapes.
- Metabolic reactions take place in highly controlled aqueous environments.
- Reactions of breakdown are called catabolism and reactions of synthesis are called anabolism.
- Biopolymers form by condensation reactions and are broken down by hydrolysis reactions.
- Photosynthesis is the synthesis of energy-rich molecules from carbon dioxide and water using light energy.
- Respiration is complex set of metabolic processes providing energy for cells.

Guidance
Intermediates of aerobic respiration and photosynthesis are not required.

Applications and skills:
- Explanation of the difference between condensation and hydrolysis reactions.
- The use of summary equations of photosynthesis and respiration to explain the potential balancing of oxygen and carbon dioxide in the atmosphere.

Biochemical reactions are organized in metabolic pathways

The scientific study of the origin of life has been described as one of the last frontiers of the life sciences, as so many questions remain unanswered. There is though general agreement that life began in an aqueous environment, and that a key event was the development of a membrane that enclosed and defined a volume of space, known as a **cell**. Within this membrane-bound environment, sequestered from the outside, specific conditions such as temperature, pH, and chemical concentrations can be generated and controlled. Cells are the basic unit of structure and function in all living things. Complex organisms contain vast numbers of cells, which together carry out all the life processes.

At any one time within the microscopic volume of a living cell, thousands of chemical reactions occur (Figure 13.1). The sum of all these reactions taking place in an organism is known as **metabolism**. This complex chemistry is dependent on a high level of order where every compound has a distinct function. Some features of metabolism are:

- Reactions are controlled in sequences and cycles known as **metabolic pathways**. The product of each step is the reactant for the next. Compounds taking part in metabolism are known as **metabolites**.
- Every reaction is controlled by a specific catalyst called an **enzyme**.
- Similar pathways and enzymes exist in a wide range of different organisms.
- Reactions can be coupled so that energy from one reaction is used to drive another.

Given the complexity of metabolism, it is useful to classify pathways according to their broad purpose. Later in this chapter, specific examples of metabolic processes will be discussed in more detail.

The term **emergent properties** is used in biology to describe the properties that result from interactions between components in cells and between cells in multicellular organisms. It is a manifestation of 'the whole is greater than the sum of the parts'.

Metabolism is the sum of the chemical reactions occurring in a living organism.

Anabolism: pathways of synthesis

The part of metabolism concerned with building up or synthesis is known as **anabolism**. The reactants are small molecules called **precursors**, and the products are larger, more complex molecules of higher energy. Anabolic pathways therefore require energy. Examples include the synthesis of proteins from amino acids, nucleic acids from nucleotides, and carbohydrates from the process of photosynthesis.

Metabolism is dependent on a regular supply of diverse nutrients in the diet. Many differences in human health across the world are the result of differences in the supply of nutritious food.

Catabolism: pathways of breakdown

Metabolic reactions of breakdown or degradation are known as **catabolism**. Catabolic reactions release energy and produce energy-poor end-products, such as carbon dioxide and water. Examples include the breakdown of glucose in respiration or the oxidation of fatty acids.

The energy from catabolic reactions is used to drive anabolic reactions. This is known as **energy coupling** and involves an intermediary energy carrier called adenosine triphosphate, which is known as **ATP**.

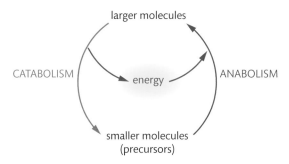

Figure 13.2 The relationship between anabolic and catabolic pathways of metabolism.

Anabolic and catabolic processes take place simultaneously in a cell, but they are separately controlled. This is possible because the metabolic pathway for the biosynthesis of a molecule is usually different from the pathway for its breakdown, and involves different enzymes. Otherwise, metabolism would involve so-called **futile cycles** where stable complex structures would not exist in cells, but would be broken down as they form.

Anabolism refers to metabolic pathways of synthesis; catabolism refers to metabolic pathways of breakdown.

451

Biomolecules are diverse organic molecules

Of the approximately 100 elements found on Earth, only 27 have been found to be essential components of living things, and the majority of these are present in very small amounts – known as **trace elements.** The molecules found in cells are mostly organic compounds containing about 96% by mass hydrogen, oxygen, carbon, and nitrogen. Sulfur, phosphorus, calcium, and iron are also present in significant amounts.

Biomolecules, the molecules present in living things, represent an immense diversity of structures. Many of them, such as proteins, nucleic acids, and polysaccharides, are **macromolecules**, having relative molecular masses of several thousand. Despite their size and complexity, macromolecules can be described relatively easily in terms of the small units from which they are made, commonly referred to as building blocks, which are linked together by covalent bonds. Most macromolecules are polymers and so the building blocks are monomers – molecules such as glucose and amino acids. Many of these monomers have functions in their own right, for example as energy carriers or molecular messengers. The reactions of build-up and breakdown of all these molecules follow a similar pattern, described below.

Condensation and hydrolysis reactions

Biopolymers are **condensation polymers**, because their synthesis involves the loss of a molecule of water for each covalent bond that forms between two monomers. An example of this, esterification, was described in Chapter 10. But in order to form a polymer, the monomers must each have *two functional groups*, which can be considered as two active ends of the molecule, so they can link together in a similar way to people forming a chain by linking hands on both sides. The reaction is catalysed by enzymes, which are often known as **polymerases**.

Note that condensation polymerization differs from addition polymerization, also described in Chapter 10. Addition reactions lead to only one product, with no elimination of a small molecule.

Figure 13.3 Condensation reactions involve loss of a molecule of water for every covalent bond formed.

The breakdown of these molecules reverses the above reaction, adding a molecule of water for each covalent bond broken. The water is split with −H and −OH attaching separately to the product molecules. These are **hydrolysis** reactions and occur during chemical **digestion**. They are catalysed by enzymes, and can also be favoured by heat and acidic or alkaline conditions.

Figure 13.4 Hydrolysis reactions involve addition of a molecule of water for every covalent bond broken.

Examples of condensation and hydrolysis reactions include the synthesis and breakdown of proteins from amino acids and polysaccharides from sugars. Lipids, although they do not form polymers, also involve condensation and hydrolysis reactions between their sub-units. These are all discussed in more detail later in this chapter. These reactions are summarized below.

The activity of biological molecules is dependent on their structures and shapes

A recurring theme in biochemistry is the relationship between molecular structure and function. In other words, molecules seem to be 'chosen' for particular tasks in cells on the basis of their chemical nature and often their three-dimensional shape. Structural molecules like collagen and cellulose are tough and insoluble, whereas a chemical messenger such as the hormone insulin must interact specifically with receptor molecules. The catalytic action of enzymes depends entirely on their ability to form a temporary binding to their substrate, while nucleic acids are able to store and transmit genetic information using chemical sequences.

Living cells transform energy

Living things absorb energy from their environment and use it to synthesize their own complex structures from simple starting molecules, and to carry out functions such as movement and reproduction. As energy is used in life processes, most of it is returned to the environment as heat.

Photosynthesis converts light energy into chemical energy

The primary source of energy for life is the Sun. Green plants (and some other organisms) are able to capture solar energy and use it to synthesize energy-rich biomolecules. This process is known as **photosynthesis**, and all organisms, directly

NATURE OF SCIENCE

As more and more data have been obtained on biochemical pathways, similar reaction patterns are seen in metabolic processes in species that may not be closely related. For this reason biochemistry is now a major part of the study of evolutionary biology. This is an example of how an interdisciplinary approach can contribute to deeper knowledge and understanding.

CHALLENGE YOURSELF

1 From a thermodynamic standpoint, what must occur while living things create molecular order using energy from their environment?

453

Photosynthesis is the synthesis of energy-rich molecules from carbon dioxide and water using light energy.

or indirectly, depend on it for their supply of food. Simply put, without photosynthesis there would be no life on Earth.

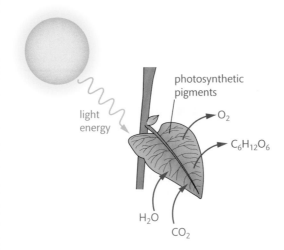

Figure 13.5 Summary of the reactants and products of photosynthesis.

The key to photosynthesis is the absorption of light by **photosynthetic pigment** molecules. The primary pigment is **chlorophyll**. The light energy trapped drives a series of redox reactions, in which – remarkably – water is split into hydrogen and oxygen. The oxygen is released as a waste product and the hydrogen ultimately reduces carbon dioxide to simple sugar molecules. This summary does not attempt to do justice to the complexity of the process, which involves many intermediates, electron carriers, and enzymes. But in essence, photosynthesis transforms the energy-poor molecules carbon dioxide and water into energy-rich sugar with the release of oxygen. The overall reaction of photosynthesis can be summarized as follows.

$$6CO_2 + 6H_2O \; \rightarrow \; \rightarrow \; \rightarrow \; C_6H_{12}O_6 + 6O_2$$

(The multiple arrows indicate that this is only a summary of the process, not a representation of a single reaction.)

Note that *respiration*, which is a biochemical process, is completely different from *breathing*, which is a physical process used to bring about gas exchange. Confusion between the two is generated by many sources, including the fact that the word for breathing is related to 'respire' in several languages, including French, Italian, and Spanish.

Respiration makes energy available for life processes

Living things obtain energy-rich molecules such as glucose either through their own process of photosynthesis, or by the intake of energy-rich molecules in food. Broadly speaking, green plants do the former and animals the latter. The release of this energy in a controlled way inside cells is known as **respiration**. It is essential to life, taking place in every living cell continuously.

Respiration is often likened to burning a fuel in oxygen, though in reality it is a much more complex and highly controlled process. But, like burning, it does involve reactions of oxidation where the amount of energy released depends on the extent of oxidation achieved. The details of respiration are complex, involving up to 50 different chemical reactions, each controlled by a specific enzyme. Although different metabolites can be used as respiratory substrates, they are usually first converted into glucose, $C_6H_{12}O_6$.

Respiration is the process of chemical breakdown of energy-rich molecules in cells with the release of energy. It takes place in all living cells all the time.

The first stage of respiration, known as **glycolysis**, is common to all cells and does not use oxygen. Only a small proportion of the energy in glucose is released, as most is trapped in the products of this stage. In the absence of oxygen, known as **anaerobic conditions**, this is the only energy released, and it is enough to keep some cells alive, temporarily in the case of muscle cells and permanently in the case of some bacteria. Products of anaerobic respiration such as lactate and ethanol are therefore energy-rich molecules (as we know from the burning of ethanol described on page 335).

In the presence of oxygen, known as **aerobic conditions**, the oxidation of glucose is complete, and much more energy is released. This is why most cells are dependent on a continuous supply of oxygen. The end products of aerobic respiration are the energy-poor molecules carbon dioxide and water.

Aerobic respiration involves a series of coupled redox reactions, where reactants are successively reduced and then re-oxidized. Ultimately, oxygen accepts electrons and is reduced to water.

The overall equation for the aerobic respiration of glucose can be represented as follows:

$$C_6H_{12}O_6 + 6O_2 \rightarrow \rightarrow \rightarrow 6CO_2 + 6H_2O$$

Multiple arrows are again used to show that this is a multi-step reaction, and the representation is a summary only. Note that the reactants and products are the same as for the combustion of glucose.

Summary of photosynthesis and respiration

Photosynthesis and respiration are metabolic redox processes. Photosynthesis is an anabolic, energy-storing process which reduces carbon dioxide to sugar. Respiration is a catabolic, energy-yielding process, which oxidizes sugar to carbon dioxide.

The products of anaerobic respiration of the single-celled fungus yeast have been used by human cultures for millennia. The release of CO_2 is used to make dough rise in baking, and the production of ethanol is the basis of all brewing.

Figure 13.6 Summary of aerobic and anaerobic respiration.

Aerobic respiration uses O_2 and completely oxidizes glucose to CO_2 and H_2O. It releases much more energy than anaerobic respiration, which occurs in the absence of oxygen.

CHALLENGE YOURSELF

2 Compare the oxidation states of carbon in $C_6H_{12}O_6$ and in CO_2 to examine the redox processes involved.

Respiration releases heat. Here water vapour is rising from decaying organic matter on an active compost heap. Micro-organisms living in the compost are releasing significant heat as a result of their high rate of respiration.

The overall chemical changes in photosynthesis and respiration are the reverse of each other – but in no way do these processes involve a reversal of their chemical steps. Yet together they provide a balance of chemicals, as the waste products of respiration are the raw materials for photosynthesis.

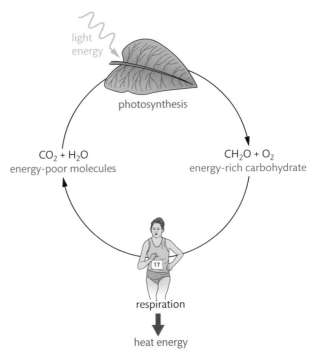

Figure 13.7 Chemical cycling and energy flow through photosynthesis and respiration.

Photosynthesis acts as a **carbon sink**, as it removes carbon dioxide from the atmosphere, while respiration and combustion, which release carbon dioxide, are **carbon sources**. Human activities such as deforestation have decreased the carbon sink, and increased the carbon source by burning fossil fuels. Consequently, there is a change in the balance of gases in the atmosphere, and the increasing level of carbon dioxide linked to climate change is a source of widespread concern.

Matter cycles and energy flows through biochemical processes.

Note in Figure 13.7 that while chemicals are cycled and reused through living things, energy flows and is ultimately lost as heat. This means that life is dependent on a continuing supply of solar energy.

Data from the Mauna Loa research station in Hawaii provide a record of atmospheric carbon dioxide concentration since 1958. Taking into account seasonal fluctuations and variances, the overall trend has been an increase in carbon dioxide levels from about 315 ppm to about 390 ppm in the last 50 years. Carbon dioxide is a greenhouse gas that absorbs and re-radiates infrared radiation, and so this dramatic increase in its concentration is widely accepted as a major factor influencing climate change.

Exercises

1   Write an equation for the hydrolysis of the molecule $C_{18}H_{32}O_{16}$ (a trisaccharide) into its monomers, which are all isomeric with glucose.

2   State the features of molecules that are able to form condensation polymers, and describe what happens during the polymerization reaction.

3   State whether the following metabolic processes are anabolic or catabolic.

   (a) protein synthesis   **(b)** oxidation of fatty acids
   (c) anaerobic respiration   **(d)** DNA replication

4   Outline the conditions required for photosynthesis to take place, and explain why it can be described as a redox process.

5   State and explain the difference in energy yield between aerobic and anaerobic respiration.

6   When comparing aerobic with anaerobic respiration in human cells, which statement is true?

   A   Both processes release CO_2.
   B   Both processes use O_2.
   C   Both processes involve oxidation of glucose.
   D   The two processes release equal amounts of energy.

Proteins and enzymes

Understandings:

- Proteins are polymers of 2-amino acids, joined by amide links (also known as peptide bonds).
- Amino acids are amphoteric and can exist as zwitterions, cations, and anions.
- Protein structures are diverse and are described at the primary, secondary, tertiary, and quaternary levels.
- A protein's three-dimensional shape determines its role in structural components or in metabolic processes.
- Most enzymes are proteins that act as catalysts by binding specifically to a substrate at the active site.
- As enzyme activity depends on the conformation, it is sensitive to changes in temperature, pH, and the presence of heavy metal ions.
- Chromatography separation is based on different physical and chemical principles.

Guidance

- *The names and structural formulas of the amino acids are given in the IB data booklet in section 33.*
- *Reference should be made to alpha helix and beta pleated sheet, and to fibrous and globular proteins with examples of each.*

Applications and skills:

- Deduction of the structural formulas of reactants and products in condensation reactions of amino acids, and hydrolysis reactions of peptides.
- Explanation of the solubilities and melting points of amino acids in terms of zwitterions.
- Application of the relationships between charge, pH, and isoelectric point for amino acids and proteins.
- Description of the four levels of protein structure, including the origin and types of bonds and interactions involved.
- Deduction and interpretation of graphs of enzyme activity involving changes in substrate concentration, pH, and temperature.
- Explanation of the processes of paper chromatography and gel electrophoresis in amino acid and protein separation and identification.

Guidance

In paper chromatography the use of R_f values and locating agents should be covered.

The functions of proteins

Proteins are in many ways the most remarkable of the biomolecules. It is estimated that as many as ten million different protein molecules may exist in nature, each with a unique structure and function. From this almost overwhelming diversity, we can classify two main types of proteins.

Fibrous proteins	Globular proteins
• structural components	• tools that operate at the molecular level – as enzymes, carriers, receptors
• elongated molecules with dominant secondary structure	• compact spherical molecules with dominant tertiary structure
• insoluble in water	• soluble in water

Fibrous proteins are responsible for structure, support, and movement, whereas globular proteins drive the reactions of metabolism. Some specific examples of each type are given on page 458.

Role of protein	Named example	Type of protein	Specific function
structure	keratin	fibrous	protective covering in hair, wool, claws
structure	collagen	fibrous	connective tissue in skin and tendons
enzyme (catalyst)	polymerase	globular	catalyses anabolic reactions such as DNA synthesis
communication	insulin	globular	controls and maintains the concentration of glucose in the blood
transport	hemoglobin	globular	carries oxygen

How can it be that this same type of molecule, the protein, is used for both the walls of the reactor and the reactions within? The answer lies in the fact that proteins are as diverse and unique in their structures as they are in their functions, and that this variety is rooted in their molecular building blocks.

The structure of proteins

Amino acids are the building blocks of proteins

Proteins are polymers – long-chain molecules – of monomer units called **amino acids**. Each amino acid contains an amino group ($-NH_2$) and an acid group ($-COOH$) bonded to the same carbon atom.

amino group   carboxylic acid group

Coloured scanning electron micrograph (SEM) of hair shafts growing from the surface of human skin. Hair is made of the fibrous protein keratin, anchored in hair follicles. The outer layer of skin consists of dead keratinized cells that detach giving this flaky appearance.

They are called 2-amino acids. Because the chain is numbered starting with the carboxylic acid group, the amino group is attached to carbon 2. This carbon atom is also bonded to a hydrogen atom and to a group usually known as 'R'. The R group differs from one amino acid to the next, and is therefore the feature that defines the amino acid. About 20 different amino acids are found in naturally occurring proteins. Each is given a standard three-letter abbreviation, for example the smallest amino acid glycine, where R = H, is known as Gly.

A complete list of all the amino acids used in proteins is given in section 33 of the IB data booklet. Amino acids can be classified according to the chemical nature of their R group, usually on the basis of their different polarities, as shown in the examples on page 459.

Type of amino acid	R group contains	Named example	Structure

non-polar / hydrophobic	hydrocarbon	alanine, Ala	H_2N — CH —COOH
			    |
			    CH_3

polar but uncharged	hydroxyl, —OH, sulfhydryl, —SH, or amide, —$CONH_2$	serine, Ser	H_2N — CH —COOH
			    |
			    CH_2 —OH

basic (positively charged at pH 6.0–8.0)	amino, —NH_2	lysine, Lys	H_2N — CH —COOH
			    |
			    CH_2 —CH_2 —CH_2 —CH_2 —NH_2

acidic (negatively charged at pH 6.0–8.0)	carboxylic acid, —COOH	aspartic acid, Asp	H_2N — CH —COOH
			    |
			    CH_2 —COOH

Amino acids are crystalline compounds with high melting points – usually above 200 °C, and they have much greater solubility in water than in non-polar solvents. In addition, amino acids usually move in an electric field. These properties are all typical of ionic compounds, and so suggest that amino acids contain charged groups. The charges are a result of acid–base behaviour, which is best explained in terms of Brønsted–Lowry theory.

In aqueous solution and in crystalline form, amino acids commonly exist with both positive and negative charges within the molecule, known as **zwitterions**. They are sometime referred to as **internal salts**, as the charges result from an internal acid–base reaction, with the transfer of a proton (H^+) from the acid –COOH group to the basic –NH_2 group in the same amino acid.

   undissociated form   zwitterion

As amino acids contain both an acidic and a basic group, they are **amphoteric** or **amphiprotic**, as described in Chapter 8. In aqueous solution they will accept and donate H^+ according to changes in the pH of the medium as shown below.

1   As an acid, donating H^+:

$$H_3N^+ - \overset{\overset{\displaystyle H}{|}}{\underset{\underset{\displaystyle R}{|}}{C}} - COO^- \; \rightleftharpoons \; H_2N - \overset{\overset{\displaystyle H}{|}}{\underset{\underset{\displaystyle R}{|}}{C}} - COO^- \; + \; H^+$$

2   As a base, accepting H^+:

$$H_3N^+ - \overset{\overset{\displaystyle H}{|}}{\underset{\underset{\displaystyle R}{|}}{C}} - COO^- \; + \; H^+ \; \rightleftharpoons \; H_3N^+ - \overset{\overset{\displaystyle H}{|}}{\underset{\underset{\displaystyle R}{|}}{C}} - COOH$$

 In addition to the 20 common amino acids of proteins, over 150 other amino acids occur in biology in different forms other than in proteins. Fungi and higher plants have a particularly large variety of non-protein amino acids, some of which are toxic to other forms of life.

 Zwitterions are neutral molecules that have unit electrical charges of opposite sign.

CHALLENGE YOURSELF

3   All amino acids except glycine are chiral, and exist in the L form in nature. By reference to section 33 of the IB data booklet, determine which two amino acids found in proteins have *two* chiral carbon atoms.

Note that in the zwitterion it is the conjugates of the acid and the base that are responsible for this property. As the pH of the medium affects the equilibrium position of these reactions, it influences the charge of an amino acid as follows:

- at high pH (low $[H^+]$), reaction 1 above is favoured as the $-NH_3^+$ group loses its H^+ and forms an anion
- at low pH (high $[H^+]$), reaction 2 above is favoured as the $-COO^-$ group gains H^+ and forms a cation.

These effects of pH on charge are summarized below. This example assumes that the R group is an uncharged group, for example the amino acid alanine.

$$
\begin{array}{ccc}
\underset{\text{cation}}{H_3N^+ - \overset{\overset{\displaystyle H}{|}}{\underset{\underset{\displaystyle CH_3}{|}}{C}} - COOH} \rightleftharpoons &
\underset{\text{neutral}}{H_3N^+ - \overset{\overset{\displaystyle H}{|}}{\underset{\underset{\displaystyle CH_3}{|}}{C}} - COO^-} \rightleftharpoons &
\underset{\text{anion}}{H_2N - \overset{\overset{\displaystyle H}{|}}{\underset{\underset{\displaystyle CH_3}{|}}{C}} - COO^-}
\end{array}
$$

ISOELECTRIC POINT

⟵ decreasing pH   increasing pH ⟶

So amino acids tend to be positively charged at low pH and negatively charged at high pH. The intermediate pH at which the amino acid is electrically neutral is known as its **isoelectric point**. With no net charge at this pH, amino acids will not move in an electric field. Also at this point, the molecules will have minimum mutual repulsion and so be the least soluble. Section 33 in the IB data booklet gives the pH of the isoelectric point of each amino acid alongside its structure, and some examples are shown in the table below.

Common name	Symbol	Structural formula	pH of isoelectric point
glycine	Gly	$H_2N - CH_2 - COOH$	6.0

alanine	Ala	$H_2N - CH - COOH$
		             $\vert$
		             CH_3
			6.0

lysine	Lys	$H_2N - CH - COOH$
		        $\vert$
		        $CH_2 - CH_2 - CH_2 - CH_2 - NH_2$
			9.7

aspartic acid	Asp	$H_2N - CH - COOH$
		        $\vert$
		        $CH_2 - COOH$
			2.8

The charge carried by an amino acid depends on the pH of the medium. The isoelectric point is the pH at which it is electrically neutral.

This shows that amino acids such as alanine and glycine, which have uncharged R groups, have the same isoelectric point of pH 6.0. But where the R group contains an acidic or a basic group, then these will also influence the charge as pH changes. This is why aspartic acid and lysine, for example, have very different isoelectric points. This difference is exploited in techniques for separating amino acids, to be discussed later in this chapter.

Like amino acids, proteins also have isoelectric points. Fresh milk has a pH of about 6.7 and at this pH the protein casein carries a negative charge and is dispersed in solution. As it sours, bacteria growing in the milk produce acids that lower the pH and so reduce the charges on the molecules. When it reaches pH 4.6 this is the isoelectric point of casein, so now the protein becomes less soluble, precipitating from solution as the familiar 'curdled milk'. This is the first step in cheese making.

A trough of curdled milk in a cheese-making factory. The curd is solidified milk formed by lowering the pH and so precipitating the protein at its isoelectric point.

Amino acids link together through condensation reactions

Amino acids are able to react together in a condensation reaction in which a molecule of water is eliminated and a new bond is formed between the acid group of one amino acid and the amino group of the other. This bond is a substituted **amide link** known as a **peptide bond**, and two amino acids linked in this way are known as a **dipeptide**. By convention the free $-NH_2$ group (known as the N-terminal) is put on the left of the sequence and the free $-COOH$ group (C-terminal) on the right.

condensation → H_2O

free amino group (N-terminal)

peptide bond

free carboxylic acid group (C-terminal)

Figure 13.8 Formation of a dipeptide by condensation of two amino acids.

We can see that the dipeptide still has a functional group at each end of the molecule, with $-NH_2$ at one end and $-COOH$ at the other. So it can react again by another condensation reaction, forming a **tripeptide** and eventually a chain of linked amino acids known as a **polypeptide**.

461

Worked example

Draw a tripeptide with the following sequence:

Cys–Val–Asn

Solution

Look up the structures (the R groups) of the amino acids in section 33 of the IB data booklet and draw them out in the same order as given in the question.

Now draw peptide bonds between the carbon of the –COOH group and the nitrogen of the –NH$_2$ group, ensuring that H$_2$O is released, and that each atom has the correct number of bonds in the final structure.

We can write a general equation for the synthesis of a polypeptide from its amino acids as follows:

repeat unit

Molecular model of the amino acid lysine NH$_2$(CH$_2$)$_4$CH(NH$_2$)COOH. Lysine is known as an **essential amino acid** because it cannot be synthesized by the body and so must be obtained in the diet. Carbon atoms are shown in blue, hydrogen in gold, oxygen in red, and nitrogen in dark blue.

In just the same way as letters linked together in different orders make different words (e.g. eat, ate, tea), so amino acids linked together in different sequences make different peptides. The three amino acids in the Worked example on page 462 could have been linked for example as: Asn–Cys–Val or Cys–Asn–Val, all of which would be different tripeptides with different properties.

The sequence in which the amino acids are linked to form the chain is of great significance as it will determine the exact nature of the polypeptide. And this is where the extraordinary variety of protein structures comes from.

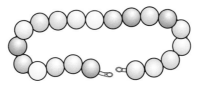

Consider making a necklace by joining together 20 different colours of beads, with each colour being used as many times as you like. In every position you would have a choice of 20 different possibilities, so just imagine how many different combinations of beads you could have. Building polypeptides from amino acids presents a similar situation – at any point in the chain there are 20 different possibilities. Even for a tripeptide there are $20 \times 20 \times 20 = 8000$ different possible combinations. But proteins are typically made from polypeptide chains with 50 or more amino acids, so the number of possible structures becomes enormous. A polypeptide with 50 amino acids has 20^{50} different possible sequences: 1.1×10^{65} variations.

We will now move on to look at how the sequence of amino acids in the polypeptide uniquely determines the structure and therefore the function of the protein. Understanding protein structure can seem quite complex, so for convenience it is divided into four levels of organization, known as primary through to quaternary.

The primary structure of proteins is the amino acid sequence

The **primary structure** of a protein refers to the number and sequence of amino acids in its polypeptide chain. Held together by peptide bonds, this forms the covalent backbone of the molecule. Interestingly, once the primary structure has been determined, all the other levels of protein structure follow – so it really does dictate the entire structure and function of the protein.

Many synthetic compounds are polyamides, formed by condensation of a carboxylic acid and an amine group. Examples include nylon and Kevlar.

Figure 13.9 Different coloured beads can be strung together in different combinations to make a wide variety of different necklaces. In a similar way, different sequences of amino acids link together to give rise to an almost infinite variety of proteins.

CHALLENGE YOURSELF

4 By reference to section 33 of the IB data booklet, determine which amino acid contains a secondary amine group. How might this affect its properties in a peptide chain?

Figure 13.10 Primary structure of a small polypeptide. Peptide bonds are highlighted in blue.

N terminal   C terminal

Cys ————— Arg ————— Val ————— Tyr ————— Ile ————— His ————— Thr ————— Phe

Sickle-cell anaemia is a condition that results from a single amino acid change in one chain of 146 amino acids in the protein hemoglobin. The resulting change in the conformation of hemoglobin means that it is not able to carry oxygen efficiently. It is a common condition in many African countries, as the altered red blood cells provide some immunity to malaria.

Often considered the father of modern molecular biology, Fred Sanger of Cambridge, England, is one of only four people to have been awarded two Nobel Prizes. In 1958 he was awarded the Chemistry Prize for establishing the sequence of the 51 amino acids in insulin chain B. This was the first protein to have its primary structure elucidated in this way and it was the culmination of 12 years of work. In 1980 Sanger shared the Nobel Prize in Chemistry for similar work on the base sequencing of nucleic acids.

So what determines the primary structure of a protein? The answer to this question when it came in the early 1960s was considered to be one of the most important discoveries of molecular biology. DNA (deoxyribose nucleic acid), which determines genetic information, acts by dictating to cells the primary structure of their proteins. In other words, the expression of genes is through the proteins that an organism synthesizes. So it is the primary structure of our proteins that gives each of us our unique genetic characteristics.

Protein sequencing is now a routine operation in biochemical research, with machines able to deduce the entire sequence of a large protein very quickly. This is a major part of **proteomics**, the study that explores the relationship between structure and function of proteins. The synthesis of new, so-called **designer proteins** through protein engineering has many applications in pharmaceutical and environmental research. Protein sequences are also the aspect of protein structure used in studies of biochemical evolution to determine the relationships between organisms.

The secondary structure of proteins is regular hydrogen bonding

The **secondary structure** refers to folding of the polypeptide chain as a result of hydrogen bonding between peptide bonds along its length. Hydrogen bonds can form between the –C=O group of one peptide bond and the –N–H group of another peptide bond further along the chain which will cause the chain to fold. The exact configuration of this will be influenced by the R groups along the chain and so differs in different proteins and even in different sections of the same protein. We can distinguish two main types of secondary structure, the α-**helix** and the β-**pleated sheet**.

The α-helix is a regular coiled configuration of the polypeptide chain resulting from hydrogen bonds forming between two peptide bonds four amino acid units apart. This twists the chain into a tightly coiled helix, much like a spiral staircase, with 3.6 amino acids per turn, as shown in Figure 13.11.

The α-helix is flexible and elastic as the intra-chain hydrogen bonds easily break and re-form as the molecule is stretched. A good example of the α-helix is found in keratins, structural proteins found in hair, skin, and claws.

Figure 13.11 α-helical secondary structure of keratin. The amino acid backbone winds in a spiral, held by hydrogen bonds shown in blue.

---- hydrogen bonds

Human hair (made of the protein keratin) grows approximately 15 cm in one year, which means that 9.5 turns of the α-helix must be produced every second.

Hair stretches to almost double its length when exposed to moist heat but contracts to its normal length on cooling, because the hydrogen bonds in the secondary structure easily break and re-form. This is why hair is often much curlier in humid conditions.

The β-pleated sheet is a structure composed of 'side by side' polypeptides which are in extended form, not tightly coiled as in the α-helix. They are arranged in pleated sheets that are cross-linked by inter-chain hydrogen bonds, as shown in Figure 13.12.

Figure 13.12 β-pleated sheet secondary structure of silk fibroin. The polypeptides run parallel to each other, held by hydrogen bonds shown in blue.

---- hydrogen bonds

A spider's web outlined with drops of morning dew. The web's fibres are made of the protein fibroin containing a β-pleated sheet secondary structure and spun from special secreting glands. A typical web may contain 20 metres of fibroin.

The β-pleated sheet is flexible but inelastic. A good example is found in fibroin, the protein in the fibres spun by spiders and silkworms and also found in the beaks and claws of birds.

Keratin and fibroin with their well-defined secondary structure are fibrous proteins. Their toughness and insolubilty in water make them ideal for their structural roles. They are simpler structures with more repetitive amino acid sequences than globular proteins, in much the same way as bricks in a building are mostly alike.

The tertiary structure of proteins is the result of interactions between the R groups

The **tertiary structure** refers to the further twisting, folding, and coiling of the polypeptide chain as a result of interactions between the R groups, known as **side chains**. The structure that results is a very specific compact three-dimensional structure, known as the protein's **conformation**. It is the most stable arrangement of the protein, taking into account all the possible interactions along the entire length of the polypeptide. Note that the interactions between the side chains are all *intra*-molecular forces, as they occur within the one polypeptide chain.

This conformation is particularly important in the globular proteins, which include all the enzymes and protein hormones. They are water soluble because their structure positions nearly all of the polar (or hydrophilic) side-chains on the outer surface of the molecules where they can interact with water, and most of the non-polar (or hydrophobic) side-chains in the interior out of contact with water. The interactions that stabilize this conformation are of the following types, summarized in Figure 13.13.

Computer artwork showing the structure of the protein albumin from human blood. The spiral regions of α-helical structure can be clearly seen as well as the overall three-dimensional conformation.

465

(a) *Hydrophobic interactions* – between non-polar side chains.
    For example, between two alkyl side chains in valine; these weak interactions, based on London (dispersion) forces between induced dipoles, produce non-polar regions in the interior of the protein.

(b) *Hydrogen bonding* – between polar side chains.
    For example, between the —CH_2OH group in serine and the —CH_2COOH group in aspartic acid.

(c) *Ionic bonding* – between side chains carrying a charge.
    For example, between the —$(CH_2)_4NH_3^+$ group in lysine and the —CH_2COO^- group in aspartic acid.

(d) *Disulfide bridges* – between the sulfur-containing amino acid cysteine.
    These are covalent bonds, and hence the strongest of these interactions.

Make sure you are clear on the difference between hydrogen bonds in the secondary structure, which form between groups in the peptide bonds, and hydrogen bonds in the tertiary structure, which form between the side chains.

Figure 13.13 Summary of the interactions that contribute to the tertiary structure of a protein.

The process of 'perming' that introduces more curls into hair involves first breaking the disulfide bridges between the cysteine residues in the keratin using a reducing agent. New disulfide bridges are formed when the hair is chemically re-oxidized while it is twisted around rollers. The size of the roller determines the position of the new disulfide bridges that form. As these are covalent bonds they do not break on normal treatments like washing and combing, and so are said to be 'permanent'. Similar processes are used in straightening curly hair.

These interactions can all be upset by changes in the medium such as to temperature, pH, or the presence of metal ions. When a protein loses its specific tertiary structure as a result of such disruptions, it is said to be **denatured**. The familiar sight of the white of an egg solidifying on heating is an example of this. Denaturation of enzymes renders them biologically inactive, which is one of the reasons why intracellular conditions must be tightly controlled. We will come back to this on page 471.

The quaternary structure of a protein is the association between different polypeptides

Some proteins comprise more than one polypeptide chain, and in these cases the association between these chains is known as the **quaternary structure**. This association involves similar forces and bonds to those found in the tertiary structure – hydrophobic interactions, hydrogen bonds, ionic bonds, and disulfide bridges.

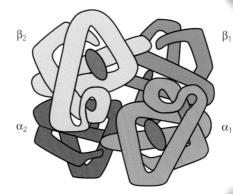

three polypeptide chains

Figure 13.14 Triple-helical quaternary structure of collagen.

β_2 β_1

α_2 α_1

Figure 13.15 Quaternary structure of hemoglobin, an assembly of four polypeptides.

For example, the protein collagen, which is found in skin and tendons and is actually the most abundant protein in the human body, is a triple helix of three polypeptide chains, with inter-chain hydrogen bonds between them. This helps to give it a stable rope-like structure that is resistant to stretching.

Another example is the protein hemoglobin, responsible for carrying oxygen in the blood, which is made up of four polypeptide chains that fit together tightly in the protein assembly.

Many proteins consist of only one polypeptide chain, and so do not have a quaternary structure.

Summary of the bonds and forces involved in protein structure

Protein structure	Nature of interactions
primary	covalent (amide/peptide) bonds between amino acids
secondary	hydrogen bonds within polypeptide chain involving groups in the peptide bonds
tertiary	interactions between side chains including hydrophobic interactions, hydrogen bonds, ionic bonds, disulfide bridges
quaternary	interactions between polypeptide chains, including the same interactions as in the tertiary structure

NATURE OF SCIENCE

Because of the almost infinite variety of protein structures, for a long time they were considered to be more likely than DNA to be the store of hereditary information. Biochemists were surprised to find from experimental results that in fact it is DNA and not protein which carries the genetic code. The evidence came from separate experiments on the ability of DNA to achieve transformation of bacteria, and on the use of radioactive isotopes to demonstrate that viruses inject DNA and not protein into their host cells. Data from both experiments were necessary for broad conclusions to be reached. Subsequent evidence proved that although proteins are not the carriers of hereditary information, they are the molecules through which it is expressed.

7 **(a)** Using the three-letter word symbols for amino acids, show all the possible tripeptides that can form from the three amino acids tyrosine, valine, and histidine.

   (b) Deduce the number of different peptides that could form from the four amino acids tyrosine, valine, histidine, and proline.

8 Consult section 33 of the IB data booklet to consider the following amino acids: leucine, glutamic acid, threonine, lysine, serine.

   Which of these amino acids:

   (a) is most likely to be found in the interior of a globular protein?
   (b) contains a secondary alcohol group?
   (c) will be negatively charged at pH 5.0?
   (d) will be positively charged at pH 7.0?

9 Explain the differences in the structure and properties of fibrous and globular proteins.

10 Hydrogen bonds occur in the secondary and the tertiary structures of proteins. Describe the different origins of these.

Enzyme action is the basis of the brewing and cheese-making industries, possibly the oldest forms of biotechnology. Cheeses and fermented drinks are often associated with specific place names, according to the different flavours produced by enzymes in local microorganisms.

Enzymes are biological catalysts that control all biochemical reactions. They are protein molecules.

Enzymes are globular proteins

The complexity of metabolism demands a highly sensitive control system which can respond to the changing needs of the cell. This is achieved through the action of **enzymes**, the biological catalysts that control every reaction in biochemistry. Because enzymes are specific for each reaction and can be individually controlled, they determine the cell's reactivity at the molecular level.

Enzymes are globular proteins, and exist in compact spherical shapes when in aqueous solution in cells. Their well-defined tertiary structure gives them a specific three-dimensional shape, which is essential for enzyme activity. Enzymes are typically relatively large molecules, containing several hundred amino acids, and some also have a quaternary structure. For example, many of the enzymes involved in the first stage of respiration are dimeric proteins, meaning they contain two polypeptide chains.

In addition, some enzymes require non-protein molecules to be bound for activity. These are known as **co-factors** and may be organic, when they are known as **coenzymes**, or inorganic, such as metal ions. Common examples include vitamins, many of which act as precursors for coenzymes.

Many serious or fatal illnesses are the results of the failure of a single enzyme. For example, the condition phenylketonuria (PKU) that can lead to mental retardation is the consequence of a malfunction in the enzyme responsible for the breakdown of the amino acid phenylalanine in the liver. This condition is the reason why many food and drinks that contain aspartame are labelled 'contains a source of phenylalanine'.

Figure 13.16 Graph showing reaction route of lower activation energy in the presence of an enzyme. This means that at a specified temperature a higher proportion of particles will have sufficient energy to react and so the overall rate of reaction is increased.

Enzymes form a complex with the substrate

Enzymes are catalysts and so increase the rate of a chemical reaction without themselves undergoing permanent chemical change. The reactant in the reaction catalysed by the enzyme is known as the **substrate**. The presence of the enzyme provides a reaction route of lower activation energy and so enables the reaction to occur more quickly at the same temperature.

The action of the enzyme is due to its ability to form a temporary binding to the substrate where it is held by relatively weak forces of attraction, forming an **enzyme–substrate complex**. This binding occurs at a small region of the enzyme known as the **active site**, which is typically a pocket or groove on the surface of the protein. The substrate is usually a much smaller molecule than the enzyme, and therefore fits within it. Formation of the complex depends on a 'chemical fit' or compatibility between the substrate and the side chains of the amino acids at the active site of the enzyme. This involves non-covalent interactions such as hydrophobic interactions, dipole–dipole attractions, hydrogen bonds, and ionic attractions. The binding in the complex puts a strain on the substrate molecule, and this facilitates the breaking and the forming of bonds. Once the substrate has reacted, the product formed no longer fits in the active site and so it detaches. The enzyme is then released unchanged and is able to catalyse further reactions.

Computer graphics representation of the enzyme lysozyme, which breaks down polysaccharides. The protein is shown in blue with its backbone traced out as the magenta ribbon. The substrate is shown in yellow bound to the active site. Note that the substrate is much smaller than the enzyme.

Figure 13.17 Enzymes operate as catalysts by forming a complex with their substrate in which the reaction occurs.

Using **E** for enzyme, **S** for substrate, and **P** for product, we can summarize the action of enzymes as follows:

$$\mathbf{E} + \mathbf{S} \rightleftharpoons \mathbf{E\text{-}S} \rightleftharpoons \mathbf{E\text{-}P} \rightleftharpoons \mathbf{E} + \mathbf{P}$$

Note that all the reactions are shown as equilibrium reactions, and so are reversible depending on the conditions.

Enzymes are specific for the reaction they catalyse

Many enzymes are known to be very specific for their substrate. For example, different proteases, enzymes that hydrolyse proteins, target only specific peptide bonds between certain amino acids. The specificity of an enzyme for its substrate results from its conformation, as this determines the arrangement of the side chains of the amino acids at its active site and therefore its ability to bind precisely with the substrate. The exact nature of the interactions leading to the enzyme–substrate complex is a subject of ongoing research.

469

NATURE OF SCIENCE

Development of enzyme theory provides a case study of how a scientific model may change over time. In 1890 the German chemist Emil Fischer proposed a model known as the **lock and key** mechanism to describe the fit between an enzyme and its substrate, and to explain the specificity of enzymes. This is illustrated in Figure 13.18. But this model cannot readily explain all aspects of enzyme inhibition, and does little to explain the catalytic action, because a lock does not change a key the way an enzyme changes a substrate. Later work on proteomics recognized that enzymes are less rigid structures than the lock and key model suggests, and in 1958, Daniel Koshland of Rockefeller University, New York, proposed a modification known as the **induced-fit** mechanism of enzyme action. This suggests that in the presence of the substrate, the active site undergoes some conformational changes, shaping itself to allow a better fit. So instead of the substrate fitting into a rigid active site, this is a more dynamic relationship where the side chains at the active site change into the precise positions that allow the binding to occur. It has been compared to putting on a rubber glove that is shaped to the specific shape of the hand as it is pulled over the fingers. It is thought that the distortion that occurs as enzyme and substrate approach may be critical to catalysis.

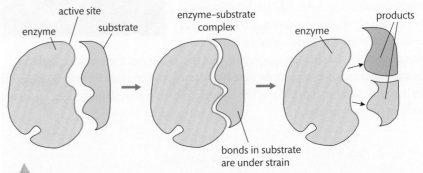

Figure 13.18 Induced fit model of enzyme action. The approach of the substrate induces a conformational change at the active site. This enables the substrate to bind and undergo reaction. As the products are released, the enzyme reverts to its original state.

More recent research suggests that enzymes may be even more flexible structures in which the active site continually reshapes by its interactions with the substrate until the time the substrate is completely bound to it. This is known as the **shifting specificity model** and recognizes the involvement of the entire enzyme molecule rather than just the active site in the catalytic event. Evidence for these developments in enzyme theory has come largely from X-ray protein crystallography, and from advances in computer modelling that enable accurate three-dimensional predictions of enzyme structure to be made.

A small group of enzymes, known as **ribozymes**, have catalytic activity in cells but are made not of protein, but of DNA. The discovery of the catalytic properties of RNA in the 1980s led to a new theory regarding the origin of life, known as the 'RNA world hypothesis'. This suggests that in early life the cell used RNA as both the genetic material and the structural and catalytic molecule, instead of dividing these functions between DNA and proteins. In this case the ribozymes that have persisted could be considered as 'living fossils' of a life based only on nucleic acids.

Enzyme kinetics indicate that saturation occurs in the formation of the complex

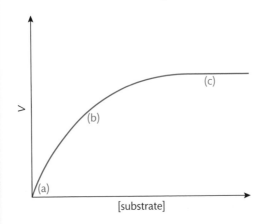

Figure 13.19 The relationship between substrate concentration and rate for an enzyme-catalysed reaction. Note the symbol *V* (velocity) is used to describe the rate of enzyme reactions.

The rate of enzyme-catalysed reactions can be followed using the same principles as those for other reactions discussed in Chapter 6. When graphs of substrate concentration against rate of reaction are plotted, the curves show the distinctive shape of **saturation**. Interpretation of these data lends support to the mechanism of enzyme action proceeding via an enzyme–substrate complex.

The following points can be deduced from the graph.

(a) At low substrate concentration, the rate of the reaction is proportional to the substrate concentration. Enzyme is available to bind to the substrate.

(b) As the substrate concentration is increased the rate decreases and is no longer proportional to the substrate concentration. Some of the enzyme has its active sites occupied by substrate and is not available.

(c) At high substrate concentration the rate is constant and independent of substrate concentration. At this point the enzyme is saturated with substrate.

All enzymes show this saturation effect, but they vary widely with respect to the substrate concentration required to produce saturation.

Enzyme activity is influenced by its physical and chemical environment

We have seen that the action of an enzyme depends on how its specific three-dimensional shape enables it to bind to the substrate. So any conditions that alter its conformation will affect its catalytic action. We will describe three of these factors here.

1 Temperature

We know from Chapter 6 that the rate of a reaction is increased by a rise in temperature due to the increase in the average kinetic energy of the particles. For enzymic reactions, this means there is an increase in the frequency of collisions between molecules of enzyme and substrate that have greater than the activation energy, leading to a higher rate of reaction. But this is only true up to a certain temperature. Beyond this, the effect of the increase in kinetic energy is to change the conformation of the protein by disrupting the bonds and forces responsible for holding it in its tertiary structure. Consequently, the enzyme is no longer able to bind the substrate at the active site and its catalytic activity is diminished. This explains the shape of the curve shown in Figure 13.20.

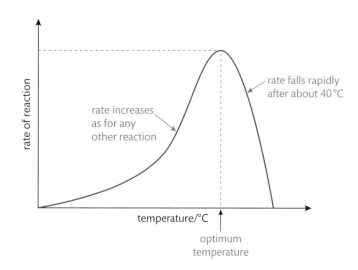

The temperature corresponding to the maximum rate of reaction for a particular enzyme is known as its **optimum temperature**. Most enzymes in the human body have an optimum value close to 37 °C, body temperature. Organisms that are adapted to very different environments, such as bacteria in hot springs or algae on glaciers, produce enzymes with optimum values closer to their ambient temperatures.

Note that loss of the tertiary structure, which is known as **denaturation**, does not mean loss of the covalent backbone of the protein molecules, which is known as **digestion**. Nonetheless, denaturation is usually an irreversible process, as you might know from the impossibility of uncooking an egg! Lowering the temperature usually causes what is called **deactivation** of an enzyme rather than denaturation. This prevents the enzyme from working but as it does not change the tertiary structure, it

(i) Enzyme names are often quite long and appear complex, but in most cases they are logically derived. The name of the substrate is followed by the type of reaction followed by the suffix –ase. So, for example, 'pyruvate dehydrogenase' acts on pyruvate to remove hydrogen; 'glucose isomerase' converts glucose into its isomer fructose.

TOK To what extent do the use of metaphors and models, such as 'lock and key' and 'induced fit', enhance our knowledge of enzyme action?

Figure 13.20 The effect of temperature on the activity of an enzyme.

The effect of temperature on enzyme activity

Full details of how to carry out this experiment with a worksheet are available on your eBook.

Coloured scanning electron micrograph of granules of biological detergents showing the enzymes encapsulated in their structure. The enzymes help break down biomolecules such as those in blood, which may stain clothing. These enzymes are often the result of protein engineering with different optimum temperatures. Synthetic enzymes are also used in biodegradable plastics and in the textiles and food industries.

is usually reversible. This is why, for example, food that has been preserved by freezing soon spoils on thawing due to resumption of microbial activities as the temperature rises.

The effect of temperature on enzymes and other proteins is one of the main reasons why controlling the temperature is so important to many organisms, and why a change in the human core temperature of a couple of degrees Celsius is usually fatal.

Figure 13.21 The influence of pH on the state of ionization of acidic and basic groups in the side chains of a protein. For simplicity the diagram shows side chains of only two amino acids, lysine (lys) and glutamic acid (glu). In lysine R = $-(CH_2)_4-NH_2$ and in glutamic acid R = $-(CH_2)_2-COOH$.

2 pH

The pH of a solution has several effects on the activity of an enzyme. It directly influences the state of ionization of acidic or basic groups in the side chains of the protein. From Le Chatelier's principle we can predict that at low pH (high $[H^+]$), acidic and basic groups become protonated, and at high pH (low $[H^+]$) they become deprotonated. The precise influence of pH depends on the R groups of the amino acids in the enzyme, and so varies in different enzymes. These changes in ionization within the protein structure alter the attractive forces stabilizing the enzyme, and crucially affect its shape and its ability to recognize the substrate.

More specifically, changes in the ionization of side chains of amino acids at the active site will affect the ability of the enzyme to form a complex with the substrate. In most cases there is a clear optimum value for pH at which the enzyme has maximum activity. The optimum pH value for an enzyme gives a clue to the likely amino acids at its active site. Unlike for temperature, different enzymes in the same organism can have a wide variation in the optimum values of their pH, as shown in Figure 13.22.

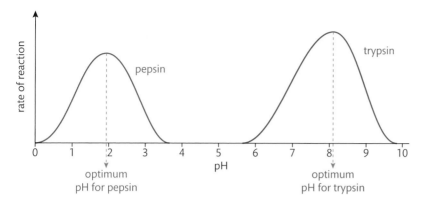

Figure 13.22 The effect of pH on two different digestive enzymes in the human body.

These differences in the pH optima of different enzymes can be an important way of controlling enzyme activity. In the example shown in Figure 13.22, the enzyme pepsin is most active in the stomach, where the pH is very low. However, it becomes inactive once it is moved with the digested food into the more alkaline environment of the intestine, where trypsin is active. Their optimum values correspond to the pH in the different regions of the digestive tract where they are active. Extremes of pH denature an enzyme in much the same way as described for high temperature; an egg which has been dropped into strong acid looks 'cooked' in the same way as if it had been heated, due to changes in the tertiary structure of its protein.

3 Heavy metal ions

Heavy metals such as lead, copper, mercury, and silver are poisonous, primarily due to their effects on enzymes. When these metals are present as positive ions, they react with sulfhydryl groups, $-SH$, in the side chains of cysteine residues in the protein, forming a covalent bond with the sulfur atom and displacing a hydrogen ion. This disrupts the folding of the protein, and may change the shape of the active site and its ability to bind substrate. This is a form of inhibition, discussed below.

cysteine residue
in protein

Ag bound to cysteine
causing conformational
change in the protein

Figure 13.23 Enzyme inhibition by Ag^+ ions. Binding of the metal to a sulfhydryl group in the amino acid cysteine may change the conformation of the enzyme at the active site.

> The optimum values of temperature and pH for an enzyme refer to the conditions where the enzyme and substrate are maximally able to bind and form a complex.

Inorganic dyes used to darken hair, such as 'Grecian Formula', contain a soluble lead salt which interacts with the sulfur atoms in the hair protein keratin to produce lead sulfide, PbS, which is black. The amount of darkening depends on the proportion of cysteine residues in the hair. Ancient Greeks used to line their waterways with lead and it was noticed that people who bathed often in this water had darker hair. Lead poisoning from the drinking water is believed to have contributed to the decline of both the Greek and the Roman empires. Concerns over the toxicity of lead salts have caused these hair dyes to be banned in many countries.

Exercises

11 **(a)** State four characteristics of enzymes.
   (b) Sketch a graph of the rate of an enzyme reaction against temperature and explain its shape.

12 Draw a graph of the rate of an enzyme reaction against substrate concentration.

13 Compare enzymes and inorganic catalysts, with reference to two similarities and three differences.

Analysis of proteins

Analysis of protein content is a major aspect of research in biochemistry. For example, clinical analysis of protein levels in body fluids can be used to confirm pregnancy or can be used to help diagnose a variety of diseases. Food analysts are interested in knowing the total concentration and type of proteins in foods, and the pharmaceutical industry often uses altered protein levels to test the efficacy of a drug.

Many different approaches and techniques are used in protein analysis. We will consider here two main aspects of this work:

• analysis of the amino acid composition of an isolated protein;
• analysis of the protein concentration of a sample.

Analysis of the amino acid composition of a protein

The first step in the analysis is to break the peptide bonds between the amino acids in the protein structure through **hydrolysis** reactions, usually using acid. These reactions reverse the condensation reactions discussed on page 453, and occur commonly in cells during enzyme-catalysed protein digestion. (Note that determination of the amino acid composition of a protein is not the same as knowing its primary structure, as the *sequence* of the amino acids will not be known.)

Figure 13.24 Hydrolysis of protein produces amino acids; condensation of amino acids produces proteins.

Separation of the resulting amino acid mixture into its components can then be achieved in two ways.

1 Chromatography

Chromatography is a useful technique for separating and identifying the components of a mixture. The basic principle is that the components have different affinities for two phases, a **stationary phase** and a **mobile phase**, and so are separated as the mobile phase moves through the stationary phase. As amino acids are colourless in solution they are usually treated with a **locating reagent** at the end of the process which makes them take on colour to aid their identification.

Paper chromatography is an example of partition chromatography, in which the components are separated on the basis of their different solubilities in the two phases. It is used mainly for qualitative analysis. The paper contains about 10% water, and this is the stationary phase. Water is adsorbed by forming hydrogen bonds with the —OH groups in the cellulose of the paper. The solvent is the mobile phase as it rises up the paper by capillary action. As it does so it dissolves the components of the mixture to different extents, so carrying them at different rates.

The procedure is simple to run. A small sample of the amino acid mixture is spotted near the bottom of the chromatographic paper, and this position, known as the **origin**, needs to be clearly marked (in pencil so as not to interfere with the experiment). The paper is then suspended in a chromatographic tank containing a small volume of solvent, ensuring that the spot is above the level of the solvent.

When measuring the distances to calculate R_f values, be careful to measure from the origin and not from the bottom of the paper. Similarly, the solvent moves as far as the solvent front, not to the top of the paper.

Separation of amino acids by chromatography

Full details of how to carry out this experiment with a worksheet are available on your eBook.

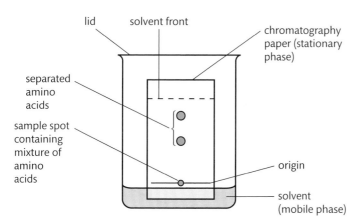

Figure 13.25 Apparatus used to separate amino acids by paper chromatography.

As the solvent rises up the paper it will pass over the spot. Amino acids in the spot will distribute themselves between the two phases and so move up the paper at different speeds. As a result they become spread out according to their different solubilities. When the solvent reaches almost to the top of the paper, its final position is marked and is known as the **solvent front**. The paper is removed from the tank and developed by spraying it with the locating reagent **ninhydrin**. Most amino acids will now appear purple and can be distinguished as separate isolated spots up the length of the paper. The final result is known as a **chromatogram**.

The position of each amino acid on the chromatogram can be represented as an R_f value (retention factor), which is calculated as shown below.

$$R_f = \frac{\text{distance moved by amino acid}}{\text{distance moved by solvent}}$$

So, for amino acid A, $R_f = \dfrac{a}{x}$

Specific amino acids have characteristic R_f values when measured under the same conditions, so can be identified by comparing the values obtained with data tables. It is helpful to spot known amino acids alongside the mixture to act as markers for the experiment.

2 Electrophoresis

Electrophoresis is a technique for the analysis and separation of a mixture based on the movement of charged particles in an electric field. As we saw on page 460, amino acids carry different charges depending on the pH, and these differences can be exploited to separate them when placed in a buffered solution at a particular pH.

- When the pH is equal to their isoelectric point, amino acids will not move as they carry no net charge.
- When the pH > their isoelectric point, the amino acids exist as anions and move to the anode.
- When the pH < their isoelectric point, the amino acids exist as cations and move to the cathode.

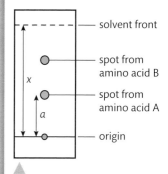

Figure 13.26 Calculation of R_f values in chromatography.

In chromatography, the R_f value can be used to identify the components of a mixture.

$$R_f = \frac{\text{distance moved by amino acid}}{\text{distance moved by solvent}}$$

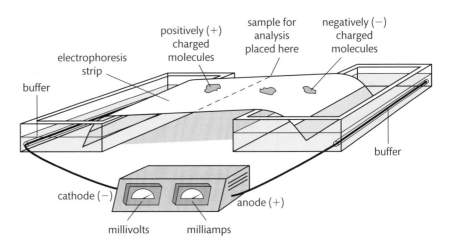

Figure 13.27 Electrophoresis apparatus for amino acid or protein separation.

The rate of movement of the ions will depend on the number of charges on the ion and the molecular mass – smaller, more highly charged ions migrate faster. The voltage used and the temperature also affect the rate of movement.

In gel electrophoresis, the medium is a gel, typically made of polyacrylamide. The amino acid mixture is placed in wells in the centre of the gel and a voltage is applied. Depending on the pH of the buffer used, different amino acids will move at different rates and in different directions towards the oppositely charged electrodes. When separation is complete they can be detected with a stain such as ninhydrin or made to fluoresce under UV light, and identified by comparison with known samples or from data tables.

Electrophoresis can also be used to separate and identify intact proteins according to their different rates of migration towards the poles.

Multi-pipette used to place protein samples into agarose gel in a buffer solution for electrophoresis. The protein molecules will separate according to their different attractions to opposite electrical poles across the polyacrylamide gel (polyacrylamide gel electrophoresis or PAGE). This technique is used to detect whether proteins associated with particular diseases are found in the blood.

Worked example

Gel electrophoresis was carried out using a buffer at pH 6.0 on a mixture of glycine, alanine, lysine, glutamic acid, and aspartic acid. Use section 33 of the IB data booklet to identify which amino acids

(a) will remain close to the origin

(b) will move fastest towards the anode

(c) will move fastest towards the cathode.

Solution

From their isoelectric points, at pH 6.0 the amino acids will exist as follows:

glycine: neutral; alanine: neutral; lysine: cation; glutamic acid: anion; aspartic acid: anion

Therefore:

(a) glycine and alanine will not move

(b) glutamic acid and aspartic acid will move towards the anode, and aspartic acid will move more quickly as it is a smaller molecule

(c) lysine will move towards the cathode.

Urine analysis using a multiple test stick against a reference chart. The pads test for pH as well as for various components of the urine. Body fluids such as urine maintain a relatively constant pH through the action of so-called pH buffers. Close control of pH is vital due to its effects on the structures of proteins including enzymes.

Exercises

14 (a) When carrying out paper chromatography on a sample of hydrolysed protein, explain why it is important to avoid handling the paper.
Make reference to section 33 in the IB data booklet to answer parts (b) and (c).

(b) Explain why in gel electrophoresis the amino acid isoleucine migrates towards the anode at high pH and towards the cathode at low pH.

(c) You are attempting to separate a mixture of glutamic acid and histidine by gel electrophoresis. Give a suggested pH for an appropriate buffer solution to use, and say in which direction each amino acid would migrate.

B.3 Lipids

Understandings:

- Fats are more reduced than carbohydrates and so yield more energy when oxidized.
- Triglycerides are produced by condensation of glycerol with three fatty acids and contain ester links. Fatty acids can be saturated, monounsaturated, or polyunsaturated.
- Phospholipids are derivatives of triglycerides.
- Hydrolysis of triglycerides and phospholipids can occur using enzymes or in alkaline or acidic conditions.
- Steroids have a characteristic fused ring structure, known as a steroidal backbone.
- Lipids act as structural components of cell membranes, in energy storage, thermal and electrical insulation, transport of lipid soluble vitamins, and as hormones.

Guidance
- The structures of the fatty acids are given in the data booklet in section 34.
- Specific named examples of fats and oils do not have to be learned.

Applications and skills:

- Deduction of the structural formulas of reactants and products in condensation and hydrolysis reactions between glycerol and fatty acids and/or phosphate.
- Prediction of the relative melting points of fats and oils from their structures.
- Comparison of the processes of hydrolytic and oxidative rancidity in fats with respect to the site of reactivity in the molecules and the conditions that favour the reaction.
- Application of the concept of iodine number to determine the unsaturation of a fat.
- Comparison of carbohydrates and lipids as energy storage molecules with respect to their solubility and energy density.
- Discussion of the impact of lipids on health, including the roles of dietary high-density lipoprotein (HDL) and low-density (LDL) cholesterol, saturated, unsaturated, and *trans* fat and the use and abuse of steroids.

Guidance
The structural differences between cis and trans fats are not required.

CHALLENGE YOURSELF

5 Even though the concept of oxidation state is of limited use in organic chemistry, predict how you would expect the oxidation state of carbon to compare in a simple carbohydrate and in a simple lipid molecule. See if you can check this with some simple examples from each group.

The term **lipid** is used as an umbrella term for a range of biomolecules such as fats and oils, steroids, and phospholipids. They are characterized by being hydrophobic or insoluble in water. They are, though, soluble in non-polar solvents, and this property is often used in extracting them from cells. Lipids contain the elements carbon, hydrogen, and oxygen, but the ratio of hydrogen to oxygen is greater than in carbohydrates – in other words they are more reduced molecules.

Functions of lipids

Lipids are essential molecules in a variety of roles in cells

Lipids contain stored energy that is released when they are broken down in the reactions of respiration in cells. Because lipids are more reduced than carbohydrates, they can effectively undergo *more* oxidation and so release *more* energy per unit mass when used as a respiratory substrate. The difference is significant: a gram of lipid releases almost twice as much energy as a gram of carbohydrate. However, partly due to their insolubility, the energy in lipids is not so readily available as it is in carbohydrates, as more reactions are involved in the breakdown. So the energy is released more slowly. The fat stores in animals, known as **adipose tissue** or **blubber**, serve as reservoirs of energy, swelling and shrinking as fat is deposited and withdrawn. Plants also sometimes store lipids for energy, for example as oils in seeds.

You are more likely to take a glucose tablet than suck a lump of cheese, for example, when you are running a marathon. But if you were going on an expedition to the Arctic, you would take lots of lipids like cheese and butter, as they make ideal storage molecules. These differences are because the energy in carbohydrates is more readily available, but lipids are a denser energy store.

Electron micrograph of lipid droplets shown in green in a fat cell. These cells form adipose tissue, which stores energy as an insulating layer of fat.

Stored fat helps to protect some body organs, such as the kidneys, and a layer of fat under the skin acts as a thermal insulator. This is why animals that live in cold climates, such as seals and polar bears, have significant fat stores. Lipids also act as electrical insulators. In nerve cells a special layer of phospholipids called the myelin sheath gives electrical insulation to the nerves, and speeds up nervous transmission.

Some hormones, such as the sex hormones testosterone and estrogen, are made of lipids in the form of steroids. Bile acids, which aid digestion of fat in the intestine, are also steroid based. In addition, lipids help to absorb fat-soluble vitamins such as A, D, E, and K.

Lipids also play an important structural role. The phospholipids are a major component of membranes that bind cells. Here they help to determine the selective transport of metabolites across cell boundaries. A different lipid molecule, cholesterol, is also important in plasma membrane structure, where it influences the fluidity and so the permeability of the membrane.

Excess lipids in the diet can have negative effects on health

Excess lipids in the diet are increasingly linked to negative effects on health. These arise largely due to their low solubility that causes some lipids to be deposited in the walls

Magnified view of a slice through an artery showing a thick deposit caused by the disease atherosclerosis. The deposit is composed of a mixture of fats, cholesterol, and dead muscle cells. It disrupts blood flow and can break off in fragments blocking smaller blood vessels, leading to strokes and heart disease.

Computer artwork of LDL (right) and HDL (left) cholesterol, the major carriers of cholesterol in the blood. The purple spheres represent cholesterol molecules which are bonded to phospholipids, shown in yellow, and protein shown as purple and pink strands. LDL cholesterol is associated with increased risk of heart disease.

TOK

Debate exists as to whether people who need two airline seats because they are obese should have to pay for this themselves or have the second seat paid for as part of a disability coverage. To what extent should health problems perceived as resulting from life-style choices be distinguished from other forms of disability?

of the main blood vessels. This can restrict blood flow, a condition known as **atherosclerosis**. It is usually associated with high blood pressure and can lead to heart disease.

In addition, because of the body's ability to convert excess fats into adipose tissue, a diet too rich in lipids can lead to the excess accumulation of body fat known as **obesity**. This is linked to many other health issues including diabetes and a variety of cancers. The molecule that is often the main culprit in circulatory diseases is **cholesterol**. It is present in the human diet, particularly from animal fat, and is also synthesized in the body. Because cholesterol is insoluble in blood, it is transported bound in different lipoproteins, the most well known of which are **LDL** (low-density lipoprotein) and **HDL** (high-density lipoprotein).

These have gained the somewhat simplistic terms 'bad cholesterol' and 'good cholesterol' respectively. The names reflect the fact that high levels of LDL cholesterol are associated with increased deposition in the walls of the arteries, while high levels of HDL cholesterol seem to protect against heart attack. It is believed that HDL tends to carry cholesterol away from the arteries, so slowing its build-up. The main sources of LDL cholesterol are saturated fats and *trans* fats, the chemical nature of which is discussed in the next section.

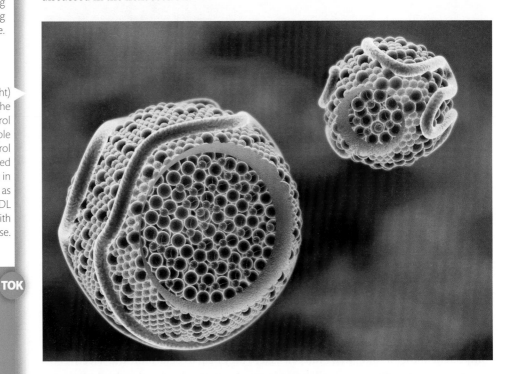

Clearly the type of fat consumed is as important as the total amount. In general an intake of poly-unsaturated fats such as those found in fish, many nuts, and corn oil is considered beneficial in lowering levels of LDL cholesterol. Also, a type of fatty acid known as omega-3-poly-unsaturated fatty acid, found for example in fish oils and flax seeds, has been shown to be linked with reduced risk of cardiovascular disease as well as with optimum neurological development. These fatty acids cannot be manufactured by the body so are known as **essential fatty acids** and must be taken in the diet.

Uses and abuses of steroids

As noted above, lipids in the form of steroids are found in some hormones. Female steroid hormones are used in contraceptive pill formulations and in HRT (hormone replacement therapy) sometimes prescribed during menopause. Possible side-effects of these steroid treatments must be monitored and ongoing research is essential to provide data about long-term usage.

Male steroid hormones are collectively called androgens, of which **testosterone** is the most important. Medical uses of testosterone include treatment of disorders of the testes and breast cancer. These hormones are also known as **anabolic steroids** due to their role in promoting tissue growth, especially of muscles. Synthetic forms of them are used medically to help gain weight after debilitating diseases. They have also been used as **performance-enhancing drugs** by athletes in sports such as weight-lifting and cycling, as they can increase strength and endurance. Their use is banned by most sporting authorities for medical and ethical reasons.

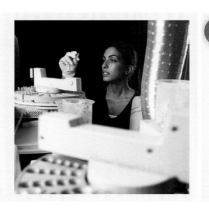

Scientist centrifuging urine samples sent for anti-doping testing at the laboratories of the Italian National Olympic Committee. The samples are analysed for performance-enhancing drugs such as anabolic steroids, using techniques such as liquid chromatography/mass spectrometry. Drug testing like this has become a focus of national and international sporting authorities and uses increasingly accurate technology. Anabolic steroids can cause changes in secondary sexual characteristics resulting from hormone imbalances, and can be associated with increased risk of liver cancer.

Structures of different lipids

The structures of the three main types of lipids – triglycerides, phospholipids, and steroids – will be considered here in turn.

Structure of triglycerides: fats and oils

Triglycerides are the major constituent of fats and oils. They are esters formed by condensation reactions between **glycerol** and **three fatty acids**.

Glycerol is a molecule with three carbon atoms, each of which has an alcohol group as shown below.

$$
\begin{array}{c}
H \\
| \\
H - C - O - H \\
| \\
H - C - O - H \\
| \\
H - C - O - H \\
| \\
H
\end{array}
$$

glycerol

The essential fatty acids linoleic acid and linolenic acid are known as omega-6 and omega-3. The names refer to the position of the first double bond in the molecule relative to the terminal –CH_3 group. This is referred to as omega (the last letter in the Greek alphabet), to represent its distance from the –COOH group. These structures are given in section 34 of the IB data booklet.

The American Food and Drug Administration (FDA) recommends that pregnant women and nursing mothers should limit their intake of fish to two servings per week, due to concerns about mercury contamination. However, studies have also shown the importance of omega-3-fatty acids, which are found in fish, for fetal health and development of the brain. The obvious tension between these opposing recommendations leaves women with a difficult choice. One possible solution is to choose fish with low mercury levels such as salmon and sardines; another is to use omega-3 fatty acid dietary supplements.

Following the guidelines in Chapter 10, see if you can give glycerol its IUPAC name? The answer is propane-1,2,3-triol; however, we will continue to refer to it as glycerol here as this name is widely used.

Fatty acids are long-chain carboxylic acids R–COOH. For example, the fatty acid palmitic acid, $C_{15}H_{31}COOH$, has the following structure:

An esterification reaction takes place between an acid –COOH group and each –OH group in glycerol, eliminating water as each ester link forms.

glycerol

So one glycerol condenses with *three* fatty acids to form the *triglyceride*.

Figure 13.29 A triglyceride.

glycerol

a triglyceride

In most natural oils and fats the three fatty acids that form one triglyceride molecule are not all the same. They can be designated R_1, R_2, and R_3 as shown in Figure 13.30.

The fatty acids differ from each other in the following two ways, which give rise to the specific properties of different fats and oils.

1 The length of their hydrocarbon chain: the most abundant fatty acids have an even number of carbon atoms with chains between 14 and 22 carbon atoms long.

2 The number and position of carbon–carbon double bonds in the hydrocarbon chain:
   • fatty acids with no double bonds are said to be **saturated**;
   • fatty acids with a single double bond are described as **mono-unsaturated**;
   • fatty acids with several double bonds are described as **poly-unsaturated**.

Because fats and oils usually contain a variety of fatty acids, they are classified according to the predominant types of unsaturation present.

Saturated fatty acids

Saturated fatty acids have the general formula $C_nH_{2n+1}COOH$. The carbon chain, made from only carbon–carbon single bonds, has tetrahedral bond angles (109.5°) which allow the molecules to pack relatively closely together. This leads to significant London (dispersion) forces between them. As a result they form saturated triglycerides with relatively high melting points that are solids at room temperature. They are known as **fats** and are derived mostly from animals. Common examples are butter and lard.

Figure 13.30 A triglyceride containing three different fatty acids.

Fatty acids with an odd number of carbon atoms are rarely found in land-based animals, but are very common in marine organisms.

Saturated fatty acids contain all single carbon–carbon bonds; unsaturated fatty acids contain one or more double carbon–carbon bonds in the hydrocarbon chain.

Figure 13.31 A saturated triglyceride.

Unsaturated fatty acids

By contrast, the unsaturated fatty acids, containing one or more carbon–carbon double bonds with 120° bond angles, have kinks in the chains that make it more difficult for the molecules to pack closely together. They form unsaturated triglycerides which have weaker intermolecular forces and lower melting points, so are liquids at room temperature. They are known as **oils**, and are found mostly in plants and fish. Common examples are corn oil and cod liver oil.

Figure 13.32 An unsaturated triglyceride. The double bonds put kinks in the hydrocarbon chains.

483

As commonly occurring fats and oils consist of a mixture of triglycerides, they usually do not have sharp melting points. Generally, the melting points increase with increasing molar mass (length of the hydrocarbon chains) and with increasing degree of saturation. The table below illustrates this by comparing the melting points of fatty acids with similar molar mass.

Fatty acid	Formula	M / g mol^{-1}	Number of double bonds	Melting point / °C	Common source	
linolenic	$C_{17}H_{29}COOH$	278	3	−11	soyabean oil	increasing saturation
linoleic	$C_{17}H_{31}COOH$	280	2	−5	corn oil	
oleic	$C_{17}H_{33}COOH$	282	1	16	olive oil	
stearic	$C_{17}H_{35}COOH$	284	0	70	beef fat	

As noted earlier, a strong correlation has been shown between diets rich in saturated fats and elevated levels of LDL cholesterol, with associated increase in the incidence of heart disease.

NATURE OF SCIENCE

Public knowledge concerning the health effects of excess lipids in the diet is the result of many published studies of long-term data. Scientists have shared their results through peer-reviewed publications and have helped to explain the links between diet and health. The widely accepted relationship between *trans* fats, excess saturated fat, and cholesterol with cardiovascular disease has helped to direct policies on food production and education.

Determination of the degree of unsaturation in a fat uses iodine

Unsaturated fatty acids are able to undergo **addition reactions** by breaking the carbon–carbon double bond(s) and adding incoming groups to the new bonding positions created on the carbon atoms. This is a characteristic reaction of alkenes, described in Chapter 10. Iodine (I_2) is able to react with unsaturated fats in this way.

The equation shows that one mole of iodine will react with each mole of double bonds in the fat. Therefore the higher the number of double bonds per molecule, the larger the amount of iodine that can react. This is expressed as the **iodine number**, defined as the number of grams of iodine which reacts with 100 grams of fat. It is therefore a measure of the amount of unsaturation in the fat.

Determination of the iodine number of a fat usually involves reacting a known amount of the fat with a known amount of iodine, and waiting for the reaction to be completed. The amount of excess iodine remaining can then be calculated by titration with $Na_2S_2O_3(aq)$, from which the reacted iodine can be determined.

Worked example

Linoleic acid has the formula $C_{18}H_{32}O_2$. Determine the iodine number of linoleic acid.

At room temperature, fats are solid and oils are liquid.

Assortment of dietary oils (liquids) and fats (solids). Oils have a lower melting point because they contain unsaturated fatty acids. These lower the level of cholesterol in the blood. ▼

The melting points of fatty acids increase with their molar mass and degree of saturation.

Solution

The formula for linoleic acid can be expressed as $C_{17}H_{31}COOH$, from which we can deduce that it has two carbon–carbon double bonds.

$\therefore$ 2 moles I_2 will react with 1 mole linoleic acid.

M(linoleic acid) = 280 g mol^{-1}

$M(I_2)$ = 254 g mol^{-1}

$\therefore$ 280 g linoleic acid reacts with (2×254) = 508 g I_2

100 g linoleic acid reacts with $\dfrac{508 \text{ g} \times 100 \text{ g}}{280 \text{ g}}$ = 181 g I_2

$\therefore$ iodine number = 181

The lower the iodine value, the higher the proportion of saturated fatty acids in the fat; the iodine number of saturated fatty acids will, of course, be zero. The table below gives some iodine values for some common fats and oils.

Fat or oil	Iodine number
soyabean oil	122–134
olive oil	80–90
bacon fat	47–67
beef fat	35–45

A similar reaction to the addition of iodine is addition of hydrogen, known as **hydrogenation**. This is sometimes carried out by the food industry to increase the saturation of oils. The process of partial hydrogenation produces *trans* fats, which are associated with some of the health problems discussed earlier.

Rancidity of fats

When fats used in the food industry are stored for long periods of time, they can undergo chemical change which causes them to become **rancid**. This is characterized by disagreeable smells, taste, texture, or appearance. There are two main causes of this.

Hydrolytic rancidity

This occurs when the fat breaks down by hydrolysis reactions, using the water present in food. The site of reactivity is the ester linkages in the triglycerides.

$$\text{fat} + 3H_2O \rightarrow \text{glycerol} + \text{fatty acid}$$

This is the reverse of the condensation reaction described on page 482. The reaction occurs more readily in the presence of heat, such as during deep-fat frying. It is also catalysed by the enzyme **lipase**, and can be favoured in the presence of certain bacteria. The rancid smell and flavour is due to the release of free fatty acids, such as butanoic and octanoic acids which are released from rancid milk. As hydrolytic rancidity is favoured by higher temperatures, it can be substantially reduced by refrigeration.

Oxidative rancidity

This occurs when unsaturated fats react with oxygen from the air. The site of reactivity is the carbon–carbon double bonds in unsaturated triglycerides. The products responsible for the rancidity are volatile aldehydes and ketones. The process, known as auto-oxidation, is often accelerated by light and enzymes or metal ions. It proceeds via a free-radical mechanism and so yields a mixture of products. Oxidative rancidity is characteristic of fats and oils that have a high proportion of carbon–carbon double bonds, such as oily fish like herring. It can be controlled, but not eliminated, by the addition of **antioxidants**.

As they cannot undergo auto-oxidation, saturated fats are more stable than unsaturated fats.

Structure of phospholipids

Phospholipids are similar to triglycerides in that they are also derived from fatty acids and glycerol, but have only two fatty acids condensed onto the glycerol molecule. The third –OH position of the glycerol has, instead, condensed with a phosphate group. Different phospholipids vary in their fatty acid chains and in the group attached to the phosphate. One of the most common phospholipids, **lecithin**, is shown in Figure 13.33.

Different cultures use varied sources of lipids and so different methods to extend their shelf-life. Examples of preservation include processing, packaging, and chemical additives.

Figure 13.33 Representations of the structure of phospholipids.

Whale oil was a traditional source of lipids for many countries, and was widely used as a food substance, a lubricant, and as a fuel for lighting. Over-harvesting of whales led to a depletion of stocks by the mid-1800s, and kerosene from crude oil became the major alternative fuel.

Phospholipids are characterized by having a polar, or hydrophilic, 'head' (the phosphate group) and two non-polar, or hydrophobic, 'tails' (the hydrocarbon chains of the fatty acids). As a result they will spontaneously form a **phospholipid bilayer** which maximizes the interactions between the polar groups and water, while creating a non-polar, hydrophobic interior.

This phospholipid bilayer provides the basis of membrane structure.

Hydrolysis of fats and phospholipids

Triglycerides and phospholipids are broken down in hydrolysis reactions to yield their component molecules. The reactions use water and can occur in acidic or in alkaline conditions, or catalysed by enzymes known as **lipases**. This occurs during the digestion of lipids in the gut, where the activity of the enzymes is controlled largely by local changes in pH. Lipid digestion is generally a slow process and may take several hours before soluble products are released. Hydrolysis reactions are also responsible for hydrolytic rancidity.

Alkaline hydrolysis produces the salt of the fatty acid and is used in the manufacture of soap. For this reason, this reaction of reverse esterification is sometimes called **saponification**.

For example,

$$\text{triglyceride of stearic acid} + 3KOH(aq) \xrightarrow{\text{alkali hydrolysis}} 3C_{17}H_{35}COO^-K^+ + \text{glycerol}$$

triglyceride of stearic acid

alkali hydrolysis

potassium stearate

glycerol

Structure of steroids

Steroids are lipids with a structure consisting of four fused rings, known as a **steroidal backbone**. One of the most important steroids is cholesterol, which has the following structure. It is given in the IB data booklet in section 34.

Cholesterol is used as a precursor in the synthesis of many biomolecules, including other steroids such as the sex hormones, bile acids, and Vitamin D. It is an essential component of cell membranes as it helps to provide fluidity and permeability to the structure. The hydroxyl group interacts with the polar head groups of phospholipids in the membrane, while the non-polar rings and hydrocarbon chain interact with the hydrophobic tails of the phospholipid bilayer. The uses, and problems, of cholesterol and other steroids were discussed earlier in this section.

487

15 A sample of fat containing 0.02 moles of fatty acid was found to react with 10.16 g of iodine. Determine the number of carbon–carbon double bonds present in the fatty acid.

16 What is meant by 'essential' fatty acids?

    A Fatty acids that form phospholipids in cell membranes.

    B Fatty acids that must be present in the diet.

    C Fatty acids that are only present in green vegetables.

    D Fatty acids that are unsaturated.

17 Explain the different chemical basis of the two types of rancidity which can occur in lipids.

B.4 Carbohydrates

Understandings:

- Carbohydrates have the general formula $C_x(H_2O)_y$.
- Haworth projections represent the cyclic structures of monosaccharides.
- Monosaccharides contain either an aldehyde group (aldose) or a ketone group (ketose) and several –OH groups.
- Straight-chain forms of sugars cyclize in solution to form ring structures containing an ether linkage.
- Glycosidic bonds form between monosaccharides forming disaccharides and polysaccharides.
- Carbohydrates are used as energy sources and energy reserves.

    Guidance

    - *The component monosaccharides of specific disaccharides and the linkage details of polysaccharides are not required.*

    - *The distinction between α- and β-forms, and the structure of cellulose is not required.*

Applications and skills:

- Deduction of the structural formulas of disaccharides and polysaccharides from given monosaccharides.
- Relationship of the properties and functions of monosaccharides and polysaccharides to their chemical structures.

    Guidance

    The straight-chain and α-ring forms of glucose and fructose are given in the data booklet in section 34.

Carbohydrates (literally *hydrated carbon*) are composed of the three elements carbon, hydrogen, and oxygen, with the hydrogen and oxygen always in the same ratio as in water i.e. 2 : 1. They therefore can be expressed by the general formula $C_x(H_2O)_y$. Note that this higher ratio of oxygen represents a more oxidized state for the carbon atoms than in lipids. There are two main types of carbohydrates – the simple sugars or **monosaccharides** and the condensation polymers of these known as **polysaccharides**.

Functions of carbohydrates

The monosaccharides, for example **glucose** and **fructose**, are readily soluble in water and are mostly taken up by cells quite rapidly. They are used as the main substrate for respiration, releasing energy for all cell processes. They also act as precursors in a large number of metabolic reactions, leading to the synthesis of other molecules such as fats, nucleic acids, and amino acids.

Polysaccharides, being insoluble, are used as the storage form of carbohydrates. Animals mostly use **glycogen** for storage of carbohydrates in the liver and muscles, while plants store **starch** in their cells. These energy reserves can be broken down into monosaccharides, which are then oxidized in respiration to release energy for the cell's activities.

Animals generally make little use of carbohydrates for structural materials, but plant cells are very dependent on carbohydrates for their structure. The polysaccharide **cellulose**, which is found in the walls of all plant cells, is claimed to be the most abundant organic compound on Earth.

Structure of carbohydrates

Monosaccharides are simple sugars

The monosaccharides are the simplest form of carbohydrates and are usually classified according to the number of carbon atoms that they contain. Some of the most common are the **triose** sugars (C3), the **pentose** sugars (C5), and the **hexose** sugars (C6). All monosaccharides can be represented by the empirical formula CH_2O. Hexose sugars, for example, all have the molecular formula $C_6H_{12}O_6$.

These sugar molecules all have two or more hydroxyl groups (–OH) and a carbonyl group (–C=O). Their large number of polar hydroxyl groups is responsible for their ready solubility in water.

Many isomers of sugars exist, representing different structural arrangements of the same number and type of atoms in different molecules. For example, $C_6H_{12}O_6$ exists in many forms including glucose and fructose. The straight-chain forms of these sugars are shown below.

glucose: an aldose sugar   fructose: a ketose sugar

In aqueous solution these sugars undergo an internal reaction resulting in the more familiar ring structures shown below.

glucose   fructose

TOK

Aspartame is an artificial sweetener, widely used in some foods and drinks. However its use is controversial, with claims and counter-claims made about its negative impact on health. What ways of knowing can be used to determine response when faced with contradictory information such as this?

Monosaccharides contain a carbonyl group and at least two hydroxyl groups. They have the empirical formula CH_2O.

The straight-chain and α-ring forms of glucose and fructose are given in section 34 of the IB data booklet so they do not have to be learned.

These representations of the ring forms of sugars are known as **Haworth projection formulas**. The edge of the ring nearest the reader is represented by bold lines, and the letter C for the carbons in the ring are usually omitted from the structure.

NATURE OF SCIENCE

The stereochemistry of carbohydrates is essential to their structural and functional roles in cells. Different representations are used to symbolize these molecular structures. Fischer projections are two-dimensional representations of three-dimensional molecules, such as shown here for the straight-chain forms of the sugars. Haworth projection formulas, on the other hand, aim to give a simple three-dimensional perspective. They are often favoured for representing cyclic structures as, by making ring carbon (and often hydrogen) atoms implicit, they help to focus on the nature and position of the substituent groups. Haworth formulas can, however, be misleading as they suggest that the five-membered ring of fructose and six-membered ring of glucose are planar, which is not the case. In reality these exist as puckered rings in different conformations which can interconvert by rotation around single bonds.

Scientists depend on models and visualizations to communicate knowledge, but it is often the case that a single representation is inadequate. Understanding can therefore be enhanced by the use of a variety of models, including computer simulations and mathematical models.

The formation of the ring in glucose and fructose makes possible another type of isomer, so-called alpha and beta forms.

Disaccharides are two simple sugars linked together

Disaccharides form by linking two monosaccharides together in a condensation reaction. A molecule of water is eliminated as an −OH group from each sugar molecule react together. The resulting bond between the monosaccharides is known as a **glycosidic link**. Disaccharides are all soluble molecules that can be hydrolysed into two monosaccharides by acid hydrolysis or by enzyme-catalysed reaction. Combining different monosaccharides will produce different disaccharides.

For example, two α-glucose molecules condense to form the disaccharide **maltose**, as shown here. The glycosidic link is known as 1–4 because C_1 in one molecule is bonded to C_4 in the other molecule. The molecular formula of maltose is $C_{12}H_{22}O_{11}$.

Worked example

Sucrose is a disaccharide of glucose and fructose, whose structures are shown below. The condensation reaction involves the –OH group at C_1 of glucose. Deduce the structural formula of sucrose.

glucose

fructose

Solution

The monosaccharides are joined by a glycosidic link as follows:

Lactose is a disaccharide found in milk. Many people suffer from 'lactose intolerance', which is usually a genetic condition, characterized by an inability to digest lactose owing to a lack of the enzyme lactase. The condition is more prevalent in many Asian and South African cultures where dairy products are less traditionally part of the adult diet. By contrast, people with ancestry in Europe, the Middle East, and parts of East Africa, where mammals are often milked for food, typically maintain lactase production throughout life.

Polysaccharides are the polymers of sugars

Polysaccharides form by repetitions of the reaction shown above, leading to a long chain of monosaccharide units held together by glycosidic bonds. Due to their large size, polysaccharides are all insoluble molecules, and so make an ideal storage form of the energy-rich carbohydrates. Cellulose forms a rigid structure which provides support to plant cells.

The most common polysaccharides are:

• starch – carbohydrate store in plants;
• glycogen – carbohydrate store in animals;
• cellulose – structural material in plants.

These are all polymers of glucose, but differ from each other in the isomer of glucose used and in the amount of cross-linking in the chain. For example, starch consists mostly of a straight-chain polymer of α-glucose with 1–4 linkages.

Sugar is an important trade product from many countries. Sugar cane is the world's largest crop, and is exported largely from tropical and sub-tropical regions of Brazil, India, China, and Thailand. Sugar beet grows only in the temperate zones of North America and Europe, though countries in these regions are usually net importers of sugar. Both crops yield sugar in the form of sucrose.

You are not expected to learn the combinations of monosaccharides in different disaccharides, but will be given this information if it is needed in an examination question.

The production of ethanol as a biofuel usually involves the fermentation of carbohydrates from crops such as corn and sugar cane. This is at the heart of the **food versus fuel** debate on land and resource use.

Worked example

Glycogen is a branched polysaccharide which contains α-glucose molecules linked with both 1–4 and 1–6 glycosidic bonds. Use the structure of α-glucose in your IB data booklet to draw a section of the molecule showing both types of linkages.

Solution

Exercises

18 (a) State the empirical formula of all monosaccharides.
(b) State and explain the difference in solubility of monosaccharides and polysaccharides.

19 The disaccharide lactose is made from the monomers shown below.

β-galactose   α-glucose

Deduce the structural and molecular formula of lactose, and name the bond between the sugars.

B.5 Vitamins

Understandings:

- Vitamins are organic micronutrients which (mostly) cannot be synthesized by the body but must be obtained from suitable food sources.
- The solubility (in water or fat) of a vitamin can be predicted from its structure.
- Most vitamins are sensitive to heat.
- Vitamin deficiencies in the diet cause particular diseases and affect millions of people worldwide.

Applications and skills:

- Comparison of the structures of vitamins A, C, and D.
- Discussion of the causes and effects of vitamin deficiencies in different countries and suggestion of solutions.

Guidance

- *The structures of vitamins A, C, and D are provided in the IB data booklet section 35.*
- *Specific food sources of vitamins or names of deficiency diseases do not have to be learned.*

Given the complexity of metabolic processes, it is not surprising that organisms need an equally complex array of molecules to maintain health, and these are known as **nutrients**. In terms of the human diet, **micronutrients** are those needed in extremely small amounts, generally less than 0.005% of body mass, quantities so small that they are usually measured in mg or μg per day. These substances are needed to enable the body to produce enzymes, hormones, and other biomolecules. As tiny as the amounts are, however, the consequences of their absence are severe and are known as **deficiency diseases**. Micronutrients include the **vitamins** and many so-called **trace minerals** such as: Fe, Cu, Zn, I, Se, Mn, Mo, Cr, Co, and B.

Vitamins are organic micronutrients

Vitamins are organic compounds, needed in small amounts for normal growth and metabolism, which (with the exception of vitamin D) are not synthesized in the body. They are usually broken down by the reactions in which they are involved, so must be taken in from suitable food sources in the diet. They are often classified according to their relative solubility in water or in lipid.

Water-soluble vitamins

Vitamins that are water soluble have polar bonds and the ability to form hydrogen bonds with water. They are transported directly in the blood, and excesses are filtered out by the kidneys and excreted. Vitamins B and C are water soluble.

Vitamin C contains several functional groups (–OH and –C=C–) that are relatively easily oxidized. This is why the vitamin is easily destroyed by most methods of food processing and storage, and is therefore best obtained from *fresh* fruits and vegetables. In general, the water-soluble vitamins are the most sensitive to heat, but other vitamins also lose some activity after being heated.

Lipid-soluble vitamins

Vitamins that are lipid soluble are mostly non-polar molecules with long hydrocarbon chains or rings. They are slower to be absorbed and excesses tend to be stored in fat tissues where they can produce serious side-effects. Vitamins A, D, E, and K are fat soluble.

British people are sometimes known as 'limies' in America, because of the earlier practice of the British Navy to supplement the diet of sailors with limes to prevent scurvy.

The structures of some important vitamins are given in section 35 of the IB data booklet, so they do not have to be learned.

NATURE OF SCIENCE

The discovery of vitamins (*vital amines*) is an example of scientists seeking a cause for specific observations. In the 1700s, many sailors on long voyages suffered from a disease known as scurvy, with symptoms of bleeding gums, poor resistance to infection, and dark spots on the skin. Although the concept of a disease resulting from the *lack* of a dietary component was not understood, it was discovered that these symptoms could be prevented by providing a nutrient that is present in citrus fruits. The vital ingredient was later identified as vitamin C. Similarly, in 1905, it was noted that the disease beriberi could be prevented by eating an ingredient in unpolished rice, later identified as vitamin B.

These and similar correlations led to the **hypothesis of deficiency diseases** – the concept that a *lack* of something in the diet could cause disease. This was formulated in 1912 and now forms the basis of much healthcare practice.

Vitamin	Structure	Solubility and properties
A, retinol		• fat soluble • hydrocarbon chain and ring are non-polar and influence the solubility more than the one –OH group • involved in the visual cycle in the eye, and particularly important for vision in low light intensity
C, ascorbic acid		• water soluble • several –OH groups enable hydrogen bonds to form with water • acts as cofactor in some enzymic reactions, and important in tissue regeneration following injury and resistance to some diseases
D, calciferol		• fat soluble • predominantly a hydrocarbon molecule with four non-polar rings and only one –OH group • chemically similar to cholesterol • stimulates the uptake of calcium ions by cells and important in the health of bones and teeth

Vitamin deficiencies are a form of malnutrition

The absence of a regular, balanced supply of the diverse nutrients needed in the diet is known as **malnutrition**. This describes a broad spectrum of conditions, including vitamin deficiency diseases, which are always associated with compromised health. The main focus of malnutrition has traditionally been the large variety of nutrient-deficiency diseases, and in particular the incidence of these in under-developed countries. But increasingly the world is seeing a dramatic increase in diseases caused by high consumption of processed, energy-dense but micronutrient-poor foods.

The causes of malnutrition arising from vitamin deficiency are varied and widespread. They include:

• lack of distribution of global resources;
• depletion of nutrients in the soil and water;
• lack of education about, or understanding of, the importance of a balanced diet;

'Freedom from hunger and malnutrition is a basic human right and their alleviation is a fundamental prerequisite for human and national development.'

World Health Organization

- over-processing of food for transport and storage;
- the use of chemical treatments such as herbicides in food production.

Vitamin A is an antioxidant and is needed for healthy eyesight. It is related to carotene and found in orange and yellow fruit and vegetables. As it is fat soluble, it has been found that it can be effectively added to margarine in a process known as **vitamin fortification**. The potential of rice as a vehicle for vitamin A fortification is also being explored, given that rice is an important staple in many countries where the prevalence of vitamin A deficiency is high. Vitamin B is a term for a group of eight distinct water-soluble vitamins, which are most commonly found in unprocessed foods such as whole grains. Their deficiency causes a range of diseases including beriberi, forms of anaemia, and mental disorders. Cereals are commonly fortified with B vitamins. As vitamin B_{12} contains cobalt, which is available only from animal sources, vegetarians and vegans may be at particular risk of deficiency. Vitamin C deficiency is characterized by lower resistance to infection and can develop into scurvy. It is best prevented by a diet rich in fresh fruits and vegetables. Vitamin D is made by the action of sunlight on the skin and is important for healthy bones.

The World Health Organization has identified vitamin A as the most important vitamin deficiency in global health terms. It is estimated that more than half of all countries, especially in Africa and South-East Asia, have a significant incidence of vitamin A deficiency, which is the leading cause of preventable blindness in children and increases the risk of disease and death from severe infections.

Food label showing fortification of foods with vitamins.

TOK
To what extent is mass medication through the food we eat an infringement of personal freedom? Are there ways of striking a balance between the claim of the scientists or government that they know what is best for health, and the right of an individual to choose what to eat?

Child suffering from rickets. Rickets is a disease in growing children in which the bones do not harden and are malformed. It is due to a deficiency in vitamin D, which is necessary for the uptake of calcium.

Exposure to sunlight is an important source of vitamin D, but it is also the case that ultraviolet light has a damaging effect on the skin and can be the cause of skin cancers. Protection from this necessitates the use of sunscreens, and those with a protection factor of 8 or greater will block UV rays that produce vitamin D. This makes it even more important to include good sources of vitamin D in the diet when sun exposure is limited in this way. Mandatory vitamin D fortification is increasing, usually applied to milk and margarine, as the vitamin is fat soluble.

In summary, there exist many possible solutions to the varying challenges of malnutrition. These include:

- the fortification of different staple foods with micronutrients;
- the availability of vitamin supplements in many forms;
- the possible improvements to nutrient content of food through genetic modification;
- increased labelling of foods with content information;
- education regarding the nature of a balanced diet and promotion of the importance of personal responsibility in dietary choices.

NATURE OF SCIENCE

The manufacture and sale of vitamin supplements is a major industry in many countries. Debate is widespread on the extent to which a balanced diet can provide sufficient quantities of vitamins, or whether supplementation is necessary for optimum health. Part of the controversy is a result of claims made by Linus Pauling in 1970 that 'megadoses' of vitamin C could be effective in preventing the common cold, and possibly certain cancers and heart disease as well. As the only person ever to have won two unshared Nobel Prizes, Pauling was a scientist and humanitarian of significant authority, and so his claims led to a surge in the sales of vitamin C. This happened despite the fact that his megavitamin claims lacked the evidence needed for acceptance by the scientific community. The existence of conflicting information and advice, and the pressure of advertising, can make it difficult for individuals to make an informed choice. Scientists have a duty to share their findings with the public in ways that help people to understand the issues and make valid judgements.

Exercises

20 Make reference to section 35 in the IB data booklet.

   (a) Identify two functional groups common to all three vitamins shown.

   (b) Identify one vitamin that is water soluble and one vitamin that is fat soluble. Explain the differences in solubility in terms of their structures and intermolecular forces.

21 Suggest ways in which vitamin deficiency diseases can be alleviated.

B.6 | Biochemistry and the environment

Understandings:

- Xenobiotics refer to chemicals that are found in an organism but which are not normally present there.
- Biodegradable/compostable plastics can be consumed or broken down by bacteria or other living organisms.
- Host–guest chemistry involves the creation of synthetic host molecules that mimic some of the actions performed by enzymes in cells, by selectively binding to specific guest species, such as toxic materials in the environment.
- Enzymes have been developed to help in the breakdown of oil spills and other industrial wastes.
- Enzymes in biological detergents can improve energy efficiency by enabling effective cleaning at lower temperatures.
- Biomagnification is the increase in concentration of a substance in a food chain.
- Green Chemistry, also called sustainable chemistry, is an approach to chemical research and engineering that seeks to minimize the production and release to the environment of hazardous substances.

Applications and skills:

- Discussion of the increasing problem of xenobiotics such as antibiotics in sewage treatment plants.
- Description of the role of starch in biodegradable plastics.
- Application of host–guest chemistry to the removal of a specific pollutant in the environment.
- Description of an example of biomagnification, including the chemical source of the substance. Examples could include heavy metals or pesticides.
- Discussion of the challenges and criteria in assessing the 'greenness' of a substance used in biochemical research, including the atom economy.

   Guidance
   - *Specific names of 'green chemicals' such as solvents are not expected.*

   - *The emphasis in explanations of host–guest chemistry should be on non-covalent bonding within the supramolecule.*

Xenobiotics: strangers to life

Xenobiotics are chemical compounds that are found in a living organism, but which are foreign to that organism. The term is also used to describe chemicals found in higher-than-normal concentrations, or compounds that are not produced naturally but only by synthetic processes – in other words chemicals that are foreign to the biosphere.

Examples of xenobiotics are:

- drugs, including antibiotics such as penicillin;
- food additives;
- pollutants, such as PCBs and dioxins;
- insecticides, such as DDT;
- heavy metals, such as mercury and lead ions;
- hormones, such as estrogens;
- plastics, such as PVC.

Within an organism, xenobiotics can have a wide variety of effects. Non-polar molecules pass relatively easily across the hydrophobic cell membranes. They enter cells where they may be modified by enzymes and then detoxified. This is how many drugs are broken down in the body. In agriculture, pesticides may be metabolized by similar processes, sometimes leading to resistance to the effect of the chemical.

However, if the xenobiotic cannot be modified in the organism it may build up in the cells. The increasing concentration of the substance in an organism is known as **bioaccumulation**. For example, mercury compounds in the form of methylmercury, which is non-polar, cross into the brain, where they build up causing mercury poisoning. Similarly, lead, in the form of tetraethyl lead from petroleum, can accumulate in fat tissues.

An increasing area of concern is the existence of **pharmaceutically active compounds** such as antibiotics, painkillers, and chemotherapy drugs in the environment. These may be discharged from industries or hospitals, or passed through the human body and released unmodified or partially metabolized in urine. Sewage treatment plants may break the xenobiotic down through bacterial action, but too often this process is incomplete. As a result, the compounds are released into the effluent, where they can be taken up by fish living downstream.

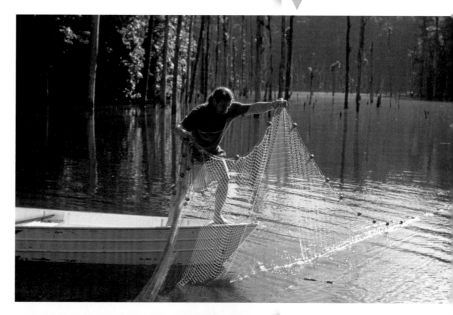

Scientist monitoring a water reservoir by sampling fish to analyse the mercury concentrations in their bodies. A nearby gold mine uses mercury to amalgamate the gold and this mercury is a xenobiotic, polluting the surrounding areas. Photographed in French Guiana.

Molecular model of a polychlorinated biphenyl (PCB) molecule. The carbon atoms in the phenyl rings are shown in blue, chlorine is shown in green, and hydrogen in white. PCBs are organic compounds that are highly stable, good insulators, and have low electrical conductivity. They were widely used in capacitors and transformers. The discovery in the 1960s that PCBs are toxic and carcinogenic and can act as **xenoestrogens** led to tight regulation of their use, but due to their stability they persist in the environment and in living tissue.

497

The waste water from sewage treatment may also contain sex hormones such as the female estrogens that have been released in human urine, particularly due to use of the synthetic contraceptive pill. There is some concern that male fish may absorb sufficient quantities of estrogens to be 'feminized', and unable to breed. Related concerns about disruptions to reproductive cycles arise from the widespread presence of so-called **xenoestrogens**, chemicals that imitate the effects of estrogen. Examples include polychlorinated biphenyls (PCBs) and bisphenol A.

 Bisphenol A is an organic compound widely used in making polymers such as the polycarbonate plastics that are used in reusable water bottles, food containers, and water pipes. Bisphenol A has become controversial because it may mimic hormones, especially estrogens, and so give rise to a range of health problems. Studies have shown that risk of the chemical leaching from the plastic is increased when it is heated, and so particular concern has been expressed about its use in babies' bottles that are routinely heated during sterilization. While debate continues about safe levels, many industries have withdrawn these products and several governments have legislation pending to limit their use.

Water bottle label showing that it does not contain bisphenol A, BPA. The chemical has been withdrawn from many applications due to concern over its xenoestrogenic properties.

Biomagnification

Although biological processes can produce many harmful substances, such as snake venom and irritants, natural toxins do not build up in the environment as they are broken down by enzymes. By contrast, some of the synthetic chemicals produced by humans are not broken down naturally as there are no enzymes to achieve this. Consequently, they build up in air, water, soil and living cells, and in some cases their concentration can increase in food webs to potentially harmful levels.

Biomagnification refers to the increase in concentration of a xenobiotic substance in a food web. It occurs when a xenobiotic cannot be metabolized, and so is taken up directly when one organism feeds on another, causing the greatest effect for animals that feed at the top of a food chain. A well-studied example of this is the insecticide DDT, dichlorodiphenyltrichloroethane.

DDT is a complex aromatic molecule, which was used to great effect starting during World War II to control the mosquitoes that are responsible for the spread of diseases such as malaria and typhus. The World Health Organization suggests that five million human lives were saved in the early years of its use. DDT is readily soluble in fat, and does not undergo metabolic breakdown. It therefore bioaccumulates in tissues and passes unchanged through food chains.

The bald eagle feeds high in the food chain and is therefore susceptible to the effects of biomagnification.

 Concerns over the environmental impact of DDT and other pesticides, particularly on bird life, were brought to the public attention through the publication of the book *Silent Spring* by American biologist Rachel Carson in 1962. This book is largely credited as launching the environmental movement that is now global in scope.

Figure 13.35 Data on DDT concentrations taken from an estuary in Long Island Sound, USA. Ospreys at the top of the chain have 10 million times the concentration of DDT present in the phytoplankton.

Figure 13.35 illustrates the biomagnification of DDT at each feeding level, known as a **trophic level**. As, for example, the small fish feed on a vast number of zooplankton, the concentrations of DDT are multiplied at each level. So the large fish and birds that feed high in the food chain accumulate elevated concentrations of DDT, as much as 10 million times the original concentration.

In the 1960s it was noticed that birds of prey, such as ospreys and peregrine falcons, suffered a serious decline in their numbers. The cause was traced to a thinning of their eggshells that made the eggs break under their parent's weight, and this was found to be due to the toxic effects of the high levels of DDT in their tissues. This and other negative environmental impacts eventually led to a ban on the use of indiscriminate spraying of DDT in many countries by the 1970s. Nonetheless, some continued use of DDT persists in vector control, particularly in countries where malaria is a serious health risk, and this remains controversial.

Other examples of bioaccumulation include organic molecules such as dioxins and PCBs, as well as heavy metals such as mercury and uranium. Data collected on these effects have been used to influence government policies and health advisories.

NATURE OF SCIENCE

It is the responsibility of scientists to consider the ways in which their research and findings impact the environment, and to find ways of amelioration. This involves risk assessment and long-term data collection. The issues presented raise ethical issues which cross national boundaries and demand international collaboration by scientists from different disciplines.

Amelioration: responses to xenobiotics

Clearly, the widespread existence of xenobiotics in organisms and in the environment is a major cause of concern for human health and for biodiversity. *Amelioration* refers to approaches that seek to lessen the problems and improve the outlook. We will consider some examples here.

Host–guest chemistry

We saw in section B.3 that enzymes and substrates form complexes as a result of molecular recognition and specific binding. The complexes are held together by forces

TOK Who should determine the balance between the individual's right to freedom from disease and society's right to freedom from environmental degradation?

Bioaccumulation refers to the build-up of a substance within an organism; biomagnification refers to the build-up of a substance in a food web.

The Stockholm Convention on Persistent Organic Pollutants (POPs) identified twelve chemicals, known as 'the dirty dozen', whose use should be banned. Although legislation to this effect now exists in many countries, many of the chemicals are stable and persist in the environment. There is concern that climate change causing melting of the polar ice is re-mobilizing some of these banned chemicals into the Arctic atmosphere.

other than covalent bonds which depend on the three-dimensional shape of the molecules. This and similar examples of molecular recognition in biological systems have inspired the development of so-called host–guest chemistry. This involves the synthesis of a **host** molecule which is able to bind non-covalently to a guest molecule, and form a **supermolecule**. In essence the host, the larger molecule, is analogous to the enzyme, and the guest to the substrate.

$$H + G \rightleftharpoons H–G$$
host guest host–guest complex

The forces within the supermolecule, like those in enzyme–substrate complexes, include ionic bonds, hydrogen bonds, van der Waals' forces, and hydrophobic interactions.

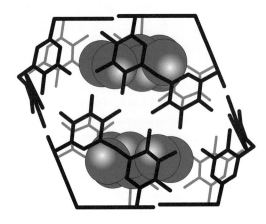

Figure 13.36 Host–guest complex showing two guest molecules (pyrene butyric acid) in blue trapped within the structure of the host molecule which is a six-chain nanocapsule held together by hydrogen bonds.

Host–guest chemistry can be applied to the removal of some xenobiotics in the environment. The xenobiotic is the guest, and its chemical features determine the synthesis of the host, which is designed to bind to it. Many host molecules have a cage-like or tube-like structure which traps the guest molecule. The technique has been used in the removal of radioactive ions such as cesium-137 from nuclear waste.

Figure 13.37 Host molecule (known as BOBCalix6) shown with a positively charged cesium ion held inside one of its cavities. This host molecule was specifically developed to bind to the cesium-137 ion, by application of the thermodynamics of ion binding.

Another example is the removal of aromatic amines, which are derived from the cosmetics industry and are known to be carcinogenic. Drugs and drug metabolites are also targets of research for suitable host molecules for their removal.

Biodegradable substances

Substances that cannot be broken down by natural processes, which mostly involve microbial action, are said to be **non-biodegradable**. Compounds in this category often contain carbon–halogen bonds or stable aromatic structures, which enzymes are not able to break. This is why many plastics, such as PVC and polystyrene, and compounds like DDT persist in the environment indefinitely.

The associations between the host and guest molecules in a supermolecule are all non-covalent.

On the other hand, a compound is **biodegradable** if it can undergo bacterial degradation into end products that are found in nature, and therefore are not harmful to the environment. Much research attention has been given to the development of biodegradable plastics, and two main types exist.

1 Plant-based hydro-biodegradable plastic

This plastic has a high starch content, and is often obtained from corn. Genetic modification of grasses may help to produce similar plastics. The breakdown is initiated by hydrolysis and produces carbon dioxide and water. Swelling of starch grains can help to break up the plastic. At high temperatures it decomposes relatively quickly, but when buried in a landfill it may take much longer to decompose and may produce methane.

Biodegradable food packaging. Apples sealed in a wrapper made from starch-based plastic. The starch used to make this packaging was sourced from a non-genetically modified crop, as seen in the 'Non GM' label.

2 Petroleum-based oxo-biodegradable plastic

This is derived from a by-product of the oil industry. Additives, often cobalt, are used to act as catalysts for the breakdown process, which can be programmed for different times depending on the use of the plastic. The plastic degrades into microfragments which are dispersed and eventually broken down by bacteria.

Plastics are sometimes described as **compostable**, which means they can be broken down in a compost pile, along with natural food products and garden waste.

Biodegradable substances are those that can be broken down in natural processes.

Waste plastic is a major international problem, and estimates suggest only 3% of plastic is recycled globally. Use of oxo-biodegradable plastics is becoming mandated in many rapidly developing countries in the Middle East and Africa to help mitigate the problems of plastic disposal. This puts pressure on other countries to use this plastic in their export goods. Some critics though express concerns over the use of artificial additives in these plastics.

Bioremediation – the use of enzymes

Although as a fossil fuel, crude oil is a natural product, it can be present in sufficient concentrations to be considered xenobiotic. This is the case, for example, when oil spills occur on land or at sea, depositing millions of litres into the adjacent environment. Organisms such as sea birds and marine mammals are then at risk from physical damage and from the toxic effects of the crude oil spill. Ways to ameliorate the impact of oil spills include the use of microorganisms which are able to break the oil down by using it as a food source and oxidize it in respiration. This is known as **bioremediation**.

As crude oil contains a large number of different compounds, many different chemical reactions are involved in its breakdown. Microorganisms have evolved different enzymes that are specific for the degradation of different hydrocarbons in the oil so breakdown of the oil takes the combined action of a community of bacteria and fungi. Most of these are found naturally in the environment.

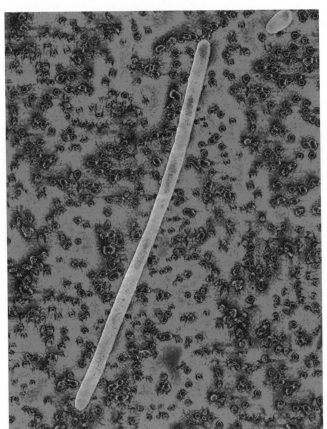

Coloured transmission electron micrograph (TEM) of an oil-degrading bacterium, shown in yellow, collected from a deep-sea oil plume in the Gulf of Mexico after the Deepwater Horizon oil spill in April 2010. This is a previously unknown species of bacteria that helped in the breakdown of oil from the spill around one kilometre below the ocean's surface.

Over time, microbes are a dependable means of breaking down oil in the environment, although some of the larger and more highly branched molecules seem resistant to breakdown by enzymes. Environmental conditions such as temperature, supply of nutrients, and availability of oxygen all influence the efficiency of the process, and in many cases the process may be too slow to prevent ecological damage. Research is ongoing to find ways to enhance the enzymic processes involved.

The use of enzymes in bioremediation also includes processes for the clean-up of industrial waste such as effluents from paper mills, textile industries, and the leather industry.

Green Chemistry

Concerns over health and environmental impact have put the chemical industry under a lot of pressure for greater accountability. New regulations and rising oil prices have contributed to the need for significant changes to be made. This has become formalized to some extent with the establishment of **Green Chemistry**, also known as **sustainable chemistry**, as a field in its own right. The term 'Green Chemistry' was first coined in 1991, and is now a recognizable and rapidly growing area of study.

In essence, Green Chemistry is chemistry for the environment. Twelve principles have been developed which cover such concepts as mimimizing production of waste, the use of safe solvents, the design of energy-efficient processes, and increasing the atom economy of processes. In other words, it seeks to reduce the footprint of chemical manufacturing processes while improving product and environmental safety. In the context of biochemical research, Green Chemistry has contributed to some innovative processes. A few examples are discussed below.

Food and drink

Carbon dioxide under pressure is known as supercritical carbon dioxide, and can penetrate into substances and act as a solvent. It is cheap and non-toxic. It is used in the extraction of caffeine in the preparation of decaffeinated coffee, replacing previously used toxic solvents. It is also used to remove fungicide contaminants from wine-bottle corks, and to pull pungent oil out of sesame seeds.

Bioplastics

Plastics derived from corn starch which has been converted into a resin by bacteria can replace traditional oil-based plastics. Genetically engineered plants such as tobacco may be able to harvest useable plastics.

Cosmetics

Production of esters for face creams has traditionally used sulfuric acid at high temperatures, but can be done using enzymes at room temperature.

Clothing industry

Enzymes can replace polluting detergents and improve energy efficiency by enabling effective cleaning at lower temperatures. Renewably sourced textile fibres such as bamboo and eucalyptus may replace synthetic materials from the petrochemical industry or fabrics such as cotton which rely on heavy use of fertilizers.

Many of the applications of Green Chemistry are still developing, and are the focus of active biochemical research. With better education, it is hoped that individuals will exert consumer choice in helping to promote some of these innovative practices. Green Chemistry provides an opportunity for the chemical industry to be both forward-looking and environmentally responsible.

Wool dyed with natural products. Green Chemistry seeks to limit the use of toxic dyes and solvents which are widely used in the textile industry.

Practice questions

1 The following table shows the melting point for a number of common fatty acids found in dietary fats and oils.

Name of acid	Formula	Structural formula	Melting point / °C
lauric	$C_{11}H_{23}COOH$	$CH_3(CH_2)_{10}COOH$	44
myristic	$C_{13}H_{27}COOH$	$CH_3(CH_2)_{12}COOH$	58
palmitic	$C_{15}H_{31}COOH$	$CH_3(CH_2)_{14}COOH$	63
stearic	$C_{17}H_{35}COOH$	$CH_3(CH_2)_{16}COOH$	70
oleic	$C_{17}H_{33}COOH$	$CH_3(CH_2)_7CH=CH(CH_2)_7COOH$	16
linoleic	$C_{17}H_{31}COOH$	$CH_3(CH_2)_4CH=CHCH_2CH=CH(CH_2)_7COOH$	−5

(a) Which of the fatty acids are solids at a room temperature of 25 °C?

(b) Describe and explain the trend in the melting points in the first four fatty acids listed.

(c) Describe and explain the pattern in the melting points of the last three acids mentioned.

2 The nature of the bonds between the monomers in proteins, carbohydrates, and lipids is as follows

	protein	*carbohydrate*	*lipid*
A	ester	amide	ether
B	amide	ether	ester
C	amide	ester	ether
D	ether	amide	ester

3 The secondary structure of a protein is determined by

A hydrophobic interactions between R groups

B hydrogen bonds between R groups of adjacent amino acids

C the sequence of amino acids in the polypeptide

D hydrogen bonds between peptide bonds

4 When the pH of the environment of a protein in changed significantly, it is said to be denatured. This is a result of

A breakage of the peptide bonds   B breakage of the disulfide links

C loss of the tertiary structure   D breakdown of the R groups

5 All of the following statements about enzymes are true **except**

A enzymes bind reversibly to their substrate   B enzymes are globular proteins

C enzymes are homogeneous catalysts   D enzymes increase the yield of product in a reaction

6 The structures of the amino acids cysteine and serine are shown in section 33 of the IB data booklet. They can react with each other to form a dipeptide.

(a) State the type of reaction occurring when amino acids react together and identify the other product of the reaction. (2)

(b) Draw the structures of the two possible dipeptides formed in the reaction between one molecule each of cysteine and serine. (2)

(c) Six tripeptides can be formed by reacting together one molecule of each of the amino acids arginine, histidine, and leucine. Predict the primary structures of these six tripeptides using the symbols shown in Section 33 of the IB data booklet to represent the amino acids. (3)

(d) When many amino acid molecules react together a protein is formed. These proteins have primary, secondary, and tertiary structures.

    (i) State the type of intermolecular force responsible for maintaining the secondary structure. (1)

    (ii) State **two** other ways in which the tertiary structure of the protein is maintained. (2)

(Total 10 marks)

7 (a) Maltose is a disaccharide of α-glucose.

    (i) Use information from section 34 of the IB data booklet to draw the structure of maltose. (3)

    (ii) Use molecular formulas to show the reaction for the breakdown of maltose into its monomers. (2)

    (iii) State the name of this type of metabolic process. (1)

(Total 6 marks)

8 The graph opposite shows the effect of temperature on the rate of a reaction catalysed by an enzyme in the human body.

(a) With reference to the structure and function of enzymes, explain the shape of the graph. (5)

(b) Describe how the graph might be different if it showed the effect of temperature on the rate of a reaction catalysed by an enzyme in a plant adapted to a very cold climate. (2)

(Total 7 marks)

9 (a) The structures of some fatty acids are given in section 34 of the IB data booklet.

    (i) Determine the iodine number of linoleic acid. (3)

    (ii) A different fatty acid known as X is isolated, and it is found to have a similar molecular mass to that of linoleic acid, but a lower iodine number. What can you conclude about its structure? (1)

    (iii) State and explain which fatty acid, linoleic acid or X, would have the higher melting point. (2)

(b) Rancidity in fats can occur as a result of two separate processes. Name these processes, and describe how they differ in the site of reactivity and the conditions that favour the reaction. (6)

(c) Compare and contrast the use of lipids and carbohydrates as a source of energy. (3)

(Total 15 marks)

10 (a) Outline the meaning of the term xenobiotic. (2)

(b) Describe the role of starch in biodegradable plastics. (2)

(c) Explain why a plastic such as PVC, poly(chloroethene), is non-biodegradable. (2)

(Total 6 marks)

11 Enzymes are proteins that can catalyse the reactions of some molecules in living matter.

The action of an enzyme is specific. Outline what is meant by the term specific and explain how an enzyme works. (You may use the symbols E for enzyme, S for substrate, and P for product) (4)

14

Option C: Energy

Essential ideas

C.1 Societies are completely dependent on energy resources. The quantity of energy is conserved in any conversion but the quality is degraded.

C.2 The energy of fossil fuels originates from solar energy that has been stored by chemical processes over time. These abundant resources are non-renewable but provide large amounts of energy due to the nature of chemical bonds in hydrocarbons.

C.3 The fusion of hydrogen nuclei in the Sun is the source of much of the energy needed for life on Earth. There are many technological challenges in replicating this process on Earth but it would offer a rich source of energy. Fission includes the splitting of a large unstable nucleus into smaller stable nuclei.

C.4 Visible light can be absorbed by molecules that have a conjugated structure with an extended system of alternating single and multiple bonds. Solar energy can be converted to chemical energy in photosynthesis.

C.5 Gases in the atmosphere that are produced by human activities are changing the climate as they are upsetting the balance between radiation entering and leaving the atmosphere.

An oil refinery. In the last 50 years oil has overtaken coal as the world's most important source of energy, however it is a limited resource, and eventually chemists will need to consider other sources of carbon.

We are completely dependent on our energy resources. Our ability to harness energy has allowed us to transform our world and give us control of what we do and when and where we do it. All this energy can be traced back to the formation of the Earth and the solar system. We are currently very dependent on the use of fossil fuels, which are a chemical store of solar energy from millions of years ago, and nuclear fuels, which are present in the earth. The energy of fossil fuels has its origins in the reorganization of electrons as they form new chemical bonds. The energy of nuclear fuels comes from mass changes in the centre of the atom as protons and neutrons adopt a more stable arrangement. Although the quantity of energy we have available to us will not change; the ability of this energy to do useful work does. Energy is constantly being degraded and so we will need to find and use alternative high-quality energy sources. The Sun again offers many options. Life itself is driven by the chemical changes of photosynthesis, which start with the electrons in a double being excited to higher energy levels. This reaction has always been the ultimate source of our food but can also be harnessed to provide biomass fuels. We can use the solar energy indirectly by capturing the kinetic energy of the winds or the potential energy of raindrops. Perhaps the most attractive, but challenging, option is to try and replicate the solar fusion reactions here on Earth, as this could meet all of our energy needs.

View from the International Space Station (ISS) of the city lights of north-western Europe. This image highlights our ability to change our planet by harnessing energy supplies. North is to the left of the photo – London is at the bottom left and Paris at the centre.

Whatever energy source we use in the future it will need to be more sustainable and environmentally friendly then those used in the last 300 years. The release of carbon atoms, which have been stored up naturally over millions of years, into the atmosphere as carbon dioxide in such a short time interval has had a significant effect on our climate. It is difficult to predict the future, but it is clear our use of energy will have to change.

C.1 Energy sources

Understandings:
- A useful energy source releases energy at a reasonable rate and produces minimal pollution.
- The quality of energy is degraded as heat is transferred to the surroundings. Energy and materials go from a concentrated into a dispersed form. The quantity of the energy available for doing work decreases.
- Renewable energy sources are naturally replenished. Non-renewable energy sources are finite.
- Energy density $= \dfrac{\text{energy released from fuel}}{\text{volume of fuel consumed}}$
- Specific energy $= \dfrac{\text{energy released from fuel}}{\text{mass of fuel consumed}}$
- The efficiency of an energy transfer $= \dfrac{\text{useful output energy}}{\text{total input energy}} \times 100\%$

Applications and skills:
- Discussion of the use of different sources of renewable and non-renewable energy.
- Determination of the energy density and specific energy of a fuel from the enthalpies of combustion, densities, and the molar mass of fuel.
- Discussion of how the choice of fuel is influenced by its energy density or specific energy.
- Determination of the efficiency of an energy transfer process from appropriate data.
- Discussion of the advantages and disadvantages of the different energy sources in C.2 through to C.5.

People use a great range of energy sources. Some of these, such as wood fire burning, are ancient technologies while others, such as nuclear power and solar cells, are very recent. Most of our energy derives from the Sun, which drives the climate and photosynthesis. Humans can harness this energy directly using photovoltaic cells or indirectly by burning fossil fuels.

Oil is the fossil fuel that currently provides the world's economy with the most energy but this will change as our finite resources run out. Fossil fuels are **non-renewable** energy sources – they are used at a rate faster than they can be replaced. Another non-renewable energy source is uranium, which gives up energy as its nuclei splits to form smaller more stable nuclei.

In this section we are going to review some basic energy concepts and consider a variety of the most important energy technologies.

A useful energy source releases energy at a reasonable rate and produces minimal pollution

Energy is defined as the ability to do work. Very little can happen without it – if we apply a force over a distance we do work – and to do this we need energy. Although our energy sources are being run down, this is not happening to the *quantity* of energy in the universe. The **conservation of energy** tells us that energy cannot be created or destroyed. It can only be converted from one form into another. The problem is that the *quality* of our energy is being degraded – if we lose energy to the environment it is no longer available to do useful work.

A room where everything is at the same temperature has low-quality energy, as there is no way that we can make the energy more spread out than it already is. Placing a piece of burning wood into the room, however, introduces some high-quality energy; the heat produced during the exothermic combustion reaction can be used to power an engine which can do useful work. During this process some of the energy will become spread out in the room where it can no longer be useful, so the quality of the energy has decreased.

Sources of energy are either hot bodies like the Sun, or objects that store high-quality potential energy, like the water in a reservoir or the chemical energy of a fossil fuel.

An energy source needs to be cheap, plentiful, and readily accessible and provide high-quality energy at a suitable rate – not too fast or too slow. It should do this in a way that has minimal effect on the environment. Rain water, for example, is generally a poor energy source; although it possesses gravitational potential energy it releases this energy at too slow a rate for it to be useful. The construction of a dam, however, allows this energy to be released at a more useful rate. A nuclear bomb, unlike a nuclear reactor, releases energy at too fast a rate for it to be used safely. Current high-quality energy sources which meet these criteria include fossil fuels, nuclear fission, electrochemical cells, solar energy, biomass, and alternative sources such as wind, waves, tidal, and hydroelectric.

The conservation of energy states that energy cannot be created or destroyed. It can only be converted from one form into another.

In any cyclical process designed to convert heat to work, some energy is always degraded. Degraded energy is energy that is no longer available for the performance of useful work.

Water droplets on a window pane. The water droplets are a source of energy but they deliver the energy at too slow a rate to be useful.

Water can give up its potential energy at a useful rate if it is stored up to be released later. This is a view of the Shasta dam, a hydroelectric power station located at Redding, California.

A **fuel** is a substance that can release energy by changing its chemical or nuclear structure. Fossil fuels release energy during a chemical reaction whereas uranium releases its energy during a fission reaction.

A fuel is a substance that can release energy by changing its chemical or nuclear structure.

509

Renewable energy sources are naturally replenished

Water will give up its energy when it is released from the dam to drive the turbines to generate hydroelectricity, but this source can be replenished by natural rainfall. It is a **renewable** source. A renewable source is one that is replenished at a rate faster than it is used. Wood for example is a renewable resource as trees can be grown to replace those chopped down to provide wood as fuel, but coal is non-renewable as it takes millions of years for fossil fuels to form.

The energy density of a fuel is the energy produced per unit volume and the specific energy is the energy produced per unit mass

In Chapter 5 we discussed the enthalpy change of combustion. This is the enthalpy change that occurs when one mole of the substance is burnt completely in an excess of oxygen under standard conditions. This is a natural choice when comparing the energy changes of different reactions but is not necessarily the most relevant when factors such as storage and transport of a fuel need to be considered.

$$\text{Energy density} = \frac{\text{energy released from fuel}}{\text{volume of fuel consumed}}$$

$$\text{Specific energy} = \frac{\text{energy released from fuel}}{\text{mass of fuel consumed}}$$

The **energy density** of a fuel is the energy produced per unit volume whereas the **specific energy** of a fuel is the energy produced per unit mass.

The two terms are related via the density of the fuel, as the following Worked example illustrates.

Worked example

The enthalpies of combustion of a range of organic compounds are given in section 13 of the IB data booklet. Calculate the specific energy and energy density of hexane from its density, which is 0.6548 g cm^{-3} under standard conditions.

Solution

Formula = C_6H_{14}

$M / \text{g mol}^{-1} = (6 \times 12.01) + (14 \times 1.01) = 86.2$

$\Delta H_c / \text{kJ mol}^{-1} = -4163$

Specific energy $/ \text{kJ g}^{-1} = \dfrac{-4163}{86.2} = 48.3$

Energy density $/ \text{kJ cm}^{-3} = 48.3 \times 0.6548 = 31.6$

The specific energies of some fuels are tabulated below.

Fuel	Specific energy / MJ kg⁻¹
fusion fuel	3×10^9
^{238}U	9×10^8
gasoline (petrol)	45.8
natural gas	55.5
coal	33.0
wood	17.0
hydrogen(g)	142

The specific energy of a fuel is the energy produced per unit mass.

Nuclear fuels have a higher energy density and specific energy than fossil fuels.

We can see that nuclear fuels have the highest specific energies and fossil fuels have higher specific energies than the related renewable sources.

The International Energy Agency is an autonomous organization which works to ensure reliable, affordable, and clean energy for its 28 member countries and beyond. The International Renewable Energy Agency (IRENA) was founded in 2009 to promote increased adoption and sustainable use of renewable energy sources (bioenergy, geothermal energy, hydropower, ocean, solar, and wind energy.

Energy conversions are never 100% efficient

A **primary source** of energy is often not used directly but converted to a **secondary source** such as electricity and some energy is inevitably lost during the conversion.

The **efficiency** of an energy transfer is defined as:

$$\text{efficiency} = \frac{\text{useful output energy}}{\text{total input energy}} \times 100$$

$$\text{efficiency} = \frac{\text{useful output energy}}{\text{total input energy}} \times 100$$

No matter how well a power plant is designed it can never convert energy from one form into another with 100% efficiency. Energy is always dissipated during energy transformations. This is a consequence of the **second law of thermodynamics**. The efficiency of different power stations depends on the design but typical values for fossil fuel power stations are tabulated below.

Fossil fuel	Typical efficiency values
gas	40–50%
oil	35–45%
coal	35–40%

The efficiency is generally less than 50% as the random motion of the heated gas particles needs to be converted into the coordinated motion of the particles in the solid turbine and some energy is inevitably lost in the process. It has been estimated that the complete conversion of 10 J of heat energy into 10 J work has about the same likelihood as a group of monkeys typing Shakespeare's complete works.

The maximum efficiency with which heat can be converted to work depends on the temperature of the heat source and the surroundings to which the heat is dissipated. A jet engine is more efficient than a car engine because it runs at a higher temperature. If an engine was operating in an environment at 0 K then all the random motion of the gases would be lost and the process would be 100% efficient, but it is impossible to achieve absolute zero.

Worked example

A coal-burning power station generates electrical power at a rate of 550×10^6 J s^{-1}. The power station has an overall efficiency of 36% for the conversion of heat into electricity.

(a) Calculate the total quantity of electrical energy generated in one year of operation.

(b) Calculate the total quantity of heat energy used in the generation of this amount of electricity.

(c) Calculate the mass of coal that will be burned in one year of operation, assuming that coal has the enthalpy of combustion of graphite.

Solution

(a) Total electrical energy in one year = $550 \times 10^6 \times 60 \times 60 \times 24 \times 365$

$$= 1.73 \times 10^{16} \text{ J}$$

(b) $\dfrac{\text{useful output energy}}{\text{total input energy}} = \dfrac{\text{useful electrical energy}}{\text{total input heat energy}} = 0.36$

$$\text{heat energy in} = \frac{\text{electrical energy generated}}{0.36}$$
$$= 4.82 \times 10^{16}\,\text{J}$$

(c) $\text{heat energy} = 4.82 \times 10^{16}\,\text{J}$
$$= 4.82 \times 10^{13}\,\text{kJ}$$

$$\text{moles of coal (or graphite)} = \frac{4.82 \times 10^{13}}{394}$$
$$= 1.22 \times 10^{11}\,\text{mol}$$

$$\text{mass} = 1.22 \times 10^{11}\,\text{mol} \times 12.01\,\text{g mol}^{-1}$$
$$= 1.47 \times 10^{12}\,\text{g}$$
$$= 1.47 \times 10^{9}\,\text{kg}$$

Cooling towers of the Ferrybridge coal-fired power station in England. A lot of low-quality energy is released into the environment in the hot steam.

CHALLENGE YOURSELF

1 1000 kJ of electrical energy are supplied every hour to a television set. 300 kJ are given out as light and 20 kJ are given out as sound. Identify an additional energy transfer process that occurs during the working of a television and calculate the energy efficiency of the television.

NATURE OF SCIENCE

Albert Szent-Györgyi said 'Discovery consists of seeing what everybody has seen and thinking what nobody has thought.' The scientific ideas behind the concepts of energy, both its quantity and its quality, arose from simple observations of the world around us. Everyone is familiar with the fact that heat is observed to go from hot to cold objects, but only a few scientists understood the significance of this. The theories relating heat and work are very broad in their application. They were originally developed in the 19th century to increase the efficiency of the steam engine – an issue of crucial economic importance at the time, as a country's power was intimately linked with its use of steam power. They can now be applied to explain many aspects of the physical world. The broad application of the theories is linked to the precise mathematical language in which they are expressed. We are able to assign numbers to the quantity and quality of energy.

TOK

The theoretical advances in understanding the relationship between heat and movement were often stimulated by political and economic considerations. Sadi Carnot's *Reflections on the Motive Power of Fire*, which was one of the most important pieces of writing on the efficiency of steam engines, was written while he was a semi-retired military officer after Napoleon's final defeat in 1815.

In what ways might social, political, cultural, and religious factors affect the types of research that are financed and undertaken, or rejected?

Exercises

1 Consider the following energy sources:

- biomass
- fossil fuels
- geothermal
- hydroelectricity
- nuclear fission
- nuclear fusion
- solar electricity
- solar heating
- tidal
- wind power

(a) Identify the sources which are derived from recent solar radiation.
(b) Identify the sources which are derived from ancient solar radiation.
(c) Identify the sources which are derived from the formation of Earth.
(d) Identify the sources which are renewable and explain your answer with reference to your answers to parts (a)–(c).

2 4.00×10^7 kJ are required to heat a home in a typical winter month.

(a) The house can be heated directly with a gas boiler burning methane gas (efficiency 85%). Calculate the mass of methane required in one month using this method of heating.
(b) The home can also be heated using electricity from a natural gas-burning power plant (efficiency 50%). Determine the mass of methane needed to generate the electricity needed to heat the house.

3 The enthalpies of combustion of methane and hydrogen are given in section 13 of the IB data booklet.

    (a) Calculate the specific energies of CH_4 and H_2.

    (b) Use the ideal gas equation to calculate the density of the two gases at s.t.p. and hence calculate the energy density of the two gases.

    (c) Identify the best fuel based on this information and discuss the practical difficulties involved in its widespread use.

C.2 Fossil fuels

Understandings:

- Fossil fuels were formed by the reduction of biological compounds that contain carbon, hydrogen, nitrogen, sulfur, and oxygen.
- Petroleum is a complex mixture of hydrocarbons that can be split by a physical process into different component parts, called fractions, by fractional distillation.
- The tendency of a fuel to auto-ignite, which leads to 'knocking' in a car engine, is related to molecular structure and measured by the octane number.
- The performance of hydrocarbons as fuels is improved by the cracking and catalytic reforming reactions.
- Coal gasification and liquefaction are chemical processes that convert coal to gaseous and liquid hydrocarbons.
- A carbon footprint is the total amount of greenhouse gases produced during human activities. It is generally expressed in equivalent tons of carbon dioxide.

Applications and skills:

- Discussion of the effect of chain length and chain branching on the octane number
- Discussion of the reforming and cracking reactions of hydrocarbons; and explanation of how these processes improve the octane number.
- Deduction of equations for cracking and reforming reactions, coal gasification, and liquefaction.
- Discussion of the advantages and disadvantages of the different fossil fuels.

Guidance
The cost of production and availability (reserves) of the fossil fuels and impact on the environment should be considered.

- Identification of the various fractions of petroleum, their relative volatility, and their uses.
- Calculations of the carbon dioxide added to the atmosphere when different fuels burn and determination of carbon footprints for different activities.

Fossil fuels were formed by the reduction of biological compounds

The fossil fuels have been described as 'sunshine in the solid, liquid, and gaseous form', as their energy comes from sunlight which was trapped by green plants millions of years ago. Fossil fuels are produced by the slow and partial decomposition of plant and animal matter that is trapped in the absence of air. Oxygen is lost from the biological molecules containing carbon, hydrogen, nitrogen, sulfur, and oxygen at a faster rate than other elements, which results in reduced biological compounds which are often hydrocarbons.

Coal is the most abundant fossil fuel

Coal is a combustible sedimentary rock formed from the remains of plant life which have been subject to geological heat and pressure. Most coal was formed during the carboniferous period (286–360 millions of years ago). The action of pressure and heat changed plant material in stages from peat to lignite to bituminous soft coal and finally to anthracite. At each stage the percentage of carbon increases. Anthracite is formed under conditions of very high heat and pressure and is almost pure carbon, but coal generally contains between 80% and 90% carbon by mass. Coal occurs in many areas, though the majority of the world's supplies are in the northern hemisphere. It is by far the most plentiful of the Earth's fossil fuels.

CHALLENGE YOURSELF

2 Suggest a source of the sulfur in coal and crude oil and explain why this is a problem.

Worked example

A number of carbon fuels are used domestically to provide heating during the winter months.

	Percentage composition				Specific energy / kJ g^{-1}
	C	H	O	N	
wood	50	6	43	1	10–13
peat	59	6	33	2	13
bituminous coal	88	5	5–15	1	30
anthracite	95	2–3	2–3	trace	31

(a) Describe the relationship between the oxygen content of a fuel and its specific energy.

(b) Describe how the composition of the fuels changes as they are exposed to high pressure.

(c) State two advantages of coal use over wood.

(d) State one advantage of the use of wood.

(e) Discuss some of the disadvantages of the use of coal.

Solution

(a) The less oxygen a compound contains the greater its specific energy.

(b) Oxygen (and water vapour) are lost.

(c) Coal is the most abundant fossil fuel and has high specific energy and energy density.

(d) It is a renewable.

(e) Difficult and expensive to mine and transport; produces sulfur oxides, which lead to acid deposition, particulates (soot), which lead to global dimming, and carbon dioxide, a greenhouse gas which leads to global warming; mining has an environmental impact.

NATURE OF SCIENCE

Coal fuelled much of the Industrial Revolution, which led to important advances in both science and technology. The development of stream power was crucial to a country's economy, but to understand the link between heat and work scientists had to unravel the nature of energy – its quality and its quantity and the underlying molecular basis for the laws governing the transfer of heat into work. Whatever the field, whether it is pure science engineering technology, there is boundless scope for creative and imaginative thinking.

Exercises

4 An analytical chemist determines the percentage composition by mass of a sample of coal.

C	H	O	N	S
84.96	5.08	7.55	0.73	1.68

(a) Determine the empirical formula of the coal.

(b) Explain how the combustion of the coal could produce acid rain. Give equations to illustrate how the elements in the coal can produce acidic gases.

5 The coal burned in a 500 MW (500×10^3 kJ s^{-1}) power station has a specific energy of 33.0 kJ g^{-1}.

(a) Determine the mass of the coal burned each second when the power station is operating at full capacity, assuming an efficiency of 38%.

(b) The empirical formula of the coal can be approximated as CH. Calculate the mass of carbon dioxide produced each second.

Crude oil is a valuable fuel and chemical feedstock

Crude oil is one of the most important raw materials in the world today. It is a complex mixture of straight-chain and branched-chain saturated alkanes, cycloalkanes, and aromatic compounds, and, in smaller quantities, compounds of nitrogen, oxygen, and sulfur which supplies us with the fuel we need for transport and electricity generation. It is also an important chemical feedstock for the production of important organic compounds such as polymers, pharmaceuticals, dyes, and solvents.

Crude oil was formed over millions of years from the remains of marine animals and plants, which were trapped under layers of rock. Under these conditions of high temperature and high pressure, organic matter decays in the presence of bacteria and the absence of oxygen. Crude oil is a limited resource and eventually reservoirs will be so depleted that chemists will need to consider other sources of carbon, both as a fuel and as a chemical feedstock.

In the last 50 years oil has overtaken coal as the world's most important source of energy. Oil and gas are easier to extract than coal since they are fluids and can be pumped up from underground reserves. It is now possible to extract oil from beneath the sea. There are risks and benefits in using oil as a source of energy or as a source of carbon to make new products.

The words used to describe the different liquid fuels can cause confusion. Petroleum is a broad category that includes both crude oil and petroleum products. The terms 'oil' and 'petroleum' are sometimes used interchangeably. In this text we have used crude oil. The liquid fuel used in cars is either called gasoline or petrol. We have used the word gasoline.

A gasoline pump supplies energy to a car at a rate of about 34 MW (34 MJ s^{-1}).

Petrochemical plants take crude oil, separate it into fractions, and process it to make useful organic compounds.

Petrol or gasoline is a highly concentrated and convenient energy source for use in transport. It could be argued, however, that burning hydrocarbons, with their resulting environmental side-effects such as smog and global warming, is a misuse of this valuable resource. When the great Russian chemist Dmitri Mendeleyev (Chapter 3, page 89) visited the oilfields of Azerbaijan at the end of the 19th century, he is said to have likened the burning of oil as a fuel to 'firing up a kitchen stove with banknotes'.

We still use about 90% of the refined product as a fuel. However, as supplies decrease, this proportion may fall. Crude oil will last longer if we conserve energy and recycle materials, such as plastics. Burning fuels derived from crude oil is the most convenient and economical option at the moment, but alternative energy sources and feedstocks may be developed.

Polymers, for example, could also be made from coal, of which there are still large reserves, and from renewable biological materials such as wood, starch, or cotton.

Crude oil needs to be refined before it is used as a fuel

Crude oil is of no use before it is **refined**. Sulfur impurities, mainly in the form of hydrogen sulfide, must first be removed as they would block the active sites of the catalysts used in later chemical processing. The acidic hydrogen sulfide is removed by dissolving it in basic potassium carbonate solution:

$$H_2S(g) + CO_3^{2-}(aq) \rightleftharpoons HS^-(aq) + HCO_3^-(aq)$$

The hydrogen sulfide can be recovered from solution by later reversing the reaction. It is burned in air to form sulfur dioxide:

$$2H_2S(g) + 3O_2(g) \rightarrow 2SO_2(g) + H_2O(l)$$

The sulfur dioxide produced can then react with more hydrogen sulfide to produce elemental sulfur:

$$2H_2S(g) + SO_2(g) \rightarrow 3S(s) + 2H_2O(l)$$

This desulfurization step also reduces acid rain pollution which would otherwise result if the sulfur was burned with the oil.

The crude oil is then separated into different **fractions** on the basis of their boiling points (Figure 14.1). In this **fractional distillation** process the crude oil is heated to a temperature of about 400 °C.

At this temperature all the different components of the mixture are vaporized and allowed to pass up a **distillation column**. The level at which the molecules condense depends on their size. The smaller molecules containing between one and four carbon atoms collect at the top as the **refinery gas** fraction. Molecules of successively larger molecular mass condense at lower levels corresponding to their higher boiling points. The different fractions and their uses are tabulated below.

Fraction	Number of carbon atoms	Use
refinery gas	1–4	fuel and as a feedstock for petrochemicals
gasoline/ naphtha	5–10	gasoline (petrol): fuel for cars naphtha: chemical feedstock
kerosene	10–16	fuel for jets, paraffin for heating
gas oil	13–25	fuel for diesel engines, power plants, and heating
residue	>25	oil-fired power stations, polishing waxes, lubricating oils, bitumen used to surface roads

The residue from a fractionating column consists of hydrocarbons with high boiling points under normal atmospheric conditions. **Vacuum distillation** can be used to vaporize these compounds and separate them at relatively low temperatures. Higher temperatures would lead to the molecules breaking up before separation takes place. The fraction with between 5 and 10 carbon atoms is the most in demand as it is used in cars. As a liquid it is convenient to handle and deliver and has a relatively low boiling point so it easy to vaporize, which assists combustion.

Figure 14.1 The fractional distillation of crude oil.

Cracking breaks down large alkanes to smaller alkanes and alkenes

Fractional distillation is a physical process and although some of the compounds distilled can be used directly, further treatment is generally needed. The demand for the different fractions does not necessarily match the amounts present in the crude oil supplied and so the hydrocarbon molecules from the crude oil need to be chemically changed. Hydrocarbons with up to 12 carbon atoms are in the most demand as they are more easily vaporized and therefore make the best fuels. The supply of these molecules can be increased by breaking down or **cracking** larger molecules. For example the cracking of heptane:

The cracking of a long hydrocarbon

$$C_7H_{16} \rightarrow \underset{\text{alkene}}{C_2H_4} + \underset{\text{alkane}}{C_5H_{12}}$$

Other examples:

$$C_{16}H_{34} \rightarrow \underset{\text{alkane}}{C_8H_{18}} + \underset{\text{alkene}}{C_8H_{16}}$$

$$C_{10}H_{22} \rightarrow \underset{\text{alkane}}{C_8H_{18}} + \underset{\text{alkene}}{C_2H_4}$$

As we can see, the reaction also produces useful alkenes (e.g. C_8H_{16} and C_2H_4), which can be used to make addition polymers and other important products.

When the process is achieved by heating the starting materials it is called **thermal cracking**. In **catalytic cracking** the use of a catalyst allows the reaction to occur at a lower temperature of 500 °C and helps to give the required product by controlling the mechanism. The reactions that occur are complicated but generally involve the formation of **carbocations** (an ion with a positively charged carbon atom), which are produced and then rearranged on the catalyst surface. Large and intermediate-sized alkanes are passed over an alumina (Al_2O_3) and silica (SiO_2) catalyst, which is in powdered form to increase its surface area. The lower temperature requires less energy and so reduces the cost of the process. Zeolites, which are naturally occurring minerals

Molecular graphics representation of the structure of the synthetic zeolite catalyst ZSM-5, showing its microchannel architecture. Zeolite minerals containing a silica-alumina crystalline structure are used as catalysts in the cracking process by which crude oil is refined.

of aluminium, silicon, and oxygen, are also good catalysts for this process as their crystal structures contain an extensive network which offers the hydrocarbons a large surface area for reaction. Some carbon is, however, formed during the process and this can coat the catalyst and stop it working. The catalyst is cleaned or regenerated by separating it from the reaction mixture using steam jets. The carbon coat is then removed by heating. The heat produced from the combustion of this carbon can be used to sustain the cracking reaction.

Catalytic cracking tends to produce branched-chain alkanes and compounds which contain the benzene ring (aromatics) – which burn more evenly in a car engine than their straight-chain isomers and are used in high-quality gasoline. This is discussed in more detail later in the chapter.

Hydrocracking can also produce compounds which can be used in high-quality gasoline. In this process a heavy hydrocarbon fraction is mixed with hydrogen at a pressure of about 80 atm ($80 \times 1.0 \times 10^5$ Pa) and cracked over palladium on a zeolite surface. A high yield of branched-chain alkanes and cycloalkanes and some aromatic compounds is produced.

Catalytic cracking uses high temperature and a catalyst to break down (crack) heavy oil fractions into lighter, more useful oils. The oil is heated to 500 °C and passed over a catalyst such as zeolite crystals. The vessel where the cracking takes places is the barrel-shaped grey one on the right.

The tendency of a fuel to auto-ignite is measured by the octane number

The four strokes of a typical gasoline engine are:

Piston position	Action
moves to increase volume of chamber	air and fuel intake
moves to decrease volume of chamber	compression stroke and spark ignition near end of compression.
moves to increase volume of chamber	expansion of gases caused by production of gases and increase temperature
moves to decrease volume of chamber	exhaust gases expelled

In the compression stroke of an internal combustion engine, a cylinder-full of fuel and air is squashed into a smaller volume and ignited with a spark plug. Some fuels auto-ignite without the need of a spark plug as the fuel–air mixture is compressed by the piston. This premature ignition is known as '**knocking**' as it gives rise to a knocking sound in the engine. Knocking reduces the efficiency of the engine as the energy of the exploding and expanding gas is not applied fully to the piston at the optimum time and can damage an engine. Straight-chain molecules have a greater tendency to knock. The branched-chain isomer of octane, 2,2,4-trimethylpentane (isooctane) does not suffer from premature ignition and is considered to be the standard by which other fuels are judged. Hence the performance of a fuel is given by its **octane number**, which is based on a scale on which the 2,2,4-trimethylpentane has a value of 100 and the straight-chain molecule heptane, which auto-ignites relatively easily, has an octane number of 0. A fuel with an octane rating of 96 burns as efficiently as a mixture of 96% 2,2,4-trimethylpentane and 4% heptane. Fuels with high octane numbers can be more highly compressed, which results in more power per piston stroke.

The octane numbers of some straight-chain alkanes are tabulated below. Note the octane number decreases with an increase in chain length.

	RON	MON	Average octane number
butane	94	89.6	92
pentane	62	62.6	62
hexane	24.8	26	25
heptane	0	0	0

The octane number of some isomers of hexane and other molecules with six carbon atoms are given in this table.

Compound	Average octane number
hexane	25
(*trans*) hex-2-ene	93
cyclohexane	83
benzene	106

From these results we can from see the following patterns:

• cyclic compounds have higher octane numbers than linear structures;
• alkenes have a higher octane number than the isomeric cycloalkane;
• aromatic compounds with the benzene ring have even higher octane numbers.

The octane number indicates the resistance of a motor fuel to knock. Octane numbers are based on a scale on which 2,2,4-trimethylpentane (isooctane) is 100 (minimal knock) and heptane is 0 (maximum knock).

The octane number of a fuel can be measured by special test engines working at different speeds (rpm = revolutions per minute).

MON: **M**otor **O**ctane **N**umber indicates the octane number measured at 900 rpm.

RON: **R**esearch **O**ctane **N**umber indicates the octane number measured at 600 rpm.

Sometimes the average of these values is reported.

Different fuel rating systems (e.g. RON, MON, or Pump Octane Number, PON) are used in different countries.

CHALLENGE YOURSELF

3 **(a)** Suggest a value for the octane number of octane.
(b) Since the octane number was developed, a number of compounds have been found with an octane number greater than 100. Predict which straight-chain alkanes have an octane number of above 100.

CHALLENGE YOURSELF

4 Use the data in the table to investigate the relationship between octane number and bond enthalpies.

Compound	Average octane number
octane	–19
2,4-dimethylhexane	65
2,2,4-trimethylpentane	100

In 1922 Thomas Midgley found that the octane number of a fuel could be increased with the addition of tetraethyl lead ($Pb(C_2H_5)_4$) and this led to the widespread use of leaded gasoline. Its use has, however, now been phased out in most countries as it both inhibits the action of catalytic convertors and is a source of lead air pollution. Lead is a heavy metal poison with cumulative neurological effects that are particularly damaging to young children. Methanol (octane number 107) and ethanol (octane number 108) are now, for example, both added to gasoline instead of tetraethyl lead.

Catalytic reforming increases the octane number of a fuel

In **catalytic reforming** the atoms in a molecule can rearrange to form a more branched chain or a cyclic or aromatic compound. The process is often referred to as plat forming if Pt is used as the catalyst, but other rare and expensive metals such as Pd, Ir, or Rh, can also be used.

Hexane, for example, can be converted to benzene and hydrogen in a **dehydrogenation** reaction:

$$C_6H_{14} \rightarrow C_6H_6 + 4H_2$$

and heptane is converted into methylbenzene and hydrogen:

$$C_7H_{16} \rightarrow C_6H_5CH_3 + 4H_2$$

The branching in a molecule can also be increased in a process called **isomerization** by heating the molecules in the presence of a catalyst such as $AlCl_3$.

Octane, for example, can be converted into 2,2,4-trimethylpentane:

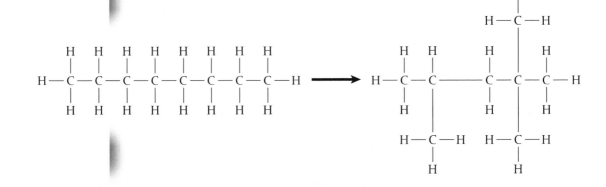

Alkylation involves the octane number by reacting lower mass alkenes with alkanes to form higher mass alkanes

The alkenes produced in the cracking process can further increase the quality of the crude oil by **alkylation**. This can be thought of as a little like the reverse of a cracking reaction in that an alkene and alkane with a short carbon chains combine together to form a high mass alkane with a branched chain. The alkane is effectively adding across the double bond in the alkene – with a hydrogen atom bonding to one of the carbons in the double bond (shown in red) and the rest of the molecule (R shown in blue) adding to the other carbon of the double bond.

The hydrogen atom (in red) bonds to the carbon atom in the double bond which has the least number of hydrogens. So 2,2,4-trimethylpentane can be produced from the reaction between methylpropane and methylpropene with an acidic catalyst.

Supplies of liquid fuels can be increased by coal liquefaction

Liquid hydrocarbon fuels can also be produced by reacting coal with hydrogen under high pressure in the presence of a catalyst. The resulting mixture of hydrocarbons can then be separated by fractional distillation. As the cost of crude oil increases as a resource this will be an increasingly economic option.

The direct conversion of coal to liquids by a hydrogenation process can be summarized by:

$$n\text{C} + (n + 1)\text{H}_2 \rightarrow \text{C}_n\text{H}_{2n + 2}$$

where $n > 4$.

The **Fischer–Tropsch** process involves using a mixture of carbon monoxide and hydrogen as feedstock and produces a variety of alkanes along with water:

$$(2n+1)\text{H}_2 + n\text{CO} \rightarrow \text{C}_n\text{H}_{(2n+2)} + n\text{H}_2\text{O}$$

The growing demand for crude oil, accompanied by the declining crude oil reserves and the concerns over energy security, has intensified the interest in direct coal liquefaction. This occurs particularly in countries which are rich in coal resources, but short of crude oil.

Exercises

6 Draw the molecular structure of 2,2,4-trimethylpentane (isooctane).

7 **(a)** Deduce an equation for the cracking of $C_{11}H_{24}$ in which an alkene and an alkane are formed in the ratio 3:1.

(b) Explain why cracking is a useful process.

(c) Although alkanes can be cracked with heat alone, it is more common for oil companies to use catalysts. Suggest two reasons for this.

8 **(a)** State the name and formula of two compounds present in gasoline.

(b) Explain how the compounds are isolated from crude oil.

(c) Explain why these components are used in gasoline.

(d) Discuss two different methods that can be used to increase the yield of gasoline from a given quantity of crude oil.

(e) State equations to represent each of these reactions.

9 Consider the following organic compounds.

- pentane
- pentene
- benzene
- cyclopentane

State the order of increasing octane number and explain your choice.

10 Consider the following organic compounds.

- pentane
- hexane
- heptane
- ethanol

State the order of increasing octane number and explain your choice.

11 Crude oil currently provides a greater percentage of the world's energy than any other energy source.

(a) State three reasons for its wide use as an energy source.

(b) Describe briefly how crude oil is formed in nature.

(c) Describe the processes by which the crude material is made ready for use.

Natural gas is mainly methane

Oil spills from oil pipelines are issues that demand international cooperation and agreement.

Methane is the primary constituent of natural gas, which also contains nitrogen and sulfur compounds (hydrogen sulfide) as impurities. Natural gas was formed millions of years ago by the action of heat, pressure, and perhaps bacteria on buried organic matter. The gas is trapped in geological formations capped by impermeable rock. It is also formed from the decomposition of crude oil and coal deposits. It can occur almost entirely on its own, dissolved under pressure in oil; or in a layer above the oil in a reservoir. Natural gas can also be found associated with coal, when it is a major hazard as it forms an explosive mixture with air.

Natural gas is the cleanest of the fossil fuels to burn due to its high H : C ratio. Impurities can easily be removed, so the combustion of natural gas produces minimal amounts of carbon monoxide, hydrocarbons, and particulates.

Aerial view of production rigs in the Vakhitovskoye natural gas field, Orenberg, Russia.

Where it is available as mains gas it flows through pipes to wherever it is needed, so little energy is used to get the gas from the ground to the consumer. Setting up such a distribution network, however, involves a massive capital investment and in some countries liquefied gas (butane or propane) is an option for domestic heating and cooking.

Worked example

Consider the following specific energies of different fuels.

Fuel	Specific energy / kJ g⁻¹	Carbon content by mass / %
coal	32	94
oil	42	83
natural gas	55	75
wood	15	70
hydrogen	142	0

(a) Suggest an explanation for the trend in specific energies between coal, oil, natural gas, and hydrogen.

(b) The choice of fuel also depends on other factors besides specific energies. One of these is the amount of carbon dioxide produced. Explain why this is an important factor to consider.

(c) Calculate the carbon dioxide production for each 1000 kJ of energy from each source and identify the best and worst fuel on this basis.

The financial costs and the political risks involved in constructing international pipelines are the main reasons why the international trade in natural gas has been relatively slow. At present most natural gas is consumed in the countries in which it is found.

Solution

(a) Hydrogen has a higher enthalpy of combustion than carbon as it forms stronger bonds with oxygen. As the percentage carbon content decreases and the hydrogen content increases the specific energy increases.

(b) Carbon dioxide is a greenhouse gas and causes global warming.

(c)

Fuel	Specific energy / kJ g⁻¹	Mass needed to produce 1000 kJ / g	Carbon content by mass / %	Carbon burnt / g	Carbon dioxide produced / g
coal	32	$=\dfrac{1000}{32}$ $= 31.3$	94	$=\dfrac{1000}{32} \times 0.94$	$=\dfrac{1000}{32} \times 0.94 \times \dfrac{44.01}{12.01}$ $= 108$
oil	42	$=\dfrac{1000}{42}$ $= 23.8$	83	$=\dfrac{1000}{42} \times 0.83$	$=\dfrac{1000}{42} \times 0.83 \times \dfrac{44.01}{12.01}$ $= 72$
natural gas	55	$=\dfrac{1000}{55}$ $= 18.2$	75	$=\dfrac{1000}{55} \times 0.75$	$=\dfrac{1000}{55} \times 0.75 \times \dfrac{44.01}{12.01}$ $= 50$
wood	15	$=\dfrac{1000}{15}$ $= 66.7$	70	$=\dfrac{1000}{15} \times 0.70$	$=\dfrac{1000}{15} \times 0.70 \times \dfrac{44.01}{12.01}$ $= 171$
hydrogen	142	$=\dfrac{1000}{142}$ $= 7.0$	0	0	0

Hydrogen is the best and coal is the worst fuel on this basis.

Supplies of methane can be increased by cracking larger hydrocarbons or from coal gasification

Coal can be converted to the more environmentally clean methane by the process of **coal gasification**. The crushed coal is mixed with superheated steam, and a mixture of carbon monoxide and hydrogen known as **synthesis gas** is produced.

$$C(s) + H_2O(l) \rightarrow CO(g) + H_2(g)$$

Synthesis gas can be used directly as a fuel. It can be processed further to make methane; it is mixed with additional hydrogen in the presence of a heated catalyst:

$$CO(g) + 3H_2(g) \rightarrow CH_4(g) + H_2O(g)$$

Synthetic natural gas can also be made by heating crushed coal in the presence of steam with a potassium hydroxide catalyst to produce methane and carbon dioxide:

$$2C(s) + 2H_2O(g) \rightarrow CH_4(g) + CO_2(g)$$

Exercises

12 Describe a process that can be used to convert a more available fossil fuel to the less available hydrocarbon-based source of energy. State equations to show how methane and pentane are formed during these processes.

13 State three reasons for not relying on carbon-containing fuels in the future.

14 Synthesis gas can be considered as carbon monoxide and hydrogen mixed in equal amounts.
   (a) Use section 13 in the IB data booklet to predict the enthalpy of combustion of a mixture which contains one mole each of two components.
   (b) Deduce how much energy could be available if the same carbon monoxide was first converted to methane, and the methane was used as a fuel.
   (c) A student wishes to compare the energy available from equal volumes of methane and synthesis gas. Predict which sample will produce the most energy and explain your choice.

15 (a) Identify the major constituent of natural gas and write a balanced chemical equation for its combustion.
   (b) Compare natural gas with other fossil fuels as a source of air pollution for a given amount of energy and account for any differences.
   (c) Compare the relative supplies of natural gas and other fossil fuels.
   (d) Suggest a process by which the natural supplies of the major component in natural gas can be increased and state the equations which describe the chemical reactions involved in the process.

The past and future of fossil fuels

As civilization has advanced, the carbon content of fuel has decreased. Coal was the fossil fuel used first. It is the most abundant and easiest to obtain of all the fossil fuels and most similar in properties to charcoal, which was generally used as a fuel by primitive cultures. Coal has generally been replaced today by gasoline and natural gas as the fuel of choice as they have higher specific energies and energy densities and are easier to transport. The two fluids, gas and oil, are also cleaner burning and produce less carbon dioxide per unit energy.

The advantages and disadvantages of the three fossil fuels are summarized on page 525.

All fossil fuels are non-renewable and produce the greenhouse gas carbon dioxide.

The choice of fossil fuel used by different countries depends on historical, geological, and technological factors. Different societies have different priorities in their energy choices.

	Coal	Crude oil	Natural gas
Advantages	• Cheap and plentiful throughout the world. • Can be converted into synthetic liquid fuels and gases. • Safer than nuclear power. • Ash produced can be used in making roads.	• Easily transported in pipelines or by tankers. • Convenient fuel for use in cars as volatile and burns easily. • Sulfur impurities can be easily removed.	• Produces fewer pollutants per unit energy. • Easily transported in pipelines and pressurized containers. • Does not contribute to acid rain. • Higher specific energy.
Disadvantages	• Produces many pollutants. • Produces CO_2, SO_2, particulates (electrostatic preceptors can remove most of these). • Difficult to transport. • Waste can lead to visual and chemical pollution. • Mining is dangerous.	• Limited lifespan and uneven world distribution. • Contributes to acid rain and global warming. • Transport can lead to pollution. • Carbon monoxide is a local pollutant produced by incomplete combustion of gasoline in internal combustion engines. • Photochemical smog produced as secondary pollutant due to reactions of the primary pollutants (nitrogen oxides and hydrocarbons) released from internal combustion engines.	• Limited supplies. • Contributes to global warming. • Risk of explosion due to leaks.

Carbon footprint

One measure of the impact our activities have on the environment is given by our **carbon footprint**. The carbon footprint is a measurement of all the greenhouse gases we individually produce. It has units of mass of carbon dioxide equivalent and depends on the amount of greenhouse gases we produce in our day-to-day activities through the use of fossil fuels such as heating, transport, and electricity.

The carbon footprint is a measure of the total amount of carbon dioxide emissions that is directly and indirectly caused by an activity or a product.

NATURE OF SCIENCE

Carbon footprint' has become a widely used term in the public debate on our responsibilities in the fight against global climate change. There is, however, limited consensus on how to quantify a carbon footprint. Some issues are

• should the carbon footprint include just carbon dioxide (CO_2) emissions or include other greenhouse gas emissions such as methane as well?

• should it be restricted to carbon-based gases or can it include substances that don't have carbon in their molecules such as dinitrogen monoxide, which is another greenhouse gas?

• should it include other gases such as carbon monoxide (CO), which is a toxic primary pollutant that can be oxidized to carbon dioxide in the atmosphere?

Words that scientists agree on which have an impact on the public must be clearly understood. Scientific discourse with the public needs to take account of this.

Worked example

In a typical winter's day 1.33×10^6 kJ of energy is needed in a home.

The specific energy densities and approximate empirical formulae of wood and coal and the efficiency of the heating systems are tabulated on page 526.

Fuel	Formula of fuel	Specific energy / kJ g^{-1}	Efficiency of heating / %
coal	CH	31	65
wood	C$_5$H$_9$O$_4$	22	70

(a) Calculate the percentage mass of carbon in the two fuels.

(b) Determine the carbon footprint from using the two forms of heating in terms of the mass of carbon dioxide produced by the two fuels.

(c) Suggest a reason why the carbon footprint calculation for wood does not give a full account of its impact on the environment.

Solution

(a)

Fuel	Formula of fuel	Percentage mass of C
coal	CH	$= \dfrac{12.01}{12.01 + 1.01} \times 100$ $= 92.2\%$
wood	C$_5$H$_9$O$_4$	$= \dfrac{5 \times 12.01}{(5 \times 12.01) + (9 \times 1.01) + (4 \times 16.00)} \times 100$ $= 45.1\%$

(b)

Fuel	Calorific content of fuel needed / kJ	Mass of fuel needed / g	Mass of carbon burned / g	Mass of CO$_2$ produced / kg
coal	$= \dfrac{1.33 \times 10^6}{0.65}$ $= 2.05 \times 10^6$	$= \dfrac{1.33 \times 10^6}{0.65 \times 31}$ $= 66\,000$	$= 0.922 \times \dfrac{1.33 \times 10^6}{0.65 \times 31}$ $= 60\,800 \; (= 60.8 \text{ kg})$	$= 60.8 \times \dfrac{44.01}{12.01}$ $= 223 \; (\text{kg})$
wood	$= \dfrac{1.33 \times 10^6}{0.70}$ $= 1.9 \times 10^6$	$= \dfrac{1.33 \times 10^6}{0.70 \times 22}$ $= 86\,400$	$= 0.451 \times \dfrac{1.33 \times 10^6}{0.70 \times 22}$ $= 38\,900 \; (= 38.9 \text{ kg})$	$= 38.9 \times \dfrac{44.01}{12.01}$ $= 142 \; (\text{kg})$

(c) Growing the trees to produce the wood absorbs carbon dioxide due to photosynthesis.

Exercises

16 (a) State three reasons why most of the world's energy consumption is provided by fossil fuels.

   (b) Identify the energy source that currently provides the greatest proportion of the world's total energy demand and explain your answer.

17 State three reasons why, worldwide, gas is preferred to oil as a fuel in power stations.

18 Oxygenates are oxygen-containing organic compounds that are added to gasoline because they have high octane numbers. Methylbenzene is an aromatic molecule which is added to gasoline because it too has a high octane number. The enthalpies of combustion of the two compounds are given in section 13 of the IB data booklet.

   (a) Calculate the mass of each fuel needed to produce 10 000 kJ of energy.

   (b) Determine the carbon footprint in terms of the mass of carbon dioxide added to the atmosphere in producing this amount of energy from the two fuels.

   (c) Suggest a second reason why oxygenates are added to gasoline.

C.3 Nuclear fusion and fission

Understandings:

Nuclear fusion
- Light nuclei can undergo fusion reactions as this increases the binding energy per nucleon.
- Fusion reactions are a promising energy source as the fuel is inexpensive and abundant, and no radioactive waste is produced.
- Absorption spectra are used to analyse the composition of stars.

Nuclear fission
- Heavy nuclei can undergo fission reactions as this increases the binding energy per nucleon.
- ^{235}U undergoes a fission chain reaction:

$$^{235}_{92}U + ^{1}_{0}n \rightarrow ^{236}_{92}U \rightarrow X + Y + \text{neutrons}$$

Guidance
The workings of a nuclear power plant are not required.

- The critical mass is the mass of fuel needed for the reaction to be self-sustaining.
- ^{239}Pu, used as a fuel in 'breeder reactors', is produced from ^{238}U by neutron capture.
- Radioactive waste may contain isotopes with long and short half-lives.

Guidance
Safety and risk issues include: health, problems associated with nuclear waste and core meltdown, and the possibility that nuclear fuels may be used in nuclear weapons.

- Half-life is the time it takes for half the number of atoms to decay.

Applications and skills:

Nuclear fusion
- Construction of nuclear equations for fusion reactions.
- Explanation of fusion reactions in terms of binding energy per nucleon.
- Explanation of the atomic absorption spectra of hydrogen and helium, including the relationships between the lines and electron transitions.

Nuclear fission
- Deduction of nuclear equations for fission reactions.

Guidance
Students are not expected to recall specific fission reactions.

- Explanation of fission reactions in terms of binding energy per nucleon.
- Discussion of the storage and disposal of nuclear waste.
- Solution of radioactive decay problems involving integral numbers of half-lives.

Guidance
The equations, $N = N_0 e^{-\lambda t}$ and $T_{\frac{1}{2}} = \dfrac{\ln 2}{\lambda}$ are given in section 1 of the IB data booklet.

Many people fear radioactivity: they associate it with the fall-out of atomic bombs or disasters such as the explosion at the Fukushima nuclear power station. It is, however, a natural process, constantly occurring all around us. It is the result of naturally unstable atomic nuclei changing into more stable ones. Nuclear reactions can also occur artificially when atoms are bombarded with protons, neutrons, or other high-energy particles. Nuclear reactions should be contrasted to chemical reactions which only involve the outer electrons of an atom. Atoms change their identity in nuclear reactions but not in chemical reactions.

As discussed in Chapter 2, atoms with different numbers of neutrons are known as isotopes. The neutrons help provide a strong nuclear force, of short range, which binds the nucleus together despite the electrical repulsion between the positively charged protons. This force is about 100 times more powerful than the electric force at such

Nuclear reactions involve the protons and neutrons in the nucleus, and the atoms may be converted to other elements. In chemical reactions only valence electrons are involved and atoms do not change their identity.

short distances and is also 'blind' to electric charge and acts equally on protons and neutrons, binding them together. In relatively light nuclei, the strong force counteracts the electric force, provided the number of neutrons and protons is about equal. In heavy nuclei, however, there have to be more neutrons than protons to combat the repulsion between protons. The extra neutrons are there because the strong force acts mainly between neighbouring protons. The electric force, on the other hand, can act over longer distances. A proton at one side of the nucleus will feel some electric repulsion from a proton at the other side, but not a strong force attraction from protons or neutrons. This means that the repulsive electric force begins to overcome the attraction of the strong force. The presence of extra neutrons dilutes the electric force and prevents the nucleus from blowing apart. The balance between the forces determines whether a particular nucleus will be stable or unstable.

When the stable nuclei of the elements are plotted on the graph of number of protons against number of neutrons they all fall in an area enclosed by two curved lines known as the **band of stability** (Figure 14.2).

When a nucleus contains either too many or too few neutrons, it is radioactive and changes to a more stable nucleus by giving out radiation. This may be of several different forms which differ in ionization and penetration abilities.

Alpha particles, emitted by nuclei with too many protons to be stable, are composed of two protons and two neutrons.

Beta particles, emitted by nuclei with too many neutrons, are electrons which have been ejected from the nucleus owing to neutron decay.

A nucleon is a proton or a neutron.

Figure 14.2 The stable nuclei of the elements all fall in an area known as the band of stability. A nucleus emits alpha radiation if it has too few neutrons (too many protons), and beta particles if it has too many neutrons.

Gamma rays are a form of electromagnetic radiation which are given out as a result of the **nucleons** reorganizing themselves.

Some particles in the particles zoo

Nuclear reactions can involve a wide range of particles and types of radiation. The positron, for example, is the antiparticle of the electron. It has the same mass as an electron but the opposite charge. When a positron collides with an electron both particles are destroyed and their mass converted to the equivalent amount of energy.

A small selection of these subatomic particles is tabulated on page 529.

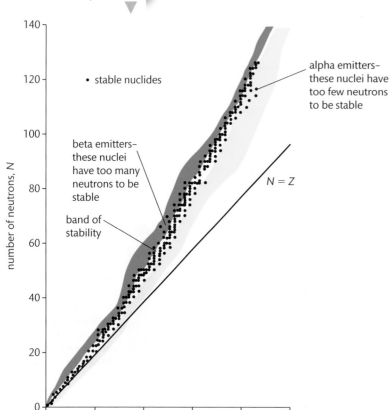

Particle/ radiation	Relative charge	Relative mass	Symbol	Description
proton	+1	1	^1_1H	hydrogen nucleus
alpha	+2	4	^4_2He	helium nucleus
beta	−1	0	$^0_{-1}e$	electron
positron	+1	0	$^0_{+1}e$	antiparticle of the electron
gamma (photon)	0	0	γ	electromagnetic wave

Note the charge does not need to be given as a superscript as it is implied in the left subscript. The alpha particle has a charge of +2 as the atomic number of helium is +2. The beta particle has a charge of −1 as it has subscript of −1.

The mass defect is the difference between the mass of the nucleus and the sum of the masses of its individual nucleons

The absolute mass of the elementary particles is given in section 4 of the IB data booklet and reproduced below.

Elementary particle	Mass / amu	Mass / kg
proton	1.008 665	1.672622×10^{-27}
neutron	1.007 265	1.674927×10^{-27}
electron	0.000 549	9.109383×10^{-31}

1 amu is defined as 1/12 of the mass of an atom of the isotope $^{12}_6C$.

$1 \text{ amu} = 1.66 \times 10^{-27} \text{ kg}$

A helium atom is made from two protons, two neutrons, and two electrons. Adding the masses of its constituent particles we have:

predicted mass of helium atom = 2(1.008665 + 1.007265 + 0.000549) amu
= 4.032958 amu

This value should be contrasted with the actual mass of a helium atom, which is 4.002603 amu. The total mass of the atom is less than the sum of the masses of the separate elementary particles. This mass difference is called the **mass defect**.

To understand the reason for this mass defect we need to bring in one of the most significant results from Einstein's Special Theory of Relativity. Einstein showed that mass and energy are equivalent and related by the famous equation $E = mc^2$. In forming a nucleus, mass appears to have been lost because it has been converted to energy which is given out as the protons and neutrons fuse together. This energy is called the **binding energy**.

Binding energy graphs can be used to understand nuclear stability

^4_2He is more stable than ^2_1H because it has a higher binding energy per nucleon. A graph of binding energy per nucleon versus mass number indicates the relative stability of the atomic nuclei.

One atom of carbon-12 has a mass of 12 amu.

The mass defect (Δm) is the difference between the mass of the nucleus and the sum of the masses of its individual nucleons.

The binding energy is the energy released when a nucleus is made from protons and neutrons or the energy required to separate a nucleus into separate nucleons.

Figure 14.3 Graph of atomic nuclei binding energies; y-axis plotted against mass number x-axis. Nuclear stability is due to the strong nuclear force overcoming the electromagnetic repulsion between the protons. Isotopes on the left of this graph undergo nuclear fusion while isotopes on the right undergo nuclear fission.

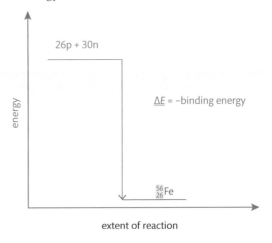

Figure 14.3 Graph of atomic nuclei binding energies; y-axis plotted against mass number x-axis. Nuclear stability is due to the strong nuclear force overcoming the electromagnetic repulsion between the protons. Isotopes on the left of this graph undergo nuclear fusion while isotopes on the right undergo nuclear fission.

The curve in the binding energy graph indicates that the binding energy per nucleon tends to increase sharply to a peak at $^{56}_{26}$Fe, which corresponds to the most stable isotope, and then gradually diminishes. As binding energy is the energy released when the nuclei are formed it is important to understand that $^{56}_{26}$Fe is the most stable nuclei because it has the *least* energy.

Figure 14.4 The binding energy is the energy released when the nucleus is formed from its constituent protons and neutrons. Fe is the most stable nucleus as it has the lowest energy.

Energy will be given out in any process that leads to an increase in the binding energy per nucleon.

Nuclear fusion, which is the joining of very light nuclei, can occur for isotopes such as deuterium, which are found to the left of the $^{56}_{26}$Fe maximum on the graph.

Nuclear fission, which is the splitting of a heavy nucleus, can occur for isotopes to the right of the $^{56}_{26}$Fe maximum, such as $^{238}_{92}$U.

Light nuclei can undergo fusion reactions as this increases the binding energy per nucleon

Nuclear fusion brings together nuclei of small or lighter elements to form heavier elements, with the release of energy. We have already considered the fusion of $^{2}_{1}$H nuclei to form $^{4}_{2}$He:

$$2\,^{2}_{1}\text{H} \rightarrow {}^{4}_{2}\text{He}$$

Note that as the number of protons has not changed, the charge, as represented by the subscripts in the formula of the different isotopes, is balanced ($2 \times 1 = 2$). Similarly the superscripts, which refer to the number of protons and neutrons, are also balanced ($2 \times 2 = 4$).

The energy of the Sun is produced from fusion reactions. The primary reaction that fuels the fires of the Sun is believed to be the fusion of four hydrogen atoms to yield one helium nucleus.

(a) Complete the reaction below by identifying a, p, and r.

$$4^1_1\text{H} \rightarrow \,^4_2\text{He} + a^r_p\text{X}$$

(b) Explain why energy is given out in the reaction.

Solution

(a) Equating the charges on both sides gives $4 = 2 + ap$

Equating the mass on both sides gives $4 = 4 + ar$

This suggests $r = 0$, $p = +1$, $a = 2$: two positrons are produced.

$$4^1_1\text{H} \rightarrow \,^4_2\text{He} + 2^0_1\text{e}$$

(b) Energy is given out in the fusion reaction because the total mass of the products is slightly less than the total mass of the reactants. Mass is converted to the equivalent amount of energy.

The elements in the stars can be identified by their absorption spectra

All objects that have a temperature above 0 K give out a range of electromagnetic radiation of different wavelengths. The amount and peak wavelength of the radiation depends on the temperature of the body. The higher the temperature, the more radiation is emitted and the shorter the wavelength of the bulk of the radiation. At the temperatures we experience on Earth most objects radiate in the infrared part of the electromagnetic spectrum, but the Sun has a sufficiently high temperature (the surface temperature is 5700 K) to give out all the colours of the spectrum. It is a source of white light with a maximum intensity occurring in the yellow region of the spectrum.

This is not the complete story, however, as the Sun is surrounded by an 'atmosphere' which is at a lower temperature than the Sun itself. The gases in this region can absorb some wavelengths of the Sun's emitted radiation, producing dark absorption lines in the spectrum. These dark bands can be used to identify elements present in the gases surrounding the Sun. The Sun's spectrum shows dark lines that represent absorbed radiation from the elements hydrogen and helium.

The absorption lines correspond to the electrons being excited from lower to higher energy levels

Hydrogen and helium atoms and helium ions are present in the outer layers of the Sun. At very high temperatures the atoms are stripped of their electrons and the intensely hot mixture of positive nuclei and free electrons is called

Diagram of the spectra of stars, showing a set of dark absorption lines which indicate the presence of certain elements, such as hydrogen and helium, in the outer atmosphere of the star. The stars from top to bottom are: Lambda Cephei, P Cygni, Beta Orionis, Alpha Canis Majoris, Alpha Canis Minoris, Alpha Aurigae, Alpha Hydrae, Alpha Orionis, Omicron Ceti, and Y Canum Venaticorum.

plasma. Hydrogen atoms and helium ions (He⁺ ions) are both one-electron systems and have similar patterns in their energy levels. As we saw in Chapter 2, the energy levels converge with increasing energy. The absorption lines in the visible region of the spectrum of hydrogen are due to the electron being excited from the $n = 2$ energy level.

The energy levels of the hydrogen atom and helium ion (He⁺ ion) are compared below.

Energy level	Energy H atom / kJ mol⁻¹	Energy He⁺ ion / kJ mol⁻¹
1	−1312.0	−5250
2	−327.5	−1310.0
3	−145.4	−581.8
4	−81.9	−327.5
5	−52.0	−209.6
∞	0	0

Note that all the energy levels have negative values as the fully ionized state with $n = \infty$ corresponds to zero energy.

The energy levels for helium have lower energy than the corresponding states for hydrogen due to increased nuclear charge which attracts the electron more closely to the nucleus.

Worked example

(a) Determine the wavelength absorbed when an electron in a helium ion is excited from the $n = 3$ to the $n = 4$ level.

(b) Identify the region of the spectrum in which this transition occurs.

Solution

(a) $\Delta E = -327.5 - -581.8 \text{ kJ mol}^{-1} = +254.3 \text{ kJ mol}^{-1}$

[convert kJ per mol to J per ion]

$$\frac{254.3 \times 10^3}{6.02 \times 10^{23}} = 4.22 \times 10^{-19} \text{ J}$$

Use the equation $E = h\nu$

$$\nu = \frac{4.22 \times 10^{-19}}{6.63 \times 10^{-34}}$$

$$= 6.37 \times 10^{14} \text{ s}^{-1}$$

Use the equation $c = \nu\lambda$

$$\lambda = \frac{3.0 \times 10^8}{6.37 \times 10^{14}}$$

$$= 4.70 \times 10^{-7} \text{ m}$$

(b) The electromagnetic spectrum is shown in section 3 of the IB data booklet. This line occurs in the visible region of the spectrum.

CHALLENGE YOURSELF

5 Compare the energy levels of the hydrogen atom and the helium ion. Explain the values of the corresponding energy levels.

Nuclear fusion as a possible source of energy

The fusion of 1 g of hydrogen will release as much energy as the combustion of 10^3 kg of coal but unfortunately there are practical difficulties in carrying out such fusion reaction on Earth. Very high temperatures are needed for the protons to have sufficient kinetic energy to overcome the mutual electrostatic repulsion and fuse together. The energy needed to initiate the uncontrolled fusion reaction in a hydrogen bomb, for example, is produced by the fission of U-235 or Pu-239. Controlled fusion reactions are more difficult as there are some technical problems:

- the production of plasma state which must be held together long enough to fuse the nuclei;
- enough energy must be produced to make the process profitable.

The hot plasma can be confined by **magnetic confinement**. Atoms of the appropriate hydrogen isotope are injected into a donut-shaped container called a **tokamak** where they are subjected to strong magnetic and electric fields. The electric field accelerates the positive ions and so increases the kinetic energy of the nuclei until the nuclei fuse. The hot matter is prevented from touching the walls of the container by the magnetic field. A metal such as sodium or lithium is then used to absorb and transfer the heat produced to a generator. The tokamak at Princeton University has achieved high enough temperatures for fusion to occur but the energy output has not yet equalled the energy input. A super-cooled magnet is used to generate the magnetic field but there are technical difficulties associated with maintaining such low temperatures near the high temperatures needed to produce the plasma state.

In the **inertial confinement** method, tiny glass spheres are filled with deuterium or a deuterium/tritium mixture at a pressure of several hundred atmospheres. The fuel pellets are then subjected to UV radiation generated by high-energy lasers. Under

Spherical ball of plasma (pink) inside the START device at Culham, England. The START (Small Tight Aspect Ratio Tokamak) device changes the shape of the plasma from a torus (ring) to a sphere.

As no single nation can solve the world's energy problems on their own, scientists from all over the world work together on the ITER project. ITER is an acronym of International Thermonuclear Experimental Reactor and Latin for 'the way' or 'the road'. This aims to harness the energy produced by the fusion of atoms to help meet mankind's energy needs.

View of Princeton University's Tokamak Fusion Test Reactor, which is being used to research nuclear fusion. Fusion requires temperatures of around 1.0×10^8 °C, where the reaction gas is in a plasma state. The aim of TFTR is to achieve fusion break-even, where the power input is balanced by the fusion energy output.

this photon bombardment the atoms are squeezed together to cause them to fuse. Molten lithium is then used to absorb the energy from fusion and transfer it to a steam generator to produce electricity. This method has not yet been found to be successful.

The advantages of nuclear fusion

There are advantages to nuclear fusion.

- The fuel is abundant: there are about 10^{23} deuterium atoms in one litre of sea water.
- Fusion is considered to be less dangerous than fusion with regard to radioactive materials: most radioactive isotopes produced by fusion have short half-lives and are therefore only a threat for a short time.
- Massive transport of radioactive materials is not required and no waste has to be stored.

Laser Megajoule fuel pellet. The Laser Megajoule (LMJ) is an experimental nuclear fusion device being built near Bordeaux, France. Its uses laser beams to heat a target to the point where fusion and power generation occurs. It uses the inertial confinement fusion (ICF) method to keep the fuel in place by spider threads.

TOK

In 1989 two respected chemists, Stanley Pons and Martin Fleishmann, claimed to have achieved a fusion reaction during a simple electrolysis experiment. The claims were dismissed by other scientific groups as the results of the experiment were not reproducible. Is it always possible to obtain replicable results in the natural sciences? Are reproducible results possible in other areas of knowledge?

Exercises

19 The hydrogen bomb is an example of uncontrolled nuclear fusion which involves two isotopes of hydrogen. Deduce the missing coefficients and species in the following equations.

(a) $^2_1H + {}^3_1H \rightarrow {}^4_2He + ...$

(b) $^4_2He + {}^{14}_7N \rightarrow {}^1_1H + ...$

20 Diagram 1 shows some of the energy levels of the hydrogen atom. Diagram 2 is a representation of part of the absorption spectrum of atomic hydrogen, with the black lines showing the absorption lines.

Diagram 1

energy / kJ mol^{-1}

- $\quad$ −51.5
- $n = 4$ $\quad$ −85.5
- $n = 3$ $\quad$ −144.5
- $n = 2$ $\quad$ −327.5
- $n = 1$ $\quad$ −1312

Diagram 2

colour	red		blue	violet
wavelength	656 mm		486 mm	434 mm

(a) Calculate the energy change that corresponds to each of the three lines.

(b) Identify the three transitions that give rise to these transitions.

(c) Explain why the lines in the absorption bands of atomic hydrogen, shown in diagram 2, converge as the wavelength of the lines decreases.

Heavy nuclei can undergo fission reactions as this increases the binding energy per nucleon

In the same way that small atoms would be expected to form larger nuclei by fusion due to their relatively low binding energy per nucleon, we expect large nuclei to break down into smaller nuclei. Nuclear fission can occur naturally, or it can be induced by bombardment with a particle such as a neutron. **Artificially induced fission** is the operating basis behind nuclear reactions, which were first observed in 1938 when two German scientists, Otto Hahn and Fritz Strassmann, discovered barium among the products formed when uranium was bombarded with neutrons. The results were explained by Lise Meitner and Otto Frisch based on Bohr's 'droplet' model of the nucleus, in which neutrons and protons are compared to the molecules in a drop of liquid. In the same way that the spherical shape of a drop distorts into a dumbbell shape and then splits into fragments when water is added, a nucleus will split when the number of neutrons is increased.

Target nucleus shown as the large circle absorbs a neutron (small circle).	Nucleus has too many neutrons and excess vibrational energy.	Vibrations produce dumb bell shape.	Repulsive forces between protons stretch the nucleus.	Fission occurs. Fragments separate and give out extra neutrons.

Figure 14.5 The water droplet model of nuclear fission.

The additional neutron causes the uranium nuclei to divide like a biological cell undergoing **fission**, with the production of energy. A wide variety of possible products can be formed when the nucleus of an atom of $^{235}_{92}U$ is struck with a neutron. For example:

$$^{235}_{92}U + ^{1}_{0}n \rightarrow ^{141}_{56}Ba + ^{92}_{36}Kr + 3\,^{1}_{0}n$$

A large amount of energy is produced as the total mass of the products is slightly less than the total mass of the reactants. The mass is converted into an equivalent amount of energy, which is given out. The neutrons released in the fission of one nucleus can trigger the fission of other uranium atoms in a **chain reaction**.

In a nuclear chain reaction, a neutron strikes a $^{235}_{92}U$ atom, splitting it into atoms of krypton and barium and releasing energy along with three neutrons, which go on to strike three more $^{235}_{92}U$ atoms. Uncontrolled chain reactions can be used in weapons. Chain reactions can be controlled using neutron-absorbing materials such as boron.

Nuclear reactors are designed to ensure that, on average, only one neutron from each reaction goes on to initiate a further reaction. If more reactions took place the chain reaction could run out of control. With less than one neutron available the number of reactions would decrease and the fission process would soon stop.

The chance that a given neutron goes on to cause a fission reaction depends on:

• the number of potential nuclei in the neutron's path;
• the speed of the neutrons.

The neutrons produced created by the fission process are generally moving too quickly to initiate further reactions and need to be slowed down by **moderators** in the reactor. The moderators slow down the neutrons sufficiently so that they are absorbed more easily by the nuclei. **Control rods** absorb neutrons. They are introduced or removed from the reactor to control the chain reaction. They are made of materials which can absorb neutrons, such as graphite and cadmium.

The critical mass is the minimum mass of fissionable material needed to sustain a chain reaction

For a fissile material to sustain a chain reaction there must be enough fissionable material to allow the neutron released in one fission process to have a good chance of finding another fissile nuclei before escaping from the bulk material. The **critical mass** is the minimum mass of a fissionable material needed to sustain a chain reaction. The exact value of the critical mass depends on the exact nature of the fuel being used and the shape of the assembly. Naturally occurring uranium contains less than 1% of $^{235}_{92}$U so enriched uranium fuel is needed to sustain the reaction. **Enrichment** is the process by which the percentage composition of $^{235}_{92}$U is increased to make nuclear fission more likely.

The critical mass is the minimum mass of a fissionable material needed to sustain a chain reaction.

$^{235}_{92}$U accounts for about 0.72% of all naturally occurring uranium.

View of the top of the reactor at a nuclear power station in Kent, England, showing a technician standing on top of the reactor charge transfer plate into which the uranium fuel rods fit.

Is it right for the small number of countries that already have nuclear capability to prevent other countries from acquiring that knowledge or technology?

Since World War II, when the destructive nature of nuclear bombs was witnessed for the first time, the threat of their use has acted as a deterrent to countries planning to act aggressively against the nuclear powers. Non-proliferation treaties have been formulated which attempt to limit nuclear technology to a small number of nations.

Uncontrolled nuclear reactions are used in nuclear weapons

When the number of neutrons is not controlled, a fission reaction can release an enormous amount of energy in a very short time. This happened when the fission bombs were dropped on Hiroshima and Nagasaki in Japan during World War II. Weapons have been designed using both $^{235}_{92}$U and $^{239}_{94}$Pu, which is a by-product of the peaceful use of $^{235}_{92}$U for energy.

Some argue against the use of nuclear power. For them, the risk of an uncontrolled nuclear reaction happening in a power station is not worth taking as it would lead to a thermal meltdown of the core and the release of dangerous radioactive material into the environment. It is also claimed that nuclear power stations could be targets for terrorist attack.

$^{239}_{94}$Pu used as a fuel in 'breeder reactors' is produced from $^{238}_{92}$U by neutron capture

Fast breeder reactors were developed because the supply of fissionable $^{235}_{92}$U is limited. Breeder reactors convert the more abundant uranium isotope $^{238}_{92}$U into fissionable $^{239}_{94}$Pu.

$^{238}_{92}$U can capture fast-moving neutrons to form the heavier uranium isotope:

$$^{238}_{92}U + ^{1}_{0}n \rightarrow ^{239}_{92}U$$

which then decays to $^{239}_{93}$Np with the emission of a beta particle:

$$^{239}_{92}U \rightarrow ^{239}_{93}Np + ^{0}_{-1}e$$

and the $^{239}_{93}$Np further decays to $^{239}_{94}$Pu with the emission of another beta particle:

$$^{239}_{93}Np \rightarrow ^{239}_{94}Pu + ^{0}_{-1}e$$

In the fast breeder reaction the $^{239}_{94}$Pu is bombarded with a neutron and undergoes a fission reaction. For example:

$$^{239}_{94}Pu + ^{1}_{0}n \rightarrow ^{145}_{56}Ba + ^{93}_{38}Sr + 2\,^{1}_{0}n$$

No moderators are needed in a plutonium reactor because plutonium requires faster neutrons for fission than $^{235}_{92}$U.

There are major concerns associated with the use of breeder reactors.

- Plutonium is toxic.
- Plutonium can be concentrated from reactor grade to weapons grade easily. It can be easily separated from the uranium isotopes as they are atoms of different elements with different chemical properties.
- Breeder reactors are less efficient than those fuelled by uranium and require liquid metals as coolants. The escape of liquid sodium from a breeder reactor and its subsequent contact with water would be disastrous.
- They could be more susceptible to accidents.
- All nuclear reactors produce radioactive by-products that are difficult to store and dispose of.

NATURE OF SCIENCE

Science is highly collaborative and the scientific community is composed of people working in science, engineering, and technology. As well as collaborating on the exchange of results, scientists work on a daily basis in collaborative groups on a small and large scale within and between disciplines and countries, facilitated even more by virtual communication. IAEA and the ITER project are examples of such large-scale collaboration.

Exercises

21 Incomplete equations for nuclear reactions of a number of different isotopes of uranium are given below.

I	$^{233}_{92}U \rightarrow {}^{4}_{2}He + W$
II	$^{235}_{92}U + {}^{1}_{0}n \rightarrow {}^{141}_{56}Ba + {}^{92}_{36}Kr + X$
III	$^{239}_{92}U \rightarrow Y + {}^{0}_{-1}e$
IV	$^{233}_{92}U + {}^{1}_{0}n \rightarrow {}^{140}_{58}Ce + Z + 2\,{}^{1}n$

(a) Identify the missing species W, X, Y, and Z.
(b) State which of the nuclear reactions above is/are used to produce electricity in nuclear power plants. Explain your choice.
(c) Explain the origin of the energy produced in the reaction identified in (b).

22 Explain why natural uranium cannot be used directly as a nuclear fuel.

Nuclear waste is still radioactive

One of the potential hazards associated with the use of nuclear energy is that the products of fission reactions are still dangerously radioactive. The neutron:proton ratio of the isotopes produced does not fall in the stability belt shown in Figure 14.3.

Some radioactive isotopes are long-lived. $^{238}_{92}U$, for example, has a half-life of 4.47×10^9 years, which is approximately the age of the Earth, so only half the $^{238}_{92}U$ that existed when the Earth formed has since decayed away. Other isotopes, such as $^{214}_{84}Po$, have half-lives of a fraction of a second. The long half-lives of certain artificially produced isotopes are of particular concern when handling radioactive waste. One by-product of nuclear reactors, $^{237}_{93}Np$, has a half-life of 2.2 million years. Any site for storing waste contaminated with such isotopes must be one that is unlikely to be disturbed in the future. Otherwise radioactive material may escape into the environment.

The half-life of radioactive isotopes

Although we cannot predict at which instant a particular nucleus will decay, the overall rate at which a collection of nuclei decays is regular and can be quantified by its **half-life**. This is the time taken for:

• half the mass of an isotope to decay;
• the concentration of an aqueous isotope to fall to half its initial value;
• the number of atoms of the isotope to fall to half their original number;
• the activity of an isotope to fall to half its initial value.

Worked example

Bismuth-212 has a half-life of 1 hour. Deduce how long it would take for 16.00 g of the isotope to decay so that only 1.00 g remained.

Solution

The half-life is the time taken for the mass to fall to half its value. Construct a table:

Time / hours	Mass of isotope remaining / g
0	16.00
1	8.00
2	4.00
3	2.00
4	1.00

The decay will take 4 hours.

A decay curve for the isotope in the Worked example is shown in Figure 14.6. It is an exponential curve and in theory never falls to zero. Radioactive decay is a first-order process.

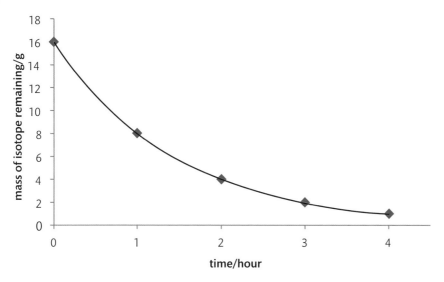

Figure 14.6 A decay curve for an isotope which has a half-life of 1 hour.

The half-life of an isotope depends intimately on the balance of forces within a nucleus.

NATURE OF SCIENCE

Carbon-14 dating

$^{14}_{6}C$ has too many neutrons to be stable. It can reduce the neutron : proton ratio when a neutron changes to a proton and an electron. The proton stays in the nucleus and changes the identity of the atom to nitrogen and the electron is ejected from the atom as a beta particle:

$$^{14}_{6}C \rightarrow {}^{14}_{7}N + {}^{0}_{-1}e$$

The relative abundance of $^{14}_{6}C$ present in living things, however, remains quite constant as the decayed atoms are continually replenished from $^{14}_{6}C$ present in carbon dioxide from the atmosphere during photosynthesis. When organisms die no more carbon is exchanged and the levels of $^{14}_{6}C$ fall due to beta decay.

This process occurs at a regular rate and can be used to date carbon-containing materials. The half-life is 5730 years, so the carbon-14 to carbon-12 ratio falls by 50% every 5730 years after the death of a living organism. This creates a timescale which allows it to be used in the dating of archaeological objects. *continued*

What is the role of evidence in justifying religious belief?

TOK

NATURE OF SCIENCE

continued

For many centuries people have believed the Turin Shroud was used to wrap the body of Jesus Christ after his death. Carbon-14 measurements have dated the shroud to have been made no earlier than 1260 ACE. The linen was found to have come from flax grown sometime between 1260 and 1390.

Scientists adopt a sceptical attitude to knowledge claims. This does not mean that they disbelieve everything, but rather that they suspend judgement until they have a good reason to believe a claim to be true or false. Such reasons are based on evidence and argument.

Nuclear waste can be high level or low level

An important aspect of the nuclear industry is the disposal of radioactive waste. The spent fuel rods from nuclear power stations are **high-level waste** whereas the containers which hold the fuel are classified as **low-level waste**. The method of disposal depends on the level of the waste and the length of time it remains active. Low-level wastes have low levels of activity and short half-lives. High-level wastes have high activity and long half-lives.

Sources and characteristics of low- and high-level waste

Nature of waste	Source	Characteristics
low level	• hospitals: items such as clothing, paper towels which are used where radioactive materials are handled • fuel containers	• activity is low • short half-life • high volume
high level	• nuclear industry: spent fuel rods • military	• activity is high • long half-life • low volume

Disposal of low-level waste

As the decay process produces heat energy, low-level waste is stored in cooling ponds of water until the activity has fallen to safe levels. The water is then passed through an ion-exchange resin, which removes the isotopes responsible for the activity, and diluted before being released into the sea. Other methods of disposal include keeping the waste in steel containers inside concrete-lined vaults.

Disposal of high-level waste

As we have seen, the products formed from nuclear reactors with long half-lives can maintain dangerously high levels of radioactivity for thousands of years. Unfortunately, there is no way to speed up the rate of the decay process. Waste disposal presents a formidable problem because products from the decay process may themselves undergo further nuclear reactions. Remotely controlled machinery removes the spent rods from the reactor and transfers them to deep pools where they are cooled by water containing a neutron absorber. The fuel rods are often cased in ceramic or glass and then packed in metal containers before being buried deep in the Earth, either in impervious granite rock or in deep unused mines. The site selected for the disposal must safely contain the material for a very long period of time and prevent it from entering the underground water supply. Because there is always the problem that land masses may move (for example, in an earthquake) and the radioactive material escape, the waste is buried in remote places that are geologically stable.

Drilling machinery being used to excavate underground boreholes into which nuclear waste may be placed. Before long-term nuclear waste is stored underground, the area must be examined for geological activity.

Used fuel cooling and storage pond. Fuel rods are placed in the storage ponds awaiting reprocessing. The spent fuel is still highly radioactive and continues to generate heat. The water absorbs the heat and shields the operators from the radiation emitted by the fuel.

Comparison between fossil fuel and nuclear power stations

Fossil fuel	Nuclear fission
ordinary chemical combustion reaction to produce heat	nuclear fission to produce heat from mass defect: $$\Delta E = \Delta mc^2$$
products are CO_2 (greenhouse gas) + SO_2 (acid rain) + particulates (global dimming)	products can be highly radioactive; no CO_2 is produced; accidents can release radioactive materials
fuel does not have to be enriched	U-235 fuel has to be enriched
fuels burnt in a furnace; requires air	fuel rods in an airtight building require neutrons
all fuel can be used up	spent fuel is highly radioactive
fly ash can be used to make roads	nuclear waste has to be stored and safely disposed of
no meltdown possible	failure of control system can lead to meltdown

Exercises

23 (a) It has been suggested that the fission products from nuclear reactions should be isolated for 10 half-lives. Calculate the fraction of a radioactive species that remains after this length of time.

(b) Deduce the percentage of the material that has decayed in this time.

24 Consider a sample of a radioactive isotope with a half-life of 19.2 s. What would its count rate be after 96 s if it started with an initial count rate of 1200 disintegrations per second?

25 One fission reaction of $^{235}_{92}U$ that can take place in a nuclear reactor can lead to the production of an atom of strontium-90 and two neutrons. Deduce the identity of the other nuclide produced.

26 Radioactive waste from nuclear power stations is often divided into high-level and low-level wastes. Describe the materials present in these wastes and the methods used for their storage and disposal.

27 It has been estimated that the $^{14}_{6}C$ in the atmosphere is responsible for producing 60 atoms of $^{14}_{7}N$ and 60 electrons every hour for each gram of carbon. This gives a disintegration rate of 60 counts hr^{-1} g^{-1}. A sample of a sea shell found near the sea shore was found to have a count rate of 4 counts hr^{-1} g^{-1}. Estimate the age of the shell.

C.4 Solar energy

Understandings:

- Light can be absorbed by chlorophyll and other pigments with a conjugated electronic structure.
- Photosynthesis converts light energy into chemical energy:

$$6CO_2 + 6H_2O \rightarrow C_6H_{12}O_6 + 6O_2$$

- Fermentation of glucose produces ethanol which can be used as a biofuel:

$$C_6H_{12}O_6 \rightarrow 2C_2H_5OH + 2CO_2$$

- Energy content of vegetable oils is similar to that of diesel fuel, but vegetable oils are not used in internal combustion engines as they are too viscous.
- Transesterification between an ester and an alcohol with a strong acid or base catalyst produces a different ester:

$$RCOOR^1 + R^2OH \rightarrow RCOOR^2 + R^1OH$$

- In the transesterification process, involving a reaction with an alcohol in the presence of a strong acid or base, the triglyceride vegetable oils are converted to a mixture mainly comprising alkyl esters and glycerol, but with some fatty acids.
- Transesterification with ethanol or methanol produces oils with lower viscosity that can be used in diesel engines.

Applications and skills:

- Identification of features of the molecules that allow them to absorb visible light.

  ### Guidance
  Only a conjugated system with alternating double bonds needs to be covered.

- Explanation of the reduced viscosity of esters produced with methanol and ethanol.
- Evaluation of the advantages and disadvantages of the use of biofuels.
- Deduction of equations for transesterification reactions.

Solar energy has been described as the ultimate energy source and we have seen that a lot of the energy we have on the Earth originates from the Sun. All our fossil fuel supplies were derived from the Sun through photosynthesis. We have seen that solar energy is produced by a series of fusion reactions which convert hydrogen to helium. About 98% of the Sun's energy is emitted in the form of heat and light and the remaining is given out as X-rays and gamma rays.

There are many advantages of solar energy.

- It will be readily available as long as we need it, is free, and requires no purification.
- It is a clean and safe form of energy. The environmental impact is relatively small, although large areas of land are needed.
- It is often available where it is needed, so no transportation is needed.
- Political problems are reduced as the Sun is available to 'all'.

The use of solar energy has, however, been limited because of some disadvantages with its use.

- Other energy sources have been relatively inexpensive.
- Solar energy is widely dispersed and so must be concentrated before it is used.
- Solar energy is not available at night when the demand it at its highest.
- As the supply varies with weather conditions and time of day, an effective method of storing solar energy is needed.

Solar energy can be collected in a number of ways:

• Thermal (passive collection): the Sun's heat is used to heat water or other objects, which are then used for other purposes.
• Thermal (active collection): the Sun's heat is used to bring about an endothermic change. The energy is then given out when the process is later reversed.
• The solar energy can be converted to chemical energy (biomass) using photosynthesis and then given out when the chemical products are used as fuels.
• The solar energy can be converted to electricity by means of photovoltaic and dye-sensitized solar (DSSC) cells.
• The solar energy can be captured indirectly in its derived forms of wind and hydroelectricity.

Light can be absorbed by chlorophyll and other pigments with a conjugated electronic structure

Photosynthesis converts about 1% of incident solar radiation into chemical energy. Some of the solar energy is reflected or used to heat the surface of the Earth. Plants do not cover the Earth's surface completely or absorb all wavelengths of light. Although an inefficient process, photosynthesis does provide a crucial route for harnessing vast amounts of the solar energy that the Earth receives.

The process begins in the chloroplasts of plant cells, which contain chlorophyll and carotenoid molecules that can absorb incoming photons and capture their energy. This energy can then be used to drive a complex sequence of redox reactions which converts carbon dioxide and water to the energy-rich glucose molecule. Leaves appear green because chlorophyll absorbs blue and red light. Carotenoid molecules absorb violet and blue light but are not as abundant as chlorophyll molecules in leaves. They only make themselves known to us in the orange/yellow leaves of autumn, when the chlorophyll molecules are decaying.

 Photosynthesis recycles all the atmospheric carbon dioxide every 300 years and all the oxygen every 2000 years.

The chromophores in the molecule absorb light

Visible light produces electronic transitions in organic molecules. The amount of light absorbed at different wavelengths depends on the molecular structure. The colour of a substance is determined by which colour(s) it transmits or reflects. This is the **complementary** colour(s) to the ones absorbed.

Worked example

The absorbance of an artificial dye is shown. Identify the wavelength which corresponds to maximum absorbance (λ_{max}) and use the colour wheel in section 17 of the IB data booklet to deduce the colour of the dye.

Solution

- The wavelength that corresponds to the maximum absorbance is 600 nm.
- Orange light is absorbed.
- The dye is blue (the complementary colour of orange).

The part of the molecule responsible for absorbing the photon of radiation is called the **chromophore**. Unsaturated groups such as $C=C$, $C=O$, $-N=N-$, and the benzene ring, are examples of chromophores. The wavelengths that correspond to the maximum absorbance for some chromophores are shown in the table.

Chromophore	λ_{max} / nm
$C=C$	175
$C=O$	190 and 280
$C=C-C=C$	210
$-NO_2$	270
	190 and 260

A compound is more likely to absorb visible light and appear coloured when it contains a **conjugated system** of alternate double and single bonds. The more extensive the conjugation the longer the wavelength of the light absorbed. Benzene is a conjugated system and so absorbs at longer wavelengths than the alkenes with a single double bond.

The relationship between the wavelength of the radiation absorbed and the length of the conjugated system can be explained using the wave model of the electron discussed in Chapter 2 (page 74). The wavelength of the light absorbed by a conjugated system increases with length in the same way, and for essentially the same reason, that a guitar string produces a lower note as its length increases.

> A conjugated system contains alternate double and single bonds. The benzene ring is a conjugated system. The wavelength of the light absorbed by an organic molecule increases with the length of the conjugated system.

Chlorophyll absorbs red and blue light

Chlorophyll contains a planar heterocyclic unit called a porphyrin whose structure consists of four pyrrole rings linked by a single bridging carbon atom (Figure 14.7). Each pyrrole ring contains four carbon atoms and one nitrogen atom.

There are two closely related forms of chlorophyll that have different R groups – chlorophyll a has a methyl (CH_3) group and chlorophyll b has an aldehyde (CHO) group.

The extensive conjugation in chlorophyll, which stretches beyond the porphyrin ring, allows it to absorb visible light. The two different forms of chlorophyll, which differ only in one group that is attached to the ring, absorb light at different wavelengths; chlorophyll a absorbs red light and chlorophyll b absorbs blue light. As the two molecules span a large region of the visible spectrum they harvest more solar energy than either would individually. Only green light is not absorbed and this is the colour that we see.

(a)

(b)

Figure 14.7 (a) The structure of a porphyrin ring. (b) The structure of chlorophyll. R = CH$_3$ (chlorophyll a) or R = CHO (chlorophyll b).

Carotenoids are the most widespread pigments in nature. A large majority are produced by algae.

Carotenoids are the most common pigments in nature

Carotenoids are the most common pigments in nature. They absorb light in the violet and green range and so range in colour from yellow to red. There are only low levels of carotenoids in grass but a large majority are produced by algae.

The majority of the carotenoids are derived from a 40-carbon polyene chain. The hydrocarbon carotenoids are known as **carotenes**. In α- and β-carotene, the chain is terminated by cyclic end-groups (Figure 14.8).

α-carotene

β-carotene

Figure 14.8 The structures of α- and β-carotene.

CHALLENGE YOURSELF

6 Study the structure of the two forms of carotene. Deduce the molecular formula of the two molecules and distinguish between them.

545

Carotenoids are structurally related to vitamin A. Vitamin A is a primary alcohol and can be oxidized to the aldehyde, retinal.

vitamin A

The conjugated system of retinal absorbs visible light. The energy gained allows retinal to change its geometry, which results in an electrical signal being sent along the optic nerve to the brain.

Exercises

28 (a) Explain why CH_2=CH—CH=CH_2 shows an absorption band at a longer wavelength than CH_3—CH=CH—CH_3.

(b) Explain why the absorption bands disappear when bromine is added.

(c) Explain why benzene is colourless and nitrobenzene is yellow.

29 A simplified colour wheel is given in section 17 of the IB data booklet. The effect of conjugation is illustrated by the spectra of the diphenylpolyenes, as shown in the table below.

Diphenylpolyenes	n	λ_{max} / nm
	2	328
	3	358
	4	394
	5	403
	6	420

(a) Describe the relationship between n and λ_{max}.

(b) Suggest which members of the series absorb in the visible region.

(c) Suggest the colour of C_6H_5—$(CH=CH)_5$—C_6H_5 and C_6H_5—$(CH=CH)_6$—C_6H_5.

(d) Explain the limitations to your answer in parts (b) and (c).

30 The spectrum of β-carotene is shown in Figure 14.9 and the structure in Figure 14.8. Explain why the molecule absorbs in the visible region of the spectra and suggest the colour of the pigment.

Figure 14.9 The spectrum of β-carotene.

Figure 14.10 The conjugated system of 4-amino benzoic acid enables it to act as a sunscreen.

Moderate exposure to UV light results in the production of the natural pigment melanin, and darkens the skin. Repeated over-exposure to the Sun, however, can cause premature ageing and increases the risk of skin cancer. Conjugated compounds can be used as sunscreens as they absorb dangerous ultraviolet radiation. For example, 4-aminobenzoic acid absorbs UV radiation at 265 nm and is a component of many sunscreens (Figure 14.10). It is also known as para-aminobenzoic acid (PABA).

Photosynthesis converts light energy into chemical energy

The energy of the excited chlorophyll molecule drives the sequence of redox reactions that is photosynthesis.

This reaction can be divided into two half reactions. One half-reaction involves the reduction of carbon dioxide to glucose:

$$6CO_2 + 24H^+ + 24e^- \rightarrow C_6H_{12}O_6 + 6H_2O$$

Twenty-four electrons are needed to reduce six molecules of carbon dioxide to one molecule of glucose as the oxidation number of each carbon decreases from +4 to 0.

The electrons are generated from the oxidation of twelve molecules of water to form oxygen. The oxidation number of twelve oxygen atoms increases from −2 to 0.

The equation for the oxidation half-reaction is:

$$12H_2O \rightarrow 6O_2 + 24H^+ + 24e^-$$

Adding the two half-reactions:

$$6CO_2 + 24H^+ + 24e^- \rightarrow C_6H_{12}O_6 + 6H_2O$$

$$12H_2O \rightarrow 6O_2 + 24H^+ + 24e^-$$

gives

$$6CO_2 + 12H_2O \rightarrow C_6H_{12}O_6 + 6H_2O + 6O_2$$

which can be simplified to:

$$6CO_2 + 6H_2O \rightarrow C_6H_{12}O_6 + 6O_2$$

The products of photosynthesis can be used for food, as a primary fuel or converted to other fuels such as ethanol. These biofuels are a renewable energy source. Wood is a form of biomass and a primary fuel but has a lower specific energy than fossil fuels due to its relatively high oxygen content.

Ethanol can be used as a biofuel

The most useful biofuels are liquids which can be used in internal combustion engines.

Ethanol can be made from biomass by fermenting plants high in starches and sugars.

$$C_6H_{12}O_6 \rightarrow 2C_2H_5OH + 2CO_2$$

This process can be carried out at approximately 37 °C in the absence of oxygen by yeast which provide an enzyme which catalyses the reaction.

Worked example

(a) State the equation for the complete combustion of ethanol.

(b) The enthalpy of combustion of ethanol is −1367 kJ mol^{-1}. Calculate the specific energy of ethanol in kJ g^{-1}.

(c) Compare this value with the corresponding value for octane and explain the difference.

Solution

(a) $C_2H_5OH(l) + 3O_2(g) \rightarrow 3H_2O(l) + 2CO_2(g)$

(b) heat produced by one mole (46.08) = -1367 kJ

$$\text{heat produced by } 1.00 \text{ g} = \frac{1367}{46.08} \text{ kJ g}^{-1}$$

$$= 29.67 \text{ kJ g}^{-1}$$

(c) heat produced by one mole (114.26) = -5470 kJ g^{-1}

$$\text{heat produced by } 1.00 \text{ g} = \frac{5470}{114.26} \text{ kJ g}^{-1}$$

$$= 47.87 \text{ kJ g}^{-1}$$

Less heat is produced per unit mass with ethanol because it is already partially oxidized.

Gasohol is a mixture of 10% ethanol and 90% unleaded gasoline. The ethanol can be produced from several types of plant material and in most cases gasohol can be substituted for gasoline with only minor changes in fuel consumption and performance. The advantages of using ethanol include:

• it is renewable;
• it has a higher octane rating than normal gasoline;
• it produces lower emissions of carbon monoxide (by up to 30%) and nitrogen oxides;
• it decreases a country's dependence on oil.

One disadvantage is that the ethanol absorbs water as it can form hydrogen bonds with the water molecules in the atmosphere. This leads to the ethanol separating from the hydrocarbon components in the fuel as well as causing corrosion.

Methanol can also be used; it is produced by heating wood in the presence of steam and limited amounts of oxygen. A mixture of hydrogen, carbon monoxide, and carbon dioxide is initially produced. The hydrogen and carbon monoxide can then react further to form the liquid fuel methanol.

Particulates in the form of soot and unburned hydrocarbons are hazardous by-products of the process and carbon monoxide is a toxic gas.

CHALLENGE YOURSELF

7 A possible incomplete equation for the conversion of wood into hydrogen, carbon monoxide, and carbon dioxide is:

$$2C_{16}H_{23}O_{11} + 19H_2O + O_2 \rightarrow xH_2 + yCO + zCO_2$$

(a) Identify the oxidation number of all the elements in the equation.
(b) Identify the elements which are oxidized and reduced in the reaction.
(c) Deduce the value of x by balancing the hydrogen atoms.
(d) Determine the value of y and z by balancing the changes of oxidation numbers and the number of carbon atoms.
(e) Deduce how many methanol molecules can be produced from one wood molecule.

Methane can be made from the bacterial breakdown of plant material in the absence of oxygen. The process can be controlled to produce a clean burning biogas like natural gas.

Carbohydrates, for example, produce a mixture which is about 50% methane:

$$C_6H_{12}O_6 \rightarrow 3CO_2 + 3CH_4$$

Fats, however, 72% methane:

$$2C_{15}H_{31}COOH + 14H_2O \rightarrow 9CO_2 + 23CH_4$$

The advantages and disadvantages of using biofuels

Advantages

• Cheap and readily available;
• if crops/trees are replanted can be a renewable sustainable source.

Disadvantages

• The production of biomass involves the use of land which could be used for other purposes, such as growing food;
• high cost of harvesting and transportation in large volumes;
• most of the land considered for biomass production would need the massive application of fertilizers;
• lower specific energy than fossil fuels;
• greenhouse gases still produced;
• biomass is not renewable if crops/trees are not replanted.

The energy content of vegetable oils

The idea of using vegetable oil as an engine fuel dates back to Rudolf Diesel (1858–1913), who used peanut oil to run his first engine at the World Exhibition in Paris in 1900. In 1911, he said, 'The diesel engine can be fed with vegetable oils and would help considerably in the development of agriculture of the countries which use it.'

Vegetable oil was, however, forgotten as a renewable source of power when the crude oil industry produced a hydrocarbon 'diesel fraction' that would power a modified 'diesel engine'. The vegetable oils are not ideal fuels. They are about 11 to 17 times more viscous than diesel fuel and have low volatility, which means they do not burn completely and form deposits in the fuel injector of diesel engines.

Vegetable oils are **esters** of **propane-1,2,3-triol (glycerol)** and long-chain carboxylic acids, called **fatty acids**.

glycerol   fatty acids   triglyceride

The triglyceride oil molecules can be thought of as having 'tuning fork' structures, with the three long limbs being the fatty acid chains. The oils are viscous as there are relatively strong van der Waals' forces between the long fatty acid limbs of each molecule.

Figure 14.11 The fatty acid chains align themselves so as to allow close packing between the oil molecules, which makes the liquid viscous.

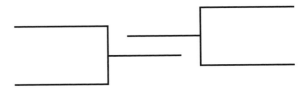

Transesterification with ethanol or methanol produces oils with lower viscosity that can be used in diesel engines

The process used to convert these oils to biodiesel is called **transesterification**, in which the triglyceride oil is reacted with methanol or ethanol to form glycerol and a methyl or ethyl ester with reduced viscosity due to the smaller size of the molecules.

The triglyceride is reacted with the alcohol in the presence of a catalyst, usually a strong base like sodium hydroxide or a strong acid. The ethanol or methanol replaces the glycerol in the oil and forms an ester with the fatty acids, and free glycerol is regenerated.

$$
\underset{\textbf{triglyceride}}{\begin{array}{c} O \\ \| \\ R_2-C-O-CH \\ \text{with } CH_2O-C-R_1 \text{ and } CH_2O-C-R_3 \end{array}}
+ 3\,C_2H_5OH \underset{\text{Catalyst}}{\overset{OH^-}{\rightleftharpoons}}
\underset{\textbf{glycerol}}{\begin{array}{c} CH_2OH \\ | \\ CHOH \\ | \\ CH_2OH \end{array}}
\underset{\textbf{ethyl esters}}{\begin{array}{c} C_2H_5-O-C-R_1 \\ C_2H_5-O-C-R_2 \\ C_2H_5-O-C-R_3 \end{array}}
$$

triglyceride   **ethanol**   **glycerol**   **ethyl esters**

The reaction is reversible, so the alcohol must be added in excess to drive the reaction towards the right, according to Le Chatelier's Principle, to ensure complete conversion. The heavier and more viscous glycerol settles out and may be purified for use in the pharmaceutical, cosmetic, or detergent industries.

The biodiesel produced is less viscous than the original oil as it is made up from smaller molecules which do not pack together so effectively, reducing the van der Waals' intermolecular forces. It is biodegradable, non-toxic, and has significantly fewer emissions when burned than crude oil-based diesel.

The oils used can either be grown specifically for the purpose, or waste oil from other sources which has been treated to remove impurities, such as free fatty acids, can be used. Blends of 20% biodiesel with 80% crude oil diesel can be used in unmodified diesel engines. Biodiesel can be used in its pure form but may require certain engine modifications to avoid maintenance and performance problems.

31 (a) Solar energy has been described as the ultimate energy source. Identify energy sources which derive from photosynthesis and other indirect sources.

   (b) Discuss the advantages and disadvantages of the use of biomass as a fuel.

32 (a) State the chemical equation for the photosynthesis of glucose.

   (b) Identify the molecule needed by plants to photosynthesize.

   (c) Identify the structural feature which allows this molecule to carry out this function.

   (d) Glucose can be converted to ethanol, which can be used as a fuel. State the name and equation of the process and describe the conditions needed.

33 (a) When biomass decomposes in the absence of oxygen, biogas is formed. Name the main gas present in biogas.

   (b) When wood and crop residues are burnt in a limited amount of oxygen, a mixture of gases known as producer gas is formed. Identify the two combustible gases present in producer gas.

   (c) When wood is burnt in an enclosed space the combustion produces harmful pollutants. Identify the pollutants.

   (d) Suggest why biomass is likely to become more important in the future as a fuel.

34 One part of the Earth's surface receives 1.25×10^6 J of solar energy. Green plants such as algae absorb 1.25×10^4 J of this energy.

   (a) Determine the percentage of the Sun's energy absorbed by green plants.

   (b) Suggest two reasons why the remainder of the Sun's energy is not absorbed by green plants.

   (c) Identify the process by which green plants use the Sun's energy to convert water and carbon dioxide into glucose and state the equation for the reaction.

   (d) State two forms of biomass which can be converted into energy.

35 State some of the advantages of using biodiesel.

C.5 Environmental impact: global warming

Understandings:

- Greenhouse gases allow the passage of incoming solar short-wavelength radiation but absorb the longer-wavelength radiation from the Earth. Some of the absorbed radiation is re-radiated back to Earth.

   ### Guidance
   Greenhouse gases to be considered are CH_4, H_2O, and CO_2.

- There is a heterogeneous equilibrium between the concentration of atmospheric carbon dioxide and aqueous carbon dioxide in the oceans.

- Greenhouse gases absorb IR radiation because there is a change in dipole moment as the bonds in the molecule stretch and bend.

- Particulates such as smoke and dust cause global dimming as they reflect sunlight, as do clouds.

Applications and skills:

- Explanation of the molecular mechanisms by which greenhouse gases absorb IR radiation.

- Discussion of the evidence for the relationship between the increased concentration of gases and global warming.

- Discussion of the sources, relative abundance, and effects of different greenhouse gases.

- Discussion of the different approaches to the control of carbon dioxide emissions.

- Discussion of pH changes in the ocean due to increased concentration of carbon dioxide in the atmosphere.

Greenhouse gases absorb the long-wavelength IR radiation from the Earth

The temperature of the Earth is maintained by a steady-state balance between the energy received from the Sun and the energy leaving the Earth and going back into space. Incoming solar radiation is in the visible and ultraviolet region. Some of this radiation is reflected back into space and some is absorbed by gases in the atmosphere. Most of the solar radiation passes through the atmosphere, however, and warms the surface of the Earth. The warm Earth surface then **radiates** some of this energy as **longer wavelength infrared** radiation which is **absorbed** by **greenhouse molecules** such as carbon dioxide and water vapour in the lower atmosphere. A covalent bond is like a spring in that it vibrates at a natural frequency. When infrared radiation has the same frequency as a covalent bond, the molecule absorbs the radiation and the bonds increase their vibrational energy. This makes the air warmer, causing it to radiate heat in turn. Some of this radiation is **re-radiated** back to the Earth's surface and some is re-radiated back into space (Figure 14.12). This natural process is called the **greenhouse effect** because the Sun's energy is absorbed in a way that is similar to the way light energy is trapped by glass in a greenhouse. The glass lets light energy in but does not let heat energy out.

Figure 14.12 The greenhouse effect is a process by which the Earth warms up. The surface of the Earth absorbs some solar radiation and re-radiates some at a longer (infrared, IR) wavelength which can be absorbed and re-radiated by gases such as carbon dioxide in the atmosphere.

some energy reflected back to space

Earth's surface heated by Sun; radiates heat back to space

solar energy passes through atmosphere

atmospheric greenhouse gases trap some of the heat

Greenhouse gases and their sources

The greenhouse effect occurs naturally but there are concerns that human activities may be increasing its effect, leading to **global warming**. Water is the main greenhouse gas owing to its great abundance, but as it is produced from natural processes, its contribution to global warming is generally not considered. The level of carbon dioxide produced from burning fossil fuels has been increasing steadily over the last 150 years. Levels of carbon dioxide have been measured at Mauna Loa in Hawaii since the International Geophysical Year in 1957 (Figure 14.13).

Avoid using journalistic terms such as 'bounce off', 'trapped', or 'reflected' when talking about the greenhouse effect.

The Mauna Loa Observatory monitors all atmospheric constituents that may contribute to climatic change, such as greenhouse gases and aerosols, and those which cause depletion of the ozone layer.

The increase in levels of carbon dioxide can be compared to changes in average global temperatures during the same period (Figure 14.14). It is estimated that carbon dioxide contributes about 50% to global warming.

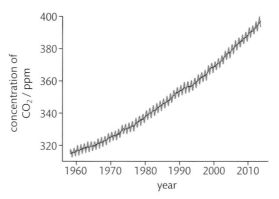

Figure 14.13 Graph showing the rising concentration of atmospheric CO_2 between 1958 and 2012 measured 4170 m up on Mauna Loa, Hawaii. The graph reveals the steady rise of CO_2 levels in the atmosphere each year due to increasing fossil fuel consumption. The regular wobbles reflect seasonal plant growth in the spring and decay in the autumn in the northern hemisphere each year.

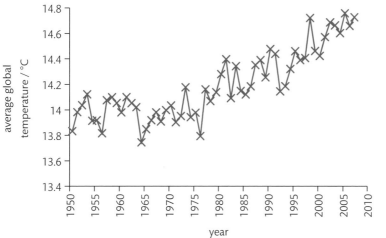

Figure 14.14 Global average temperatures from 1950 to 2007.

Not all gases are equally effective at absorbing infrared radiation. The ability to absorb infrared radiation depends on the change in dipole moment that occurs as a molecule vibrates. Symmetric non-polar diatomic molecules such as N_2 and O_2 are not greenhouse gases as they do not absorb infrared radiation. The ability of a gas to absorb infrared is quantified by what is known as the **greenhouse factor**, which compares the ability of a substance to absorb infrared to carbon dioxide's ability to do so. Ten molecules of water, for example, have the same global warming effect as one molecule of carbon dioxide, while one molecule of methane has the same effect as 30 molecules of carbon dioxide.

Gas	Main source	Greenhouse factor	Relative abundance / %	Overall contribution to increased global warming / %
water (H_2O)	evaporation of oceans and lakes	0.1	0.10	–
carbon dioxide (CO_2)	increased levels owing to combustion of fossil fuels and biomass	1	0.036	50
methane (CH_4)	anaerobic decay of organic matter; increased levels caused by intensive farming	30	0.0017	18
dinitrogen oxide (N_2O)	increased levels due to use of artificial fertilizers, needed for example in increased production of biomass	160	0.0003	6

NATURE OF SCIENCE

The graph below demonstrates the correlation between carbon dioxide levels and temperature through the last glacial cycle. The upper curve shows CO_2 concentration in parts per million while the lower curve is a reconstruction of atmospheric temperature from measurements of the isotope deuterium. Both are plotted against age, measured in thousands of years before the present (BP), with the present at the far left.

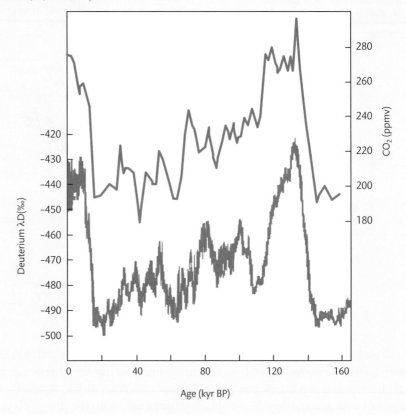

Figure 14.15 The graph showing the correlation between carbon dioxide levels and temperature through the last glacial cycle.

The data are not enough to prove the causal link between CO_2 concentration and temperature. Both changes could be due to changes in a third variable.

The ideas of correlation and cause are very important in science. A correlation is a statistical link or association between one variable and another. A strong correlation (positive or negative) between one factor and another suggests some sort of causal relationship between the two factors but more evidence is usually required before scientists accept the idea of a causal relationship. To establish a causal relationship, scientists need to have a plausible scientific mechanism linking the factors. This has been proposed in the case of the greenhouse effect. Ideally, however, the relationship between the variables needs to be experimentally investigated with all other possible key variables being controlled. This is often impossible; levels of carbon dioxide cannot be added to the environment in such a controlled way and so we need to rely on computer models.

Influence of increasing amounts of greenhouse gases on the atmosphere

There is now little doubt that since the 19th century the amount of carbon dioxide and other anthropogenic greenhouse gases in the atmosphere have increased dramatically and the average temperature of the Earth has also increased, even if rather erratically. It has been suggested that levels of carbon dioxide will double in about 100 years.

Allowing for the effect of all the gases, the temperature of the Earth could rise by 2 °C within 50 years. There are three likely effects resulting from this:

• changes in agriculture such as crop yields;
• changes in biodistribution due to desertification and loss of cold water fish habitats;
• rising sea levels because of thermal expansion and the melting of polar ice caps and glaciers.

There is a heterogeneous equilibrium between atmospheric carbon dioxide and aqueous carbon dioxide in the oceans

About 50% of the carbon dioxide produced by the combustion of fossil fuels is absorbed by plants during photosynthesis or dissolved by the oceans. There is a heterogeneous equilibrium between concentrations of atmospheric carbon dioxide and aqueous carbon dioxide in the oceans.

$$CO_2(g) \rightleftharpoons CO_2(aq)$$

The carbon dioxide reacts with the water to form carbonic acid:

$$CO_2(aq) + H_2O(l) \rightleftharpoons H_2CO_3(aq)$$

The carbonic acid then reacts to form hydogencarbonates or carbonates:

$$H_2CO_3(aq) \rightleftharpoons H^+(aq) + HCO_3^-(aq)$$

$$HCO_3^-(aq) \rightleftharpoons H^+(aq) + CO_3^{2-}(aq)$$

This leads to higher ocean acidity, mainly near the surface, where the carbon dioxide is absorbed. This higher acidity inhibits shell growth in marine animals and is suspected to be a cause of reproductive disorders in some fish.

Since 1850, glaciers have been in retreat worldwide. It is thought that global warming has accelerated this trend in recent years.

Ocean acidification affects shell-forming animals

Over the past 300 million years, oceans have been slightly basic, with pH levels averaging about 8.2. Today, the pH has decreased to around 8.1. This drop of 0.1 represents a 25% increase in acidity. If the levels of carbon dioxide continue to increase, the pH of the oceans could fall further, affecting shell-forming animals such as corals, oysters, shrimp, and lobster.

CHALLENGE YOURSELF

8 Shell formation occurs mainly near the ocean's surface as the water at lower depths is colder and under more pressure. Explain this statement with reference to the relative solubility of calcium carbonate and calcium hydrogencarbonate.

Exercises

36 (a) Suggest why the first measurements of CO_2 levels were taken at Mauna Loa in Hawaii and at the South Pole.
(b) In 1959 the concentration of carbon dioxide was 316 ppm. In 2007 the reading was 384 ppm. Calculate the percentage increase in CO_2 levels between 1959 and 2007.
(c) Identify the major source of the increased CO_2 during this period.
(d) Explain the annual fluctuations in carbon dioxide levels.
(e) Identify two different means by which CO_2 can be removed from the atmosphere naturally and give a balanced equation for both of these.
(f) Suggest how the depletion of tropical forests can lead to an increase in carbon dioxide levels.
(g) Describe how CO_2 interacts with infrared radiation on the molecular level.

37 Carbon dioxide is about 50 times more soluble in water than oxygen and about 100 times more soluble than nitrogen.

(a) Explain the relatively high solubility of carbon dioxide.

(b) Predict the sign of the enthalpy change of solution of carbon dioxide and deduce how its solubility changes with an increase in temperature.

(c) It has been suggested that the high levels of carbon dioxide could lead to a positive feedback process whereby increases in global temperatures are amplified and rise out of control. Suggest a possible mechanism for this positive feedback process.

(d) Suggest how the photosynthesis of phytoplankton could lead to a negative feedback process in which increases in temperature are reduced.

38 The formation of sea shells can be described by the following reaction.

$$Ca^{2+}(aq) + CO_3^{2-}(aq) \rightarrow CaCO_3(s)$$

Explain how the formation of sea shells reduces atmospheric levels of carbon dioxide.

39 Explain how a fall in pH from 8.2 to 8.1 represents a 25% increase in acidity.

Global dimming

As we can see, the pattern in global temperatures is complicated. The fall in temperatures during the 1960s, for example, has been linked to the increase in particulates produced by volcanic activity during this period. Particulates can lower the temperature by scattering light so that less radiation reaches the Earth. This effect is called **global dimming** and first came to scientists' attention when pan evaporation rates were measured in the 1950s: less water than expected was evaporating from a full pan of water, suggesting the amount of solar radiation reaching the Earth was decreasing.

The incomplete combustion coal, oil, and wood produces tiny airborne particles of soot, ash, sulfur compounds, and other pollutants which reflect sunlight back into space, preventing it reaching the Earth's surface. The particles also act as nucleating agents for the formation of water droplets. Polluted clouds are more reflective than unpolluted clouds as they contain more water droplets. It is suggested that global dimming has limited the full effects of the global warming. A reduction in particulate pollution could lead to even larger global temperature increases than initially predicted.

NATURE OF SCIENCE

The factors affecting the temperature of the planet are very complex and interrelated. Scientists make mathematical models to predict the outcome of possible futures. The energy flow for the Earth and atmosphere is complicated, however. Computer simulations that model the climate of the Earth must take all factors into consideration. One concerned group, 'Climate prediction', have been doing calculations on thousands of computers in homes and schools all around the world to gain the power needed to run their computer model.

Three strategies for reducing carbon dioxide levels

There are essentially three strategies for reducing carbon dioxide levels in the atmosphere:

Strategy	Action
increased energy efficiency and conservation	• use of insulation and more efficient appliances • reducing personal energy use by turning off lights and electronics when not in use • reducing distance travelled in vehicles or using more efficient modes of transport such as hybrid cars or public transport

Strategy	Action
reduced dependence on carbon-based energy resources	• use alternative sources such as solar, wind, geothermal, hydropower, wave, tidal, or nuclear power • use reduced-carbon fuels such as natural gas • the potential use of biomass depends on the processes by which it is converted to energy
capture and storage of carbon from fossil fuels or from the atmosphere	• carbon dioxide can be removed from the atmosphere and stored within plants and soil, supporting the plants • alternatively, carbon dioxide can be captured either before or after fossil fuel is burned and then be stored (sequestered) within the Earth • reduce deforestation and plant more trees

NATURE OF SCIENCE

The study of global warming encompasses a broad range of concepts and ideas and is trans-disciplinary. As well as collaborating on the exchange of results, scientists work on a daily basis in collaborative groups on a small and large scale within and between disciplines, laboratories, organizations, and countries, facilitated even more by virtual communication. The IPCC is officially composed of about 2500 scientists. They produce reports summarizing the work of many more scientists from all around the world. Some of their work has been controversial and aroused strong emotions amongst scientists and the public.

Some people question the reality of climate change and question the motives of scientists who have 'exaggerated' the problem. How do we assess the evidence collected and the models used to predict the impact of human activities? What effect does a highly sensitive political context have on objectivity? Can politicians exploit the ambiguity of conclusions coming from the scientific community for their own ends?

The first world climate conference in 1979 recognized the need for action against climate change. The Intergovernmental Panel on Climate Change was set up by the United Nations in 1988. Since then there have been a number of agreements and commitments for action. The 2007 Nobel Peace Prize was awarded to the IPCC and Al Gore (former Vice President of the United States, 1993–2001).

Exercises

40 (a) Carbon dioxide contributes to the greenhouse effect. Identify one natural source of this gas.
   (b) Identify a second carbon-containing greenhouse gas and state its source.
   (c) Identify an air pollutant that counteracts the greenhouse effect and describe how it achieves this.
   (d) Using carbon dioxide as an example, explain how greenhouse gases contribute to global warming.
   (e) Describe the effects of global warming.

41 (a) Describe the greenhouse effect in terms of radiations of different wavelengths.
   (b) Water vapour acts as a greenhouse gas. State the main natural and artificial sources of water vapour in the atmosphere.
   (c) Discuss the relative contributions of carbon dioxide and methane to the greenhouse effect.

42 Particulates are a type of primary air pollutant produced in several industries by the burning of fuels.

   (a) State one type of fuel that is very likely to produce particulates when burned.
   (b) Deduce the equation for a combustion reaction of methane in which particulates are formed.

When describing the greenhouse effect, do not base the whole of your answer only on rising sea levels and their causes. The effects on climate, agriculture, and biodiversity and so on should also be included.

Practice questions

1 It is now widely accepted that the increased production of carbon dioxide is leading to global warming.

   (a) Describe how carbon dioxide acts as a greenhouse gas. (2)
   (b) Discuss the influence of increasing amounts of greenhouse gases on the environment. (3)

   (Total 5 marks)

2 High-level and low-level wastes are two types of radioactive waste. Compare the half-lives and the methods of disposal of the two types of waste. (3)

3 The initial products of the fractional distillation of oil often undergo cracking. State the major reason for catalytic cracking. (2)

4 Compare the processes of nuclear fission and nuclear fusion. (2)

5 The half-life of $^{234}_{92}Ra$ is 1600 years. Determine the length of time taken for 93.75% of the radium to disintegrate. (2)

6 (a) Explain what is meant by 'degraded energy'. (2)

(b) A nuclear power station uses $^{235}_{92}U$ as fuel. Outline how the fuel produces energy. (4)

(c) Explain what is meant by the critical mass of a fissile material. (1)

(Total 7 marks)

7 (a) Most of the world's energy comes from fossil fuels. State two reasons for this. (2)

(b) Define the term 'specific energy'. (1)

(c) Identify a fuel which has a higher specific energy than fossil fuels. (1)

(d) A natural gas power station has an output power of 600×10^6 J s^{-1} and an overall efficiency of 30%. The specific energy density of the fuel is 60×10^3 kJ g^{-1}. Determine the rate of consumption of natural gas in the power station. (3)

(Total 7 marks)

8 (a) Determine the percentage of carbon by mass in the fuels coal (CH), gasoline (C_8H_{18}), and natural gas (CH_4). (1)

(b) Suggest two reasons why coal has been replaced by gasoline and natural gas today as the fuel of choice. (2)

(c) One fuel that has been proposed as a replacement for carbon-containing substances is hydrogen. State two advantages of using hydrogen as a fuel. (2)

(Total 5 marks)

9 The enthalpies of combustion of propane and butane are given in section 13 of the IB data booklet.

(a) Calculate the specific energies of C_3H_8 and C_4H_{10}. (2)

(b) Use the ideal gas equation to calculate the density of the two gases at s.t.p. and hence calculate the energy density of the two gases. (3)

(Total 5 marks)

10 (a) State the name of the process by which green plants capture the Sun's energy and convert carbon dioxide and water into glucose. (1)

(b) Identify a molecule in plants which absorbs sunlight and explain how it is able to carry out this function with reference to its molecular structure. (2)

(c) State the half-equation in which oxygen is oxidized from carbon dioxide to glucose. (1)

(d) State the overall equation for the full redox reaction. (1)

(e) Glucose can be converted into ethanol, which can be used in fuel cells.

    (i) Identify this process by name and write the equation for the chemical reaction. (2)

    (ii) Determine the thermodynamic efficiency of a fuel cell fuelled by ethanol. (3)

(Total 10 marks)

11 Consider the following organic compounds.

- ethanol
- pentane
- hexane
- benzene

(a) Explain the term octane number. (2)

(b) State the order of increasing octane number and explain your choice. (4)

(Total 6 marks)

12 $^{235}_{92}$U decays by alpha decay emitting a helium nucleus.

    (a) Deduce the identity of the decay product. (2)

    (b) Deduce the time it takes for 75% of the sample to decay. (2)

                         (Total 4 marks)

13 (a) Discuss the effects of fossil fuel use on the environment. (3)

    (b) Suggest steps that could be taken to reduce these effects. (6)

    (c) The average cost of gasoline varies dramatically from country to country. Discuss the implications of this for the average carbon footprint. (3)

                        (Total 12 marks)

14 (a) State the name and formula of two compounds present in gasoline. (2)

    (b) Describe and explain the process by which these compounds are obtained from crude oil. (4)

    (c) Describe a method that can be used to increase the yield of gasoline from a given quantity of crude oil that contains $C_{14}H_{30}$. (2)

                        (Total 8 marks)

15 (a) Use section 13 of the IB data booklet to calculate the specific energy of methane and methanol. (2)

    (b) Deduce the average oxidation number of carbon in the two compounds. (1)

    (c) Suggest a possible relationship between the oxidation number and specific energy. (1)

    (d) Calculate the specific energy of glucose and discuss the validity of your hypothesis. (3)

                        (Total 7 marks)

16 Vegetable oils have a similar energy content to diesel fuel.

    (a) Explain why vegetable oils are not used in internal combustion engines. (2)

    (b) Describe the process by which vegetable oils are converted to more useful fuels. (2)

                        (Total 4 marks)

To access weblinks on the topics covered in this chapter, please go to www.pearsonhotlinks.com and enter the ISBN or title of this book.

15

Option D: Medicinal chemistry

Essential ideas

D.1 Medicines and drugs have a variety of different effects on the functioning of the body.

D.2 Natural products with useful medicinal properties can be chemically altered to produce more potent and safe medicines.

D.3 Potent medical drugs prepared by chemical modification of natural products can be addictive and become substances of abuse.

D.4 Excess stomach acid is a common problem that can be alleviated by compounds that increase the stomach pH by neutralizing or reducing its secretion.

D.5 Antiviral medications have recently been developed for some viral infections while others are still being researched.

D.6 The synthesis, isolation and administration of medications can have an effect on the environment.

For thousands of years it has been known that chemicals with medical properties are found in extracts of animal organs, plant tissue, and minerals found in the local environment. In many cultures this knowledge has been passed from generation to generation within communities, and continues to be an important aspect of health management for many people today.

The 20th century saw a major new development in healthcare with the production of synthetic molecules specifically for the treatment of illnesses. Without question, this has been one of the most significant achievements of the last 100 years. The development of targeted drugs and vaccines has meant that smallpox has been eradicated, millions of people have survived infections such as malaria and tuberculosis, and other diseases like polio are on their way to extinction. Untold numbers of people owe their lives to the action of medicines.

But at the same time – and as with many other great innovations – the pharmaceutical industry has brought new challenges.

- Abuses, excesses, and the problem of antibiotic resistance have to be faced.
- Nuclear medicine contributes greatly to diagnosis and therapy especially of cancer, but raises new issues of radiation hazard and disposal.
- The appearance of new diseases such as avian flu highlights the need for the industry to be proactive in developing new drugs – the AIDS pandemic is a reminder of what happens when the spread of an infectious disease is not checked.

Computer model showing the structure of anaesthetic drug molecules on the lower left and right, bound to a protein molecule shown in grey. The protein has five sub-units and acts as an ion channel. The binding of the drug to the surface of the protein inhibits its action, and this helps to induce and maintain general anaesthesia during surgery. Research and development in drug design often focuses on the chemical interactions between drugs and specific receptor target molecules in the body.

Digital composite image showing a biochemist using a virtual reality system to investigate molecular interactions. The large purple ribbon-like molecule is an enzyme of HIV and the blue helical object is half of a section of DNA. This system allows researchers to manipulate computer-generated stereo images of molecules to study their interactions. This is one approach used in structure-based drug design.

In addition, there are huge discrepancies in the availability of drugs in different parts of the world, leading to continued suffering and death from diseases for which effective treatments exist.

In this chapter we study applications of chemistry in drug design, development, and administration by some case-study examples. Note that a knowledge of organic chemistry from Chapter 10 is important to help you interpret this information fully.

D.1 Pharmaceutical products and drug action

Understandings:

- In animal studies, the therapeutic index is the lethal dose of a drug for 50% of the population (LD_{50}) divided by the minimum effective dose for 50% of the population (ED_{50}).
- In humans, the therapeutic index is the toxic dose of a drug for 50% of the population (TD_{50}) divided by the minimum effective dose for 50% of the population (ED_{50}).
- For ethical and economic reasons, animal and human tests of drugs (for LD_{50}/ED_{50} and TD_{50}/ED_{50} respectively) should be kept to a minimum.
- The therapeutic window is the range of dosages between the minimum amount of the drug that produces the desired effect and a medically unacceptable adverse effect.
- Dosage, tolerance, addiction, and side-effects are considerations of drug administration.
- Bioavailability is the fraction of the administered dosage that reaches the target part of the human body.
- The main steps in the development of synthetic drugs include identifying the need and structure, synthesis, yield, and extraction.
- Drug–receptor interactions are based on the structure of the drug and the site of activity.

Applications and skills:

- Discussion of experimental foundations for therapeutic index and therapeutic window through both animal and human studies.
- Discussion of drug administration methods.
- Comparison of how functional groups, polarity, and medicinal administration can affect bioavailability.

Coloured scanning electron micrograph of bacteria, shown in yellow, in the blood alongside red blood cells and a white blood cell. The white blood cell will destroy the bacteria, protecting the body from disease.

The human body has many natural systems of defence

The functioning of the human body involves an incredibly intricate balance of thousands of different reactions occurring simultaneously. The sum of all these processes is known as **metabolism**. Inevitably, this complex system can suffer from many types of defect and breakdown, through injury, through genetically or environmentally caused abnormalities, and through accumulated changes with age. In addition, we are constantly under attack from microorganisms which can enter the body, alter its functioning, and so cause disease.

Happily, the human body is well equipped with equally complex systems of defence and healing processes. Rather like in a battle of war, we describe attacking microorganisms as **invaders** and the body's responses as different **lines of defence**, activated as the invaders penetrate more deeply. Often the responses of the body manifest themselves as symptoms of disease. For example, we may experience fever as the body raises its temperature to fight a bacterial infection. Although these symptoms generally need to be monitored, they are not usually themselves cause for concern.

When considering how best to fight disease, it is essential that we keep the focus on maximizing the effectiveness of the body's natural defence systems. At best, medicines work by supplementing our natural healing processes.

Computer artwork of the inflammatory response. Bacteria, shown in gold, are seen entering the body through a cut in the skin, and the blood capillary beneath the site of entry is releasing white blood cells, shown in purple and green, into the tissue. These cells will destroy the bacteria and activate the immune response.

Medicines and drugs: some terminology

The terms 'medicines' and 'drugs' are sometimes used interchangeably, and sometimes have slightly different meanings in different parts of the world. They are most clearly defined as follows.

- **Drug**: a chemical that affects how the body works. This includes changes for the better *and* for the worse. The term is sometimes associated with substances which are illegal in many countries, such as cocaine, ecstasy, and heroin, but it has a broader meaning.
- **Medicine**: a substance that improves health. Medicines, which may be natural or synthetic, therefore contain beneficial drugs. Synthetic medicines also contain other ingredients, which are non-active but help in the presentation and administration of the drug. The beneficial effect of a medicine is known as its **therapeutic** effect.

The therapeutic effect is the beneficial effect of a medical treatment.

NATURE OF SCIENCE

The placebo effect – the power of suggestion – is a well-documented phenomenon. It occurs when patients gain therapeutic effect from their belief that they have been given a useful drug, even when they have not. Although there is no rigorous explanation for this effect, it is generally accepted that about one-third of a control group taking a placebo show some improvements. This fact is used in double-blind tests in all major clinical trials as discussed on page 569.

To establish a causal link between the placebo and therapeutic effect, scientists need to establish a mechanism. This needs experimental evidence and data which are objective and reproducible. But studies on the placebo effect are fraught with subjectivity and difficulties of interpretation. Other factors could have contributed to the claimed therapeutic effects, such as spontaneous improvement, fluctuation of symptoms, answers of politeness, and patient misjudgement, and these all need to be accounted for by control experiments. Without a scientific explanation, the placebo effect continues to be somewhat controversial.

The word *placebo* is Latin for 'I will please'. The term *nocebo*, Latin for 'I will harm', is sometimes used to describe a condition worsened by a belief that a drug used is harmful. One example is a person dying of fright after being bitten by a non-venomous snake.

Drugs can be administered in different ways

The way a drug is delivered to the patient's body depends on many factors. These include the chemical nature of the drug, the condition of the patient, and the most effective way of getting the drug to the target organ. For example, some chemicals, including proteins such as insulin, are decomposed by the action of the digestive enzymes in the gut, so they cannot be administered as pills, but must instead be injected directly into the blood. Likewise, a patient in a coma might be unable to swallow an ingested pill so the drug must be delivered in another way.

The following methods are all used to administer drugs.

Method of administering drug	Description	Example
oral	taken by mouth	tablets, capsules, pills, liquids
inhalation	vapour breathed in; smoking	medications for respiratory conditions such as asthma; some drugs of abuse such as nicotine and cocaine
skin patches	absorbed directly from the skin into the blood	some hormone treatments, e.g. estrogen, nicotine patches
suppositories	inserted into the rectum	treatment of digestive illnesses and haemorrhoids
eye or ear drops	liquids delivered directly to the opening	treatments of infections of the eye or ear
parenteral: by injection (see Figure 15.1)	intramuscular (into muscle)	many vaccines
	intravenous (into the blood, the fastest method of injection)	local anaesthetics
	subcutaneous (under the skin)	dental injections

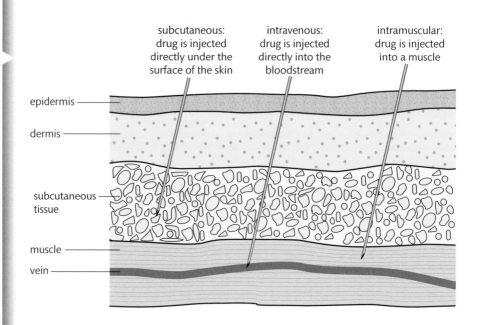

Figure 15.1 Different parenteral methods for the administration of drugs.

Bioavailability of drugs: the amount that reaches the target

Not all of an administered drug reaches its target in the body. This is because the drug may be broken down in metabolic processes or may be incompletely absorbed into the blood. The fraction of an administered drug that reaches the blood supply is known as its **bioavailability**. By this definition, drugs that are administered by intravenous methods have a bioavailability of 100%, so this is used as the basis of comparison.

Bioavailability is the fraction of the administered dosage that reaches the bloodstream.

Bioavailability is an important consideration when considering how much of a drug to administer, known as the **dosage**.

Figure 15.2 shows a typical result of the bioavailability of a drug taken orally, compared with the same amount of the same drug taken intravenously.

Factors that influence bioavailability are discussed below.

Figure 15.2 Bioavailability of a drug when administered orally and intravenously. The absolute bioavailability is calculated from the ratio of the areas under the two curves.

Administration of the drug

The relatively low bioavailability of a drug taken orally, shown in Figure 15.2, is known as the **first-pass effect**, and means that as little as 20–40% of an orally ingested drug may reach the bloodstream. This is because after swallowing, these drugs pass into the digestive system where biological catalysts known as **enzymes** may alter them chemically. Once absorbed from the digestive sytem, they are passed in the blood to the liver where further metabolic breakdown reactions occur.

Other methods of drug administration avoid the first-pass effect as they provide more direct routes into the bloodstream. So in general an oral dose of a drug needs to be about four times higher than the dosage of the same drug administered intravenously. The strong analgesic morphine has a bioavailability of only about 30% when taken orally as the remainder is metabolized by the liver. For more effective pain management, morphine is therefore administered intravenously.

The solubility of the drug

Water solubility is important for circulation in the aqueous solution in the blood, but lipid solubility helps in the passage of the drug through membranes during absorption. Codeine is more lipid soluble than morphine as it is a less polar molecule (as can be seen on page 583), and has a bioavailability of about 90%.

Functional groups in the drug

Functional groups in the drug can also influence bioavailability, particularly acid–base groups. The pK_a and pK_b values of these groups in the molecule will determine the charges carried on the drug at different pH values, and therefore its reactivity and solubility in different parts of the body.

Physiological effects of drugs are complex

Because of the complexity of metabolism, a drug will interact in many different ways and produce more than one physiological effect. The situation is made more complicated by the fact that different individuals respond in different ways to administered drugs. Healthcare providers therefore need to keep several considerations in mind when prescribing drugs and evaluating an individual's reponse to the medication.

Syringe attached to a cannula in a patient's hand to administer the painkilling drug morphine intravenously during surgery.

Side-effects

The overall effects of a drug in the body can be classified as follows:

physiological effects of drug in body

therapeutic effect
the intended
physiological effect

side-effects
unintended
physiological effects

Side-effects are defined as physiological effects which are not intended, and they vary greatly from one drug to another, and with the same drug in different people. Sometimes side-effects may be beneficial, such as the fact that aspirin, taken for pain relief, helps protect against heart disease. Other times the side-effects may be relatively benign, such as causing drowsiness, nausea, or constipation. But of greater concern are side-effects which are much more adverse, such as causing damage to organs. The impact of these side-effects must be evaluated throughout the drug treatment. Patients must also be made aware of the possible side-effects of a drug to help in monitoring the treatment and to make possible adjustments in lifestyle. For example, in some cases this will mean not driving or operating machinery. One of the most dramatic – and tragic – examples of adverse side-effects was the deformities produced in unborn children resulting from the thalidomide drug. This is discussed on page 570.

Tolerance and addiction

When a person is given repeated doses of a drug, **tolerance** can develop, which means a reduced response to the drug. So higher doses are needed to produce the same effect, and this increases the chances of toxic side-effects. The mechanism by which tolerance to a drug develops is not always understood – it could be that the body has become able to metabolize and break down the drug more efficiently, or that the drug receptors in cells become less effective. For some drugs, tolerance develops to one effect of the drug and not to other effects.

A related but different condition is **dependence** or **addiction**. This occurs when a patient becomes dependent on the drug in order to feel normal, and suffers from **withdrawal symptoms** if the drug is not taken. Symptoms can be mild, such as headaches suffered on withdrawal from dependence on caffeine, or serious if the drug is toxic or shows tolerance, such as opiates, alcohol, and barbiturates.

Dosage

The **dosing regime** for a drug refers to the specific quantity of drug to be taken at one time, and the frequency of administration. Calculations of dosage must take bioavailability into account, as well as possible side-effects and potential problems of tolerance and addiction. Determining appropriate dosage is usually quite difficult as there are so many variables involved – for example the age, sex, and weight of the patient, as well as factors such as diet and environment. Interactions with other drugs must also be considered. Ideally the dosage should result in constant levels of the drug in the blood, but this is almost impossible to achieve other than by a continuous, intravenous drip. Other methods of administration will inevitably lead to fluctuations in the blood drug level between doses. The important thing is that the concentration

---

Tolerance occurs when repeated doses of a drug result in smaller physiological effects.

Addiction occurs when the dependency on a drug leads to withdrawal symptoms if it is withheld.

It is possible to experience addiction even to one's own hormones and neurotransmitters (chemicals used for communication). For example, some people are addicted to exercise as this leads to the release of chemicals that can produce a 'high'. Susceptible people are driven to exercise increasingly, and they suffer withdrawal symptoms such as depression if they cannot fulfil this need.

in the bloodstream must remain within a certain range: above this range, unacceptable side-effects may occur, below it there may not be effective therapeutic outcomes. This target range is known as the **therapeutic window**.

The range of concentrations that defines the therapeutic window varies greatly from one drug to the next. For drugs that have a small therapeutic window, drug levels in the blood must be monitored closely to maintain effective dosing without giving a toxic dose.

The therapeutic window can be quantified as the **therapeutic index (TI)**. This is the ratio of the dose that produces toxicity to the dose that produces a clinically effective response in a population. The relevant terms in the equation are:

- The minimum effective dose, ED_{50}, is the dose that produces therapeutic effect in 50% of the population.
- The lethal dose, LD_{50}, is the dose that is lethal to 50% of the population. This is used in animal trials.
- The toxic dose, TD_{50}, is the dose that is toxic to 50% of the population. This is used in human studies.

In animal studies lethal doses are determined; however, in human trials the upper limit is the toxic dose. This means that the therapeutic index is defined differently in the two groups:

- in animals $TI = \dfrac{LD_{50}}{ED_{50}}$

- in humans $TI = \dfrac{TD_{50}}{ED_{50}}$

The therapeutic index is a measure of a drug's safety because a higher value indicates a wide margin between doses that are effective and doses that are toxic. A low therapeutic index means a low margin of safety, where a slight change in the dose may produce an undesirable adverse side-effect.

Some examples of the relative values of the therapeutic index of some common drugs are compared in the table below.

> The therapeutic window is the range of a drug's concentration in the blood between the minimum amount that produces its therapeutic effect and a medically unacceptable adverse effect.

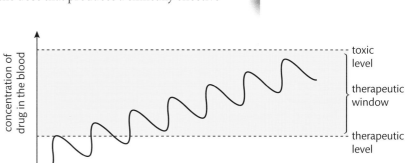

Figure 15.3 The therapeutic window.

Figure 15.4 The therapeutic index is determined from data on the responses of the population to different dosages of the drug.

Drug	Therapeutic effect	Therapeutic index (TI)
penicillin	antibiotic	
morphine	analgesic	
cocaine	stimulant	increasing value of therapeutic index
ethanol	depressant	
warfarin	anticoagulant in blood	

Penicillin has a high therapeutic index, and is therefore quite forgiving in terms of the dose administered. This means it is safe if taken in higher doses than that required for therapeutic effect. On the other hand, warfarin, with a very low therapeutic index, has a low margin of safety and the correct dosage is crucial. The difference in the therapeutic window of these two drugs is shown in Figure 15.5. In general, drugs with a low therapeutic index are those where bioavailability critically alters the therapeutic effects.

Figure 15.5 Therapeutic index of (a) penicillin and (b) warfarin.

Drug action depends on interactions with receptors

The activity of most drugs is determined by their ability to bind to a specific receptor in the body. Receptors are usually proteins, which includes enzymes, chemical structures on cell membranes, or DNA. The binding of the drug prevents or inhibits the normal biological activity, and so interrupts the development of disease. Drug–receptor interactions depend on a 'chemical fit' between the drug and receptor – in general the better the fit, the greater the activity of the drug. The binding of drug and receptor usually involves different types of non-covalent bonding, such as ionic bonds, hydrogen bonds, van der Waals' forces, and hydrophobic interactions.

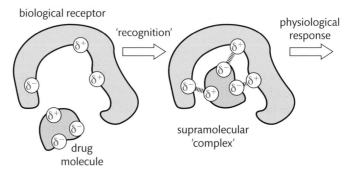

Figure 15.6 A drug often combines with a receptor through hydrogen bonding to form a supramolecular complex.

Understanding drug–receptor interactions has made an important contribution to advances in approaches to drug design.

Supramolecular chemistry refers to the properties of assemblies of two or more molecules held together by intermolecular forces, most importantly hydrogen bonding. It involves molecular recognition by the different components, known as **host–guest** interactions. In addition to its applications in drug design, it is the subject of research for developing chemical sensors to act as a 'chemical nose' and extract specific substances from mixtures such as caffeine from coffee, urea from the blood in kidney machines, and heavy metals from industrial waste.

The development of new synthetic drugs is a long and costly process

Pharmaceutical companies and research groups are constantly developing new drugs, seeking those that are more effective and have fewer toxic side-effects than pre-existing drugs for the same condition. In addition, there is demand for drugs for new conditions such as new viral strains of flu. Every new drug developed represents a major investment of cost, and so the industry is very selective in its focus. Consequently, a large amount of research goes into drugs for conditions such as obesity, depression, cancer, cardiovascular disease, and ulcers, which are prevalent in the developed world where the market can support the cost. Much less attention and fewer resources are given to researching drugs for conditions such as tropical diseases prevalent in the developing world.

 Malaria is a disease that is both curable and preventable. But a child dies of malaria every 10 seconds; more than one million people die of malaria every year. Why do you think this is?

Most countries have stringent controls over the development and licensing of drugs. For every new drug that reaches the market, thousands of candidate molecules fail to meet the criteria and are rejected. The average time for development of a drug from its first identification to the market is about 10–12 years.

Figure 15.7 Stages in the discovery and development of a new medicine.

Knowledge of drug–receptor interactions has revolutionized the process by which new drugs are developed. Most research now focuses on identifying a suitable molecular target in the body and designing a drug to interact with it. This approach, known as **rational drug design**, is very different from the time when pharmaceutical companies worked mostly on a 'trial and error' basis, starting with a natural remedy and trying to improve on nature with no real insight into the mechanism of the action of the drug at the molecular level.

Once a target molecule has been identified, the next step is to find a lead compound – one that shows the desired pharmaceutical activity which will be used as a start for the drug design and development process. (Note: 'lead' here is pronounced to rhyme with 'need', not the element Pb!). Lead compounds are often derived from plants, for example, an anti-cancer agent extracted from yew trees led to the development of Taxol, and digitalis extracted from the foxglove flower led to heart medications. Microorganisms too have provided rich sources of lead compounds, particularly in the development of antibiotics.

The effectiveness of the lead compound is optimized by synthesizing and testing many chemically related compounds known as **analogues**. A process called **combinatorial**

John le Carré's novel *The Constant Gardener* is a fictional tale of drug trials administered by a large pharmaceutical company on AIDS patients in Kenya. It touches on issues such as drug side-effects and synergies, client selection for trials, the drive for profit by the pharmaceutical industry, and the role of government and NGO pharmaceutical watchdogs. Although it is not based on facts of a specific case, it raises some relevant questions and is a good read. It is also available as a movie.

chemistry enables the production and testing of vast numbers of candidate medicines in a very short time. Following extensive laboratory tests, a potential medicine is then tested on animals, under strict legislative control. For ethical and economical reasons, animal and human testing of drugs should be kept to a minimum. Data on the safety and effectiveness of a drug enable researchers to predict the clinical therapeutic index of a drug candidate at an early stage. From this, the value of the therapeutic index for humans and the dose to be administered in human trials are determined.

Figure 15.7 shows that there are usually three phases to the subsequent human trials, involving an increasing number of patients. The effectiveness of the drug is judged by the relative improvement in the patients who had received the real medication as compared with those on placebo in Phase III.

Today many countries maintain post-marketing safety surveillance programmes for all approved drugs, and databases are available detailing adverse drug reactions. This has sometimes led to the withdrawal of a drug from the market after years of usage.

 During the early 1960s the drug thalidomide was marketed, initially in Germany, and prescribed to pregnant women in many countries to help with 'morning sickness' in their early months of pregnancy. Tragically, the drug had devastating effects on the development of the fetus, and up to 12 000 children were born with severe birth defects, most notably missing or malformed limbs, and many more did not survive infancy. By the time the deformities in the newborns were linked with the thalidomide drug, it had been widely marketed in at least 46 countries. This tragedy has led to the addition of further regulatory steps in drug licensing.

 The thalidomide drug was never marketed in the USA because of the intervention of Frances Kelsey, a pharmacologist working at the Food and Drug Administration (FDA). Despite pressure from thalidomide's manufacturer and the fact that it was already approved in over 20 countries, she registered concerns about the drug's ability to cross the placenta into the fetal blood. Her insistence that further tests be carried out was dramatically vindicated when the effects of thalidomide became known. For her insightful work in averting a similar tragedy in the USA she was given a Distinguished Federal Service Award by President Kennedy.

 TOK All drugs carry risks as well as benefits. Who should ultimately be responsible for assessing the risk-to-benefit ratio of a drug in an individual – the pharmaceutical company, a government watch body, the doctor, or the patient?

Close-up of the deformed hand and forearm of a 'thalidomide baby'. Thalidomide is a sedative drug that was administered to many pregnant women in the 1960s. It was withdrawn from the market after it was found to cause serious fetal abnormalities. This tragedy led to major changes in drug testing protocols.

Exercises

1 List the three different ways in which drugs can be injected into the body. Predict, giving a reason, which of the three methods will result in the drug having the most rapid effect.

2 State what is meant by *tolerance* towards a drug and explain why it is potentially dangerous.

3 **(a)** Explain why the therapeutic index is defined differently in animal studies and in humans.
  (b) Outline the factors that must be considered when determining the dosage of a drug.
  (c) Why can it be challenging to determine the dosage of a drug that has a low therapeutic index?

4 Describe three factors that influence the bioavailability of a drug.

Quick reference for functional group identities

In the following sections on different classes of drugs, reference will be made to the functional groups of the molecules which are generally associated with their activity. It is important that you can recognize and identify these groups in different molecules. Some, but not all, of them were introduced in Chapter 10, so a brief summary of the important ones found in drugs is given here. (Note that R and R′ refer to carbon containing or alkyl groups.)

Structure of functional group	Name of functional group	Structure of functional group	Name of functional group
$\text{C}=\text{C}$	alkenyl	$R-N\begin{smallmatrix}H\\H\end{smallmatrix}$	primary amino
$-\text{C}-\text{OH}$	hydroxyl	$R-N\begin{smallmatrix}H\\R'\end{smallmatrix}$	secondary amino
$\text{C}=\text{O}$ (R, R′)	ketone	$R-N\begin{smallmatrix}R''\\R'\end{smallmatrix}$	tertiary amino
(benzene ring with substituent)	arene	$-\text{C}=\text{O}$, $\text{N}-\text{H}$, H	carboxyamide
$-\text{C}\begin{smallmatrix}\text{O}\\\text{OH}\end{smallmatrix}$	carboxylic acid	$-\text{C}\begin{smallmatrix}\text{O}\\\text{O}-R\end{smallmatrix}$	ester
$R-\text{O}-R'$	ether	(six-membered ring with N)	a heterocyclic ring, containing atoms other than C, usually N

> **!** It is easy to confuse *amine* and *amide*. Amines are organic derivatives of ammonia, NH_3. In amides, the N is attached to a carbonyl carbon ($-\text{C}=\text{O}$), so these are derivatives of carboxylic acids. There is no $-\text{C}=\text{O}$ group in amines.

D.2 Aspirin and penicillin

Understandings:

Aspirin
- Mild analgesics function by intercepting the pain stimulus at the source, often by interfering with the production of substances that cause pain, swelling, or fever.
- Aspirin is prepared from salicylic acid.
- Aspirin can be used as an anticoagulant, in prevention of the recurrence of heart attacks and strokes, and as a prophylactic.

Penicillin
- Penicillins are antibiotics produced by fungi.
- A beta-lactam ring is a part of the core structure of penicillins.
- Some antibiotics work by preventing cross-linking of the bacterial cell walls.
- Modifying the side-chain results in penicillins that are more resistant to the penicillinase enzyme.

Applications and skills:

Aspirin

- Description of the use of salicylic acid and its derivatives as mild analgesics.
- Explanation of the synthesis of aspirin from salicylic acid, including yield, purity by recrystallization, and characterization using IR and melting point.
- Discussion of the synergistic effects of aspirin with alcohol.
- Discussion of how aspirin can be chemically modified into a salt to increase its aqueous solubility and how this facilitates its bioavailability.

Penicillin

- Discussion of the effects of chemically modifying the side-chain of penicillins.
- Discussion of the importance of patient compliance and the effects of the over-prescription of penicillin.
- Explanation of the importance of the beta-lactam ring on the action of penicillin.

Guidance

- Students should be aware of the ability of acidic (carboxylic) and basic (amino) groups to form ionic salts, for example soluble aspirin.
- Structures of aspirin and penicillin are available in the data booklet in section 37.

Conceptual artwork of a person suffering from a headache showing inflamed blood vessels and nerves around the brain. Analgesics work in different ways to block the pathway between the source of pain and perception by the brain.

Aspirin: a mild analgesic

Our body's ability to perceive pain is one of our very best defence mechanisms. We act immediately to try to eliminate the source of pain – and so act to reduce further damage to ourselves. Removing our hand from a hot plate, being aware that a sharp object has pierced our skin, or being virtually incapable of moving a broken limb are all examples of our innate abilities to protect ourselves.

But we all know that the sensation of pain is unpleasant – at best. At worst, it can dominate the senses and cause a debilitating effect, especially as many people have medical conditions that result in chronic pain. And so the need exists for painkillers, a class of drugs known as **analgesics**. Note though that pain is a symptom of a bigger problem – an injury or a disease – and therefore long-term relief is dependent on treating the underlying cause.

It is estimated that chronic pain afflicts about 20% of the population of developed countries. Musculoskeletal and joint disorders and neck and back pain accounts for most of this, with headaches, migraines, and cancer accounting for most of the remainder.

perception of pain
site of strong analgesics

pain signal

pain receptors
site of injury
site of mild analgesics
source of pain

Figure 15.8 Pathways of pain in the body. Different types of analgesic have different sites of action.

Pain is detected as a sensation by the brain when nerve messages are sent from various **pain receptors** located around the body. These receptors are themselves stimulated by chemicals known as **prostaglandins**, which are released from cells damaged by thermal, mechanical, or chemical energy. Once released, prostaglandins also mediate the **inflammatory response** by causing the dilation (widening) of blood vessels near the site of injury. In turn this can lead to swelling and increased pain. In addition, prostaglandins have an effect on the temperature regulation of the body that may result in increased temperature known as **fever**.

To be effective, a painkiller must intercept or block this pathway somewhere between the source of pain and the receptors in the brain.

Aspirin and non-steroidal anti-inflammatory drugs (NSAIDs) such as ibuprofen are **mild analgesics**. They act by preventing stimulation of the nerve endings at the site of pain and inhibit the release of prostaglandins from the site of injury. This gives relief to inflammation and fever as well as to pain. Because these analgesics do not interfere with the functioning of the brain, they are also known as **non-narcotics**.

Development of aspirin

From the time of Hippocrates in about 400 BCE it was known that chewing willow bark could give relief to pain and fever. But it was not until the early 1800s that it was demonstrated that the active ingredient in the bark is salicin, which is converted to **salicylic acid** in the body (*salix* is the Latin name for willow). Although salicylic acid proved to be effective in treating pain, it tasted awful and caused the patient to vomit.

In 1890 the Bayer Company in Germany made an ester derivative of salicylic acid, which was more palatable and less irritable to the body, while still effective as an analgesic. It was named **aspirin**, in recognition of the plant spirea which produces a similar compound. Aspirin manufacture began that year, and it became one of the first drugs to enter into common usage. Today it continues to hold its place as the most widely used drug in the world, with an estimated production of over 100 billion standard tablets every year. It is widely used in the treatment of headache, toothache, and sore throat. Also, because it is effective in reducing fever, known as an **antipyretic**, and inflammation, it is used to provide relief from rheumatic pain and arthritis.

The synthesis of aspirin

Salicylic acid, 2-hydroxybenzoic acid, is converted into aspirin through esterification, which is a condensation reaction. The process usually uses ethanoic anhydride, $(CH_3CO)_2O$, and can be represented as follows.

salicylic acid   ethanoic anhydride   aspirin   ethanoic acid

Concentrated sulfuric acid or phosphoric acid is added to the reactants and the mixture is warmed gently. The aspirin product must then be isolated and purified from the mixture.

Mild analgesics block sensation of pain at the source.

TOK It could be argued that whereas mild analgesics seek to eliminate pain at the source, strong analgesics only alter our ability to perceive pain. Do these two approaches depend only on sense perception or also on other ways of knowing?

Figure 15.9 The structure of salicylic acid (2-hydroxybenzoic acid).

The name 'Aspirin' was originally a trademark belonging to the pharmaceutical company Bayer. After Germany lost World War I, Bayer was forced to surrender this trademark (and also the one for 'Heroin') to the UK, France, Russia, and the USA as part of the reparations of the Treaty of Versailles in 1919.

Figure 15.10 The structure of aspirin (2-ethanoyloxybenzene-carboxylic acid or acetylsalicylic acid, ASA).

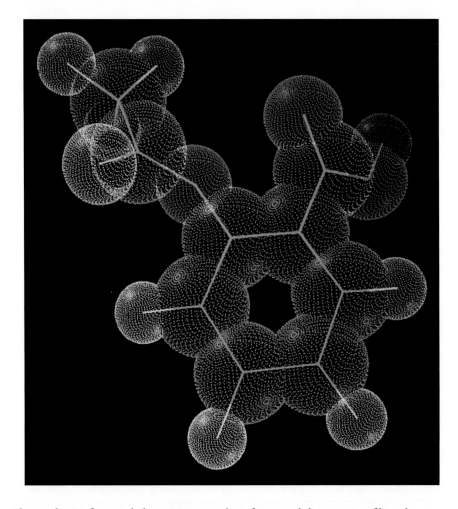

Computer graphic of a molecule of aspirin, 2-ethanoyloxybenzenecarboxylic acid. The carboxylic acid group, −COOH, is shown top right and the ester group, −COOCH₃, top left. The ester group is introduced by reaction of salicylic acid, 2-hydroxybenzoic acid, with ethanoic anhydride in an esterification reaction.

Magnified view through a lens of a melting point determination in a melting point apparatus. The crystals of the sample in the tube are slowly heated electrically until they melt, and the temperature is obtained from a thermometer. Several readings will be averaged and compared with standard literature values to determine the purity of the sample.

The product is first cooled to cause crystals to form, and then suction filtered and washed with chilled water. Aspirin has a very low solubility in water at low temperature, so this process removes the soluble acids while not leading to the loss of the aspirin product.

Purification involves a technique known as **recrystallization**. This involves dissolving the impure crystals in a minimum volume of hot ethanol, which is a better solvent for the impurities than for the aspirin product. A saturated solution of aspirin is formed. As this solution is then cooled *slowly*, the solubility of the aspirin decreases and it crystallizes out of solution first. It can be separated by filtration, as the impurities and unreacted salicylic acid remain in solution.

The purity of the product can be confirmed by **melting point determination**. Pure substances have well-defined melting points which are altered by the presence of impurities. Special apparatus is usually used to carry out this determination and the results are compared with data. Pure aspirin has a melting point of 138–140 °C, and salicylic acid has a melting point of 159 °C. A mixture would have a lower and less well-defined melting point.

The yield can be calculated from the stoichiometry of the reaction, using the mass of salicylic acid used and the mass of product obtained. See Exercise 5 on page 577.

Infrared (IR) spectroscopy can be used in the characterization of aspirin and related molecules. As described in Chapter 11, page 370, the absorption of particular wavenumbers of IR radiation helps to identify the presence of certain functional groups in a molecule. Characteristic IR absorption bands are given in section 26 of the IB data booklet.

The infrared spectra of salicylic acid and aspirin are shown in Figure 15.11.

Figure 15.11 IR spectra of (a) salicylic acid and (b) aspirin.

Comparisons of the spectra reveal similarities and differences between the two molecules. The major similarities in the spectra are:

- strong peaks from 1050 to 1410 cm^{-1} due to C–O in alcohol/ester;
- strong peaks from 1700 to 1750 cm^{-1} due to C=O in carboxylic acid;
- both have broad peaks from 2500 to 3000 cm^{-1} due to OH in carboxylic acid;
- both have peaks from 2850 to 3090 cm^{-1} due to C–H (overlapping the broad –OH peak).

The major differences in the spectra are:

- a second peak from 1700 to 1750 cm^{-1} due to the presence of an ester group in aspirin;
- a peak from 3200 to 3600 cm^{-1} in salicylic acid due to the presence of its –OH group; this peak is not present in the aspirin spectrum.

Physiological effects of aspirin

In 1982 the British chemist John Vane won the Nobel Prize in Medicine for his discovery that aspirin works by blocking the synthesis of prostaglandins. This finding explains the analgesic effects of aspirin, as well as its effectiveness in reducing fever and inflammation, and some of its significant side-effects. The latter can be both positive and negative, as discussed below.

Aspirin is an **anticoagulant**, meaning it reduces the ability of the blood to clot. This makes it useful in the treatment of patients at risk from heart attacks and strokes.

Many people use a low daily dose of aspirin as a prophylactic for this purpose. But this same side-effect means that aspirin is not suitable (and could be potentially dangerous) if taken by a person whose blood does not clot easily, or for use following surgery when blood clotting must be allowed to occur. Recent research has also shown that regular intake of a low dose of aspirin may reduce the risk of colon cancer, although additional data are needed before aspirin is routinely recommended for this use.

Negative side-effects of aspirin include irritation and even ulceration of the stomach and duodenum, possibly leading to bleeding. A large number of people, especially those prone to asthma, are also allergic to aspirin, so it must be used with caution. It is not recommended for children under 12 because its use has been linked to Reye's syndrome, a rare and potentially fatal liver and brain disorder.

The physiological effects of aspirin are more acute when it is taken with ethanol in alcoholic drinks. This effect is known as **synergy**, and means that care must be taken when consuming alcoholic drinks alongside medication. The synergistic effects of ethanol and aspirin can cause increased bleeding of the stomach lining and increased risk of ulcers.

Modification of aspirin for absorption and distribution

Aspirin is available in many formulations, which include various coatings and buffering components. These can delay the activity of the aspirin until it is in the small intestine to help alleviate some of its side-effects.

Aspirin is taken orally and transported in the plasma of the blood in aqueous solution. It has a low solubility in water as it is a largely non-polar molecule. Its bioavailability can be increased by increasing its solubility in water through chemical modification. This involves reacting aspirin with an alkali such as NaOH or $NaHCO_3$, so that it forms an ionic salt.

aspirin is not
very soluble

sodium salt of aspirin
is more soluble
sodium 2-ethanoyloxybenzenecarboxylate

Formulations that contain the salt of the acid are known as **soluble aspirin** or **dispersible aspirin**.

A **prophylactic** refers to a medical treatment that is taken to prevent disease. This is in contrast to drugs which are administered in response to the symptoms of disease.

Drugs which contain an acidic or a basic group can be chemically modified to form an ionic salt which increases their aqueous solubility.

Soluble aspirin is dissolved in water and taken into the body by drinking. The increased aqueous solubility of the drug is the result of converting the carboxylic acid group into an ionic salt.

Exercises

5 **(a)** Aspirin is prepared by reacting salicylic acid with excess ethanoic anhydride. In an experiment, 50.05 g of salicylic acid was converted into 55.45 g of aspirin. What was the percentage yield?

(b) How could you check the purity of your product?

6 Describe how chemical modification of aspirin can increase its bioavailability.

7 **(a)** Aspirin is described as a *mild analgesic* and as an *anticoagulant*. Explain the meaning of these two terms.

(b) Why can it be dangerous to consume alcoholic drinks when taking aspirin medication?

Penicillin: an early antibiotic

The discovery of antibiotics

The first example of a chemical used to kill pathogens came from the observation that certain dyes used in the dyestuffs industry were able to kill some microorganisms. It led in 1891 to the treatment of malaria using methylene blue. Paul Ehrlich of Berlin (page 582) introduced the concept of a 'magic bullet', a chemical designed to target a specific disease but not touch the host cells, and successfully treated syphilis patients with an arsenical drug. Systematic screening for other potential antimicrobials led to the discovery of the sulfonamide drugs, such as Prontosil® in 1933, with their seemingly miraculous ability to cure septicaemia. By 1940, the use of sulfonamides had dramatically reduced the number of deaths of mothers in childbirth.

However, it was the discovery of the chemicals known as **penicillins** that truly revolutionized modern medicine, as this gave birth to drugs now known as **antibiotics**. These are chemicals, usually produced by microorganisms, which have action against other microorganisms. Their discovery is generally credited to Alexander Fleming, who was a Scottish microbiologist, working in 1928 on bacteria cultures. He noticed that a fungus (or mould) known as *Penicillium notatum* had contaminated some of his cultures, and was therefore about to discard them as spoiled. However, his eye was drawn to the fact that the mould had generated a clear region around it where no bacterial colonies were growing. He concluded that something produced by the mould was specifically inhibiting the bacterial growth. Fleming published his findings, but as he and his collaborators were not chemists, they did not pursue the work of isolating and identifying the active ingredient.

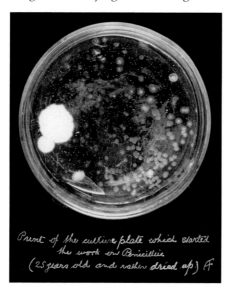

NATURE OF SCIENCE

The aspirin story started with anecdotal evidence that extracts from willow tree bark gave relief from pain. From this, scientists progressed to isolate the active ingredient, and later to modify its structure and demonstrate a mechanism for its action. The discovery, synthesis, and development of aspirin at all stages shows the importance of observations and the replication of data.

Fleming's original culture plate of the fungus *Penicillium notatum*, photographed 25 years after the discovery in 1928. The clear region around the fungus where bacterial growth is inhibited can be clearly seen.

During World War II, when penicillin supply could not meet demand, it was a common practice to collect the urine from patients being treated to isolate and reuse the penicillin it contained. It was estimated that as much as 80% of early penicillin formulations was lost from the body in the urine.

Dorothy Hodgkin (1910–1994), the British X-ray crystallographer who discovered the structures of penicillin, vitamin B12, and insulin. She was awarded the Nobel Prize in Chemistry in 1964.

NATURE OF SCIENCE

The story of Fleming's discovery of penicillin is often described as serendipitous – a fortunate discovery made by chance or by accident. But it was more than that. Would not the majority of people who noticed the plates were contaminated simply have thrown them away, likely disappointed at the 'failed experiment'? The difference was that Fleming had the insight to observe the plates carefully and ask the right questions about why a clear ring appeared around the fungal growth. Scientists are trained to be observant and to seek explanations for what they see, and this must include the unexpected. As Louis Pasteur once famously said, 'Chance favours only the prepared mind'. Consider to what extent scientific discoveries are only possible to scientists who are trained in the principles of observation and interpretation.

In the early 1940s, the Australian bacteriologist Howard Florey and German-born biochemist Ernst Chain, working in Oxford, England, picked up the research and successfully isolated penicillin as the antibacterial agent produced by the penicillium mould. It was used for the first time in human trials in 1941 – in the midst of World War II when there was an unprecedented demand for such a treatment for bacterial infections resulting from war wounds. Its rapid development and distribution is known to have saved thousands of lives in the later years of the war. For their work in discovering penicillin, Fleming, Florey, and Chain shared the Nobel Prize in Medicine in 1945.

The main research and production of penicillin was moved to the USA in 1941 to protect it from the bombs attacking Britain during the war. Large-scale production methods were developed using deep fermentation tanks containing corn steep liquor with sterile air being forced through.

The action of penicillin

The isolation and development of penicillin occurred, however, before there was any understanding of its chemical structure or its mode of action. It was the work of British biochemist Dorothy Hodgkin in 1945 using X-ray crystallography that determined the structure of **penicillin G**, the major constituent of the mould extract.

The structure of penicillin can be considered as a dipeptide formed from two amino acids, cysteine and valine. The molecule contains a nucleus of a five-membered ring containing a sulfur atom known as thiazolidine, attached to a four-membered ring containing a cyclic amide group, known as **beta-lactam**. This ring consists of one nitrogen and three carbon atoms, and is the part of the molecule responsible for its antibacterial properties.

Figure 15.12 Structure of penicillin, showing its beta-lactam ring in red. The R group varies in different penicillins but activity of the drug depends on the intact ring.

cysteine   valine   penicillin

This structure is highly unusual as beta-lactam rings were unknown before the discovery of penicillin. The bond angles in this ring are reduced to about 90°, despite the fact that the atoms in the ring seek to form bonds with angles of 120° and 109.5°

respectively. This puts a strain on the bonds, effectively weakening them. Consequently the ring breaks relatively easily, and this is the key to the molecule's biological activity.

The action of these beta-lactam antibiotics is to disrupt the formation of cell walls of bacteria by inhibiting a key bacterial enzyme, **transpeptidase**. As the drug approaches the enzyme, the high reactivity of the amide group in the ring causes it to bind irreversibly near the active site of the enzyme as the ring breaks. Inactivation of the enzyme in this way blocks the process of cell wall construction within the bacterium because it prevents polypeptide cross-links from forming between the mucopeptide chains. Without these strengthening links, the cell wall is unable to support the bacterium, and so it bursts and dies.

Penicillin's action is effective against a wide range of bacteria, many of which are responsible for infections of the ear, nose, throat, and mouth as well as sites of infection from wounds.

enzyme
transpeptidase (E)

enzyme trapped
and deactivated

Figure 15.13 The action of penicillin. By means of its highly reactive beta-lactam ring, the antibiotic binds and deactivates the transpeptidase enzyme. This leads to a halting of bacterial cell wall construction causing bacterial death.

Bacterial cell walls are chemically quite distinct from cell walls in plants and cell membranes in plants and animals. The polypeptide chains used to build the cross-links to strengthen the bacterial cell wall contain the amino acid d-alanine. Only its optical isomer, l-alanine, is found in humans. So penicillin selectively targets bacteria and is generally not toxic to animals.

Coloured scanning electron micrograph of *Penicillium* sp. growing on bread. This is the mould that is used to produce the antibiotic penicillin.

A disadvantage of penicillin G is that it is broken down by stomach acid, and so has to be injected directly into the blood. Different forms of penicillin have been developed by modifying the side chain (the part denoted as 'R' in Figures 15.12 and 15.13), and these enable the drug to retain its activity even when ingested in pill form. The use of penicillin is limited by the significant number of people who suffer from allergic responses to it.

Ring strain in the beta-lactam ring is responsible for the activity of penicillins.

Antibiotic resistance: bacteria fight back

Confirmation that the beta-lactam ring is crucial to penicillin's antibacterial action comes from studies that show the drug loses all activity when this ring is broken. This is what happens in the presence of some bacteria which show **antibacterial resistance**.

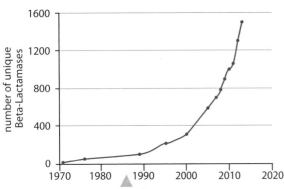

Figure 15.14 A graph showing the rapid increase in the number of different β-lactamase enzymes identified since 1970.

Bacterial resistance to penicillin – and also to other antibiotics – has become a major problem in modern medicine. This was observed as early as the 1940s when penicillin proved to be ineffective against some populations of bacteria. It is now known that these resistant bacteria produce an enzyme, **penicillinase** or **beta-lactamase**, which can open penicillin's four-membered ring and render it inactive. The spread of these resistant bacteria in a population is increased by exposure to the antibiotic, as this wipes out the non-resistant strains and so gives the resistant forms a competitive advantage.

Responses to the challenge of antibiotic resistance to penicillin include the following.

• The synthesis of different forms of penicillin which are able to withstand the action of penicillinase. These include methicillin, which has now largely been replaced by oxacillin, due to the spread of methicillin-resistant bacteria.

Figure 15.15 The structures of (a) methicillin and (b) oxacillin. Both drugs are made by modifying the side chains in penicillin (denoted by R in Figures 15.12 and 15.13, and shown in green here). These modifications make the drug resistant to the penicillinase enzyme.

• These two penicillin derivatives still have the beta-lactam ring, but have modified side-chains which prevent the binding of the penicillinase enzyme, and so protect the ring from cleavage before it finds its target.

• The control and restriction of the use of antibiotics by legislation to make them prescription-only drugs. In addition, doctors are encourged not to over-prescribe antibiotics when other treatments can be effective.

• The education of patients in the importance of completing the full course of treatment with an antibiotic, referred to as 'patient compliance'. This is essential to prevent resistant bacteria prolonging the disease or spreading into the community.

The problems of antibiotic-resistant bacteria are discussed further on page 606.

Exercises

8 (a) With reference to the structure given in section 37 of the IB data booklet, determine the molecular formula of penicillin.

(b) Mark on the molecule where the side chain can be modified and explain why this is done.

(c) Refer to the part of the molecule responsible for its antibiotic properties, and explain the basis of its mode of action.

9 Discuss three ways in which human activities have caused an increase in the resistance to penicillin in bacteria populations.

Understandings:

- The ability of a drug to cross the blood–brain barrier depends on its chemical structure and solubility in water and lipids.
- Opiates are natural narcotic analgesics that are derived from the opium poppy.
- Morphine and codeine are used as strong analgesics. Strong analgesics work by temporarily bonding to receptor sites in the brain, preventing the transmission of pain impulses without depressing the central nervous system.
- Medical use and addictive properties of opiate compounds are related to the presence of opioid receptors in the brain.

Applications and skills:

- Explanation of the synthesis of codeine and diamorphine from morphine.
- Description and explanation of the use of strong analgesics.
- Comparison of the structures of morphine, codeine, and diamorphine (heroin).
- Discussion of the advantages and disadvantages of using morphine and its derivatives as strong analgesics.
- Discussion of side-effects and addiction to opiate compounds.
- Explanation of the increased potency of diamorphine compared to morphine based on their chemical structure and solubility.

Guidance
Structures of morphine, codeine, and diamorphine can be found in the data booklet in section 37.

The opiates bind to receptor sites in the brain

We have seen that aspirin acts as a mild analgesic. A completely different group of compounds, the **opiates** (also known as **opioids**), act as **strong analgesics**. This means that they kill pain by preventing the transmission of pain impulses in the brain, rather than at the source (see Figure 15.8 on page 572).

Opiates are natural analgesics that are derived from **opium**, which is found in poppy seeds. The first records of cultivation of the opium poppy go back to Mesopotamia more than 5000 years ago. This crop has had a very long, complex, and bloody history. It seems likely that no chemical product ever has been responsible for more wars, economic fortunes, and legislative changes, and this is still the case today.

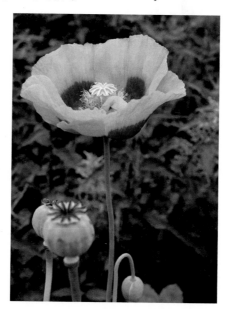

Flower and seed head of *Papaver somniferum*, the opium poppy.

The analgesic properties of the opiates arise because we possess so-called **opioid receptors** in the brain to which they bind temporarily. This binding blocks the transmission of impulses between brain cells that would signal pain. In other words, strong anlgesics interfere with the *perception* of pain without depressing the central nervous system.

581

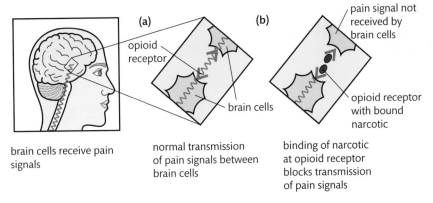

Figure 15.16 The action of strong analgesics is to bind at opioid receptors in the brain cells and so block the transmission of pain signals.

(a)

opioid receptor

brain cells

brain cells receive pain signals

normal transmission of pain signals between brain cells

(b)

pain signal not received by brain cells

opioid receptor with bound narcotic

binding of narcotic at opioid receptor blocks transmission of pain signals

Because these analgesics act on the brain, they may cause possible changes in behaviour and mood, so they are also known as **narcotics**. Opioids are the most effective painkillers for severe pain, but due to their side-effects and potential problems with dependence, their usage must be monitored through medical supervision.

Strong analgesics must enter the brain

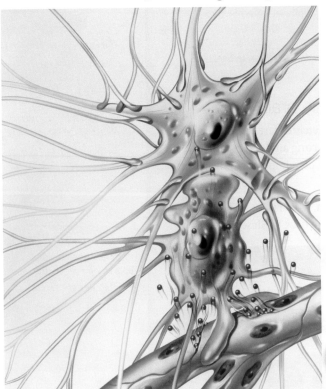

Illustration of the transmission of a drug from a blood capillary into a nerve cell of the brain. Small molecules which leave the blood, shown as blue spheres, have to pass through the cell shown in orange which supports and selectively screens molecules from the nerve cell of the brain, shown in green. This blood–brain barrier stops harmful molecules from reaching the brain. Molecules which are more non-polar such as heroin are able to cross this barrier more easily.

The target for the opiates is the brain. This presents a challenge as the brain is surrounded by a membrane-bound structure, known as the **blood–brain barrier**, which protects it by restricting the chemicals that can enter from the blood. Like all membranes, this structure is made largely of lipids which are non-polar molecules. The blood–brain barrier is therefore a hydrophobic, non-polar environment, not easily crossed by polar molecules. For a drug to penetrate this barrier and enter the brain, it will be more effective when it itself is non-polar and lipid-soluble.

The analgesic properties of the opiates depend largely on their ability to move from the blood, where aqueous solubility is important, into the brain where lipid solubility is important to cross the barrier. The solubilities of the drugs are determined by their chemical structure.

The blood–brain barrier was first discovered by the German scientist Paul Ehrlich in the late 19th century, when he observed that a blue dye introduced into the blood of an animal coloured all its organs blue except the brain. Later experiments involved injecting the dye into the spinal fluid, when it was found that the brain became dyed but the rest of the body did not. This tight control over the movement of substances between fluids in the brain and blood vessels helps to protect the brain. But one of the challenges in treating brain diseases such as tumours involves outwitting this natural defence of the brain so that it will allow therapeutic chemicals to enter.

The structures and synthesis of opiods

The narcotic drugs derived from opium are primarily morphine and its derivatives.

We will consider three of these here: **codeine**, **morphine**, and **diamorphine** (known as **heroin**).

The structure and effects of these drugs are compared in the table below.

	Codeine	Morphine	Diamorphine (heroin)
Structure			
Functional groups	• arene • ether (2) • alkenyl • hydroxyl (1) • tertiary amino	• arene • ether • alkenyl • hydroxyl (2) • tertiary amino	• arene • ether • alkenyl • ester (ethanoate) (2) • tertiary amino
Obtained from	raw opium (0.5%) usually prepared from morphine	raw opium (10%)	found in opium, but usually obtained by reaction of morphine
Therapeutic uses	• sometimes used in a preparation with a non-narcotic drug such as aspirin or paracetamol in the second stage of the pain management ladder • also used in cough medications and in the short-term treatment of diarrhoea	• used in the management of severe pain, such as in advanced cancer • can be habit forming and can lead to dependence, so use must be regulated by a medical professional	• used medically only in a few countries legally for the relief of severe pain • the most rapidly acting and the most abused narcotic • initially produces euphoric effects, but very high potential for causing addiction and increasing tolerance • dependence leads to withdrawal symptoms and many associated problems

Notice that these three drugs have a common basic structure that accounts for their similar properties, as well as some different functional groups. Morphine is the principal drug derived from opium. When administered through intravenous injection it has about six times the bioavailability as when taken orally. The two –OH groups in morphine give it some polarity which limits its ability to cross the blood–brain barrier.

Codeine is found at low levels in opium but is more commonly prepared from morphine. It is therefore known as a **semi-synthetic** drug. The reaction converts one of the –OH groups into the methyl ether, so is known as methylation. This change makes codeine a less polar molecule than morphine and so it can cross the blood–brain barrier more easily. However, the conversion also causes a significant drop in the binding at the opioid receptors, which makes codeine a weaker analgesic than morphine.

The process used in the methylation of morphine to form codeine has evolved over time. The reaction was first carried out in 1881 by reacting morphine with methyl iodide (CH_3I) in alkaline solution:

morphine + CH_3I + KOH Æ codeine + KI + H_2O

But the reaction is inhibited by the water released. Later methods involve the use of methylbenzene ($C_6H_5CH_3$) which acts to remove water from the reaction mixture by distillation.

Diamorphine (heroin) is produced from morphine by an esterification reaction in which both –OH groups are converted into ethanoate (ester) groups by reaction with ethanoic acid (CH_3COOH) or ethanoic anhydride ($(CH_3CO)_2O$). This reduces the polarity significantly, making diamorphine much more lipid soluble than morphine and so more able to cross the blood–brain barrier. This is why it is faster acting than the other opioid drugs.

The synthesis of codeine and diamorphine from morphine is summarized below.

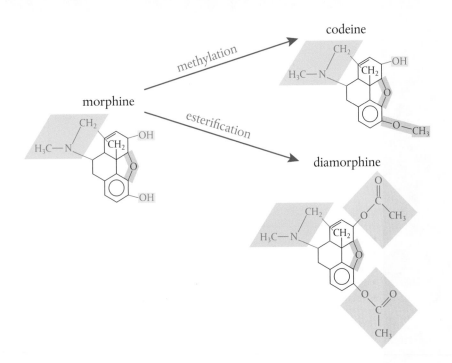

As a result of their structures and solubilities, these three drugs differ in their effectiveness as follows:

- codeine: increasing strength as analgesic
- morphine: increasing narcotic effects
- diamorphine: increasing side-effects

So diamorphine has a much greater potency than morphine, reaching the brain cells faster and in higher concentration. It is more active by a factor of two. Note that this also applies to its greater side-effects as well as to its characteristics of tolerance and dependence. Inside the brain diamorphine must undergo metabolic change before it can act at the opioid receptors. The ester links are broken by enzymes called **esterases**. For this reason diamorphine is described as a **pro-drug**, meaning that its metabolic products, mostly morphine, actually bring about its effects. The molecular structure of diamorphine can be thought of as a way of 'packaging' the morphine so that it can reach its target more efficiently.

Another derivative of morphine known as 6-acetylmorphine, which contains the ester link at only one of the positions, is even more potent than heroin as it does not need to undergo this hydrolysis reaction before interacting with the brain cells. It is produced as a metabolite from heroin in the body, but due to its high activity it is an extremely dangerous drug when taken in pure form.

Morphine is a chiral molecule, which means it can exist as two so-called optical isomers which differ from each other in the spatial arrangements of their atoms. It exists naturally as a single isomer (–). When it was first synthesized it was made as a mixture of the two isomers. When these were separated and tested, it was found that the (+) form, which does not occur in nature, has no analgesic activity.

The so-called opium wars involving China, Britain, France, and India in the late 19th century erupted from trade disputes involving opium. They ended in the imposition of several treaties by western countries on China, including the yielding of Hong Kong to Britain, which ended in 1997. Opium production continues to be a major, if illegal, crop, particularly in South West Asia. Afghanistan produces most of the world's opiates, and increasingly is processing more of the crop into heroin within the country. According to a United Nations (UN) report in 2013, the cultivation of opium has beeen steadily increasing in Afghanistan, despite eradication attempts and UN-backed incentive programmes to reduce production.

NATURE OF SCIENCE

The analgesic action of opium derivatives has been known for hundreds of years, well in advance of an understanding of their effects. Morphine was first isolated in 1803, and was administered during the American Civil War in the 1860s. As there was little useful information available on dosage, side-effects, and dependence, its use caused the deaths and addiction of many soldiers. Diamorphine went on the market in 1898, marketed as 'heroin' because it was believed to be the 'heroic' drug that would banish pain forever. It had to be withdrawn from general distribution 5 years later when its addictive properties became evident. Over time, this 'hit and miss' approach to pain management has evolved into official protocols with clear guidelines. This has been possible because data on the action of opiates have been widely collected and shared, so that their uses and potential problems have been more fully evaluated. Data collection and analysis of trends and causal links is an ongoing aspect of medical science.

Advantages and disadvantages of using strong analgesics

Pain management

The World Health Organization (WHO) has developed a three-step 'analgesic ladder' to be a simple guideline to encourage better global standards of pain management:

1   use mild analgesics;
2   add a weak opioid such as codeine or tramadol;
3   in severe intractable pain, use strong opioids such as morphine, methadone, or possibly diamorphine.

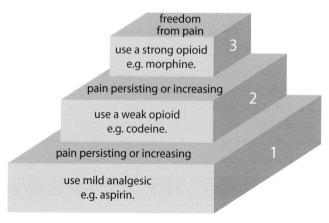

In step 3, cases of severe pain, intravenous morphine is the most widely used analgesic. In some places, notably the UK and a few European countries, diamorphine (heroin) is available as a legally prescribed, controlled drug.

TOK A UN source states that farmers can earn as much as $203 per kg for harvested opium, while only 43 c per kg for wheat or $1.25 per kg for rice. Do national and international counter-narcotics programmes have responsibilities to these farmers? Would it be more ethical for these agencies to buy rather than burn the opium crops?

Despite the fact that cost-effective methods of pain control exist, they are not widely used everywhere. There are cultural, societal, political, and economic factors that influence the availability of painkillers globally. Recognizing this as a deep problem, coalitions of doctors in many countries are pushing towards the goal of making access to pain management a universal human right.

Figure 15.17 The WHO three-step analgesic ladder.

Side-effects

Strong analgesics have several other effects that can sometimes be used for therapeutic purposes, but sometimes are considered adverse side-effects. They include:

- constipation;
- suppression of the cough reflex;
- constriction of the pupil in the eye;
- narcotic effects, which are discussed below.

The constipating effects of mild opioids are sometimes used in medication. A mixture of kaolin and morphine is used to treat cases of diarrhoea, as the morphine reduces the muscle contractions in the lower gut and so slows down the passage of faecal matter. It is not used as a painkiller in this context.

Heroin user slumped after injecting himself with diamorphine. The tourniquet around his arm is used to make the veins stand out to ease injection. Heroin, a strong analgesic, is a highly addictive drug with powerful narcotic effects.

Narcotic effects and addiction

The word 'narcotic' is derived from a Greek word meaning numbness or stupor. Narcotics depress brain function, induce sleep, and are potentially addictive. Diamorphine is the most potent narcotic, causing the problem of heroin addiction.

In the short term, heroin induces a feeling of well-being and contentment, as it causes a dulling of pain and a lessening of fear and tension. There is often a feeling of euphoria in the initial stages after intake. But relatively quickly, heroin users start to show dependence, so they cannot function properly without the drug and suffer from withdrawal symptoms such as cold sweats and anxiety when it is withheld. This is compounded by an increasing tolerance to the drug, so higher doses are needed to bring about relief. In most countries access to the drug usually involves dealing in an illegal market, and the cost of the supply is often beyond the individual's means. This in turn may lead to crime and other social problems. As the drug is taken by injection, the user commonly picks up infections such as HIV and hepatitis from unclean needles. In short, the life of the heroin addict is usually profoundly altered by the drug.

Helping heroin addicts to break their dependence is a slow and difficult process. Sometimes an alternate analgesic, **methadone**, is administered. Methadone is taken orally and has a longer duration of action. This can reduce drug craving and prevent symptoms of withdrawal. Although its use is controversial in some countries, research has shown that methadone maintenance is an effective treatment for opioid dependence and has substantially reduced the death rates of addicts receiving it.

TOK

Laws often exist to protect people from things that can do them harm – such as making it compulsory to wear a seat belt in a car or banning certain chemical substances. Some argue that these laws impinge on personal rights and freedoms; others argue that they validate the rights to safety of society at large. To what extent do you think these points of view are in opposition with each other?

Exercises

10 Codeine, morphine, and heroin are described as strong analgesics.

    (a) State two functional groups common to codeine, morphine, and heroin.

    (b) A patient has been prescribed morphine following surgery. State the main effect and a major side-effect she will experience.

11 By reference to its chemical structure, explain why diamorphine is more potent in its action as a strong analgesic than morphine.

12 The medical use of diamorphine is allowed only in some countries. Give arguments in favour and against its legal controlled use.

D.4 pH regulation of the stomach

Understandings:

- Non-specific reactions, such as the use of antacids, are those that work to reduce the excess stomach acid.
- Active metabolites are the active forms of a drug after it has been processed by the body.

Applications and skills:

- Explanation of how excess acidity in the stomach can be reduced by the use of different bases.
- Construction and balancing of equations for neutralization reactions and the stoichiometric application of these equations.
- Solving buffer problems using the Henderson–Hasselbalch equation.
- Explanation of how compounds such as ranitidine (Zantac) can be used to inhibit stomach acid production.
- Explanation of how compounds like omeprazole (Prilosec) and esomeprazole (Nexium) can be used to suppress acid secretion in the stomach.

Guidance

- *Antacid compounds should include calcium hydroxide, magnesium hydroxide, aluminium hydroxide, sodium carbonate, and sodium bicarbonate (sodium hydrogencarbonate).*
- *Structures for ranitidine, omeprazole, and esomeprazole can be found in the data booklet in section 37.*

Excess acidity in the stomach is potentially harmful

The body keeps a tight control over the pH in cells and extra-cellular fluids, as changes in the H^+ concentration have significant effects on the activity of many molecules, especially enzymes. The gastro-intestinal tract, or **gut**, generates and maintains different pH environments along its length, which play an important role in controlling the activity of digestive enzymes.

The stomach is unusual in that it generates a pH as low as 1–2 by the production of hydrochloric acid, HCl. The acid is released from specialized cells called **parietal cells** in gastric glands in the lining of the stomach wall.

The acid environment not only kills bacteria that may have been ingested with food, but also provides the optimum environment for the action of its digestive enzymes. However, some factors, such as excess alcohol, smoking, caffeine, stress, and some anti-inflammatory drugs, can cause excess production of this acidic secretion, known as **gastric juice**. This can lead to the following problems:

- acid indigestion – feeling of discomfort from too much acid in the stomach;
- heartburn – acid from the stomach rising into the oesophagus (often called acid reflux);
- ulcer – damage to the lining of the gut wall, resulting in loss of tissue and inflammation.

The term **dyspepsia** is used to refer to feelings of pain and discomfort in the upper abdomen, which include indigestion and heartburn.

Illustration of a raft of foaming antacid on top of the contents of a human stomach. Heartburn is caused by a rising of the stomach's acidic contents into the oesophagus, shown in the upper centre, causing inflammation and a sense of pain. Antacids neutralize the acid to bring relief.

Ulcers can occur in different regions of the gut, and there are distinct differences in the relative frequency of occurrence of the different types of ulcer. For example, in the British population duodenal ulcers are more common, whereas in Japan gastric ulcers predominate. The reasons for the different occurrences are probably based on diet, but there are other possible causes, including genetics.

NATURE OF SCIENCE

The study of dyspepsia provides a good example of what scientists call *cause and effect*. Excess stomach acid (cause) brings about the symptoms of indigestion and heartburn (effect). The relationship is known as a causal relationship because a mechanism exists to explain the link between the variables. (This is different from a correlation, which is a mutual relationship between two variables that lacks a linking mechanism. For example, in the last 50 years there has been an increase in both atmospheric CO_2 and in obesity – but there is no mechanism to suggest that obesity is the *cause* of this atmospheric change. Correlation does not always imply causation.)

Understanding the cause and effect relationship of excess stomach acid and dyspepsia leads to two different approaches to the treatment:

1 reduce or remove the cause

2 ameliorate the effects.

False-colour double contrast X-ray showing a duodenal ulcer as the oval pink feature in the upper centre-right. Ulcers can cause severe pain. Healing is promoted by antibiotics and by drugs that block the secretion of acid.

Some drugs work to prevent the production of excess acid

In the early 1980s, a surprising discovery was made. Researchers in Australia identified a bacterium, known as *Helicobacter pylori*, that was shown to be a cause of stomach ulcers and linked to the risk of developing stomach cancer. The *Helicobacter* burrows into the mucus lining of the stomach, causing inflammation. This leads to loss of mechanisms that protect the stomach wall from its hostile acidic contents, and so tissue breakdown occurs. Conditions such as chronic inflammation and ulcers were not previously thought to be related to microorganisms, and so the discovery of *Helicobacter* led to significant changes in treatment regimens. Antibiotics are now frequently prescribed for these conditions, and used in combination with the drugs that reduce acid secretion (described below).

The presence of *Helicobacter* in the stomach can be tested using a breathalyser. The patient is given a drink containing urea which has been labelled with non-radioactive carbon-13. If present, the bacteria will break down the urea, causing the release of carbon-13 labelled CO_2 in the breath.

H$_2$-receptor antagonists

The body is equipped with complex mechanisms to protect it from the self-harm that could result from uncontrolled release of stomach acid. Together these mechanisms ensure that gastric juice is released only when required – stimulated by the presence of food and distension (stretching) of the stomach walls. Several transmitters and chemical messengers called hormones are involved, and of these **histamine** is of specific interest.

Histamine has the structure shown in Figure 15.18.

Figure 15.18 The structure of histamine, a chemical transmitter in the body that stimulates stomach acid production by binding at H$_2$ receptors.

Histamine has different functions in the body and several different receptor sites. In the stomach it stimulates secretion of stomach acid by interacting at receptors known as H_2 (not to be confused with hydrogen gas!) in the parietal cells in the gastric glands. This histamine interaction initiates a sequence of events, leading to the release of acid into the stomach lumen. This suggests that a possible target for a drug which will reduce stomach acid secretion would be to block the histamine–H_2 interaction. Drugs which do this and which compete with histamine for binding at the H_2 receptors are known as **H_2-receptor antagonists**.

Ranitidine (Zantac) is an example of an H_2-receptor antagonist drug. It was developed from analogues of histamine using knowledge of the H_2-receptor structure, and refined from earlier drugs to increase its potency. In many countries it is available as an over-the-counter drug, but higher dosages need prescription.

Figure 15.19 The structure of ranitidine (Zantac), an H_2-antagonist that inhibits stomach acid production.

Zantac is quite widely used, but in many cases has been superseded by the proton pump inhibitors described below.

Proton pump inhibitors

In the last step of gastric acid secretion, the parietal cells in the gastric glands pump protons (H^+) across their membranes and into the lumen of the stomach. For each H^+ ion pumped into the lumen, one K^+ ion is pumped in the opposite direction so there is no charge build-up. Movement of the ions occurs against their concentration gradients and so requires energy. This is provided by the hydrolysis of an energy carrier known as ATP, using the enzyme ATPase which is embedded in the cell membrane. The enzyme is therefore known as the **H^+/K^+ ATPase** or simply as a **gastric proton pump**.

Drugs which inhibit the proton pump will directly prevent the release of acid into the stomach lumen. The first proton pump inhibitor was omeprazole, marketed as Prilosec, which was followed by the release of esomeprazole or Nexium when the patent for Prilosec expired in 2001. These drugs, shown in Figure 15.20, are amongst the world's most largely used medications.

Nexium pills, showing their distinctive purple colour with racing stripes. Prilosec was the original purple pill marketed by AstraZeneca, and this design was modified with the launch of Nexium to suggest its increased potency. Prilosec and Nexium are both proton pump inhibitors that reduce the secretion of stomach acid, but scientists are divided on their relative effectiveness.

(a)

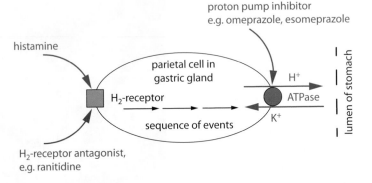

(b)

Figure 15.20 Proton pump inhibitor drugs (a) omeprazole (Prilosec) and (b) esomeprazole (Nexium).

NATURE OF SCIENCE

If you study the formulas of omeprazole and esomeprazole, which can also be found in section 37 of the IB data booklet, you could be forgiven for thinking they look the same. They are in fact the same structure. Like many drugs, they exist as isomers *R* and *S* which differ in their spatial arrangement, known as optical isomers. Omeprazole is a racemic mixture of the *R* and *S* forms, whereas esomeprazole is only the *S* form (*es*-omeprazole). There is evidence that the *S* form has greater potency as a proton pump inhibitor, leading to claims that this molecule alone, marketed as Nexium, is more effective than equivalent amounts of Prilosec. This is reflected in the higher price of Nexium. There are, however, counter claims that this is simply a marketing strategy, as in fact the two enantiomers interconvert in the body and so the drugs are equally effective. Medical doctors often face a choice when prescribing medicines, and conflicting information such as this makes it difficult. The situation demands data, the lifeblood of science, and this needs to be as objective and free from bias as possible.

Summary of the action of H₂-receptor antagonists and proton pump inhibitors in reducing stomach acid secretion

Figure 15.21 Summary of the targets of drugs that reduce the production of stomach acid.

Antacids are weak bases which neutralize excess acid

Drugs to help combat excess stomach acid are known as **antacids**. They work by neutralizing the hydrochloric acid, so relieving the symptoms. Antacids are usually *weakly* basic compounds, often metal oxides, hydroxides, carbonates, or hydrogencarbonates. Strong bases cannot be used because they are caustic and would cause direct harm to the stomach. The antacids used do not directly coat the ulcer or induce healing, but according to the dictum 'no acid, no ulcer', they do allow the stomach lining time to mend. Antacids are used for a wide variety of non-specific digestive disorders.

Antacids which contain metal hydroxides include calcium hydroxide, magnesium hydroxide, and aluminium hydroxide. These neutralize hydrochloric acid with the formation of a salt and water, as shown on page 591:

Investigation of the effectiveness of antacids

Full details of how to carry out this experiment with a worksheet are available on your eBook.

- calcium hydroxide, $Ca(OH)_2$

$$Ca(OH)_2(aq) + 2HCl(aq) \rightarrow CaCl_2(aq) + 2H_2O(l)$$

- magnesium hydroxide, $Mg(OH)_2$

$$Mg(OH)_2(aq) + 2HCl(aq) \rightarrow MgCl_2(aq) + 2H_2O(l)$$

- aluminium hydroxide, $Al(OH)_3$

$$Al(OH)_3(aq) + 3HCl(aq) \rightarrow AlCl_3(aq) + 3H_2O(l)$$

Several antacid formulations contain both aluminium and magnesium compounds, as they complement each other well. Magnesium salts tend to be faster acting, but aluminium compounds, because they dissolve more slowly, tend to provide longer-lasting relief. In addition, magnesium salts tend to act as a laxative, whereas aluminium salts cause constipation. Aluminium has been linked with the development of Alzheimer's disease, and although this is by no means proven, many people carefully limit its intake.

Antacids which contain metal carbonates and hydrogencarbonates include sodium carbonate and sodium hydrogencarbonate. These neutralize hydrochloric acid with the formation of a salt, water, and carbon dioxide, as shown below:

- sodium hydrogencarbonate, $NaHCO_3$

$$NaHCO_3(aq) + HCl(aq) \rightarrow NaCl(aq) + H_2O(l) + CO_2(g)$$

- sodium carbonate, Na_2CO_3

$$Na_2CO_3(aq) + 2HCl(aq) \rightarrow 2NaCl(aq) + H_2O(l) + CO_2(g)$$

The gas released can cause bloating of the stomach and flatulence. To reduce this side-effect, antifoaming agents are often added to the fomulation. Some antacids also contain alginates which float to the top of the stomach, forming a 'raft' which acts as a barrier preventing reflux into the oesophagus.

Note that because antacids change the pH of the stomach, they can alter other chemical reactions, including the absorption of other drugs. Although they are over-the-counter drugs, they should not be taken for an extended period without medical supervision.

pH and buffering

As we noted, biological systems are very sensitive to changes in pH. This is why complex systems exist in cells to help to prevent major fluctuations in the pH. Buffers resist the change in the pH of a solution on the addition of small amounts of acid or base, and can be prepared to operate at a wide range of pH.

A buffer solution is resistant to changes in pH on the addition of small amounts of acid or alkali.

The pH of a buffer solution, that is its H^+ concentration, will depend on the interactions among its components. We will consider here an acidic buffer made of the generic weak acid HA and its salt MA.

The equilibria that exist in the buffer will be as follows.

1 weak acid: $\quad\quad\quad\quad HA(aq) \rightleftharpoons H^+(aq) + A^-(aq)$

2 salt: $\quad\quad\quad\quad\quad\quad MA(aq) \rightarrow M^+(aq) + A^-(aq)$

An antacid tablet dissolving in a glass of water. The fizzing is due to the release of carbon dioxide as the sodium carbonate reacts with water. Antacids neutralize stomach acid and so relieve the symptoms of indigestion, heartburn, or stomach ulcer.

CHALLENGE YOURSELF

2 Why do sodium carbonate and sodium hydrogencarbonate react as weak bases? Consider possible hydrolysis reactions of their conjugate ions.

Remember from Chapter 8:

acid + base $\rightarrow$ salt + H_2O

acid + carbonate/ hydrogencarbonate $\rightarrow$ salt + H_2O + CO_2

In stoichiometry questions concerning antacids, remember that the molar ratio of antacid to acid will vary with different antacids. So make sure you are basing your answer on the correct balanced equation.

pH testing equipment used to diagnose oesophageal reflux disease. The tubes contain water and buffer solution used to calibrate the sensors and recorder shown at the bottom.

We can make two approximations, based on some assumptions about these reactions, which will help to make the calculations easier.

1 The dissociation of the weak acid is so small that it can be considered to be negligible. The equilibrium lies so far to the left that we can make the approximation:

$$[HA]_{initial} \approx [HA]_{equilibrium}$$

2 The salt is considered to be fully dissociated into its ions. The equilibrium lies so far to the right that we can make the approximation:

$$[MA]_{initial} \approx [A^-]_{equilibrium}$$

From the approximations justified above and using equilibrium law, we can derive equations that enable us to calculate the pH of a buffer from the initial concentrations of the acid (or base) and salt. These equations are known as the Henderson–Hasselbalch equations, and they are given in section 1 of the IB data booklet.

For acidic buffer solutions:

$$pH = pK_a + \log_{10} \frac{[salt]}{[acid]}$$

For basic buffer solutions the equivalent equations are:

$$pOH = pK_b + \log_{10} \frac{[salt]}{[base]} \qquad (pOH = -\log_{10}[OH^-])$$

where pK_a and pK_b are respectively derived from the acid dissociation constant and the base dissociation constant, K_a and K_b. Values for these constants for common acids and bases are given in section 21 of the IB data booklet.

The beauty of these expressions is that they enable us to know the pH of a buffer solution directly from

- the K_a or K_b values of its component acid or base and
- the ratio of initial concentrations of acid and salt used to prepare the buffer.

$$pH = pK_a + \log_{10} \frac{[salt]}{[acid]}$$

$$pOH = pK_b + \log_{10} \frac{[salt]}{[base]}$$

Joseph Henderson (1878–1942) was an American biochemist, who developed equations showing that acid–base balance in the blood is regulated by buffers. Karl Hasselbalch (1874–1962), a Danish chemist and a pioneer in the use of pH measurement in medicine, converted the equations to logarithmic form in his work on studying acidosis in the blood. We now know that different buffers in the blood work together to keep the pH tightly controlled at 7.4. Fluctuation in this value is so crucial that pH levels below 7.0 (acidosis) and above 7.8 (alkalosis) are, in the words of the medical profession, 'incompatible with life'.

Worked example

Calculate the pH of a buffer solution at 298 K, prepared by mixing 25 cm³ of 0.10 mol dm⁻³ ethanoic acid (CH₃COOH) with 25 cm³ of 0.10 cm³ sodium ethanoate (Na⁺CH₃COO⁻). K_a of CH₃COOH = 1.8×10^{-5} at 298 K.

Solution

pK_a of $CH_3COOH = -\log_{10}(1.8 \times 10^{-5}) = 4.74$

As there are equal volumes and concentrations of CH_3COOH and $NaCH_3COO$, then [acid] = [salt].

$$pH = pK_a + \log_{10}\frac{[salt]}{[acid]} = 4.74 + \log_{10}(1) = 4.74 + 0 = 4.74$$

(Note that $\log_{10}(1) = 0$)

This example shows that when a buffer solution contains equal amounts in moles of acid and salt (or base and salt), the last term in the Henderson–Hasselbalch expression becomes zero, so $pH = pK_a$ (or $pOH = pK_b$). This relationship is extremely useful when it comes to preparing buffers of a specified pH. All we have to do is choose an acid with a pK_a value close to the required pH and then, if necessary, adjust the concentrations of acid and salt accordingly.

The buffer solution can be prepared by reacting the acid with enough strong alkali to convert one half of the acid into salt.

> In a buffer solution when [acid] = [salt], pH = pK_a
>
> When [base] = [salt], pOH = pK_b.

Worked example

How would you prepare a buffer solution of pH 3.75 starting with methanoic acid (HCOOH) and NaOH?

Solution

From the IB data booklet, pK_a (HCOOH) = 3.75, so a buffer with equal amounts in moles of this acid and its salt (Na^+HCOO^-) will have pH = 3.75.

This equimolar solution is prepared by reacting the acid with enough NaOH so that one half of the acid is converted into salt and therefore $[HCOOH] = [HCOO^-]$.

Alternatively, the buffer can be prepared by mixing the acid directly with an appropriate amount of its salt.

Worked example

How much 0.10 mol dm^{-3} butanoic acid solution and solid potassium butanoate should be used to make 1.00 dm^3 of pH 5.00 buffer solution? State the assumptions made in the calculation.

Solution

From the IB data booklet, butanoic acid $pK_a = 4.83$.

$$pH = pK_a + \log_{10}\frac{[A^-]}{[HA]}$$

$$5.00 - 4.83 = \log_{10}\frac{[butanoate\ ion]}{0.10\ mol\ dm^{-3}}$$

Take anti-logs of both sides:

$$10^{0.17} = \frac{[butanoate\ ion]}{0.10\ mol\ dm^{-3}} = 1.5$$

[butanoate ion] = 0.15 mol dm^{-3}

The molar mass of potassium butanoate is 126.12 g mol^{-1}

1.00 dm^3 of 0.15 mol dm^{-3} solution = 0.15 mol × 126.12 g mol^{-1} = 19 g

So 19 g potassium butanoate should be added to 1.00 dm^3 of 0.10 mol dm^{-3} butanoic acid.

The following assumptions were made:

- [butanoate ion]$_{equilibrium}$ = [potassium butanoate]$_{initial}$
- [butanoic acid]$_{equilibrium}$ = [butanoic acid]$_{initial}$
- no volume change occurs on mixing the solution

Exercises

13 Suggest why the action of drugs in lowering the production of stomach acid is considered to be indirect in the case of H_2-receptor antagonists, but direct in the case of gastric proton pump inhibitors.

14 Magnesium hydroxide and aluminium hydroxide can act as antacids.

   (a) Write an equation for the reaction of hydrochloric acid with each of these antacids.
   (b) Identify which antacid neutralizes the greater amount of acid if 0.1 mol of each antacid is used.
   (c) Explain why potassium hydroxide is not used as an antacid.

15 **(a)** 100 cm^3 of a buffer is prepared which contains 0.100 mol dm^{-3} butanoic acid and 0.200 mol dm^{-3} sodium butanoate. What is the pH of this buffer? The pK_a of butanoic acid is 4.82.
   (b) How would the pH of the buffer alter if 20 cm^3 of distilled water was added to the original solution?

D.5 Antiviral medications

Understandings:
- Viruses lack a cell structure and so are more difficult to target with drugs than bacteria.
- Antiviral drugs may work by altering the cell's genetic material so that the virus cannot use it to multiply. Alternatively, they may prevent the viruses from multiplying by blocking enzyme activity within the host cell.

Applications and skills:
- Explanation of the different ways in which antiviral medications work.
- Description of how viruses differ from bacteria.
- Explanation of how oseltamivir (Tamiflu) and zanamivir (Relenza) work as preventative agents against flu viruses.
- Comparison of the structures of oseltamivir and zanamivir.
- Discussion of the difficulties associated with solving the AIDS problem.

   Guidance
   Structures for oseltamivir and zanamivir can be found in the IB data booklet in section 37.

Viruses: nature's most successful parasites

Figure 15.22 shows that viruses come in different shapes and sizes and are all extremely small. Their diameters range from 20 to 300 nm, which means that they are **sub-microscopic**. In other words they cannot be studied with a light microscope, but only with an electron microscope.

Viruses are such small and simple structures that there is debate about whether they can be classified as living organisms in their own right. They contain only two main components, protein and nucleic acid (either RNA or DNA), have no cellular structure, and are only capable of reproducing inside another living cell. In all these ways they are different from bacteria, which have a complex cellular structure and the ability to survive and reproduce independently from other living cells.

Viruses are in fact the original hijackers – they literally take over the functioning of another cell, the so-called **host cell**, and use it to carry out their own reproduction. The host cell's components are used in the assembly of new viral particles and in the process the cell eventually dies, releasing thousands of viral particles into the organism. Viruses are usually somewhat specific for their host, and different strains exist that infect bacteria, plants, and animals.

Figure 15.22 Examples of viruses.

T4 bacteriophage
DNA
protein coat
sheath
baseplate
tail fibre
100 nm

HIV virus with its lipid envelope
lipid envelope
viral proteins incorporated in envelope
viral RNA
core proteins
25 nm

The war against viruses

The body's defence system usually responds to viral infections by producing specific **antibodies**, which act against a virus in the **immune response**. This often leads to protection, known as **immunity**, against repeated infections with the same virus. But sometimes the virus is not completely eradicated from the body and remains dormant in cells. This can cause a flare-up on another occasion, such as some herpes infections which cause cold sores. Another example is the chicken pox virus that can cause the different disease shingles years after the original infection.

Despite the body's defences, viral infections claim the lives of millions of people each year and are responsible for an even greater number of illnesses, many of them serious. Diseases such as measles, meningitis, and polio are caused by viruses, as are more recent diseases

The words *virus* and *infection* have been adopted in technological jargon to describe a type of malicious software that inserts itself into computer files and replicates, usually causing harm to the system. Does the use of these terms depend on a knowledge of their biological origin? To what extent is knowledge implicit in language?

Artwork of a SARS virus particle inside a cell. SARS (severe acute respiratory syndrome) is an often fatal lung disease that first appeared in China in late 2002 and spread rapidly through the world via air travel. The virus is related to the type that causes the common cold. Like all viruses it cannot replicate by itself but instead uses the machinery of the host cell to produce more copies of itself.

Antibiotics are effective against bacteria but not against viruses.

595

such as AIDS, ebola, and avian flu. The development of effective treatments against
viruses is therefore one of the most pressing challenges of modern medicine.

such as AIDS, ebola, and avian flu. The development of effective treatments against
viruses is therefore one of the most pressing challenges of modern medicine.

Treating viral infections is particularly difficult because the viruses live within host
cells and so cannot be easily targeted. Antibiotics such as penicillin are effective
against bacteria, because they can target a structure such as a cell wall – but there are
no equivalent structures to target in viruses. This is why antibiotics are not effective
against viruses. In a sense viruses are so stripped-down structurally that there is little
for a drug to target.

Another problem is the speed at which viruses can multiply, so that they are often
spread through the organism by the time that symptoms appear. In addition, virus
particles have a tendency to **mutate** rapidly, which means that they make small
changes in their genetic material, and this changes their susceptibility to drugs.

There have, though, been successes in the treatment of viral infections. Vaccines were
first introduced in the 18th century, and today are a major aspect of preventative
healthcare, known as **prophylactic** treatment. Vaccines work by stimulating the
body to prepare specific antibodies which can give immunity. Successful vaccination
programmes have reduced the incidence of diseases such as cholera, polio, and
measles. In 1980 the World Health Organization declared that smallpox has been
eradicated from all parts of the world.

NATURE OF SCIENCE

Edward Jenner (1749–1823) pioneered the work that eventually led to the global eradication
of the devastating disease smallpox. Yet his methods would not stand the test of today's ethical
standards for scientific experimentation. Jenner observed that people who suffered from the
relatively mild disease cowpox did not seem to contract smallpox (a more serious disease).
He tested his theory on an eight-year-old boy by first injecting him with pus from a cowpox
pustule, and when the boy had recovered from cowpox, injected him with pus from a smallpox
pustule. The boy did not develop smallpox. When he was told he needed more proof, Jenner
repeated the practice on more children, including his own baby son. Despite the evidence,
Jenner's work was slow to be accepted as many people found the idea of innoculating the
body with disease to be repulsive. But eventually the results spoke for themselves, and the use
of vaccination became widespread.

Jenner used intuition and careful observation to design a process that he believed would
be beneficial to others. Consider other cases where scientists may have had to balance the
courage of their convictions with contrary public perception.

Mutations in a virus can, however, limit the effectiveness of some vaccines. For example,
flu vaccines are useful only against the known strains, and as these change through
mutation, different vaccines usually have to be prepared and administered every year.

The main strategy to treat viral infections is the administration of specific medicines
known as **antivirals**. These all interfere in some way with the viral life cycle and so
prevent the release of new viral particles from the cell. Some antivirals work by altering
the cell's DNA, its genetic material, so that the virus cannot use it to multiply. Others
block enzyme activity within the host cell which prevents the virus from reproducing.
One reasonably effective antiviral drug is Amantadine which has a cage like structure
and causes changes in the cell membrane that prevent the entry of a virus into the host
cell. It is therefore best used as a prophylactic treatment or given before the infection
has spread widely – a difficult task given the speed at which infections can strike.

Some recent advances in the development of antivirals for the flu virus are discussed in
the next section.

Polio is a highly infectious
disease caused by a virus
which invades the nervous
system. It most commonly
affects children under five
years old, leaving many
who survived crippled
and paralysed. There is
no cure, but there are
effective vaccines, which
have been available since
the 1950s. Immunization
programmes have
eradicated polio from
most of the world, but the
disease is still endemic in
Afghanistan, Nigeria, and
Pakistan. The Global Polio
Eradication Initiative was
launched in 1988 and
tracks all new cases on a
weekly basis. Its goal is to
eradicate polio worldwide
by immunizing every child
until transmission stops.

The word *vaccine* is
derived from the Latin
word *vacca* for cow. It
was first used by Edward
Jenner in 1798 in the
context of his work on
cowpox and smallpox.

Flu viruses: a case study in antivirals

Influenza, commonly known as the flu, is such a common disease that most of us can expect to experience it during our lives. Its symptoms include chills, headache, sore throat, and weakness, but it can develop into much more serious illnesses such as pneumonia. Flu infections can be particularly serious in the elderly and those with compromised immune systems. It is estimated that about half a million people die of flu every year, and there are constant fears of a global outbreak, known as a **pandemic**.

In November 1918, the same month in which World War I ended, a flu pandemic started in which 20 million people died in less than 2 years. It is believed that the outbreak started with a relatively harmless strain of flu that slowly evolved into a very virulent strain. Its effects were global, with large numbers of casualties in the Pacific region, Africa, and North America. It is considered to be the worst pandemic of all time, often referred to as the 'Spanish flu'.

Flu is caused by two main types of virus known as influenza A and B. They are spherical viruses and have RNA as their genetic material. Flu viruses have specific proteins on their surface, of which two play a key role in their life cycle.

1 **Hemagglutinin (H)** is a glycoprotein that enables the viral particle to 'dock' with the host cell before it enters.

2 **Neuraminidase (N)** is an enzyme that catalyses a cleavage reaction which allows the new viral particles to escape from the host cell and spread infection. The enzyme snips off a type of sugar molecule, sialic acid, from glycoproteins on the surface of the host cell membrane.

Computer artwork of the action of an antiviral drug, shown in blue, blocking an ion channel in the viral surface. This prevents the release of the viral genetic material into the host cell, and so interrupts the viral replication and infection cycle. Viral surface proteins are shown in red and yellow in the background.

Cut-away computer artwork of an influenza virus particle. The surface shows two types of protein spike, hemagglutinin shown in red, and neuraminidase (shown in yellow). These determine the strain of virus and are essential to its life cycle. Other viral proteins are shown in purple, and the genetic material, RNA, is shown in yellow in the core.

These two molecules come in a variety of subunits which control the infectivity of the virus. The naming system of viruses such as H1N1 and H5N1, refers to the different forms of these molecules that are present.

In 2009 a new strain of the influenza A virus, known as H1N1, was identified as causing flu infections. As people had little natural immunity to this strain, the infection spread globally causing serious illness and death, and the World Health Organization (WHO) declared it a pandemic. The alert was lifted in 2010 when the number of infections had declined steeply. Debate continues on whether the pandemic designation was an exaggerated response, possibly triggered by economic interests in increased sales of vaccines and antivirals. It is believed that more than 250 000 people died of the disease, mostly in Africa and South-East Asia.

Figure 15.23 Summary of the life cycle of the flu virus showing the roles of hemagglutinin and neuraminidase.

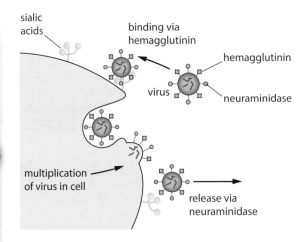

sialic acids

binding via hemagglutinin

hemagglutinin

virus

neuraminidase

multiplication of virus in cell

release via neuraminidase

The action of hemagglutinin and neuraminidase is shown in Figure 15.23.

If the action of either of these viral proteins was affected, it would evidently interrupt the viral life cycle. Of the two, neuraminidase seems to be a better target for drug design and so it has become a focus for research.

As an enzyme, neuraminidase binds to its reactant sialic acid, the **substrate**, at a specific region known as the **active site**. It is this binding between enzyme and substrate that gives the catalytic action, as it provides a reaction pathway of lower activation energy. Chemicals that interfere with this binding are called **inhibitors** and usually have a specific fit with the enzyme.

The three-dimensional structure of neuraminidase became known through X-ray crystallography in 1993, including details on its active site. This enabled researchers to design a molecule which could bind at the active site and so block the binding of substrate and act as an inhibitor.

The first neuraminidase inhibitors were designed by a team in Australia, and led to the production of zanamivir (Relenza), which was approved for use in 2000. It was closely followed by the production of oseltamivir (Tamiflu). As can be seen in Figure 15.24 and the table on page 599, both drugs have a chemical structure similar to sialic acid and so are able to bind at the active site in neuraminidase. This class of drug is active against both influenza A and B viruses. Tamiflu and Relenza are claimed to reduce the symptoms of flu and shorten the time of its effects, but must be taken within 48 hours of the appearance of symptoms.

It may be of help to you to learn a little bit more about enzymes – read pages 468–473 in the Biochemistry option chapter.

Oseltamivir (Tamiflu) and zanamivir (Relenza) are both neuraminidase inhibitors that prevent the release of new viral particles from infected cells.

Molecular model of the neuraminidase enzyme found on the surface of the influenza virus, in a complex with the drug oseltamivir. Binding of the drug at the enzyme's active site inhibits its action, and so prevents the release of new viral particles from the host cell.

HO   COOH
C
OH   O
H
H₂C   C   C
         OH
H   OH
OH   OH   HN
         C
      H₃C   O

Figure 15.24 The structure of the neuraminidase substrate sialic acid, showing the similarity of its structure to that of the inhibitors oseltamivir and zanamivir.

CHALLENGE YOURSELF

3 Suggest why neuraminidase inhibitors can be described as *competitive* inhibitors.

The table below compares and contrasts the two drugs Tamiflu and Relenza.

	Oseltamivir (Tamiflu)	Zanamivir (Relenza)
Structure	(structure diagram)	(structure diagram)
Functional groups	alkenyl ether primary amino carboxyamide ester	alkenyl ether primary amino carboxyamide carboxylic acid hydroxyl (3)
Drug action	neuraminidase inhibitor	neuraminidase inhibitor
Administration	orally	inhalation
Resistance to drug	some rare strains of flu virus have shown resistance	no resistance reported
Counter-effects	nausea, vomiting	possible asthma

Antiretroviral drugs are expensive and so have been very poorly distributed in the countries where they are generally needed the most. The Clinton Health Access Initiative Foundation (CHAI) began as a campaign to address the HIV/AIDS crisis in the developing world and strengthen health systems there. A major achievement is that nearly six million people now have access to HIV medications at costs reduced to about $200 per person per year. This includes a large number of HIV-positive children who were previously left untreated. It is estimated that one child dies every two minutes from mother to child transmission of HIV, and global efforts are focused on preventing this, especially in Cambodia, Ethiopia, Lesotho, Malawi, Tanzania, and Vietnam.

The structures of oseltamivir and zanamivir are given in section 37 of the IB data booklet.

Computer artwork of HIV replication. The viral particles, shown in green, surround the white blood cell, shown in blue, and attach to its surface using specific proteins for recognition. Viral RNA, shown in pink, is then injected into the cell and using reverse transcriptase synthesizes DNA which integrates into the host's chromosome. This can be seen in the white cell nucleus in the centre. New viral particles are assembled within the cell and are shown at the bottom budding from the cell, taking part of the membrane as an envelope.

AIDS: a viral pandemic

The condition known as **AIDS**, acquired immune deficiency syndrome, caused by the human immunodeficiency virus (HIV), was first diagnosed in humans in 1981. The infection is transmitted from person to person through sexual or parenteral exposure to fluids such as blood, semen, and mucus that contain HIV. The disease AIDS is characterized by a failure of the immune system, so that the body falls prey to life-threatening opportunistic infections such as pneumonia and forms of cancer. The infection has spread at an alarming rate through the global population and it is estimated that approximately 33 million people are currently **HIV positive**, with a likelihood of developing AIDS. Although cases have been reported in all regions of the world, a very high proportion of people who are HIV positive live in sub-Saharan Africa.

HIV primarily infects vital white blood cells in the immune system. These cells are called **CD4$^+$ T cells**. The virus binds to specific receptor proteins on the cell surface and then penetrates the cell. HIV is a **retrovirus**, which means that its genetic material is in the form of RNA rather than DNA. The virus releases its RNA into the cell and the enzyme **reverse transcriptase** controls the synthesis of viral DNA from this RNA. The viral DNA integrates into the cell's own DNA and replicates with it when the cell divides. Viral particles are produced within the host cell, and are released in large numbers when the cell dies.

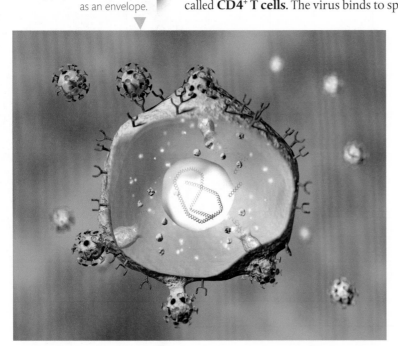

The fight against HIV infection

There are three main reasons why HIV is proving even more challenging than other viruses to defeat.

1 The virus destroys helper T cells, the very cells in the immune system that should be defending the body against the virus.

2 The virus tends to mutate very rapidly, even within a patient. It is thought that there is more variation in HIV in a single patient than in the influenza virus worldwide in a year. These variations mean that the virus 'escapes' the immune response, so the patient has to make a response to the new virus.

3 The virus often lies dormant within host cells, so the immune system has nothing to respond to.

Despite the challenges, great progress has been made in the development of specific antivirals for HIV infection. The drugs are known as **antiretroviral drugs**, **ARV**s, and about 20 of these are now commonly available. Although these drugs do not cure the patient, they can give lasting suppression of the HIV infection. This means that with appropriate treatments, HIV infection can be considered as a potentially chronic disease rather than as a fatal disease. Antiretroviral treatment during pregnancy can also effectively prevent transmission of the disease from mother to child.

Antiretroviral drugs target and interrupt the following different stages in the HIV life cycle:

• binding and fusion of the virus to the receptor on the CD4 cell membrane;
• reverse transcription of viral RNA to DNA in the host cell;
• integration of viral DNA into the host chromosome;
• release of new viral particles by budding from the host cell surface.

Of these targets, inhibitors of the viral enzyme reverse transcriptase are the most widespread, and include drugs such as AZT, also known as zidovudine, which was the first antiretroviral drug to be approved. It has been found that the best results occur when a combination of different ARVs is used. Combination treatments typically include two different reverse transcriptase inhibitors plus a third drug, all of which can be taken as a single pill once daily. The cost for most combination treatments is approximately $12 000 per patient per year.

Molecular model of the HIV enzyme reverse transcriptase complexed with the inhibitor efavirenz. Binding of the inhibitor to the enzyme prevents HIV reproducing in the host cell. Efavirenz is therefore an effective antiretroviral drug that reduces the spread of HIV infection.

The development of ARVs is a field which is advancing rapidly as more drugs become available. Medical doctors must consider how to tailor a prescription to individual patients, who may benefit from different regimens of different drugs. Considerations of side-effects, potency, expense, convenience, and prevention of transmission must all be weighed. ARV treatments generally need to be sustained throughout life.

Intense research on developing a vaccine for HIV/AIDS is ongoing. There are some hopes that a therapeutic vaccine may be possible to help control the infection in people who are HIV-positive. But the development of a preventative vaccine that would give immunity to people who are HIV-negative has so far not been possible. This is mainly because of the problem of the variable nature of the virus within cells, and the fact that the immune response seems to act too slowly in the case of HIV infection.

NATURE OF SCIENCE

The development of effective antivirals is a good example of the interdisciplinary nature of many scientific endeavours. Technological advances in the areas of electron microscopy and X-ray crystallography have provided insights into structures that could not otherwise be known. Advances in molecular biology have helped explain the role of viral proteins and genetic material in the viral life cycle. This cumulative knowledge has helped to drive research in the pharmaceutical industry, resulting in the availability of effective new drugs for many diseases. At best, science is a collaborative process in which findings from different disciplines contribute to the achievement of a common goal.

Exercises

16 Why are viral infections not able to be treated with antibiotics?

17 With reference to the structure of the influenza virus, explain why it is possible to suffer from flu several times during a lifetime.

18 Explain why the antivirals Tamiflu and Relenza must be taken within a very short time after the appearance of the symptoms of flu.

19 Discuss some of the challenges and successes in the global response to the AIDS pandemic.

D.6 Environmental impact of some medications

Understandings:
- High-level waste (HLW) is waste that gives off large amounts of ionizing radiation for a long time.
- Low-level waste (LLW) is waste that gives off small amounts of ionizing radiation for a short time.
- Antibiotic resistance occurs when microorganisms become resistant to antibacterials.

Applications and skills:
- Description of the environmental impact of medical nuclear waste disposal.
- Discussion of environmental issues related to left-over solvents.
- Explanation of the dangers of antibiotic waste, from improper drug disposal and animal waste, and the development of antibiotic resistance.
- Discussion of the basics of Green Chemistry (sustainable chemistry) processes.
- Explanation of how Green Chemistry was used to develop the precursor for Tamiflu (oseltamivir).

Guidance
The structure of oseltamivir is provided in the data booklet in section 37.

In this chapter we have explored many of the ways in which modern medicine has made significant contributions to advances in human health. Better diagnosis and treatments of many conditions have led to improvements in the quality of life, and increases in longevity in many parts of the world.

A recurring theme has been an awareness of how side-effects of medications may directly impact health. Consequently, side-effects to the patient are monitored and negative effects avoided wherever possible. In a parallel way, the activities of the pharmaceutical industry in drug preparation, administration, and disposal produce side-effects in the environment. Many of these are negative and potentially damaging to human health. It is thus equally important that these environmental side-effects are monitored, with policies and procedures put in place to minimize their negative impact. Failure to do so would be self-defeating, as the quality of the environment is critical to the health of all living things.

In this last section, we will look at some of the challenges and possible solutions to the environmental impact of the medical industry, including the role of Green Chemistry. This branch of chemistry, also known as Sustainable Chemistry, has developed since 1991, and focuses on 12 principles. These principles cover concepts such as avoiding waste, maximizing the amount of raw material that ends up in the product, and the use of safe solvents. In essence, Green Chemistry seeks to reduce the footprint of chemical manufacturing processes while improving product and environmental safety. As we will see, it has many applications in the pharmaceutical industry.

The 12 principles of Green Chemistry are given in the Appendix on pages 612–613. You do not need to learn these, but you may find it useful to refer to them in this study.

Water pollution monitoring in Gujarat, India. A scientist collects a sample of polluted water as it pours from a pipe into a shallow ditch. The water has been stained dark yellow by the presence of poisonous organochloride chemicals, especially 2,6-dichlorobenzenamine and 2,4,5-trichlorobenzene which are used in the pharmaceutical industry. In this major industrial area, wastes are often disposed of by dumping them in any convenient open space or watercourse.

Solvent waste: the major emission of the drug industry

Most drugs are complex molecules, so their synthesis and extraction involves multiple steps. In many parts of this process, organic solvents are used. These may be toxic and are often left over at the end of the synthesis, leading to problems of disposal. It is estimated that up to 80% of the mass of reactants that does not end up in the pharmaceutical product is due to solvents, including water. Disposal of solvents often involves incineration, which can release toxins into the environment. Overall solvents are by far the biggest contributor to the emissions of the pharmaceutical industry.

Solvent use is therefore a serious concern in the pharmaceutical industry. The suitability of solvents can be assessed by three factors:

1   toxicity to workers – whether the solvent is carcinogenic (cancer causing) or associated with other health issues;
2   safety of the process – whether the solvent is highly flammable, explosive, or can cause toxic by-products;
3   harm to the environment – whether the solvent will contaminate soil and ground water, cause ozone depletion, or contribute to greenhouse gas formation when released or burned.

On the basis of these criteria, examples of some common solvents can be classified as preferred or undesirable as shown on page 604.

Preferred solvents

water, H_2O

ethanol, C_2H_5OH

2-propanol, $CH_3CH(OH)CH_3$

propanone, CH_3COCH_3

ethyl ethanoate, $CH_3COOC_2H_5$

Undesirable solvents

dichloromethane, CH_2Cl_2

methanal, HCHO

tetrachloromethane, CCl_4

diethyl ether, $C_2H_5OC_2H_5$

benzene, C_6H_6

It can be seen that chlorinated compounds, ethers, and many aromatic compounds are considered problematic, and should wherever possible be replaced by water, alcohols, or possibly esters.

Apparatus for supercritical extraction of compounds from plants. The extraction occurs at high pressure and temperature using carbon dioxide as a solvent, known as supercritical carbon dioxide, and avoids the use of environmentally harmful solvents. Photographed in the Green Chemistry research group laboratory in the University of York, UK.

▼

One of the principles of Green Chemistry is the use of *safer solvents and to avoid the use of auxiliaries where possible*. Water is clearly the safest solvent for the environment, and supercritical carbon dioxide (CO_2 under pressure) can also be used in some processes. Another principle of Green Chemistry is to *prevent waste*. Pharmaceutical companies are finding ways to reduce and reuse solvents in the synthesis process, so that there is less waste released into the environment. Detailed analysis of the entire energy costs has shown that solvent recycling programmes can run at significantly lower costs than the total cost of the production of new solvent and burning of waste. Case-studied examples include the production of the arthritis drug Celebrex by Pfizer, where scenarios with and without solvent recycling were rigorously compared.

Left-over organic solvents are the major emission of the pharmaceutical industry. Solvent recycling can substantially cut emissions to air, water, and soil.

The International Atomic Energy Agency (IAEA) provides recommendations for the classification of nuclear waste, but the actual definition of low-level waste is set by individual countries. As the level of activity for this waste is usually quite variable, there may be some radioactive components in the mixture that have relatively high activity.

Nuclear waste: an increasing problem in the drug industry

The use of nuclear chemistry in the diagnosis and treatment of disease is a rapidly expanding area of medicine. Many of the techniques used are associated with some radioactive waste, which can potentially be hazardous to living things and the environment. Disposal of medical nuclear waste is therefore a growing problem that must be faced by the medical industry.

The method of disposal used depends on the level of waste and the length of time it remains radioactive, which is determined by its half-life.

- **High-level waste** gives off large amounts of ionizing radiation for a long time. The isotopes have long half-lives.
- **Low-level waste** gives off small amounts of ionizing radiation for a short time. The isotopes have short half-lives.

Most of the waste generated by nuclear medicines is low-level waste. It includes items such as clothing, protective shoe covers, paper towels, and implements that have become contaminated with radioactive material. Disposal of this low-level waste usually involves first interim storage in sealed containers that are safe, secure, and environmentally sound. The radioactivity typically decays in hours or days, and the waste can then be disposed of by conventional means – compaction, landfill, or sewers for liquids.

Spent isotopes from medical diagnosis techniques may generate some high-level waste, although this amount is quite small relative to the amount of high-level waste from spent fuel rods generated by the nuclear energy industry. The medical waste is often toxic as well as radioactive, and can have damaging effects in the environment.

Disposal of high-level waste is a complex problem because products of the decay process may themselves be radioactive and continue to emit ionizing radiation. The decay processes also often emit significant heat. High-level waste is usually stored first under water in reinforced cooling ponds for 5 to 10 years, and then transferred to dry storage in heavily shielded structures, often buried deep in the Earth. It is essential to prevent the radioactive waste from entering the underground water supply.

Innovations in Green Chemistry may help to reduce nuclear waste, for example by extracting enriched uranium from incinerator ash using supercritical carbon dioxide.

An alternative innovative approach is to reduce the use of radioactive isotopes in diagnosis, by replacing them with fluorescent dyes. This has given promising results in some early trials and has substantially reduced the radioactive waste.

Antibiotic waste: are we killing the cures?

The problem of antibiotic-resistant bacteria, which we discussed with respect to penicillin on page 580, applies to most other antibiotics as well. This presents a major challenge to modern medicine, as many antibiotics are simply no longer effective as therapeutic agents against bacterial infections.

NATURE OF SCIENCE

Scientific innovations sometimes bring unintended burdens as well as benefits to society. This is certainly the case with some of the environmental impacts of the pharmaceutical industry. The responsibility to ameliorate the effects then falls to the scientists, who often must work in cooperation with governments and regulatory authorities. While scientific advances are clearly the source of some of these issues, it is also scientific developments that will most appropriately address the concerns.

Antibiotic resistance has become a major problem with some strains of tuberculosis (TB), and treatment now requiring the use of several different antibiotics together. It is estimated that today 1 in 7 new TB cases is resistant to the drugs most commonly used to treat it. Antibiotic-resistant TB bacteria have been identified in many countries and are a particular concern in Russia, India, South Africa, and Peru. Antibiotic resistance must be faced on a global scale, as no country can protect itself from the importation of resistant pathogens through travel and trade.

Coloured scanning electron micrograph (SEM) of methicillin-resistant *Staphylococcus aureus*, known as MRSA. The bacteria are shown here in yellow on the microscopic fibres of a wound dressing. These bacteria are a major problem in hospitals because they are resistant to many commonly prescribed antibiotics. They can cause wound infections, pneumonia, and blood poisoning in vulnerable people, such as those who have recently had surgery.

Hospitals often face a particular problem in dealing with antibiotic-resistant bacteria. So-called **superbugs** are bacteria such as methicillin-resistant *Staphylococcus aureus* (MRSA) that carry several resistant genes, and cause infections that are extremely difficult to treat. Extensive use of **broad-spectrum antibiotics**, that is those that are used against a wide range of bacteria, has also enabled infections such as *Clostridium difficile* to thrive.

Antibiotic resistance arises by genetic mutation in bacteria and would normally account for a very small proportion of the population. But increased exposure to the antibiotic dramatically increases the number of resistant organisms, as it effectively kills off the competition. The spread of antibiotic resistance can be traced to the beginning of the large-scale commercial production and distribution of antibiotics. It is estimated that over the last 50 years, millions of tonnes of antibiotic compounds have been released into the biosphere. Perhaps surprisingly, less than half of these antibiotics produced are used for treatment of disease in humans. Other uses include:

- therapeutic use in aquaculture and household pets;
- growth promotion and prophylactic use in animal livestock;
- pest control in agriculture;
- sanitizers in toiletries and household cleaning products;
- sterilization and culture selection in research and industry.

The use of antibiotics in animal feeds is worth particular note. The drugs are given to lower the incidence of disease in the stock as a precautionary measure, in other words administered to healthy animals. The antibiotics pass through animal waste into the soil and water and so enter the human food chain, where they increase exposure of bacteria to the antibiotic.

Another source of antibiotics in the environment is through improper drug disposal. Expired, unused antibiotics are frequently discarded by households and by the medical profession, and this can result in contamination of surface, ground, and drinking water supplies. Studies have also shown that in some countries, effluent from pharamaceutical production plants can be contaminated with antibiotics.

There are no simple solutions to the problem of antibiotic-resistant bacteria. Strict measures of infection control and antibiotic use are a global priority. These must be backed up by efforts to minimize release of antibiotics into the environment, including the destruction of their activity before disposal. Individuals can contribute to the solution by avoiding overuse, and complying with instructions to complete a prescribed dose.

Obtaining the Tamiflu precursor: a Green Chemistry case study

Oseltamivir (Tamiflu), described on pages 598–599, is an antiviral that may lessen the spread of the flu virus within the body by preventing the release of new viral particles from their host cells. The drug has attracted particular attention as it is the only orally administered antiviral that may be effective in cases of H5N1 (avian flu) infection.

The key precursor for the synthesis of Tamiflu is **shikimic acid**, or its salt shikimate, with the structure shown below.

This compound is found in low concentrations in many plants, but the Chinese star anise, *Illicium verum*, which grows in Vietnam and South-West China, has been a favoured source. Shikimate is found in the star-shaped fruit of the tree, and can be extracted in a lengthy chemical process. But the low yields from this process are blamed for the worldwide shortage of Tamiflu in 2005, and again during the flu pandemic of 2009 when many governments stock-piled the drug.

The term *selection pressure* is used in evolutionary biology to refer to situations such as the effect of antibiotics in increasing the population of antibiotic-resistant bacteria.

The spread of antibiotic-resistant bacteria is primarily the result of the overuse of antibiotics.

There are significant differences in the availability and regulation of antibiotic use in different countries. Whether the drugs are available over-the-counter or only by prescription varies, as does the cost of supply. There have also been concerns that outdated antibiotics that are no longer effective or approved have been distributed in developing nations. These factors can impact human health directly, and also indirectly through the spread of antibiotic-resistant bacteria.

TOK Which ways of knowing can we use to guide us in making decisions when there may be conflicting ethical concerns?

Fruits of Chinese star anise, *Illicium verum*, which are a source of the Tamiflu precursor shikimate. The fruits also contain products used in herbal medicine, and have been intensely harvested. propellants.

There are therefore active efforts worldwide to prospect for alternate sources of the shikimate precursor. Some of the promising developments in this field, which are all applications of Green Chemistry, include the following.

- The production of shikimate from fermentation reactions of genetically engineered bacteria. This process has been developed by the pharmaceutical company Roche.
- The harvesting of shikimate from the needles of several varieties of pine trees. Even though yields are quite low, the needles represent a plentiful resource.
- The extraction of shikimate from suspension cultures of the Indian sweetgum tree. This is an inexpensive natural source and does not involve genetic manipulation.

Green Chemistry success stories in the pharmaceutical industry

At first glance, the principles of Green Chemistry seem to be rather obvious common sense statements rather than innovative ideas. Maybe this is their very strength. By putting the focus on prevention rather than amelioration and on reduction rather than excess, Green Chemistry principles have challenged the status quo of many chemical processes.

The following are some examples of Green Chemistry success stories in the pharmaceutical industry, which illustrate some of the principles.

- The production of the drug Viagra by Pfizer uses a modified reaction route that produces just a quarter of the waste of the original process. It reduces the amount of solvent and avoids the use of toxic and hazardous reagents.
- The synthesis of the anti-inflammatory drug ibuprofen has been altered from a six-step to a three-step reaction route. This has increased the atom economy of the process from 40% to 77% and reduced the energy demand.
- Synthesis of the analgesic drug Lyrica was modified to use a natural reagent of an enzyme with water as a solvent to reduce the use of non-renewable organic materials. This has eliminated the emissions of more than 3 million tonnes of CO_2 compared with the original process.

The challenge to scientists is to consider the environmental footprint of an *entire* chemical process from cradle to grave. The use of safer chemicals and solvents, shorter synthesis pathways and renewable resources in production, and the recycling and treatment of waste are all part of this.

These are just examples chosen to illustrate some of the principles, and do not have to be known specifically. Keep your eyes open for other examples in the news.

Exercises

20 Describe some of the problems caused by left-over solvents in the pharmaceutical industry.

21 State some of the sources of low-level radioactive waste arising from nuclear medicine, and explain how this must be treated.

22 'The very success of antibiotics in fighting disease has led to the widespread emergence of resistant strains, which today threatens their very usefulness.' Discuss this statement.

23 What is meant by 'patient compliance' in the context of antibiotic prescriptions?

24 Outline the general processes that should be followed to promote Green Chemistry in the manufacture of drugs.

1   Bioavailability refers to the percentage of a dose of a drug that reaches the bloodstream. This will be influenced by all of the following factors **except**

   A   breakdown of the drug by HCl in the stomach

   B   solubility of the drug in aqueous solution

   C   solubility of the blood in non-polar solvents

   D   binding of the drug to carrier molecules

2   If antacids were prepared each containing 0.1 mole of the following compounds, which would neutralize the greatest amount of HCl?

   A   magnesium hydroxide   B   aluminium hydroxide

   C   sodium hydrogencarbonate   D   calcium carbonate

3   When the action of mild and strong analgesics is compared, which statement is true?

   A   Mild analgesics stimulate the production of prostaglandins at the site of injury.

   B   Strong analgesics prevent the production of prostaglandins at the site of injury.

   C   Mild analgesics block the transmission of pain signals between nerve cells.

   D   Strong analgesics bind to opioid receptors in the brain.

4   Ethanol is said to have synergistic effects with some other drugs. Which of the following follows from this?

   A   Higher doses of the other drugs must be taken in the presence of ethanol.

   B   Ethanol consumption should be limited in the presence of these other drugs.

   C   The effects of intoxication due to ethanol will be decreased in the presence of these other drugs.

   D   Tolerance to ethanol will be increased in the presence of these other drugs.

5   Which of the following is the best description of bacterial resistance to penicillin?

   A   Resistant bacteria are able to produce the enzyme transpeptidase.

   B   Resistant bacteria lack the enzyme transpeptidase.

   C   Resistant bacteria are able to produce the enzyme beta-lactamase.

   D   Resistant bacteria lack the enzyme beta-lactamase.

6   The conversion of morphine into heroin produces a stronger analgesic. This is because

   A   heroin has a stronger affinity for the opioid receptors in the brain

   B   morphine is broken down in the body more quickly

   C   heroin is more able to cross the blood–brain barrier as it is more non-polar

   D   morphine must undergo hydrolysis before it can react in the body

7   Antibiotics treat infections by stopping the growth of bacteria or destroying them.

   (a) Identify the side-chain by drawing a circle around the side-chain in the structure of benzylpenicillin given below. (The structure of penicillin is given in section 37 of the IB data booklet.)   (1)

(b) Discuss **two** problems associated with the over-prescription of penicillin and explain how these are overcome. (3)

(Total 4 marks)

8 Two substances commonly used in antacid tablets are magnesium hydroxide and aluminium hydroxide.

(a) State an equation to represent a neutralization reaction with one of the above antacids. (1)

(b) State and explain whether 0.1 mol of magnesium hydroxide is more effective or less effective than 0.1 mol of aluminium hydroxide. (1)

(Total 2 marks)

9 (a) State **two** differences in structure between viruses and bacteria. (2)

(b) Describe **two** ways in which antiviral drugs work. (2)

(c) Discuss **two** difficulties associated with the development of drugs for the effective treatment of AIDS. (2)

(Total 6 marks)

10 Morphine is a strong analgesic which is administered parenterally.

(a) Explain why morphine is normally injected intravenously. (1)

(b) Diamorphine (heroin) is a more effective painkiller than morphine. The structures of morphine and diamorphine are shown in section 37 of the IB data booklet. Explain at the molecular level why diamorphine is absorbed into fatty tissue more rapidly than morphine. (2)

(Total 3 marks)

11 During drug development, trials are conducted to determine the therapeutic window. Explain the meaning of the term 'therapeutic window' and discuss its importance in drug administration. (4)

12 Examples of strong analgesics are morphine, codeine, and diamorphine (heroin). Their structures are shown in section 37 of the IB data booklet.

(a) Identify **two** functional groups present in all three of these analgesics. (2)

(b) Identify **one** functional group present in morphine, but not in diamorphine. (1)

(c) State the name of the type of chemical reaction which is used to convert morphine into diamorphine. (1)

(Total 4 marks)

13 The first penicillin to be used was benzylpenicillin (Penicillin G), and its structure is shown below.

(a) Explain how penicillins are able to act as antibacterials. (2)

(b) Modern penicillins have a similar structure to Penicillin G but a different side-chain. State **two** advantages of modifying the side-chain. (2)

(c) The active part of penicillins is the beta-lactam ring. Determine the functional group present in the beta-lactam ring and explain why the ring is important in the functioning of penicillin as an antibacterial. (3)

(Total 7 marks)

14 Drugs can be prescribed for treating various diseases and assisting in healing the human body; however, any drug presents potential risks. The properties of three drugs are summarized below.

Drug	Physiological effect	Side-effects	Therapeutic window
A	high	severe	medium
B	moderate	moderate	narrow
C	low	minimal	wide

Suggest which drug (**A**, **B**, or **C**) could be

(a) considered safe enough to be taken by patients without supervision. (1)

(b) administered **only** by qualified staff. (1)

(c) used **only** in a medical emergency. (1)

(Total 3 marks)

15 The effectiveness of a drug depends on the method of administration.

(a) One method of injecting drugs into the body results in the drug having a very rapid effect. State the method and explain its rapid action. (2)

(b) List the **two** other methods which can be used to inject drugs into the body. (1)

(c) Identify the method of administration used to treat respiratory diseases such as asthma. (1)

(Total 4 marks)

 To access weblinks on the topics covered in this chapter, please go to www.pearsonhotlinks.com and enter the ISBN or title of this book.

The twelve principles of green chemistry:

1 Prevention

It is better to prevent waste than to treat or clean up waste after it has been created.

2 Atom economy

Synthetic methods should be designed to maximize the incorporation of all materials used in the process into the final product.

3 Less hazardous chemical synthesis

Whenever practicable, synthetic methods should be designed to use and generate substances that possess little or no toxicity to people or the environment.

4 Designing safer chemicals

Chemical products should be designed to effect their desired function while minimizing their toxicity.

5 Safer solvents and auxiliaries

The use of auxiliary substances (e.g. solvents or separation agents) should be made unnecessary whenever possible and innocuous when used.

6 Design for energy efficiency

Energy requirements of chemical processes should be recognized for their environmental and economic impacts and should be minimized. If possible, synthetic methods should be conducted at ambient temperature and pressure.

7 Use of renewable feedstocks

A raw material or feedstock should be renewable rather than depleting whenever technically and economically practicable.

8 Reduce derivatives

Unnecessary derivatization (use of blocking groups, protection/de-protection, and temporary modification of physical/chemical processes) should be minimized or avoided if possible, because such steps require additional reagents and can generate waste.

9 Catalysis

Catalytic reagents (as selective as possible) are superior to stoichiometric reagents.

10 Design for degradation

Chemical products should be designed so that at the end of their function they break down into innocuous degradation products and do not persist in the environment.

11 Real-time analysis for pollution prevention

Analytical methods need to be further developed to allow for real-time, in-process monitoring and control prior to the formation of hazardous substances.

12 Inherently safer chemistry for accident prevention

Substances and the form of a substance used in a chemical process should be chosen to minimize the potential for chemical accidents, including releases, explosions, and fires.

Experimental work is an integral part of chemistry

Chemistry is an experimental science. During your IB chemistry course your learning will involve a significant amount of laboratory work. This will help you to understand some of the concepts, teach you important skills, and give you opportunities to extend your knowledge through investigations. And it is often the best part about studying chemistry!

Laboratory work usually involves 'hands-on' experimental work, which leads to the collection of **primary data**. These are data obtained directly, such as by measuring changes in a variable during an experiment or by collecting information through surveys or observations. **Secondary data** refers to data obtained from another source, such as via reference material or third-party results. The source of secondary data must always be cited in a report. Analysis of secondary data can also form an important part of experimental work.

Much of your laboratory work is likely to involve communication technology, through the use of data-logging devices and software such as spreadsheets, databases, and graph-plotting programs. The use of simulations and the development and analysis of models are also important skills.

Health, safety, and the environment

Considerations of health and safety are a crucial aspect of experimental work. The best sources of information for carrying out risk assessments are **MSDS, material safety datasheets**, which should be available whenever you are handling chemicals. The Laboratory Safety Institute (LSI) has developed useful guidelines on laboratory practice, which are summarized in the IB Chemistry guide. It is also important that you consider the environmental effects of your work in the laboratory and learn safe procedures for the storage, use, and disposal of chemicals. Micro-scale chemistry and Green Chemistry both present opportunities to limit the waste and environmental impact of your work.

International hazard symbols used in laboratories ensure that safety information is conveyed irrespective of the working language.

continued

continued ....

From top left to bottom right, the symbols represent:

- dangerous to the environment
- toxic
- gas under pressure
- corrosive
- explosive
- flammable
- caution – used for less serious health hazards like skin irritation
- oxidizing
- biohazards.

Practical skills

The choice of apparatus for carrying out reactions and for accurate measurement involves considerations of safety, efficiency, precision, and availability. The list below summarizes some of the most important skills for practical chemistry; it is hoped you will become familiar with these either through direct experimentation, through demonstration, or through simulation/virtual experimentation.

- choice of glassware for different tasks/measurements
- collection of gases by displacement of water
- accurate measurement of mass using a balance, including heating to constant mass
- precipitation and gravimetric analysis
- use of filtration apparatus, possibly including suction
- use of pipette with filler, and burette
- titration techniques including acid–base and redox
- preparation of standardized solutions and serial dilutions
- safe choice and practices for heating chemicals
- calorimetry
- use of pH meter and indicators
- use of probes for data-logging
- construction of voltaic and electrolytic cells
- use of colorimeter/spectrophotometer
- use of molecular models
- use of separating funnel and decantation
- simple distillation and reflux techniques
- recrystallization and melting point determination
- use of a centrifuge
- paper chromatography and TLC plates with R_f calculations
- preparation and use of standard curves for calibration and determination of concentration.

TOK It is now possible to observe and carry out many virtual experiments electronically. Are there ways of knowing that cannot be used in this medium? Do you think the quality of the learning that takes place is different in a virtual versus a real environment?

Assessment of experimental work

In addition to supporting your learning throughout the course, experimental work also forms part of the assessment of the IB programme. In Section A of Paper 3, questions will test your understanding of laboratory procedures and applications. The table below shows the experiments that are specified as part of the course, so be sure that you are familiar with these.

Sub-topic	Page number	Experiment
1.2 The mole concept	22	The obtaining and use of experimental data for deriving empirical formulas from reactions involving mass changes
1.3 Reacting masses and volumes	49	Use of the experimental method of titration to calculate the concentration of a solution by reference to a standard solution
1.3 Reacting masses and volumes	43	Obtaining and use of experimental values to calculate the molar mass of a gas from the ideal gas equation
5.1 Measuring energy changes	173	A calorimetry experiment for an enthalpy of reaction should be covered and the results evaluated
8.2 Properties of acids and bases	248	Students should have experience of acid–base titrations with different indicators
8.3 The pH scale	251	Students should be familiar with the use of a pH meter and universal indicator
9.2 Electrochemical cells	287	Performance of laboratory experiments involving a typical voltaic cell using two metal/metal ion half-cells
10.1 Fundamentals of organic chemistry	317	Construction of 3D models (real or virtual) of organic molecules

Experimental work is also the focus of the Internal Assessment component, discussed in the next chapter.

The investigation

During your two-year IB chemistry course, you are expected to carry out an individual scientific investigation, sometimes known as an **exploration**. This must be written up as a full report, and contributes to your final assessment on the course.

The investigation will be based on a topic of your own interest, and have a purposeful research question and scientific rationale. Your approach and methodology may rely on the collection of primary data through experimental work, or it may involve analysis of secondary data. Possibilities include the use of spreadsheets for analysis and modelling, extraction and analysis of data from a database, or the use of open-ended simulations. The investigation may also use a mix of approaches and data sources. In all cases, the investigation is marked according to the same five criteria, which are summarized below. Note the following general points:

- The written investigation is marked by your teacher (internally).
- The reports of a sample of students from your class will be re-marked by the IB, a process known as moderation, which ensures that the same standards are applied across all candidates.
- The mark awarded for your investigation contributes 20% towards your final IB result.
- The investigation is expected to take approximately 10 hours to complete.
- The investigation should be about 6 to 12 pages in length in regular font size.
- The investigation can be based on a topic within the course content, or it can be on extension material beyond the topic specifications in the IB Chemistry guide.

The investigation should provide clear evidence of the knowledge and skills that you have acquired with respect to the Nature of Science, and an awareness of the aims of the course. You also have the opportunity here to demonstrate the attributes of the IB learner profile.

The assessment criteria

The investigation will be marked using a best-fit approach to match the level of work with the descriptors given as mark bands. Each criterion is marked separately, and makes a specific contribution to the final mark out of 24 (later scaled to 20% of the overall IB assessment), as shown below.

	Personal engagement	Exploration	Analysis	Evaluation	Communication
mark out of 24	2	6	6	6	4
% of IA mark	8%	25%	25%	25%	17%

The marking descriptors for each criterion are shown below, with some additional notes for guidance. You are strongly recommended to focus only on the descriptor of the highest level in each case, shown in red here – there is no point in aiming for less!

Personal engagement

Mark	Descriptor
0	The student's report does not reach a standard described by the descriptors below.
1	**The evidence of personal engagement with the exploration is limited with little independent thinking, initiative, or creativity.** The justification given for choosing the research question and/or the topic under investigation does not demonstrate **personal significance, interest, or curiosity**. There is little evidence of **personal input and initiative** in the designing, implementation, or presentation of the investigation.
2	**The evidence of personal engagement with the exploration is clear with significant independent thinking, initiative, or creativity.** The justification given for choosing the research question and/or the topic under investigation demonstrates **personal significance, interest, or curiosity**. There is evidence of **personal input and initiative** in the designing, implementation, or presentation of the investigation.

Your report should include some background to the choice of your investigation and what inspired you in the planning. Maybe it was something you thought about in class, or during an experiment, or something you read? You will be credited for an investigation that is innovative and somewhat unique, that shows evidence of independent thinking and creativity in any or all stages. Try to demonstrate personal interest and genuine enthusiasm in your report.

Exploration

Mark	Descriptor
0	The student's report does not reach a standard described by the descriptors below.
1–2	The topic of the investigation is identified and a research question of some relevance is **stated but it is not focused**. The background information provided for the investigation is **superficial** or of limited relevance and does not aid the understanding of the context of the investigation. The methodology of the investigation is only appropriate to address the research question to a very limited extent since it takes into consideration few of the significant factors that may influence the relevance, reliability, and sufficiency of the collected data. The report shows evidence of limited awareness of the significant safety, ethical, or environmental issues that are **relevant to the methodology of the investigation***.
3–4	The topic of the investigation is identified and a relevant but not fully focused research question is described. The background information provided for the investigation is mainly appropriate and relevant and aids the understanding of the context of the investigation. The methodology of the investigation is mainly appropriate to address the research question but has limitations since it takes into consideration only some of the significant factors that may influence the relevance, reliability, and sufficiency of the collected data. The report shows evidence of some awareness of the significant safety, ethical, or environmental issues that are **relevant to the methodology of the investigation***.
5–6	The topic of the investigation is identified and a relevant and fully focused research question is clearly described. The background information provided for the investigation is entirely appropriate and relevant and enhances the understanding of the context of the investigation. The methodology of the investigation is highly appropriate to address the research question because it takes into consideration all, or nearly all, of the significant factors that may influence the relevance, reliability, and sufficiency of the collected data. The report shows evidence of full awareness of the significant safety, ethical, or environmental issues that are **relevant to the methodology of the investigation.***

* This indicator should only be applied when appropriate to the investigation.

Your report must have a clearly stated and focused research question, and give the scientific context of the work. This means relating it to your knowledge of the topic studied. The methodology used must show how relevant data are collected, taking into account factors that influence reliability of results. Consider control variables, choice of apparatus, and how many data will be sufficient for useful analysis. Note that five data points are usually considered necessary to establish a trend line. Where appropriate, make sure you have demonstrated awareness of related health, safety, and environmental issues. References to sources must, of course, be properly quoted.

Analysis

Mark	Descriptor
0	The student's report does not reach a standard described by the descriptors below.
1–2	The report includes **insufficient relevant** raw data to support a valid conclusion to the research question. Some **basic** data processing is carried out but is either too **inaccurate or too insufficient to lead to a valid** conclusion. The report shows evidence of little consideration of the impact of measurement uncertainty on the analysis. The processed data are incorrectly or insufficiently interpreted so that the conclusion is invalid or very incomplete.
3–4	The report includes relevant but incomplete quantitative and qualitative raw data that could support a simple or partially valid conclusion to the research question. Appropriate and sufficient data processing is carried out that could lead to a broadly valid conclusion but there are significant inaccuracies and inconsistencies in the processing. The report shows evidence of some consideration of the impact of measurement uncertainty on the analysis. The processed data are interpreted so that a broadly valid but incomplete or limited conclusion to the research question can be deduced.
5–6	The report includes sufficient relevant quantitative and qualitative raw data that could support a detailed and valid conclusion to the research question. Appropriate and sufficient data processing is carried out with **the accuracy** required to enable a conclusion to the research question to be drawn that is fully **consistent** with the experimental data. The report shows evidence of full and appropriate consideration of the impact of measurement uncertainty on the analysis. The processed data are correctly interpreted so that a completely valid and detailed conclusion to the research question can be deduced.

In this part of the report you must record data, both qualitative and quantitative, and demonstrate how the data are processed. This includes showing accuracy in calculations, the correct use of units, and consideration of the impact of error propagation. Data should be tabulated where possible. Graphs must be clearly titled, have appropriate scales and labelled axes with units, and show accurately plotted data points. Suitable best-fit lines or curves need to be marked distinctly. Your processed data need to be interpreted carefully in the context of the research question to develop a valid conclusion.

Evaluation

Mark	Descriptor
0	The student's report does not reach a standard described by the descriptors below.
1–2	A conclusion is **outlined** which is not relevant to the research question or is not supported by the data presented. The conclusion makes superficial comparison to the accepted scientific context. Strengths and weaknesses of the investigation, such as limitations of the data and sources of error, are **outlined** but are restricted to an **account of the practical or procedural issues** faced. The student has **outlined** very few realistic and relevant suggestions for the improvement and extension of the investigation.
3–4	A conclusion is **described** which is relevant to the research question and supported by the data presented. A conclusion is described which makes some relevant comparison to the accepted scientific context. Strengths and weaknesses of the investigation, such as limitations of the data and sources of error, are **described** and provide evidence of some awareness of the **methodological issues*** involved in establishing the conclusion. The student has **described** some realistic and relevant suggestions for the improvement and extension of the investigation.
5–6	A detailed conclusion is **described and justified** which is entirely relevant to the research question and fully supported by the data presented. A conclusion is correctly **described and justified** through relevant comparison to the accepted scientific context. Strengths and weaknesses of the investigation, such as limitations of the data and sources of error, are **discussed** and provide evidence of a clear understanding of the **methodological issues** involved in establishing the conclusion. The student has **discussed** realistic and relevant suggestions for the improvement and extension of the investigation.

* The report shows evidence of full awareness of the significant safety, ethical or environmental issues that are **relevant to the methodology of the investigation**.

You must give a conclusion that is both justified by the results presented, and puts the findings in a broader context. This involves comparison with literature values and accepted data sources. This is a good place to show off your relevant scientific knowledge, and you should aim to include molecular level explanations for your findings where possible. Full consideration of errors is essential, and should lead you to evaluate the methodology chosen and suggest relevant modifications. Make sure the modifications are specific to the weaknesses identified. A table with three columns can help you to keep this part of the report focused, as shown in the example below:

Error/design limitation	Impact on results	Suggested modification
some of the CO_2 collected by displacement of water may have dissolved in the water	volume of CO_2 measured is less than the volume released by the reaction	collect gas over warm water to reduce it solubility

Communication

Mark	Descriptor
0	The student's report does not reach a standard described by the descriptors below.
1–2	**The presentation of the investigation is unclear, making it difficult to understand the focus, process, and outcomes.** The report is not well structured and is unclear: the necessary information on focus, process, and outcomes is missing or is presented in an incoherent or disorganized way. The understanding of the focus, process, and outcomes of the investigation is obscured by the presence of inappropriate or irrelevant information. There are many errors in the use of subject-specific terminology and conventions*.

3–4	**The presentation of the investigation is clear. Any errors do not hamper understanding of the focus, process, and outcomes.** The report is well structured and clear: the necessary information on focus, process, and outcomes is present and presented in a coherent way. The report is relevant and concise thereby facilitating a ready understanding of the focus, process, and outcomes of the investigation. The use of subject-specific terminology and conventions is appropriate and correct. Any errors do not hamper understanding.

* For example, incorrect/missing labelling of graphs, tables, images; use of units, decimal places.

A good scientific report communicates in clear and concise language with no superfluous comments. There is no fixed narrative style or outline of sub-headings expected, but your report should follow a logical sequence and make correct use of the subject-specific terms. Scientific journal articles provide a good source of ideas for how to structure your report. This criterion will be judged holistically on the overall report.

Making the most of your Internal Assessment opportunity

1 Start early

Your school will give guidance on when you are expected to work on your investigation and will probably issue internal deadlines. But you can start thinking about possible topics from the beginning of the course, and research ideas and approaches. Keep a record of your resources and outlines, and allow your ideas to develop as your knowledge grows in the course.

2 Be aware of the criteria

As you choose your research question and design your investigation, keep a close eye on the assessment criteria as given here. Remember the marks you are given are determined by how well your work matches these specific descriptors, so keep checking.

3 Seek and follow feedback

Your teacher may give you some guidance on your early ideas and suggest modifications. Don't be afraid to ask for help as you develop your plan, as this may well make your work more efficient and will not affect your assessment.

4 Be enthusiastic!

This is your chance to put the Nature of Science into action. You are in charge of your choice of topic, and have the flexibility here to be creative, so enjoy it fully.

Theory of knowledge

Introduction

In TOK you are encouraged to think critically about the process of knowing. Which ways of knowing do you use to justify your chemical knowledge? Does chemistry give you a 'true' picture of reality? How does the knowledge you gain in your chemistry class differ from that gained in other subjects? What are the ethical implications of technological developments in the subject? Chemistry has been hugely successful in giving us explanations of the material world and has also made a significant contribution to improving our quality of life, but does it offer certainty?

Ways of knowing: perception

What does the figure on the right represent?

To many people this is simply a circle and a hexagon, but to an IB chemistry student it should have more significance. It can be interpreted as a benzene ring for example. How you choose to interpret the picture will depend on the context in which it is presented and your prior knowledge. This illustrates an important point: perception is an active process, which includes an element of personal interpretation.

Chemistry and technology

Chemistry deals with **empirical knowledge**. This is knowledge acquired by the senses, enhanced, if necessary, by technology. We are now able to see things which are beyond the direct limits of our senses. Look at the photograph below. Is this what a metal surface really looks like?

The scientific method

Should the natural sciences be regarded more as a method or more as a system of knowledge?

Richard Feynman (1918–1988), one of the great physicists of the 20th century, gave the following description of the scientific method:

> " In general we look for a new law by the following process. First we guess it. Then we compute the consequences of the guesses to see what would be implied if the law was right. If it disagrees with experiment, it is wrong. In that simple statement is the key to science … It does not make any difference how smart you are, or what is your name – if it disagrees with experiment it is wrong … It is true that one has to check a little to check that one is wrong. "

During your IB chemistry course, you are continually challenged to think about the Nature of Science. To what extent is Feynman's view of the scientific method still a valid description today? Does a single method adequately describe scientific studies in all disciplines from astronomy to geology? Could you

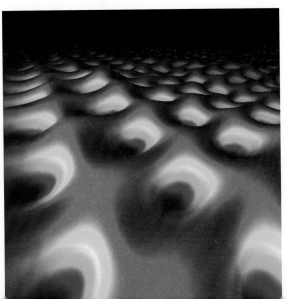

This picture is obtained by firing a beam of polarized ^{3}He atoms towards a metal surface. The metal can be seen as a lattice of positive metal ions (blue) in a sea of electrons (red).

use your experience in the chemistry laboratory or on the group 4 project to write your own definition of the scientific method?

Ways of knowing: induction (reason)

How do individual observations lead to theories and scientific laws of nature? Imagine an experiment in which you test the pH of some aqueous solutions of different oxides.

Oxide	Acid/alkali
$Na_2O(s)$	alkali
$MgO(s)$	alkali
$CO_2(g)$	acid
$SO_2(g)$	acid
$CaO(s)$	alkali
$N_2O_5(g)$	acid

Two possible explanations which fit the pattern are:

• All solid oxides are alkalis. All gaseous oxides are acidic.
• All metal oxides are alkalis. All non-metal oxides are acidic.

We have used **induction** to draw the two general conclusions. Inductive logic allows us to move from specific instances to a general conclusion. Although it appeals to common sense, it is logically flawed. Both conclusions are equally valid, based on the evidence, but both conclusions could be wrong. Just because something has happened many times in the past does not prove that it will happen in the future. This is the **problem of induction**. The philosopher Bertrand Russell illustrated the danger of generalization by considering the case of the philosophical turkey. The bird reasoned that since he had been fed by the farmer every morning, he always would be. Sadly, this turkey discovered the problem with induction on Thanksgiving Day! Are you acting in the same way as the turkey when you draw conclusions in your experimental work?

How do we justify the use of induction? Consider the following form of reasoning.

• On Monday I used induction and it worked.
• On Tuesday I used induction and it worked.
• On Wednesday I used induction and it worked.
• On Thursday I used induction and it worked.
• On Friday I used induction and it worked.
• Therefore I know that induction works.

What form of reasoning is used here to justify induction?

Karl Popper (1902–1994) realized that scientific verification doesn't actually prove anything and decided that science finds theories, not by verifying statements, but by **falsifying** them. Popper believed that even when a scientific theory had been successfully and repeatedly tested, it was not necessarily true. Instead, it had simply not yet been proved false. Observing a million white swans does not prove that all swans are white, but the first time we see a black swan, we can firmly disprove the theory.

No matter how many times we record in our notebooks the observation of a white swan, we get no closer to proving the universal statement that all swans are white. Black swans inhabit lakes, rivers, and coastal areas in Australia.

Ways of knowing: deduction (reason)

Deductive logic allows us to move from general statements to specific examples.

The conclusion of deductive logic must be true if the general statements on which it is based are correct. Deductive reasoning is the foundation of mathematics. We can use this reasoning to test our scientific hypotheses. Consider again the pH of the oxides tabulated earlier. The two competing hypotheses could be distinguished by considering the pH of a non-metal oxide such as phosphorus oxide, which is a solid at room temperature. If we use the two hypotheses as starting points (**premises**), they lead to two different conclusions using deductive reasoning.

• All solid oxides are alkalis.
• Phosphorus oxide is solid.

Therefore: phosphorus oxide is an alkali.

OR

• All non-metal oxides are acidic.
• Phosphorus oxide is a non-metal oxide.

Therefore: phosphorus oxide is an acid.

When the pH of phosphorus oxide solution is tested and shown to be an acid we can be certain that the first hypothesis is false, but we cannot be sure that the second is definitely true.

If it survives repeated tests, it may, however, become accepted as scientific truth, but this is not certain. No matter how many tests a hypothesis survives, we will never prove that it is true in the same way as mathematical proof is true. All scientific knowledge is provisional.

There are still problems, however, with this view of science. When your results don't match up with the expected values in a chemistry investigation, do you abandon the accepted theories or do you explain the differences as being due to experimental error, faulty instruments, or contaminated chemicals?

How have scientists and philosophers made use of Karl Popper's ideas? Are we any closer to proving scientific principles are 'true'?

When are you justified in dismissing a data point which does not fit the general pattern?

Same data, different hypothesis

It is always possible to think of other hypotheses that are consistent with the given set of data. The hypothesis: 'Oxides with one oxygen in the formula are alkalis, oxides with more than one oxygen are acids' also fits the data presented. For the same reason, an infinite number of patterns can be found to fit the same experimental data.

 The curve and straight line in the graph both fit the experimental data.

You may argue that the straight line in the graph above is more suitable as it is simpler, but on what grounds do we base the assumption that simplicity is a criterion for truth? The idea that the simplest explanations are the best is inspired by the principle – named after the medieval philosopher William of Occam – known as Occam's razor.

Rejecting anomalous results: confirmation bias

We often dismiss results which don't fit the expected pattern because of experimental error. In the example below, is it reasonable to reject the point not on the line?

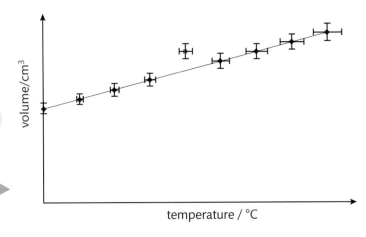

Are the models and theories that scientists use merely pragmatic instruments or do they actually describe the natural world?

Scientists use models to clarify certain features and relationships. They can become more and more sophisticated but they can never become the real thing. Models are just a representation of reality. The methane molecule, for example, can be represented in a number of forms. All these models of methane are based on the Bohr model of the atom discussed in Chapter 2. Although this is one of the most successful scientific models, it is not complete as it fails to explain the electron arrangement of atoms after calcium in the Periodic Table. To explain the chemistry of all the elements, a more sophisticated model that involves considering an electron as a wave is needed.

need imagination to form a mental representation of something when it is beyond sense experience. Imagination is also associated with creativity, problem-solving, and originality; all key skills of the scientists.

The wave–particle duality of the electron illustrates a general knowledge issue. Two sources of knowledge can often give conflicting results and it is for us to see if the conflict is real or a limitation of our ways of knowing.

Different models of the methane molecule.

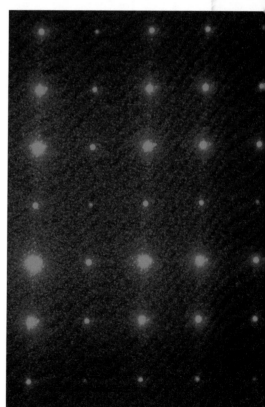

This is a diffraction grating pattern formed by laser light (red), which has passed through an array of crossed gratings. Light is generally considered as a wave.

The evidence for the wave nature of electrons comes from the diffraction pattern observed when a beam of electrons is passed through a metal structure, which is similar to that observed when light is passed through a diffraction grating (see right). We now recognize that the 'true' nature of the electron, or indeed anything, cannot be completely described by a single model. Both the wave model and the particle model are needed. This should not surprise us as models are often based on our everyday experience which does not apply to the small scale of the atom. To understand nature at this level, scientists must go beyond their experience and use their imagination. Scientists

This is an electron diffraction pattern of a binary alloy of 90% titanium and 10% nickel. The pattern can be explained by considering an electron as a wave.

Science and pseudoscience: alchemy and homeopathy

If you have ever dropped sugar into a glass of a carbonated water you will have noticed that it fizzes. Can you offer an explanation for this?

If someone suggested that it was because there was an 'evil demon' present in the drink who was responding angrily to being assaulted by sugar granules you would probably reject this as a non-scientific explanation, but what makes this non-scientific? A scientific theory must be testable. It is difficult to imagine an experiment which could be designed to prove the 'evil demon' theory *false*. A theory that can be used to explain everything explains nothing.

It is worth reflecting, however, that many of the experimental techniques of chemistry have their origins in the pseudoscience of alchemy.

The alchemist's hunt for the Philosopher's Stone, which was believed to give eternal life and could turn base metals into gold, seems very naïve to us now, but how do you think our chemical knowledge will be viewed 500 years on?

Add sugar to any of these drinks and awake an evil demon! ▶

A page from a treatise on alchemy written by Zosimus of Panapolitus (4th century). Some of the equipment drawn is found in a modern chemistry laboratory.

In 1661, with the publication of *The Sceptical Chemist*, Robert Boyle established chemistry as a separate science. He is famous for *Boyle's law*, which states the relationship between pressure and volume for a fixed mass of gas.

 There are a number of activities that are claimed by those who practise them to be scientific, such as astrology, homeopathy, and crystology. The label 'science' can add authority to the claims, but how do we distinguish a genuine science from a fake or **pseudoscience**?

 Ernest Rutherford, the father of nuclear physics, described himself as an alchemist as he was able to change one element into another by nuclear reactions.

A web and hierarchy of disciplines

The IB Diploma programme refers to group 4 as 'Sciences', while the Theory of Knowledge programme refers to two separate areas of knowledge, the human sciences and the natural sciences, which broadly represent groups 3 and 4 respectively. What is the distinction between these two areas of knowledge? Can you think of subjects that might be classified in either group? The IB course 'computer science' has at different times been classified as a group 3 subject (individuals and societies), a group 5 subject (mathematics) but now is part of group 4. What arguments can be made for placing it in these different categories?

Is it possible to place the different scientific disciplines in a hierarchy and which criteria would you use for your choice? Chemical theories can help our understanding of biology: for example, hydrogen bonding explains the double helix structure of DNA. But much of chemistry relies on physics: for example, hydrogen bonding is explained in terms of electrostatic attraction.

Is this direction of explanation ever reversed? The view that one subject can be explained in terms of the components of another is called **reductionism**. Is physics in some way 'better' than the other sciences? Where would you place mathematics, which has been described as both the queen and servant of the sciences in this hierarchy? Our knowledge of the Periodic Table and atomic structure suggests that there are limits to the number of elements in nature. Is chemistry in some way the most complete science? Which of the natural sciences is most clearly based on direct observation?

How does chemical knowledge change with time?

We have seen that the inductive and falsification theories of science give an incomplete description of how science progresses. An alternative view was offered by Thomas Kuhn (1922–1996). Kuhn suggested that science does not develop by the orderly accumulation of facts and theories, but by dramatic revolutions which he called **paradigm shifts**. In this context, a paradigm can be thought of as a model or world view accepted by the scientific community. Kuhn distinguished between periods of **normal science** in which new discoveries are placed within the current paradigm and **extraordinary science** which produces results which do not fit the current paradigm. Isaac Newton, John Dalton, Charles Darwin, and Albert Einstein are all revolutionary scientists who changed the way we look at the world by proposing new paradigms.

The idea of a paradigm shift can be illustrated by considering the picture below.

In one paradigm, the picture can be interpreted as a duck; in another paradigm, it can be interpreted as a rabbit. Turn the page through 90° and experience a paradigm shift.

As Kuhn says 'What were ducks in the scientists' world before the revolution, are rabbits afterwards …'

Atomic theory is one of the most important paradigms of chemistry. Dalton's model of the atom as being indivisible collapsed with the discovery of the proton, neutron, and electron.

Paradigm shifts: phlogiston theory and the discovery of oxygen

When a solid such as magnesium burns, it crumbles into an ash. It seems quite natural to assume that the metal is giving something off as it burns. It was originally believed that all flammable materials contain phlogiston (a word derived from the Greek for flame), which was absorbed by the air as substances burn. In this theory, substances stop burning when all the phlogiston has been released or when the air is saturated with the phlogiston released. The crisis for the paradigm occurred when careful

According to the phlogiston paradigm, a substance is released into the air when a candle burns. We now know that the carbon and hydrogen in the candle combine with oxygen in the air to form carbon dioxide and water.

measurements showed that a mass increase occurred during combustion. Some explained this result within the phlogiston paradigm by suggesting that phlogiston could have a negative mass but that explanation was rejected in favour of the modern oxygen theory of combustion.

As substances burn more brightly in oxygen, the gas was originally called 'dephlogisticated air' by Joseph Priestley, one of the scientists credited with its discovery. However, the discovery of oxygen made the term 'phlogiston' meaningless.

A widely held stereotype of scientific progress is that of an idealistic young innovator challenging the ideas of the establishment. This is rationalized in Kuhn's model of science because individual scientists are often reluctant to make such leaps. So what is the role of creative thinking in scientific progress? The need to be a risk taker and think out of the box is emphasized by Richard Feynman: 'One of the ways of stopping science would be to only experiment in the region where you know the law'.

Max Planck said 'A new scientific theory does not triumph by convincing its opponents and making them see the light, but rather because its opponents eventually die out and a new generation grows up that is familiar with it'.

Shared and personal knowledge

The subject of chemistry has a body of highly structured and systematic shared knowledge. It is the work of many individuals and is in a sense anonymous – although there would have been no Hamlet without Shakespeare, atomic theory would have been developed without Dalton. While individuals can and do contribute to this body of knowledge, their work is subject to peer review and their experimental results need to be replicated by others if they are going to be accepted by the scientific community.

We all, however, have difference experiences of chemistry, and this gives us personal knowledge of the subject. This includes procedural knowledge of how to do something such as a titration. Personal knowledge can be formed from a number of ways of knowing such as our memories, our experimental observations, and the significance we associate with different ideas. Like public knowledge, personal knowledge also evolves with time. What you now know about the atom is quite different to what you knew five years ago. Personal knowledge, unlike public knowledge, can be forgotten!

Ways of knowing: language

The language of alchemy was cryptic and secretive as the knowledge it communicated was thought to be too powerful to share with the general public. The names of many chemicals were derived from their natural origin and were not related to their composition.

The language of modern chemistry, by contrast, is precise, and is an effective tool for thought. When asked to draw the different isomers of C_7H_{16} it is very easy to draw the same structure twice. The IUPAC nomenclature, however, allows you to distinguish the different isomers.

heptane	2-methylhexane	3-methylhexane
2,2-dimethylpentane	2,3-dimethylpentane	2,4-dimethylpentane
3,3-dimethylpentane	3-ethylpentane	2,2,3-trimethylbutane

The nine isomers of C_7H_{16}. The names help you to distinguish the different structures.

The use of oxidation numbers has also allowed us to develop a systematic nomenclature for naming inorganic substances.

Chemistry, of course, also has its own universal language. Balanced equations allow us to use mathematics to solve chemical problems. The ability to attach numbers to substances allows the chemist to use mathematics as a precise tool to investigate the material world. Language should be a tool and not an obstacle to knowledge.

Measurement: the observer effect

Measurement has allowed the chemist to attach numbers to the properties of materials, but the act of measurement can change the property being measured. Adding a thermometer to a hot beaker of water, for example, will cause the temperature to decrease slightly and adding an acid–base indicator, which is itself a weak acid, will slightly change the pH of the solution.

Generally, such effects can be ignored, as measures are taken to minimize them. Only a few drops of indicator are used, for example, and thermometers are designed to have a low heat capacity. The **observer effect** can cause significant problems at the atomic scale, however, which led the physicist Werner Heisenberg (1901–1976) to comment: 'What we observe is not nature itself but nature exposed to our mode of questioning'. The observer effect is also significant in the human sciences. Can your school director observe a 'normal' chemistry class?

Knowledge and belief

It should be clear from the previous discussion that science does not offer complete certainty and absolute truth. Do you *know* that sodium chloride is made up from Na^+ and Cl^- ions or do you simply *believe* this to be the case? What is needed to change a belief into knowledge?

Chemistry and ethics

Progress in science and technology affects our lives. Often these effects are positive – drugs and medicines have made our lives safer, and the development of new materials has made our lives more comfortable – but technological developments can also bring suffering and injustice. Industry and technology have had a negative impact on the environment. How do we decide what is the right and wrong use of science? These are ethical questions. There is often disagreement about what is 'right' and ideas of what is considered to be acceptable often change over time. Ethical issues raise difficult questions about risk versus benefits. In many cases, the science is so new that judging long-term benefits and risks is difficult. Developments in chemistry can create new ethical issues. There are also more direct concerns about how scientists should conduct their work. Scientists generally work in communities, not in isolation, and are expected to report their results honestly and openly in an atmosphere of trust. Science is, however, a human endeavour and scientists, like the rest of humanity, can be motivated by envy, vanity, and ambition.

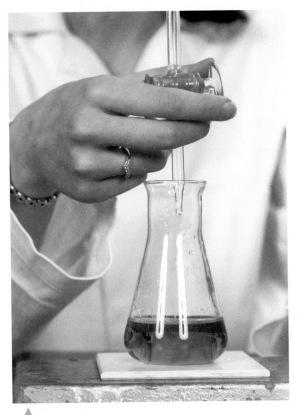

Methyl orange is a weak acid. The addition of the indicator will change the pH of the solution it is measuring.

The dangers of dioxin pollution were discussed in Chapter 12. Dioxin toxicity research has involved tests on rats. Are such tests ethically justified?

Is science, or ought it to be, value-free? Some would argue that it is the aim of science to describe the world as it is and not as it should be. The natural sciences and ethics are different areas of knowledge which use different ways of knowing to answer different questions. It is for society to decide what to do with scientific issues – that is the moral question.

Some people do, however, fear the consequence of scientists 'interfering with nature'. The arguments for and against the use of genetically modified foods, for example, are still the subject of lively debate. Who decides what is and what is not a legitimate area of scientific research? The scientific community or society at large? The fear of scientific discoveries is, of course, understandable. As discussed in Chapter 15, scientists believed that thalidomide was so safe that it was prescribed to pregnant women to control morning sickness, with tragic consequences. Who is responsible when things go wrong?

Ways of knowing: imagination

E. J. Corey, a Nobel prize winning work pioneer on organic syntheses, wrote:

> " The synthetic chemist is more than a logician and strategist; he is an explorer strongly influenced to speculate, to imagine and even to create. "

Our imagination can help us to solve problems and develop original ideas. We may use imagination to make connections between separate ideas, to build models or create theories. But to what extent should we trust our imagination, given that is derived in the mind rather than through sense perception? Can imagination reveal truths that reality hides? What other examples of the discoveries of chemists described in this book illustrate the importance of imagination?

The knowledge framework in chemistry

An area of knowledge can be characterized by a knowledge framework which provides a tool for comparing different areas of knowledge.

Scope/applications	Concepts/language
Chemistry is about understanding the nature of matter and its interactions. It helps us understand and control the material world and can be used to improve human life. Chemistry is a central science which has applications in the biological, material, and environmental sciences. There are ethical considerations that limit its scope of inquiry. Chemicals can damage our environment and be used as weapons.	Chemical knowledge is shared using natural languages in books, journals, and meetings. Chemical equations and mathematics are used to formulate and solve quantitative problems. Key chemical concepts include mass, charge, bonding and structure, and energy. Everyday metaphors are used to understand the microscopic world; atoms can be thought of as billiard balls and electrons as waves. Units and chemical nomenclature are required to communicate shared knowledge precisely.

Methodology

Chemists follow a scientific methodology with an emphasis on experimental work. Results are explained using theories and models and evaluated by peer review. Many ways of knowing are involved in the sciences. Intuition and creativity are needed to produce hypotheses and reason to provide coherent explanations. Knowledge is shared using natural language and problems formulated and solved using chemical symbols and mathematical language. Observations and measurements are made using sense perception, and emotion can provide the personal motivation for a scientist to focus on a particular area of research. The scientific approach assumes that the material world behaves in a coherent way and is rationally comprehensible. Experimental results and well-established theories count as facts and explanations which reduce chemical change and structure to simple, well-understood concepts such as mass, charge, and attractive and repulsive forces. Models can be used to simplify a problem to simple cause and effect relationships. The scope of the subject is limited by the dangerous nature of some substances to the individual and the environment.

Historical development

Many of the techniques of chemistry originate from alchemy. Lavoisier attached numbers to substances and helped chemistry develop as a physical science. Mendeleyev's Periodic Table systematized a mass of chemical information, and Atomic Theory explained the structure of the Periodic Table and the nature of chemical interactions. It was originally believed that a 'vital force' was needed to explain organic chemistry but we now realize that it fits in with the rest of our chemical understanding.

Links to personal knowledge

Our shared chemical knowledge has grown from the personal knowledge of individuals such as Boyle, Avogadro, Mendeleyev, Dalton, Bohr, Lewis, Gibbs, Brønsted, Lowry, and Kebulé. Their contributions have made the subject more systematic and coherent. Individual chemists have to take some responsibility for the consequences of their work. They must use their knowledge responsibly and consider the full implications of their work.

Chemistry and TOK assessment

In your TOK essays, you are expected to make connections between the knowledge issues raised and your own experiences as a learner. It is helpful to support your argument with examples drawn from your IB diploma courses as well as from other sources. In your TOK presentations, you are asked to apply your TOK thinking skills to a contemporary issue. This can be an opportunity, for example, to reflect on the moral and ethical implications of scientific developments. Your chemistry course offers a wide range of experiences for reflection.

Some examples of prescribed essay titles for you to consider

- What similarities and differences are there between historical and scientific explanations? (May 2010)

- A model is a simplified representation of some aspect of the world. In what ways may models help or hinder the search for knowledge? (May 2011)
- What is it about theories in the human and natural sciences that makes them convincing? (May 2012)
- In what ways may disagreement aid the pursuit of knowledge in the natural and human sciences? (May 2013)
- 'Knowledge is nothing more than the systematic organization of facts.' Discuss this statement in relation to two areas of knowledge. (May 2014)
- 'That which is accepted as knowledge today is sometimes discarded tomorrow.' Consider knowledge issues raised by this statement in two areas of knowledge. (May 2014)

The Extended Essay is a compulsory part of the IB Diploma. It is an independent 40-hour research project in an IB subject of your choice. The final essay is up to 4000 words of formally presented, structured writing. The marks awarded for the Extended Essay and TOK are combined to give a maximum of three bonus points.

An Extended Essay in chemistry must have a clear chemical emphasis and not be more closely related to another subject. For example, a chemistry Extended Essay in an area such as biochemistry will be assessed on its chemical and not its biological content. It should include chemical principles and theory.

The best chemistry Extended Essays are often based on experiments carried out in a school laboratory.

Some advice

Before you start

Read a copy of the subject-specific details of an Extended Essay in chemistry, including the assessment criteria. Read some previous essays and try to identify their strengths and weaknesses. Draw up a list of possible research questions including the techniques you would use to address these questions. Many of the best essays are written by students investigating relatively simple phenomena using apparatus and materials that can be found in most school laboratories.

You may find it useful to consider some of the following techniques when planning your research; it is often appropriate to use a combination of two or more of these approaches:

• titration: acid–base or redox
• chromatography: paper, partition, thin-layer, column

- electrophoresis
- spectrophotometry
- measuring mass or volume changes
- calorimetry
- qualitative and quantitative analysis
- separation and purification techniques in organic chemistry
- use of data-logging probes for some of the above.

Think carefully about which technique(s) you will be using when planning your research. Acid–base and redox titrations, for example, can be used to analyse a range of problems.

The research question

The research question is the key to a successful Extended Essay. You should choose a topic that interests you as you will be spending 40 hours on this. Your question must be sharply focused. For example, *'What is the ratio of oxygen and chlorine produced at the anode during the electrolysis of different concentrated solutions of aqueous sodium chloride solution?'* is better than *'What happens during the electrolysis of salt?'*

The research process

- Safety is a priority. Don't do anything in the laboratory without checking with your supervisor.

- Use a range of resources to find out what others have done in the area. Textbooks or the internet should never be the only source of information.

- Keep written records of everything that you do and make a note of all references, including the date when internet sites were accessed so that you can build up your footnotes and bibliography as you go along.

- Record all experimental data, including the dates when the experiments were performed and any uncertainties in your measurements. In your preliminary investigations, write down any problems and challenges you encountered and record any modifications. Use your imagination to design new equipment if necessary.

While writing the essay

Make sure that you address your stated research question and the Extended Essay assessment criteria.

- Include explanations of any theory not covered in the IB subject guide, including the chemistry of any specialized techniques you have used.

- Use the appropriate chemical language and make sure that all chemical equations are balanced.

- Include sufficient details of any experimental procedure to allow others to repeat the work.

- Check any calculations and make sure that all experimental data are presented correctly.

- Discuss the limitations of the experimental method and any systematic errors.

- Consider any questions which are unresolved at the end of your research and suggest new questions and areas for possible further investigation.

- Let your enthusiasm and interest for the topic show and emphasize clearly your own personal contribution.

- Ensure that your word count is close to 4000. You will often find you can cut quite a number of words as you polish your essay at the end.

After completing the essay

- Check and proofread the final version carefully.
- Use the assessment criteria to grade your essay. Are you satisfied with the grade you award yourself?

The assessment criteria

All Extended Essays are assessed according to five criteria, labelled A–E. Each criterion has several descriptors corresponding to different achievement levels. By judging which of these levels most closely matches the work in the essay, the appropriate mark is assigned for each criterion. The final grade awarded for the essay is determined by totalling these five marks. The maximum number of marks available is 34.

The table below gives the descriptor for the highest achievement level for each criterion together with the maximum number of marks available.

The Extended Essay criteria and advice to achieve high marks for each criterion

Criterion and marks	Assessment focus	Advice/questions to ask yourself
A: Focus and method – 6 marks • Topic • Research question • Methodology	Assesses the explanation of the focus of the research (this includes the topic and the research question), how the research will be undertaken, and how this focus is maintained throughout the essay.	Your research question must be formulated as a question, and given context by researching the existing literature. The methodology could include practical work in the laboratory or be based on secondary sources. The rationale for choosing an experimental procedure should be clearly explained.
B: Knowledge and understanding – 6 marks • Context • Subject-specific terminology and concepts	Assesses the extent to which the research relates to chemistry, and additionally the way in which this knowledge and understanding is demonstrated through the use of appropriate terminology and concepts.	Does the essay focus on the chemistry aspect of the investigation? You are expected to apply your chemical knowledge appropriately and explain the underlying principles behind your research question and methodology. You should use acknowledged scientific sources and they should be relevant and effectively referenced. You must try to maintain a consistent linguistic style and use chemical. nomenclature and terminology, including chemical and structural formulas, balanced equations with state symbols, significant figures and SI units.
C: Critical thinking – 12 marks • Research • Analysis • Discussion and evaluation	Assesses the extent to which critical thinking skills has been used to analyse and evaluate the research undertaken.	Does your data support and clarify your argument? Your analysis could include data tables, graphs, mathematical transformations, and statistical analysis. The rationale behind any statistical test should be explained and the significance of the results discussed. You should avoid investigations with a large number of variables as they can be unfocused and incoherent. Any limitations of your investigation including poor experimental design, systematic errors and any unresolved issues should be discussed. You must comment on the quality, balance and quantity of your sources and the validity and reliability of your data, including the uncertainties of any measurements. You should suggest ways in which the investigation could be extended.

Criterion and marks	Assessment focus	Advice/questions to ask yourself
D: Presentation – 4 marks • Structure • Layout	Assesses the extent to which the presentation follows the standard format expected from academic writing and the extent to which this aids communication.	Does your presentation conform to accepted academic standards? The use of numbered and headed paragraphs helps you clearly present your argument. Only use charts, images or tables if they contribute towards your argument. Large tables of primary raw data collected should be labelled and put in an appendix. Graphs or charts showing processed data should highlight only the most pertinent aspects and you should avoid the use of excessive graphs, charts and tables as they hinder communication. When your experimental procedure is long or complex it can be placed in the appendix and summarized in the body of the essay. This summary should however include all the key elements that contribute to the quality of the investigation. Similarly include sample calculations in the text to illustrate how your data was processed. A bibliography is essential and any unoriginal material must be carefully acknowledged otherwise it will be considered as a case of possible academic misconduct.
E: Engagement – 6 marks • Process • Research focus	This assesses your engagement with your research focus and the research process.	You are expected to reflect on the decision-making and planning process during your investigation. You must explain why you chose your question and the methodology used. You must complete a 'Reflections on Planning and Progress Form' (RPPF) which should refer to: • the approach and strategies you chose, and their relative success • the 'Approaches to Learning' skills you have developed, and their effectiveness • how the research process has changed your conceptual understandings • how you responded to unexpected challenges • how additional questions emerged during the research process • what you would do differently if you were given the opportunity to repeat the process. Your reflections should be personal and demonstrate that you have learned from the experience. You should show evidence of your thinking, creativity and originality.

Bibliography and references

It is required that you acknowledge all sources of information and ideas in an approved academic manner. Essays that omit a bibliography or that do not give references are unacceptable. Your supervisor or school librarian will be able to give you advice on which format to follow. One acceptable format is:

Author(s), Year, *Title*, Place of Publication, Publisher.

C. Brown and M. Ford, 2014, *Standard Level Chemistry 2nd edition*, UK, Pearson Baccalaureate.

Internet references should include the title of the extract used as well as the website address, the date it was accessed, and, if possible, the author. You should always exercise caution when using information from websites that do not give references or that cannot be cross-checked against other sources. The more important a particular point is to the essay, the more the quality of its source needs to be evaluated. There websites available online which can assist you in these tasks.

Viva voce

Remember to use a range of resources including the internet and any libraries available.

After you have handed in the final version you will be given a short interview or *viva voce* by your supervisor, who is required to write a report on your project. This is an opportunity to discuss the successes and challenges of the project and for you to reflect on what you have learned from the experience.

World Studies Extended Essay

As you think about topics for an Extended Essay in chemistry, it may be that you find an area of current global interest, which overlaps with another subject. In this case, it may be appropriate to submit the essay as World Studies, which is a separate IB Extended Essay subject. An essay in World Studies must have the following characteristics:

• it must focus on an *issue of contemporary global significance*;
• it must involve an in-depth *interdisciplinary study*, making reference to at least two IB subjects.

The approach to a World Studies Extended Essay is to identify a global issue and find a local example that lends itself to research and analysis, using the methodologies of two different subjects. This gives a grounded appreciation and understanding of the issue under study. As part of the research, you are encouraged to keep records of your thoughts and ideas in the 'researchers reflection space'. This helps to show development in your global perspective and some of the challenges in the research.

Areas of study which could have chemical content include:

- environmental and/or economic sustainability

- health and development

- science, technology and society.

The Extended Essay process is one on the most distinctive features of the Diploma programme and is a great preparation for your further studies. Enjoy it!

During the course

Take responsibility for your own learning. When you finish your study of a particular topic in class, that is a good time to check that you have covered and understood everything detailed by the IB that can be assessed. This information is shown at the start of each sub-section in the book in two pale-yellow boxes, *Understandings* and *Applications and skills*, as shown in the examples below. The notes on *Guidance* direct you to the IB data booklet or help explain the detail required.

Understandings:

- Qualitative data include all non-numerical information obtained from observations not from measurement.
- Quantitative data are obtained from measurements, and are always associated with random errors/uncertainties, determined by the apparatus, and by human limitations such as reaction times.

Guidance:
SI units should be used throughout the programme.

Applications and skills:

- Distinction between random errors and systematic errors.
- Record uncertainties in all measurements as a range (±) to an appropriate precision.
- Discussion of ways to reduce uncertainties in an experiment.
- Propagation of uncertainties in processed data, including the use of percentage uncertainties.
- Discussion of systematic errors in all experimental work, their impact on the results, and how they can be reduced.
- Estimation of whether a particular source of error is likely to have a major or minor effect on the final result.
- Calculation of percentage error when the experimental result can be compared with a theoretical or accepted result.

Guidance
- *Note that the data value must be recorded to the same precision as the random error.*
- *The number of significant figures in a result is based on the figures given in the data. When adding or subtracting, the answer should be given to the least number of decimal places. When multiplying or dividing the final answer is given to the least number of significant figures.*

Check that you have completed all the *Exercises* at the end of each sub-topic, and checked your answers with those given on the eText.

Exercises

36 Identify the bonds which will produce strong absorptions in the IR region of the electromagnetic spectrum.

   I $C-O$ bond
   II $C=C$ bond
   III $C=O$

  A I and II only   **B** I and III only   **C** II and III only   **D** I, II, and III

37 State what occurs at the molecular level when IR radiation is absorbed.

Spend extra time on parts of the course where you are less confident of your knowledge and understanding. Use additional sources of information such as other books, journals, movies, and the web links in this book to help to spark your curiosity, deepen your understanding, and grasp the wider contexts of the topic. The more you do, the more you will enjoy the course and the more successful you will be.

The *Practice questions* at the end of each chapter are mostly IB questions from recent IB examination papers, so they are a very good way of testing yourself at the end of each topic. The answers used by examiners in marking the papers are also given on the eText.

1 What is the electron configuration of the Cr^{2+} ion?

   A [Ar] $3d^5 4s^1$ **B** [Ar] $3d^3 4s^1$ **C** [Ar] $3d^6 4s^1$ **D** [Ar] $3d^4 4s^0$

2 What is the relative atomic mass of an element with the following mass spectrum?

   A 24   **B** 25   **C** 26   **D** 27

You will also be assessed on experimental work through the Internal Assessment, and by some short questions on experimental work in Paper 3. The best way to prepare for this is to take a lively interest in the laboratory work throughout the course and always relate it to the theory.

Preparing for the examination

Organize your time for review well ahead of the examination date, planning on a topic by topic basis. While you are studying make sure that you test yourself as you go – being able to recognize the content on the page is very different from being able to produce it yourself on blank paper. Effective revision generally involves using lots of scrap paper for testing your knowledge and understanding. Practise writing balanced equations, drawing diagrams, structural formulas, and so on.

Try to make your studying cumulative; this means building up a connected picture of knowledge and understanding by seeing how the topics are inter-related and reinforcing the same concepts. It can feel a bit like doing a jigsaw, where the more you have done the easier it gets to add in the new pieces.

There is no choice of questions in the examination, so make sure that you do not miss anything out. When you have finished your review of a particular topic, it is a good idea to test yourself with IB questions and time yourself according to how much time you are given for each type of question.

In the examination

The external assessment of Standard Level Chemistry consists of three examination papers, as follows.

	% of total mark	Duration / hours	Description of examination
Paper 1	20	¾	30 multiple-choice questions
Paper 2	40	1¼	Short-answer and extended-response questions on Topics 1–11
Paper 3	20	1	Section A: one data-based question and several short-answer questions on experimental work. Section B: Short-answer and extended-response questions from one option

Paper 1: Multiple-choice questions on Topics 1–11 (Chapters 1–11)

You are not allowed to use your calculator or the IB data booklet in this paper, but you are given a copy of the Periodic Table. The questions will give you any other data that you need, and any calculations will be straightforward.

There is no penalty for wrong answers so make sure that you do not leave any blanks. Read *all* the given answers A–D for each question. It is likely that more than one answer is close to being correct but you must choose the best answer available.

Paper 2: Written answers on Topics 1–11 (Chapters 1–11)

Paper 3: Written answers on laboratory work and the options (Chapters 12–15)

You are given 5 minutes reading time for Paper 2 and Paper 3. There is no choice of question in either paper; you are expected to answer *all questions*. You are allowed to use a calculator and will be provided with a copy of the IB data booklet.

- Note the number of marks given in brackets for each part of a question and use this to guide you in the detail required. In general, one mark represents one specific fact or answer.
- Take note of the **command terms** used in the questions as these also give an important clue about exactly what is required. It is a good idea to underline the command terms on the question paper to help you focus your answer.
- Sometimes questions include several different instructions, and it can be easy to miss a part of the question; avoid this by crossing off the parts of the question on the paper as you go, much as you cross items off a shopping list so you can see what you might have missed.

Remember these questions are testing your knowledge and understanding of *chemistry*, so be sure to give as much relevant detail as you can, with equations and specific examples wherever possible. The examiner can only give you credit for what you write down so do not assume anything. Show off!

It is essential that you show all your workings in calculations very clearly. Also pay attention to significant figures and include units in your answers. When a question has several parts which all follow on from each other, you will not be penalized more than once for the same mistake. So, for example, if you make a mistake in part (a) of a question, but then use that wrong answer in a correct method in part (b), you will still get full marks for part (b) – *provided that your method was clear*. So never give up! (This is known as 'error carried forward' in examiner-speak, and is shown as ECF in the mark schemes.)

In Paper 3 make sure that you follow the guidelines on the front of the paper. After section A turn to the option you have studied in section B, and do not be distracted by the other questions on the paper.